MASTERING
CISCO ROUTERS

MASTERING™
CISCO® ROUTERS

Chris Brenton
with Network Designs by Andrew Hamilton
and Gary Kessler

SYBEX®

San Francisco • Paris • Düsseldorf • Soest • London

Associate Publishers: Guy Hart-Davis, Neil Edde
Contracts and Licensing Manager: Kristine O'Callaghan
Acquisitions & Developmental Editor: Brenda Frink
Editor: Nancy Conner
Project Editor: Colleen Wheeler Strand
Production Editors: Jennifer Durning, Judith Hibbard
Technical Editor: Dana Gelinas
Book Designers: Patrick Dintino, Catalin Dulfu,
Franz Baumhackl
Graphic Illustrator: Tony Jonick
Electronic Publishing Specialist: Nila Nichols
Proofreaders: Laurie O'Connell, Suzanne Stein
Indexer: Ted Laux
Cover Designer: Design Site
Cover Illustrator/Photographer: Sergei Loobkoff,
Design Site

Library of Congress Card Number: 99-69915

ISBN: 0-7821-2643-X

Manufactured in the United States of America

10 9 8 7 6 5 4 3 2

*This book is dedicated to
Shelby Morgan Brenton.
Thank you for being
Daddy's little muse.*

ACKNOWLEDGMENTS

I think that my favorite part of writing is being able to generate the acknowledgments because it gives me an opportunity to thank all of the wonderful people who have made this book possible by sharing their time and effort.

Let me start by saying thank you to Guy Hart-Davis. The old text butcher himself has been a strong influence on my writing since my very first book. It's kind of bizarre for me to think that this may be our last book project together, as Guy has moved on to other opportunities. At the very least, the offer to Guy of a few home brews on the front porch still stands.

Thank you as well to Brenda Frink for all the help with developing the material and to Colleen Wheeler Strand (the Cisco Router Diva) for using only a small stick in her role as keeper of the project schedule. In fact, I owe Colleen a double helping of gratitude for writing the certification chapter. Her witty style makes her material a wonderful asset to the book.

Speaking of contributing authors, thanks to Andy and Kess for their great work on the design case studies. It's great knowing guru types in the industry who have a few free clock cycles to share and teach what they know. Thanks as well to Dana Gelinas and Deb Tuttle for providing technical editing and support. It's nice to have tech editors who can point out my stupider mistakes without picking on me too heavily about it. Thanks as well to the Sybex crew of Judith Hibbard, Jennifer Durning, Nila Nichols, and Tony Jonick for all their behind-the-scenes work in pulling this book together.

I also owe another heartfelt thank you to Nancy Conner for continuing to be the world's greatest editor. Her attention to detail, diligence in reviewing the material, helpful suggestions, and all-around wonderful personality make her a pleasure to work with. I know I would not be as happy with the final material of this book if not for her help and valued input.

On a technical note, I would like to thank Tina Bird (the VPN Diva), Ron Hallam, Jim Oliver, Gene Garceau, and Geoff Shaw who each helped to contribute to the content of this book in some way, shape, or form.

While not direct contributors, each of the following individuals has had a strong influence on keeping me challenged technically and thus sharp enough to generate material that (I hope) people find useful. Thanks to Lance Spitzner who has the best security white paper sites on the net, J.D. Glaser who makes the best security tools on the planet, Stephen Northcutt with all of his great community work through SANS, Dave Elfering, Joe Prest, Kathy Hickey, William Stearns, Gerry Fowley, Alice Peal, Michael Wright, Jerry Buote, George Cybenko, and the whole Dartmouth College security crew.

On a personal note, I would like to thank Sean Tangney, Chris Tuttle, Al and Maria Goodniss, Linda Catterson, Toby Miller, Sheila O'Donnell, Patricia Kennedy, and the ultimate best bud and nag, Sue Rotchford, for being cool individuals to bounce ideas off of or just to hang out with and pretend the whole computer thing never really happened.

On a family note, I would like to thank my parents Al and Carolee Brenton for buying me that first computer and not shipping me off to military school. Hopefully, you feel your persistence and patience finally paid off. Thanks as well to my sister Kym and brother-in-law Brian Frasier for being very cool people and making a difference in the lives of all of the kids who are lucky enough to be around them. Thanks also to my son Skylar for showing me that some of the greatest joys in life can be found in an empty cardboard box or a roll of refrigerated cookie dough.

Finally, thanks to my wonderful wife, soul mate, and best friend Andrea. The fact that you would let me turn our lives upside down again by writing a book during a pregnancy is a testimony to your sheer tolerance and fortitude. Thank you for putting up with all the long hours and multiple, half-completed house projects. This book never would have been finished without your loving support.

CONTENTS AT A GLANCE

CONTENTS

10   Creating a Bastion Router   349

11   Virtual Private Networking   369

12 Managing Cisco Routers 413

13 Network Case Studies 447

INTRODUCTION

I t can be argued that no company has dominated its own little portion of computer networking as completely as Cisco Systems. Market research has estimated that 80 percent of the Internet runs on Cisco hardware. This is an amazing statistic when you consider the number of manufacturers vying for market share in this arena. To put this number in perspective, imagine that eight out of every 10 cars on the highway today were produced by a single car manufacturer.

Why is Cisco hardware so popular? First and foremost is reliability. In my time, I've installed probably hundreds of Cisco routers. Out of all of these installations, I've seen maybe three or four of these routers fail within the first three years. This means that when you invest in a Cisco router, you can be relatively certain that it will continue to perform for many years.

Another strength is a plethora of features. Cisco routers support a wide range of networking protocols, as well as many options. Along with the expected routing functionality, you can choose to implement packet filtering, network address translation, quality of service, and even virtual private networking. Cisco is constantly adding new features to its router product line to make these devices even more valuable to an organization's core infrastructure.

You also have many different router models to choose from. Cisco offers a wide range of router products that can fill the requirements of the small home office, the large WAN infrastructure, and everything in between. You can choose between models that have integrated communication ports and models that accept module cards that let you customize the router to your communication needs. If you go the module route, you can choose between routers that will accept only a single module to routers that will accept as many as 16 different module cards. Clearly, there is a Cisco router to fit every need.

Of course, you don't have to learn a new set of commands as you move from the lower-end models to the top-of-the-line routers. All Cisco routers are based on the Cisco Internetwork Operating System (IOS). This means that the commands you use to manage a low-end Cisco 800 router are identical to the commands you use on the top-of-the-line Cisco 12000. This helps to cut the learning curve: Knowing how to work with one router product allows you to feel comfortable when working with the rest.

Cisco routers are also easy to work with. When you purchase a Cisco router, you get a free copy of the Router Software Loader and ConfigMaker. These products make upgrading and configuring your router a simple task. For example, with ConfigMaker, you simply draw a picture of your network and the software automatically takes care of the proper configuration settings. For the more hands-on types, you can choose to configure the router through the command line or an HTML interface.

Finally, Cisco takes router performance and security very seriously. This is probably one of the main reasons that so many Internet routers have the Cisco label. If Internet connectivity has become a critical business function, you need to know that the device providing this connectivity can do so in a reliable fashion. Cisco has proved over the years that its line of router products can do just that.

What This Book Covers

Chapter 1 starts you off with the basic technologies of network communications. We'll look at how information is packaged and transmitted between network systems. We'll also cover a range of connectivity options and the strengths and weaknesses of each.

In Chapter 2, you'll learn about logical topologies. We'll cover an assortment of LAN and WAN topologies and discuss the strengths and weaknesses of each. In particular, the discussion on Ethernet includes a good primer on how to measure and calculate your network's performance. This can be extremely helpful when planning for your network's growth.

Chapter 3 discusses network protocols. Included are TCP/IP, IPX, AppleTalk, and NetBIOS/NetBEUI. Since a router needs to know how to handle each of these protocols, we go into some depth on network addressing, address discovery, and transport layer services. The efficiency of each of these protocols is also compared.

Bridging and switching are the focus of Chapter 4. Since most environments that use routers will also use bridges or switches, you need a good understanding of how these devices work in order to integrate the technologies. This chapter also includes a number of design examples in which you must decide whether bridging or switching is a proper fit for the environment.

Chapter 5 covers the fundamentals of routing. We'll look at the available options for propagating network address information throughout your infrastructure. We'll also compare and contrast the strengths and weaknesses of each of these options. You'll even reconsider some design examples to see when routing can control traffic more effectively than bridging and switching.

In Chapter 6, we discuss the specific routing protocols you will need to manage your network infrastructure. We consider routing protocol options for TCP/IP, IPX, AppleTalk, and NetBIOS in depth. We'll even start looking at how routing protocols are configured on a Cisco router.

Ready to go hands on with a Cisco router and start learning the IOS command set? Chapter 7 teaches basic operations like how to access help and how to get assistance in determining proper command syntax. For those who do not like working with a command line interface, the HTTP interface is covered, as well.

In Chapter 8, you'll learn how to determine which features you require when ordering your Cisco router. We'll also cover how to go about installing the operating system on your router after it has arrived. Finally, we'll discuss the different options available to you in loading and managing your configuration files.

Chapter 9 is all about packet filtering. You'll learn how a packet filter works and how to use this feature to control traffic effectively. We'll discuss standard access lists, extended access lists, and even Cisco's new reflexive filters. We'll close out the chapter by looking at some design examples that use packet filtering to control traffic in TCP/IP, IPX, and AppleTalk environments.

Router security is featured in Chapter 10. Because many routers live outside the protective circle of a firewall, we'll look at all the precautionary steps you can take to make sure that your router remains secure.

In Chapter 11, you'll learn all about virtual private networking. We'll start by discussing the importance of authentication and encryption and how to use these technologies to build a secure tunnel between two sites. We'll look at the options available to you in setting up a VPN and cover a design example using Cisco router hardware.

Chapter 12 discusses how best to manage your router infrastructure. Keeping tabs on the health of your routers is a critical step in insuring that network performance remains at an optimal level. We'll cover how to collect log entries and statistics from your routers, as well as how to perform proper backups in case the worst ever occurs.

In Chapter 13, you'll get into the basics of network design. We'll start by looking at a set of business requirements and follow the design process all the way through to deployment. Each design example includes the necessary router configuration files, so you can even adapt these designs to your own environment.

Chapter 14 continues with additional case studies on how to formulate a proper network design. The designs in this chapter have been generated by two other authors. This helps to spice things up a bit and gives you a different perspective on how to resolve problems through the design process.

Finally, Chapter 15 discusses Cisco certification and the options available to you. You'll learn about the different levels of certification, as well as the requirements for each. While getting certified is not an easy process, the benefits that certification can bestow are well worth the effort.

Who Should Read This Book

With all the Cisco books on the market today, why pick up this one? While most Cisco books are specifically geared toward earning a certification, this book focuses on the individual who needs to get up to speed quickly on deploying and managing Cisco routers. So, while a CCNA book may focus on the actual router configuration and a CCDA book on design, this book melds these two topics in an attempt to give you a complete set of tools for both laying out and deploying your infrastructure.

True, you may very well be able to pass your CCNA or CCDA based on the material presented in this book. I can guarantee, however, that you will not see a sufficient number of exam questions on TFTP to make it worth the heavy coverage it has received in these pages. If, on the other hand, you are actually deploying a large number of routers, the material presented on how and when to use TFTP, as well as how to configure it on multiple operating systems, will be extremely valuable to you.

The focus here is on getting the job done. I've made few assumptions about the reader's prior knowledge. This means that the book includes enough background theory to get the truly green up to speed. For those who are a bit more seasoned, feel free to skip the introductory information and get right to the meat of the book. If you've been assigned the task of redesigning your company's network, you may want to jump right into the design examples to start getting a few ideas.

If you have any questions or comments regarding any of the material in this book, feel free to e-mail me at cbrenton@sover.net.

CHAPTER 1

Communication Basics

Before we can discuss routers and how they work, we first need to cover the basics. In this chapter, we will look at the fundamentals of network communications and how data is moved between systems. While the communication process is cloaked from the typical end user, a savvy network engineer must be armed with this information in order to be an effective troubleshooter.

We will start by looking at analog and digital signaling. All network communications rely on one of these transmission methods for moving information. We will then look at the kinds of problems that can occur during attempts to transmit information and how you can minimize the effects of these problems.

From there, we will talk about the core infrastructure of a network. We'll look at how systems get connected and exactly how digital or analog signaling is used to move information between systems. Finally, we'll map out the entire process of a communication session using the OSI model as a guide, so you can better understand exactly what is occurring on your network.

Analog and Digital Transmissions

There are two ways data can be communicated:

- Through analog transmissions
- Through digital transmissions

An *analog transmission* is a signal that can vary either in power level (known as *amplitude*) or in the number of times this power level changes in a fixed period (known as *frequency*). An analog transmission can have a nearly infinite number of permissible values over a given range. For example, we use analog signals in order to communicate verbally. Our voice boxes vibrate the air at different frequencies and amplitudes. These vibrations are received by the eardrum and interpreted as words. Subtle changes in tone or volume can dramatically change the meaning of what we say.

Figure 1.1 shows an example of an analog transmission. Notice the amplitude each time the waveform peaks. Each of the three amplitude levels could be used to convey different information, such as alphanumeric characters. This makes for a very efficient way to communicate information, as each wave cycle can be used to convey additional information. In a perfect world, analog might be the ideal way to convey information.

FIGURE 1.1

An example of an analog transmission plotted over time

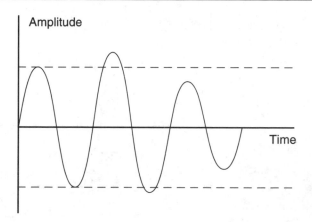

 NOTE Frequency is measured in cycles per second, or *hertz* (Hz). If Figure 1.1 were measured over a period of one second, it would be identified as a frequency of three cycles per second or 3Hz.

The problem with analog transmissions is that they are very susceptible to *noise*, or interference. Noise is the addition of unwanted signal information. It can result in a number of data retransmissions, slowing down the rate of information transfer. Think of having a conversation in a crowded room with lots of people talking. With all of this background noise going on, it can become difficult to distinguish between your discussion and the others taking place within the room. Data retransmissions are signaled by phrases such as "What?" and "What did you say?" This slows down the rate of information transfer.

Figure 1.2 shows an example of an analog signal in a noisy circuit. Note that it is now more difficult to determine the precise amplitude of each waveform. This can result in incorrect information being transmitted or in requiring the correct information to be resent.

FIGURE 1.2

An analog transmission on a noisy circuit

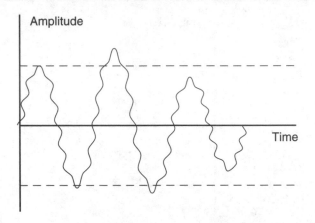

To the rescue come *digital transmissions*. Digital communications are based on the binary system: Only two pieces of information are ever transmitted, a 1 or a 0. In an electrical circuit, a 0 is usually represented by a voltage of zero volts and a 1 is represented by five volts. This is radically different from analog transmissions, which can have an infinite number of possible values. These 1s and 0s are then strung together in certain patterns to convey information. For example, the binary equivalent of the letter *A* is 01000001.

Each individual signal or digital pulse is referred to as a *bit*. When eight bits are strung together (like our binary equivalent of *A*), it is referred to as a *byte*. The byte is considered to be the base unit when dealing with digital communications. Each byte relays one complete piece of information, such as the letter *A*.

 NOTE Digital communication is analogous to Morse code or the early telegraph system: Certain patterns of pulses are used to represent different letters of the alphabet.

If you examine Figure 1.3, you'll note that our waveform has changed shape. It is no longer a free-flowing series of arcs but now follows a rigid and predictable format.

FIGURE 1.3

A digital transmission plotted over time

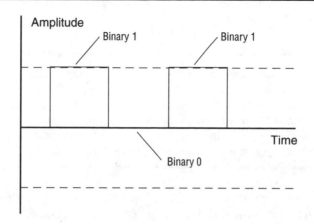

Because this waveform is so predictable and the variation between acceptable values is so great, it is now much easier to determine which values are being transmitted. As shown in Figure 1.4, even when there is noise in the circuit, you can still see which part of the signal is a binary 1 and which part is a 0.

FIGURE 1.4

A digital transmission on a noisy circuit

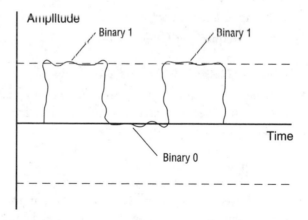

This simple format, which allows digital communication to be so noise resistant, can also be its biggest drawback. The information for the ASCII character *A* can be transmitted with a single analog wave or vibration, but transmitting the binary or digital equivalent requires eight separate waves or vibrations (to transmit 01000001). Despite this inherent drawback, it is usually much more efficient to use digital communications whenever possible. Analog circuits require more overhead in order to detect and correct noisy transmissions. This is why most modern networks use digital communications.

 NOTE *Overhead* is the amount of additional information that must be transmitted on a circuit to insure that the receiving system gets the correct data and that the data is free of errors. Typically, when a circuit requires more overhead, less bandwidth is available to transmit the actual data. This is like the packaging used when something is shipped to you in a box. You didn't *want* hundreds of little Styrofoam peanuts, but they're there in the box taking up space to insure your item is delivered safely.

Another big plus for digital communications is that computers process information in digital format. If you use analog communications to transfer information from one computer to another, you need some form of converter (such as a modem or a codex) at each end of the circuit to translate the information from digital to analog and then back to digital again.

Sources of Noise

So where does noise come from? Noise can be broken down into two categories:

- Electromagnetic interference (EMI)
- Radio frequency interference (RFI)

Electromagnetic Interference (EMI)

EMI is produced by circuits that use an alternating signal like analog or digital communications (referred to as an *alternating current* or an *AC circuit*). EMI is not produced by circuits that contain a consistent power level (referred to as a *direct current* or a *DC circuit*).

For example, if you could slice one of the wires coming from a car battery and watch the electrons moving down the wire (kids: don't try this at home), you would see a steady stream of power moving evenly and uniformly down the cable. The power level would never change; it would stay at a constant 12 volts. A car battery is an example of a DC circuit because the power level remains stable.

Now, let's say you could slice the wire to a household lamp and try the same experiment (kids: *definitely* do not try this at home!). You would now see that, depending on the point in time when you measured the voltage on the wire, it would read anywhere between –120 volts and +120 volts. The voltage level of the circuit is constantly changing. Plotted over time, the voltage level would resemble the analog signal shown earlier in Figure 1.1.

If you were to watch the flow of electrons now in the AC wire, you would notice something very interesting. As the voltage changes and the current flows down the wire, the electrons tend to ride predominantly on the surface of the wire. The center point of the wire would show almost no electron movement at all. If you increased the frequency of the power cycle, more and more of the electrons would travel on the surface of the wire instead of at the core. This effect is somewhat similar to what happens to a water skier—the faster the boat travels, the closer to the top of the water the skier rides.

As the frequency of the power cycle increases, energy begins to radiate at a 90° angle to the flow of current. Just as a water skier will push out wakes or waves, so too will energy move out from the center core of the wire. This radiation is in a direct relationship with the signal on the wire: If the voltage level or the frequency is increased, the amount of energy radiated will also increase (see Figure 1.5).

FIGURE 1.5

A conductor carrying an AC signal radiating EMI

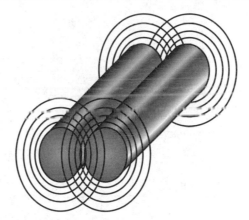

Copper wire conducting AC signal

This energy has magnetic properties and is the basis of how electromagnets and transformers operate. The downside to all of this is that the electromagnetic radiation can introduce an electrical signal into another wire if one is nearby. This interference either adds to or subtracts from the existing signal and is considered to be noise. EMI is the most common type of interference encountered on local area networks and can be produced by everything from fluorescent lights to network cables to heavy machinery. EMI also causes signal loss. Any energy that is dissipated as EMI is energy that can no longer be used to carry the signal down the wire.

Radio Frequency Interference (RFI)

Radio frequency interference (RFI) can be produced when two signals have similar properties. The waveforms can join together, changing the frequency or amplitude of the resulting signal. This is why geographically close radio stations do not transmit on adjacent frequencies. If they did, a radio might not be able to receive the weaker of the two stations.

For an example, examine Image 1 in Figure 1.6. Assume that this is a communication signal we are transmitting between two systems. Now, let's assume that Image 2 is RFI that has been introduced to the circuit. These two signals would combine to produce the transmission shown in Image 3. Note that this is so far off from our original signal that our data would probably be incomprehensible.

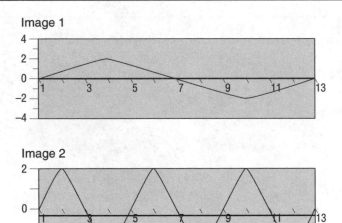

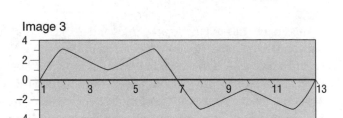

The most common source of RFI in networking is caused by a condition known as *reflection*. Reflection occurs when a signal is reflected back upon itself by some component along its connection path. For example, a faulty connector within a circuit may reflect back some of the signal's energy to the original transmitting host. This is why all end points in a network must be capable not only of receiving the signal, but also of absorbing all of the signal's energy.

Communication Synchronization

Another important property in communications is letting the receiving system know when to expect data transmissions. If a receiving system cannot determine the beginning of a transmission, that system may mistake the beginning of a transmission for the middle or vice versa. This is true for both analog and digital communications.

Time Division

One way to achieve proper signal timing is to have the systems synchronize their communications so that each transmits data at a predetermined time. For example, the two systems may agree to take turns transmitting for one second each and then pass control over to the other system (similar to the give-and-take of a human conversation). This type of communication is known as *time division*, because the window of time when transmission is allowed is divided between the two systems.

While this type of negotiation is simple and straightforward, it has a number of inherent flaws. First, if a station has nothing to say, its time slice will be wasted while the second station sits by idly, waiting to transmit additional information. Also, if the stations' clocks are slightly different, the two systems will eventually fall out of sync and will smother each other's communication. Finally, consider what happens when further stations are plugged into the same circuit and have something to say: The time slices *could* be renegotiated, but this will severely diminish the amount of data that can be transmitted on this circuit in a timely fashion.

Despite its weaknesses, time division communication is used quite effectively by many wide area network (WAN) technologies. This is because a WAN circuit is typically between only two hosts. This eliminates the problem of trying to scale time division to many systems. Also, the fact that time division allocates bandwidth in such a predictable manner allows it to be an effective means of transmitting time-sensitive data such as video or voice.

The Preamble

To resolve the scaling problems with time division, many networking technologies communicate using a *preamble*: a defined series of communication pulses that tell all receiving stations, "Get ready—I've got something to say."

Using a preamble allows systems on the network to take a more ad hoc approach to communications. Instead of having to wait for their time slots to arrive, systems are allowed to attempt transmission any time data must be conveyed. The preamble insures that all stations are able to sync up and receive the data in the same time measure that it was sent. This is just like a band's lead singer or drummer calling out the beat to lead into the start of a song, making sure all band members start the first note at exactly the same time and are in sync with each other.

Because a station sends a preamble only when it needs to transmit data, this eliminates dead-air time by leaving the circuit open for systems that need it. Also, keeping the data transmission bursts fairly small resolves the issue of systems falling out of sync due to time variations, because the stations can resync their times during each data delivery.

Understanding Topologies

The *topology* of a network is the set of rules for physically connecting and communicating on a given network medium. When you decide on a particular topology for connecting your network systems, you will need to follow a number of specifications that tell you how the systems need to be wired together, what type of connectors to use, and even how these systems must speak to each other on the wire.

Topology is broken down into two categories:

- Physical
- Logical

Physical Topology

Physical topology refers to how the transmission media are wired together. There are four types of physical topology:

- Bus
- Star
- Ring
- Point to point

Bus Topology

The *bus* topology is the common configuration for Thinnet wiring. Systems attached to the bus are connected in a series type of connection. All systems are connected via a single long cable run and tap in via T connectors. Figure 1.7 shows an example of a bus topology.

FIGURE 1.7

An example of a bus topology

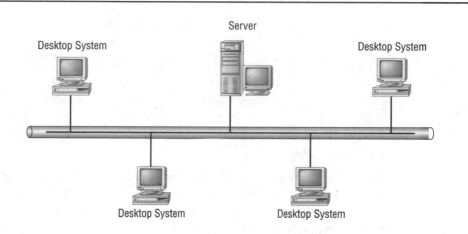

All systems connect to the same logical cable length.

Star Topology

The *star* topology is the common configuration of twisted-pair wiring. Each system is connected to a central device, such as a hub or a switch. Only one system is connected to each physical wire run. These hubs and switches can then be linked together to form larger networks. Figure 1.8 shows an example of a star topology.

FIGURE 1.8

*An example of a
star topology*

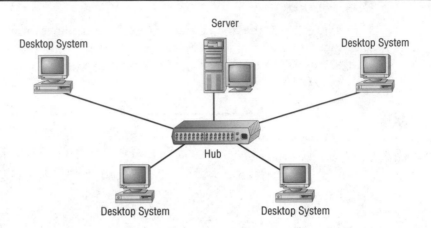

Ring Topology

The *ring* configuration is commonly used in token-based communications such as FDDI. The output data port (Tx for *transmit*) is connected to the input data port (Rx for *receive*) of the next station along the ring. This continues until the last station connects its output data port to the input data port of the first system, forming a complete ring. Figure 1.9 is an example of a ring topology.

FIGURE 1.9

*An example of a
ring topology*

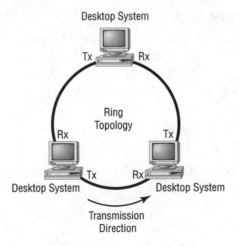

Point to Point

A *point-to-point* connection is commonly used in WAN configurations or in home networks with only two computers. With point to point, only two systems are connected to the physical medium. Fiber cable is commonly deployed in a point-to-point fashion. Twisted pair can also be configured for point-to-point connections by using a *cross cable*. A cross cable is simply a twisted-pair cable that has the transmit and receive pairs switched at one end.

Desktop System   Desktop System

NOTE   The transmission medium is separate from the physical topology. The examples I've just given are what you will commonly run into in the field, but they are not hard-and-fast rules. For example, even though fiber is commonly used in a ring topology, you can use it in a star or even a bus topology.

Physical Topologies and Cisco Routers

So what role does the physical topology play in deploying your Cisco routers? You need to determine up front what kind of physical topology you will be using in order to insure that you order a model which supports the right type of connectors.

For example, let's say you decide to use fiber optic cables to connect your Cisco router in order to support long cable runs. Cisco routers support two types of fiber optic connectors: SMA and FDDI. An *SMA connector* is commonly used in point-to-point applications. The *FDDI connector*, however, is commonly used in ring topologies. You need to determine which physical topology you will be using before selecting a Cisco model.

Logical Topology

A *logical topology* describes the communication rules each station should use when communicating on a network. For example, the specifications of the logical topology describe how each station should determine whether it's OK to transmit data, and what a station should do if it tries to transmit data at the same time as another station. The logical topology's job is to insure that information gets transferred as quickly and with as few errors as possible. Think of a discussion group moderator and you'll get the idea. The moderator insures that each person in the group gets a turn to speak. The moderator also insures that if two individuals try to speak at the same time, one gets priority and the other waits his or her turn.

So how are physical and logical topologies related? Any given logical topology will operate only on specific physical topologies. For example, Ethernet will operate on a bus, star, or point-to-point physical topology, but it will not work on a ring. The FDDI specification will function on a ring or a star topology but not on a bus or a point to point. Once you have determined which logical topology you will use, you can then go about selecting your physical topology.

Logical topologies are defined by the Institute of Electrical and Electronics Engineers (IEEE). The IEEE is a not-for-profit organization that consists of an assembly of companies and private individuals within the networking industry. The members of the IEEE work together to define specifications, preventing any single company from claiming ownership of the technology and helping to insure that products from multiple vendors will interoperate successfully in a network.

Table 1.1 shows the most common network specifications.

TABLE 1.1: COMMON IEEE NETWORK SPECIFICATIONS

Specification	Defines
IEEE 802.1	VLANs and bridging
IEEE 802.2	Logical link control (LLC)
IEEE 802.3	10Mb Ethernet
IEEE 802.3u	100Mb Ethernet
IEEE 802.3x	Full-duplex Ethernet
IEEE 802.3z	1Gb Ethernet
IEEE 802.5	Token Ring
IEEE 802.7	Broadband
IEEE 802.11	Wireless LANs
IEEE 802.12	Demand priority
IEEE 802.14	Cable modem
IEEE 802.16	Broadband wireless

As a major player in the internetworking arena, Cisco has taken an active role in finalizing many of the specifications shown in Table 1.1. This not only helps to insure that Cisco products adhere to the IEEE specifications; it also helps to insure that support can be included as soon as a specification is ready for general consumption.

Connection Types

Every logical topology uses one of three methods for creating the connections between end stations:

- Circuit switching
- Message switching
- Packet switching

Circuit Switching

Circuit switching means that when data needs to be transferred from one node to another, a dedicated connection is created between the two systems. Bandwidth is dedicated to this communication session and remains available until the connection is no longer required. A regular telephone call uses circuit switching. When you place a call, a connection is set up between your phone and the one you are calling. This connection remains in effect until you finish your call and hang up. Figure 1.11 illustrates a circuit-switched network. The best route is selected, and bandwidth is dedicated to this communication session the entire length of the circuit, remaining in place until no longer needed. All data follows the same path.

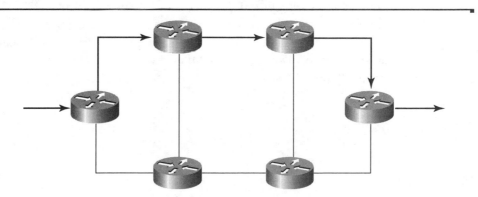

Circuit-switched networks are useful for delivering information that must be received in the order it was sent. For example, applications such as real-time audio and video cannot tolerate the delays incurred in reassembling the data in the correct order. While circuit switching insures that data is delivered as quickly as possible by dedicating a connection to the task, it can also be wasteful compared to other types of connections, because the circuit will remain active even if the end stations are not currently transmitting.

Examples of circuit-switched networks include the following:

- Asynchronous Transfer Mode (ATM)
- Analog dial-up line (public telephone network)
- ISDN
- Leased line
- T1

Message Switching

Message switching means that a *store-and-forward* type of connection is set up between connectivity devices along the message path. The first device creates a connection to the next and transmits the entire message. Once this transmission is complete, the connection is torn down, and the second device repeats the process if required.

The delivery of e-mail is a good example of message switching. As you type in your e-mail message, your computer queues the information until you are done. When you hit the Send button, your system delivers your message in its entirety to your local post office, which again queues the message. Your post office then contacts the post office of the person to whom you have addressed the message. Again, the message is delivered in its entirety and queued by the receiving system. Finally, the remote post office delivers your message to its intended recipient using the same process.

Figure 1.12 illustrates a message-switched network. While all the data still follows the same path, only one portion of the network is dedicated to delivering this data at any given time.

FIGURE 1.12

*An example of a
message-switched
network*

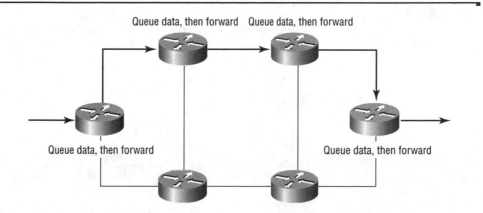

None of the logical topologies covered in this book uses message switching for the delivery of data. In part, this is because message switching increases the memory and processing requirements on interim hardware in order to store the information prior to delivery.

Packet Switching

The final method for connecting end stations is *packet switching*. This method is by far the most widely used in current networking topologies. Within a packet-switching network, each individual frame can follow a different path to its final destination. Because each frame can follow a different path, frames may or may not be received in the same order they were transmitted. To correct this problem, the receiving station uses the sequence numbers on the frames to reassemble the data in the correct order.

Note the operative phrase "can follow a different path." Other factors, such as the routing protocol, play a part in determining whether this feature is exploited. For now, however, it is enough to realize that in a packet-switched network all the data may not follow the same path.

Figure 1.13 illustrates a packet-switched network. Data is allowed to follow any path to its destination. Packet switching does not require that any bandwidth be reserved for this transmission.

FIGURE 1.13

*An example of a
packet-switched
network*

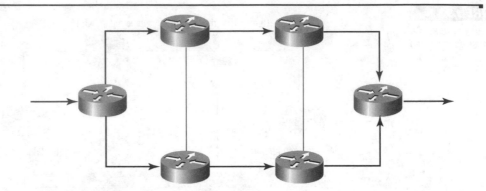

Packet-switched networks are useful for transmitting regular network data. This
includes storing files, printing, or cruising the Web. In short, all the activities you
would normally associate with network usage will run fine in a packet-switched network. While packet switching is a poor choice for the delivery of live audio and video,
it is extremely efficient for delivering information that is not time sensitive, because it
does not require dedicating bandwidth to the delivery of information. Other nodes
are capable of sharing the available bandwidth as required.

Here are some examples of packet-switched networks:

- All Ethernet topologies
- FDDI
- Frame Relay and X.25

Data Packaging

So far, we have talked about analog and digital signaling. We have also talked about
physical and logical topologies and how they are used to tie our network together. It
is now time to combine signaling with topologies in an attempt to transmit information between two systems.

When data is moved along a network, it is packaged inside a delivery envelope
known as a *frame*. Frames are topology specific. An Ethernet frame needs to convey
different information than a Token Ring or an ATM frame. Since Ethernet is by far the
most popular topology, we will cover it in detail here.

Ethernet Frames

An *Ethernet frame* is a set of digital pulses transmitted onto the transmission media in order to convey information. An Ethernet frame can be anywhere from 64 to 1,518 bytes in size (a byte being 8 digital pulses or bits) and is organized into four sections:

- Preamble
- Header
- Date
- Frame check sequence (FCS)

Preamble

Discussed earlier in this chapter, the preamble is used to synchronize communications between multiple systems along the same logical network. In an Ethernet environment, systems may begin transmitting at any time. The preamble allows systems receiving the transmission to get ready for the actual flow of data. An Ethernet preamble is eight bytes long.

 NOTE Because the preamble is considered part of the communication process and not part of the actual information being transferred, it is not usually included when measuring a frame's size.

Header

A *header* always contains information about who sent the frame and where it is going. It may also contain other information, such as how many bytes the frame contains; this is called the *length field* and is used for error correction. If the receiving station measures the frame to be a different size than that indicated in the length field, it asks the transmitting system to send a new frame. If the length field is not used, the header may instead contain a *type field* that describes what type of Ethernet frame it is.

 NOTE The header size is always 14 bytes.

Data

The *data* section of the frame contains the actual data the station needs to transmit, as well as any protocol information, such as source and destination IP addresses. The data field can be anywhere from 46 to 1,500 bytes in size. If a station has more than 1,500 bytes of information to transfer, it will break up the information over multiple frames and identify the proper order by using *sequence numbers*. Sequence numbers identify the order in which the destination system should reassemble the data. This sequence information is also stored in the data portion of the frame.

If the frame does not have 46 bytes' worth of information to convey, the station pads the end of this section by filling it in with 1 (remember that digital connections use binary numbers). Depending on the frame type, this section may also contain additional information describing what protocol or method of communication the systems are using.

Frame Check Sequence (FCS)

The *frame check sequence* insures that the data received is actually the data sent. The transmitting system processes the FCS portion of the frame through an algorithm called a *cyclic redundancy check* (CRC). This CRC takes the values of the above fields and creates a four-byte number. When the destination system receives the frame, it runs the same CRC and compares it to the value within this field. If the destination system finds a match, it assumes the frame is free of errors and processes the information. If the comparison fails, the destination station assumes that something happened to the frame during its travels and requests the transmitting system to send another copy of the frame.

 NOTE The FCS size is always four bytes.

The Frame Header Section

Now that we have a better understanding of what an Ethernet frame is, let's take a closer look at the header section. The header information is ultimately responsible for identifying who sent the data and where the sender wanted it to go.

The header contains two fields to identify the source and the destination of the transmission. These are the *node addresses* of both the source and destination systems. This number is also referred to as the *media access control* (MAC) address. The node address is a unique number that is used to serialize network devices (like network cards or networking hardware) and is a unique identifier that distinguishes a given network device from any other network device in the world. No two network devices should ever be assigned the same number. Think of this number as equivalent to a telephone number. Every home with a telephone has a unique telephone number, so that the telephone company knows where to direct the call. In this same fashion, a local system will use the destination system's MAC address to send the frame to the proper system.

NOTE The MAC address has nothing to do with Apple's computers and is always capitalized. It is the number used by each system attached to the network (PCs and Macs included) to uniquely identify itself.

The MAC address is a six-byte, 12-digit hexadecimal number that is broken up into two parts. The first half of the address is the manufacturer's identifier. A manufacturer is assigned a range of MAC addresses to use when serializing its devices. Some of the more prominent MAC addresses appear in Table 1.2.

TABLE 1.2: COMMON MAC ADDRESSES

First Three Bytes of MAC Address	Manufacturer
00000C	Cisco
0000A2	Bay Networks
0080D3	Shiva
00AA00	Intel
02608C	3Com
080009	Hewlett-Packard
080020	Sun
08005A	IBM

TIP The first three bytes of the MAC address can be a good troubleshooting aid. If you are investigating a problem, try to determine the source MAC address. Knowing who made the device may put you a little closer to determining which system is giving you trouble. For example, if the first three bytes are 00000C, you know you need to focus your attention on any Cisco devices on your network.

The second half of the MAC address is the serial number the manufacturer has assigned to the device.

One address worthy of note is FF-FF-FF-FF-FF-FF. This is referred to as a *broadcast address*. A broadcast address is special: It means that all systems receiving this packet should read the included data. If a system sees a frame that has been sent to the broadcast address, it will read the frame and process the data if it can.

 NOTE You should never encounter a frame that has a broadcast address in the source node field. The Ethernet specifications do not include any conditions where the broadcast address should be placed in the source node field.

Note that we already have address information and the capability of transferring information on our Ethernet network, yet we've made no mention of protocols. The reasons for this will become clearer in the next section when we discuss the Address Resolution Protocol (ARP). For now, remember that every system on our Ethernet segment sees every packet and needs to look at that packet to see whether or not the packet is addressed to that system.

If I am using a PC that only speaks IPX to a NetWare server, and somewhere on my network are two Apple computers speaking AppleTalk, my system still sees those frames and needs to look at every one of them to determine whether it needs to read the data within the frame. The fact that my system speaks a different protocol makes no difference. The Ethernet communication rules require that every computer on the segment look at every packet.

 NOTE Ethernet communication rules are discussed in greater detail in Chapter 2.

That a computer must dedicate some CPU time to analyzing frames on a network may seem a minor point, but it isn't: If the network is busy, a workstation can appear to respond sluggishly, even though it is not intentionally transmitting or receiving network data.

Here's one last point about Ethernet frames before we move on. We have seen that each frame contains a 14-byte header and a four-byte FCS. These field lengths are fixed and never change. The sum of the two is 18 bytes. The data field, however, is allowed to vary from 46 to 1,500 bytes. This is where our minimum and maximum frame sizes come from:

```
46 + 18 = 64 bytes (minimum frame size)
1,500 + 18 = 1,518 bytes (maximum frame size)
```

The Address Resolution Protocol

How do you find the destination MAC address so that you can send data to a system? After all, network cards do not ship with telephone books. Finding a MAC address is done with a special frame referred to as an *address resolution protocol* (ARP) frame. ARP functions differently depending on which protocol you're using (such as IPX, IP, Net-BEUI, and so on).

For an example, see Figure 1.14. This is a decode of the initial packet from a system that wishes to send information to another system on the same network. Notice the information included within the decode. The transmitting system knows the IP address of the destination system, but it does not know the destination MAC address. Without this address, local delivery of data is not possible. ARP is used when a system needs to discover the destination system's MAC address.

NOTE A frame *decode* is the process of converting a binary frame transmission to a format that can be understood by a human being. Typically, this is done using a network analyzer.

FIGURE 1.14

A transmitting system attempting to discover the destination system's MAC address

No.	Source	Destination	Layer	Summary	Size	Interpacket	Absolute Time
1	Herne	Broadcast	arp	Req by 10.1.1.132 for 10.1.1.10	64	0 µs	10:17:42 AM
2	Skylar	Herne	arp	Reply 10.1.1.10=0000C0A7F49A	64	575 µs	10:17:42 AM
3	Herne	Skylar	icmp	Type=Echo Request	78	269 µs	10:17:42 AM
4	Skylar	Herne	icmp	Type=Echo Reply	78	2 ms	10:17:42 AM

```
Packet Number : 1              10:17:42 AM
Length : 64 bytes
ether: =================== Ethernet Datalink Layer ====================
       Station: Herne ----> Broadcast
       Type: 0x0806 (ARP)
  arp: =================== Address Resolution Protocol ===============
       Hardware: Ethernet
       Protocol: 0x0800 (IP)
       Operation: ARP Request
       Hardware adress length: 6
       Protocol address length: 4
       Sender Hardware Address: 00-00-E8-2F-77-2A
       Sender Protocol Address: 10.1.1.132
       Target Hardware Address: 00-00-00-00-00-00
       Target Protocol Address: 10.1.1.10
```

Keep in mind that ARP is only for local communications. When a packet of data crosses a router, the Ethernet header will be rewritten so that the source MAC address is that of the router, not the transmitting system. This means that a new ARP request may need to be generated.

ARP in Action

Figure 1.15 shows how this works. Our transmitting system (Fritz) needs to deliver some information to the destination system (Wren). Since Wren is not on the same subnet as Fritz, Fritz transmits an ARP in order to discover the MAC address of Port A on the local router. Once Fritz knows this address, Fritz transmits its data to the router.

FIGURE 1.15

MAC addresses are used for local communications only.

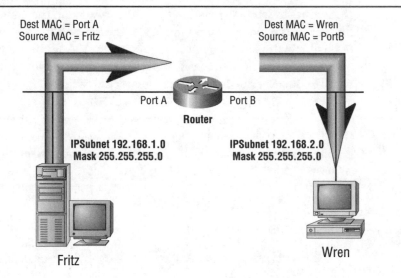

Our router will then need to send an ARP from Port B in order to discover the MAC address of Wren. Once Wren replies to this ARP request, the router will strip off the Ethernet frame from Fritz's data and create a new one. The router replaces the source MAC address (originally Fritz's MAC address) with the MAC address of Port B. It will also replace the destination MAC address (originally Port A) with the MAC address of Wren.

NOTE When Fritz realized that Wren was not on the same subnet, he went looking for a router. We will discuss why in greater detail when we discuss networking protocols. For now, it is simply enough to understand that when two systems are in the same logical network, the MAC address is used to move data between systems.

The ARP Cache

All systems are capable of caching information learned through ARP requests. For example, if a few seconds later Fritz wishes to send another packet of data to Wren, he would not have to transmit a new ARP request for the router's MAC address, as this value would be saved in memory. This memory area is referred to as the *ARP cache*.

ARP cache entries are retained for up to 60 seconds. After that, they are typically flushed out and must again be learned through a new ARP request. It is also possible to create static ARP entries, which creates a permanent entry in the ARP cache table. This way, a system is no longer required to transmit ARP requests for nodes with a static entry.

For example, we could create a static ARP entry for the router on Fritz's machine so that it would no longer have to transmit an ARP request when looking for this device. The only problem would occur if the router's MAC address changed. If the router were to fail and you had to replace it with a new one, you would also have to go back to Fritz's system and modify the static ARP entry, because the new router would have a different MAC address.

The OSI Model

In 1977, the International Organization of Standards (IOS) developed the *Open Systems Interconnection Reference Model* (OSI model) to help improve communications between different vendors' systems. The IOS was a committee representing many different organizations, whose goal was not to favor a specific method of communication but to develop a set of guidelines that would allow vendors to insure that their products would interoperate.

The IOS was setting out to simplify communications between systems. Many events must take place in order to insure that data first reaches the correct system and is then passed along to the correct application in a usable format. A set of rules was required to break down the communication process into a simple set of building blocks.

Simplifying a Complex Process

An analogy to the OSI model would be the process of building a house. While the final product may seem a complex piece of work, it is much simpler when it is broken down into manageable sections.

A good house starts with a foundation. There are rules that define how wide the foundation wall must be, as well as how far below the frost line it needs to sit. After that, the house is framed off. Again, there are rules to define how thick the lumber must be and how far each piece of framing can span without support. Once the house is framed, there is a defined process for putting on a roof, adding walls, and even connecting the electrical system and plumbing.

By breaking down this complicated process into small, manageable sections, building a house becomes easier. This breakdown also makes it easier to define who is responsible for which section. For example, the electrical contractor's responsibilities include running wires and adding electrical outlets, but not shingling the roof.

The entire structure becomes an interwoven tapestry, with each piece relying on the others. For example, the frame of our house requires a solid foundation. Without it, the frame will eventually buckle and fall. The frame may also require that load-bearing walls be placed in certain areas of the house in order to insure that the frame does not fall in on itself.

The OSI model strives to set up similar kinds of definitions and dependencies. Each portion of the communication process becomes a separate building block. This makes it easier to determine what each portion of the communication process is required to do. It also helps to define how each piece will be connected to the others.

The OSI Layers Defined

The OSI model consists of a set of seven layers. Each layer describes how its portion of the communication process should function, as well as how it will interface with the layers directly above it, below it, and adjacent to it on other systems. This allows a vendor to create a product that operates on a certain level and to be sure it will operate in the widest range of applications. If the vendor's product follows a specific layer's guidelines, it should be able to communicate with products, created by other vendors, that operate at adjacent layers.

To return to our house analogy for just a moment, think of the lumberyard that supplies main support beams used in house construction. As long as the yard follows the guidelines for thickness and material, builders can expect beams to function correctly in any house that has a proper foundation structure.

Figure 1.16 represents the OSI model in all its glory. Let's take the layers one at a time to determine the functionality expected of each.

FIGURE 1.16

The OSI model

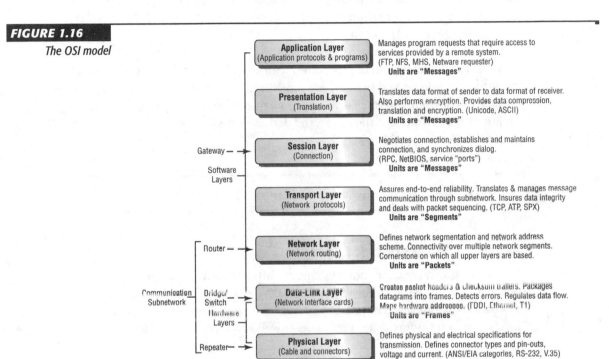

| | | Application Layer (Application protocols & programs) | Manages program requests that require access to services provided by a remote system. (FTP, NFS, MHS, Netware requester) **Units are "Messages"** |

Application Layer (Application protocols & programs) — Manages program requests that require access to services provided by a remote system. (FTP, NFS, MHS, Netware requester) **Units are "Messages"**

Presentation Layer (Translation) — Translates data format of sender to data format of receiver. Also performs encryption. Provides data compression, translation and encryption. (Unicode, ASCII) **Units are "Messages"**

Gateway —

Software Layers

Session Layer (Connection) — Negotiates connection, establishes and maintains connection, and synchronizes dialog. (RPC, NetBIOS, service "ports") **Units are "Messages"**

Transport Layer (Network protocols) — Assures end-to-end reliability. Translates & manages message communication through subnetwork. Insures data integrity and deals with packet sequencing. (TCP, ATP, SPX) **Units are "Segments"**

Router —

Network Layer (Network routing) — Defines network segmentation and network address scheme. Connectivity over multiple network segments. Cornerstone on which all upper layers are based. **Units are "Packets"**

Communication Subnetwork

Bridge/ Switch

Hardware Layers

Data-Link Layer (Network interface cards) — Creates packet headers & checksum trailers. Packages datagrams into frames. Detects errors. Regulates data flow. Maps hardware addresses. (FDDI, Ethernet, T1) **Units are "Frames"**

Repeater —

Physical Layer (Cable and connectors) — Defines physical and electrical specifications for transmission. Defines connector types and pin-outs, voltage and current. (ANSI/EIA categories, RS-232, V.35) **Units are "Bits"**

Layer 1: The Physical Layer

The *Physical layer* describes the specifications of our transmission media, connectors, and signal pulses. Choosing to use analog or digital signaling would be considered a Physical layer specification. So would the medium that carries these signals, such as twisted pair, fiber, or even the atmosphere.

Network hubs and repeaters are referred to as Physical layer devices. This is because they are little more than signal amplifiers. All of a hub's functionality is defined within the first layer of the OSI model.

Layer 2: The Data-Link Layer

The *Data-Link layer* describes the specifications for topologies and the communication between local systems. Ethernet is a good example of a Data-Link layer specification because it is capable of functioning with multiple Physical layer specifications (such as twisted pair and fiber cabling) as well as with multiple Network layer specifications (such as IP, IPX, and AppleTalk).

The Data-Link layer is the "door between worlds," connecting the physical aspects of the network (cables and digital pulses) with the abstract world of software and data streams. Bridges and switches are considered data-link devices because they are capable of controlling traffic based on topology address information. For example, in an Ethernet environment the source and destination MAC addresses can be used to control traffic flow.

 NOTE Topologies such as Ethernet are discussed in Chapter 2.

Layer 3: The Network Layer

The *Network layer* describes how systems on different network segments find each other; it also defines network addresses. IP, IPX, and AppleTalk's Datagram Delivery Protocol (DDP) are all examples of Network layer specifications because they define a mechanism for finding distant resources as well as addressing individual systems.

 NOTE Protocols are discussed in Chapter 3.

Layer 4: The Transport Layer

The *Transport layer* deals with the actual manipulation of your data and prepares it for delivery through the network. If your data is too large for a single frame, the Transport layer breaks it up into smaller pieces and assigns *sequence numbers*. Sequence numbers allow the Transport layer on the receiving system to reassemble the data into its original content. While the Data-Link layer performs a CRC check on all frames, the Transport layer can act as a backup check to insure that all the data was received and is usable.

Examples of Transport layer functionality would be IP's Transmission Control Protocol (TCP), User Datagram Protocol (UDP), IPX's Sequence Packet Exchange (SPX), and AppleTalk's AppleTalk Transaction Protocol (ATP). Note that these specifications also have components that would be considered part of the Session layer, as well.

 NOTE Transport layer functionality is discussed further in the "Transport Layer Services" section of this chapter.

Layer 5: The Session Layer

The *Session layer* deals with establishing and maintaining a connection between two or more systems. It insures that a query for a specific type of service is made correctly. For example, if you try to access a system with your Web browser, the Session layers on both systems work together to insure you receive HTML pages and not e-mail. If a system is running multiple network applications, it is up to the Session layer to keep these communications orderly and to insure that incoming data is directed to the correct application.

Layer 6: The Presentation Layer

The *Presentation layer* insures that data is received in a format that is usable to applications running on the system. For example, if you are communicating over the Internet using encrypted communications, the Presentation layer would be responsible for encrypting and decrypting this information. Most Web browsers support this kind of functionality for performing financial transactions over the Internet. Data and language translations also occur at this level.

Layer 7: The Application Layer

The label *Application layer* is a bit misleading, because this term does not describe the actual program that a user may be running on his system. Rather, this is the layer that is responsible for determining when access to network resources is required. For example, Microsoft Word does not function at the Application layer of the OSI model. If a user tries to retrieve a document from her home directory on a server, however, the Application layer networking software is responsible for delivering her request to the remote system.

NOTE In geek lingo, the layers are *numbered* in the order I've described them. If I were to state that switches function at layer 2 of the OSI model, you would interpret this to mean that switches work within the guidelines provided by the Data-Link layer of the OSI model.

How the OSI Model Works

When data is transmitted between systems, it is the job of each OSI layer to communicate with

- The layer above it
- The layer below it
- The adjacent layer on the remote system

For example, the Network layer on a transmitting host should be able to communicate with its Data-Link and Transport layer counterparts. It should also be able to communicate with the Network layer on the remote system.

Let's look at an example to see how these layers work together. Assume you're using your word processor program, and you want to retrieve a file called `resume.txt` from your home directory on a remote server. The networking software running on your system would react similarly to the description that follows.

Formulating a File Request

The Application layer detects that you are requesting information from a remote file system. It formulates a request to that system that `resume.txt` should be read from disk. Once it has created this request, the Application layer passes the request to the Presentation layer for further processing.

The Presentation layer determines whether it needs to encrypt this request or perform any type of data translation. Once this has been determined and completed, the Presentation layer then adds any information it needs to pass along to the Presentation layer on the server and forwards the packet down to the Session layer.

The Session layer checks which application is requesting the information and verifies the service being requested from the server (file access). The Session layer adds information to the request to insure that the remote system knows how to handle this request. Then, it passes all this information along to the Transport layer.

The Transport layer insures that it has a reliable connection to the server and begins the process of breaking down all the information so that it can be packaged into frames. If more than one frame is required, the information is split up and each block of information is assigned a sequence number. These sequenced chunks of information are passed one at a time to the Network layer.

The Network layer receives the blocks of information from the Transport layer and adds the network address for both the local workstation and the server. This happens to each block before it is passed down to the Data-Link layer.

At the Data-Link layer, the blocks are packaged into individual frames. Note that all the information added by each of the previous layers (as well as the actual file request) must fit into the 46- to 1,500-byte data field of the Ethernet frame. This is shown in Figure 1.17. The Data-Link layer then adds a frame header, which consists of the source and destination MAC addresses, and uses this information (along with the contents of the data field) to create a CRC trailer. The Data-Link layer is then responsible for transmitting the frame according to the topology rules in use on the network. Depending on the topology, this could mean listening for a quiet moment on the network, waiting for a token, or waiting for a specific time division before transmitting the frame.

FIGURE 1.17

The location of each layer's information within our frame

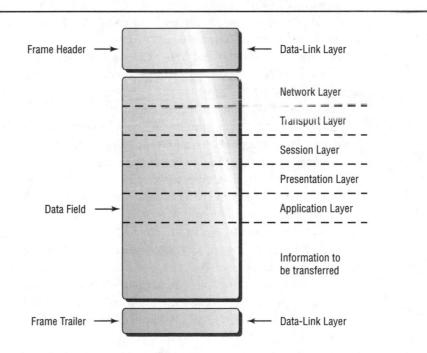

NOTE The Physical layer does not add any information to the frame.

The Physical layer is responsible for carrying the information from the source system to its destination. Because the Physical layer has no knowledge of frames, it is simply passing along the digital signal pulses transmitted by the Data-Link layer. The Physical layer is the medium by which a connection is made between the two systems; it is responsible for carrying the signal to the Data-Link layer on the remote system.

Our workstation has successfully formulated our data request ("Send me a copy of `resume.txt`") and transmitted it to the server. At this point, the server follows a similar process, but in reverse.

Receiving Data on the Server

The Data-Link layer on the server receives the transmitted frame. It notes that the MAC address in the destination field of the header is its own and recognizes that it needs to process this request. It performs a CRC check on the frame and compares the results to the value stored in the frame trailer. If these values match, the Data-Link layer strips off the header and trailer and passes the data field up to the Network layer. If the values do not match, the Data-Link layer sends a request to the source system asking that another frame be sent.

The Network layer on the server will analyze the information recorded by the Network layer on the workstation. It will note that the destination software address is its own. Once this analysis is complete, the Network layer removes information related to this level and passes the remainder up to the Transport layer.

The Transport layer receives the information and analyzes the information recorded by the Transport layer on the workstation. If it finds that packet sequencing was used, it will queue any information it receives until all the data has been received. If any of the data is missing, the Transport layer will use the sequence information to formulate a reply to the workstation, requesting that this piece of data be sent again. Once all the data has been received, the Transport layer will strip out any transport information and pass the full request up to the Session layer.

The Session layer will receive the information and verify that it is from a valid connection. If the check is positive, the Session layer strips out any session information and passes the request up to Presentation layer.

The Presentation layer receives the frame and analyzes the information recorded by the Presentation layer on the workstation. It then performs any translation or decryption required. Once translation or decryption has been completed, it strips out the Presentation layer information and passes the request up to the Application layer.

The Application layer insures that the correct process running on the server receives the request for data. Because this is a file request, it is passed to whichever process is responsible for access to the file system.

This process then reads the requested file and passes the information back to the Application layer. At this point, the entire process of passing the information through each of the layers would repeat. If you're amazed that the requested file is retrievable in anything less than a standard coffee break, then you have a pretty good idea of the magnitude of what happens when you request a simple file.

Cisco Routers and the OSI Model

Since a router controls traffic at the Network layer, it is considered an OSI layer 3 device. A Cisco router does offer, however, some higher-level services. For example, a Cisco router can control traffic flow using information contained in the Transport and Session layers. You can also use Telnet to remotely access the router. Telnet would be considered a function of layer 7 on the OSI model.

 NOTE While a router is predominately a layer 3 device, do not forget about the additional functionality that has been included. This will become especially important when it comes time to focus on security.

Transport Layer Services

Now we can get our information from point A to point B, regardless of whether the systems are located on the same logical network. This raises the question, "Once we get there, how do we carry on a proper conversation?" This is where the Transport layer comes in.

The Transport layer is where we begin to set down the rules of communication etiquette. It's not enough that we can get this information from one system to another; we also have to insure that both systems are operating at the same level of decorum.

As an analogy, let's say you pull up to the finest restaurant in the city in your GMC Pacer and proceed to the front door donning your best set of leather chaps, Harley jacket, and bandanna. Once inside, you greet the maitre d' by stating, "Yo, wimp, gimme a table and some grub, NOW!" Surprisingly, you're escorted out of the restaurant at gunpoint. What went wrong? Why, you used improper etiquette, of course. Everyone knows the correct term is not "grub" but "escargots."

You can avoid such verbal breakdown, as well as those in network communications, by insuring that all parties involved are conversing at the same level of etiquette. There are two forms of network communication etiquette:

- Connection-oriented
- Connectionless

Connection-Oriented Communication

A *connection-oriented communication* exchanges control information, called a *handshake*, before transmitting data. The Transport layer uses the handshake to insure that the destination system is ready to receive information. A connection-oriented exchange will also insure that data is transmitted and received in its original order.

Modems are heavy users of connection-oriented communications, as they need to negotiate a connection speed before sending any information. In networking, this functionality is accomplished through the use of a Transport layer field, which is referred to as a *flag* in the IP and AT world, or as the *connection control field* under IPX. Only connection-oriented communications use these fields. When IP is the underlying routing protocol, TCP is used to create connection-oriented communications. IPX uses SPX, and AppleTalk uses ATP to provide this functionality. As a communication session is started, the Application layer (not necessarily the program you are using) will specify whether it needs to use a connection-oriented protocol. Telnet is just such an application. When a Telnet session is started, the Application layer will request TCP as its transport service to better insure reliability of the connection. Let's look at how this session is established to see how a handshake works.

The TCP Three-Packet Handshake

At your workstation, you type in **telnet thor.foobar.com** to establish a remote connection to that system. As the request is passed down through the Transport layer, TCP is selected to connect the two systems so that a connection-oriented communication can be established. The Transport layer sets the synchronization (SYN) flag to 1 and leaves all other flags at 0. IP uses multiple flag fields and uses the binary system to set values. This means that the only possible values of an IP flag are 1 and 0. IPX and AT use a hexadecimal value, as their frames only contain one flag field. This allows the one field to contain more than two values.

By setting SYN to 1 and all other fields to 0, you let the system on the other end (`thor.foobar.com`) know that you wish to establish a new communication session with the system. This request is then passed down the remaining OSI layers, across the wire to the remote system, and then up through its OSI layers.

If the Telnet service is available on the remote system, the request is acknowledged and sent back down the stack until it reaches the Transport layer. The Transport layer then sets the SYN flag to 1 as did the originating system, but it will also set the acknowledgment (ACK) flag to 1, as well. This lets the originating system know that its transmission was received and that it's OK to send data. The request is then passed down the stack and over the wire back to the original system.

The original system then sets the SYN flag to 0 and the ACK flag to 1 and transfers this frame back to Thor. This lets Thor know, "I'm acknowledging your acknowledgment and I'm about to send data." At this point data is transferred, with each system required to acknowledge each packet it receives. Figure 1.18 shows a Telnet session from the system Loki to the system Thor. Each line represents a different frame that has been transmitted from one system to the other. Source and destination systems are identified, as well as some summary information about the frame. Notice that the first three frames are identified as TCP frames, not Telnet, and that they perform the handshaking described above. Once TCP establishes the connection-oriented connection, Telnet can step in to transfer the data required. The TCP frames that appear later in the conversation are for acknowledgment purposes. Remember that with a connection-oriented protocol, every frame must be acknowledged. If the frame was a request for information, the reply can be in the form of delivering the requested information.

FIGURE 1.18

An example of a connection-oriented communication

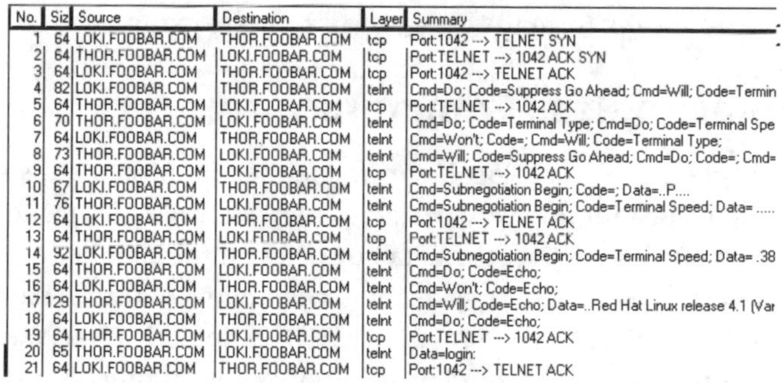

No.	Siz	Source	Destination	Layer	Summary
1	64	LOKI.FOOBAR.COM	THOR.FOOBAR.COM	tcp	Port:1042 ---> TELNET SYN
2	64	THOR.FOOBAR.COM	LOKI.FOOBAR.COM	tcp	Port:TELNET ---> 1042 ACK SYN
3	64	LOKI.FOOBAR.COM	THOR.FOOBAR.COM	tcp	Port:1042 ---> TELNET ACK
4	82	LOKI.FOOBAR.COM	THOR.FOOBAR.COM	telnt	Cmd=Do; Code=Suppress Go Ahead; Cmd=Will; Code=Termin
5	64	THOR.FOOBAR.COM	LOKI.FOOBAR.COM	tcp	Port:TELNET ---> 1042 ACK
6	70	THOR.FOOBAR.COM	LOKI.FOOBAR.COM	telnt	Cmd=Do; Code=Terminal Type; Cmd=Do; Code=Terminal Spe
7	64	LOKI.FOOBAR.COM	THOR.FOOBAR.COM	telnt	Cmd=Won't; Code=; Cmd=Will; Code=Terminal Type;
8	73	THOR.FOOBAR.COM	LOKI.FOOBAR.COM	telnt	Cmd=Will; Code=Suppress Go Ahead; Cmd=Do; Code=; Cmd=
9	64	THOR.FOOBAR.COM	LOKI.FOOBAR.COM	tcp	Port:TELNET ---> 1042 ACK
10	67	LOKI.FOOBAR.COM	THOR.FOOBAR.COM	telnt	Cmd=Subnegotiation Begin; Code=; Data=..P....
11	76	THOR.FOOBAR.COM	LOKI.FOOBAR.COM	telnt	Cmd=Subnegotiation Begin; Code=Terminal Speed; Data= .....
12	64	LOKI.FOOBAR.COM	THOR.FOOBAR.COM	tcp	Port:1042 ---> TELNET ACK
13	64	THOR.FOOBAR.COM	LOKI.FOOBAR.COM	top	Port:TELNET ---> 1042 ACK
14	92	LOKI.FOOBAR.COM	THOR.FOOBAR.COM	telnt	Cmd=Subnegotiation Begin; Code=Terminal Speed; Data= .38
15	64	LOKI.FOOBAR.COM	THOR.FOOBAR.COM	telnt	Cmd=Do; Code=Echo;
16	64	LOKI.FOOBAR.COM	THOR.FOOBAR.COM	telnt	Cmd=Won't; Code=Echo;
17	129	THOR.FOOBAR.COM	LOKI.FOOBAR.COM	telnt	Cmd=Will; Code=Echo; Data=..Red Hat Linux release 4.1 (Var
18	64	LOKI.FOOBAR.COM	THOR.FOOBAR.COM	telnt	Cmd=Do; Code=Echo;
19	64	THOR.FOOBAR.COM	LOKI.FOOBAR.COM	tcp	Port:TELNET ---> 1042 ACK
20	65	THOR.FOOBAR.COM	LOKI.FOOBAR.COM	telnt	Data=login:
21	64	LOKI.FOOBAR.COM	THOR.FOOBAR.COM	tcp	Port:1042 ---> TELNET ACK

A Connection-Oriented Analogy

In case you're still a bit fuzzy on handshaking and connection-oriented communications, let's look at an analogy. Let's say you call a friend to inform him you'll be having a network Quake party on Saturday night and that he should come by with his laptop. You follow these steps:

- You dial your friend's phone number (SYN=1, ACK=0).
- Your friend answers the phone and says, "Hello" (SYN=1, ACK=1).
- You reply by saying, "Hi Fred, this is Dave" (SYN=0, ACK=1).

You would then proceed to transfer your data about your upcoming party. Every time you pause, your friend would either transfer back information ("Yes, I'm free Saturday night") or send some form of acknowledgment (ACK) to let you know he has not yet hung up.

When the conversation is complete, you would both tear down the connection by saying goodbye, which is a handshake to let each other know that the conversation is complete and that it's OK to hang up the phone.

The purpose of connection-oriented communications is simple. They provide a reliable communication session when the underlying layers may be considered less than stable. Insuring reliable connectivity at the Transport layer helps to speed up communication when data becomes lost. This is because the data does not have to be passed all the way up to the Application layer before a retransmission frame is created and sent. While this is important in modem communications, where a small amount of noise or a crossed line can kill a communication session, it is not as useful with network-based communication. TCP and SPX originate from the days when the Physical and Data-Link layers could not always be relied on to successfully transmit information. These days, this is less of a concern because reliability has increased dramatically from the earlier years of networking.

Connectionless Communication

A *connectionless* protocol requires neither an initial handshake nor that acknowledgments be sent for every packet. When you use a connectionless transport, it makes its best effort to deliver the data but relies on the stability of the underlying layers, as well as Application layer acknowledgments, to insure that the data is delivered reliably. IP's User Datagram Protocol (UDP) and IPX's NetWare Core Protocol (NCP) are examples of connectionless transports. Both protocols rely on connectionless communications to transfer routing and server information, as well. Although AppleTalk does not utilize any connectionless communications for creating data sessions, AppleTalk does use connectionless communications when advertising servers with its Name Binding Protocol (NBP).

NOTE Broadcasts are always transmitted using a connectionless transport.

A Connectionless Example

As an example of connectionless communications, check out the *Network File System* (NFS) session in Figure 1.19. NFS is a service that allows file sharing over IP. Its older versions used UDP as the underlying transport protocol. Note that all data acknowledgments are in the form of a request for additional information. The destination system (Thor) assumes that the last packet was received if the source system (Loki) requests additional information. Conversely, if Loki does not receive a reply from Thor for information it has requested, NFS takes care of requesting the information again. As long as you have a stable connection that does not require a large number of retransmissions, this is a very efficient method of communicating because it does not generate unnecessary acknowledgments.

FIGURE 1.19

NFS uses UDP to create a connectionless session.

No.	Size	Source	Destination	Layer	Summary
1	198	LOKI.FOOBAR.COM	THOR.FOOBAR.COM	nfs	Call Lookup ???/games.tar.gz
2	174	THOR.FOOBAR.COM	LOKI.FOOBAR.COM	nfs	Reply Lookup for games.tar.gz
3	182	LOKI.FOOBAR.COM	THOR.FOOBAR.COM	nfs	Call Get File Attributes for games.tar.gz
4	142	THOR.FOOBAR.COM	LOKI.FOOBAR.COM	nfs	Reply Get File Attributes
5	154	LOKI.FOOBAR.COM	THOR.FOOBAR.COM	nfs	Call Read From File games.tar.gz; Offset 0, 1024 bytes
6	1,170	THOR.FOOBAR.COM	LOKI.FOOBAR.COM	nfs	Reply Read From File; 1024 bytes
7	194	LOKI.FOOBAR.COM	THOR.FOOBAR.COM	nfs	Call Read From File games.tar.gz; Offset 1024; 1024 bytes
8	1,170	THOR.FOOBAR.COM	LOKI.FOOBAR.COM	nfs	Reply Read From File; 1024 bytes
9	194	LOKI.FOOBAR.COM	THOR.FOOBAR.COM	nfs	Call Read From File games.tar.gz; Offset 2048; 1024 bytes
10	1,170	THOR.FOOBAR.COM	LOKI.FOOBAR.COM	nfs	Reply Read From File; 1024 bytes
11	194	LOKI.FOOBAR.COM	THOR.FOOBAR.COM	nfs	Call Read From File games.tar.gz; Offset 3072; 1024 bytes
12	1,170	THOR.FOOBAR.COM	LOKI.FOOBAR.COM	nfs	Reply Read From File; 1024 bytes
13	194	LOKI.FOOBAR.COM	THOR.FOOBAR.COM	nfs	Call Read From File games.tar.gz; Offset 4096; 1024 bytes
14	1,170	THOR.FOOBAR.COM	LOKI.FOOBAR.COM	nfs	Reply Read From File; 1024 bytes
15	194	LOKI.FOOBAR.COM	THOR.FOOBAR.COM	nfs	Call Read From File games.tar.gz; Offset 5120; 1024 bytes
16	1,170	THOR.FOOBAR.COM	LOKI.FOOBAR.COM	nfs	Reply Read From File; 1024 bytes
17	194	LOKI.FOOBAR.COM	THOR.FOOBAR.COM	nfs	Call Read From File games.tar.gz; Offset 6144; 1024 bytes
18	1,170	THOR.FOOBAR.COM	LOKI.FOOBAR.COM	nfs	Reply Read From File; 1024 bytes
19	194	LOKI.FOOBAR.COM	THOR.FOOBAR.COM	nfs	Call Read From File games.tar.gz; Offset 7168; 1024 bytes
20	1,170	THOR.FOOBAR.COM	LOKI.FOOBAR.COM	nfs	Reply Read From File; 1024 bytes
21	194	LOKI.FOOBAR.COM	THOR.FOOBAR.COM	nfs	Call Read From File games.tar.gz; Offset 8192; 1024 bytes
22	1,170	THOR.FOOBAR.COM	LOKI.FOOBAR.COM	nfs	Reply Read From File; 1024 bytes
23	194	LOKI.FOOBAR.COM	THOR.FOOBAR.COM	nfs	Call Read From File games.tar.gz; Offset 9216; 1024 bytes

A Connectionless Analogy

Let's look at another analogy to see how this type of communication differs from the connection-oriented one described earlier. Again, let's say you call Fred to inform him you'll be having a network Quake party on Saturday night and that he should come by with his laptop. You call Fred's number, but this time you get his answering machine. You leave a detailed message indicating when the party will take place and what he should bring. Unlike the first call, which Fred himself answered, you are now relying on

- Your ability to dial the correct phone number, as you did not reach your friend to confirm that this number was in fact his

- The fact that the phone company did not drop your phone connection in the middle of your message (answering machines do not ACK—unless, of course, you talk until the beep cuts you off)

- The answering machine's proper recording of the message—without eating the tape

- The ability of Fred's cat to discern between the tape and a ball of yarn

- The absence of a power failure (which would cause the machine to lose the message)

- Fred's retrieval of this message between the time of your call and the date of the party

As you can see, you have no real confirmation that your friend will actually receive the message. You are counting on the power company, the answering machine, and so on, to enable Fred to receive your message in a timely manner. If you wanted to insure the reliability of this data transmission, you could send an Application layer acknowledgment request in the form of "Please RSVP by Thursday." If you did not get a response by then, you could try transmitting the data again.

The benefit of a connectionless protocol is that it allows for a bit more freedom when determining how nitpicky the systems must be to insure proper data delivery. As you will find in our discussion of IPX, this can be leveraged so that many frames of useful information can be sent before an acknowledgment of their receipt is required.

Connection-Oriented vs. Connectionless

So which is a better transport to use? Unfortunately, the answer is whichever one your Application layer specifies. If Telnet wants TCP, you cannot force it to use UDP. Even if you could, the receiving system would be expecting a TCP handshake.

When a network program is initially coded, it is up to the programmers to choose which transport the program will support. Most applications today use a connection-oriented transport. There are a couple of reasons for this.

The first reason involves conditions at the time of development. Telnet has been around for so long that TCP was the appropriate transport at the time of development. Networking was still a very unstable animal back then. Trying to switch over to

UDP now is possible but would cause a complete mess as some systems are upgraded before others.

The other reason is a misunderstanding about when a connection-oriented protocol is required. A programmer who is faced with using a *reliable* or an *unreliable* transport for moving data will usually choose the former—without regard as to how inefficient this may make the communication session. Many programmers simply look at the term "unreliable" and shy away. If the programmer does not, certainly her pointy-haired boss will.

Summary

In this chapter, we covered the basics of network communication. We discussed the principles of transmission as well as how information gets transmitted from one system to another. We also discussed how the OSI model can help to simplify the somewhat complex process of network communication.

In the next chapter, we will take a closer look at logical topologies. We will look at the available options for both LAN and WAN applications, and how to choose the right topology for your specific needs.

CHAPTER 2

Understanding Logical Topologies

I n this chapter, we will discuss the different logical topologies available for hooking up your network. These topologies are broken up into two categories:

- Those used for connecting a local area network (LAN)
- Those used for connecting a wide area network (WAN)

We will start by looking at available LAN options.

Local Area Network Topologies

Local area network (LAN) topologies are network configurations that are confined to a small area, such as a single physical location. LAN topologies are focused on delivering data to many systems within a small geographical area.

Ethernet Networks

Ethernet is by far the most popular networking topology. Its ability to support a wide range of cable types, low-cost hardware, and plug-and-play connectivity has caused it to find its way into more corporate and home networks than any other topology.

Ethernet's communication rules are called *Carrier Sense Multiple Access with Collision Detection* (CSMA/CD). This is a mouthful, but it's simple enough to interpret when you break it down:

Carrier Sense   All Ethernet stations are required to listen to the wire if they are not currently transmitting. By "listen," I mean that the station should be constantly monitoring the network to see if any other stations are currently sending data. By monitoring the transmissions of other stations, a station can tell if the network is open or in use. This way, the station does not just blindly transfer information and interfere with other stations. Being in a constant listening mode means that the station is ready when another station wants to send it data.

Multiple Access   More than two stations can be connected to the same network, and all stations are allowed to transmit whenever the network is free. As we discussed in Chapter 1, it is far more efficient to allow stations to transmit only when they need to than it is to assign each system a time block in which it is allowed to transmit. Multiple access also scales much more easily as you add more stations to the network.

Collision Detection   This answers the question, "What happens if two systems think the circuit is free and try to transmit data at the same time?" When two stations transmit simultaneously, a *collision* takes place. A collision is similar to RFI interference, and the resulting transmission becomes mangled and useless for carrying data. As a station transmits data, it watches the signal on the wire to insure that what is received is identical to what is being transmitted. If it detects a difference in signaling, the workstation assumes that a collision has taken place. The station will back off, wait for a random period of time, and then retransmit.

Each station is responsible for determining its own random waiting period before retransmission. This helps to insure that each station is waiting for a different period of time, avoiding another collision. In the unlikely event that a second collision does occur (that is, the station backs off but is again involved in a collision), each station is required to double its waiting period before trying again. When two or more consecutive collisions take place, it is called a *multiple collision*.

While collisions are a normal part of Ethernet communications and are expected to happen from time to time, multiple collisions can be a sign that there is a problem with the network (for example, that there is a bad network card or that the network is carrying too much traffic). If a station is involved in 15 consecutive collisions, it will give up trying to transmit the frame and will return an error to the application that was attempting to transmit data.

If you were to chart CSMA/CD, it would look something like Figure 2.1.

 NOTE   A *collision domain* is a collection of systems that have the potential to collide with each other's transmissions.

FIGURE 2.1

Flowchart of Ethernet communication rules

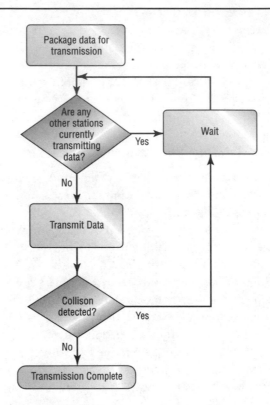

Half Duplex

Collisions are a by-product of the fact that most network communications take place in a *half-duplex* mode. This means that while any one system is transmitting data, every other system must be in a listening mode. This is like Citizens Band (CB) radio communications—whenever one person is communicating, that person effectively "owns" the channel. If another individual tries to transmit at the same time, the two signals will interfere with each other. In order for a conversation to take place, everyone must communicate in an orderly fashion by taking turns. Only one person can transmit at any given time.

Full Duplex

Full duplex allows communications to take place in both directions simultaneously. A telephone conversation is an example of a full-duplex communication. Both parties can send information at the same time (although the louder person's information usually comes through more clearly). The catch to full duplex is that only two systems can be attached to any one logical segment. Still, full duplex can potentially double the amount of data a system can process. With full duplex, a server with a 10Mbps Ethernet connection has the potential to process 20Mbps of information (transmitting 10Mbps and receiving 10Mbps). The operative word here is "potential," because it is a rare situation that would allow a full-duplex connection to reach full speed in both directions. I'll cover this in greater detail later in Chapter 4.

10Mb Ethernet

10Mb Ethernet is the oldest member of the Ethernet family. Developed in the late 1970s by Xerox, it later evolved into the IEEE specification 802.3 (pronounced *eight oh two dot three*). Its flexibility, high transmission rate (at the time, anyway), and nonproprietary nature quickly made it the networking topology of choice for many network administrators.

10Mb stands for the transmission speed of 10 megabits per second (Mbps). This means that 10Mb Ethernet is capable of transferring 10,000,000 bits (or 1,250,000 bytes) from one network station to another in a one-second period of time. This is under ideal conditions, however, and your mileage may vary. Note that 10Mb does not translate into a 10-megabyte (MB) transfer rate but rather to 1.25 megabytes per second (MBps). This confusion arises from the fact that some people refer to this topology as *10 Meg Ethernet*, which makes it sound as though the phrase refers to 10MB instead of 10Mb.

Measuring Throughput

The CSMA/CD nature of Ethernet means that most networks will begin to show a degradation in performance at 40–50 percent (4,000,000 to 5,000,000 bits per second) of maximum throughput. By the time 90-percent utilization is reached, response time is usually so slow that applications begin to time out. The percentage of maximum throughput is called the *utilization rate*. For example, if you were to take a measurement and note that 7,500,000 bits of data were passing by on the network, you could refer to this as a 75-percent utilization rate (7,500,000/10,000,000 × 100).

High utilization can be a bad thing. Every station must monitor the network for traffic before transmitting. The more traffic on the network, the longer a station has to wait before it can transmit its frame. This can make network response appear sluggish. Also, because more stations are trying to get their information out, there is an increased chance of collision. While collisions are a normal part of Ethernet transmissions, they slow down the transfer of information even more.

Another common measurement of throughput is *frame rate*, or the number of frames that pass from one station to another in a one-second period of time (frames per second, or fps). The relationship between frame rate and utilization is directly related to the size of the frames.

As I mentioned earlier, a legal Ethernet frame can be anywhere from 64 to 1,518 bytes in length. This means that a 10Mbps Ethernet segment experiencing 100-percent utilization of 1,518 byte frames would have a frame rate of approximately 813fps. Written out mathematically, it would look something like this:

```
(10,000,000/8)/(1,518 + 8 + 12) = 813fps
```

- The (10,000,000/8) portion converts the maximum transfer rate in bits to bytes. This way, the unit of measure is consistent throughout the formula, because our frame size is in bytes, as well.

- 1,518 is the size of the frame as stated in our example.

- We add 8 to this because of the preamble. As I mentioned in Chapter 1, the preamble is technically not considered part of the frame, but it does use up bandwidth on our media.

- The 12 is due to station listening time. As you saw earlier, CSMA/CD requires each station to monitor the network for other transmitting stations before sending data.

The preamble and the listening time would be considered overhead on this circuit. They represent 20 bytes' worth of bandwidth that is lost every time a packet is transmitted. You can see a breakdown of maximum fps based on frame size in Table 2.1.

TABLE 2.1: FRAME RATE BASED ON PACKET SIZE	
Frame Size in Bytes	**Number of Frames at 100-Percent Utilization**
64	14,881
256	4,529
512	2,350
1,024	1,197
1,518	813

This breakdown brings up an interesting question: Which is more efficient, many small frames or fewer larger ones? As you saw earlier, transmitting Ethernet frames requires a certain amount of overhead because of listening time and the preamble. If we multiply the size of the data field (frame size minus the header and FCS) by the number of frames transmitted, we can get a rough idea of what our potential throughput of raw data would be, as you can see in Table 2.2.

TABLE 2.2: RAW TRANSFER RATE BASED ON PACKET SIZE

Data Field Size Times Frame Rate	Bytes of Data per Second
46 × 14,881	684,526
238 × 4,529	1,077,902
494 × 2,350	1,160,900
1,006 × 1,197	1,276,002
1,500 × 813	1,219,500

As you can see, the frame size can make a dramatic difference in the amount of information the network is capable of transferring. Using the largest possible frame size, we can move 1.2 megabytes per second of data along the network. At the smallest frame size, this transfer rate is cut almost in half, to 685 kilobytes per second (KBps).

 NOTE Some of the factors that go into controlling a network's average frame size are protocol selection and regulating the amount of broadcast traffic. A Cisco router, by default, filters out broadcasts from being propagated across a network.

So which is a better measuring stick of network health: frame rate or utilization? While both are important, utilization is the meter that tells you how much of your bandwidth is currently in use, and the percentage of bandwidth in use dictates whether a network responds quickly to requests or appears to slow down application speed. The key is the frame size. I've seen networks running at 1,100fps that appear to crawl, while others sustain 3,000 or more fps with no noticeable performance degradation. When utilization levels consistently range from 30 percent to 50 percent, it may be time to further segment the network or look to faster topologies like 100Mb Ethernet.

Appropriate Applications

10Mb Ethernet is appropriate for the following applications:

Small office environments   If your environment is, say, a small law office or accounting firm, then 10Mb Ethernet may be all you need. The average workstation bus is only capable of processing data at a rate of 3Mbps to 5Mbps, so in light-traffic environments, the network is definitely not the performance gate.

 TIP The *performance gate* of a system is considered to be that portion of the configuration that supports the lowest level of throughput. For example, if you have two computers that can process data at 20Mb, and they are connected by a network that supports only 10Mb communications, the network would be the performance gate because it is capable of processing the least amount of data.

Workstation connections   If you have a large environment (100 or more nodes), 10Mb Ethernet may still be sufficient for workstation connection. There are devices available that allow you to run your servers on one topology (such as 100Mb Ethernet) and your workstations on another. This type of configuration is usually sufficient when you are dealing with simple word processing and spreadsheet files, but there are more nodes doing it. If you have a few workstations with higher data transfer needs (such as graphics development), they can be placed on the faster topology, as well.

Topology Rules

Table 2.3 summarizes the topology rules for 10Mb Ethernet.

TABLE 2.3: TOPOLOGY RULES FOR 10Mb ETHERNET

Item	Rules
Maximum cable lengths	Thinnet: 600 ft
	Twisted pair: 325 ft
	Fiber: 3,000 ft
Minimum cable lengths	Thinnet: 1.5 ft

Continued ▶

TABLE 2.3: TOPOLOGY RULES FOR 10Mb ETHERNET (CONTINUED)	
Item	**Rules**
Maximum number of stations per cable	Thinnet: 30 Twisted pair: 2 Fiber: 2
Maximum number of stations per logical network	1,024
Maximum number of segments	5 segments, only three of which are populated
Maximum overall length of logical network	3,000 ft

100Mb Ethernet

100Mb Ethernet is the natural progression from 10Mb Ethernet. Communication is still CSMA/CD, only faster. The time between digital pulses is condensed, and the time a system is required to wait and listen is shorter. The result is a tenfold increase in throughput. Because 100Mb Ethernet is an extension of 10Mb Ethernet, the IEEE simply extended the original Ethernet specification and dubbed this topology IEEE 802.3u. The *u* is used for revision control and indicates that this specification has simply been appended to the original 802.3 specification.

There are currently two implementations of 100Mb Ethernet:

- 100Tx
- 100T4

100Tx is the older of the two and by far the more widely used. 100T4 has the additional benefit of working with CAT3 twisted-pair cabling, while 100Tx requires CAT5.

 WARNING 100Tx and 100T4 are not directly compatible: For example, you cannot use 100T4 network cards with a 100Tx hub and expect them to work. When purchasing hardware for a 100Mb Ethernet network, make sure you know what you're getting.

The improvements offered by 100Mb Ethernet do not come without a price, however. The shorter transmission times mean that the overall cable lengths for 100Mb Ethernet must be shorter than for 10Mb Ethernet.

Appropriate Applications

The appropriate applications for 100Mb Ethernet are the following:

High-end workstations   If your environment includes end users who process large graphic files or compile code over the network, 100Mb Ethernet may be just the trick to improve performance. These stations usually have a high-performance bus that allows them to process data at a rate of 10Mb to 20Mb. While such data rates would overwhelm 10Mb Ethernet, 100Mb gives a bit more breathing room. The additional bandwidth may be just the thing to improve network response time.

 WARNING   A word of caution: Some of the newer desktop machines use the same technology as server-class machines. A busy 100Mb segment can easily move the performance gate from the network to the server itself. As a result, the server cannot keep up with the rate of file requests and responds by crashing or by losing data. You will need to insure that your server is up to the task of servicing a 100Mb network. RAID level 5 (RAID is short for *Redundant Array of Inexpensive Disks*) and other *go fast* technologies go a long way toward insuring that a server will remain stable at these higher data rates.

Backbones and server connections   As I mentioned in the section on 10Mb Ethernet, a larger environment (100 or more nodes) may benefit from leaving the user community at 10Mb but upgrading the servers to 100Mb. Busy, non-populated segments that connect office floors or departments could benefit from the performance increase, as well.

Topology Rules

Table 2.4 shows the topology rules for 100Mb Ethernet.

TABLE 2.4: TOPOLOGY RULES FOR 100Mb ETHERNET

Item	Rules
Maximum cable lengths	Twisted pair: 325 ft
	Fiber: 650 ft
Minimum cable lengths	None
Maximum number of stations per cable	Twisted pair: 2
	Fiber: 2

Continued ▶

TABLE 2.4: TOPOLOGY RULES FOR 100Mb ETHERNET (CONTINUED)	
Item	**Rules**
Maximum number of stations per logical network	1,024
Maximum number of segments	2
Maximum overall length of logical network	650 ft

1Gbps Ethernet

Network transmission speeds are definitely on the rise. It was not until June of 1995 that the IEEE gave its full blessing to the final specification of 100Mb Ethernet. By July of 1996, the IEEE was back in committee appointing a task force to create specifications for 1Gbps Ethernet. This task force has been dubbed 802.3z, as the specification is expected to simply be a natural progression from the original Ethernet standards. This new specification has received phenomenal support: As of this writing, more than 80 organizations have joined the Gigabit Ethernet Alliance. The "need for speed" has truly taken hold.

The 1Gbps Ethernet specification is 10 times faster than 100Mb Ethernet and is meant to be in direct competition with Asynchronous Transfer Mode (ATM) on local area networks. ATM, which has been in development for a number of years, currently has the potential of supporting data rates up to 622Mb. Lack of agreement between vendors has delayed approval of final specifications for ATM, so it appears that 1Gbps Ethernet may become a fully integrated topology before ATM.

Even though 1Gbps Ethernet appears to be following in the footsteps of its predecessors, there is one change of focus. While 10Mb and 100Mb Ethernet have been implemented mostly on twisted-pair cabling, 1Gbps Ethernet is made to run over fiber. Concessions have been made to leverage existing twisted-pair cable runs from wiring closets out to the desktop, but the majority of the cabling will need to be fiber.

The reasoning for this is twofold:

- First, the current specification has adopted the communication properties of Fiber Channel, which was developed for fiber optic cable.

- Second, propagation delay is a factor. 1Gbps Ethernet represents a 100× increase in transmission speed over 10Mb Ethernet. This means that it can tolerate only a minimal amount of propagation. Fiber is a perfect mate for this technology, as its propagation delay is very close to zero.

Appropriate Applications

The best fit for 1Gb Ethernet is a backbone connection on medium to large networks. This is especially true when the desktop systems are already running at 100Mb. A small number of 1Gb Ethernet NICs have been produced, which are designed to run in high-end servers.

 WARNING   My earlier cautions about making sure that servers are up to handling this high rate of data apply even more with 1Gb transmission speeds. Only a top-of-the-line server specifically designed for this rate of data processing can ever hope to keep up in a busy environment.

Topology Rules

These rules are subject to change as work continues on the 802.3z specification. Changes and improvements may be made over time.

Table 2.5 shows the topology rules for Gigabit Ethernet.

TABLE 2.5: TOPOLOGY RULES FOR GIGABIT ETHERNET	
Item	**Rules**
Maximum cable lengths	Fiber: 1,640 ft
	Twisted pair: Currently 82 ft, possibly increasing to 325 ft later
Minimum cable lengths	None
Maximum number of stations per cable	Twisted pair: 2
	Fiber: 2
Maximum number of stations per logical network	Still under development; should be 1,024
Maximum number of segments	Still under development; should be 1 or 2
Maximum overall length of logical network	Will be media dependent

This concludes our discussion of purely Ethernet-based topologies. Next, we will explore other options, besides CSMA/CD, that are available for constructing a network topology.

FDDI

Fiber Distributed Data Interface (FDDI) was the first of the popular networking topologies to reach 100Mb throughput. For a number of years, if you needed 100Mb performance, FDDI was the only way to go. While other topologies have caught up in raw throughput, FDDI offers benefits in network stability and fault tolerance that still make it a good choice. While the transmission medium of choice for FDDI is fiber, the specification also makes concessions for running CAT5 out to the desktop.

FDDI supports two physical topologies: ring and star. Ring is far more widely implemented than star because it allows the use of FDDI's fault-tolerant features. FDDI's ring topology is similar to IBM's legacy Token Ring topology, but with an additional ring that has been added for redundancy. This second ring is normally dormant and is only used if a failure occurs in the primary ring.

Figure 2.2 shows FDDI networks with star and ring physical topologies. As a ring, FDDI can recover from a cable failure by activating the secondary ring. This redundancy is lost when FDDI is implemented in a star topology or when the ring is operated in full-duplex mode.

FIGURE 2.2

An example of an FDDI network, including star and ring physical topologies

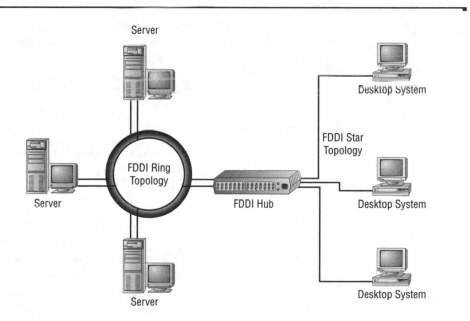

Token Passing

FDDI has also borrowed Token Ring's method of data transmission. A single frame, called a *token*, is passed around the ring from station to station. When a station has data to transmit, it grabs the token and transmits a frame of data in its place. This frame then travels around the ring until it is received by the destination node to which it was addressed. The destination station then makes a copy of the frame and continues to forward it along the ring, setting the Frame Copied Indicator (FCI) bit. When the station that originally transmitted the frame receives the frame back and sees that the FCI bit has been set, it assumes the transmission has been successful. It then removes the frame from the ring and transmits the token in its place. The next station wishing to transmit data will then grab the token and repeat the process.

Token communications have some inherent advantages over Ethernet. The first is the ability to support a larger frame size of 4,096 bytes. As you will recall from our discussion about frame size versus network utilization, the larger the average frame size, the more data that can be transmitted in a given period of time due to reduced overhead.

NOTE   Token passing is also a bit more orderly then Ethernet's CSMA/CD method of communication. It tends to perform better as higher utilization levels are achieved. This makes it an ideal choice when you are expecting to move very large data files over the network.

Dual-Attach Stations

You'll remember from our discussion on ring topologies in Chapter 1 that each station gets its output data port (Tx) connected to the input data port (Rx) of its downstream neighbor. This continues around the ring until the last station connects its Tx port to the Rx port of the first station.

This rule applies to FDDI topology, as well, except that an FDDI station will have a second set of transmit-and-receive ports for the second ring. On the second ring, the Rx port of a station connects to the Tx port of its downstream neighbor. This dual set of transmit-and-receive ports is why these stations are referred to as *dual-attach stations* (DAS). To avoid confusion, these ports are grouped by destination and labeled A and B. This yields four wires (two sets) to deal with instead of eight (four sets). When connecting DAS systems, you attach connection A to connection B of its downstream neighbor. This simplifies wiring and avoids cross-connecting the rings.

Figure 2.3 illustrates FDDI dual-attach stations. Note that each node connects to both rings in case of a failure.

An example of FDDI dual-attach stations

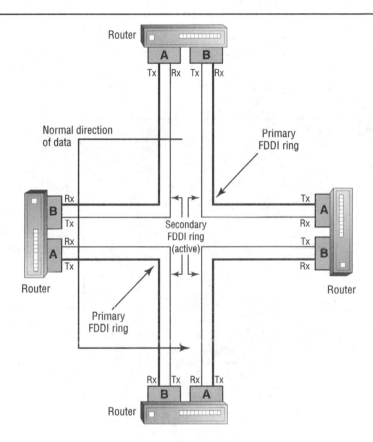

Stations are connected in this fashion to guard against cable or hardware failure. Let's assume that you have a cable failure between two of the routers shown in Figure 2.3. When this cable failure occurs, the system immediately downstream from the failure will quickly realize that it is no longer receiving data. It then begins to send out a special maintenance packet called a *beacon*. A beacon is the method used by token stations to inform other systems around the ring that it has detected a problem. A beacon frame is a system's way of saying, "Hey, I think there is a problem between me and my upstream neighbor, because I am no longer receiving data from him." The station would then initialize its connection on the secondary ring so that it would now send and receive data on connector A.

The beacon packet would continue to be forwarded until it reached the beaconing system's upstream neighbor. This upstream neighbor would then initialize its connection to the secondary ring by sending and receiving on connector B. This, in effect, isolates the problem area and returns normal connectivity. When the beaconing station begins to receive its own beacons, it ceases transmission, and ring operation returns to normal. The final transmission path would resemble the network shown in Figure 2.4. By using beacon frames, the systems on the network can determine the failure area and isolate it by activating the secondary ring.

FIGURE 2.4

How FDDI DAS stations recover from a cable failure

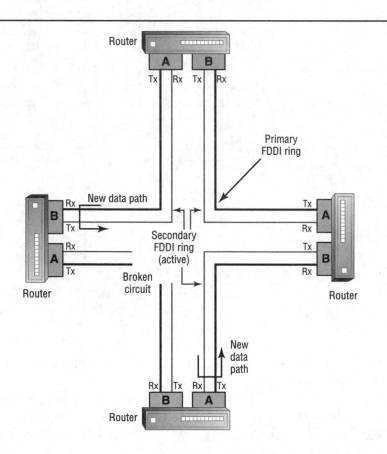

NOTE If this had in fact been a hardware failure caused by a fault in the upstream neighbor and that system was unable to initialize the secondary ring, the faulty system's upstream neighbor would have detected this and stepped in to close the ring. This would isolate the problem hardware but allow the rest of the network to continue to function.

The DAS stations would continue to monitor the faulty links until connectivity appears to be restored. If the link passes an integrity test, the primary ring returns to full operation, and the secondary ring again goes dormant. This type of network fault tolerance can be deemed critical in environments where connectivity must be maintained seven days a week, 24 hours a day (called *7 by 24 operation*). This functionality is what still makes FDDI the most fault-tolerant networking topology available today for local area networks.

If fault tolerance is not required, most FDDI hardware will allow you to simultaneously activate both the primary and secondary ring. This provides full duplex communication with a potential of 200Mb throughput. The tradeoff is that you lose fault tolerance.

One drawback to this dual-ring design is that distance specifications are half of what is usually supported by fiber cable. This is because when a ring fails, the effective ring size can double (because the effective ring size is the primary ring size plus the secondary ring size). However, given the exceptional distance specification of fiber cable, this is rarely a problem.

DAC and SAS

FDDI also supports a star topology for connecting systems that do not require this level of fault tolerance. Devices called *dual-attach concentrators* (DAC) are connected to the ring topology, providing multiple *single-attach station* (SAS) connections. SAS connections are typically used for end-user workstations. These stations are usually not deemed critical and can endure short periods of downtime due to cable or hardware failures. While DAS and DAC connections must be made with fiber, SAS connections can be fiber or category 5 twisted pair. Figure 2.5 shows a network using a mixture of DAS, DAC, and SAS connections. The ring topology is deployed in the area requiring fault tolerance (server connections), while the less critical workstations are connected as a star.

FIGURE 2.5

FDDI DAC connecting
SAS systems to
the ring

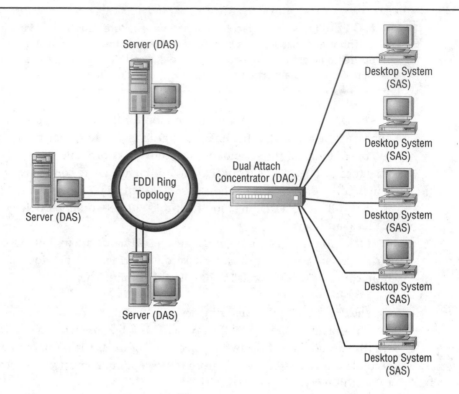

FDDI Drawbacks

Despite its fault tolerance and high efficiency in transferring data, FDDI has suffered from lack of deployment. This is partially due to the fact that equipment costs for an FDDI network are far more expensive than an Ethernet counterpart. For example, an FDDI network card will set you back $200 or more, while a top-of-the-line Ethernet card is no more than $75.

Since FDDI has not done well at gaining the interest of the networking community, there is little drive to further the specification. For example, while Ethernet has already been pushed up to 1Gb, there is no effort in the works to do the same with FDDI. This means that if you deploy FDDI on your network, you may end up with a technology that is incapable of keeping up with your growing bandwidth demands.

Appropriate Applications

The most appropriate applications for FDDI are

- Servers
- Backbones

Because of its high level of fault tolerance, FDDI is a wonderful fit for server rooms and for connecting workgroup clusters. Its resilience to cable and hardware failures makes for a stable environment.

FDDI has been around for a while, so you should have little trouble finding hardware vendors and support. Because it is a more efficient topology than Ethernet, it can keep up when connected to multiple 100Tx segments.

Topology Rules

Table 2.6 shows the topology rules for FDDI.

TABLE 2.6: TOPOLOGY RULES FOR FDDI

Item	Rules
Maximum cable lengths	CAT 5 twisted pair: 325 ft
	Fiber: 1.2 miles
Minimum cable lengths	None
Maximum number of stations per cable	Ring topology: 500
	Star: 2
Maximum number of stations per logical network	500
Maximum number of segments	Gated by performance
Maximum overall length of logical network	62 miles

ATM

Asynchronous Transfer Mode (ATM) is probably the most elusive and least understood of all network topologies. ATM was conceived in 1983 by AT&T Bell Labs, but it took nearly 10 years before an official forum was created to try to mature this technology into a production-quality topology. It then took the ATM forum another four years (until June, 1995) just to release its first specification for ATM LAN emulation (LANE). In November of 1996, the much anticipated LANE 2 was released, only to be found lacking much-needed features such as scalability and multiprotocol support. This spec was then revamped in February, 1999. To add insult to injury, some LANE 1–compliant hardware was incapable of supporting LANE 2. Pioneers of this slow-moving technology found themselves replacing some very expensive hardware just to stay current.

With this kind of a track record, why has ATM captured so much attention? Because ATM has the potential of providing high data rates and quality of service, as well as blurring the line between local and wide area networks.

Understanding ATM

ATM represents a significant change in network design. To start, ATM does not vary its frame size like Ethernet or token-based topologies. Instead, ATM uses a fixed packet size of 48 bytes (referred to as a *cell*) for all communications. This fixed size allows for a more predictable traffic rate than networks with variable-length packets. By regulating the number of packets that flow between connections, ATM can accurately predict and closely control bandwidth utilization. The drawback to this fixed packet size, of course, is increased overhead. As you saw in our discussion of 10Mb Ethernet, smaller packets mean a less efficient data transfer and more network bottlenecks. An ATM cell is roughly 3 percent of the size of a full Ethernet frame and 1 percent of the size of an FDDI frame.

To quantify this loss in performance, when 155Mb ATM is deployed on a LAN to handle normal network traffic (file access and printing, for example), it provides less throughput than 100Mb Ethernet. Although some of this loss is due to protocol translation (described below), a good portion of it is due to the smaller frame size.

Another significant difference is how ATM stations communicate with each other. While other topologies rely on upper-layer protocols like IPX and IP to route information between logical networks, ATM uses permanent virtual connections (PVCs) and switched virtual connections (SVCs) between communicating stations. *Virtual connections* (VCs) are logical communication channels between end stations—logical because this circuit is created along shared media that may also contain other virtual connections providing a circuit between other end stations. You can see this in Figure 2.6. Although the circuits must share available bandwidth along the media, communications are kept separate from each other through the use of connection identifiers. This is very similar to Frame Relay (discussed in the "Frame Relay/X.25" section of this chapter), but it is the complete opposite of Ethernet, where every station shares a single circuit along the media and is required to listen to packet transmissions between other stations.

FIGURE 2.6

Virtual connections through an ATM network

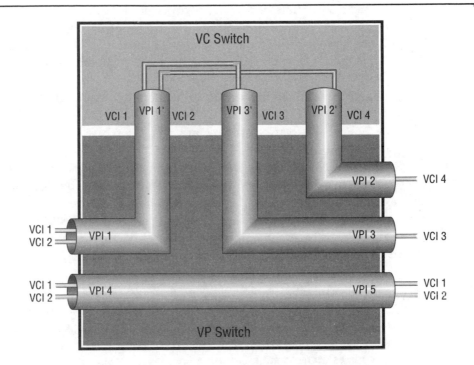

ATM is a connection-oriented topology. This means that a connection or VC circuit must be established between the source and destination stations before data transfer. Again, this is in contrast to other topologies like Ethernet, which simply transmit the data onto the wire and rely on networking hardware to route the information to its destination network. With ATM connectivity, devices on the network called *ATM switches* maintain tables with the identifications of all end stations. When a station needs to transmit data, it issues a maintenance packet called a *virtual path identifier* (VPI) that propagates out into the network, setting up a virtual connection between the two systems. The purpose of the VPI is to create a circuit-switched connection between the two systems and insure that each portion of the path along the way has enough available bandwidth to carry the signal. Once this circuit is complete, data transmission may begin.

 NOTE We'll discuss routing information between logical networks in greater detail in Chapter 6.

A big plus to this type of connectivity is quality of service (QoS). If the bandwidth demands of the application can be identified before setting up the virtual connection, the VPI can reserve the required bandwidth and only pick routes that can support the required transmission rate. In effect, this a form of automatic load balancing of the network.

This type of connectivity is nearly identical to the connectivity of the public telephone network (PTN). When you dial a telephone number, a signal similar to a VPI goes out over the network, setting up a connection between your phone and the phone at the number you just dialed. This is accomplished in that brief period of time between when you dial the number and when you hear that first ring. If there is a problem in a direct-line connection between you and the destination number (for example, if there is a broken connection or if there is currently heavy usage), the network will switch you to an alternate circuit path that is free. When the circuit is complete, your call goes through, and the phone rings on the other end. When your call is complete, the circuit is torn down and the bandwidth is made available to other users.

Because ATM functions similarly to the PTN, it is an ideal candidate for large networks. ATM is able to leverage the largest existing network in the world (PTN) by integrating without translation or modification. A connection can be made from LAN to WAN to LAN using strictly ATM. The PTN becomes a seamless extension of the local network, as no translation is required.

Let's say you have two Ethernet LANs connected by a frame relay WAN. Let's also assume you wish to send a frame of data from one Ethernet network to the other. With this configuration, your network will require additional hardware at both ends of the WAN to translate between the two topologies. Your frame will undergo translation as it enters the WAN, and then again when it leaves the WAN to be transmitted onto the other Ethernet segment. If you replace this configuration with ATM, no translation is required because ATM can be supported on both the LAN and the WAN.

ATM Drawbacks

Currently there are some problems with this configuration. To start, ATM wants to handle all of the end-to-end connections. This is the same type of functionality provided by existing upper-layer protocols like IPX and IP. Methods for incorporating these existing protocols with ATM have met with a number of delays. For example, LANE 2 was supposed to include changes to the frame header to support multiple protocols, but this feature was dropped from the specification by the time it was released. Such configuration problems are not an issue in an ATM-only environment, but they can make incorporating ATM functionality into an existing network infrastructure difficult at best.

Another drawback to ATM is the *node maps* maintained by ATM switches. These node maps are what allow VPIs to create paths from one end station to another. There is currently no auto-discovery method for creating these tables in PVC circuits; these tables must be maintained manually. This can make maintaining a network with many nodes a real nightmare. While SVCs do not have this limitation, there is no guarantee that the circuit will be able to allocate the full bandwidth required by the end station if a WAN connection is required. If you have ever tried to make a phone call during peak hours and received a busy circuit signal, you have experienced this phenomenon. If the connection is not permanent, there is no guarantee it will be there 100 percent of the time. In some environments (such as money transfers or credit checks), this kind of unpredictability is unacceptable.

As if all this were not confusing enough, a number of ATM vendors have grown weary of waiting for specification drafts to add functionality to their networking hardware. To compensate, they have developed proprietary implementations of this functionality that may or may not work with equipment from other vendors. In effect, you could end up locked into a single vendor for all your ATM needs. This has created a real "buyer beware" environment for those who purchase network components. As an example, when LANE 2 was released, some ATM vendors could provide the additional functionality it supported with a simple software upgrade to existing hardware; other vendors, however, could not provide this level of support—and customers found themselves in the position of needing to replace some very expensive hardware to gain the additional functionality.

Appropriate Applications

ATM specifications are still in a state of flux. While the technology shows great promise, it is difficult to recommend it for any application at the time of this writing. There are still a number of bugs that need to be shaken out of this technology. With the recent adoption of 1Gb Ethernet, it is questionable whether ATM will receive the resources and attention it so desperately needs to be molded into a stable production topology.

Most network managers have decided to err on the side of caution by letting others ride out ATM's bumpy road ahead, adopting a wait-and-see policy. ATM's greatest benefits will be in backbone implementations—the last place a seasoned network person wants to introduce a metamorphosing technology.

Wide Area Network Topologies

Wide area network (WAN) topologies are network configurations designed to carry data over a great distance. Unlike LANs, which are designed to deliver data between many systems, WAN topologies are usually point to point. *Point to point* means that the technology was developed to support only two nodes sending and receiving data. It is expected that if multiple nodes need access to the WAN, a LAN will be placed behind it to accommodate this functionality.

Figure 2.7 displays this type of connectivity. The only devices communicating directly on the WAN are the two routers. The routers provide connectivity from a single point to another. Any other devices that need to use the WAN must communicate through the two routers.

FIGURE 2.7

Only two devices (routers) are directly communicating on the WAN.

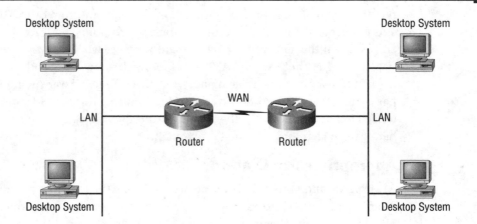

Local Exchange Carriers

A *local exchange carrier* is an organization capable of providing WAN services on a local level. Since a majority of these are public telephone companies (such as the regional Bell companies), a local exchange carrier is sometimes referred to as a *telco*. Most local exchange carriers can provide WAN connectivity from 56K to 622Mb.

For an exchange carrier to handle your WAN needs, you first need to get your data to the carrier. This is done by running a connection between you and the closest local exchange carrier facility, commonly referred to as a *central office* or CO. The local exchange carrier will take care of installing a circuit between its facility and yours. Somewhere within your facility is a point referred to as the *demarc* (demarcation point). This is the point to which the local carrier guarantees service. You want to make sure that this point is as close to your networking hardware as possible, because it identifies the point where the local exchange carrier's responsibility ends. If the connection is active up to the demarc, but you're still having connectivity problems, most local exchange carriers will be of little help.

For example, if your demarc is in the same room as your servers and network hardware, it's a straightforward process to isolate a connectivity problem (it's either the WAN link or in the hardware). If your demarc is in another building or 20 floors away, you have an additional length of cable to add to the equation. To compound the problem, you may find that no one wishes to take ownership of a problem caused by that cable. Does it belong to the exchange carrier? The building owner? Your organization? By locating the demarc in the same room as your network hardware, you remove this gray area.

Geographically Large WANs

If you are establishing a WAN that connects to a local geographical location, all you may need is to have the same local exchange carrier wire up to the other site. If the connection is required to span a large distance, however, you will probably need to involve a long-distance carrier. Long-distance carriers like AT&T, Sprint, and MCI connect to the local carrier at a location called the *Point of Presence* (POP). A POP is simply telephone-speak for the point where the networks for the local exchange carrier and the long distance carrier meet. Most large towns will have at least one POP; major cities will have quite a few. An example of how each exchange carrier would be responsible for a portion of your circuit is shown in Figure 2.8.

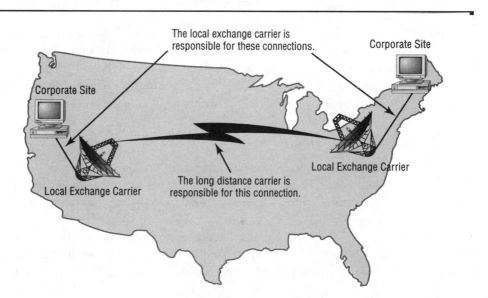

FIGURE 2.8

WAN requiring multiple exchange carriers

The local exchange carrier is responsible for these connections.

Corporate Site

Corporate Site

Local Exchange Carrier

Local Exchange Carrier

The long distance carrier is responsible for this connection.

If all this sounds a bit complex—well, it can be. But most long distance carriers have revamped their service departments and are willing to take care of the setup for you. They will take care of contacting all local exchange carriers involved and schedule the wiring and testing for you.

WAN Options

WAN technologies fall into one of three categories. Before deciding which WAN technology to use, you need to evaluate how you plan to use the circuit and what kind of data will be transmitted. You must also take a good look at what your bandwidth requirements will be.

Bandwidth on demand   This includes technologies such as dial-up analog and ISDN. These technologies are best used when WAN connectivity requirements are sporadic. For example, bandwidth on demand can be used effectively to provide fault tolerance for a WAN circuit which utilizes some other method of connectivity. If the main link goes down, dial on demand can step in to provide a short-term solution.

Private circuits   These are useful when security is an issue. You may also need a private circuit if you require QoS for time-sensitive applications. Leased lines, T1, and T3 are considered private circuit topologies.

Shared media   This is useful when QoS is not so critical but cost is a major factor. For example, Frame Relay is a shared-media topology and has experienced phenomenal growth due to its cost savings over private circuit topologies. It is estimated that a majority of corporate WAN data now runs across Frame Relay.

One thing that can be confusing is that even if you go with a shared-media solution, you still need a private circuit to connect you to a CO. For example, your WAN may be based on Frame Relay, but you will probably use a T1 or DSL circuit to connect you to the frame cloud. So, the real difference between private circuits and shared media is the method of connectivity used beyond the CO.

Dial-Up Analog

Dial-up analog connections use the same PTN that your telephone uses to create end-to-end connections. The largest data communications use of this network is using a modem (short for *modulator/demodulator*) to dial up the phone number you wish to contact.

Unfortunately, the public telephone network was originally designed to carry voice, which does not require a large amount of bandwidth. This is why modem connections are in the kilobit range instead of the megabit range. Because it was easier to service voice with an analog connection, the telephone network was originally designed to be analog, not digital. These analog lines are referred to as *plain old telephone service* (POTS).

A modem takes the digital signals from a computer and converts them to analog. This analog signal is then transmitted over the dial-up line to the POP, where it is converted back to a digital signal. Even though analog is still used to connect to people's homes, most of the connections between POPs have been upgraded to digital.

So our modem's signal has been returned to a digital format. It travels over the backbone to the destination POP where it is again translated into an analog signal. The analog signal travels down the POTS on the other side to the receiving modem.

Analog transmission rates peak at around 9600bps. Despite this limitation, modem vendors have been able to push raw throughput to 28.8Kbps and even 56Kbps by leveraging technologies such as frequency shifting or phase shifting. Include data compression, and this rate can be as high as 115Kbps. 115Kbps is not the true transfer rate—it is the effective rate through the use of compression. For example, a 33.6K modem may be able to achieve a throughput rate of 115Kbps through the use of compression, but the raw transfer rate is still 33.6Kbps.

NOTE *Frequency shifting* and *phase shifting* involve using more than one carrier wave to transmit a signal. *Compression* involves removing redundant characters from the data before transmission.

Limiting the speed of a modem is the noise created when the signal is translated between the digital and analog formats. The faster a connection, the more susceptible it becomes to errors from interference by noise. Modem manufacturers walk a fine line: They must make modems transfer data as fast as possible, but not so fast that noise begins to generate errors. 56K modems get around this noise problem by eliminating some of these translations, thus reducing the amount of noise generated on the circuit.

How 56K Is Achieved

56K modems function under the principle that converting information from digital to analog creates more noise than translating it from analog to digital. In order for a 56K modem to work properly, the signal cannot go through any digital-to-analog conversions once it leaves the modem. The theory is that if the destination system has a digital connection to its local POP, no digital-to-analog conversions are required (besides for the modem itself).

For example, let's assume you are using a 56K modem to call your Internet Service Provider (ISP). This ISP maintains a T1 digital connection to its local POP for dial-in access. This connection leads directly into the ISP's network, which is also digital.

When the signal leaves your modem, it is converted from digital to analog. The signal then travels down the POTS to the POP, where it is converted back to a digital signal. This signal travels down a digital backbone to the ISP's POP. Until now, the functionality has been identical to a regular modem connection. Once the signal leaves the ISP's POP, however, it does not need to be converted. Because the ISP maintains a digital connection, the signal can remain digital from your POP all the way into the ISP's network. This eliminates the need to perform any digital-to-analog conversions once the signal has left the modem.

Dial-Up Analog Drawbacks

There are a few caveats about using this type of connection. First, you cannot put a 56K modem on each end and expect a 56K connection. Doing so would require the use of POTS on each end that need to perform a digital-to-analog conversion by the destination POP. Special hardware is required on the receiving end to accommodate a digital connection to the POP (such as the T1 mentioned above).

 NOTE When two 56K modems are connected via POTS, the connection speed drops to the highest level the two modems can negotiate, usually between 22K and 33.6K.

The second issue is that this connection speed assumes that near-perfect phone conditions and wiring exist, which is rarely the case. Even if the receiving station is outfitted for a digital connection, expect a 56K modem to connect between 45K and 53K. Also, this connection speed is only available for downstream traffic (from the ISP to your modem). Upstream traffic is limited to 33.6K.

In a business environment, dial-up analog is good for load balancing; you can also use it as a backup connection to some other WAN topology. Cisco routers include the ability to switch over to a secondary means of connection if the primary means of connection fails. For example, a company may rely on a Frame Relay circuit to connect a remote office site but have an analog dial-up connection configured in case the Frame Relay fails.

Appropriate Applications

The following are appropriate applications for dial-up analog:

- Home access to the Internet
- Home access to the corporate network

- Remote management of network hardware
- Backup connectivity for other WAN services

ISDN

Integrated Services Digital Network (ISDN) is the digital alternative to the analog PTN. There are two levels of service available:

- Basic Rate Interface (BRI)
- Primary Rate Interface (PRI)

Basic Rate ISDN comprises two 64Kb channels, called B channels (*bearer* channels), and one 16Kb channel, called a D channel (*data* channel). The two B channels are used for transmitting data. The D channel is used for overhead in maintaining the connection. *Primary Rate ISDN* includes 23 B channels and one D channel and has the effective throughput of a T1 connection (1.544Mb).

Understanding ISDN

An ISDN line uses separate telephone numbers for each channel, just as an analog dial-up connection does for each line. For example, a BRI connection would have two separate phone numbers, one for each B channel. Because the two channels are completely separate, ISDN can load-balance a connection by using the second line only when required or by leaving it open for other communications.

For example, let's say you're using your ISDN connection to cruise the Internet. You're buzzing around from Web page to Web page. At this point, you most likely only have one B channel active, for an effective throughput rate of 64Kb. You then run across a site that has every Dilbert comic from the last three years located in a single 450MB zip file. Interested in cubicle art, you click the link and start downloading the file. At some predetermined point in the communication, the second B channel will kick in, increasing the transfer rate to 128Kb. This effectively cuts the downloading time by nearly half. When the large file transfer is complete, the second B channel drops, and your effective throughput rate returns to 64Kb.

As mentioned, this second channel can also be used for completely separate communications, as well, both inbound and outbound. While cruising the Web on the first B channel, you could also be carrying on a telephone conversation or sending (or receiving) a fax on the second B channel.

Because ISDN uses digital transmissions, it is typically a more stable connection than analog. Connectivity is provided by an ISDN card that fits into your PC or by a piece of hardware that you can connect to your network. The network version allows anyone on the network to open an ISDN connection through the device. Connection times are near instantaneous. This is a good thing, as a connection can easily be established before a network connection can time out. The delays imposed in setting up an analog modem connection make this type of connectivity impractical if not impossible. In effect, ISDN can serve up bandwidth on demand, leaving the connection closed when not in use.

Avoid Getting Bitten by ISDN

Unfortunately, bandwidth on demand has led to some abuses of ISDN. Small companies have been sucked in by the glamour of ISDN, hoping that a pay-as-you-go structure would be more economical than a full-time connection—only to get burned when they receive the telephone bill.

As mentioned, ISDN is capable of doing load balancing by bringing up the second B channel when needed. This is usually configured as a balance between time and current throughput. We want the second line to kick in under heavy traffic loads—but not so quickly that it responds to small files, being used for a few seconds and then not at all. Conversely, we do not want the second line to kick it in too late, because it would then do very little to improve file transfer time.

At the other end of the transmission, we want to tear that second connection down as quickly as possible when it is no longer needed. We do not want to tear it down too quickly, however, as the user may have a number of files to transfer, which would just cause the line to be brought back up again immediately.

This is also somewhat true for the initial B channel. Initialization is easy: You bring up the channel when it is needed. The question is, when do you tear it down? In the Web example above, if you tear the connection down too quickly, you will end up bringing the line back up every time the user clicks a new link.

Here's the kicker. ISDN costs anywhere from two to eight times what you would pay for an analog line. This varies with your local exchange carrier but should get you into the ballpark of what ISDN will cost. Like an analog call, the first minute of an ISDN call is typically far more expensive than the minutes that follow. The result is that if you are tearing down and bringing up lines continuously, you could end up paying $1 or more per minute. I know of a few companies that have been shocked to receive a first-month phone bill of more than $4,500. This is over twice what they would have paid for a T1 sporting 1.544Mb bandwidth!

ISDN Drawbacks

If you are using ISDN for Internet connectivity, keep in mind that the connection can only be established from your end. While this is not a problem if you are connecting from a single system and relying on your provider for services such as e-mail, it can cause problems if you are trying to connect your company's network to the Internet. Services such as e-mail and domain name services (DNS) need to be able to create connections bi-directionally. If someone on the Internet needs to send your company e-mail, your e-mail system needs to be constantly reachable. Because ISDN connections are constantly brought up and torn down, your mail system may or may not be reachable. This can cause e-mail to be delayed or, even worse, undeliverable.

If your ISP offers ISDN network connections, make sure it can host your Web server, reply to any DNS requests for you, and queue your e-mail until your connection is brought back up online. You should also make sure that the ISP's method of transferring your e-mail to your local site is supported by your e-mail gateway. For example, some ISPs expect your e-mail system to use the `finger` command to trigger e-mail delivery. This command is supported by very few mail gateways.

Such one-way connectivity can also cause problems if you are using ISDN to connect a remote office. Keep in mind that you must specifically design the circuit so that it may be initiated from either side (possibly by using two dial-up numbers). Otherwise, your home office may not be able to contact the remote network unless the connection has already been initiated by the remote office.

Because ISDN is digital, it is not directly compatible with devices such as analog phones and faxes. These devices must be replaced with their digital counterparts or run through a *coder/decoder* (codec). A codec converts the analog signal from these devices to digital.

Appropriate Applications

These are the most appropriate applications for ISDN:

- Home access to the corporate network
- Corporate access to the Internet when only a few users need access
- Backup connectivity for other WAN services
- Connectivity to small remote-office sites

Leased Lines

Leased lines are dedicated analog or digital circuits that you pay for on a flat-rate basis. This means that whether or not you use the circuit, you are paying a fixed monthly fee. Of course, this also means that there are no surprises due to heavy usage. Leased lines are point-to-point connections—they are used to connect one geographical location to another. You cannot dial a phone number and point them to a new destination.

There are two common ways leased lines are deployed:

- The leased line constitutes the entire length of the connection between the two geographic locations.
- The leased line is used for the connection from each location to its local exchange carrier. Connectivity between the two exchange carriers is then provided by some other technology, like Frame Relay.

Analog leased lines are *conditioned* to facilitate a lower error rate than would normally be achieved with a dial-up line. Conditioning helps to remove noise from the circuit, which allows the connection to be used with less overhead for error correction. Digital leased lines are also referred to as *digital data service lines* and are available with bandwidths up to 56K. With analog leased lines, you may still use a modem. Digital data service lines require a channel service unit/data service unit, or CSU/DSU. They also require some form of data-terminating equipment (DTE)—typically a router—to regulate traffic flow across the line. The DTE connects to the CSU/DSU via an RS232 serial connector, or possibly an RS449 connector for 56K connections. Digital data services are full duplexed, meaning that data transmissions are bi-directional, flowing in both directions at the same time.

Analog leased lines are used very little today. They were popular back in the main-frame days when they were used for connecting dumb-terminal users at remote sites. Digital leased lines are usually sufficient for connecting small companies to the Internet or providing connectivity for remote offices.

 NOTE A leased line is not expandable. To provide more bandwidth, you must replace the line with a T1 (discussed in the next section).

Appropriate Applications

The following are appropriate applications for leased lines:

- Connecting remote sites to the corporate office when bandwidth requirements are small
- Providing Internet connectivity for small offices
- Carrying voice or data

T1

A *T1* is a full-duplex signal over four-conductor twisted-pair cabling. This wire pair terminates in a receptacle that resembles the square phone jacks used in older homes. T1s are used for dedicated point-to-point connections in the same way that leased lines are. Bandwidth on a T1 is available in increments from 64Kb up to 1.544Mb.

Time Division

T1s use *time division* to break the two wire pairs up into 24 separate channels. Time division is the allotment of available bandwidth based on time increments. In the case of a T1 circuit, each channel is allowed to transmit for 5.2 microseconds (μs). This is the amount of time a T1 requires to transmit 8 bits (or 1 byte) of information. At the end of 5.2 μs, the channel must stop transmitting and relinquish control of the circuit to the next channel. If the channel has additional information to transmit, it must wait 119.8 μs—the amount of time it takes to cycle through the other 23 channels until it is that channel's turn to transmit again.

To determine the available bandwidth on each channel, you must first determine the time division *sample rate*. The sample rate is the number of times each channel is allowed to transmit in a one-second period. Since each channel is allowed to transmit for 5.2 μs before releasing control to the next channel, you can determine the number of transmissions per second by using the following calculation:

```
1 (second) / .0000052 (transmit time per channel) = 192,398 transmissions
per second
```

This is the total number of transmissions possible in one second along a T1 line.

These 192,398 transmissions are then broken up equally over the 24 channels:

```
192,398 (transmissions) / 24 (the number of channels) = 8,000
```

Each of the 24 channels is allowed to transmit 8,000 times per second. This is the sample rate—the number of times per second that each channel is sampled or checked to see if it needs to transmit data.

To determine the available bandwidth per channel, multiply the sample rate by the amount of data you can transmit in each sample period:

```
8 bits × 8000 samples per second = 64Kbps
```

The short answer to all this number-crunching is that each of the 24 channels on a T1 line is capable of moving 64Kb worth of data per second.

With 24 active channels, the full bandwidth available on a T1 is

```
64 Kbps × 24 = 1.536Mbps
```

NOTE You'll notice that we ended up with 8Kbps unaccounted for from the 1.544Mbps bandwidth mentioned in the first paragraph of this section (1544Kbps − 1536Kbps = 8Kbps). This 8Kbps is overhead that goes toward managing the connections. So while a T1 is able to move 1.544Mb of information per second, only 1.536Mb can be actual data.

Fractional T1

The nice thing about this setup is that an exchange carrier will lease you individual channels of this T1, based on your bandwidth requirements. This is called a *fractional T1*. If you only need 512Kb, for example, then you only need to lease eight channels. In the long term, this can save you a considerable amount of money over leasing a full T1. Fractional T1 can be an ideal solution if your company only needs 64 or 128Kb now but may want to upgrade to a larger pipe later. By initially connecting via a fractional T1 instead of a leased line, you will not need to rewire—you can simply turn on additional channels.

These 24 channels can also be broken up and dedicated to different services. For example, you can dedicate three channels to data and one channel to voice. In this way, a single connection can provide connectivity for multiple services. By combining these services over a single T1, your organization can achieve a lower communication cost than by using separate wiring for each.

How Much Does a T1 Cost?

The cost of a T1 is based on bandwidth requirements and the distance to your local exchange carrier. The typical cost for a T1 can be anywhere from $800 to $2200 per month. Consult your local exchange carrier for its price structure.

Appropriate Applications

The following are appropriate applications for T1 lines:

- Connecting remote sites to the corporate office when you require a large amount of bandwidth

- Providing Internet connectivity for all but the largest offices

- Carrying multiple voice and data lines to reduce cost

T3

A *T3* is little more than 28 T1 circuits tied together. This results in 672 separate channels producing just under 45Mb worth of data throughput. Because of the increased bandwidth, T3s are wired using fiber optic cable rather than twisted pair.

Just like their T1 counterparts, T3s can be used for carrying a mixture of voice and data. You can also choose to lease a fractional T3 if 45Mb is beyond your data requirements. The appropriate applications for a T3 circuit are identical to a T1, except T3s have the ability to service much higher bandwidth demands.

DSL

DSL is an abbreviation for *digital subscriber line* technology. DSL is used to connect a customer site to the local CO. The term *last-mile technology* is used to describe DSL, as it is only used for the connection between the site and the CO. Figure 2.9 shows an example configuration. DSL is used to tie each end of the connection to the local POP. The connection between COs needs to be supplied through some other technology (Frame Relay, T1, vendor network, and so on). Notice that you are not required to use DSL on both ends. For example, in Figure 2.9 the corporate office could be using a T1 to connect to its local POP, while the remote office uses DSL.

FIGURE 2.9

DSL is last-mile technology.

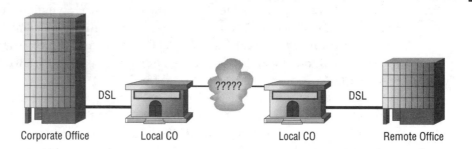

| Corporate Office | Local CO | | Local CO | Remote Office |

The term DSL actually combines a number of standards. This is why you may see it referred to as *x*DSL from time to time: Each of the different standards uses a different first letter. ADSL is the most widely implemented standard, but VDSL is new and gaining in popularity. Table 2.7 shows a list of popular DSL standards and the transmission speeds they support.

TABLE 2.7: DIFFERENT TYPES OF DSL

xDSL type	Meaning	Speeds
ADSL	Asymmetric DSL	Downstream: 1.5–6Mbps
		Upstream: 64–384Kbps
HDSL	High-speed DSL	Downstream: 128Kbps–1.5Mbps
		Upstream: same
IDSL	(AIX proprietary)	Downstream: 1.1Mbps
		Upstream: same
RADSL	Rate-adaptive DSL	Downstream: 6.1Mbps
		Upstream: 1.5Mbps
SDSL	Symmetric DSL	Downstream: 128Kbps–1.5Mbps
		Upstream: same
VDSL	Very high bit-rate DSL	Downstream: 51Mbps
		Upstream: 1.6–2.3Mbps

Why Is DSL Asymmetrical?

You may have noticed in Table 2.7 that DSL is not usually symmetrical in providing bandwidth. In other words, unlike a T1, which can provide the same bandwidth in both directions, DSL typically supports a faster downstream speed (traffic flowing from the CO to the site) than it does an upstream speed (traffic flowing from the site to the CO).

The reason for this is EMI. The large bundle of copper wires at the CO is very susceptible to EMI because the wires are in close proximity to each other. This creates a condition known as *near-end crosstalk* (NEXT). Since the customer site does not usually have such a large bundle of wires, NEXT isn't a problem and the bandwidth is greater in that direction (from the CO to the site).

This is fine if you're using DSL to access the Internet, since a site will commonly download more information than it uploads. For example, when you connect to a Web server, you transmit upstream a very small request, but the resulting downstream traffic may consist of text, multiple graphics, program code, and so on. On average, Internet users will receive eight times as much information as they transmit.

The asymmetrical nature of DSL can be a problem, however, if you are connecting remote offices. To refer back to Figure 2.9, what is upstream traffic on one DSL circuit will end up being downstream traffic on the other DSL circuit. When considering DSL for remote offices, make sure you include a traffic study to insure adequate bandwidth in both directions.

Interestingly, it's the asymmetrical nature of DSL which has caused it to be exempted from tariff charges. If this functionality changes, it is quite possible that the technology may be subjected to the same regulations which keep existing WAN technologies (T1, leased lines) so expensive.

The Appeal of DSL

Why is DSL so appealing? DSL has a number of things going for it. To start, it will work over the POTS wiring that exists in every home or business today. While this means you don't have to wire a new circuit, you'll probably need to set up a site visit to test circuit conditions. This usually requires less lead time, however, than having a full wire run installed—so deployment times are quicker.

POTS was originally designed to carry only voice. With this in mind, both ends of the connection were set to work at a signaling rate of 3–4KHz. While this is sufficient for voice transmissions, it limits data to 33.6Kbps upstream and about 52Kbps downstream, under ideal conditions. When a circuit is used for DSL, the signaling is increased to the 1.1MHz range. The faster signaling rate allows more data bits to be transferred each second, thus resulting in much higher bandwidth potential.

Unlike analog dial-up or ISDN, DSL provides a full-time connection. This eliminates all pay-by-usage charges that are usually associated with on-demand WAN technologies. Also, DSL is extremely fast. Speeds start at 64Kb and go as high as 6Mb (equivalent to just under four T1s combined), depending on the technology being used and the line quality.

While cable modems sometimes boast faster access speeds than DSL, they cannot guarantee bandwidth. This is because cable networks are shared media similar to Ethernet. DSL does not have this limitation because each connection going back to the CO is a dedicated circuit. This helps to insure that an organization is receiving the bandwidth it is paying for.

 NOTE DSL only guarantees bandwidth back to the CO. It is the responsibility of the technology bridging the gap between the COs to guarantee bandwidth over the WAN backbone. For example, if Frame Relay is used, you must negotiate a bandwidth guarantee over the frame, as well, in order to insure quality of service over the entire link.

Finally, DSL is being deployed at a very low cost. It is not uncommon to be able to purchase 384Kb worth of bandwidth at around $150 per month. This is roughly one-quarter to one-sixth of the cost of an equivalent fractional T1—which can result in a substantial monthly cost savings for the circuit. Also, many DSL vendors have developed their own backbones free of tariff charges, allowing them to be extremely cost effective over the telco alternatives.

DSL Drawbacks

DSL has three major drawbacks:

- Availability
- Distance
- Line quality

DSL is just starting to make its way into the public eye. For that reason, it is not available in all areas. Expect to see availability in the major metropolitan areas right now, with support moving out into less populated areas over the next two years. Before you decide to use DSL, you should first find out if it is even an option.

DSL also suffers from significant distance limitations. As a rule of thumb, sites must be within three miles of their CO in order to utilize DSL. VDSL requires fiber within 1,000 feet of the site location, which could be a CO or a local loop. Many common telco practices can limit this distance even further.

For example, many circuits are run through copper loops extended through the use of loading coils. These loading coils are nothing more sophisticated than big iron doughnuts that add inductance to the twisted pair to counteract the effects of the added distance on signal loss. There are also local loops that have been extended by some other active equipment, known generically as *line extenders*. Finally, there are loops that consist of copper pairs branching off into sub-loops with what are known as *bridge taps*. This is typically done to avoid the need to run new twisted pair all the way back to the central office. While all of this works fine for voice connections, this equipment can combine to reduce the effective distance of DSL. When in doubt, work with a provider and perform a line test before committing to deployment.

Line quality plays a big part in how much access speed you can get via a DSL connection. You may find that while a provider is capable of setting you up with DSL service, you may not be able to achieve the levels of bandwidth you require. Line quality and distance play a big part in determining how much bandwidth is available. For example, a poor ADSL circuit may be only capable of providing 128Kbps, even though the specification is much higher.

Appropriate Applications

The following are appropriate applications for DSL:

- Home Internet access
- Internet access for a small to medium-sized organization
- Last-mile connection for remote field offices

Frame Relay/X.25

Frame Relay and *X.25* are packet-switched technologies. Because data on a packet-switched network is capable of following any available circuit path, such networks are represented by clouds in graphical presentations, as you can see in Figure 2.10.

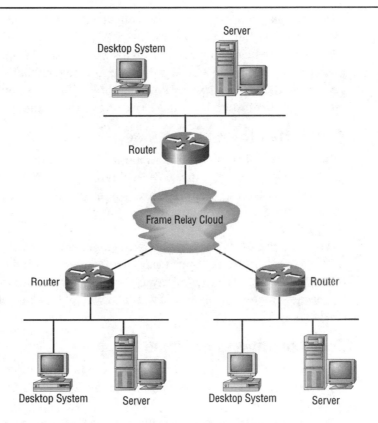

Both topologies must be configured as *permanent virtual circuits* (PVCs), meaning that all data entering the cloud at point A is automatically forwarded to point B. These end points are defined at the time the you lease the service, using Data Link Connection Identifier (DLCI) numbers.

Before a packet of data destined for a remote network enters the Frame Relay cloud, the router encapsulates it in a Frame Relay frame. The header of this frame contains the DLCI number for the PVC circuit. This allows the packet to be properly routed through the frame. When the packet reaches the remote network, the router strips off the Frame Relay information and delivers the packet to the local LAN.

NOTE The packet-switched network is a shared medium. Your exchange carrier uses the same network for all PVCs it leases out. In effect, you are sharing available bandwidth with every one of its clients. While this does not provide the truly private connection supplied by a leased line, it does help to keep down the costs of available bandwidth.

Frame Relay supports data transmission rates of 56K to 1.544Mb. Frame Relay is identical to and built upon the original X.25 specification, except that X.25 is analog, whereas Frame Relay is digital. As a digital transmission, Frame Relay requires less overhead for error correction and thus supports higher bandwidths than X.25 (X.25 only supports 56Kb). These topologies are an excellent example of how you can get more usable bandwidth by simply switching from analog to digital communications.

Committed Information Rate

When you order Frame Relay, the amount of bandwidth you purchase is based on a *committed information rate* (CIR). The CIR is the minimum amount of bandwidth your exchange carrier will guarantee as available at any given time. Many carriers will allow you to burst above that rate, depending on how much traffic is currently being passed through the cloud.

For example, let's say that you order a Frame Relay circuit with a CIR of 128Kb. If traffic is light within the Frame Relay cloud, you may be able to achieve momentary burst rates of 150Kb to 190Kb. Because Frame Relay has become popular, however, it has become more difficult to find windows where these higher transfer rates are available.

Cost Advantages of Frame Relay

For large WAN environments, Frame Relay can be far more cost effective than dedicated circuits. This is because you can run multiple PVCs through a single WAN connection.

For example, let's say you have four remote sites that require a 56Kb connection to the home office. If you were to construct this network out of dedicated circuits, you would require a 56Kb connection at each of the remote sites, as well as four 56Kb connections running into the main office.

With Frame Relay, however, you could replace the four dedicated connections at the main office with one fractional T1 connection and simply activate four channels of the T1 circuit to accept the data. By requiring only a single circuit at the main site, you can reduce your WAN costs.

In fact, there is nothing that says the CIR at the main office must equal the CIR value of all your remote sites. For example, let's assume that the connections to your remote site are used strictly for transferring e-mail. If bandwidth requirements are low, you may be able to drop the CIR at the main office from 256Kb to 128Kb. As long as the combined traffic to your four remote sites never exceeds 128Kb, you would not even notice a drop in performance. This would reduce your WAN costs even further.

X.25 is a mature technology with worldwide connectivity. Frame Relay is a bit newer and, as such, not as widely deployed. Most implementations should be able to utilize the benefits of Frame Relay. If you're running a truly global network, however, you may be stuck with X.25 in some areas.

 NOTE To connect to a Frame Relay or X.25 network, you must have a leased line or T1 wired between your organization and your local exchange carrier. From there, the circuit enters the cloud instead of following a dedicated path.

Appropriate Applications

The following are appropriate applications for Frame Relay and X.25:

- Connecting remote sites to the corporate office when you only require data connectivity
- Carrying data that is not time sensitive (not voice or video)

SONET

SONET, or *Synchronous Optical Network*, is available in bandwidths from 64Kb to 2.4Gbps (yes, Gb *is* gigabit). SONET uses time division (the same as a T1) over fiber and is being billed as the next-generation replacement to the T1. SONET has some additional benefits that certainly make this a possibility.

The first benefit that SONET offers is direct support of the ATM topology. If ATM technology should ever take off on the LAN, SONET will be poised to extend the boundaries of ATM LAN networks by providing transparent support over the WAN. This, in effect, helps to blur the line between LAN and WAN by utilizing similar communication rules across the entire transmission domain. If ATM has been deployed on the LAN, SONET is the ideal medium to utilize ATM over the WAN, as well. This removes the usual requirement of translating between LAN and WAN topologies.

SONET is also in a much better position than ATM to support global networks. One drawback to the T1 is that it is deployed in North America only. Most countries follow Conference and European Posts and Telecommunications Standards, which specify an E1 carrier, which is not directly compatible with a T1 carrier. SONET is a much closer match to the European optical WAN specification called Synchronous Digital Hierarchy. When you're implementing a large global network, you can encounter many problems between the services offered by U.S. and European carriers. SONET is an approach that tries to close some of these gaps.

SONET supports private virtual channels and will transmit ATM, as well as ISDN, natively; this removes the translation requirement between LAN and WAN topologies.

Appropriate Applications

The following are appropriate applications for SONET:

- Connecting large metropolitan networks
- Providing Internet connectivity for large global companies
- Providing Network backbones for Internet Service Providers
- Carrying voice and data via ATM from LAN to WAN to LAN

Summary

In this chapter, we discussed the LAN and WAN topologies available for configuring your network. We looked at the strengths and weaknesses of each, as well as examples of situations in which these topologies are commonly deployed.

The topology is only half of the picture, however. In the next chapter, we will discuss the protocols you will need to use in order to carry your data along a specified topology.

CHAPTER 3

Protocols

A *protocol* is a set of communication rules deployed over a given topology. To refer back to the OSI model, a protocol typically specifies all communication rules from the Network layer (OSI layer 3) to the Application layer (OSI layer 7).

Cisco routers are capable of supporting a variety of different protocols. The most popular are covered in this chapter.

The Internet Protocol Suite (IP)

The IP suite has become something of a network administrator's tool kit. When using dissimilar systems, administrators tend to turn to IP for providing connectivity. IP has its roots in the UNIX operating system. It was this NOS that first leveraged the flexibility and diversity of services that IP can offer. This was a perfect match, because both were designed to provide a plethora of services.

 WARNING The IP suite's versatility does not come without a price, however—in order to insure its correct implementation, it requires a higher level of administrator expertise and management than any of the other protocols we will discuss.

Figure 3.1 diagrams how different portions of the IP suite match up to the OSI model. This really is not an exact match, because the IP protocol predates the development of this model. As we continue through this chapter, we will continue to refer back to the OSI model in order to provide a quick reference about how each of the pieces in our communication puzzle fit together. If you do not recognize all the pieces outlined in the diagram, don't worry; we will cover them later in this chapter.

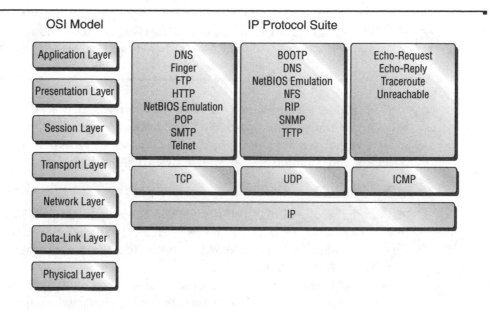

IP Address Conventions

IP logical network segments are referred to as *subnets*. A proper subnet address is made up of four blocks of numbers separated by periods. Each of these number blocks is called a *byte*. Values for each of these bytes can range from 0 to 255. When you're writing a subnet, a trailing *0* implies reference to an entire network segment. For example, when I write 192.168.175.0, it is assumed that I am referring to the entire IP subnet, whose address is 192.168.175. If I write 10.0.0.0, it is assumed that I am referring to the entire IP subnet whose address is 10.

When writing an IP address for a server or workstation (referred to as an *IP host*), you replace the 0 field with a number to uniquely identify that system on the IP subnet. Values for these numbers can range from 1 to 254. For example, given the IP subnet 192.168.175.0, the first system on this network may receive the address 192.168.175.1, the next may receive 192.1168.175.2, and so on. In our subnet 10 example, the first IP host may be 10.0.0.1, the next may be 10.0.0.2, and so on. On an IP subnet, every host must be assigned a unique IP address. If not, communications can become crossed and information delivered to the wrong system.

NOTE The assigning of unique IP addresses is analogous to the assigning of Social Security numbers to individuals. If two people were assigned the same number, it would be extremely difficult to straighten out their tax information.

IP host addresses are referred to as *unicast* addresses, as they are designed for point-to-point communications. When unicast addresses are used, only a single system is expected to receive and process the data. There are other types of addresses, called *broadcasts* and *multicasts*, which we will cover later in this chapter.

Why 0–255?

You may be asking yourself, "Why are only numbers up to 255 valid? Why can't I use 999?" The fact that each set of numbers is referred to as a byte provides a strong clue. The reason that numbers beyond 255 are not valid is that we are dealing with decimal equivalents to binary numbers.

You may remember from our discussion of digital communications in Chapter 1 that a byte is made up of eight bits. Since we are talking digital, each bit has one of two possible values: 0 or 1. So, from a binary perspective, each of our bytes can range in value from 00000000 to 11111111.

Now examine Figure 3.2. Each of our eight binary bits has an equivalent decimal value. This allows us to convert between the two numbering systems. For example, a binary value of 00000001 is equal to the decimal number 1. The binary value 10000000 is equal to the decimal number 128.

FIGURE 3.2

Each binary bit has a decimal equivalent.

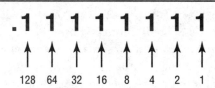

Notice that the values of the binary bits are cumulative. This means that not only can I express each of the decimal values shown in Figure 3.2; I can express sum values, as well. For example, 10000001 would be equivalent to a decimal 129; 10000010 would be a decimal 130; and 10000011 would be equivalent to a decimal 132.

So to return to our original question of why 255 is the magic number, we need to do a little math. Using Figure 3.2 as a guide,

```
binary 11111111 = decimal 128 + 64 + 32 + 16 + 8 + 4 + 2 + 1 = 255
```

This calculation shows that 255 is the highest decimal equivalent to an eight-bit binary value.

The reason that most people express IP addresses in decimal instead of binary is that it is much easier for humans to read and remember. For example, unless you are a serious bit weenie, it is much easier to remember that your IP address is 192.168.100.150 than to try to remember that it's 11000000.10101000.01100100.10010110.

Subnet Masks

Each IP address contains two parts:

- One that refers to the network segment
- One that refers to the host

We now have a small problem. By simply looking at an IP host address, it can be difficult to determine which part of the address refers to the network and which part refers to the host. For example, if I say that my IP address is 10.73.201.5, the combinations shown in Table 3.1 are possible.

TABLE 3.1: IDENTIFYING THE HOST AND NETWORK PORTIONS OF THE ADDRESS	
Network Portion of the Address	**Host Portion of the Address**
10	73.201.5
10.73	201.5
10.72.201	5

This is where the *subnet mask* is used. A subnet mask, listed along with an address, allows you to tell which portion of the host address identifies the network and which portion identifies the host. The subnet mask follows the same format as an IP host address, consisting of four bytes separated by periods. In a standard subnet mask (we will talk about variable-length subnet masking in a moment), the only values used are 255 and 0. A 255 denotes the network portion of the address, while a 0 denotes the host portion.

Given the above host address, our options would be those shown in Table 3.2.

TABLE 3.2: THE SUBNET MASK IDENTIFIES THE HOST AND NETWORK PORTIONS OF THE ADDRESS.

Decimal Subnet Mask	Network Portion	Host Portion
255.0.0.0	10	73.201.5
255.255.0.0	10.73	201.5
255.255.255.0	10.73.201	5

Clearly, if you are going to identify an IP host properly, you must know both the IP address and the subnet mask. It is important that a consistent subnet mask be used on all IP hosts to preclude routing conflicts. An IP host with an incorrect subnet mask may not be able to determine which other systems occupy the same logical network.

For example, assume you have a subnet of 10.73.0.0. All systems on this network should be using a mask value of 255.255.0.0. Now, let's say the host at 10.73.1.25 has an incorrect mask value set of 255.255.255.0. What happens when 10.73.1.25 tries to talk to other systems on the 10.73.0.0 network?

Because of the process IP uses to determine which systems are on the same subnet and which hosts are remote, this host would only be able to talk to other systems with an address of 10.73.1.*x*. This is because our improperly configured host thinks the local subnet address is 10.73.1.0, not 10.73.0.0. This means that the host will assume that any system with an address of 10.73.0.*x* or 10.73.2.*x*–10.73.255.*x* is located on a remote network.

Figure 3.3 shows IP's transmission decision table. Note that the subnet mask which has been assigned to the local system plays an important role in determining which hosts are on the same subnet and which hosts can only be reached through a local router.

 TIP A Cisco router can be configured to hide connectivity problems when you have hosts with incorrect subnet mask values. Of course, the proper fix is to insure that you use a consistent subnet mask on all of your systems.

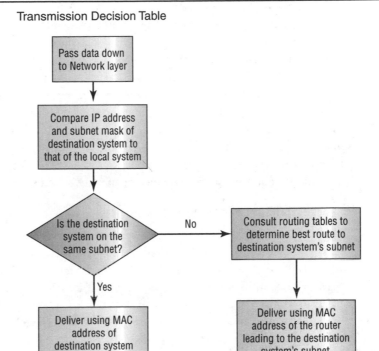

Transmission Decision Table

Why is subnetting even used? Because every network has different requirements for the number of hosts that must be supported on any given network. By adjusting the subnet mask, I can increase or decrease the number of hosts supported on any given subnet by using up a portion of the network space. Table 3.3 shows how the maximum numbers of networks and subnet hosts change as the subnet mask is adjusted. The quantities reflect the segmentation of a single address: for example, 10.0.0.0, 11.0.0.0, 12.0.0.0, and so on.

TABLE 3.3: TOTAL NETWORKS AND HOSTS AVAILABLE WITH EACH MASK VALUE

Subnet Mask	Maximum Number of Networks	Maximum Number of Hosts
255.0.0.0	1	16,581,373
255.255.0.0	255	65,023
255.255.255.0	65,025	254

If you decide to use the address range of 10.0.0.0 for your IP addresses, you can use the subnet mask to customize the number of available hosts based on your network requirements. If you have few subnets with many hosts on each, you may want to use a subnet mask of 255.255.0.0. This would support 255 subnets (10.1.0.0– 10.254.0.0), with a maximum of 65,023 hosts on each.

If you're responsible for a large number of subnets, each with a small number of hosts, you may want to use a subnet mask of 255.255.255.0. This would support 65,025 subnets (10.0.0.0–10.254.254.0), with a maximum of 254 hosts on each. The choice is yours to make—however, keep in mind that you should always plan for growth. The chore of changing the subnet mask on 250 or more hosts simply because you ran out of address space is a time-consuming one at best.

Subnet Mask Shorthand

One thing you can say about true geeks is that they will cut corners whenever possible. We've determined how important it is to know the subnet mask value in association with the IP address. The problem is that writing 255.255.255.0 with every address can be quite time consuming. With this in mind, a method of expressing the subnet mask with only a few characters was developed.

I stated that IP addresses and subnet masks are based on the binary system. The shorthand method involves using a division symbol (/) followed by a count of the number of bits in the subnet mask. Table 3.4 shows some possible values.

TABLE 3.4: OPTIONS FOR EXPRESSING THE SUBNET MASK

Decimal Mask	Binary Value	Shorthand
255.0.0.0	11111111.0.0.0	/8
255.255.0.0	11111111.11111111.0.0	/16
255.255.255.0	11111111.11111111.11111111.0	/24

Instead of having to write your local IP address as 192.168.1.25 with a mask of 255.255.255.0, you can simply write 192.168.1.25/24. This is because the mask value is using 24 bits to describe the network portion of the address. This method of describing the mask reduces the amount of work required to properly express the address.

Registered IP Addresses

While you can select any random IP range to assign to your network, you may want to plan ahead for Internet connectivity and use a set of registered IP addresses. The *InterNIC* is the authority responsible for assigning and registering IP addresses when an organization wishes to communicate on the Internet. The InterNIC tracks which organizations are assigned which IP addresses to insure that there are no conflicts. If two organizations inadvertently try to use the same subnet numbers, routing errors will occur. If you assign random IP addresses to your network and later wish to connect to the Internet, you may find yourself reconfiguring your address range.

Before you connect through your Internet Service Provider, you may need to fill out a number of forms documenting your current network configuration, as well as the amount of network growth you expect over the next five years. Based on this information, your ISP will assign one or more IP subnet numbers to your organization.

The InterNIC has broken up the available IP subnets into different classes: *A*, *B*, and *C*. The class determines the size of your organization's address space. Table 3.5 defines these classes.

TABLE 3.5: ADDRESS CLASSES AND THEIR RANGES		
Address Class	**Address Range**	**Assumed Subnet Mask**
A	1.0.0.0 126.0.0.0	255.0.0.0
B	128.0.0.0–191.0.0.0	255.255.0.0
C	192.0.0.0–223.0.0.0	255.255.255.0

For example, let's assume you're bringing a major telecommunications company onto the Internet for the first time. Your company has an extremely large worldwide network. Given the size of your network, the InterNIC may see fit to assign you a class A address. Let's say they assign you the address 10.0.0.0. This gives you control of the range of values between 10.0.0.0 and 10.255.255.255.

 NOTE Most organizations no longer assign legal IP addresses to their internal systems. Private address space is used, which is covered later in this section.

While the subnet mask 255.0.0.0 is assumed, you are actually free to break up this range any way you see fit. A class A subnet mask will only support a single logical subnet. If you have more than one logical subnet, you will need to change your subnet mask to accommodate the additional networks. Also, you may not be required to support up to 16,581,373 hosts on a single subnet. (If you do have that many hosts on a single subnet, you have much bigger problems than just assigning IP addresses!)

For example, you could choose to use a class B subnet mask of 255.255.0.0 to subnet the range given to you by the InterNIC. This would support 255 subnets, allowing you to use the values 10.0.0.0–10.254.0.0 for your subnet range. Each subnet would be capable of supporting 65,023 hosts.

Figure 3.4 shows how the subnet portion of the address changes whenever a router is crossed. Any given logical subnet is the area confined within your routers.

FIGURE 3.4

A small section of what your telecommunications network may look like if you are using a class B address

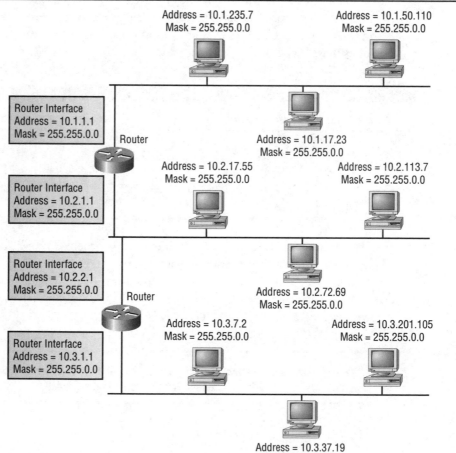

Address = 10.1.235.7
Mask = 255.255.0.0

Address = 10.1.50.110
Mask = 255.255.0.0

Router Interface
Address = 10.1.1.1
Mask = 255.255.0.0

Router

Address = 10.1.17.23
Mask = 255.255.0.0

Address = 10.2.17.55
Mask = 255.255.0.0

Address = 10.2.113.7
Mask = 255.255.0.0

Router Interface
Address = 10.2.1.1
Mask = 255.255.0.0

Router Interface
Address = 10.2.2.1
Mask = 255.255.0.0

Router

Address = 10.2.72.69
Mask = 255.255.0.0

Address = 10.3.7.2
Mask = 255.255.0.0

Address = 10.3.201.105
Mask = 255.255.0.0

Router Interface
Address = 10.3.1.1
Mask = 255.255.0.0

Address = 10.3.37.19
Mask = 255.255.0.0

You could also choose to use a class C subnet mask of 255.255.255.0. This would support up to 65,025 subnets, allowing you to use the values 10.0.0.0–10.254.254.0 for your subnet range. Each subnet could have a maximum of 254 hosts. Figure 3.5 shows your network renumber for a class C subnet mask.

When you are assigned a class B subnet, your choices are similar to using a class A subnet, but they are somewhat more limited. Let's assume that your telecommunications company is really not quite so large. Perhaps it serves only a specific country or region. In this case, the InterNIC may assign you a class B address. For our example, let's say it assigns the address 172.25.0.0 to your organization.

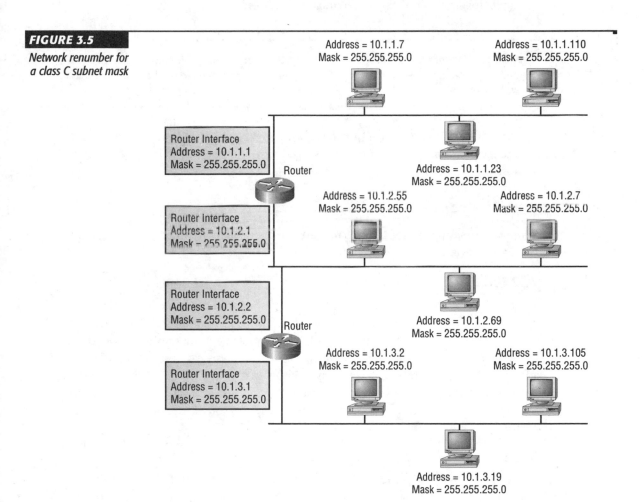

FIGURE 3.5

Network renumber for a class C subnet mask

Address = 10.1.1.7
Mask = 255.255.255.0

Address = 10.1.1.110
Mask = 255.255.255.0

Router Interface
Address = 10.1.1.1
Mask = 255.255.255.0

Router

Address = 10.1.1.23
Mask = 255.255.255.0

Address = 10.1.2.55
Mask = 255.255.255.0

Address = 10.1.2.7
Mask = 255.255.255.0

Router Interface
Address = 10.1.2.1
Mask – 255.255.255.0

Router Interface
Address = 10.1.2.2
Mask = 255.255.255.0

Router

Address = 10.1.2.69
Mask = 255.255.255.0

Address = 10.1.3.2
Mask = 255.255.255.0

Address = 10.1.3.105
Mask = 255.255.255.0

Router Interface
Address = 10.1.3.1
Mask = 255.255.255.0

Address = 10.1.3.19
Mask = 255.255.255.0

Given this class B address, you can choose to use a class B subnet mask of 255.255.0.0, which would yield a single logical network with 65,025 hosts. If you need to support more than one logical subnet, you could opt to use a class C subnet mask of 255.255.255.0. This would support 255 networks, with 254 hosts on each.

Finally, let's assume that you are registering a small company with only 75 computers. In this case, your ISP may issue a class C address, such as 192.168.10.0. With this address, you can only support a single network with up to 254 hosts. If this network is actually made up of two logical subnets, you may have to request a second subnet from your ISP. This address may be sequential (as in 192.168.11.0), or it could end up being in a completely different address range.

 NOTE The InterNIC no longer handles address space requests for fewer than 16 subnets. If you need addressing for fewer than 16 subnets, you will need to obtain the address space from your ISP.

You may note that the class C address range stops at 223.0.0.0 instead of 254.0.0.0. This range of addresses is reserved for a special purpose that we will cover in the next section.

Special Addresses

There are some special IP addresses that are not assigned by the InterNIC for regular use. Each of these addresses is defined here.

127.0.0.1

Referred to as a *loopback address*, 127.0.0.1 is a test address automatically assigned to every IP host, regardless of the operating system on which it is loaded. This address is useful when insuring that the IP protocol stack is loaded and functioning properly. If a system is not communicating with other network systems, you can try to ping the address 127.0.0.1. If this is successful, you know that your IP stack is functioning properly and that the problem may be related to your network card or cabling. If the attempt is unsuccessful, you know that your problem is software related and that the protocol stack is at fault.

Broadcast Address

In the examples already discussed, we noted that 255 is not a valid IP host address value. This is because the address is reserved for network broadcasts. If you send information to the address 192.168.11.255, you are effectively sending information to every host on the network 192.168.11.0. Broadcasts are useful when a system needs to convey information but is unsure of the destination system's address. For example, when a router sends a Routing Information Protocol (RIP) packet, it will address the packet to the broadcast address to insure that all routers located on the network segment will receive the information.

 NOTE   A broadcast is local to the subnet and is typically not propagated by routers.

There is a special type of broadcast referred to as an *all-network broadcast* that always has the destination address of 255.255.255.255. This type of broadcast is used when a system does not know the local IP subnet address. For example, there is a process that allows systems to learn which IP address they should use during startup by querying a server. Upon initial boot, the system may have no idea what the IP address of this system may be (or what the local subnet address is, for that matter). The 255.255.255.255 broadcast allows this system to send out a request for an IP address without knowing anything about the current IP addressing.

Multicast Addresses

There is another address type I haven't mentioned yet, called the class D or *multicast* address range. This class includes IP addresses in the range of 224.0.0.0–239.255.255.0. Multicast is a special kind of information delivery designed to let one IP host efficiently deliver information to multiple recipients on remote networks. Multicast is based on configuring the routers on the network with *address mapping tables*. These tables tell the router which unicast address to forward information to, based on the transmission to a specific multicast address. When a host transmits to a multicast address, routers on the local subnet pick up the transmission and search their mapping tables for a match to this address. If a router finds a match, the router will forward the information to all the destination hosts listed in the table. Let's take a look at an example to see how this works.

Let's say you are designing a network for a large commercial television organization. This organization would like to develop a special service for delivering time-sensitive news to its affiliates. The organization would like you to work the following criteria into the design:

- All information should be transmittable from a single system.

- There are well over 3,000 nodes that will require the delivery of the newsfeeds.

- Because the information is timely and updated frequently, delivery should be as fast as possible.

- A minimal amount of bandwidth should be used, because most links are Frame Relay, operating at only 56Kbps.

Figure 3.6 shows a small portion of how your network might appear. (This figure represents only a small portion of the network, as there are over 3,000 end stations.)

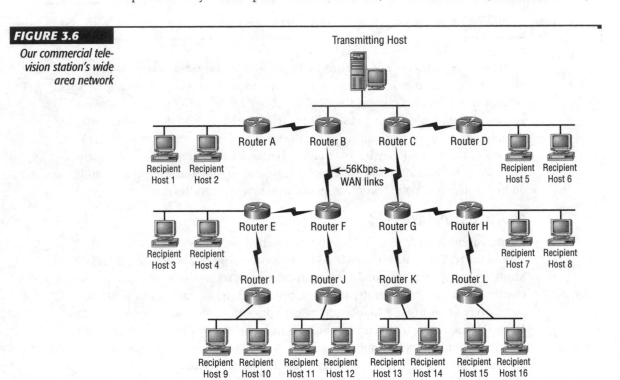

FIGURE 3.6

Our commercial tele-vision station's wide area network

Let's review our two other types of communications to see how they would affect this network.

Unicast   Our regular point-to-point communication is unicast. It would require our transmitting host to establish an individual communication session with each recipient host. This immediately raises two problems. The first is traffic. If your transmitting host is required to set up a communication session with 3,000 receiving hosts (including transmissions and acknowledgments), the amount of traffic generated would quickly saturate the network. The second problem is time. It will take your transmitting host a certain amount of time to run through all 3,000 hosts when delivering information. If there are frequent news updates, the delivery time may make it difficult for the host to keep up.

Broadcast   Broadcasts are delivered either to all hosts located on the same local subnet or to all hosts on the entire network (if the router is configured to forward broadcasts). Again, we have two problems. The first is performance. Given the network design, you would need to use all-network broadcasts. This would produce dismal network performance because the network would be saturated with broadcasts. The second problem is security. Because broadcasts will be propagated to all networks indiscriminately, your news information potentially could find itself on networks where it does not belong.

Given these descriptions, multicasting would be the most efficient means of transmitting our newsfeeds along this network. Let's apply some multicast tables to the routers to see how this would work. You can see the results in Table 3.6.

TABLE 3.6: MULTICAST ROUTING TABLE

Router	Destination Address	Forward to
A	224.10.10.5	Hosts 1 & 2
B	224.10.10.5	Routers A & F
C	224.10.10.5	Routers D & G
D	224.10.10.5	Hosts 5 & 6
E	224.10.10.5	Hosts 3 & 4
F	224.10.10.5	Routers E & J
G	224.10.10.5	Routers H & K
H	224.10.10.5	Hosts 7 & 8
I	224.10.10.5	Hosts 9 & 10
J	224.10.10.5	Hosts 11 & 12
K	224.10.10.5	Hosts 13 & 14
L	224.10.10.5	Hosts 15 & 16

According to Table 3.6, when Router B receives a packet for the destination multicast address of 224.10.10.5, it knows to forward the information to Routers A and F. When Router A receives the packet, it looks up the source address in its table, which tells it to forward the information to Hosts 1 and 2. This type of propagation continues down through the network until all the hosts have received the information.

Benefits of Multicast Addresses

There are a couple of points worth noting about this type of communication. First, the single source host can communicate efficiently with a large number of recipients. It is only required to transmit the data once; the tables on the routers take care of propagating the information as required. This spreads out the overhead required to communicate with each of our 3,000 recipient systems.

A second benefit to this type of communication is that you are creating very little traffic along your WAN links. For example, Router B is only required to generate a single communication session along each of its 56Kbps connections. If a retransmission is required, the request can go back to the previous router in the chain. The request is not required to return all the way back to the source system. Again, this cuts down on the amount of traffic along your slow links.

Because of the one-shot data transmission and light network traffic, you can deliver information in a timely manner. No single network device is required to communicate with all systems on the network. This overhead is spread out over multiple routers and network connections. This means that your source system is immediately free to transmit new information as required.

Multicast Drawbacks

There are some drawbacks to this type of communication, however, that make it applicable only in specific situations. First, in order for multicasting to work properly, your routers must be reconfigured so that they know what information must be forwarded where. If the destination is dynamic or random, it will be nearly impossible to keep up with the table changes.

Second, multicast communication is in a single direction only. The destination systems are not able to relay information back to the source system. This means that software such as Web browsers or FTP clients will not work.

Private Address Space

The InterNIC has reserved certain IP addresses for general use; their use does not need InterNIC approval. While these addresses may be used freely by any organization, they cannot be used for Internet communications. They will never be assigned to an organization by the InterNIC and thus anyone may use them for internal use only. Table 3.7 shows which IP address ranges are considered reserved.

TABLE 3.7: PRIVATE ADDRESS SPACE RANGES	
Starting Address	**Ending Address**
10.0.0.0	10.255.255.255
172.16.0.0	172.31.255.255
192.168.0.0	192.168.255.255

The use of private addresses has come about as a result of the depletion of registered addresses. As more and more organizations connect to the Internet, the pool of legal IP addresses available for Internet connectivity has shrunken dramatically. Private addresses are available for use when an IP subnet does not need Internet connectivity or when a *network address translation* (NAT) device will be used.

A NAT device is a network system capable of changing packets from one IP address to another. For example, a large network that requires a class A address could use the reserved address range of 10.0.0.0 when assigning IP addresses to internal hosts. When Internet access is required, a NAT device would then intercept these communications and map these addresses to a smaller legal subnet address. If multiple class A addresses are mapped to a single host address, the NAT device uses port numbers to keep the communication sessions orderly. This allows a small legal address range to easily support a large number of hosts. Because the NAT device must sit between the internal network and the Internet, its functionality has been incorporated into many of the top firewalling products.

 NOTE Cisco routers are capable of performing network address translation.

Variable-Length Subnet Masking

All of our IP examples until now have used standard subnet masks. By standard, I mean that the mask has had two possible values: 0 or 255. While this is fine in most situations, sometimes you need a little more control over your address range.

For example, let's say that you administer a very busy 80-node network, and as part of traffic control you have created two separate subnets with a router in between. An example of this network is shown in Figure 3.7. Let's also assume that your organization has decided to connect to the Internet but does not want to use address translation because of certain services you wish to support. You want every internal host to receive a valid IP address. You find an Internet Service Provider (ISP) and file all the required paperwork with the ISP in order to get connected.

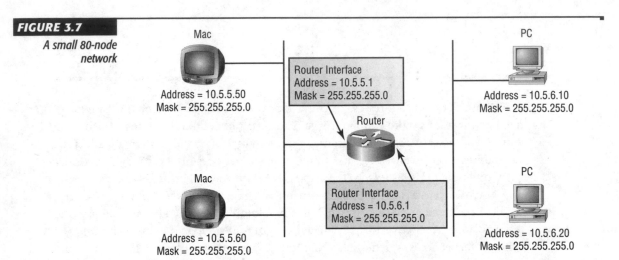

FIGURE 3.7

A small 80-node network

You find, however, that because your network is considered quite small, your ISP is only willing to give you one valid class C address. This leaves you with four options:

- Find another ISP that will give you two valid addresses

- Only allow one of your subnets to have Internet access

- Combine your two logical subnets into one and live with the performance degradation

- Apply a variable-length subnet mask

A *variable-length subnet mask* (VLSM) lets you take a single network address and break it up into multiple subnets. This is done by using some other value for the mask's bytes besides 0 or 255. A value of 255 indicates that the corresponding section of the IP address should be considered part of the network address. A value of 0 denotes that the number is unique to one specific host. By using values between 0 and 255 for the final byte in the mask, you can set a portion of it aside as being part of the network address and another portion as belonging to the host. Sound confusing? It can be. VLSM is considered one of the most difficult theories to grasp in IP networking. Let's continue with our example to help clarify this concept.

Using VSLM

Let's assume that the address assigned to you is 192.168.50.0. If you use a standard subnet mask of 255.255.255.0, you can configure a single subnet with 254 hosts.

If you change your subnet mask to 255.255.255.128, you have effectively split your network in half. Each of your two new networks can use roughly half of the host addresses available between 1 and 254. Table 3.8 shows your new configuration. Figure 3.8 shows this configuration applied to your network.

TABLE 3.8: USING VLSM

Network	Subnet Mask	First Host Address	Last Host Address	Broadcast Address
192.168.50.0	255.255.255.128	192.168.50.1	192.168.50.126	192.168.50.127
192.168.50.128	255.255.255.128	192.168.50.129	192.168.50.254	192.168.50.255

FIGURE 3.8

Network example with a variable-length sub-net mask applied

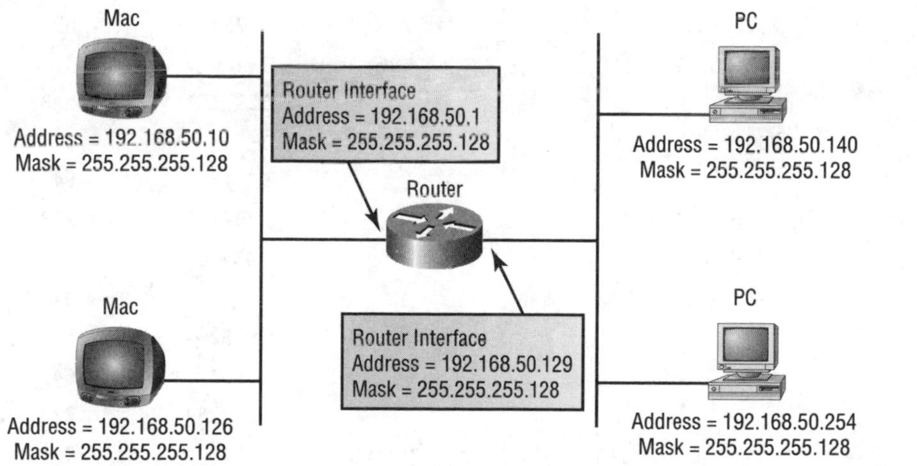

A couple of changes are worth noting here. Because of our variable-length subnet mask, 127 is now considered to be the broadcast address for our first subnet. Also, 128 is now considered a valid network address number, just like 0. This reinforces my earlier comment that an IP address is really meaningless unless you know the subnet mask, as well. With a standard subnet mask, 127 and 128 would signify specific hosts. Here, they indicate a broadcast address and your entire second network, respectively.

Where do these VLSM values come from? Remember that earlier in this chapter we discussed that IP addresses and subnet masks are based on the binary number system. When you indicate a mask value of 255.255.255.128, you are saying that the first three bytes are all considered to be part of the network address. In the last byte, the highest-order bit (decimal value of 128) is part of the network address, while the remaining seven bits are part of the host address. In shorthand, the address would be expressed as /25.

Table 3.9 depicts some potential variable-length subnet masks, as well as their effect on an IP address range. To save space, I've abbreviated masks that create more than four subnets. Only the first three subnets and the last are defined here. Given this information, it should be a simple matter to calculate the values for the subnets not listed. All address values are for the final byte in an IP address, because this is the only value that changes.

TABLE 3.9: COMMON VLSM VALUES

Mask	Number of Subnets	Hosts per Subnet	Available Host Address Ranges	Network Address Value	Broadcast Address Value
255.255.255.0	1	254	1–254	0	255
255.255.255.128	2	126	1–126	0	127
			129–254	128	255
255.255.255.192	4	62	1–62	0	63
			65–126	64	127
			129–190	128	191
			193–254	192	255
255.255.255.224	8	30	1–30	0	31
			33–62	32	63
			65–94	64	95
			225–254	224	255
255.255.255.240	16	14	1–14	0	15
			17–30	16	31
			33–46	32	47
			241–254	240	255
255.255.255.248	32	6	1–6	0	7
			9–14	8	15
			17–22	16	23
			249–254	248	255

Continued ▶

TABLE 3.9: COMMON VLSM VALUES (CONTINUED)					
Mask	Number of Subnets	Hosts per Subnet	Available Host Address Ranges	Network Address Value	Broadcast Address Value
255.255.255.252	64	2	1–2	0	3
			5–6	4	7
			9–10	8	11
			253–254	252	255
255.255.255.254	128	0	0	0	0

The first entry in Table 3.9 is your standard class C subnet mask. This creates only one logical subnet. The final nonstandard mask, 255.255.255.254, creates 128 subnets, but none can support any hosts. This means your largest *useful* subnet mask is 255.255.255.252. Because only two hosts are supported, this mask is typically used on WAN links where the only devices on the segment are the routers at both ends of the link.

You can also mix and match different subnet masks within the same IP address range. For example, let's say that you have a single subnet with approximately 100 hosts and four other subnets with 20 hosts on each. This gives you a total of five subnets to address. The closest match in the above table is 255.255.255.224, which will yield eight subnets. The problem is that this mask can only support 30 hosts per subnet.

The answer is to use a 255.255.255.128 subnet for half of your address range and 255.255.255.224 for the other half. This will let you break up your range into a total of five subnets. You could use the mask of 255.255.255.128 to reserve the first half of your available host addresses for the 100-host segment. You could break up the remaining half of your address range using a mask of 255.255.255.224 to create four additional segments supporting 30 hosts each.

Table 3.10 shows the breakdown of the address range using these masks. Let's assume that the class C address you're subnetting is 192.168.200.0.

TABLE 3.10: SUBNETTING THE NETWORK WITH VLSM				
Mask	Network Address	First Host Address	Last Host Address	Broadcast Address
255.255.255.128	192.168.200.0	192.168.200.1	192.168.200.126	192.168.200.127
255.255.255.224	192.168.200.128	192.168.200.129	192.168.200.158	192.168.200.159

Continued ▶

TABLE 3.10: SUBNETTING THE NETWORK WITH VLSM (CONTINUED)

Mask	Network Address	First Host Address	Last Host Address	Broadcast Address
255.255.255.224	192.168.200.160	192.168.200.161	192.168.200.190	192.168.200.191
255.255.255.224	192.168.200.192	192.168.200.193	192.168.200.222	192.168.200.223
255.255.255.224	192.168.200.224	192.168.200.225	192.168.200.254	192.168.200.255

Figure 3.9 shows this address scheme applied to a network. By mixing your subnet masks, you can achieve the most efficient use of a single address range.

FIGURE 3.9

Using a mixture of subnet masks to support multiple subnets with a varying number of hosts

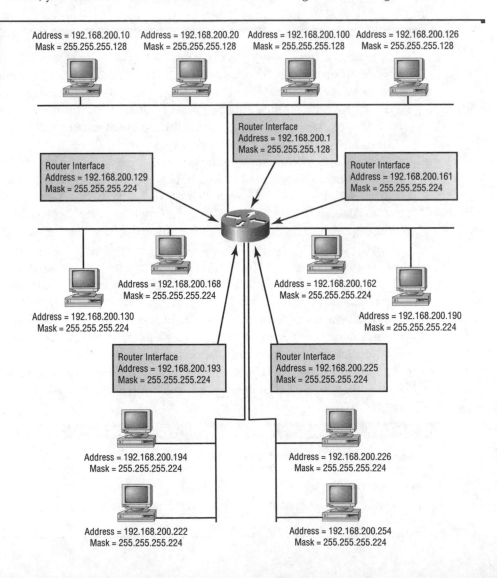

Lost Address Space

As Table 3.10 shows, each time you further subnet your address, the number of supportable hosts decreases. For example, while a class C subnet will support 254 hosts, a variable-length subnet mask of 255.255.255.248 will only support 192 (32 subnets of six hosts each). This is because each time you further divide your address, you lose two potential host numbers: one to identify the network address and one to identify the broadcast address.

Also, the original Request for Comments (RFC 950), which defined how IP subnets should be created, required that the first and last subnet created by a variable-length subnet mask be ignored. According to this requirement, while a mask of 255.255.255.248 would create 32 subnets, only 30 of them would be legal. This would drop the number of supported hosts to 180 (30 legal subnets with six hosts each).

Luckily, a later RFC (1878) redefined this specification so that it is indeed legal to use the first and last subnets. Collectively, these two subnets are known as *subnet zero*, and quite a bit of confusion exists about whether they are legal to use. Many people do not realize that a later RFC was released approving their use.

 TIP By default, a Cisco router will not accept subnet zero addresses. In order to use this address space, you must issue the command `ip subnet-zero`.

Address Discovery

IP uses the *Address Resolution Protocol* (ARP) to perform the delivery of data. All local delivery is performed using the destination system's media access control (MAC) number. ARP is used by a transmitting system to map the destination system's IP address to its MAC address.

For example, let's say you are using your favorite Web browser, and you enter the following URL:

`http://www.cisco.com`

Your system will first use the Domain Name Service (DNS) to map the host www.cisco.com to an IP address. Your system then compares this IP address to its own, to see whether the system is located on the same subnet. At this point, one of two things will happen:

- If the system is local, your computer will ARP (send an Address Resolution Protocol packet) for the destination system's MAC address.
- If the system is on another subnet, your computer will ARP for the MAC address of the local router.

NOTE You can read a detailed description of DNS later in this chapter.

ARP is simply a local broadcast frame that states, "If you are using this IP address, please reply." The frame contains the IP address for which it needs to find a MAC address. The Ethernet portion of the frame header will contain your system's MAC address in the source field and a broadcast address of FFFFFFFFFFFF in the destination field.

When the system using the IP address replies, saying, "I'm here," the frame it sends you will contain the system's MAC address in the Ethernet source field. Now your system can associate the IP address with a MAC address and perform a local delivery. Your system will also cache this information in its *ARP table*. This way, if you need to send this system more information, it already knows the local address.

ARP can also be used to avoid IP address conflicts. The typical modern network operating system will now ARP during startup to insure that another system is not already using its IP address. Before assuming that it can use a specific IP address, the machine will ARP for the address on the local subnet. If it does not receive a reply, it assumes that the address is free to use. If it does receive a reply, it will display an error message and disable IP networking. This process helps to insure that no two machines try to share the same IP address.

Transport Layer Services

Chapter 1 contains a detailed description of IP's TCP and UDP Transport layer services, so I will add only a simple review here.

Transmission Control Protocol (TCP)

TCP is IP's connection-oriented transport. It is used when an application wants the Transport layer to insure that the destination system has received all packets correctly. In a TCP transmission, the receiving system must acknowledge every packet it receives.

User Datagram Protocol (UDP)

UDP is IP's connectionless transport. UDP is used when an application is capable of insuring that the destination system has received all packets. If a packet is missed, it is the application—not UDP—that is responsible for realizing that a packet was missed and retransmitting the data. Due to its reduced overhead, UDP has the potential to transmit more information with fewer packets than TCP.

IP Services

We can find our remote system and insure that both systems are using the same level of communications. The question now is how to tell the server what we want. While computers are powerful tools—capable of processing many requests per second—they still have a problem with the phrase, "You know what I mean?" This is why we need a way to let a system know exactly what we want from it. It would be a real bummer to connect to a slick new Web site, only to have the server start spewing e-mail or routing information at you because it had no idea what you were looking for.

To make sure the computer knows what we want from it, we need to look to the Session layer.

 NOTE   You may recall from our discussion of the Session layer in Chapter 1 that this layer is responsible for insuring that requests for service are formulated properly.

What's an IP Service?

A *service* is a process or application that runs on a server and provides some benefit to a network user. E-mail is a good example of a value-added service. A system may queue your e-mail messages until you connect to the system with a mail client in order to read them. File and print sharing are two additional examples of network services.

Services are accessed by connecting to a specific port or socket. Think of ports as virtual mail slots on the system, and you'll get the idea. A separate mail slot (port number) is designated for each service or application running on the system. When a user wishes to access a service, the Session layer is responsible for insuring that the request reaches the correct mail slot or port number.

To connect to a service, you need to know the port number it is listening on. This is where the concept of *well known ports* comes into play. Well known ports are de facto standards used to insure that everyone can access services on other machines without needing to guess which port number is used by the service. For example, there is nothing stopping you from setting up a Web server on port 573, provided that the port is not in use by some other service. The problem is that people will expect the service to be available on port 80 and may be unable to find it.

NOTE De facto standard means that it is a standard by popularity; it is not a rule or law.

Ports 0–1023 are defined by the Internet Assigned Numbers Authority (IANA) for most well known services. While ports have been assigned up to 7200, it is the ports below 1024 that make up the bulk of Internet communications. These assignments are not hard and fast rules but guides to insure that everyone offers public services on the same port. For example, if you want to access Microsoft's Web page, you can assume that Microsoft offers the service on port 80, because this is the well known port for that service.

Reply Ports

When a system requests information, the system not only specifies the port it wishes to access but also which port should be used for returning the requested information. Port numbers for this task are selected from 1024 to 65535 and are referred to as *upper port numbers* or *reply ports*.

To illustrate how this works, let's review the Telnet session shown in Figure 3.10. When Loki attempts to set up a Telnet session with Thor, it will do so by accessing port 23 on that system (port 23 is the well known service port for Telnet). If you look at frame 2, you can see that Thor is sending the acknowledgment (ACK) back on port 1042. This is because the session information in the original frame that Loki sent Thor specified a reply port of 1042 and a destination port of 23. The destination port identifies where the frame was going (port 23 on Thor), while the reply port identifies which port should be used when sending replies (port 1042 on Loki). Port 23 is our well known service port, while port 1042 is our upper port number used for the reply.

 NOTE Reply ports are also known as *source ports*.

Upper reply ports are assigned on the fly. Depending on the operating system, they may be selected sequentially or randomly.

FIGURE 3.10

A Telnet session from
Loki to Thor

No.	Siz	Source	Destination	Layer	Summary
1	64	LOKI.FOOBAR.COM	THOR.FOOBAR.COM	tcp	Port:1042 ---> TELNET SYN
2	64	THOR.FOOBAR.COM	LOKI.FOOBAR.COM	tcp	Port:TELNET ---> 1042 ACK SYN
3	64	LOKI.FOOBAR.COM	THOR.FOOBAR.COM	tcp	Port:1042 ---> TELNET ACK
4	82	LOKI.FOOBAR.COM	THOR.FOOBAR.COM	telnt	Cmd=Do; Code=Suppress Go Ahead; Cmd=Will; Code=Termin
5	64	THOR.FOOBAR.COM	LOKI.FOOBAR.COM	tcp	Port:TELNET ---> 1042 ACK
6	70	THOR.FOOBAR.COM	LOKI.FOOBAR.COM	telnt	Cmd=Do; Code=Terminal Type; Cmd=Do; Code=Terminal Spe
7	64	LOKI.FOOBAR.COM	THOR.FOOBAR.COM	telnt	Cmd=Won't; Code=; Cmd=Will; Code=Terminal Type;
8	73	THOR.FOOBAR.COM	LOKI.FOOBAR.COM	telnt	Cmd=Will; Code=Suppress Go Ahead; Cmd=Do; Code=; Cmd=
9	64	THOR.FOOBAR.COM	LOKI.FOOBAR.COM	tcp	Port:TELNET ---> 1042 ACK
10	67	LOKI.FOOBAR.COM	THOR.FOOBAR.COM	telnt	Cmd=Subnegotiation Begin; Code=; Data=..P....
11	76	THOR.FOOBAR.COM	LOKI.FOOBAR.COM	telnt	Cmd=Subnegotiation Begin; Code=Terminal Speed; Data= .....
12	64	LOKI.FOOBAR.COM	THOR.FOOBAR.COM	tcp	Port:1042 ---> TELNET ACK
13	64	THOR.FOOBAR.COM	LOKI.FOOBAR.COM	tcp	Port:TELNET ---> 1042 ACK
14	92	LOKI.FOOBAR.COM	THOR.FOOBAR.COM	telnt	Cmd=Subnegotiation Begin; Code=Terminal Speed; Data= .38
15	64	THOR.FOOBAR.COM	LOKI.FOOBAR.COM	telnt	Cmd=Do; Code=Echo;
16	64	LOKI.FOOBAR.COM	THOR.FOOBAR.COM	telnt	Cmd=Won't; Code=Echo;
17	129	THOR.FOOBAR.COM	LOKI.FOOBAR.COM	telnt	Cmd=Will; Code=Echo; Data=..Red Hat Linux release 4.1 (Var
18	64	LOKI.FOOBAR.COM	THOR.FOOBAR.COM	telnt	Cmd=Do; Code=Echo;
19	64	THOR.FOOBAR.COM	LOKI.FOOBAR.COM	tcp	Port:TELNET ---> 1042 ACK
20	65	THOR.FOOBAR.COM	LOKI.FOOBAR.COM	telnt	Data=login:
21	64	LOKI.FOOBAR.COM	THOR.FOOBAR.COM	tcp	Port:1042 ---> TELNET ACK

Identifying Multiple Sessions

Reply ports are also used to distinctly identify similar sessions between systems. For example, let's build on Figure 3.10. We already have one Telnet session running from Loki to Thor. What happens if four or five more sessions are created? All sessions have the following information in common:

Source IP address   10.2.2.20 (loki.foobar.com)

Destination IP address   10.2.2.10 (thor.foobar.com)

Destination port   23 (well known port for Telnet)

The source ports remain distinctive in order to identify each individual session. Our first connection has already specified a source port of 1042 for its connection. Each sequential Telnet session that is established after that would be assigned some other upper port number to uniquely identify it. The actual numbers assigned would be based on what was not currently being used by the source system. For example, ports 1118, 1398, 4023, and 6025 may be used as source ports for the next four sessions. The actual reply port number does not really matter, only that it can uniquely identify that specific session between the two systems.

IP Application Services

Many application services are designed to use IP as a transport. Some are designed to aid the end user in transferring information, while others have been created to support the functionality of IP itself. Services commonly used on a Cisco router are described in this section, including the transport used for data delivery and the well known port number assigned to the service.

Boot Protocol (*bootp*) and Dynamic Host Configuration Protocol (DHCP)

There are three methods of assigning IP addresses to host systems:

Manual   The user manually configures an IP host to use a specific address.

Automatic   A server automatically assigns a specific address to a host during startup.

Dynamic   A server dynamically assigns free addresses from a pool to hosts during startup.

Manual is the most time consuming but the most fault tolerant. It requires that each IP host be configured with all the information the system requires to communicate using IP. Manual is the most appropriate method to use for systems that must maintain the same IP address or for systems that must be accessible even when the IP address server may be down. Web servers, mail servers, and any other servers that provide IP services are usually manually configured for IP communications.

Bootp supports automatic address assignment. A table is maintained on the bootp server, listing each host's MAC number. Each entry also contains the IP address to be used by the system. When the bootp server receives a request for an IP address, it refers to its table and looks for the sending system's MAC number, returning the appropriate IP address for that system. While this makes management a little simpler (because all administration can be performed from a central system), the process is still time-consuming because each MAC address must be recorded. It also does nothing to free up IP address space that may not be in use.

DHCP supports both automatic and dynamic IP address assignments. When addresses are dynamically assigned, the server issues IP addresses to host systems from a pool of available numbers. The benefit of dynamic assignment over automatic is that only the hosts that require an IP address have one assigned. When a host system no longer needs its IP address, the IP address can be returned to the pool to be issued to another host.

 NOTE   The amount of time a host retains a specific IP address is called the *lease period*. A short lease period insures that only systems requiring an IP address have one assigned. When IP is used only occasionally, a small pool of addresses can support a large number of hosts.

The other benefit of DHCP is that the server can send more than just address information. The remote host can also be configured with its host name, default router, domain name, local DNS server, and so on. This allows an administrator to remotely configure IP services to a large number of hosts with a minimal amount of work. A single DHCP server is capable of servicing multiple subnets.

The only drawbacks to DHCP are the following:

- Increased broadcast traffic (clients send an all-network broadcast when they need an address)

- Address space stability if the DHCP server is shut down

On many systems, the tables tracking who has been assigned which addresses are saved in memory only. When the system goes down, this table is lost. When you restart the system, it's possible that IP addresses may be assigned to systems that were already leased to another system before the shutdown. If this happens, you may need to renew the lease on all systems or wait until the lease time expires.

 NOTE Both bootp and DHCP use UDP as their communication transport. Clients transmit address requests from a source port of 68 to a destination port of 67.

Domain Name Service (DNS)

DNS is responsible for mapping host names to IP addresses and vice versa. It is the service that allows you to connect to Cisco's Web server by entering www.cisco.com instead of having to remember the system's IP address. All IP packet delivery is done with addresses, not names. While IP systems do not use names when transferring information, names are easier for people to remember. DNS was developed to make reaching remote systems simpler. DNS allows a person to enter an easy-to-remember name, while allowing the computer to translate this into the address information it needs to deliver the requested data.

DNS follows a hierarchical, distributed structure. No single DNS server is responsible for keeping track of every host name on the Internet. Each system is responsible for only a portion of the framework.

Figure 3.11 shows an example of how DNS is structured. Visually, it resembles a number of trees strapped to a pole and hanging upside down. The pole is not meant to represent the backbone of the Internet; it simply indicates that there is DNS connectivity among the different domains. The systems located just below the pole are referred to as the *root name servers*. Each root name server is responsible for one or more top-level domains. The top-level domains are the .com, .edu, .org, .mil, or .gov found at the end of a domain name. Every domain that ends in .com, for example, is said to be part of the same top-level domain.

FIGURE 3.11

The hierarchical structure of DNS

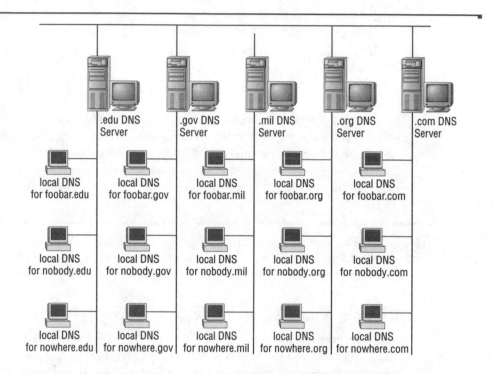

The root name servers are responsible for keeping track of the DNS servers for each subdomain within a top-level domain. They do not know about individual systems within each subdomain, only the DNS servers that are responsible for them.

Each subdomain DNS server is responsible for tracking the IP addresses for all the hosts within its domain.

Let's walk through an example to see how it works. Let's assume that you're part of the foobar.com domain. Let's also assume that you're running a Web browser and have entered the following URL:

http://www.cisco.com

Your system will first check its DNS cache (if it has one) to see if it knows the IP address for www.cisco.com. If it does not, it forms a *DNS query* (a DNS query is simply a request for IP information) and asks one of the DNS servers within the foobar.com domain for the address. Let's assume that the system it queries is ns.foobar.com.

If ns.foobar.com does not have this information cached, it also forms a DNS query and forwards the request to the root name server responsible for the top-level domain .com, because this is where the Cisco domain is located.

The root name server will consult its tables and form a reply similar to this: "I do not know the IP address for www.cisco.com. I do, however, know that ns.cisco.com is responsible for all the hosts within the cisco.com domain. Its IP address is 10.5.5.1. Please forward your query to that system."

Ns.foobar.com now knows that if it needs to find a system with the cisco.com domain, it must ask ns.cisco.com. It caches this information and forwards the request to ns.cisco.com.

Ns.cisco.com will, in turn, consult its tables and look up the IP address for www.cisco.com. Ns.cisco.com will then forward this information to ns.foobar.com. Ns.foobar.com will cache this information and forward the answer to your system. Your system would now use this IP address information to reach the remote Web server.

If you think that there is a whole lot of querying going on, then you have a good understanding of the process. The additional traffic is highly preferable, however, to the amount of overhead that would be required to allow a single system to maintain the DNS information for every system on the Internet.

As you may have noticed, DNS makes effective use of caching information during queries. This helps to reduce traffic when you're looking up popular sites. For example, if someone else within foobar.com now attempted to reach www.cisco.com, the IP address for this system has been cached by ns.foobar.com. It can now answer this query directly.

The amount of time that ns.foobar.com remembers this information is determined by the *time to live* (TTL) set for this address. The TTL is set by the administrator responsible for managing the remote name server (in this case, ns.cisco.com). If www.cisco.com is a stable system, this value may be set high, such as 30 days. If the IP address for www.cisco.com is likely to change frequently, the TTL may be set to a lower value, such as a few hours.

 NOTE   DNS uses TCP and UDP transports when communicating. Both use a destination port of 53.

File Transfer Protocol (FTP)

In all of the services discussed so far, the source system would create a single service connection to the destination system when accessing a specific service. Unless multiple users requested this service, only a single connection session was required.

FTP is used to transfer file information from one system to another. FTP uses TCP as its transport and ports 20 and 21 for communication. Port 21 is used to transfer session information (user name, password, commands), while port 20 is referred to as the *data port* and is used to transfer the actual file.

Figure 3.12 shows an FTP command session between two systems (Loki is connecting to Thor). Notice the three-packet TCP handshake at the beginning of the session, which was described in the section on connection-oriented communications in Chapter 1. All communications are using a destination port of 21, which is referred to as the *FTP session port*. Port 1038 is the random upper port used by Loki when receiving replies. This connection was initiated by Loki on port 1038 to Thor at port 21.

FIGURE 3.12

An FTP command session between two systems

No.	Size	Source	Destination	Layer	Summary
1	64	LOKI.FOOBAR.COM	THOR.FOOBAR.COM	tcp	Port:1038 ---> FTP SYN
2	64	THOR.FOOBAR.COM	LOKI.FOOBAR.COM	tcp	Port:FTP ---> 1038 ACK SYN
3	64	LOKI.FOOBAR.COM	THOR.FOOBAR.COM	tcp	Port:1038 ---> FTP ACK
4	164	THOR.FOOBAR.COM	LOKI.FOOBAR.COM	ftp	Reply:(Service ready for new user.)
5	64	LOKI.FOOBAR.COM	THOR.FOOBAR.COM	tcp	Port:1038 ---> FTP ACK
6	73	LOKI.FOOBAR.COM	THOR.FOOBAR.COM	ftp	Command=USER(User Name)
7	64	THOR.FOOBAR.COM	LOKI.FOOBAR.COM	tcp	Port:FTP ---> 1038 ACK
8	95	THOR.FOOBAR.COM	LOKI.FOOBAR.COM	ftp	Reply:(User name okay, need password.)
9	64	LOKI.FOOBAR.COM	THOR.FOOBAR.COM	tcp	Port:1038 ---> FTP ACK
10	71	LOKI.FOOBAR.COM	THOR.FOOBAR.COM	ftp	Command=PASS(Password)
11	64	THOR.FOOBAR.COM	LOKI.FOOBAR.COM	tcp	Port:FTP ---> 1038 ACK
12	88	THOR.FOOBAR.COM	LOKI.FOOBAR.COM	ftp	Reply:(User logged in, proceed.)
13	64	LOKI.FOOBAR.COM	THOR.FOOBAR.COM	ftp	Command=SYST(System Operating System Type)
14	77	THOR.FOOBAR.COM	LOKI.FOOBAR.COM	ftp	Reply:(Name system type.)
15	64	LOKI.FOOBAR.COM	THOR.FOOBAR.COM	tcp	Port:1038 ---> FTP ACK
17	66	LOKI.FOOBAR.COM	THOR.FOOBAR.COM	ftp	Command=TYPE(Representation Type)
18	78	THOR.FOOBAR.COM	LOKI.FOOBAR.COM	ftp	Reply:(Command okay.)
19	64	LOKI.FOOBAR.COM	THOR.FOOBAR.COM	tcp	Port:1038 ---> FTP ACK

Figure 3.13 shows Loki initiating a file transfer from Thor. Lines 7, 8, and 9 show the TCP three-packet handshake. Lines 10–24 show the actual data transfer. We needed to perform another three-packet handshake because communication is being established between a new set of ports.

This is where things get a bit weird. Loki and Thor still have an active session on ports 1038 and 21, as indicated in Figure 3.12. Figure 3.13 is a second, separate session running parallel to the one shown in Figure 3.12. This second session is initiated in order to transfer the actual file or data.

FIGURE 3.13

An FTP data session

No.	Size	Source	Destination	Layer	Summary
2	66	LOKI.FOOBAR.COM	THOR.FOOBAR.COM	ftp	Command=TYPE(Representation Type)
3	78	THOR.FOOBAR.COM	LOKI.FOOBAR.COM	ftp	Reply:(Command okay.)
4	79	LOKI.FOOBAR.COM	THOR.FOOBAR.COM	ftp	Command=PORT(Data Port)
5	88	THOR.FOOBAR.COM	LOKI.FOOBAR.COM	ftp	Reply:(Command okay.)
6	77	LOKI.FOOBAR.COM	THOR.FOOBAR.COM	ftp	Command=RETR(Retrieve File)
7	64	THOR.FOOBAR.COM	LOKI.FOOBAR.COM	tcp	Port:FTP-DATA ---> 1037 SYN
8	64	LOKI.FOOBAR.COM	THOR.FOOBAR.COM	tcp	Port:1037 ---> FTP-DATA ACK SYN
9	64	THOR.FOOBAR.COM	LOKI.FOOBAR.COM	tcp	Port:FTP-DATA ---> 1037 ACK
10	132	THOR.FOOBAR.COM	LOKI.FOOBAR.COM	ftp	Reply:(File status okay; about to open data connection.)
11	1,518	THOR.FOOBAR.COM	LOKI.FOOBAR.COM	tcp	Port:FTP-DATA ---> 1037 ACK
12	1,518	THOR.FOOBAR.COM	LOKI.FOOBAR.COM	tcp	Port:FTP-DATA ---> 1037 ACK
13	64	LOKI.FOOBAR.COM	THOR.FOOBAR.COM	tcp	Port:1037 ---> FTP-DATA ACK
14	1,518	THOR.FOOBAR.COM	LOKI.FOOBAR.COM	tcp	Port:FTP-DATA ---> 1037 ACK
15	1,518	THOR.FOOBAR.COM	LOKI.FOOBAR.COM	tcp	Port:FTP-DATA ---> 1037 ACK
16	1,518	THOR.FOOBAR.COM	LOKI.FOOBAR.COM	tcp	Port:FTP-DATA ---> 1037 ACK
17	64	LOKI.FOOBAR.COM	THOR.FOOBAR.COM	tcp	Port:1037 ---> FTP-DATA ACK
18	64	LOKI.FOOBAR.COM	THOR.FOOBAR.COM	tcp	Port:1034 ---> FTP ACK
19	1,518	THOR.FOOBAR.COM	LOKI.FOOBAR.COM	tcp	Port:FTP-DATA ---> 1037 ACK PUSH
20	1,518	THOR.FOOBAR.COM	LOKI.FOOBAR.COM	tcp	Port:FTP-DATA ---> 1037 ACK
21	1,518	THOR.FOOBAR.COM	LOKI.FOOBAR.COM	tcp	Port:FTP-DATA ---> 1037 ACK
22	1,518	THOR.FOOBAR.COM	LOKI.FOOBAR.COM	tcp	Port:FTP-DATA ---> 1037 ACK
23	64	LOKI.FOOBAR.COM	THOR.FOOBAR.COM	tcp	Port:1037 ---> FTP-DATA ACK
24	1,518	THOR.FOOBAR.COM	LOKI.FOOBAR.COM	tcp	Port:FTP-DATA ---> 1037 ACK

There is something else a bit odd about this connection: Look closely at line number 7. Thor—not Loki—is actually initiating the TCP three-packet handshake in order to transfer the file information. While Loki was responsible for initiating the original FTP command session to port 21, Thor is the one actually initiating the FTP data session.

This means that in order to support active FTP sessions to the Internet, we must allow connections to be established from Internet hosts on port 20 to our internal network. This will become important later on when we talk about using a router to filter traffic in Chapter 9, the chapter on access lists.

Passive FTP

There is also a second type of FTP transfer known as *passive FTP* (PASV FTP). Passive FTP is identical to active FTP in terms of sending commands over port 21. The difference between PASV FTP and active FTP lies in how the data session gets initiated. PASV FTP is the mode supported by most Web browsers.

Before transferring data, a client can request PASV mode transmission. If the FTP server acknowledges this request, the client is allowed to initiate the TCP three-packet handshake for data transfer, instead of the server. Figure 3.14 shows a capture of two systems using PASV FTP. Packet 21 shows This_Workstation (or FTP client) requesting that PASV FTP be used. In packet 22, the FTP server responds, stating that PASV mode is supported.

FIGURE 3.14

A passive-mode FTP session

No.	Source	Destination	Layer	Summary	Size	Interpacke	Absolute Time
5	00A0C9898D21	This_Workstation	tcp	Port:FTP ---> 1138 ACK SYN	64	176 ms	11:17:52 AM
6	This_Workstation	00A0C9898D21	tcp	Port:1138 ---> FTP ACK	64	529 µs	11:17:52 AM
7	00A0C9898D21	This_Workstation	ftp	Reply:(Service ready for new user.)	104	96 ms	11:17:53 AM
8	This_Workstation	00A0C9898D21	ftp	Command=USER(User Name)	74	34 ms	11:17:53 AM
9	00A0C9898D21	This_Workstation	ftp	Reply:(User name okay, need password.)	130	94 ms	11:17:53 AM
10	This_Workstation	00A0C9898D21	tcp	Port:1138 ---> FTP ACK	64	129 ms	11:17:53 AM
11	This_Workstation	00A0C9898D21	ftp	Command=PASS(Password)	73	61 ms	11:17:53 AM
12	00A0C9898D21	This_Workstation	ftp		89	90 ms	11:17:53 AM
13	This_Workstation	00A0C9898D21	tcp	Port:1138 ---> FTP ACK	64	142 ms	11:17:53 AM
14	00A0C9898D21	This_Workstation	ftp	Unknown FTP Code	266	84 ms	11:17:53 AM
15	This_Workstation	00A0C9898D21	ftp	Command=REST(Restart at Marker)	66	29 ms	11:17:53 AM
16	00A0C9898D21	This_Workstation	ftp	Reply:(Requested file action pending further information.)	80	83 ms	11:17:53 AM
17	This_Workstation	00A0C9898D21	ftp	Command=SYST(System Operating System Type)	64	17 ms	11:17:53 AM
18	00A0C9898D21	This_Workstation	ftp	Reply:(Name system type.)	86	84 ms	11:17:53 AM
19	This_Workstation	00A0C9898D21	ftp	Command=PWD(Print Working Directory)	64	26 ms	11:17:53 AM
20	00A0C9898D21	This_Workstation	ftp	Reply:(PATHNAME created.)	89	82 ms	11:17:53 AM
21	This_Workstation	00A0C9898D21	ftp	Command=PASV(Passive Listen)	64	39 ms	11:17:54 AM
22	00A0C9898D21	This_Workstation	ftp	Reply:(Entering passive mode (h1,h2,h3,h4,p1,p2).)	109	86 ms	11:17:54 AM
23	This_Workstation	00A0C9898D21	tcp	Port:1139 ---> 3323 SYN	64	101 ms	11:17:54 AM
24	This_Workstation	00A0C9898D21	tcp	Port:1138 ---> FTP ACK	64	52 ms	11:17:54 AM
25	00A0C9898D21	This_Workstation	tcp	Port:3323 ---> 1139 ACK SYN	64	30 ms	11:17:54 AM
26	This_Workstation	00A0C9898D21	tcp	Port:1139 ---> 3323 ACK	64	469 µs	11:17:54 AM
27	This_Workstation	00A0C9898D21	ftp	Command=TYPE(Representation Type)	66	36 ms	11:17:54 AM
28	00A0C9898D21	This_Workstation	ftp	Reply:(Command okay.)	78	95 ms	11:17:54 AM
29	This_Workstation	00A0C9898D21	ftp	Command=Unknown Command	66	22 ms	11:17:54 AM
30	00A0C9898D21	This_Workstation	ftp	Reply:(Syntax error, command unrecognized or too long.)	96	81 ms	11:17:54 AM
31	This_Workstation	00A0C9898D21	ftp	Command=Unknown Command	66	38 ms	11:17:54 AM
32	00A0C9898D21	This_Workstation	ftp	Reply:(Syntax error, command unrecognized or too long.)	96	83 ms	11:17:54 AM
33	This_Workstation	00A0C9898D21	ftp	Command=CWD(Change to Working Directory)	65	23 ms	11:17:54 AM
34	00A0C9898D21	This_Workstation	ftp	Reply:(Requested file action okay, completed.)	87	87 ms	11:17:54 AM
35	This_Workstation	00A0C9898D21	ftp	Command=LIST(List Information of)	64	18 ms	11:17:54 AM
36	00A0C9898D21	This_Workstation	ftp	Reply:(Data connection already open; transfer starting.)	112	85 ms	11:17:54 AM
37	00A0C9898D21	This_Workstation	tcp	Port:3323 ---> 1139 ACK PUSH	1,312	51 ms	11:17:54 AM
38	00A0C9898D21	This_Workstation	tcp	Port:3323 ---> 1139 ACK FIN	64	381 µs	11:17:54 AM

Notice what occurs in packet 23. Our FTP client initiates the TCP three-packet handshake in order to transfer data. This means that we are no longer required to allow connections to be established from Internet hosts on port 20 to our internal network just to be able to support FTP. It also means, however, that in order to support PASV FTP, we must allow outbound sessions to be established on all ports above 1023. Again, we will revisit the problems this can cause later on in the book, when we discuss using your router to filter traffic in the access lists chapter.

 NOTE FTP uses the TCP transport for all communications. Commands are sent over port 21, while data uses port 20.

Hypertext Transfer Protocol (HTTP)

HTTP is used in communications between Web browsers and Web servers. It differs from most services in that it does not create and maintain a single session while a user is retrieving information from a server. Every request for information—whether it is text, graphics, or sound—creates a separate session, which is terminated once that request is completed. A Web page with lots of graphics must have multiple simultaneous connections created in order to be loaded onto a browser.

Since version 1, HTTP has included Multipurpose Internet Mail Extensions (MIME) to support the negotiation of data types. This has helped HTTP to become a truly cross-platform service, as MIME allows the Web browser to tell the server the types of file format it can support. It also allows the server to alert the Web browser about what type of data it is about to receive. This allows the browser to select the correct, platform-specific viewing or playing software for the data it is about to receive.

Many Cisco routers include an HTTP management interface. This means that you can perform many administrative tasks using any modern Web browser.

NOTE   HTTP uses the TCP transport and a destination port of 80 when communicating.

Simple Network Management Protocol (SNMP)

SNMP is used both to monitor and control network devices. The monitoring or controlling station is referred to as the *SNMP management station*. The network devices to be controlled are required to run *SNMP agents*. The agents and the management station work together to give the network administrator a central point of control over the network.

NOTE   The SNMP agent provides the link into the networking device. The device can be a manageable hub, a router, or even a server. The agent uses both static and dynamic information when reporting to the management station.

The *static information* is data stored within the device in order to identify it uniquely. For example, the administrator may choose to store the device's physical location and serial number as part of the SNMP static information. This makes it easier to identify which device you're working with from the SNMP management station.

The *dynamic information* is data that pertains to the current state of the device. For example, port status on a hub would be considered dynamic information because the port may be enabled or disabled, depending on whether it is functioning properly.

The SNMP management station is the central console used to control all network devices that have SNMP agents. The management station first learns about a network device through a *management information base* (MIB). The MIB is a piece of software supplied by the network device vendor, usually on floppy disk. When the MIB is added to the management station, the MIB teaches the station about the network device. This helps to insure that SNMP management stations created by one vendor will operate properly with network devices produced by another.

Information is usually collected by the SNMP management station by *polling*. The SNMP management station will issue queries at predetermined intervals in order to check the status of each network device. SNMP only supports two commands for collecting information: get and getnext. The get command allows the management station to retrieve information on a specific operating parameter. For example, it may query a router to report on the current status of one of its ports. The getnext command is used when a complete status will be collected from a device. Instead of forcing the SNMP management station to issue a series of specific get commands, getnext can be used to retrieve sequentially each piece of information a device can report on.

SNMP also allows for controlling network devices through the command set. The set command can be used to alter some of the operational parameters on a network device. For example, if the above get command reported that port two on the router was disabled, you could issue a set command to the router to enable the port.

SNMP typically does not offer the same range of control as a network device's management utility. For example, while you may be able to turn ports on and off on your router, you would probably be unable to initialize IP networking and assign an IP address to the port. The amount of control available through SNMP is limited by the commands included in the vendor's MIB, as well as by the command structure of SNMP itself. The operative word in SNMP is "simple." SNMP provides only a minimal amount of control over network devices.

While most reporting is done via the SNMP management station's polling of network devices, SNMP does allow network devices to report critical events immediately back to the management station. These messages are called *traps*. Traps are sent when an event occurs that is too important to wait until the device is again polled. For example, your router may send a trap to the SNMP management console if it has just been power cycled. Because this event will have a grave impact on network connectivity, it is reported to the SNMP management station immediately, instead of waiting for the device to be polled again.

 NOTE SNMP uses the UDP transport and destination ports 161 and 162 when communicating.

Telnet

Telnet is used when a remote communication session is required with some other system on the network. Its functionality is similar to a mainframe terminal or a remote control session. The local system becomes little more than a dumb terminal, providing system updates only. The remote system supplies the file system and all processing time required when running programs.

 NOTE Telnet uses the TCP transport and destination port 23 when creating a communication session.

Trivial File Transfer Protocol (TFTP)

Think of *TFTP* as a "lite" version of FTP, and you will be on the right track. TFTP is a very simplistic protocol which is used for transferring file information—no more, no less. You cannot authenticate different users via TFTP, nor can you list directories or available files in the server. TFTP is designed to be a quick and dirty method of moving file info from point A to point B with very few frills.

One of the best uses of TFTP is loading or backing up your router configuration files. For example, let's say you administer a router with more than 16 ports and a very detailed configuration. Manually restoring the configuration from scratch could take an hour or more. Of course, this assumes that you have been diligent in documenting the configuration.

To back up your configuration using TFTP, issue this command

```
copy running-config tftp
```

and enter the name of the file you wish to use, as well as the IP address of your TFTP server.

If you ever need to restore this configuration file, simply enter the complementary command:

```
copy tftp running-config
```

You will be prompted for the TFTP server's IP address, the name of the file, and confirmation.

 NOTE Don't worry about the specifics of the TFTP commands just yet. For now, simply realize that it can be a powerful tool which is very easy to use. We will cover TFTP in greater detail in Chapter 8: "Installing Cisco IOS."

TFTP is extremely useful in large environments when you need to keep track of multiple configuration files. Since the command is so easy to use, it helps to insure that backups are performed whenever configuration changes are made. It also helps when making modifications, because the Cisco router configuration files are straight ASCII text. Simply modify the configuration using your favorite ASCII editor and use TFTP to upload your changes.

 NOTE TFTP uses the UDP transport and destination port 69 when creating a communication session.

WHOIS

WHOIS is a utility used to gathering information about a specific domain. The utility usually connects to the system rs.internic.net and displays administrative contact information, as well as the root servers for a domain.

This is useful when you wish to find out what organization is using a particular domain name. For example, typing the command

    whois sun.com

will produce the following information regarding the domain:

    Sun Microsystems Inc. (SUN)   SUN.COM   192.9.9.1
    Sun Microsystems, Inc. (SUN-DOM)   SUN.COM

If you performed a further search by entering the command

    whois sun-dom

you would find additional information:

    Sun Microsystems, Inc. (SUN-DOM)
    2550 Garcia Avenue
    Mountain View, CA 94043

    Domain Name: SUN.COM

    Administrative Contact, Technical Contact, Zone Contact:
    Lowe, Fredrick (FL59) Fred.Lowe@SUN.COM
    408-276-4199

    Record last updated on 21-Nov-96.
    Record created on 19-Mar-86.

```
Database last updated on 16-Jun-97 05:26:09 EDT.

Domain servers in listed order:

NS.SUN.COM        192.9.9.3
VGR.ARL.MIL       128.63.2.6, 128.63.16.6, 128.63.4.4


The InterNIC Registration Services Host contains ONLY Internet Information
(Networks, ASN's, Domains, and POC's).
Please use the whois server at nic.ddn.mil for MILNET Information.
```

WHOIS can be an extremely powerful troubleshooting tool: You now know who is responsible for maintaining the domain, how to contact them, and which systems are considered primary name servers. You could then use a DNS tool such as nslookup to find the IP addresses of Sun's mail systems or even its Web server.

 NOTE WHOIS uses the TCP transport and destination port 43 when creating a communication session.

Internetwork Packet Exchange (IPX)

In 1986 Novell released NetWare 2 and with it the *IPX* protocol. Based on Xerox's Xerox Network System (XNS) protocol, IPX is highly optimized and designed to provide efficient network communications. With the release of such enhancements as Large Internet Protocol (LIP) and burst mode, IPX has arguably become the most efficient protocol in use today. Figure 3.15 is a graphic representation of how the pieces of the IPX protocol suite match up to the OSI model.

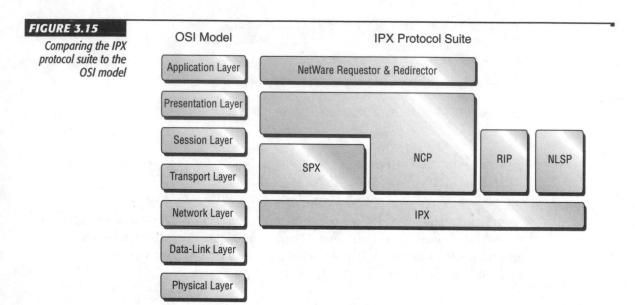

IPX Network Addressing

If IP addressing has left you a bit confused, then you'll love the simplicity of IPX. IPX uses an eight-bit hexadecimal network address, which means that values from 0 to 9 and A to F are valid. The only exceptions are 00000000 and FFFFFFFF: the former because it is a null value and the latter because it is considered a broadcast address.

Devices on the network which will be performing routing services (this includes NetWare servers, even if they have only one NIC) must be manually configured with their network addresses. All other devices are capable of auto-configuring their network addresses during startup.

Figure 3.16 shows the initial packet sent by an IPX workstation to discover the local network address. In this case, the workstation sends a Server Advertisement Protocol (SAP) packet, but some client software (such as Microsoft's) may send a Routing Information Protocol (RIP) packet, instead. In either case, the handshake is similar. If you look closely, you'll see that the source and destination network addresses are set to 0. This is because the workstation does not yet know where it is located. This also means that the client expects the server to be on the same logical network. If this is not the case, local routers must be configured to act as a proxy so that the router can return an appropriate reply.

FIGURE 3.16

A Windows 95 work-station with Client32 attempting to discover what IPX network segment it is on

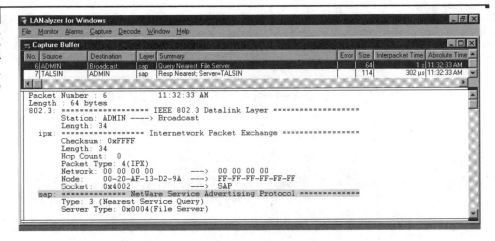

Figure 3.17 shows the server's response to the client. Notice that the address values are now filled in. Our workstation will record the value in the destination network address field and use it during all future communications.

FIGURE 3.17

The server Talsin's response to the SAP packet

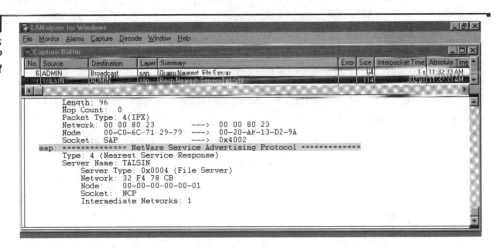

Figure 3.18 shows the very next packet sent by the Admin workstation. Notice that the address field is filled in. Our workstation now knows the local network address (00008023) and will use this address during all future communications. With a simple exchange of only two frames, our workstation is now ready to properly communicate on the network.

FIGURE 3.18

The Admin workstation has now learned the address of the local network.

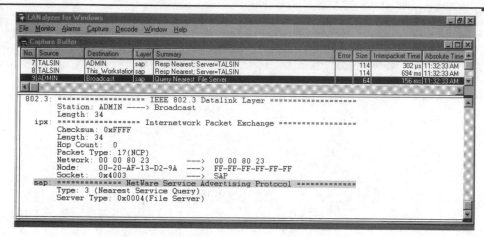

```
LANalyzer for Windows
File  Monitor  Alarms  Capture  Decode  Window  Help

Capture Buffer
No. Source      Destination      Layer  Summary                              Error  Size  Interpacket Time  Absolute Time
 7  TALSIN      ADMIN            sap    Resp Nearest; Server=TALSIN                 114    302 µs           11:32:33 AM
 8  TALSIN      This_Workstation sap    Resp Nearest; Server=TALSIN                 114    694 ms           11:32:33 AM
 9  ADMIN       Broadcast        sap    Query Nearest; File Server                   64    156 ms           11:32:33 AM

802.3: ==================== IEEE 802.3 Datalink Layer ====================
       Station: ADMIN ----> Broadcast
       Length: 34
  ipx: ==================== Internetwork Packet Exchange ====================
       Checksum: 0xFFFF
       Length: 34
       Hop Count:  0
       Packet Type: 17(NCP)
       Network: 00 00 80 23        --->  00 00 80 23
       Node:    00-20-AF-13-D2-9A  --->  FF-FF-FF-FF-FF-FF
       Socket:  0x4003             --->  SAP
  sap: ============== NetWare Service Advertising Protocol ==============
       Type: 3 (Nearest Service Query)
       Server Type: 0x0004(File Server)
```

You may recall from our discussion of IP that each station requires a unique network address to avoid communication conflicts. The same is true with IPX. Our Admin workstation will simply append its MAC address to the end of the local network number. Its full address will become 00008023:0020AF13D29A. Because every network device is required to have a unique MAC number, there should be no possibility that this address will conflict with another system.

Transport Layer Services

IPX uses three separate transports when sending and receiving data:

- IPX
- Sequence Packet Exchange (SPX and SPX II)
- NetWare Core Protocol (NCP)

Each has its own responsibilities when conducting IPX communications.

IPX

IPX is the foundation of the IPX protocol suite. All communications take place on top of IPX. Each frame contains a 30-byte section following the frame header, which contains all the information required to route and identify the frame.

IPX is a connectionless protocol, meaning that it does not require a handshake prior to data transmission. It also does not require packet acknowledgments. This means that it has no way to guarantee the final delivery of data. Also, IPX does not guarantee sequential delivery, which means that packets can be received in any order.

Sound like a pretty poor protocol? Actually, it is quite the opposite. IPX is specifically designed to do only one thing well—route information. It does not concern itself with things like acknowledgments and packet sequencing, leaving such things to the upper layers to deal with. By leaving the scope of IPX fairly loose, the door is left open to optimize communications.

For example, burst mode (which we will discuss later in this section) allows for the sending of multiple frames before an acknowledgment is sent. If IPX had been designed to require an acknowledgment after each frame, burst mode would not be possible without a ground-up revamping of the entire protocol suite. This, of course, would lead to backwards-compatibility problems; it would be difficult to keep the new and old specifications compatible.

Because IPX is a loose specification and acknowledgments are handled at a higher communication layer, IPX did not need to change when burst mode was introduced. This allowed older systems to continue to function as they always did while the newer software was deployed on the same network.

The only drawback to this type of design is that acknowledgments must be passed further up the stack in order to be verified. Because this means that additional communication layers become involved during a retransmission of a frame, the system uses more resources and takes longer to send a replacement. Figure 3.19 shows why this occurs. If a protocol requires an acknowledgment of successful frames at the Network layer, as in Protocol A, it can respond with a replacement frame quickly, using a minimal amount of CPU time. If acknowledgments are handled at a higher layer, as in Protocol B, the replacement frame requires more processing than it did with Protocol A, because it needs to be handled by additional layers.

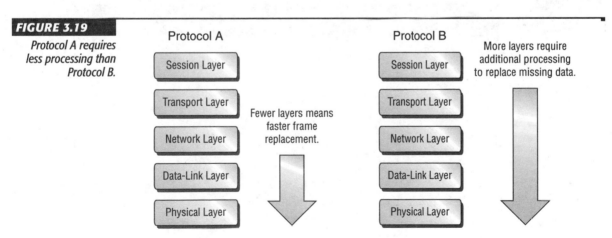

FIGURE 3.19

Protocol A requires less processing than Protocol B.

How much of an effect this has depends on the stability of the network. If errors are few and far between, the ratio of retransmissions to the amount of data moved becomes negligible. Modern networks can be very stable when designed and installed properly.

IPX supports both unicast and broadcast frames. It does not support multicast at this time. A *raw* IPX packet (meaning no other transport is used) will have an IPX type field value of 0 or 4.

 NOTE   The IPX type field is different from the type field used by some frame headers. The IPX type field is located in the data portion of the frame, not in the frame header.

SPX

SPX is the connection-oriented portion of the IPX protocol suite. SPX does not replace IPX but communicates just above it. All SPX frames still include an IPX header section. As shown in Figure 3.20, the SPX header follows the IPX header within the data portion of a frame. SPX packets are identified by an IPX packet type value of 5. Notice that we have an Ethernet section (identified as 802.3), an IPX section, an SPX section, and then Data. Because our Ethernet frame has a fixed header length, which includes the information required for local delivery, the IPX and SPX fields are stored in the data section of the frame.

FIGURE 3.20

A packet decode of an SPX frame

```
LANalyzer for Windows                                                    _ 8 X
File  Monitor  Alarms  Capture  Decode  Window  Help
Capture Buffer (Filtered)                                                _ □ X
     Packet Number : 1             7:13:39 AM
     Length : 98 bytes
     802.3: =================== IEEE 802.3 Datalink Layer ===================
            Station: TALSIN ----> ADMIN
            Length: 80
       ipx: ================== Internetwork Packet Exchange =================
            Checksum: 0xFFFF
            Length: 80
            Hop Count:  1
            Packet Type: 5(SPX/SPXII)
            Network: 32 F4 78 CB       --->  00 00 80 23
            Node:    00-00-00-00-00-01  --->  00-20-AF-13-D2-9A
            Socket:  NW 386            --->  0x4010
       spx: =========== NetWare Sequenced Packet Exchange Protocol ===========
            Connection Control: 0x40 (Send ACK; )
            Datastream Type: 0
            Source Connection ID: 712
            Destination Connection ID: 61579
            Sequence Number: 543
            Acknowledge Number: 10
            Allocation Number: 10
     Data:
         0: 26 00 01 90 B3 8C 01 01 1C 00 00 00 08 01 7C 05  |&.............|.
        10: 14 00 DB 0C DB 0C B2 0C B2 0C B1 0C B1 0C B0 0C  |...............
        20: B0 0C 20 0C 20 0C                                |. . .
```

SPX communications handshake before the data transmission and require an acknowledgment for each frame of data sent. SPX sequences transmitted frames (notice the sequence number in the SPX section of Figure 3.20) and insures that they are received in the proper order. Because of its connection-oriented nature, SPX supports unicast communications only.

Figure 3.21 shows an SPX session in progress. This is an *Rconsole* connection between a workstation and a server. Rconsole is a NetWare utility that allows a remote control session to be set up from the workstation to the server. All information that is shown on the server's monitor is also displayed through the Rconsole session window. In our example, the session has been idle long enough for the server's screen saver to be activated. The screen saver is simply a blank screen with an ASCII character snake moving randomly around the screen. The busier the server's CPU, the longer the tail is on the snake.

TIP   Have a look at the "ping pong" effect between data transmission and acknowledgments (ACK). We are transmitting four frames per second just watching the screen saver snake move around the screen! To avoid unnecessary traffic, Rconsole sessions should be shut down when not in use.

FIGURE 3.21

An SPX session in progress

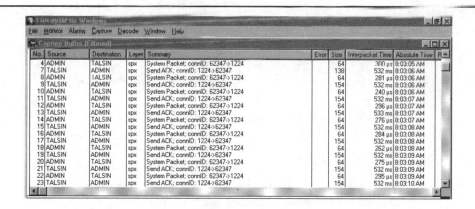

There are actually two separate versions of SPX: SPX and SPX II. The previous descriptions apply to both specifications. The original SPX has been available since NetWare version 2. SPX II was introduced with NetWare 4.

Novell's First SPX Implementation

The original SPX protocol uses 12 bytes within the data field and has a maximum Ethernet frame size of 576 bytes. If you refer to Figure 3.22, you'll see that this only leaves 516 bytes free to carry actual data. Combine this with SPX's requirement for an acknowledgment after each frame transmission, and we have a horribly inefficient means of communication.

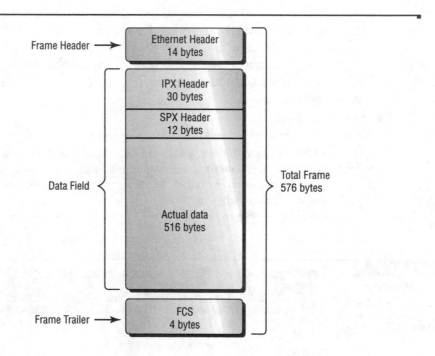

FIGURE 3.22

Only 516 bytes are available to carry data.

Why all the overhead and the smaller packet size? The overhead is used to insure proper delivery of every single frame. SPX was not designed for everyday communications; it is reserved for those special situations in which a stable connection is preferable to speed. For example, when the Rconsole session described earlier is created, stability while controlling the server is far more important than speed. SPX was spawned in the days of Thinnet and Thicknet wiring, as well as 1200Bps modems with minimal error correction. This is why it is so uptight about insuring that all the data is received in one piece. In the old days, the Physical layer of networks was not as stable as it is today. In situations in which the stability of the circuit between the two communicating systems is questionable, SPX is the best method available to insure that data is sent in one piece.

As for its puny frame size, before 1992 IPX would negotiate a frame size of 576 bytes if the server and client were not on the same logical network. By fixing the SPX frame at 576 bytes, this negotiation was not required. This was corrected when Novell released LIP (described later in this section).

Because of these issues, SPX should be avoided in stable network environments whenever possible. Its small frame size (size *does* matter in networking) and connection-oriented nature can generate an excessive number of frames in medium to large environments. The following is a list of common software known to use SPX:

- Rconsole
- Pserver
- Lotus Notes, when IPX is selected as the transport
- SAA Gateway, when IPX is selected as the transport
- Many client/server database programs

In many cases, the administrator has a choice of not using SPX. For example, Notes can be run over IP, as well, and operates much more efficiently.

SPX II

SPX II fixed many of the problems with SPX while still maintaining a connection-oriented session. The packet size was increased to support the maximum allowable frame size per the topology in use. In the case of Ethernet, this means that a frame can be as large as 1,518 bytes.

SPX II also assumes that the Physical layer connecting the two systems is a bit more stable than it used to be. With this in mind, SPX II supports a method of communication known as *windowing*. With SPX, a frame must be acknowledged before the next one can be sent. SPX II lets multiple frames be outstanding without receiving an acknowledgment. The number of packets that can be outstanding is called the *window size*. While the window size is negotiated using the allocation number field within the SPX II header, the window size is not allowed to exceed 10 outstanding packets at any given time.

SPX II will use the sequence numbers and negative acknowledgments (NAK) to recover lost frames during a communication session. When a frame is lost, the receiving system will send a NAK that identifies the sequence number of the missing frame to the transmitting system. This allows the transmitting system to resend just the missing piece of information.

SPX II is a big improvement in communication efficiency over SPX. Some backup software vendors have developed *push agents* which allow their software to leverage SPX II during server-to-server backups. Cheyenne's ARCserve and Seagate's Backup Exec are two popular examples.

NCP

The *NetWare Core Protocol* (NCP) is appropriately named, because it is the transport responsible for a majority of IPX communications. NCP defines the structure of requests and responses as they apply to most NetWare communications. The packet type field with the IPX header section has a value of 17 when NCP is used. The NCP header follows the IPX header, as well as the SPX header, if one is required.

NCP uses a type field to identify the purpose of the information contained within the data field of the frame. Because a NetWare environment uses black-and-white definitions of a "client" and a "server" (for example, you cannot sit at the server console and access files located on a logged-in client), the type field is labeled according to the kind of system that originated the information. If the frame originates from a client, the field is referred to as *request type*. If the frame comes from a server, the field is called *reply type*. The most common NCP communication types are listed in Tables 3.11 and 3.12.

TABLE 3.11: CLIENT REQUEST TYPES	
Type Value	**Description**
1111	Used before authentication to request a server connection.
2222	Manipulation or information request. Most commonly used during directory listings, path searches, file and directory creation or deletion, or when trustee right information is required or must be set.
5555	Destroy connection. Most commonly used when the server that replies to the initial Get nearest server request is not the server the client wishes to authenticate with. This removes the client's connection and frees it up for another client. Connections identified as "not logged in" are clients that have not yet sent a type 5555 request.

TABLE 3.12: SERVER REPLY TYPES	
Type Value	**Description**
3333	Information reply. A type 3333 reply is always preceded by a client sending a type 2222 request.
9999	Request pending, no ECB timeout. A type 9999 reply is a server's way of saying "She can't take any more speed, Captain! The emergency bypass control of the matter/anti-matter integrator is going to fuse!" When a server replies with a type 9999 NCP frame, it is telling the client that its buffer for accepting inbound requests is currently full. It needs to process the pending requests before it can accept any more from the client.

NOTE There is a single NCP type that is used by both the client and the server. An NCP type 7777 is used during all packet burst communications. This includes requests, acknowledgments, and actual data transfers.

In addition to NCP types, other fields are used to further identify the purpose of a frame. All NCP frames include a *function code* and *subfunction code* field, as well. Novell has specified a number of codes to provide more granularity in identifying a frame's purpose beyond that provided by the NCP type field.

For example, Figure 3.23 shows a decode of the NCP portion of a frame. The request type field (which is the second line of the NCP header) has a value of 2222, so we know it is a client requesting manipulation or information regarding a file or directory. If we look at the value of the data field at the bottom of the figure, it is identified as *temp*. The question is "What is 'temp,' and what do we want to do with it?"

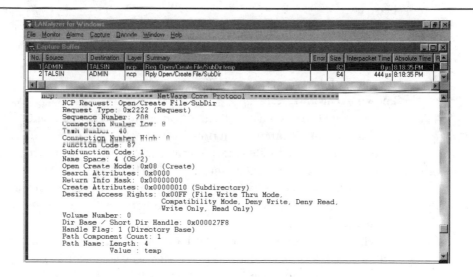

This is where the function code and subfunction code fields come in handy. Novell has defined a request type of 2222, with a function code of 87 and a subfunction code of 1, as a request to open or create a file or directory.

So now we know that we need to open or create a file or directory named `temp`. While we're a bit closer, it's still not clear what precise action our workstation is requesting of the server. While all NCP frames contain a function code and a subfunction code, other fields are used only as required.

This particular frame has an open create mode field, which identifies whether we want to open or create the value in the data field (`temp`). A value of 8 tells us we wish to create it. There is also a create attributes field, which identifies with a value of 10 that `temp` is a directory.

Through the use of these five fields, we now know that `temp` is a directory we wish to create at our current location. While cryptic for the average network geek to read, control fields are an efficient, space-saving means of relaying information. In most situations, only the type, function, and subfunction fields are required. When this is true, only eight bytes of frame space are needed to identify the requested service. Novell has categorized over 350 services using these three fields.

Large Internet Protocol (LIP)   This protocol was added to the functionality of NCP back in 1992. Before then, a client would limit the size of its frames to 576 bytes when it detected a router between itself and the server. LIP allows a client to communicate with the server using the maximum allowable frame size (1,518 bytes for Ethernet), even when the hop count field indicates that there are one or more routers in between.

Burst Mode   This is arguably the single biggest improvement that Novell has made to the NCP transport. In short, *burst mode* allows a system using NCP to send multiple frames of data without having to acknowledge the receipt of each one. It also allows the communicating systems to adjust the wait time between frame transmissions, known as the *interpacket gap*.

Figure 3.24 shows burst mode in action. Frame 112 is the client Admin requesting 28,720 bytes of file information from the server Talsin. Frames 113–133 show Talsin replying with the requested file information. Note that the only required acknowledgment is when Admin requests another 29,084 bytes in frame 134. What would normally require 42 frames to transfer (between data transfers and acknowledgments) is completed in just 22 frames. This is approximately a 50-percent reduction in network traffic!

When a client and a server are both capable of burst-mode communications, they will negotiate how many packets to transfer between acknowledgments (*burst packet count*), and how long to wait between transmissions (*interpacket gap*). During the course of their communication, these values will be adjusted as required. For example, in Figure 3.24 you saw that our server was able to successfully transfer 28,720 bytes to our client in burst mode. When our client requested additional file information in frame 134, it pushed the envelope a bit and requested 29,084 bytes. This would continue until an error occurs or until the maximum burst mode size is reached.

FIGURE 3.24

A NCP client and
server communicating
in burst mode. Note
that an acknowledg-
ment is not required
until all the requested
file information is
transferred.

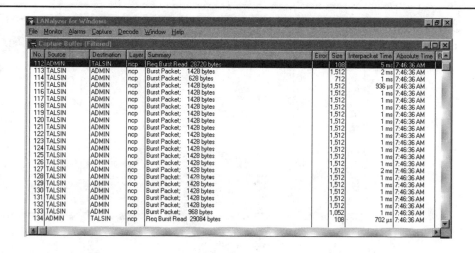

Figure 3.25 shows what happens when a burst mode session is unsuccessful. In frame 185, the client Admin is notifying the server Talsin that it missed 4,284 bytes' worth of information. Frames 186–189 show the server replying with the requested information. Note that these four frames total 4,284 bytes exactly.

It is extremely interesting (if you are a wire geek, that is) to look at Admin's next request for data in frame 190. The client is only requesting 14,724 bytes of information. This is exactly half the amount of file information it requested in frame 163. Because an error was encountered, the client has decided to back off on the number of burst packets in order to avoid future problems. If this transfer is successful, it may again negotiate a slightly larger number of burst packets until it finds the maximum number of frames that can be transferred without error.

This intelligent tuning allows the two systems to optimize their communication based on the current network conditions. The healthier the network, the more information can be transferred between acknowledgments, and the less time each system is required to wait between transmissions.

Just how fast can you go? Figure 3.26 shows burst mode pushed just about to its limit. The client has requested a write request of 65,024 with an interpacket gap of 2 ms. This is a 10MBps Ethernet segment. A faster pipe will be able to produce a lower gap time.

FIGURE 3.25

A burst mode communication recovering from a transmission error. Only the missing data needs to be retransmitted.

LANalyzer for Windows

File Monitor Alarms Capture Decode Window Help

Capture Buffer (Filtered)

No.	Source	Destination	Layer	Summary	Error	Size	Interpacket Time	Absolute Time	R
163	ADMIN	TALSIN	ncp	Req Burst Read 29448 bytes		108	6 ms	7:46:37 AM	
164	TALSIN	ADMIN	ncp	Burst Packet; 1428 bytes		1,512	2 ms	7:46:37 AM	
165	TALSIN	ADMIN	ncp	Burst Packet; 1140 bytes		1,224	1 ms	7:46:37 AM	
166	TALSIN	ADMIN	ncp	Burst Packet; 1428 bytes		1,512	2 ms	7:46:37 AM	
167	TALSIN	ADMIN	ncp	Burst Packet; 1428 bytes		1,512	1 ms	7:46:37 AM	
168	TALSIN	ADMIN	ncp	Burst Packet; 1240 bytes		1,324	1 ms	7:46:37 AM	
169	TALSIN	ADMIN	ncp	Burst Packet; 1428 bytes		1,512	1 ms	7:46:37 AM	
170	TALSIN	ADMIN	ncp	Burst Packet; 1428 bytes		1,512	1 ms	7:46:37 AM	
171	TALSIN	ADMIN	ncp	Burst Packet; 1428 bytes		1,512	1 ms	7:46:37 AM	
172	TALSIN	ADMIN	ncp	Burst Packet; 1428 bytes		1,512	1 ms	7:46:37 AM	
173	TALSIN	ADMIN	ncp	Burst Packet; 1428 bytes		1,512	1 ms	7:46:37 AM	
174	TALSIN	ADMIN	ncp	Burst Packet; 1428 bytes		1,512	1 ms	7:46:37 AM	
175	TALSIN	ADMIN	ncp	Burst Packet; 1428 bytes		1,512	1 ms	7:46:37 AM	
176	TALSIN	ADMIN	ncp	Burst Packet; 1428 bytes		1,512	1 ms	7:46:37 AM	
177	TALSIN	ADMIN	ncp	Burst Packet; 1428 bytes		1,512	1 ms	7:46:37 AM	
178	TALSIN	ADMIN	ncp	Burst Packet; 1428 bytes		1,512	1 ms	7:46:37 AM	
179	TALSIN	ADMIN	ncp	Burst Packet; 1428 bytes		1,512	1 ms	7:46:37 AM	
180	TALSIN	ADMIN	ncp	Burst Packet; 1428 bytes		1,512	1 ms	7:46:37 AM	
181	TALSIN	ADMIN	ncp	Burst Packet; 1428 bytes		1,512	1 ms	7:46:37 AM	
182	TALSIN	ADMIN	ncp	Burst Packet; 1428 bytes		1,512	1 ms	7:46:37 AM	
183	TALSIN	ADMIN	ncp	Burst Packet; 1428 bytes		1,512	1 ms	7:46:37 AM	
184	TALSIN	ADMIN	ncp	Burst Packet; 1372 bytes		1,456	1 ms	7:46:37 AM	
185	ADMIN	TALSIN	ncp	Burst System Packet; 4284 bytes missing		96	916 µs	7:46:37 AM	
186	TALSIN	ADMIN	ncp	Burst Packet; 1428 bytes		1,512	2 ms	7:46:37 AM	
187	TALSIN	ADMIN	ncp	Burst Packet; 1240 bytes		1,324	1 ms	7:46:37 AM	
188	TALSIN	ADMIN	ncp	Burst Packet; 188 bytes		272	927 µs	7:46:37 AM	
189	TALSIN	ADMIN	ncp	Burst Packet; 1428 bytes		1,512	962 µs	7:46:37 AM	
190	ADMIN	TALSIN	ncp	Req Burst Read 14724 bytes		108	979 µs	7:46:37 AM	

FIGURE 3.26

Burst mode pushed to the max. Forty-five burst packets will be transmitted before an acknowledgment is required.

LANalyzer for Windows

File Monitor Alarms Capture Decode Window Help

Capture Buffer

No.	Source	Destination	Layer	Summary	Error	Size	Interpacket Time	Absolute Time	R
31	ADMIN	TALSIN	ncp	Req Burst Write 65024 bytes		1,512	3 ms	6:51:26 PM	
32	ADMIN	TALSIN	ncp	Burst Packet; 1428 bytes		1,512	2 ms	6:51:26 PM	
33	ADMIN	TALSIN	ncp	Burst Packet; 1428 bytes		1,512	2 ms	6:51:26 PM	
34	ADMIN	TALSIN	ncp	Burst Packet; 1428 bytes		1,512	2 ms	6:51:26 PM	
35	ADMIN	TALSIN	ncp	Burst Packet; 1428 bytes		1,512	2 ms	6:51:26 PM	
36	ADMIN	TALSIN	ncp	Burst Packet; 1428 bytes		1,512	2 ms	6:51:26 PM	
37	ADMIN	TALSIN	ncp	Burst Packet; 1428 bytes		1,512	2 ms	6:51:26 PM	
38	ADMIN	TALSIN	ncp	Burst Packet; 1428 bytes		1,512	2 ms	6:51:26 PM	
39	ADMIN	TALSIN	ncp	Burst Packet; 1428 bytes		1,512	2 ms	6:51:26 PM	
40	ADMIN	TALSIN	ncp	Burst Packet; 1428 bytes		1,512	2 ms	6:51:26 PM	
41	ADMIN	TALSIN	ncp	Burst Packet; 1428 bytes		1,512	2 ms	6:51:26 PM	
42	ADMIN	TALSIN	ncp	Burst Packet; 1428 bytes		1,512	2 ms	6:51:26 PM	
43	ADMIN	TALSIN	ncp	Burst Packet; 1428 bytes		1,512	2 ms	6:51:26 PM	
44	ADMIN	TALSIN	ncp	Burst Packet; 1428 bytes		1,512	2 ms	6:51:26 PM	
45	ADMIN	TALSIN	ncp	Burst Packet; 1428 bytes		1,512	2 ms	6:51:26 PM	
46	ADMIN	TALSIN	ncp	Burst Packet; 1428 bytes		1,512	2 ms	6:51:26 PM	
47	ADMIN	TALSIN	ncp	Burst Packet; 1428 bytes		1,512	2 ms	6:51:26 PM	
48	ADMIN	TALSIN	ncp	Burst Packet; 1428 bytes		1,512	2 ms	6:51:26 PM	
49	ADMIN	TALSIN	ncp	Burst Packet; 1428 bytes		1,512	2 ms	6:51:26 PM	
50	ADMIN	TALSIN	ncp	Burst Packet; 1428 bytes		1,512	2 ms	6:51:26 PM	
51	ADMIN	TALSIN	ncp	Burst Packet; 1428 bytes		1,512	2 ms	6:51:26 PM	
52	ADMIN	TALSIN	ncp	Burst Packet; 1428 bytes		1,512	2 ms	6:51:26 PM	
53	ADMIN	TALSIN	ncp	Burst Packet; 1428 bytes		1,512	2 ms	6:51:26 PM	
54	ADMIN	TALSIN	ncp	Burst Packet; 1428 bytes		1,512	2 ms	6:51:26 PM	
55	ADMIN	TALSIN	ncp	Burst Packet; 1428 bytes		1,512	2 ms	6:51:26 PM	
56	ADMIN	TALSIN	ncp	Burst Packet; 1428 bytes		1,512	2 ms	6:51:26 PM	
57	ADMIN	TALSIN	ncp	Burst Packet; 1428 bytes		1,512	2 ms	6:51:26 PM	
58	ADMIN	TALSIN	ncp	Burst Packet; 1428 bytes		1,512	2 ms	6:51:26 PM	
59	ADMIN	TALSIN	ncp	Burst Packet; 1428 bytes		1,512	2 ms	6:51:26 PM	
60	ADMIN	TALSIN	ncp	Burst Packet; 1428 bytes		1,512	2 ms	6:51:26 PM	
61	ADMIN	TALSIN	ncp	Burst Packet; 1428 bytes		1,512	2 ms	6:51:26 PM	
62	ADMIN	TALSIN	ncp	Burst Packet; 1428 bytes		1,512	2 ms	6:51:26 PM	

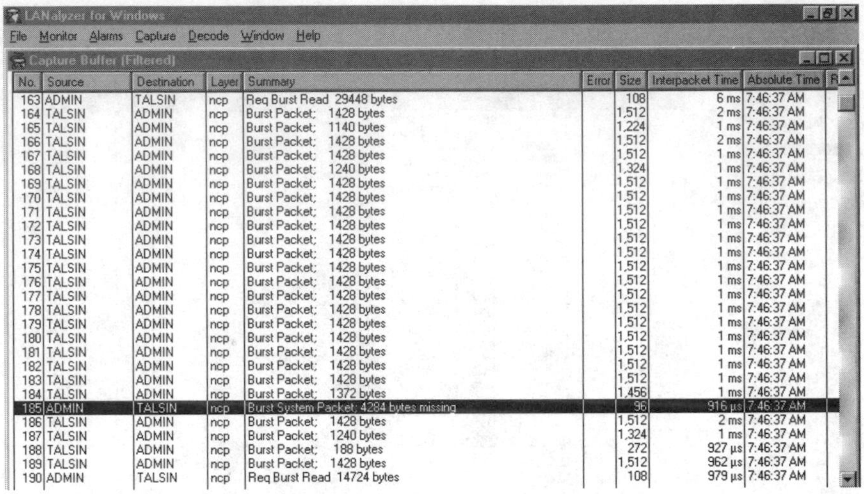

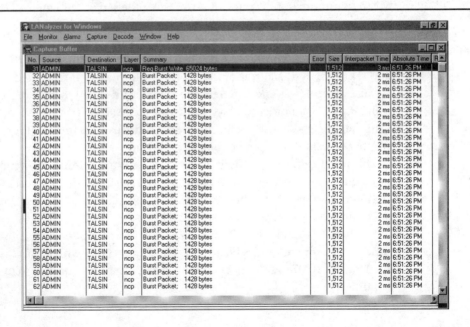

How does this translate into actual improvements in network performance? Table 3.13 tells the story. Identical network and computer configurations were used in each example. The only difference was whether burst mode was turned on or off. The data

in question is a 5MB .zip file. This test is prejudiced toward measuring the raw transfer rate of a file; your mileage may vary. No animals were harmed while performing this test.

TABLE 3.13: NETWORK PERFORMANCE WITH AND WITHOUT BURST MODE

Connection Mode	File Transfer Time	Number of Frames Required
Burst mode enabled	6 seconds	3,946
Burst mode disabled	12 seconds	7,790

As you can see, burst mode can have a dramatic effect on the time and number of frames it takes to transfer a file. Since regular network usage is a mixture of file transfers and other activities, the net effect of enabling burst mode on a network is usually quite a bit less than an improvement by a factor of two. Still, it's hard to beat free bandwidth.

IPX Application Layer Services

IPX uses the term *sockets* instead of ports to identify Application layer services. While not nearly as diverse as IP, there are a few commonly used socket numbers worth noting; you can see these in Table 3.14. IPX socket number are identified in a hex format.

TABLE 3.14: COMMON IPX SOCKETS

Socket	Service	Description
0451	NCP	NetWare Core Protocol
0452	SAP	Service Advertising Protocol
0453	RIP	Routing Information Protocol
0455	NetBIOS	NetBIOS over IPX
0456	Diag. Packet	Server diagnostic packet
0457	Serial # check	License serial number check between servers
4000–8000	Reply	Upper reply socket randomly assigned by client
5100	Descent	Default for multi-player updates
869C	Id games	Default for DOOM2, Heretic, and so on
26000	Quake	Default for multi-player updates

SAP frames are used to advertise the services available from each IPX system on the network. The NetWare display servers command will list each server on the network, once for each service it provides. This is why some NetWare servers may appear multiple times within a server list. Table 3.15 lists the most common services available on an IPX network. SAP types are identified in hex format.

TABLE 3.15: IPX SERVICES AND THEIR SAP VALUE	
SAP Type	**Service**
0004	File server
0047	Print server
0278	NDS server
026B	Time Sync server

Network Basic Input/Output System (NetBIOS)

Developed by IBM for its PC Network LAN, *NetBIOS* was created to be an application program interface (API). NetBIOS is designed to be a *front end* for carrying out interapplication communications: NetBIOS defines the interface to the network protocol, not the protocol itself. At the time of development, it was assumed that the application accessing NetBIOS would be responsible for defining the protocols required for transmitting the information.

Figure 3.27 is a graphic representation of NetBIOS and some of its related components as they compare to the OSI model. NetBIOS provides Transport and Session layer services only. It does not provide networking services, which means that NetBIOS is a *non-routable protocol*. If a network is broken up by one or more routers, NetBIOS does not have the ability to reach nodes located on remote segments.

 TIP Routers cannot pass NetBIOS traffic unless bridging mode is enabled.

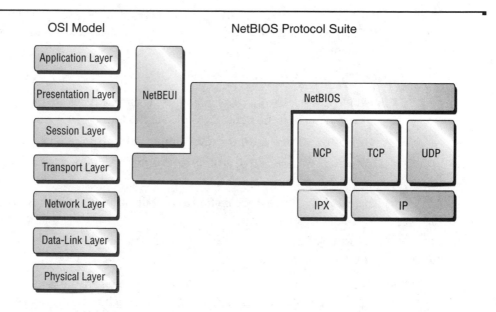

FIGURE 3.27

NetBIOS as it compares to the OSI model

NetBIOS has very loose specifications for the Presentation and Application layers. No standard structure or format is specified. This has led to the pairing of NetBIOS with other protocols such as NetBEUI, which can provide a precise specification. It has also led to incompatibility problems, as vendors were left to create proprietary implementations. Artisoft's LANtastic is a good example of a system that communicates using a proprietary NetBIOS implementation and cannot communicate with other NetBIOS systems.

NetBIOS is designed to allow all nodes on a network to communicate on an equal basis. This is also known as *peer-to-peer networking*. All NetBIOS systems can share local files and access shared files on remote systems. This model is the exact opposite of those discussed under IPX and NCP.

NetBIOS Addressing

Each machine on a NetBIOS network receives a unique name. This name can be up to 16 characters long but must not start with an asterisk (*). NetBIOS uses this name to discover a system's media access control number. Once the MAC address is known, all local transmissions will take place using this address. A system's NetBIOS name is very similar to a system's host name under IP. In a mixed-protocol environment, these two names are usually kept the same.

When a NetBIOS system first initializes on a network, it is required to register its NetBIOS name. How the registration process takes place depends upon the *node type* of the system.

Node Types

NetBIOS identifies four different node types. The node types are categorized by how they resolve names on the network. These are the four types of nodes:

b-nodes   These use broadcast communications to resolve names.

p-nodes   These use point-to-point communications with a name server to resolve names.

m-nodes   These first function as b-nodes and then, if necessary, function as p-nodes to resolve names.

h-nodes   These first function as p-nodes and then, if necessary, function as b-nodes to resolve names.

b-nodes   A *b-node* system uses broadcasts for name registration and resolution. Figure 3.28 shows a b-node system named Fenrus, which is in the process of powering up. When NetBIOS is initialized, the system broadcasts the name it wishes to use.

A b-node NetBIOS system registering the name it wishes to use

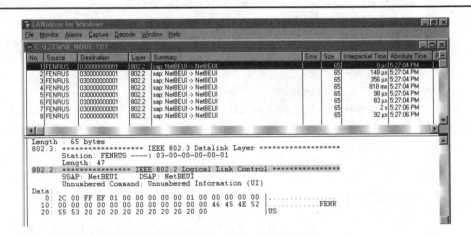

If the station receives no response, it assumes that the name is not in use and will begin identifying itself as Fenrus. If the name Fenrus is in use by another system, the station will receive a *name challenge*. A name challenge lets the broadcasting system know that the name is already in use. Names are registered on a first come, first served basis. Because NetBIOS names must be unique, a system should back off and never register a NetBIOS name for which it has received a challenge.

WARNING It is possible to force a workstation to register a name even after it has received a challenge. This should never be done in a production environment, because it will affect connectivity to the system that originally registered the name.

A b-node system will also broadcast when it is performing a *discovery*. A discovery is performed when one system wishes to connect to another but does not know the destination system's network address. The system will broadcast a discovery message asking the destination system to reply with its address. Once a b-node system finds the address of the system it wishes to contact, it will begin communicating in a unicast mode.

Returning to Figure 3.28, notice the destination broadcast address. This is not the typical broadcast address of FFFFFFFFFFFF that you'd normally see. 030000000001 is actually a multicast address used only by NetBIOS systems operating in broadcast mode. There are two major benefits to this mode of operation:

- Non-NetBIOS systems are not required to process this multicast. It will be viewed as a unicast frame by other systems.

- The only systems that will interpret this frame as a broadcast are the ones that need to process it, anyway. All b-node systems must be involved in each name registration and discovery message.

So while b-node communications say they are broadcast based, they are actually multicast based and are not as bad as the typical network broadcast. Still, if we can remove our workstations from the registration and discovery process, it will free up bandwidth and CPU cycles to perform other functions.

p-nodes When *p-nodes* are used, a central system, referred to as a NetBIOS Name Server (NBNS), tracks the registration of NetBIOS names. A p-node system does not need to broadcast during startup; it simply sends a unicast query to the NBNS to find out whether the name it wishes to register is already in use.

Likewise, when the system needs to discover another system, it will again contact the NBNS with a unicast query. This communication method eliminates the need for network broadcasts during registration and discovery, preventing all systems from being involved in each of these queries.

The drawback to using p-nodes is that each system needs to be preconfigured with the network address of the NBNS. It also relies on the NBNS being online and functional to support all NetBIOS communications. If the NBNS goes down, discovery is no longer possible. Another problem with the NBNS crashing is that it could lose all p-node table information regarding systems that had been registered before the crash. If this occurs, a second system could conceivably register a name that is already in use.

 NOTE B-node and p-node systems are not compatible. A b-node system will not register or discover through an NBNS, and a p-node system will ignore any NetBIOS broadcasts it receives from a b-node system.

To get around some of the problems with both p-node and b-node systems, m-node and h-node systems provide a mixture of the functionality supported by each.

m-nodes An *m-node* system will broadcast when performing registration and discovery. If the discovery should happen to fail, the m-node will then act like a p-node and query the local NBNS. While adding a bit of versatility, this does not really address many of the problems noted with b-node and p-node operation.

h-nodes An *h-node* system will first register and discover through an NBNS in the same manner that a p-node does. If either of these two processes fail, it will drop back to b-node and use broadcasts to perform registration and discovery.

This mode of operation offers the best of both worlds. The h-node will first communicate using unicast transmissions. This helps to limit the number of broadcasts being transmitted on your network. If this should fail (for example, if the NBNS is offline), the system can recover by communicating in broadcast mode.

When you use Microsoft's DHCP services, you can configure the node operation of Windows NetBIOS/IP systems as you desire. Operating as a b-node is the default for Microsoft Windows systems, as well as SAMBA. When you run NetBIOS over IP and use Windows Internet Name Service (WINS), the Microsoft Windows default changes to h-node. WINS is Microsoft's implementation of an NBNS. We will discuss WINS further in Chapter 6, as we get into the dilemma of trying to pass NetBIOS traffic over a router.

Session and Transport Layer Support

NetBIOS supports three types of communication services:

- Name
- Datagram
- Session

I've explained the name service already in the last section. A NetBIOS system uses the name service when it needs to register or discover a name.

Datagram is NetBIOS's connectionless service for data delivery. While it is arguably faster than session, it provides no error correction and no guarantee of final delivery. If the receiving system is offline or busy, any data sent is lost. Datagram supports both unicast- and broadcast-based communications.

Datagram supports the following four API calls:

Send   Send message using unicast communications

Send Broadcast   Send message using broadcast communications

Receive   Receive unicast message

Receive Broadcast   Receive broadcast message

Session is NetBIOS's connection-oriented data delivery service. It handshakes before transmitting data but provides no flow control. Session provides error correction but can only guarantee delivery on the first 64kb of a message. All session communications are unicast in nature.

Session supports the following API calls:

Call   Initialize a session with a listening system

Listen   Accept sessions attempting a call

Hangup   Normal session termination

Send   Transmit one message up to 131,071 bytes in length

Receive   Receive message

Session Status   Report on all current sessions

NetBIOS Extended User Interface (NetBEUI)

Designed for LANManager in 1985 by IBM, *NetBEUI* formalizes the transport framework left a bit vague by NetBIOS. NetBEUI specifies how the upper-layer software should send and receive messages when NetBIOS is the transport.

Like NetBIOS, NetBEUI is not routable. It is optimized for the same single-segment networks with 200 nodes or less. The current version of NetBEUI is 3, which fixes the problems encountered by earlier versions in the following ways:

- Can exceed 254 sessions limit over a single NIC
- Has better memory optimization
- Has self-tuning to optimize local communications
- Offers slightly better WAN performance

Except for a few missing API calls, NetBEUI 3 is fully compatible with NetBIOS 3.

Despite its limitations, NetBEUI has been implemented on a number of platforms. It is supported by all of Microsoft's Windows operating systems, LANManager, WARP, and Pathworks.

AppleTalk

AppleTalk was developed by Apple Computers in 1984 as a means of connecting its Macintosh and Apple II computers on an Ethernet network. AppleTalk should not be confused with LocalTalk, which was also developed by Apple but was a Data-Link layer protocol designed to run on a proprietary bus topology (that is, not Ethernet). These are two separate protocols. While AppleTalk includes support for various flavors of UNIX, DEC VAX, and even DOS systems, it is primarily used to provide connectivity for the Mac.

In 1989 Apple produced AppleTalk Phase II, which is the current revision. Phase II offered solutions to a number of problems with Phase I, most notably these:

- Increased the number of supported hosts beyond 254 per network segment
- Allowed for more than one Zone Name to be used per network
- Improved coexistence when other protocols are used on the same network
- Included support for ring topologies

Figure 3.29 is a graphic representation of the AppleTalk protocol suite and how it compares to the OSI model.

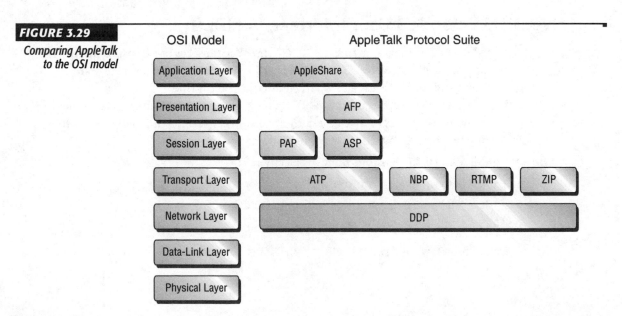

FIGURE 3.29

Comparing AppleTalk to the OSI model

Address Space

AppleTalk Phase II supports the use of extended network numbers. Numbers can range from 1 through 65,279. Network addresses are assigned in ranges, so starting and stopping values must be specified. An AppleTalk host is dynamically assigned a node address within the specified range. Valid node addresses are 1–254. Table 3.16 shows some potential numbering schemes.

TABLE 3.16: SAMPLE APPLETALK RANGE VALUES			
Network Range	**First Node Addresses**	**Last Node Address**	**Number of Hosts Supported**
1–1	1.1	1.254	254
200–201	200.1	201.254	508
65100–65200	65100.1	65200.254	50,800

Unlike IP, AppleTalk does not use address classes or subnet masks. This gives the administrator the freedom to adjust the network range values as required for a growing network. If you need to support an additional 254 hosts, simply increase the network range. After rebooting, AppleTalk nodes will automatically take advantage of the additional address space.

There are two categories of AppleTalk nodes:

Seeding These systems have their network range preconfigured and are responsible for advertising this network range to other systems.

Non-seeding These systems have their network range set to 0-0, which tells them to discover the real network range during startup. Once the system knows the network range, it will attempt to register a valid node address within the range.

This setup has a few major advantages. The first is that only one system (usually a router) must be configured with the network range. This saves the administrator a lot of leg work, because she does not have to touch each system before communicating on the network. This minimizes administration: Most users on the system can learn their addresses dynamically.

AppleTalk has shortened the discovery process by allowing a non-seed host to remember its last node address. When the system initializes, it first insures that the network range has not changed. If it has not (which is usually the case), it tries to use its old node address. If it receives a challenge from another node using this address, it will then go back through the discovery process to find a free address.

When Ease of Use Can Lead to Additional Work

The big drawback to AppleTalk addressing is that it does not accept changes very easily. If a network address range is changed, other systems on the network will challenge this new address, stating that the old range is the correct one. It is for this reason that *all* AppleTalk devices (hosts, servers, printers, and so on) must be shut down while the change takes place. Once the devices power up, they will accept the new address range, and all will be happy.

Clearly, this does not bode well for large environments. If you have 1,000 or more AppleTalk hosts, it may be nearly impossible to shut down every system. I was once in a situation in which we needed to make AppleTalk network changes on a 250-node network. The changes had to be completed by the end of the weekend.

Although we thought we had powered down every AppleTalk device within the building, it became apparent that we had not. Our new network ranges were not being accepted. A walk through the building confirmed that there were some inaccessible areas that probably had AppleTalk devices.

We did, however, have access to all the hub closets and quickly identified which hub ports were still active. The solution? We unplugged every connection that still had a link light. This disconnected the remaining AppleTalk systems from the network, which allowed us to make our changes successfully. On Monday morning, when we again had access to these locked areas, we simply shut down the remaining systems and reconnected them to the network.

Local Frame Delivery

Just like the other protocols we have discussed, AppleTalk uses a network card's MAC address when delivering frames to systems located on the same network range. AppleTalk uses the AppleTalk Address Resolution Protocol (AARP) to discover these addresses.

AARP functions in the same fashion as IP's ARP protocol. AARP will send out a network broadcast containing the node address of the system it needs to send information to. When the system replies, the value in the Ethernet source address field can now be used for local delivery.

AARP will cache this information in its *address mapping table* (AMT). The AMT serves the same purpose as IP's ARP cache, mapping MAC addresses to node addresses. This allows the system to refer to the table instead of issuing another AARP when it again needs to send this system data.

Zone Names

Zone names allow for the assignment of a useful name to a specified network range. Zone assignments are made as part of the seeding system's configuration. Every AppleTalk network range must be assigned at least one zone name, which is known as the *primary zone*. You can assign *secondary zones* to the network range as required.

Through the use of zones, resources can be logically grouped for easier access. For example, let's assume that you have a large network with many remote sites. The office located in Boston, MA, could be assigned the primary zone name of Boston. If a user is looking for a network resource (server, printer, and so on) located at the Boston office, he can logically assume that he should look in the Boston zone.

Secondary zones could also be assigned to provide even greater resolution. For example, let's assume that you create secondary zones under Boston called HR, Sales, and Dilbert. If a Human Resources person needs to print a document, she can probably assume that the closest printer to her location is in the HR zone. Salespeople's resources could be located in the Sales zone, and upper management would keep their resources in the Dilbert zone (don't worry, they probably wouldn't get it, anyway).

The *Zone Information Protocol* (ZIP) is used when a network address need to be mapped to a zone name. The *Name Binding Protocol* (NBP) is used when a zone name must be mapped to a network address. It is also used to translate host names into node addresses.

Network Layer Services

Network layer services are provided by the *Datagram Delivery Protocol* (DDP). DDP is similar to IPX in that it is the foundation on which all AppleTalk communications travel. The DDP header appears at the beginning of the data portion of the frame.

DDP is a connectionless protocol which performs no handshaking and requires no acknowledgments. Like IPX, it is happy to deliver information, but it makes no guarantee that the information will arrive at its final destination. That responsibility is left to the upper layers.

DDP does not support packet sequencing. As such, it can make no guarantee that frames will be delivered in order. Again, this is left to the upper-layer protocols.

Transport and Session Layer Services

AppleTalk uses a number of different protocols to maintain transport and session communications. The most important is the AppleTalk Transaction Protocol, because it is used by all file and print sharing.

AppleTalk Transaction Protocol

Transport layer services are provided by the *AppleTalk Transaction Protocol* (ATP). ATP is a connection-oriented protocol which supports packet sequencing. ATP differs from most transport protocols in that it is transaction-based, not byte-stream–based. A transaction consists of a request from client followed by a response by a server. Requests and responses are tracked through the use of a transaction ID number, as you can see in Figure 3.30.

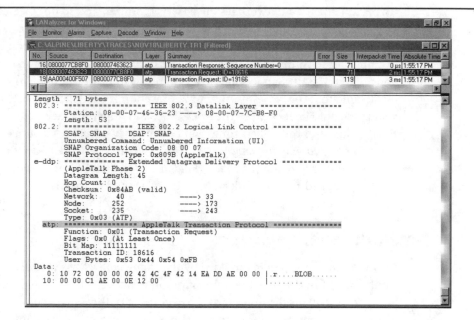

ATP also takes care of packet fragmentation and reassembly. In order to insure proper tracking of each transaction, messages are limited to eight frames. Each frame can contain no more than 578 bytes of data. This means that the maximum frame size with header information is limited to 625 bytes.

AppleTalk Session Protocol

The *AppleTalk Session Protocol* (ASP) is a client of ATP and works with it to provide connectivity for file share access. As a Session layer protocol, it is responsible for negotiating a connection when a client wishes to access files on a server. This is not to say that it takes care of authentication; it is simply responsible for establishing the connection between the two systems. The upper layers are actually responsible for the authentication process.

ASP is also responsible for maintaining the connection once it is established. ASP makes sure that queries and command sets are in an acceptable format for the upper-layer services. ASP is also responsible for properly terminating a connection when the session is complete.

Printer Access Protocol

The *Printer Access Protocol* (PAP) performs exactly the same services as ASP, except it is responsible for printer access. It takes care of sessions between printers located directly in the network, as well as printers that are being shared by host systems.

Upper-Layer Services

AppleTalk supports two upper-layer services:

- The AppleTalk Filing Protocol, which takes care of file requests on both clients and servers
- AppleShare, which provides remote file and printer services to network clients

AppleTalk Filing Protocol

The *AppleTalk Filing Protocol* (AFP) provides transparent access to both local and remote file systems. It is designed to make dealing with remote file systems just as easy as it is to deal with the files on your local drive. AFP also takes care of authentication when remote file systems are requested.

When a user issues a file access command, AFP determines whether the request involves local or remote file access. If the access is local, the request is passed along to the local operating system (usually System 7). If remote file access is requested, AFP passes the request down through ASP and across the network to the server. AFP on the server accepts the request (if authentication is accepted) and passes it along to Apple-Share.

If the remote file system is not compatible (System 7 uses a special file system which requires a fork file and a data file for each piece of information), AFP takes care of translating the two file formats, if it can. AFP then takes care of returning the information to the requesting client.

AppleShare

AppleShare is the roof that sits on top of the AppleTalk protocol suite. It is the application that coordinates file and printer access through the lower layers. AppleShare has three major components:

AppleShare File Server　This works with AFP to allow users to remotely access and save their files. AppleShare is responsible for registering users and mapping them to their appropriate volumes and directories.

AppleShare Print Server　This works with NBP and PAP to allow users to access printers remotely. When a user selects a printer, NBP is used to find the remote printer's node address and PAP is used to send it data. AppleShare is responsible for spooling the print job before sending it to the printer. AppleShare uses the PostScript Command set when communicating with a printer.

AppleShare PC　This allows a network client using a DOS-based file system to access and exchange files with a Macintosh server. AppleShare takes care of all the conversion requirements between the two dissimilar file systems.

Summary

This completes our discussion of the major protocol suites. Hopefully, at this point your eyes are not too bloodshot—there is a lot of information to digest in this chapter. For those who prefer a more hands-on approach, feel free to refer back to this section as we discuss protocol configurations later in the book. This may help to reinforce any portions of this chapter that did not quite sink in.

While this book is primarily about routing, we are going to take a slight detour in the next chapter to talk about bridging and switching. Cisco has begun shipping a number of products that include both switching and routing ability. With this in mind, an understanding of these technologies can be extremely beneficial.

CHAPTER **4**

Bridging and Switching

Back in the old days (a couple of years ago), hardware was very departmentalized. Bridges bridged traffic, switches switched, and routers routed. This made for very specialized hardware, and the world was a simpler place to live in.

The problem was that these devices were not very versatile. What if you needed switching speed on your backbone but also needed to route the traffic in order to improve segmentation? The need for flexibility has spawned the development of infrastructure devices that include all this functionality.

With this in mind, we are going to take a quick look at bridging and switching technology before jumping back into routing. Since many Cisco models include these technologies, you need to understand them in order to decide when to bridge, when to switch, when to route, and when to use a combination of the three.

Bridges

A *bridge* is typically a small box with two network connectors that attach to two separate portions of the network. A bridge boosts the electrical properties of the transmission in a way similar to a hub, but it also looks at the frames of data, allowing it to control traffic flow. A common bridge is shown in Figure 4.1. A *forward* light flashes whenever the bridge needs to pass traffic.

FIGURE 4.1

A common bridge

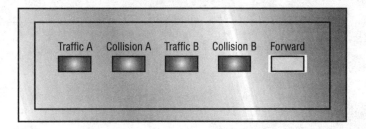

In our discussion of Ethernet in Chapter 1, I introduced the concept of a data frame and described the information contained within the frame header. Bridges put this header information to use by monitoring the source and destination MAC address on each frame of data. By monitoring the source address, the bridge learns the location of each network system. It will construct a table, listing which MAC addresses are directly accessible by each of its ports. It will then use that information to play traffic cop and regulate the flow of data on the network. Let's look at an example.

A Bridge Example

Take a look at the network in Figure 4.2. Betty needs to send data to the server Thoth. Because everyone on the network is required to monitor the network, Betty first listens for the transmissions of other stations. If the wire is free, Betty will then transmit a frame of data. The bridge is also watching for traffic and will look at the source address in the header of Betty's frame. Because it is unsure which port the system with MAC address 00C08BBE0052 (Thoth) is connected to, the bridge amplifies the signal and retransmits it out port B. Note that until now the bridge's functionality is very similar to that of a hub. The bridge does a little extra, however; it has learned that Betty is attached to port A and creates a table entry with her MAC address.

FIGURE 4.2

Betty transmits data to the server Thoth by putting Thoth's MAC address into the destination field of the frame.

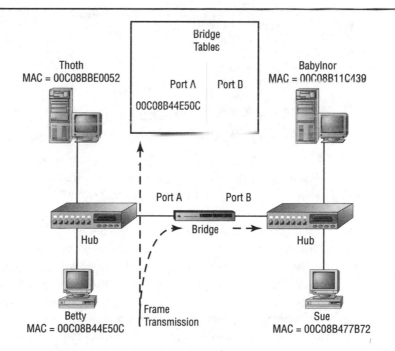

When Thoth replies to Betty's request, as shown in Figure 4.3, the bridge will look again at the destination address in the frame of data. This time, however, it finds a match in its table, noting that Betty is also attached to port A. Because it knows that

Betty can receive this information directly, it drops the frame and blocks it from being transmitted from port B. The bridge will also make a new table entry for Thoth, recording the MAC address as being off port A.

Thoth's reply to Betty's message

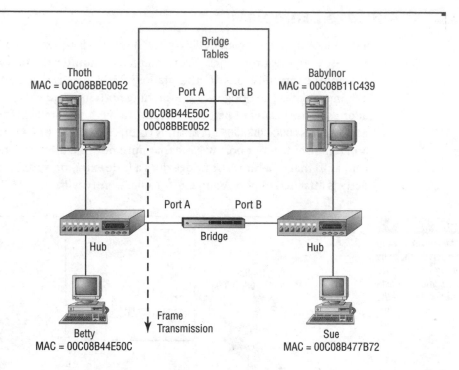

For as long as the bridge remembers each station's MAC address, all communications between Betty and Thoth will be isolated from Sue and Babylnor. *Traffic isolation* is a powerful feature because it means that systems on both sides of the bridge can be carrying on conversations at the same time, effectively doubling the available bandwidth. The bridge insures that communications on both sides stay isolated, as if they were not even connected. Because stations cannot see transmissions on the other side of the bridge, they assume that the network is free and send their data.

Each system only needs to contend for bandwidth with systems on its own segment. This means that there is no way for a station to have a collision outside of its segment. Thus, these segments are referred to as *collision domains*, as shown in Figure 4.4. Notice that one port on each side of the bridge is part of each collision domain. This is because each of its ports will contend for bandwidth with the systems it is directly connected to. Because the bridge isolates traffic within each collision domain, there is no way for separated systems' signals to collide. The effect is a doubling of potential bandwidth.

FIGURE 4.4

Two separate collision domains

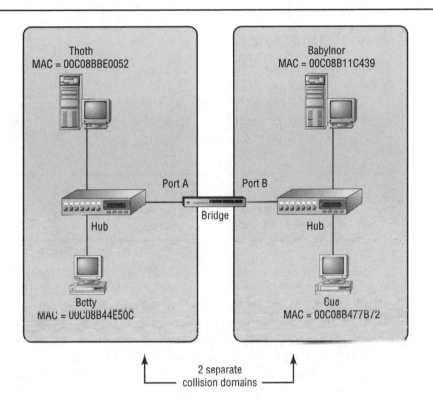

Thoth
MAC = 00C08BBE0052

Babylnor
MAC = 00C08B11C439

Port A

Port B

Bridge

Hub

Hub

Bctty
MAC = 00C08B44E50C

Cuo
MAC = 00C08B477B72

2 separate
collision domains

What happens when traffic needs to traverse the bridge? As you've seen, when a bridge is unsure of a system's location, it will always pass the packet along, just in case. Once the bridge learns that the system is in fact located off its other port, it will continue to pass the frame along as required.

This example is specific to two stations carrying on a data exchange. As I mentioned in our discussion of Ethernet frames, there is a special destination address referred to as a *broadcast address*. Broadcasts contain information required by multiple stations on the network. Broadcast frames are typically used by upper-layer protocols like IPX and IP to relay network and server information. For this reason, a bridge will always pass a broadcast frame and will not bother making a table entry for it.

NOTE Since a system will never use a multicast address in the source MAC field, multicast traffic is handled similarly to broadcasts.

Protocol Independence

Bridges are *protocol independent*. This means that it does not matter whether you're running AppleTalk, IPX, IP, NetBEUI or any other 802.3-compliant method of communicating. All a bridge cares about is the source and destination MAC addresses present in any valid Ethernet frame. Protocol independence can come in handy if you're using a protocol that receives limited hardware support, like Banyan's VINES.

 NOTE Since a bridge works at the topology layer, network addresses are the same off each port. For example, if the network off port A is 192.168.1.0, that same subnet address must be used off port B, as well.

Some bridges can analyze the frame check sequence (FCS) located in the trailer of the frame. As I mentioned before, the FCS contains the cyclic redundancy check (CRC), which is an algorithm used to determine whether the frame is intact or has become damaged during transmission. If FCS checking is enabled, the bridge will perform its own CRC check on the frame and compare the value to what is contained in the FCS field of each frame before forwarding the frame along. If a frame fails the CRC comparison, the bridge contacts the transmitting system and asks it to send a new copy of the frame.

 TIP If you commonly have a lot of CRC errors on your network, this check feature may be useful because it keeps the frame from being passed to the destination system, which would then find the CRC failure and would need to request a new frame itself. By letting the bridge do it, you cut down on the bandwidth used by the bad frame and the resulting request to only a single collision domain.

If you do not see a lot of errors, you may want to keep this feature disabled, as it does require some additional overhead on the bridge. If you do see a lot of errors (if, say, 1 percent of your traffic is bad CRC frames), enable this feature. Then, set out to determine and eliminate the cause of these errors.

NOTE Excessive CRC failures are usually caused by a bad network interface card.

The Spanning Tree Protocol

Bridges can communicate with each other via a set of rules called the *Spanning Tree protocol*. The Spanning Tree protocol is used to configure default paths dynamically when two or more bridges are connected in parallel to each other.

Bridge Looping Causes Problems

The Spanning Tree protocol helps to avoid a situation called *bridge looping*. To get an idea of how bridge looping works, let's look at an example.

Given a network layout similar to our last example, let's say that you decide to add a second bridge for redundancy. That way, if someone spills coffee on the first bridge and it quickly dies in a shower of sparks, the second bridge can continue to provide connectivity between the two collision domains. The configuration would look something like Figure 4.5.

FIGURE 4.5

Two bridges connected parallel to each other create a redundant link between the two collision domains.

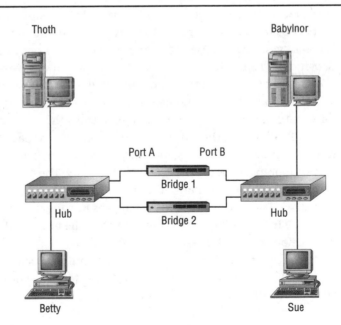

If both bridges are active, something curious happens. If Betty sends a frame of data to Thoth, both bridges would initially detect the frame and be unsure of where Thoth is located, so they would both transmit the data to the other segment and make an entry for Betty in their tables, placing her off port A.

 NOTE   When both bridges detect the frame and transmit the data to the other segment, two separate copies of the frame have been transmitted to the other collision domain (off port B).

As each bridge detects the frame sent by the other on the port B collision domain, each would assume that this is a new attempt by Betty to send Thoth a frame of data. Because both bridges would still be unsure of where Thoth is located, they would pass the frame back to the collision domain off port A. Each bridge would also assume that Betty has now moved to the other collision domain and would incorrectly list that system as being off port B.

We now have a couple of problems. First, we have three identical frames (one from Betty and one from each bridge) floating around off port A, when there should only be one frame. Instead of improving our traffic pattern, the bridges have tripled our frame rate on this segment. Second, because Betty is now incorrectly listed as being off port B, any data transmitted to Betty by Babylnor and Sue would be blocked by both bridges, each incorrectly assuming that Betty is on the same local segment as Babylnor and Sue. The result is that Betty cannot receive any data sent to her from stations off port B because neither bridge will forward the information.

At this point, the entire situation repeats itself. Each bridge detects the frame transmission of the other off port A. Each retransmits the frame onto the segment attached to port B and moves the entry for Betty's MAC address back to port A. Betty can now receive data across the bridge, but only until the tables are incorrectly reset again.

This looping effect is called *counting to infinity*. The bridges will continue to pass the frame back and forth until the end of time or until the bridge's power plug is pulled, whichever comes first. This happens because the bridge has no way to identify duplicate frames. When analyzing the frame, the bridge only looks at the source and destination MAC addresses. It's beyond the scope of a bridge's functionality to perform some sort of check to determine whether it has seen a particular frame before; attempting to do so would severely degrade a bridge's performance, causing it to become a bottleneck on the network.

Now, take this situation with Betty's system and multiply it by a network full of systems. It's easy to see how two misconfigured bridges could easily bring an entire network to its knees.

Eliminating Bridging Loops with the Spanning Tree Protocol

To the rescue comes the Spanning Tree protocol. This protocol allows bridges to communicate with each other and learn where they are in relation to one another. If a bridge is configured to use the Spanning Tree protocol, it will transmit a maintenance frame on startup called a *Bridge Protocol Data Unit* (BPDU). This frame contains an ID number for the bridge and is transmitted on all the bridge's ports. This ID number is a combination of a number preset by the network administrator and the device's MAC address. For example, an ID number of 0100000C3BAE72 would be a priority setting of 01 with a MAC address of 00 00 0C 3B AE 72.

If the Spanning Tree protocol were used in the example we've been discussing, both bridges would transmit BPDUs from each of their ports. Each bridge would receive a BPDU from the other bridge on both of its ports and realize that the two devices are hooked up in parallel. They would then compare their BPDUs to see which bridge has the lower ID number. The bridge with the lower ID number would become active, while the other would enter a standby mode. In standby mode, the second bridge monitors the first bridge to insure that it is continually passing frames. The second bridge would remain in standby mode until it detects that the first bridge is no longer passing frames. If the first bridge were to drop offline, the second bridge would step in to supply connectivity. Because there is only one active path for the frames to follow, bridge looping is eliminated.

 TIP A bridge's ID is prefixed by a number that you can assign. If you prefer to use one bridge over another, you can assign it a lower number (like 01) to insure that it initiates as the active bridge. Acceptable values are 01–FF in hexadecimal.

About the only drawback to the Spanning Tree protocol is that the switchover occurs so quickly that you will probably never know the bridge has failed unless you are monitoring the devices.

Monitoring Traffic in a Bridged Environment

While bridges have many benefits, they do have one minor drawback. If you are trying to monitor your network's health with some sort of network analyzer, a bridge will block you from ever seeing a full picture. An analyzer relies on being able to detect each frame in order to collect statistics. When you use a bridge, your view is limited to the collision domain to which you are connected. If you have a single bridge installed and you want to monitor all traffic on your network, you will need to purchase a second analyzer and keep one hooked up to each collision domain.

 TIP Some analyzers allow you to install probes on each of your logical segments that will forward traffic statistics back to a central console.

Switches

Switches are the marriage of hub and bridge technology. They look like stackable hubs, having multiple RJ45 connectors for connecting network systems. Instead of being a dumb amplifier like a hub, however, switches function as though they have a miniature bridge built into each port. A switch will keep track of the MAC addresses attached to each of its ports and will forward traffic destined for a certain address only to the port to which it is attached.

Figure 4.6 shows a switched environment in which the device will learn the position of each system once a single frame transmission occurs (this is identical to a bridge). Assuming that each system has already transmitted at least one frame, we now find that at exactly the same instant Station 1 needs to send data to Server 1, Station 2 needs to send data to Server 2, and Station 3 needs to send data to Server 3.

There are some interesting things about this situation. For example, each wire run involves only the switch and the station attached to it. Since each port of the switch acts like a bridge, we have a unique collision domain off each port of the switch.

The only traffic seen by the workstations and servers consists of frames specifically sent to them or the broadcast address. The result is that all three stations are able to transmit at exactly the same time. This is a powerful feature that goes a long way toward increasing potential bandwidth. Given our example, if this is a 10Mbps topology, the effective throughput has just increased by a factor of 3. This is because all three sets of systems can carry on their conversations simultaneously, as the switch isolates them from each other. While it is still technically 10Mbps Ethernet, potential throughput has increased to 30Mbps.

FIGURE 4.6

A switch installation showing three work-stations and three servers that must communicate

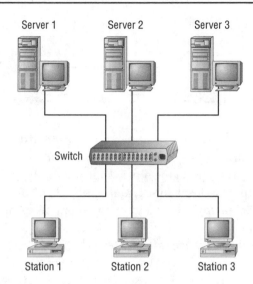

Because each collision domain is limited to only two devices (the switch and the system attached), you could completely eliminate the chance of any collisions if you could come up with some way to keep these two systems from stepping on each other's transmissions.

Full-Duplex Operation

This is where *full-duplex operation* comes into play. Full duplex under Ethernet changes the communication rules by telling a system that it is OK to receive different data from what it is currently transmitting. Each of the two systems has exclusive access to a pair of wires in order to transmit data. This is shown in Figure 4.7. Notice that each system has a wire pair that it can use for transmitting data and another pair that it can use for receiving data. Since there is no chance of a signal collision, both systems are free to transmit whenever they need to.

 NOTE   Keep in mind that the physical wiring is identical for both full- and half-duplex mode. The only difference is the communication rules. Since there are only two systems in the collision domain, each system can safely transmit simultaneously without fear of a collision.

FIGURE 4.7

Full duplex is possible
because each system
has a dedicated
transmit-and-
receive pair.

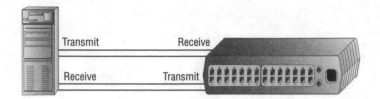

The result is that each system can transmit data without having to worry about pesky collisions. A system can continually transmit 10Mbps on one wire pair while receiving 10Mbps on the other. Applying this to our network example, our potential throughput has just jumped from 30Mbps to 60Mbps! Our topology has not changed—we are achieving these bandwidth potentials using standard 10Mbps Ethernet hardware.

Note the operative word "potential." This is because it would be an extremely rare situation for these six systems to transmit this much data simultaneously. Still, having exclusive wire access is a great way to insure that a system can transmit whenever it needs to. If applied only to servers, full-duplex operation gives these systems a bit of an edge in keeping up with requests from multiple clients. The result is a governing effect, allocating more bandwidth to the server than the workstations. This will help the server keep up with the additional frames it will see now that each workstation has its own 10Mbps pipe.

Full-Duplex Auto-Detection

Some network cards have a feature that allows them to *auto-detect* when full-duplex operation may be used. You should disable this feature and specifically configure the card for the correct mode of operation (full or half duplex). I have seen situations in which the first or second computer booted on the network will assume that it has exclusive access to a collision domain and will switch to full-duplex mode. The computer will not realize that it is connected through a shared hub. This works fine until the rest of the network's systems begin to power up. The result is that one station will be attempting to transmit and receive data simultaneously, making the entire network crawl to a halt as each non-full-duplex system assumes that multiple collisions are taking place. This can be a difficult problem to diagnose. The only clue is that the collision light on the hub will be lit up like a Christmas tree.

I have also seen situations in which a NIC is unable to detect full-duplex operation even though it is hooked up directly to a switch. I've even seen specific models of switches that have difficulty detecting full-duplex mode with specific NIC vendors.

The old adage, "If you want something done right, do it yourself," definitely applies to setting the proper duplex-operation mode. Best to set it yourself and know that it is correct.

Modes of Operation

Switches have two modes of operation:

- Cut through
- Store and forward

Cut-Through Mode

In *cut-through mode*, the switch receives only the first 14 bytes of the frame (just the header) and will immediately begin to decide where the frame should be sent. In cut-through mode, a switch can begin transmitting the frame on the destination port before it receives the frame in its entirety; this results in extremely fast switching times with a minimal amount of latency added to the circuit. The greatest benefits of cut-through mode are in quiet or full-duplex environments, where it is unlikely that the switch will need to pause before transmission.

The benefits of cut-through mode diminish as traffic levels increase. If use is high, the switch will probably not be able to transmit the frame onto a collision domain before receiving it in its entirety, anyway.

Also, you cannot use cut-though mode if you are passing frames between different topology speeds: for example, if you have some systems connecting at 10Mb while others connect at 100Mb. This is because the whole frame must be queued before it can be forwarded over a different speed topology. In such cases, you will need to use store-and-forward mode.

Store-and-Forward Mode

Store-and-forward mode requires the switch to read the entire frame into memory before transmission. While reading the entire frame adds a bit of a delay, store-and-forward mode definitely has its advantages. Like a bridge, a switch in store-and-forward mode can check the FCS field for CRC errors; this insures that bad frames are not propagated across the network. Another cool feature is that store-and-forward mode gives the switch the ability to support multiple topologies. A server could be connected to a 100Mbps port while all the workstations are connected to 10Mbps ports, making it easy for the server to keep up with data requests from multiple workstations and speeding overall network performance.

Store-and-forward switching is always used with mixed topologies because it insures that the switch has the entire frame available before the switch attempts a transmission. In cut-through mode, because a switch can begin transmitting a frame before receiving it in its entirety, problems may arise in a mixed-speed situation. Let's say a frame is received on a 10Mbps port and it is addressed to a system on the 100Mbps port. In cut-through mode, the switch would immediately begin delivery on the faster segment. This can be a problem because the switch could potentially transmit all the frame information it has received on the faster segment and then have to pause and wait for the delivery of the rest of the frame information. Obviously, this would cause communication problems on the faster segment.

Avoiding Switch Overload

Take care to not overload the switch with excessive traffic. Let's look at an extreme example of how switch overload can occur.

Assume that you have an old 386 server running NetWare 2.15. Because the system has continued to function, it has pretty much been ignored over the years. Your users, however, have been complaining about how slow their system is and claiming they require dual-processor Pentium III machines with PCI buses and every go-fast computer part you can think of (insert a Tim Allen grunt here).

You decide to upgrade your network infrastructure by replacing your old hub with a brand-new switch. You swap in the new device, connect all systems, put the workstations in full-duplex mode (the server has an old card that does not support this feature), and wait for your users to begin working. A curious thing occurs—network performance actually gets worse! Why did this happen? To answer this question, let's look at what was probably going on before you installed the switch.

How Switch Overload Can Occur

When you use a network hub, all systems are in direct communication with each other. This means that the topology speed limits the maximum amount of information that can be transmitted at any given time. The nice thing about this situation is that it is self-regulating. Granted, network performance can be a bit sluggish, but it helps to keep any one system from becoming overloaded (although overload can still occur).

Now, let's drop the switch back in and see what happened. In full-duplex mode, each workstation assumed that it had full bandwidth available and would transmit information whenever it needed to. Because each workstation never had to contend for bandwidth, it could send more information in a given period of time than it could before the switch was installed. The switch would then attempt to deliver these frames of data to the server.

As the pipe leading to the server becomes overloaded (we have multiple 10Mb full-duplex connections trying to send data to a half-duplex 10Mb connection), the switch begins to queue up packets sent by the workstations. If the server's pipe cannot catch up eventually with the frames stored in the switch's queue (which it probably cannot, given our example), the frames will eventually fill up the switch's memory pool. Once this occurs, any new frames transmitted to the switch have nowhere to be stored and subsequently are ignored. In short, the switch is throwing away information because it has nowhere to store it.

To make matters even worse, the workstations will eventually time out waiting for a reply to the frames the switch threw away; this causes them to transmit the same information again, compounding the bottleneck.

This is a good example of why it is important to maintain a balance on your network and insure that you know the impact of any hardware you install. While this example may seem a bit extreme, it is not too far off from a real-life network situation I had to diagnose.

 TIP Some switches handle queued frames better than others. When shopping for a switch, pay close attention to the backplane speed, because this regulates how quickly the switch can forward traffic. You should also note the size of the memory pool used to queue frames before delivery.

VLAN Technology

Switching introduces a new technology referred to as the *virtual local area network* (VLAN). Software running on the switch lets you set up connectivity parameters for connected systems by workgroup instead of by geographical location. The switch's administrator can organize port transmissions logically to group connectivity according to each user's requirements. The "virtual" part of it is that these workgroups can span multiple physical network segments. By assigning all switch ports that connect to PCs used by accounting personnel to the same workgroup, for example, you can create a virtual accounting network.

Let's take a look at a more detailed example of how this works.

A VLAN Example

Let's say that you have two groups of users who work exclusively with each other and a particular server. You could create two VLANs, isolating the traffic so that all communications remain within the group. While a switch will do this anyway for point-to-point communications, the addition of the VLANs will block broadcast traffic, as well. This isolation will help to reduce unnecessary traffic even further.

 TIP VLAN technology is designed to improve performance, not to provide a security perimeter. If you need to fully isolate two segments, use two physical switches.

There may be a problem with this setup, however. What if the two servers are running NetWare 4.11 and need to exchange NDS information with each other? The solution is to add a third VLAN that includes only the servers. VLANs can overlap as circumstances require. This overlap allows server broadcasts to reach all members of the workgroup, as well as the other server. Workstations located in the other workgroup do not see these broadcasts and thus are safeguarded from this additional traffic. Your network would look something like Figure 4.8.

FIGURE 4.8

VLAN implementation in a small networking environment

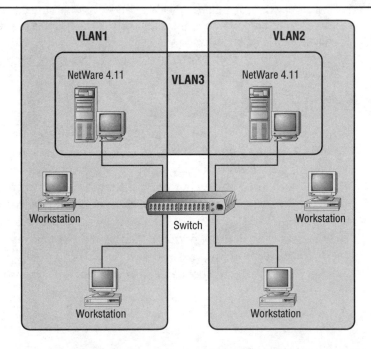

While the true benefits of VLANs may not be apparent immediately, let's increase the scale of the network and watch what happens. Figure 4.9 shows an organization that occupies a number of floors in a building. If each department is confined to each floor, then your network design may be fine as is.

FIGURE 4.9

A large network using switches to connect to the backbone

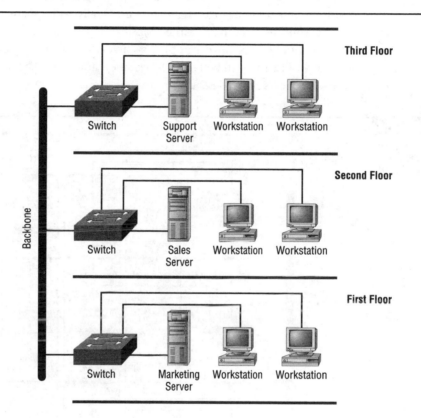

 NOTE A *backbone* is a network segment used to connect other segments that contain end users. It usually runs a faster topology than the populated segments in order to keep up with the larger bandwidth demands it may experience.

Unfortunately, rarely will you have your users so neatly segregated, and workgroups can find themselves spread out over a wide area. If the marketing server is located on the first floor, then any marketing personnel who need to access it will find themselves traversing the backbone on a regular basis. Let's assume that this situation is true for other departments, as well.

Because there is no way to organize workgroups geographically, network broadcasts must be propagated to every corner of the network because valid users could be located anywhere; this can make for a very busy network.

Now let's create some virtual networks and see what happens. If you use VLANs to segment, your network traffic can be confined to each individual workgroup, even though members of each workgroup are spread throughout the building. This confinement would give you better traffic isolation and thus better network performance. Figure 4.10 shows how you could group these users.

FIGURE 4.10

A large network using VLANs to better isolate network traffic

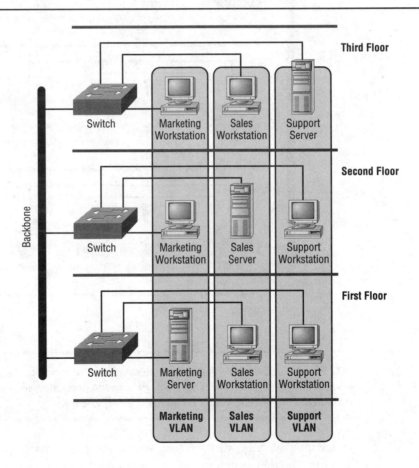

While you may be able to wire each user physically to the floor where his server is located, this could be impractical. Besides the fact that this kind of wiring could create a spaghetti nightmare, what happens when a user moves down the hall? Then you would have to rewire her new office space to connect to her server location, and you might also have to rewire her old office if a user from another department moves in. With a VLAN, this type of relocation would mean a simple configuration change through the switch's management software.

VLAN Drawbacks

VLANs do have a few drawbacks. The first is that the scalability just noted is usually vendor specific. There are a number of different ways virtual LANs are created. You may find that some vendor implementations will not work with others. While this discrepancy should correct itself over the next few years, you should be conscious of this limitation for now.

Also, segmentation is very specific. Each user is completely isolated to working only within his workgroup. While this was acceptable in the examples just discussed, what if all users need to share access to multiple servers or require access to the Internet? In these situations, you would need VLAN routers to connect separate VLANs. Depending on the switch model, this routing functionality may or may not be included.

 TIP As with any technology, make sure you know exactly how you plan to use it and that it does in fact support your intended use before you make any hardware purchases. To take poetic liberty with an old carpenter's saying: Research twice and purchase once.

One final drawback to VLANs is that they can be very high maintenance. If you have a large network with each user connected to a single switch port, it will take some time to get all the ports configured correctly, and you will have to make changes whenever a user moves. Plan on gaining an intimate knowledge of the administration software.

Trunking

One of the problems with a switched environment is that it can saturate a network's backbone. Since a switch provides dedicated bandwidth to each system, a higher rate of throughput is required along common links in order to keep up with the increased traffic flow. In other words, a network backbone must be able to support a higher level of throughput than what is offered to each individual system, in order to insure that it does not become a performance gate.

Of course, the obvious solution is to use a faster topology on the backbone. For example, you could run 10Mb Ethernet to the desktop, 100Mb to your servers, and 1Gb along the network backbone. The problem here is what happens if 1Gb Ethernet is outside of your price range, your switch does not support it, or—even worse—the distance requirements of your backbone prohibit 1Gb use.

In these situations, circuit *trunking* can be extremely useful. Trunking allows you to take multiple switch ports and group them together in order to produce a higher rate of bandwidth. In the Cisco world, trunking is commonly referred to as *Fast Ether-Channel*. Fast EtherChannel allows you to group together up to four 100Mb Ethernet channels in order to increase the amount of bandwidth available on your backbone.

For example, examine the two Catalyst 5000 switches shown in Figure 4.11. Both switches are providing 100Mb connectivity to a number of systems. Due to work-flow patterns, users on one switch commonly need to access resources located on the other. If the backbone connection between the two switches were a single 100Mb connection, it would be possible for a single user to saturate the backbone.

FIGURE 4.11

Two switches trunked together

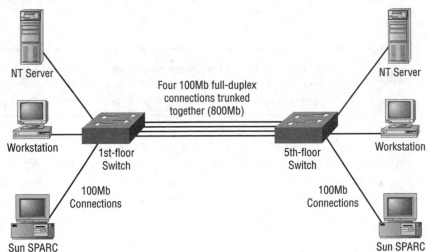

Fast EtherChannel allows you to bond up to four consecutive 100Mb Ethernet connections into a single circuit. The resulting link has the aggregated bandwidth of these four circuits combined. Since all four circuits can be run in full-duplex mode, the available bandwidth along this backbone connection is 800Mb. To review the math:

```
100Mb × 2 (full duplex) × 4 (circuits) = 800Mb
```

This allows you to support a higher backbone speed without having to upgrade to 1Gb Ethernet. The additional bonus is that you have removed a single point of failure for this link. If any one of your circuit paths should fail, the remaining circuits would continue passing traffic at a lower level of available bandwidth. This makes trunking not only cost effective but fault tolerant, as well.

 NOTE When you enable trunking, you automatically disable the Spanning Tree protocol on the trunked ports. This is to insure that all trunked ports remain active and capable of forwarding traffic at the same time.

Spanning Tree and Switches

Spanning Tree with switches is similar to Spanning Tree with bridges; the big difference is that a switch has many more ports to worry about. This greatly increases the potential to run into circuit loops with a single device. For this reason, Spanning Tree can be even more useful in a switched environment than it is in a bridged environment.

Since a bridge is a two-port device, the chances that a network administrator will connect two ports to the same logical circuit are minimal (note that the operative word is "minimal"—not "impossible"). Switches are a different animal, however, and there are in fact situations in which you might actually want to create redundant circuits.

For example, let's say you have a network similar to the one shown in Figure 4.12. You wish to double up on the physical connection between the switch and the hubs in case one of these links should fail. While you cannot do this to increase performance (you need a switch at both ends to trunk traffic), this would provide an alternate circuit path in case one of the links failed.

FIGURE 4.12

*Using redundant
wiring to increase fault
tolerance*

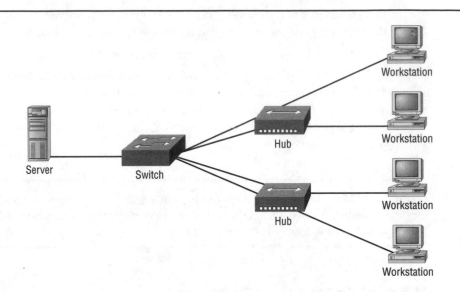

Of course, the problem here is that we have created a circuit loop. Similar to the network shown in Figure 4.5, there are now two switch ports replicating traffic throughout your network. To resolve this issue, you can use the Spanning Tree protocol to place one of the switch ports in standby mode. This way, it will begin passing traffic only if the first link should fail.

While in the bridge world we had the ability to set priorities for certain bridges, in the switch world we can also set priorities for different ports. You can do this by using the `set spantree` command in order to adjust the *port priority* value. When two ports are connected to the same logical circuit, the port with the lower port priority will be the one to forward traffic. If both ports have the same priority, the assigned port number value will be used. For example, if ports 2 and 3 have the same port priority and are connected to the same logical circuit, port 2 will be chosen to forward traffic.

 NOTE Valid values for the port priority are 0–63.

Monitoring Traffic

One of the biggest problems with switches is that they make it extremely difficult to monitor your network. When all systems were connected to a single collision domain, you simply plugged in your analyzer and started capturing traffic. With a switch, however, each system is on its own, unique collision domain. In order to collect statistics for a particular system, your analyzer must be plugged in to the same switch port as the system you wish to monitor.

Of course, this is not always practical and can be extremely time consuming if you have many systems to monitor. For this reason, most switches let you configure a *monitoring port*. A monitoring port allows you to tell the switch, "Send a copy of all traffic headed in and out of port X to the port where the analyzer is plugged in." In this way, you can change the port you are monitoring through a simple software change. This is still not as simple as plugging in your analyzer and just grabbing all traffic, but that's one of the prices we have paid for advancement.

 TIP One trick is to monitor the statistics gathered by the switch itself in order to identify the best collision domains to monitor. For example, if your switch reports that it is seeing a lot of CRC errors off port 7, you know that it may be a good idea to use your analyzer on port 7 to get a better picture of what might be going wrong.

Designing Networks with Bridges and Switches

Let's look at four sample networks and determine which would benefit the most by the use of bridging or switching. Note that we're focusing on the network infrastructure, not on the actual operating systems or the functionality of the protocols being used.

The Examples

As you read each example, see whether (and why) you think bridging or switching would be a good idea before you read on.

Example 1: 25 Engineers

Our first example is a group of 25 engineers using SGI UNIX workstations. Each engineer uses his or her machine to write code and create images for computer games. As part of the software development process, the engineers need to exchange file information with each other. They are not broken up into defined workgroups, as all development is a collaborative effort. Each engineer may need to share files with any one of the other engineers at any given time. The data transfers between systems can also be quite intensive, as large graphic files are used and source code is compiled over the network. Figure 4.13 depicts our first example.

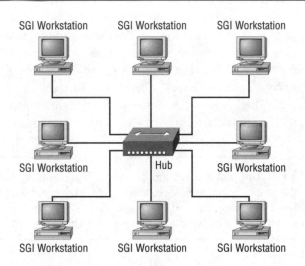

Example 2: Multiple Servers and Protocols

Our second example is a small advertising firm with about 50 employees. They have three servers: one NetWare, one Mac, and one UNIX. Fifteen of the 50 use Mac workstations to do graphic design work which involves moving some average-size image files. All files are stored on the Mac server using Apple's native AppleTalk protocol. The remaining 35 users perform mostly administrative tasks and connect with the NetWare system via the IPX protocol for file and print services. All users run IP, as well, to connect to the UNIX system for e-mail and Internet access. Figure 4.14 depicts our second example.

FIGURE 4.14

Example 2: Network with multiple server types and protocols

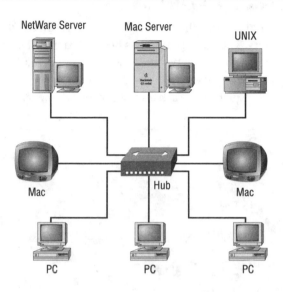

Example 3: Three NT Servers

Our third example includes 100 users with three NT servers. Fifty of these users use one of the servers for file and print services. The remaining 50 use the second server for the same. The third system runs the company's mail program and needs to be accessed by everyone. NetBEUI is used to access all servers. Figure 4.15 shows our third example.

FIGURE 4.15

Example 3: Network with users neatly broken up by workgroup; everyone needs access to mail

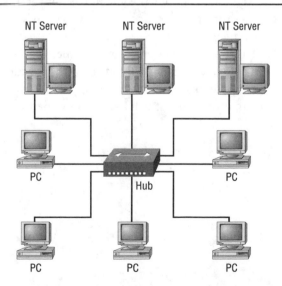

Example 4: WAN Link

Our final example includes two separate NT networks which currently have no connectivity. The organization has decided to install a leased line in order to provide file sharing between the two networks. Each network uses NetBIOS/IP as a protocol and consists of approximately 100 users. Your job is to recommend the type of device that should be placed on each end of the leased line. Figure 4.16 shows our fourth example.

FIGURE 4.16

Example 4: Two remote networks which will be connected via a leased line circuit

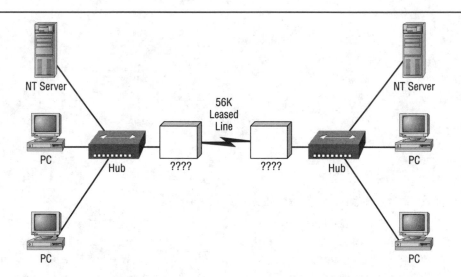

In the first three examples, the users are complaining about slow network response time. In the final example, the circuit has not yet been installed, so there are no metrics to determine performance. As always, cost is a factor and you will need to justify any hardware purchases.

While the task of redesigning each of these networks may seem a bit overwhelming, think of what we have learned about the functionality of bridges and switches and try to apply their traffic-isolation features to each example. Move systems around as required, if you think it will help improve performance.

NOTE Feel free to stop and ponder for a moment before reading on. It's important for a successful network engineer to have good problem-solving skills and to be analytical. Learning the theory of how network systems work is the easy part. Applying it on a daily basis is the real challenge.

Evaluating the Case Studies

When is it a good idea to deploy bridging or switching? Let's revisit our four example networks, shown in Figures 4.13–4.16, to see where it makes sense.

Example 1: 25 Engineers

Our first example is clearly not a good choice for implementing a bridge. Because everyone shares files with everyone else, there is no way to group traffic into logical collision domains. Bridging would be of very little use in this environment.

However, our group of 25 engineers would be a great fit for switching technology. Let's say you installed a single backbone switch and gave each engineer his or her own port connection. When one engineer shares files with another, the traffic generated would stay isolated from the remaining systems. If each system is outfitted with a 100Mbps card, the potential bandwidth would be in the 1.2Gbps range. In fact, because there is only one system per port, you could utilize full-duplex connections and up the potential bandwidth to the 2.4Gbps range.

 NOTE Increasing the potential bandwidth to the 2.4Gbps range could yield up to a 2,400-percent improvement in available bandwidth. Not bad for replacing a single piece of hardware!

Example 2: Multiple Servers and Protocols

Our second example shows a bit more potential for using a bridge. Users are somewhat broken up into workgroups because administration mostly uses the NetWare server and graphic design mostly accesses the Mac server. If you were to separate these workgroups with bridges, putting the UNIX system in the middle, as shown in Figure 4.17, you may be able to isolate enough traffic to improve network performance.

FIGURE 4.17

A potential network design for Example 2's advertising firm

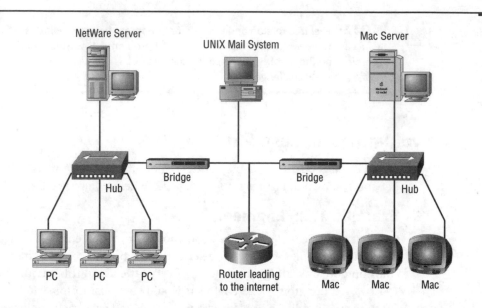

The only caveat here is that you have three different protocols in use. As you saw earlier, protocols use the broadcast address to relay information concerning servers and networks. Also, as we discussed in the section on Ethernet, all stations are required to process a frame that contains a broadcast address in the MAC destination field, whether or not the receiving station is currently using the same protocol as the station that transmitted the frame. Of course, if the receiving station does not understand the protocol being used, the frame is discarded because the information has no relevance. However, it still takes time and CPU cycles for the system to determine that it did not actually need this information.

Clearly, if you could isolate the protocols from the stations that do not need to see them, you may well be able to increase overall performance even more. Because bridging is protocol-stupid and cannot provide this functionality (bridges forward all broadcasts), you may be better off waiting to see if another technology would be a better fit. Unfortunately, you cannot simply disconnect the networks from each other because they still need to share the UNIX system for mail and have access to the Internet.

If you use a switch, there are two potential network layouts to investigate. The first is to use VLANs and segregate traffic by workgroup. Each virtual LAN would include the users and their server. The UNIX system and the Internet connection would be overlapped by both VLANs, as shared access is required for both. Your network design may appear similar to that shown in Figure 4.18.

FIGURE 4.18

A potential network design for our advertising firm's network using VLANs

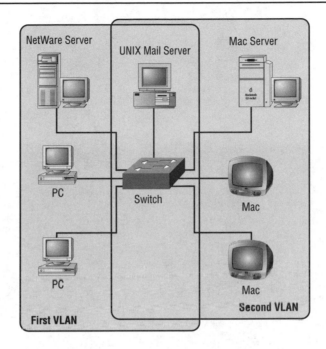

While this design would yield an increase in network performance, it does have a few minor drawbacks. The first is that switches with VLAN support are expensive, running between $200 and $400 per port. An organization as small as our advertising firm might consider this cost excessive. The fact that bandwidth requirements would not be considered excessive would make this cost outlay even more difficult to justify. Also, networks this small generally have poor network support. Even if such organizations do staff a LAN administrator, the administrator is usually focused on supporting the end users. The added task of supporting VLAN tables may be beyond the organization's skill set.

The second option would be to use the switch as the network backbone, with hubs cascaded from it to support small user groups. Servers could receive a dedicated connection and be connected in full-duplex mode. A potential design appears in Figure 4.19.

FIGURE 4.19

Another potential design for our advertising network

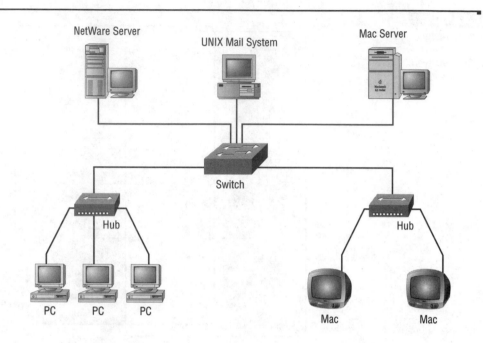

This option may be more desirable because it can be supported by a switch with a minimal number of ports—and thus reduce the cost. It also reduces the maintenance requirements, as you did not need to create any VLANs. The only real drawback is that there is no broadcast isolation between different protocols.

NOTE This option would not help with the protocol broadcast issue.

Example 3: Three NT Servers

Our third example looks like a good fit for bridging. It has a similar layout to Example 2 but no multiple protocols to worry about. Users are broken up into two distinct workgroups but have a common need to share mail. If you install two bridges, as shown in Figure 4.20, you set up three distinct collision domains. This isolates the workgroups from each other and even isolates file and print traffic from the mail server. Overall, bridging looks like a good fit for improving performance on this network.

Another plus is the protocol-independence functionality of a bridge. As mentioned in Chapter 3, NetBEUI is a non-routable protocol. This means that the traffic is incapable of crossing a router. Since a bridge works at the topology level, it is capable of controlling NetBEUI traffic flow.

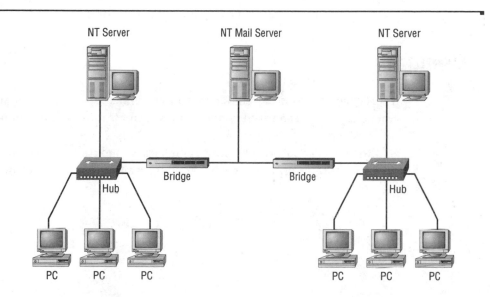

If you implemented a switch, this example network would benefit in much the same way as in Example 2. If you gave each of the three NT servers its own port and cascaded hubs from the switch for the user community, you would strike the best balance between cost and performance. A switch would cost a bit more than the bridge solution discussed above, but it would allow for greater flexibility. When bridging the network, each collision domain consisted of 50 users each. There was no easy way to segment the users even further. With a switch, you could simply cascade an additional hub off a free hub port and migrate some of the users over to it. Power users could even be assigned their own switch ports.

Example 4: WAN Link

Our fourth example looks like another poor fit for bridging. The protocol in use is NetBIOS/IP. As mentioned in Chapter 3, this protocol generates a lot of broadcasts. If you used bridges on both ends of the leased line, the limited bandwidth of the circuit would quickly become saturated from the broadcasting of more than 200 systems. There would be little bandwidth available for actual data.

Trying to use switching in this example would yield the same problems as trying to use a bridge. Since broadcast traffic would not be blocked, the limited bandwidth along the link would quickly become saturated.

Clearly, none of the networking technologies we have discussed so far would be an adequate fit for this configuration. We will come back to this example later in the book, once we have evaluated a few more potential solutions.

Summary

In this chapter, we discussed bridging and switching. We looked at the strengths and weaknesses of each and even pondered how each fits into a number of potential network designs.

In the next chapter, we will jump right back into routing. We will discuss what routing is, how it works, and what options are available for mapping out our networks.

CHAPTER 5

Routing

This chapter introduces the core material of this book: routers and how they function. We will start with a general review of protocols and the need for network addressing. We will then discuss a number of different ways to implement routing. Finally, we'll close the chapter by looking at a number of different network designs to see if routing would be a good fit for a particular environment.

Protocol Review

As I mentioned in Chapter 3, protocols define a set of address rules that provide the means for networking systems to be grouped by geographical area and common wiring. To indicate that it is part of a specific group, each of these systems is assigned an identical network address.

Network addresses are kind of like zip codes. Let's assume someone mails a letter and the front of the envelope simply reads: Frieda Babcock, Maple Road. If this letter were mailed within a very small town and if Frieda is a local resident, the letter would probably be delivered properly (just like using MAC addresses on a LAN).

If the letter were mailed in a city like Boston or New York, however, the Post Office where it lands would have no clue where to send it (although postal workers would probably get a good laugh). Without a zip code, the Post Office might not even attempt delivery. The zip code provides a way to specify the general geographical area where this letter is to be delivered. The postal worker processing the letter is not required to know exactly where Maple Road is located. He simply looks at the zip code and forwards the letter to the Post Office responsible for this code. It is up to the local Post Office to know the location of Maple Road and use this information to deliver the letter.

Protocol network addresses operate in a similar fashion. A protocol-aware device will add the network address of the device it wishes to reach to the data field of a frame. It will also record its own network address, in case the remote system needs to send a reply.

This is where a router comes in. A router will maintain a table of all known networks. It will use these tables to help forward information to its final destination. Let's walk through an example to see how a routed network operates.

A Routed Network Example

Let's assume that you have a network similar to the one shown in Figure 5.1. System B needs to transmit information to System F.

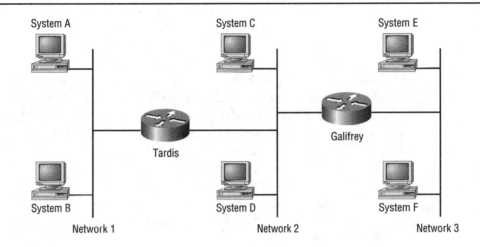

System B begins by comparing its network address to that of System F. If there is a match, System B assumes that System F is local and attempts to deliver the information directly. If the network addresses are different (as they are in our example), System B broadcasts a *route request* query to see if any other systems on its network segment (Network 1) know how to get to the destination system's network (Network 3). A route request is essentially a request for directions. It's a networked system's way of asking, "How do I get there from here?"

Because Tardis is a router, it maintains tables of all known networks. Tardis knows it can get to Network 3 by delivering information to Galifrey. Tardis sends this information to System B as a reply to its routing request. Because this is the only reply System B receives to its routing request, it assumes that Tardis is the only route. System B then adds the delivery information for System F (its network and MAC addresses) to the data and creates a frame using Tardis's MAC address as the destination. It does this because Tardis indicated in its reply that it knew the way to Network 3. System B is sending the frame to Tardis because it assumes that Tardis will take care of forwarding it to the destination network.

Once Tardis receives the frame, it performs a CRC check to insure the integrity of the data. If the frame checks out, Tardis then completely strips off the header and trailer. It then creates a new frame around the data by creating a new CRC, adding its

MAC address to the source address field and putting Galifrey's MAC address in the destination field.

While all this stripping and recreating seems like a lot of work, it is a necessary part of this type of communication. Remember that routers are placed at the borders of a network segment. The CRC check is performed to insure that bad frames are not propagated throughout the network. The header information is stripped away because it is only applicable on Network 1. When Tardis goes to transmit the frame on Network 2, the original source and destination MAC addresses have no meaning. This is why Tardis must replace these values with others that are valid for Network 2.

Because the majority of the header (12 of the 14 bytes) needs to be replaced anyway, it is easier to simply strip the header completely away and create a new one from scratch. As for stripping off the trailer, once the source and destination MAC addresses change, the original CRC value is no longer valid. This is why the router must strip it off and create a new one.

 NOTE A data field that contains protocol information is called a *packet*. While this term is sometimes used interchangeably with the term *frame*, a packet in fact only describes a portion of a frame.

So Tardis has created a new frame around the packet and is ready to transmit it. Tardis looks at the destination and has no idea who System F is, but it does know it can get to Network 3 by delivering the frame to Galifrey. Tardis then transmits the frame onto Network 2. Galifrey receives the frame and processes it in a similar fashion to Tardis, checking the CRC and stripping off the header and trailer.

At this point, however, Galifrey realizes that it has a local connection to System F because they are both connected to Network 3. It builds a new frame around the packet and, instead of needing to refer to a table, simply delivers the frame directly.

Protocol Specificity

In order for a router to provide this type of functionality, it must understand the rules for the protocol being used. This means that a router is *protocol specific*. Unlike a bridge, which will handle any valid protocols that you throw at it, a router must be specifically designed to support both the topology and the protocol being used. For example, if your network contains Banyan VINES systems, your router may be required to support the VINES IP protocol.

WARNING All this functionality comes at a cost. Legacy routers (as opposed to ASIC or switch routers) are typically poor performers when compared to bridges and switches. This is due to the overhead involved with removing and recreating the frame.

Routers can be a powerful tool for controlling the flow of traffic on your network. If you have a network segment that is using IPX and IP but only IP is approved for use on the company backbone, enable IP support only on your router. The router will ignore any IPX traffic it receives.

A wonderful feature of routers is their ability to block the flow of broadcasts between network segments. As I mentioned in Chapter 3, broadcasts are frames that contain all *F*s for the destination MAC address. Because any point on the other side of the router is a new network, these frames are blocked.

 NOTE There is a counterpart to this, called an *all-network broadcast,* that contains all *F*s in both the network and MAC address fields. These frames are used to broadcast to local networks when the network address is not known. Routers will block these all-network broadcasts by default, as well.

Most routers also have the ability to filter out certain traffic. For example, let's say your company enters into a partnership with another organization. You need to access services on this new network, but you do not want to allow your partner to access your servers. To accomplish this, simply install a router between the two networks and configure it to filter out any network information that would normally be propagated from your network to your partner's, as well as any inbound sessions.

 NOTE Packet filtering is discussed in Chapter 9.

Bridging and Routing Compared

Table 5.1 shows the differences between bridges and routers, and how they handle traffic. While a bridge or switch can usually forward traffic faster than a router, a router gives you a greater level of traffic control.

TABLE 5.1: COMPARING BRIDGES AND ROUTERS	
A Bridge or Switch:	**A Router:**
Uses the same network address off all ports	Uses different network addresses off all ports
Builds tables based on MAC address	Builds tables based on network address
Forwards broadcast traffic	Blocks broadcast traffic
Forwards traffic to unknown addresses	Blocks traffic to unknown addresses
Does not modify frame	Creates a new header and trailer
Can forward traffic based on the frame header	Must always queue traffic before forwarding

Routers

As you saw in Figure 5.1, routers are used to connect logical networks. This is why they are sometimes referred to in the IP world as *gateways*. Figure 5.2 shows the effect of adding a router to a network. Protocols on either side of the device must use a unique logical network address. Information destined for a non-local system must be routed to the logical network on which the system resides. The act of traversing a router from one logical network to another is called a *hop*. When a protocol hops a router, it must use a unique logical network address on each side.

How do systems on one logical network segment find out which other logical segments exist on the network? Routers can use network address information that has been manually programmed into the device, or dynamic information learned from other routers in order to create a blueprint of the network. This blueprint is commonly referred to as a *routing table*.

NOTE   Routing tables tell the router which logical networks are available to deliver information to and which routers can forward information to those networks.

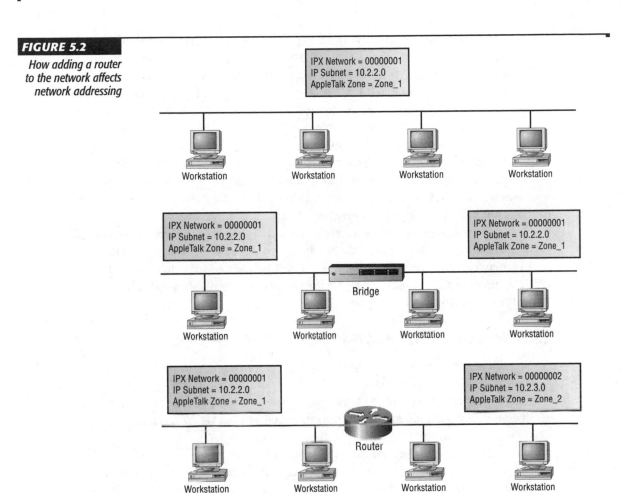

FIGURE 5.2

How adding a router to the network affects network addressing

What's in a Routing Table?

While the contents of a routing table may sound rather complex, the information is actually quite simple and easy to read. The following is an example of a simple routing table from a Cisco router:

```
192.168.10.0/24 is directly connected, Ethernet0
192.168.5.4/30 is directly connected, Serial0
192.168.2.0/24 via 192.168.10.254
192.168.3.0/24 via 192.168.10.254
0.0.0.0/0 [1/0] via 192.168.5.5
```

The first two entries identify the locally connected networks. This tells the router that any packets headed to the 192.168.10.0/24 or the 192.168.5.4/30 network can be delivered directly. The next two entries tell the router that if it needs to forward packets to the 192.168.2.0/24 or 192.168.3.0/24 networks, the router should forward the packets to the router located at IP address 192.168.10.254. Because of the information in the first routing table entry, the router knows that 192.168.10.254 is located off the local router's Ethernet port.

The last line of the routing table is the default route entry. This entry tells the router to forward all traffic headed to an undefined network to the router at IP address 192.168.5.5. In other words, this line directs, "If the destination network does not have a routing table entry, send the packet to 192.168.5.5."

Routing table entries are processed in "first fit" order. For example, even though 192.168.2.0/24 could technically be considered to be part of 0.0.0.0/0 (all IP unicast networks), packets headed to this network would be forwarded to 192.168.10.254 instead of 192.168.5.5 because the specific entry forwarding all 192.168.2.0/24 traffic to 192.168.10.254 appears first.

The *traceroute* Command

You can see one example of how the routing information of multiple routers fits together in Figure 5.3, which shows the output of running the traceroute command (renamed tracert on Windows systems). The traceroute command is an IP tool for documenting the subnets that must be traversed as a packet travels from one logical network to another.

The left-hand column indicates the number of networks, so we must travel over 12 subnets to reach www.sun.com. If you subtract 1 from this, you get the hop count, because 12 subnets would require 11 routers to separate them. The next three columns measure the link speed for three consecutive tries. This is the amount of time it took the frame to travel from one router to the next. An asterisk (*) indicates that the attempt was not replied to in a reasonable amount of time. Links that display high numbers or asterisks are indications of a slow topology (such as a 28.8 dial-up connection) or heavy traffic. The final column identifies the name of the router we had to hop, as well as its IP address.

*Using Traceroute to
document a
network path*

```
C:\>tracert www.sun.com

Tracing route to www.sun.com [192.9.9.100]
over a maximum of 30 hops:

  1    *         *         *       Request timed out.
  2   197 ms    193 ms    195 ms   gis-gate.gis.net [206.42.64.1]
  3   204 ms    212 ms    204 ms   agis-gis.boston1.agis.net [206.185.153.25]
  4   209 ms    205 ms    207 ms   a2-0.1022.washington1.agis.net [206.185.153.210

  5   229 ms    222 ms    278 ms   maeeast-1.bbnplanet.net [192.41.177.1]
  6   258 ms    332 ms    252 ms   collegepk-br2.bbnplanet.net [4.0.1.17]
  7   364 ms    372 ms    360 ms   collegepk-br1.bbnplanet.net [128.167.253.5]
  8   290 ms    252 ms    256 ms   chicago2-br1.bbnplanet.net [4.0.1.5]
  9   317 ms    300 ms    307 ms   paloalto-br1.bbnplanet.net [4.0.1.1]
 10   329 ms    333 ms    305 ms   paloalto-cr5.bbnplanet.net [131.119.0.205]
 11   315 ms    285 ms    312 ms   sun2.bbnplanet.net [131.119.28.98]
 12   308 ms    306 ms    309 ms   www.sun.com [192.9.9.100]

Trace complete.

C:\>
```

 TIP   Traceroute is an excellent diagnostic tool when you are having trouble connecting to a server on a remote network. Because it can be used to map networks, many network administrators do not allow Traceroute traffic into their network from the Internet.

Routing Tables

Don't confuse the output of the `traceroute` command with an actual routing table. The output is simply the path my data followed to get from Point A to Point B (Point B being www.sun.com). As an analogy, think of a routing table as being like a road map. A road map shows all the streets in a local city or town in much the same way a router table keeps track of all the local networks. Now, think of the directions you may give a friend to get to your house based on this map (follow Oak street to Pine and then take a left on Elm). These directions are synonymous with the output of the `traceroute` command. It does not show you the entire map, just how to get to a specific location.

Without having some method for each of these routers to communicate and let each other know who is connected where, communication between logical networks would be impossible.

There are three different methods used for routing information from one network to another:

- Static

- Distance vector

- Link state

While each routing protocol has its own ways of providing routing functionality, each implementation can be broken down into one of these three categories. As the network administrator, it is your job to define which routing method will be used by each of the routers on your network.

Static Routing

Static routing is the simplest method of getting information from one system to another. Used mostly in IP networks, a static route defines a specific router to be the point leading to a specific network. Static routing does not use dynamic information; it relies on information programmed into each router by the network administrator. This, of course, assumes that you can predefine all the logical networks you will wish to communicate with. When this is not feasible (for example, when you are communicating on the Internet), you may designate a single router as a default to receive all traffic destined for networks that have not been predefined. Most workstations use static routing and receive an entry for the default router only.

For example, let's assume I configure my system to have a default route that points to the router Galifrey. As my system passes information through the Network layer, it will analyze the logical network of the destination system. If the target is located on the same logical network, the Data-Link layer adds the MAC address of that system and transmits the frame onto the wire. If the system is located on some other logical network, the Data-Link layer will use the MAC address for Galifrey and transmit the frame to it. Galifrey is then responsible for insuring that the frame makes it to its final destination.

The benefits to this type of routing are simplicity and low overhead. My workstation does not need to know or care about what other logical networks may be available and how to get to them. It has only two possibilities to worry about—deliver locally or deliver to Galifrey. This can be useful when there is only one possible route to all other networks. For example, most organizations have only one Internet connection. Setting up a static route that points all IP traffic to the router that borders this connection may be the easiest way to insure that all frames are delivered properly. Because all my routing information is preconfigured, my routers do not need to share route information with other routers. Each router is only concerned with forwarding information to its next default route. I do not need to have any dynamic routing information propagated through my network, because each router has been preset as to where it should forward information.

Static routing has a few obvious drawbacks, however. What happens, for example, if I have multiple routers connected to my logical network segment, and the traffic actually needs to traverse one of the other routers? As you can see in Figure 5.4, the frame would still be delivered to Galifrey, which must then process the frame and pass it along to Tardis. Not only have I required Galifrey to process a frame that it did not need to see, I have doubled my network traffic (one frame to Galifrey, one frame to Tardis).

FIGURE 5.4

With static routing, the default router forwards all non-local frames.

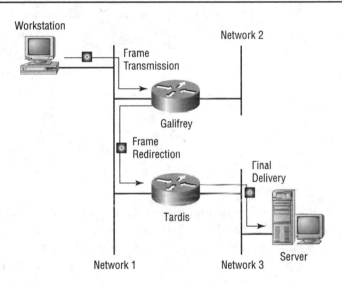

If this happens only occasionally, it would probably not be a problem. If, however, I typically see a large amount of traffic destined for the network on the other side of Tardis, I could potentially overload Galifrey. In the latter situation, a single default route is not recommended. Use a more detailed static routing table or a routing method capable of advertising route information.

NOTE When a router (such as Galifrey) needs to redirect traffic, it will issue a *redirect request* to the transmitting host. This request asks the workstation to send data directly to Tardis, but some workstations may ignore this request.

Another problem with static routing is that it usually nullifies any attempts to add *redundant routes*. Redundant routes help to insure that remote networks remain reachable when a single hardware device fails. For example, in Figure 5.5, I have two routers hooked up in parallel. The theory is that if one router dies, the other can continue to pass traffic to the remote network.

FIGURE 5.5

Two parallel routers:
Hermes and Bridgett

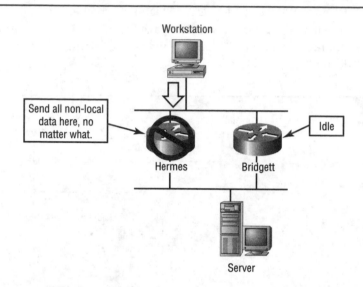

If I have set up Hermes as the default router and it drops offline, Bridgett will not be able to automatically step in. Because my systems are configured to send all non-local traffic to Hermes by default, they will not know that Bridgett is capable of supplying the same connectivity as Hermes. They will continue to attempt delivery to Hermes and will eventually fail with a "Remote network unreachable" error. In order to let them know that Bridgett supplies the same connectivity as Hermes, I would have to reconfigure each system by changing the default route to point at Bridgett instead of Hermes. Because manual intervention is needed to recover from a network failure, using static routes neutralizes the benefit provided by redundant routes.

 TIP Some routers allow you to define more than one static route. This provides for fail over if the first route is unusable.

While static routing is easy to use, it does suffer from some drawbacks that limit its application. When redundant paths are provided, or even when multiple routers are used on the same logical network, you may find it more beneficial to use a routing method that can exchange dynamic routing information. RIP allows routing tables to be developed on the fly, which can compensate for hardware failures. Both distance vector and link state routing use RIP frames to insure that routing tables stay up to date.

Distance Vector Routing

Distance vector is the oldest and most popular way to create routing tables. The Routing Information Protocol (RIP) is based on distance vector. IP and IPX each has its own variation of RIP.

Distance vector routers build their tables based on secondhand information. A router will look at the tables being advertised by other routers and simply add 1 to the advertised hop values to create its own table. With distance vector, every router will broadcast its routing table once per minute.

Propagating Network Information with Distance Vector

Figure 5.6 shows how propagation of network information works with distance vector.

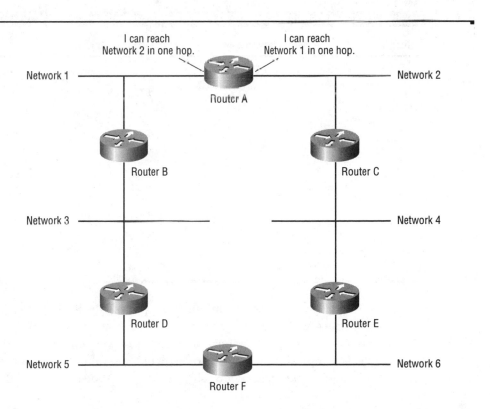

FIGURE 5.6

A routed network about to build its routing tables dynamically

I can reach Network 2 in one hop.

I can reach Network 1 in one hop.

Network 1 — Router A — Network 2

Router B   Router C

Network 3 — — Network 4

Router D   Router E

Network 5 — Router F — Network 6

Router A has just come online. Because the two attached networks (1 and 2) have been programmed into it, Router A immediately adds these to its routing table, assigning a hop value of 1 to each. The hop value is 1 instead of 0 because this information is relative to other attached networks, not the router. For example, if the router is advertising the route to Network 1 on Network 2, then one hop is appropriate, because any system sending information to Network 1 from Network 2 would have to travel one hop (the router itself) to get there. A router usually does not advertise routing information about a directly attached network on that network itself. This means that the router should not transmit a RIP frame stating, "I can reach Network 1 in one hop," on Network 1 itself.

Router A sends out two RIP packets, one on each network, to let any other devices know about the connectivity it can provide. When Routers B and C receive these packets, they reply with RIP packets of their own. Remember that the network is already up and running. This means that all the other routers have already had an opportunity to build their tables. From these other RIP packets, Router A collects the information shown in Table 5.2.

TABLE 5.2: ROUTING INFORMATION RECEIVED BY ROUTER A		
Router	**Network**	**Hops to Get There**
B	3	1
B	5	2
B	6	3
B	4	4
B	2	5
C	4	1
C	6	2
C	5	3
C	3	4
C	1	5

Router A then analyzes this information, picking the lowest hop count to each network in order to build its own routing table. Routes that require a larger hop count are not discarded but are retained in case an alternate route is required due to link failure. The router simply ignores these higher hop values during normal operation. Once complete, the table appears similar to what's shown in Table 5.3.

TABLE 5.3: ROUTER A'S ROUTING TABLE

Network	Hops to Get There	Next Router
1	1	Direct connection
2	1	Direct connection
3	2	B
4	2	C
5	3	B
6	3	C

All we've done is to pick the lowest hop count to each network and add 1 to the advertised value. Once the table is complete, Router A will again broadcast two RIP packets, incorporating this new information.

Now that Routers B and C have noted that there is a new router on the network, they must reevaluate their routing tables, as well. Before Router A came online, the routing table for Router B would have looked like Table 5.4.

TABLE 5.4: ROUTER B'S ROUTING TABLE BEFORE ROUTER A INITIALIZES

Network	Hops to Get There	Next Router
1	1	Direct connection
2	5	D
3	1	Direct connection
4	4	D
5	2	D
6	3	D

Now that Router A is online, Router B modifies its table to reflect the new routing information that Router B learned from Router A. Router B's new routing table is shown in Table 5.5.

TABLE 5.5: ROUTER B'S ROUTING TABLE AFTER ROUTER A INITIALIZES

Network	Hops to Get There	Next Router
1	1	Direct connection
2	2	A
3	1	Direct connection
4	3	A
5	2	D
6	3	D

It takes two RIP packets on the same logical network to get to this point. The first time Router A sent a RIP to Router B, it only knew about the networks it was directly connected to. Only after Router C sent a reply RIP to Router A did Router A realize that it had a path to Networks 4, 6, 5, and 3 (in that order) through Router C. This required Router A to send a second RIP packet to Router B, incorporating this new information.

Router C would go through a similar process, adjusting its table according to the information it receives from Router A. Again, it requires two RIP frames on the same logical network to yield a complete view of our entire network so that Router C can complete the changes to its tables.

These changes would then begin to propagate throughout our network. Router B would update Router D when A first comes online and then again when it completes its tables. This activity continues until all the routers have an accurate view of our new network layout. The amount of time that is required for all our routers to complete their table changes is known as the *time to convergence*. The convergence time is important because our routing table is in a state of flux until all our routers become stabilized with their new tables.

 WARNING Keep in mind that in a large network, convergence time can be quite long, as RIP updates are only sent once or twice per minute.

Distance Vector Routing Problems

Note that this table has been almost completely built on secondhand information. Any route that a router reports with a hop count greater than 1 is based on what it has learned from another router. When Router B tells Router A that it can reach Network 5 in two hops or Network 6 in three, it is fully trusting the accuracy of the information it has received from Router D. If as a child you ever played the telephone game (in which each person in a line receives a whispered message and tries to convey it verbatim to the next), you quickly learned that secondhand information is not always as accurate as it appears to be.

Figure 5.7 shows a pretty simple network layout. It consists of four logical networks separated by three routers. Once the point of convergence is reached, each router will have created a routing table as shown in the diagram.

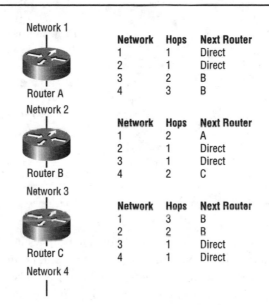

Network 1 — Router A — Network 2

Network	Hops	Next Router
1	1	Direct
2	1	Direct
3	2	B
4	3	B

Network 2 — Router B — Network 3

Network	Hops	Next Router
1	2	A
2	1	Direct
3	1	Direct
4	2	C

Network 3 — Router C — Network 4

Network	Hops	Next Router
1	3	B
2	2	B
3	1	Direct
4	1	Direct

Now, let's assume that Router C dies a fiery death and drops offline. This will make Network 4 unreachable by all other network segments. Once Router B realizes that Router C is offline, it will review the RIP information it has received in the past, looking for an alternate route. This is where distance vector routing starts to break down. Because Router A has been advertising that it can get to Network 4 in three hops, Router B simply adds 1 to this value and assumes that it can now reach Network 4 through Router A. Relying on secondhand information causes problems because, of course, Router B can't reach Network 4 through Router A, now that router C is offline.

As shown in Figure 5.8, Router B would begin to advertise that it can now reach Network 4 in four hops. Remember that RIP frames do not identify *how* a router will get to a remote network, only that it *can* and how many hops it will take to get there. Without knowing how Router A plans to reach Network 4, Router B has no idea that Router A is basing its route information on the tables it originally received from Router B.

FIGURE 5.8

Router B incorrectly believes that it can now reach Network 4 through Router A and updates its tables accordingly.

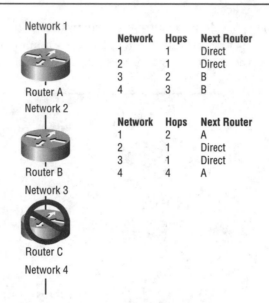

Network	Hops	Next Router
1	1	Direct
2	1	Direct
3	2	B
4	3	B

Network	Hops	Next Router
1	2	A
2	1	Direct
3	1	Direct
4	4	A

Router A would receive a RIP update from Router B and realize that it has increased the hop count to Network 4 from two to four. Router A would then adjust its table accordingly and begin to advertise that it now takes five hops to reach Network 4. It would again RIP, and Router B would again increase the hop count to Network 4 by one.

 NOTE This phenomenon is called *count to infinity* because if left unchecked, both routers would continue to increase their hop counts forever. Because of this problem, distance vector routing limits the maximum hop count to 15. Any route that is 16 or more hops away is considered unreachable and is subsequently removed from the routing table. This allows our two routers to figure out in a reasonable amount of time that Network 4 can no longer be reached.

"Reasonable" is a subjective term, however. Remember that RIP updates are sent out once only or twice per minute. This means that a minute or more may pass before our routers buy a clue and realize that Network 4 is gone. With a technology that measures frame transmissions in the microsecond range, a few minutes is plenty of time to wreak havoc on communications. For example, let's look at what is taking place on Network 2 while the routers are trying to converge.

Once Router C has dropped offline, Router B assumes that it has an alternate route to Network 4 through Router A. Any packets that Router B receives are checked for errors and passed along to Router A. When Router A receives the frame, it performs an error check again. It then refers to its tables and realizes it needs to forward the frame to Router B in order to reach Network 4. Router B would again receive the frame and send it back to Router A.

This is called a *routing loop*. Each router plays hot potato with the frame, assuming the other is responsible for its delivery, and passing it back and forth. While our example describes only one frame, imagine the amount of bandwidth lost if there is a considerable amount of traffic destined for Network 4. With all these frames looping between the two routers, there would be very little bandwidth available on Network 2 for other systems that need to transmit information.

Fortunately, the Network layer has a way to eliminate this problem, as well. As each router handles the frame, it is required to decrease a hop counter value within the frame by 1. When a router receives a frame that has a hop count value of 0, it discards the frame and transmits an "ICMP destination unreachable" message back to the original host. This removes lost frames from the wire and lets the transmitting system know that it cannot reach the destination host it was trying to communicate with. When RIP is used as the network's routing protocol, the hop counter starts at a value of 16.

While this 16-hop limitation is not a problem for the average corporate network, it can be a severe limitation in larger networks. For example, if you look back at Figure 5.3, you'll recall that we needed to hop 11 routers in order to reach Sun Microsystems' Web server. This is very close to distance vector's 15-hop maximum. If RIP were used throughout the Internet, many resources would be unreachable from certain areas of the Internet.

 NOTE   The combination of all the previously mentioned limitations spawned the development of link state routing.

Link State Routing

Link state routers function similarly to distance vector, but with a few notable exceptions. Most importantly, link state routers use only firsthand information when developing their routing tables. Not only does this help to eliminate routing errors, it drops the time to convergence to nearly zero. Imagine that our network in Figure 5.6 has been upgraded to using a link state routing protocol. Now, let's bring Router A online and watch what happens.

Propagating Network Information with Link State

As Router A powers up, it sends out a type of routing packet referred to as a *hello*. The hello packet is simply an introduction that states, "Greetings! I am a new router on this network; is there anybody out there?" This packet is transmitted on both its ports and will be responded to by Routers B and C.

Once Router A receives a reply from Routers B and C, it creates a *link state protocol* (LSP) frame and transmits it to Routers B and C. An LSP frame is a routing maintenance frame that contains the following information:

- The router's name or identification
- The networks it is attached to
- The hop count or cost of getting to each network
- Any other routers on each network that responded to its hello frame

Routers B and C then make a copy of Router A's LSP frame and forward the information along through the network. Each router receiving the frame copies it and passes it along. With link state routing, each router maintains a copy of every other router's LSP frame. The router can use this information to diagram the network and thus build routing tables. Because each LSP frame contains only the route information that is local to each router that sent it, this network map is created strictly from firsthand information. A router will simply fit the LSP puzzle pieces together until its network picture is complete.

Router A then makes an LSP frame request from either Router B or C. Because each router has a copy of all LSP frames, either router is capable of supplying a copy from every router on the network. This avoids making Router A request this information from each router individually, thus saving bandwidth. Once an LSP network is up and running, updates are usually transmitted only every two hours or whenever a change takes place (such as when a router goes offline). This makes link state routing an effective solution for networks that utilize *bandwidth-on-demand* WAN connections, such as analog dial-up or ISDN. While a distance vector network would require the link to be brought up once or more per minute in order to transfer route information, link state would only need to bring this link up once every two hours.

 TIP Even in a non-WAN environment, link state is a great way to save bandwidth. The RIP packets sent by a distance vector router have a broadcast address in the destination MAC field. This means that once per minute, every station is required to analyze every RIP packet—whether it needs the information or not. Link state routing protocols typically rely on multicast or unicast transmissions. This means that they are far less likely to rob workstations of precious CPU cycles.

Convergence Time with Link State

Our link state network is up and running. Note that Routers B and C were not required to recompute their routing tables. They simply added the new piece from Router A and continued to pass traffic. This is why convergence time is nearly zero. The only change required of each router is adding the new piece to its table. Unlike distance vector, updates were not required in order to normalize the routing table. Router B did not need a second packet from Router A, telling it what networks were available through Router C. Router B simply added Router A's LSP information to its existing table and was already aware of the links.

Load Balancing

This brings us to an interesting point. Take another look at Figure 5.6: What if someone on Network 3 needs to send information to a system on Network 2? Obviously, the host on Network 3 would simply pass the information to Router A, because Router A is reporting that it is only two hops away from Network 2. This is in contrast to Router C, which would require four hops.

Now let's say that Network 1 is a 300bps analog dial-up connection (hey, it still works) while Networks 2–6 are 1Gbps Ethernet. What would happen then? Unfortunately, with most distance vector routing protocols, the host on Network 3 would still attempt to deliver the information through Router A. Because hop count is typically used as the sole means of selecting the best route, the link speed would not be taken into consideration. Thus, the route with the lowest hop count gets the frame.

This is where *load balancing* comes in. Load balancing introduces the concepts of *link speed* and *segment congestion* to determine which route is best. A routing protocol that takes this information into consideration along with hop count is much better suited to make an informed decision about where to route traffic. Most link state routing protocols are capable of doing some level of load balancing.

The combination of link response time and hop count is referred to as *cost*. What's nice about load balancing is that it is dynamic. If a router notes that the cost along a certain path is increasing, it can divert traffic to a different path to avoid an overload. The cost of a certain path can (and does) change with traffic load. The more information passing along a specific logical network segment, the higher the cost associated with using that link. Conversely, the faster the topology used by a logical network segment, the lower the cost. For example, a 100Mbps Ethernet segment would have a lower cost value than an identical link operating at 10Mbps.

 NOTE It is possible to do load balancing using either distance vector or link state routing protocols. Load balancing is implementation specific. This means that the actual design of the routing protocol itself determines whether load balancing is possible, not the fact that it may be distance vector or link state. Because link state routing has such a low convergence time, it is much better suited than distance vector to do load balancing. For this reason, most routing protocols capable of performing load balancing are based on link state.

Recovering from a Router Failure in a Link State Environment

Finally, let's revisit Figure 5.7 to look at how link state routing reacts when a router goes offline. Again, for the purpose of this example, let's assume that our routing protocol has been upgraded from distance vector to link state. Let's also assume that our routing tables have been created and that traffic is passing normally.

If Router C is shut down normally, it will transmit a maintenance frame (known as a *dying gasp*) to Router B, informing Router B that Router C is about to go offline. Router B then deletes the copy of Router C's LSP frame that it has been maintaining and forwards this information to Router A. Both routers now have a valid copy of the new network layout and realize that Network 4 is no longer reachable. If Router C is not brought down gracefully but again dies a fiery death, there will be a short delay before Router B realizes that Router C is no longer acknowledging packets being sent to it. At this point, Router B realizes that Router C is offline. It then deletes Router C's LSP frame from its table and forwards the change along to Router A. Again, both systems have a valid copy of the new network layout. Because we are dealing with strictly firsthand information, there are none of the pesky count-to-infinity problems that we experienced with distance vector. Our router tables are accurate and our network is functioning with a minimal amount of updating. This allows link state to traverse a larger number of network segments. The typical maximum is 127 hops, but this number can be less, depending on the implementation.

 NOTE Even though link state routing is less susceptible to count-to-infinity problems than distance vector, it's still possible that an administrator could accidentally configure a routing loop. This is why link state uses a hop count. It's a final sanity check to insure that every packet that becomes lost has some graceful way of being removed from the wire.

Layer 3 Switching

By now, you should have a clear understanding of the differences between a switch and a router, so let's look at a technology that, on the surface, appears to mesh the two. *Layer 3 switching*, *switch routing*, and *router switching* are all terms used interchangeably to describe the same device.

What exactly is a switch router? The device is not quite as revolutionary as it might sound. In fact, switch routers are more an evolution of existing router technology. The association with the word "switch" is more for marketing appeal, to emphasize the increase in raw throughput these devices can provide.

Switch routers typically (but not always) perform the same functions as a standard router. When a switch router receives a frame of data, it buffers the frame into memory and performs a CRC check. Then, it strips the topology frame off the data packet. Just like a regular router, a switch router will reference its routing table to determine the best route of delivery, repackage the data packet into a frame, and send it on its merry way.

How, then, is a switch router different from a standard router? The answer lies under the hood of the device. Processing is provided by application-specific integrated circuit (ASIC) hardware. With a standard router, all processing is typically performed by a single reduced instruction set computer (RISC) processor. In a switch router, components are dedicated to performing specific tasks within the routing process. The result is a dramatic increase in throughput.

TIP When push comes to shove, there is no functionality difference between a legacy router which utilizes a single processor and a switch router which uses ASIC processing. The only difference between the two is raw throughput. This makes switch routers an ideal solution on network backbones when high bandwidth is a necessity. When dealing with slower WAN links, a single processor router is typically more than sufficient.

Cisco implements layer 3 switching via an optional *route switch module*, which is available for many of its high-end switches. When the switch has been configured with multiple VLANs, the route switch module provides routing connectivity among them. The benefit of using the route switch module over a conventional router is increased performance. Cisco route switch modules are capable of passing 150 million packets or more per second. This packet rate is more than 1,000 times faster than the average router!

Designing Networks with Routers

Let's return to the case studies we examined in Chapter 4, in order to get a feel for when it is appropriate to implement routing. We'll start by reviewing the information we gathered about each environment.

The Examples

As you read each example, see whether (and why) you think routing or switch routing would be a good idea before you read on. Don't be concerned if you think you already resolved the design using bridging or switching. One task of this exercise is to realize that, sometimes, a given problem has more than one solution. The trick is picking the best solution.

Example 1: 25 Engineers

The first example is a group of 25 engineers using SGI UNIX workstations. Each engineer must exchange file information with the others. Figure 5.9 depicts this first example.

Example 2: Multiple Servers and Protocols

The second example is a small advertising firm with about 50 employees, using NetWare, Mac, and UNIX. All users run IP to connect to the UNIX system for e-mail and Internet access. Figure 5.10 shows our second example.

FIGURE 5.9

Example 1: Network with 25 engineers (eight shown here) who need to share file information between their systems

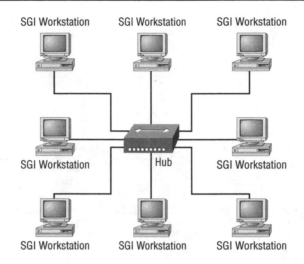

FIGURE 5.10

Example 2: Network with multiple server types and protocols

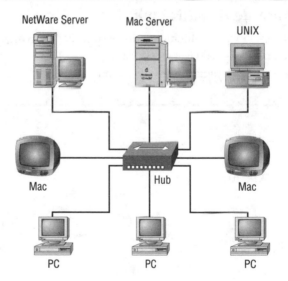

Example 3: Three NT Servers

Our third example includes 100 users with three NT servers. NetBEUI is used to access all servers. Figure 5.11 shows our third example.

FIGURE 5.11

*Example 3: Network
with users neatly bro-
ken up by workgroup;
everyone needs access
to mail*

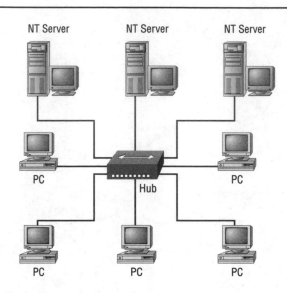

Example 4: WAN Link

Our final example includes two separate NT networks in need of a WAN connection. Each network uses NetBIOS/IP as a protocol and consists of approximately 100 users. Figure 5.12 depicts our fourth example.

FIGURE 5.12

*Example 4: Two
remote networks which
will be connected via a
leased line circuit*

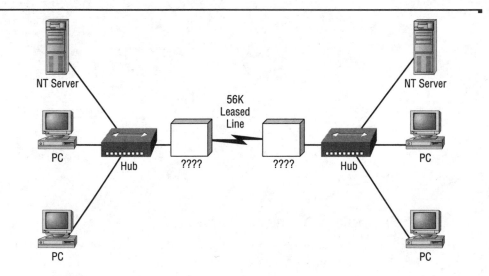

Evaluating the Case Studies

In each example, consider whether routing or switch routing could be used to make cost-effective improvements in network performance.

Example 1: 25 Engineers

Our first example is clearly a no go. Due to the unpredictable nature of traffic flow, a router would be of very little use in this situation. Each of the 25 engineers might need to communicate with any other at any given time. There are no clear boundary lines to make network segmentation effective.

Example 2: Multiple Servers and Protocols

The second network shows more promise. It has two of the main ingredients that make routing an interesting choice: multiple protocols and the need for traffic isolation. If you were to configure the network as shown in Figure 5.13, you'd now be able to do the following:

- Isolate IPX and AppleTalk traffic by simply not passing them across the router
- Support IP traffic throughout the network, while still isolating each workgroup from the traffic generated by the other
- Add a second line of defense between internal systems and the Internet

FIGURE 5.13

The accounting network is segmented with a router.

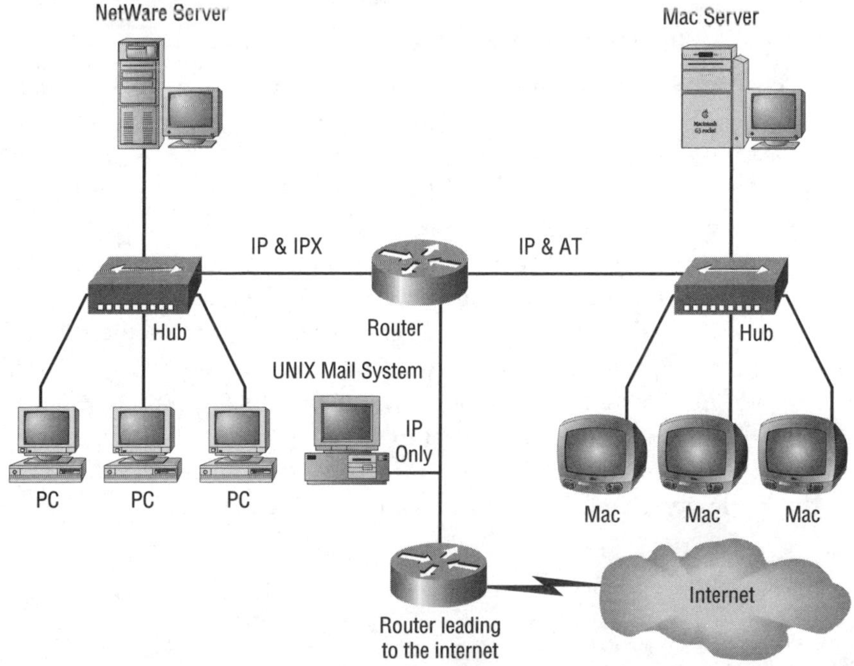

In fact, a switch router may be just what you need to really beef up performance. Both hubs and the router could be replaced by a layer 3 switch. This would provide each workstation with a dedicated 10Mb connection while the servers are run at 100Mb, allowing the servers to service multiple workstation requests more quickly.

Further, you could create three different VLANs:

- One for the NetWare segment
- One for the Mac
- One for the UNIX and Internet connections

A switch router would provide the same protocol and broadcast isolation as its low-speed counterpart, while providing a faster forwarding rate for the IP traffic that needs to pass between VLANs.

The final metric in deciding whether you are better off using a router or a switch router in this example is "How much performance can you afford?" While a switch router would dramatically increase performance, it would also increase cost by a factor of 10.

Example 3: Three NT Servers

Our third example is a bit of a trick question. While on the surface it seems to be a similar configuration to Example 2, we are only using a single protocol for communication. Further, the protocol in use is NetBEUI, which is a non-routable protocol. If you were to install a router or switch router at any point in this network, communication would be blocked. Clearly a router solution is not the way to go with this network.

Example 4: WAN Link

Our WAN connection shows some promise for using some kind of router. The main objective is isolating the WAN so that unnecessary traffic, such as broadcasts, does not "leak" across the WAN and consume bandwidth. Since a router will block all traffic that is not specifically targeted at the remote network, routing is a good choice for controlling traffic that passes across the WAN.

The question now becomes "Should we use regular routers or switch routers?" Since WAN connections tend to be far slower than their LAN counterparts, it does not make sense to pay the extra bucks for a set of switch routers. A regular router is more than capable of keeping up with full T1 or fractional T3 speeds. Since the WAN is the performance gate, most of the switch router's capabilities would go to waste.

The final question is what to do about routing. You can go with statically assigning routes or an IP-based dynamic routing protocol. The deciding factor here is how stable the IP addressing scheme is on both LANs.

For example, what if the Admin on the first network decides to completely change his IP addressing or perhaps add two or three new subnets to his network? Unless he remains in close contact with the Admin on the second network, this change could break connectivity between the two networks.

If you are dealing with stable networks that experience few changes, static routing may be the way to go, because it will reduce traffic on the WAN. If, however, either network is prone to changes, it may be better to go with a dynamic protocol.

Variations

You may have noticed that one of the examples had multiple answers. We did not even get into the possibilities of mixing and matching different technologies! This is because we are trying to make a judgment based on a very limited amount of information. While some of these examples appear to be toss-ups in terms of which technology is the best fit, if you dig deeply enough, you may find some little tidbit that will tip the scales in one direction or the other. For example, we never mentioned whether all employees use the network at the same time or whether network use is broken up over different daily shifts. This could dramatically change the traffic patterns—and thus our network requirements. Don't take anything for granted.

Summary

In this chapter, we reviewed how protocols use their addressing schemes to find systems located on remote networks. We introduced the concept of routing and described how to build routing tables both statically and dynamically. Finally, we revisited our case studies from Chapter 4 in order to see when routing is appropriate.

In the next chapter, we will dive into routing a bit more deeply. Now that we understand the theory of routing, we'll look at what routing options are available with each of our protocols.

CHAPTER <u>6</u>

Routing Protocols

I n Chapter 5, we discussed routing theory and how it works. Now we will look at how this theory has been implemented with various networking protocols. IP and IPX have multiple routing options. AppleTalk, on the other hand, only supports a single routing protocol. Since NetBIOS is non-routable, it relies on IP and IPX to get it from network to network. At the end of this chapter, we will look at a Cisco-specific routing protocol that is capable of maintaining the routing tables for all these protocols with a single set of updates.

Routing with IP

IP supports both static and dynamic routing between subnets. These may be used exclusively or in combination on any given network. When you use dynamic routing, both distance vector and link state options are available. Let's take a look at how each method is implemented when communicating with IP.

Static Routing

Static routing is when the path from one subnet to another is programmed into a networking device. This is done by defining the route a data stream must pass through when traveling to a remote subnet. With Cisco routers, an administrator manually enters the route using the `ip route` command. The syntax for this command is as follows:

```
ip route network mask gateway
```

Here's an example of the command in use:

```
ip route 10.3.3.0 255.255.255.0 10.2.50.5 1
```

 NOTE Proper syntax and commands are discussed in more detail in Chapter 7.

This command line would add an entry to a router that states, "When communicating with any system on the subnet 10.3.3.0, forward all packets through the router located at 10.2.50.5." The command assumes that the router located at 10.2.50.5 is on the local subnet and knows how to reach the network 10.3.3.0. While the mask is optional, the `ip route` command will assign a subnet mask based on the class of the IP subnet address. In the example just shown, `ip route` would assign a class A mask of 255.0.0.0 (because 10.3.3.0 falls between 1.0.0.0 and 126.0.0.0), which would be incorrect.

NOTE If you are unsure of the address class of a particular route, and therefore unsure what mask value will be automatically assigned, make sure you specify the correct mask value.

In order to delete static routes, simply precede the `ip route` statement with the `no` command. For example, to remove the static route in the example, you would enter

```
no ip route 10.3.3.0 255.255.255.0 10.2.50.5 1
```

The `ip route` command also allows the definition of a *default route*. A default route tells a router to forward all traffic bound for any remote subnet to a specific IP address. The default route is a catchall for any subnets that are not specifically defined. For example, the router that borders your Internet connection probably uses a default route. This entry tells the router to send all traffic destined to an unknown address down your WAN link to your ISP. This keeps you from having to define every Internet subnet on your router.

When defining a default route, you use the same syntax as noted previously, except the destination subnet is identified as 0.0.0.0. Think of this address as a wildcard entry and you'll get the idea. Having all 0s tells the router that this entry will match every IP subnet address. Here's an example of the command in use:

```
ip route 0.0.0.0 10.2.50.1
```

NOTE A router will always process the default route entry last. This insures that if you have a route defined for a specific subnet, the router will use the specific entry. The default route is only used when all other possibilities are exhausted.

Static routing is the most common configuration used in small networks or when only one possible path to a destination exists. Static routing frees the router from having to maintain dynamic tables, thus requiring less memory and CPU power. Static routing generates the least amount of traffic because it does not require that routing updates be propagated throughout the network. It also requires the greatest amount of administration, however, because each router must be configured manually with its own routing table.

Dynamic Routing

IP supports a number of dynamic routing protocols based on both distance vector and link state. Dynamic routing allows a network to learn which subnets are available and how to reach them. This is particularly useful when more than one path is available between subnets. The ability of a network to deal with routing changes is highly dependent on the routing protocol in use.

Routing Information Protocol (RIP 1)

RIP was first developed in 1980 by Xerox for use with its Xerox Network System (XNS) protocol. RIP saw its first use with IP in 1982 when it was adapted and shipped with BSD UNIX. After 1982, different UNIX vendors began shipping slightly different versions of RIP, causing incompatibility problems. This was all tied together in 1988 with the release of RFC 1058, which defined a common structure for RIP. Even though RIP is the oldest IP routing protocol, it is still widely used today.

RIP is a distance vector protocol, which gives it a slow convergence time and makes it prone to routing errors. It can route information for no more than 16 hops and bases its routing decisions strictly on hop count. It cannot intelligently load-balance traffic by using such variables as link speed and traffic load.

RIP is also one of the easiest routing protocols to use and configure. Simply enable RIP, define the networks you wish to advertise, and the protocol will propagate route information through the use of RIP broadcasts. For example, let's assume you wish to enable RIP on a router directly connected to the networks 192.168.1.0 and 192.168.2.0. You would use these commands:

```
router rip
network 192.168.1.0
network 192.168.2.0
```

 NOTE While RIP is a somewhat noisy protocol, sending routing updates every 60 seconds, this amount of traffic is usually negligible on a small network.

RIP is best suited for small networks (10–12 subnets or fewer) or for networking environments where redundant links do not operate at different speeds. In larger environments, RIP can cause broadcast storms as each router attempts to propagate its table information throughout the network. When redundant routes are available, RIP cannot analyze cost or make use of the multiple paths for load balancing. Secondary routes are only used when the primary route fails. In each of these situations, it is better to use one of the link state protocols described below.

TIP The original implementation of RIP does not support multiple subnet masks. RIP assumes that all subnets on the network use a mask value identical to the one in use by the router.

Routing Information Protocol, Version 2 (RIP 2)

Because of its many drawbacks, RIP has been updated in order to provide some of the additional functionality required in a modern networking environment. While these improvements are helpful, you must insure that all of your routing devices support RIP 2. If the configuration only refers to "RIP," you can assume it means the original RIP implementation.

As I mentioned, RIP 2 adds a number of needed improvements. These additions include support for variable length subnet masking and limited authentication ability. RIP 2 will even use multicasting for propagating route updates.

Unfortunately, RIP 2 still has quite a few drawbacks. It still shares RIP 1's 16-hop distance limitation, as well as its slow convergence time. Worse yet, RIP 2 continues to use hop count as its only metric, so values such as link speed and congestion are not used in making routing decisions. While RIP 2 is an improvement over the original version, it is not quite as effective as other routing protocols, such as OSPF (discussed later in this chapter).

Exterior Gateway Protocol (EGP)

EGP is another distance vector protocol that was developed in the mid-1980s, as the Internet began to grow beyond the bounds of what could be easily supported by RIP. EGP introduced the concept of *autonomous systems* (AS) as a way to reduce the amount of routing information propagated between networks.

 NOTE An AS is a collection of subnets that are all administered by the same group or organization. Typically, this would be an entire domain, but an AS can be divided even further for larger networks. By "domains" I mean the domain names issued by the InterNIC, not a Microsoft NT domain.

EGP reduces the amount of information propagated by advertising *reachability* information only. Instead of advertising hop information, an EGP router simply lists all the networks it is responsible for within its autonomous system. In Figure 6.1, you can see three AS groups connected by a backbone. Each EGP router transmits reachability information only along the backbone. This tells the other EGP routers, "If you need to send information to one of these subnets, forward the frame to me and I'll take care of delivery." This reduces the amount of information that must be propagated along the backbone. Because a single router is responsible for delivery to any given subnet, hop counts do not need to be calculated during a failure; either the subnet is reachable or it is not. This limitation on the information being sent helps to eliminate convergence problems along the backbone.

FIGURE 6.1

EGP used to propagate information between autonomous systems

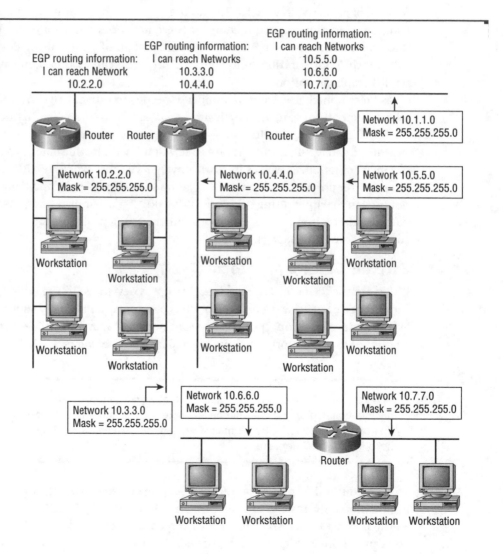

Inside each AS, another routing protocol such as RIP can be used to insure delivery and provide secondary routing paths as required. EGP simply eliminates the need to send this RIP information along the backbone.

The biggest drawback to EGP is that it relies on a hierarchical design with all traffic passing through a single point. Not only does this create a single point of failure, it eliminates the ability to perform load balancing through alternate links. You must also configure EGP routers to reflect which subnets they are responsible for.

NOTE While EGP was extremely useful in its prime, the explosive growth of the Internet has rendered it somewhat dated. Use of EGP has been on the decline due to some of the more advanced link state protocols that are now available.

Open Shortest Path First (OSPF)

OSPF was the first protocol to integrate both internal and external autonomous system updates into a single IP routing protocol. Like EGP, you can configure OSPF to exchange only reachability information along a network backbone. Unlike EGP, however, you can also configure it to provide full routing table information within each autonomous system. This eliminates the need to run two separate routing protocols, one for inside the AS and one for outside. As a link state protocol, OSPF provides low convergence times and excellent route selection metrics.

Area IDs OSPF can be configured to act as an interior or exterior routing protocol through the use of *area IDs*. Area IDs allow you define portions of the network which should exchange routing information. A router is required to maintain a separate database for each area ID it is connected to.

For example, look at the diagram in Figure 6.2. In this figure you can see two groups of four routers connected by a common backbone. Each of the two routers directly connected to the backbone has each of its two interfaces connected to different area IDs. Router interfaces within the same area ID are considered to be *neighbors* and are capable of exchanging update information.

FIGURE 6.2

*Two sets of four
routers exchanging
information via OSPF*

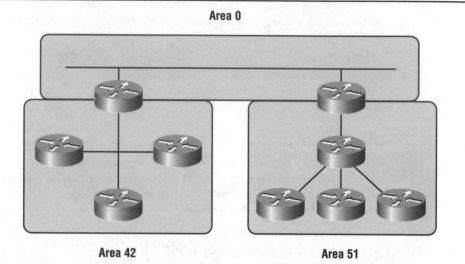

Each router directly connected to the backbone would be required to maintain two OSPF databases, one for each area it is connected to. This means that each router would also have two different sets of neighbors. Routers that connect to multiple areas are known as *border routers*. The remaining three routers in each of the two groups have all their interfaces within a single area. Routers that are only part of a single area are called *internal routers*.

Enabling OSPF   In order to use OSPF, you must first tell the router to enable OSPF processing and then assign each of your interfaces to an area ID. You would use these commands to configure the top left router in Figure 6.2:

```
router ospf 99
network 192.168.1.0 0.0.0.255 area 0
network 192.168.2.0 0.0.0.255 area 42
```

The first line enables OSPF and assigns it a *process ID*. The process ID is simply an identification number; it allows you to run multiple instances of OSPF. Unless you have an extremely large network, a single instance of OSPF should be sufficient.

The next two lines define networks to which the router is directly attached and assigns the networks to a specific area. What may look a little strange is the value 0.0.0.255. This is not a subnet mask; rather, it's a pattern match. We will discuss pattern matches in greater detail in the chapter on access lists. For now, it is sufficient to understand that this pattern will match all hosts on the 192.168.1.0 and 192.168.2.0 networks, respectively.

OSPF Authentication OSPF has support for authentication: Routers must supply a password in order to participate in routing updates. Authentication helps to insure that a rogue system cannot propagate information which might corrupt the current routing table or breach network security. By default, authentication is not enabled. You do have the option, however, of using clear-text passwords or Message Digest (MD5) authentication, which supports encryption.

Clear-Text Passwords To enable clear-text passwords, add the following command when enabling OSPF:

```
area <area-ID> authentication
```

If you combined this command with the previous commands, you would get this:

```
router ospf 99
network 192.168.1.0 0.0.0.255 area 0
network 192.168.2.0 0.0.0.255 area 42
area 0 authentication
area 42 authentication
```

Next, go into configuration mode for each of the interfaces and type the following command:

```
ip ospf authentication-key <key>
```

For the interface that faces the backbone, you would type:

```
ip ospf authentication-key aunk243
```

with aunk243 being the password to use within area 0. All routers wishing to participate in routing updates within this area must be configured to use the same password.

MD5 Authentication Of course, the biggest problem with using clear-text passwords is that anyone capable of sniffing the network will be able to capture the password. When security is a must, you are better off using MD5 authentication. Configuring MD5 is very similar to configuring clear-text passwords. The difference is that you simply specify MD5 encryption. When you're setting up OSPF, add this command:

```
area <area-ID> authentication message-digest
```

while using the following to configure each interface:

```
ip ospf message-digest-key <keyid> md5 <key>
```

So if you wanted to use MD5 instead of clear-text passwords along the backbone, the command would look like this:

```
ip ospf message-digest-key 10 md5 aunk243
```

Later, if you decide to change your password, a Cisco router will transmit OSPF updates using both the new and the old keys. This will continue until all routers within the area have been updated with the new password value. Without this feature, you would be required to update all routers within the same area at exactly the same time in order to avoid authentication failures and disruption of the routing table.

Why OSPF? Since OSPF is a link state protocol, internal AS routing decisions are based on such metrics as link speed and traffic load. When redundant paths exist, OSPF can help you to better utilize the bandwidth available along each path. The link state implementation also means that OSPF has a very low convergence time when network components fail.

Unlike RIP 1, OSPF deals effectively with variable-length subnet masking. This can be extremely useful when you need to deploy the same routing protocol across both your LAN and WAN. For example, consider Figure 6.3. This network is using four different subnet mask values in order to conserve address space. While OSPF would operate effectively in this environment, RIP 1 would generate routing errors.

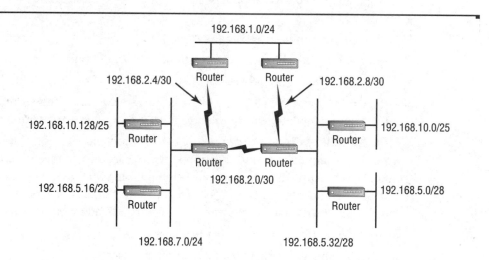

FIGURE 6.3

A network using variable mask values

192.168.1.0/24

192.168.2.4/30 — Router   Router — 192.168.2.8/30

192.168.10.128/25 — Router

Router   Router

192.168.10.0/25 — Router

192.168.2.0/30

192.168.5.16/28 — Router

192.168.5.0/28 — Router

192.168.7.0/24   192.168.5.32/28

 TIP The combination of effective bandwidth utilization, quick convergence time, authentication, and variable-length mask support make OSPF a very effective routing protocol for nearly any environment. When you need to use dynamic IP routing, OSPF is usually your best bet.

Border Gateway Protocol (BGP)

BGP is designed to be used both inside and between autonomous systems. The brainchild of Cisco Systems, BGP is the routing protocol that glues most of the Internet's backbone together. BGP comes in two flavors:

Internal Border Gateway Protocol (IBGP)   This is used when two routers that are part of the same autonomous system must exchange information.

External Border Gateway Protocol (EBGP)   This is used between routers of different autonomous systems.

On a BGP network, each autonomous system is assigned a unique group number. Each router must be configured with a table defining its neighbors' IP addresses and autonomous system group numbers. A router will assume that any neighbor with the same group number is part of the same autonomous system and thus is responsible for the same group of subnets. This allows for the use of multiple paths and provides a greater degree of flexibility over EGP or OSPF in backbone areas. Neighboring routers communicate using unicast TCP connections instead of simply broadcasting table information.

As a link state protocol, BGP can leverage these multiple paths by providing load balancing based on link speed, Internetwork delay, and available bandwidth. This allows for the most efficient use of network resources when multiple paths are available along a backbone connection.

The biggest drawback to using BGP as an internal routing protocol is that BGP is not supported by any network operating systems. If you are running dynamic routing on your internal systems, you will need to include a second routing protocol, such as OSPF.

IPX Routing

IPX supports static, distance vector, and link state routing. Unlike IP, with its plethora of dynamic routing choices, IPX only has one distance vector and one link state routing protocol. Distance vector routing is supported with RIP, and link state routing is provided by the NetWare Link State Protocol (NLSP).

RIP

As with RIP under the IP protocol suite, RIP under IPX is based on the distance vector routing information protocol developed for XNS. This is why it is prone to the same problems and limitations as its IP counterpart:

- Routing tables are built on secondhand information.
- Time to convergence is long, due to slow propagation.
- During convergence, the routing table is susceptible to errors and loops.
- Maximum hop count is 15 in order to counteract the count-to-infinity problem.

Typically, you will only want to use RIP if you have older NetWare servers that will not communicate using NLSP. Remember that many print and communication servers which communicate via IPX must also be able to participate in route updates. Before migrating from RIP, you should make sure that these devices are NLSP compatible, as well.

NLSP

NetWare's link state protocol is a vast improvement over RIP. As with most LSP protocols, it sports the following features:

- Only firsthand information is used to build routing tables.
- Minimal convergence time means a reduced chance of routing errors.
- Less network traffic is required to keep routing tables up to date.
- Most communications are unicast, not broadcast-based.
- Traffic load balancing is based on utilization and link speed.
- Maximum hop count is 128.

NetWare NLSP routers retain backwards compatibility by transmitting RIP as well as NLSP packets on segments where RIP-only devices are detected. Without this type of backwards compatibility, a RIP device would see the server during its initialization and add it to its routing table. It would then remove the entry three minutes later, because NLSP routing information is broadcast not once per minute but every two hours or when a change takes place. This would cause the RIP-only device to assume that the NLSP system is no longer available.

Routing with NetBIOS

When routers must be crossed, NetBIOS needs to be run on top of IPX or IP. Only when a NetBIOS packet is encapsulated within an IPX or IP packet can it traverse routers. This inadequacy can severely limit NetBIOS's ability to scale in larger networks. NetBIOS was originally designed to operate on single-segment LANs with 200 nodes or fewer.

NetBIOS over IPX

IPX supports the encapsulation of NetBIOS messages. When a NetBIOS message is contained within an IPX packet, the type field is set to a hexadecimal value of 14 and uses a socket of 0455. When NetBIOS is encapsulated within IPX and it is passed across a router, it is commonly referred to as *type-20 propagation*. This because the type field value of 14 converts to a decimal value of 20.

 TIP   Cisco routers block NetBIOS/IPX packets by default. You must enable type-20 propagation on each interface in order to pass this traffic.

Figure 6.4 shows a NetBIOS name claim (registration) encapsulated with an IPX packet. The NetBIOS header follows the IPX header within the data portion of the frame. Our IPX header has not only identified our IPX network number (8023), it has correctly flagged the packet type as NetBIOS (Packet Type 20).

Notice that the station destination address is the broadcast address. This means that our NetBIOS message will now have to be processed by every system on the local network, regardless of whether a system communicates using NetBIOS. Needless to say, this communication method is highly inefficient because it drains CPU time from every system on the wire.

In fact, by enabling type-20 propagation on the router, you are telling the router to forward these broadcast packets to other networks. This means that CPU time will be drained from systems on these other networks, as well. Because of NetBIOS/IPX's ability drain network resources, it has an extremely low maximum hop count of eight hops. As the packet is passing the router, the hop value will be decreased by 1, and the packet will be propagated until the hop count value reaches 0.

FIGURE 6.4

A NetBIOS message encapsulated within an IPX packet

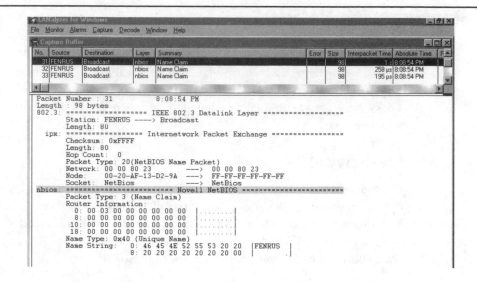

NetBIOS over IP

IP also supports the encapsulation of NetBIOS messages. UDP is used to support broadcast messages, while TCP takes care of unicast transmissions. Ports 137–139 are used for all communications. The NetBIOS header information immediately follows the TCP or UDP header within the frame.

 NOTE NetBIOS/IP b-node (broadcast-based) systems cannot communicate with systems on remote subnets by host name unless the b-node system has an LMHOSTS entry for the remote system.

With IP as the underlying transport, p-node systems can be supported for communications across a router. A good example of this type of functionality is Microsoft's WINS.

Figure 6.5 shows an example of a WINS implementation. Each WINS server acts as a NetBIOS Name Server (NBNS) for each of the p-node systems on its local subnet by maintaining a table of each system's NetBIOS name. In addition, the server also stores each system's IP address.

FIGURE 6.5

*Sample network with
three WINS servers,
one located on each
subnet*

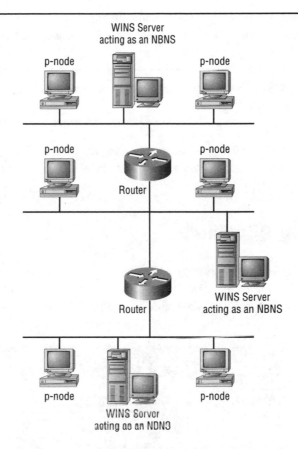

Each WINS server periodically updates the other WINS servers with a copy of its table. The result is a dynamic listing which maps NetBIOS names to IP addresses for every system on the network. Each of the three WINS systems then stores a copy of the table.

When a p-node system needs the address of another NetBIOS system, it sends a discovery packet to its local WINS server. If the system in question happens to be located on a remote subnet, the WINS server returns the remote system's IP address. This allows the remote system to be discovered without propagating broadcast frames throughout the network. When h-nodes are used, the functionality is identical.

When you run NetBIOS over IP, you can use a *NetBIOS scope* to group systems together. A NetBIOS scope is a group of computers among which a registered NetBIOS name is known. The scope identifier functions similarly to the domain name used with DNS under IP. A system's NetBIOS name must be unique within a specific scope.

WINS server will propagate name information within a specific scope. A *scope identifier* is a unique character string by which the scope is known.

 NOTE Systems from one scope ID are unable to communicate with systems of another scope ID.

NetBIOS over IP is outlined in great detail in Requests for Comments (RFCs) 1001 and 1002. RFC 1001 provides an overview of this functionality, while 1002 has been written in greater detail.

AppleTalk Routing

AppleTalk supports static and only a single dynamic routing protocol. The *Routing Table Maintenance Protocol* (RTMP) is a distance vector protocol used to maintain the network address tables. Figure 6.6 is a packet decode of an RTMP frame.

FIGURE 6.6

A router using RTMP to broadcast its known routes

```
LANalyzer for Windows                                                    _ 8 X
File  Monitor  Alarms  Capture  Decode  Window  Help
E:\HOME\LAPTOP\ALPINE\LIBERTY\TRACES\NOV18\LIBERTY.TR1 [Filtered]        _ 0 X
Packet Number : 775            1:55:18 PM
Length : 622 bytes
802.3: ================= IEEE 802.3 Datalink Layer =================
       Station: AA-00-04-00-F5-07 ----> ATalk_Bcast
       Length: 604
802.2: ================= IEEE 802.2 Logical Link Control =============
       SSAP: SNAP    DSAP: SNAP
       Unnumbered Command: Unnumbered Information (UI)
       SNAP Organization Code: 08 00 07
       SNAP Protocol Type: 0x809B (AppleTalk)
e-ddp: ============= Extended Datagram Delivery Protocol ============
       (AppleTalk Phase 2)
       Datagram Length: 596
       Hop Count: 0
       Checksum: 0x0000 (not used)
       Network:    31            ----> 0
       Node:       107           ----> 255 (Broadcast)
       Socket:       1 RTMP      ----> 1   RTMP
       Type: 0x01 (RTMP)
rtmp:  ============= Routing Table Maintenance Protocol =============
       Sender's network number: 31
       ID length: 8   Sender's node ID: 107
       Network Range:   31 -   40    Distance: 0
       RTMP version: 0x82
       Network Range: 14921 - 14921  Distance: 2
       Network Range: 14922 - 14922  Distance: 1
       Network Range: 14941 - 14941  Distance: 3
       Network Range: 14942 - 14942  Distance: 2
       Network Range: 14961 - 14961  Distance: 3
       Network Range: 14962 - 14962  Distance: 2
       Network Range: 14981 - 14981  Distance: 3
       Network Range: 14982 - 14982  Distance: 2
       Network Range: 15002 - 15002  Distance: 1
       Network Range: 15041 - 15041  Distance: 2
       Network Range: 15042 - 15042  Distance: 1
```

Note the RTMP information listed at the bottom of Figure 6.6. It contains the tell-tale signs of a router handing out secondhand information and thus using a distance vector protocol. If this were a link state routing protocol, we would not require a "distance" value since link state routers only report firsthand information.

As a distance vector routing protocol, RTMP is susceptible to all the previously mentioned problems encountered when using secondhand routing information. The only difference is that RTMP broadcasts routing updates every 30 seconds instead of once per minute. While this gives it a faster convergence time, it also makes it twice as noisy as most distance vector routing protocols.

At the time of this writing, Apple has not announced any plans to update AppleTalk to include link state routing.

Protocol-Independent Routing

Just when you get everything nicely packaged, someone has to come along and open up the flaps. Until now, each routing protocol we have discussed has been based on a specific protocol. For example, OSPF will only run on IP, NLSP will only run on IPX, and so on. This means that if you are running multiple protocols, you need to implement multiple ways of keeping your routing table up to date for each protocol.

This is where Cisco's *Enhanced Interior Gateway Routing Protocol* (EIGRP) comes into play. EIGRP is capable of maintaining route information for IP, IPX, and AppleTalk with only a single set of updates. This can result in a dramatic reduction in bandwidth utilization along slow circuits, such as WAN connections.

EIGRP is a link state protocol. This means that convergence time is kept to a minimum. Although load balancing is not supported, EIGRP can transmit partial updates when links fail so that bandwidth utilization by the routing protocol itself is kept to a minimum. Periodic updates are not required: EIGRP will only transmit information when the network configuration changes. This helps to make the protocol extremely efficient and an excellent choice for slow links which are required to support multiple protocols.

The biggest drawback of EIGRP is that it is only supported by Cisco routers. This means that if you have an environment of mixed router vendors, EIGRP can be a little more difficult to implement. When communicating with non-Cisco routers, EIGRP supports the following:

- IP: RIP, OSPF, BGP
- IPX: RIP
- AT: RTMP

If one of your Cisco routers needs to exchange IP routing information with a 3COM router, the interface on the same subnet as the 3COM must be configured to use RIP, OSPF, or BGP. Of course, this means that the 3COM must also be using RIP, OSPF, or BGP. This will allow the Cisco router to be updated by the 3COM and in turn advertise these routes using EIGRP.

This is the best use of EIGRP:

- Across a WAN with Cisco routers at both ends
- When load balancing is not required
- When multiple protocols are supported
- When bandwidth utilization is kept to a minimum

Summary

In this chapter, we discussed which routing protocols are available to each of our networking protocols. We discussed the strengths and weaknesses of each and suggested guidelines for implementation.

Now, let's get hands-on with a Cisco router. In the next chapter, we will discuss how to use the Cisco command-line interface. We will look at commands you can use to configure and to monitor the status of your router.

CHAPTER 7

Cisco IOS

Cisco routers are extremely flexible devices. The number of configurable options can be downright daunting. For example, the *Cisco IOS Software Command Summary* (referred to humorously as the "pocket guide") is 8.5" × 11" and approximately 900 pages long. Keep in mind this is a "summary," not a fully detailed manual. Not exactly something you can toss in the shirt pocket!

Online Help

With so many commands to use, even the most seasoned Cisco professional can forget the exact syntax of a command from time to time. That is why Cisco IOS includes an extensive online help system. From any prompt or position in a command entry, you can enter a question mark (?) to get a list of your available options.

For example, let's say that you are working with a particular interface and need to add a secondary IP address, but you cannot remember the exact syntax to use. Simply use online help to walk you through the process.

This is a very abbreviated version of the output you would receive:

```
router(config-if)#?
Interface configuration commands:
  apollo      Apollo interface subcommands
  appletalk   Appletalk interface subcommands
  arp         Set arp type (arpa, probe, snap) or timeout
  ip          Interface Internet Protocol config commands
```

What's important here is that the online help is telling you that any command used to configure IP information should begin with the command ip.

Let's assume this jogs a few gray cells and you remember that the first switch starts with the letter *a*, but now you can't remember the full name of the switch. To receive a more focused help display, simply add this to your command:

```
router(config-if)#ip a?
access-group accounting address authentication

router(config-if)#ip a
```

Notice that the online help has produced four possible switches. Since you are trying to set a secondary address, the address switch looks like the best option. Also, notice that when the prompt is returned, ip a is already filled in. This lets you reenter the command without having to retype it.

TIP Cisco IOS allows you to use an abridged command structure. This means you only need to type in enough of the command to distinguish it from other possible entries. For example, instead of typing **ip address**, you could type **ip addr** or even **ip ad**; either of these provides enough input to distinguish the command from other possibilities.

You now have two pieces of the puzzle. You know the command starts with ip address, but you don't know the other switches needed to complete the command. Again, you can simply fall back on online help:

```
router(config-if)#ip address ?
 A.B.C.D    IP address
 negotiated IP Address negotiated over PPP

router(config-if)#ip address
```

Your options are either to enter a static IP address or to tell the system to negotiate one during connection. Since you are looking to assign a second address, you would enter it here and follow it with a question mark to see what other input is needed:

```
router(config-if)#ip address 192.168.254.2 ?
 A.B.C.D IP subnet mask

router(config-if)#ip address 192.168.254.2
```

Only one option is available: to enter the subnet mask for this network. Enter that and again use online help to see whether additional switches are required:

```
router(config-if)#ip address 192.168.254.2 255.255.255.0 ?
 secondary Make this IP address a secondary address
 <cr>

router(config-if)#ip address 192.168.254.2 255.255.255.0
```

Again, you have two options. The <cr> means that you can press the Enter key and execute the command as is. This, however, would change the IP address assigned to this interface to the value entered in this command. If you complete the command with the switch secondary, the value entered will become an additional IP address for this interface. Since this is what you want, add the secondary switch.

Now you need to know whether you have all the information you need to complete the command. Use the online help one last time to check:

```
router(config-if)#ip address 192.168.254.2 255.255.255.0 secondary ?
 <cr>

router(config-if)#ip address 192.168.254.2 255.255.255.0 secondary
```

The only available option is to press Enter. This tells you that the command will require no additional input. Since the online help has already retyped the current command at the prompt, just press the Enter key to execute this change.

Online help can even be useful when you've tried to execute a command using the wrong syntax. For example, let's say you entered the preceding command but forgot to include the subnet mask value. In this case, you would see the following:

```
router(config-if)#ip address 192.168.254.2 secondary
                         ^                          ^
% Invalid input detected at '^' marker.

router(config-if)#
```

Note that the router is telling you that it cannot accept the command secondary. This is useful because it tells you exactly where you have entered something incorrectly in the command. You know that the ip address 192.168.254.2 portion of the command is correct; the keyword secondary is the problem. To find out what input the router is expecting, you could replace the command secondary with a question mark just as you did earlier:

```
router(config-if)#ip address 192.168.254.2 ?
  A.B.C.D IP subnet mask
```

Online help provides valuable guidance as you work through the command structure. While you still need a firm understanding of Cisco IOS, the help screens can get you through when you forget the exact syntax of what you wish to do.

Modes of Operation

By default, Cisco routers offer two levels of command access:

- Non-privilege mode
- Privilege mode

Non-privilege mode offers a limited number of command options. Available commands in non-privilege mode are restricted to those that will show the status of the router and allow the user to perform simple connectivity checks.

Privilege mode provides the full Cisco IOS command set. Along with all the non-privilege mode commands, privilege mode allows the user to perform configuration changes and to access flash and PC card storage.

Non-privilege Mode

Non-privilege mode is the first mode of operation you reach when connecting to a Cisco router. If you are running a direct console session, you are placed in non-privilege mode automatically (assuming that a console password has not been set). If you are connecting to the router via a Telnet session, you are first prompted for a terminal password.

 TIP A Cisco router will deny all Telnet session attempts if a terminal password has not been set.

A Cisco router changes the terminal prompt depending on the mode of operation you are currently using. The prompt always starts with the name of the router and ends with some special sequence to let you know where you are. For example, when you are in non-privilege mode, the prompt will appear as follows:

```
Router>
```

where the word *Router* would be replaced by the name you have specified for the router. The greater-than sign (>) lets you know you are working in non-privilege mode.

Non-privilege Mode Commands

As you just saw, non-privilege mode commands are limited to connectivity testing and router statistics. You are not allowed to make changes to the router's configuration in non-privilege mode.

While the reduced command set in non-privilege mode may seem limiting, it can actually be quite useful. For example, you might wish to grant network administrators access to the router for connectivity testing but not let them to make changes. To do this, simply restrict the administrators' access to non-privilege mode. Without the privilege mode password, they can only check connectivity; they cannot even retrieve a copy of the router's current configuration.

Table 7.1 lists some of the most useful commands available when working in non-privilege mode.

TABLE 7.1: NON-PRIVILEGE MODE COMMANDS

Command	Description
enable	Enter privilege mode
exit/logout	Close current session and exit
login	Enter privilege mode as a specific user
ping	Send an echo request to a remote host
show	Review information on different router operations
systat	Show terminal connections
telnet	Open a session to a remote host
terminal	Change terminal settings
traceroute	Trace the route to a remote host

Some of these non-privilege commands will accept additional switches. For example, the show command supports the additional parameters shown in Table 7.2.

TABLE 7.2: AVAILABLE SWITCHES WITH THE SHOW COMMAND

Command	Description
access-lists	Display any access list entries
appletalk	Show statistics for the AppleTalk protocol
arp	Show contents of the ARP cache
frame-relay	Display Frame Relay statistics
history	Review the last 10 commands entered
hosts	Show host file entries
interface	Show statistics for a specific interface
ip	Show statistics for the IP protocol
ipx	Show statistics for the IPX protocol
users	Display active terminal sessions
version	Display bootstrap, IOS, memory, and interface information

In fact, some of the switches will support additional switches. For example, the command

```
show ip traffic
```

will display cumulative IP traffic statistics. Entering the command

```
show ip traffic interface ethernet 0
```

will limit the reported traffic statistics to only the first Ethernet interface.

 TIP   Clearly, there are many possible variations with each IOS command. If you are not sure which switches are available, simply use the online help (?) to get a list of available options.

When Non-privilege Access Is Useful

Imagine that you are the network administrator for the environment shown in Figure 7.1. While there are multiple system administrators who are savvy about NT, you are the only person who understands the Cisco IOS command set. By providing the NT administrators with non-privilege access to their routers, you can allow them to perform simple connectivity checks without taking the chance that they will break the router configuration.

Let's assume that Alice, the NT administrator in Boston, is having trouble connecting to the corporate network. Her server can ping the local router, but she cannot ping the servers on the corporate backbone.

The first thing Alice could do is telnet to her local 2501 router. If she receives a password prompt, she knows that Ethernet connectivity to the router is working and that the router is powered up and functioning.

Once Alice authenticates, she is placed in non-privilege mode. From here, she can check a few things to make sure that the router is working properly. The first thing Alice can check is whether the serial interface leading to the frame relay network is functioning properly:

```
router>show interface s0
Serial0 is up, line protocol is up
```

FIGURE 7.1

Troubleshooting from non-privilege mode

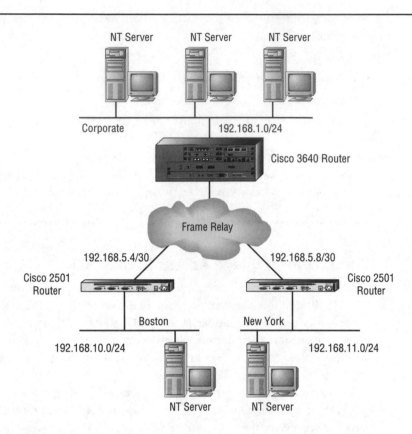

The show interface command actually returns a lot more information than this (which would probably be meaningless to an NT administrator). What is important here is that the serial interface is reported as up, which means it is functioning properly. Line protocol is also reported as up, which means data is flowing across the Frame Relay network.

The next thing Alice could try is to ping one of the corporate NT servers from the router itself:

```
shelby>ping 192.168.1.10

Type escape sequence to abort.
Sending 5, 100-byte ICMP Echos to 192.168.1.10, timeout is 2 seconds:
!!!!!
Success rate is 100 percent (5/5), round-trip min/avg/max = 8/10/12 ms
```

This has yielded a very valuable clue. Alice can reach the server from the local router, but not from the local network. This leaves us with two possible solutions to the problem:

- Traffic is being filtered via access lists.
- The remote router (3640) or NT server does not know how to reach the 192.168.10.0 network.

The first solution is rather complex and will be covered in greater detail in Chapter 9. Let's assume that Alice has entered the command

```
shelby>show access-lists
```

and received no data back, which indicates that the local router does not have any access lists installed.

The next step would be to check routing. Although we can assume that routing is working on the local 2501 router since it's possible to ping the NT servers from this location, it does not hurt to check. Alice would type the following:

```
shelby>show ip route
Codes: C - connected, S - static, I - IGRP, R - RIP, M - mobile, B - BGP
    D - EIGRP, EX - EIGRP external, O - OSPF, IA - OSPF inter area
    N1 - OSPF NSSA external type 1, N2 - OSPF NSSA external type 2
    E1 - OSPF external type 1, E2 - OSPF external type 2, E - EGP
    i - IS-IS, L1 - IS-IS level-1, L2 - IS-IS level-2, * - candidate default
    U - per-user static route, o - ODR

Gateway of last resort is 192.168.5.5 to network 0.0.0.0

C  192.168.10.0/24 is directly connected, Ethernet0
C  192.168.5.4/30 is directly connected, Serial0
S* 0.0.0.0/0 [1/0] via 192.168.5.5
```

The show ip route command returns some very useful information. First, it produces a code legend to describe where all of the route information originated. For example, any route listed with the code C has been learned because the router is directly connected to this subnet. Any route entry listed with the code S is a static route that was manually entered at the router.

The local routing table has a single static entry, which points the default route to the serial interface on the 3640 router. Since all other networks are reachable through this interface, we know that the local routing configuration is set up properly.

So your NT administrator has verified that connectivity up to the Frame Relay cloud is working. If Alice has non-privilege access to the 3640, she can perform some testing on that router, as well. Still in non-privilege mode on the 2501, Alice could enter

```
shelby>telnet 192.168.5.5
```

This would allow her to establish a session with the 3640 router. Let's assume that Alice has non-privilege access to this router, as well. The first thing she could do is verify that the 3640's routing table is set up properly:

```
shelby>show ip route
Codes: C - connected, S - static, I - IGRP, R - RIP, M - mobile, B - BGP
       D - EIGRP, EX - EIGRP external, O - OSPF, IA - OSPF inter area
       N1 - OSPF NSSA external type 1, N2 - OSPF NSSA external type 2
       E1 - OSPF external type 1, E2 - OSPF external type 2, E - EGP
       i - IS-IS, L1 - IS-IS level-1, L2 - IS-IS level-2, * - candidate default
       U - per-user static route, o - ODR

Gateway of last resort is not set

C  192.168.1.0/24 is directly connected, Ethernet0
C  192.168.5.4/30 is directly connected, Serial0.1
C  192.168.5.8/30 is directly connected, Serial0.2
```

Something in this information should jump out at you pretty quickly: The 3640 router has no route information to get to the 192.168.10.0 network. In fact, it is missing an entry for the 192.168.11.0 network, as well. Any reply trying to head back to these networks would make it as far as the 3640 router and then get dropped because this router does not know how to reach these networks. This means that when Alice tried to ping the corporate NT servers, the echo request most likely made it to the target server. The responding echo request, however, got lost in transit because it had no route to make it back.

By providing your NT administrator with only non-privilege mode access, you allowed her to do much of the troubleshooting for you without fear of her breaking the router. Instead of simply reporting, "The network is down," your NT administrator can tell you, "There is a problem with the routing table on the 3640." This can be a real time saver when you're trying to diagnose the root cause of the problem.

Privilege Mode

A user must enter non-privilege mode before entering privilege mode. Privilege mode, by default, is the big kahuna. At this level of access, a user is free to change or even delete any configuration parameters. You enter privilege mode by entering this command:

```
enable
password: privilege_password
```

NOTE Since you use the command `enable` to gain privilege access, this mode is sometimes referred to as *enable mode*.

Privilege Mode Commands

All Cisco IOS commands are accessible from privilege mode. A superset of the non-privilege mode commands is made available. For example, not only can you check the router's status, you can also make any required changes to correct any detected problems.

NOTE For the rest of this book, we will focus on working in privilege mode.

Privilege Mode Command Prompts

Like non-privilege mode, privilege mode has its own unique prompt to let you know when you are working in this mode. The router's name is followed by a pound sign (#), so the prompt will look something like this:

```
router#
```

Privilege mode actually has a number of different command modes, each identified by a unique prompt. All are based on the privilege-mode prompt, but each adds information to help you identify which command mode you are using. Some of the most common command modes are shown in Table 7.3.

TABLE 7.3: COMMAND MODE PROMPTS

Prompt	Description	How to Get There
router(boot)	Boot mode	Boot router from backup ROM image.
router(config)#	Global configuration mode	Type **config term** from privilege mode.

Continued ▶

TABLE 7.3: COMMAND MODE PROMPTS (CONTINUED)		
Prompt	Description	How to Get There
router(config-if)#	Interface configuration mode	Type **interface (*interface name*)** from global config mode.
router(config-subif)#	Sub-interface configuration mode	Type **interface (*sub-interface name*)** from global or interface config mode.
router(config-ext-nacl)#	Named access list configuration mode	Type **ip access-list extended (*ACL name*)** from global config mode.
router(config-line)#	Line configuration mode	Type **line *(terminal(s) to configure)*** from global config mode.
router(config-router)#	Router configuration mode; used to enable routing protocols	Type **router (*route protocol*)** from global config mode.
>	ROM mode	Press the Break key within 60 seconds of booting the router.

Most of the command modes in Table 7.3 are accessible once you enter global configuration mode. To get to global configuration mode from privilege mode, type the following:

```
router#configure terminal
Enter configuration commands, one per line. End with CNTL/Z.
router(config)#
```

Remember that you only need to type enough of the command to distinguish it from other possible entries. This means that you could have just as easily entered **config term** or even **conf t** to enter global configuration mode. From global configuration mode, you could then enter any of the other configuration modes indicated in Table 7.3.

Once you are done working in each of these modes, you can back out in one of two ways:

- Type **exit**, which will bring you back one level. So if you are in interface configuration mode and type the command **exit**, you will be placed in global configuration mode. Typing **exit** again will then place you in privilege mode.

- Use Ctrl+Z to move out of any configuration mode and place yourself directly in privilege mode. This is useful if you have completed any configuration changes and wish to return directly to privilege mode to either log off the system or check the running configuration.

Configuration Basics

In this section, we will cover some of the fundamental commands used in configuring a Cisco router. The purpose of this section is to not only describe how to use these commands, but to get you used to working with the Cisco router *command line interface* (CLI).

Working with the Command Line Interface

Cisco IOS provides you with a number of tools to simplify the process of working with the command line interface. One such tool is the Tab key, which you can use to fill in the remaining letters for a particular command line switch. This can be useful when you are using abridged commands and want to make sure your switches are correct.

For example, typing

```
shelby(config-if)#ip ad<TAB>
```

would result in this:

```
shelby(config-if)#ip address
```

Notice that the remaining characters in "address" have been filled in for you. You can now press **?** for online help or continue to add switches to the command.

NOTE Whenever you enter a portion of the switch, you can use the Tab key to fill in the remaining characters.

You can also use the up and down arrows to navigate the command line history. For example, pressing the up arrow twice will retrieve the second-to-last command you typed at the prompt. History is mode-sensitive, meaning that if you are in enable mode and press the up arrow, you can review the last 10 commands typed while in enable mode. This is true even if you briefly moved to global configuration mode. If you return to global configuration mode and press the up arrow, you will be looking at the last 10 commands you typed while in this mode.

NOTE History is session-specific. This means that you cannot review commands entered during a previous console or Telnet session.

There are a number of key combinations that can make navigating commands much easier, as well. For example, pressing Ctrl+A will move the cursor to the beginning of a command. Pressing Ctrl+E will move the cursor to the end of the command line. Both of these commands come in handy if you are retrieving commands from history and need to modify them before executing them.

Finally, as you saw in the last section, you can use Ctrl+Z to exit any configuration mode and return to privilege mode. This saves you from having to type **exit** one or more times.

Deleting or Negating Commands

Cisco IOS uses a very simple syntax for deleting commands. Simply use the same syntax you used to create the command, but append the no switch to the front of it.

For example, when adding a secondary IP address to an interface, we used the following command from interface configuration mode:

```
ip address 192.168.254.2 255.255.255.0 secondary
```

Let's assume that this was a mistake, and you now wish to remove the address. To do so, simply return to interface configuration mode and enter this command:

```
no ip address 192.168.254.2 255.255.255.0 secondary
```

This will remove the IP address entry from the running configuration. If you need to change the startup configuration as well, simply save your changes:

```
shelby#copy running startup
```

Be careful when using the no command because it can sometimes have a greater effect than expected. For example, entering the command

```
access-list 101 deny TCP any 200.200.200.1 0.0.0.0 eq 23
```

would create a filter which prevents anyone from using Telnet to connect to the host located at 200.200.200.1. However, entering the command

```
no access-list 101 deny TCP any 200.200.200.1 0.0.0.0 eq 23
```

would negate not only this command, but every filter associated with access list 101. This is because Cisco IOS does not allow you to delete line items within a numbered access list. You have to delete the entire group and start from scratch.

 NOTE   For more information on access lists, see Chapter 9.

Note that if you were entering this command from the command line and using the context-sensitive help, you would have seen this:

```
shelby(config)#no access-list 101 ?
 <cr>

shelby(config)#no access-list 101
```

Note that IOS does not expect any additional commands after the access list number. This implies that you cannot delete a specific entry, just the whole group.

Also note that when you entered

```
no access-list 101 deny TCP any 200.200.200.1 0.0.0.0 eq 23
```

an error code was not returned. This is because everything after 101 was simply ignored.

 TIP When using the no command to negate entries, make sure you do so carefully. Using the context-sensitive help can be a great way to avoid mistakes when deleting commands from the system.

Managing the Configuration

Of course, an important part of working with a Cisco router is the ability to retrieve, review, and save configuration files. Needless to say, it is difficult to manage a device if you do not know how it is configured.

A Cisco router maintains two distinct configuration files:

Running-config   Configuration currently being used by the router

Startup-config   Configuration loaded at startup

While it may seem logical that these files would be identical, this is not always the case.

How Your Changes Are Applied

When you enter configuration mode and make changes to your router, you are only modifying the running configuration. This is why any changes you make take effect immediately. The startup configuration is not modified until you manually save these changes. Until you specifically enter the command to overwrite the startup configuration with the contents of the running configuration, the settings in the two configuration files will be different.

To understand why IOS does this, imagine the following: You manage the infrastructure of a large environment which includes many small field offices connected to the corporate network via a WAN. Field-office employees use the WAN to access a central database which is critical to the company's day-to-day operations.

One day, while working on the network you inadvertently change the configuration on one of the field office's routers so that it can no longer communicate with the corporate network. Of course, this also means that you can't establish a command session with the device in order to fix the problem.

You now have a few options:

- Go home quickly and deny all knowledge of the problem or how it could have been caused (sun spots, maybe?)

- Visit the Monster Board and start sending out your résumé

- Find a salesperson in the remote office who just happens to carry a console cable and can be walked through fixing the problem over the phone (maybe the guy who keeps getting infected with the Melissa virus?)

- Continue racking up those frequent-flier miles on the next red-eye

Of course, if the remote router is a Cisco and you have not yet manually saved your changes (which is very likely, since the change killed your command session), you could simply have someone power cycle the router (salespeople can usually operate a power switch), which would restore the original configuration. This will get you back up and running in short order.

So the requirement of manually saving your changes in order to modify the startup configuration is actually a feature. This allows you to recover quickly if the worst occurs. Of course, it also means you need to make sure that you save your changes once you know the router is performing correctly.

Viewing Startup Configuration

To view the configuration that the router will use at startup, use the show startup-config command from privilege mode. Your output will look similar to the following:

```
shelby#show startup-config
Using 1175 out of 32762 bytes
!
version 12.0
service timestamps debug uptime
service timestamps log uptime
!
hostname shelby
```

```
!
no logging console
enable secret 5 $1$NFrn$4m6BGqPue2ScpJaoR2npUO
enable password secretpass
!
ip subnet-zero
ip host gwen 192.168.0.28
ip host shelby 192.168.0.254
ip domain-name fubar.com
ip name-server 192.168.0.1
clock timezone EST -5
!
!
!
interface Ethernet0
 ip address 192.168.0.254 255.255.255.0
 no ip directed-broadcast
 no ip route-cache
 no ip mroute-cache
 no mop enabled
!
interface Serial0
 ip address 192.168.254.1 255.255.255.0
 no ip directed-broadcast
 no ip route-cache
 no ip mroute-cache
!
interface Serial1
 no ip address
 no ip directed-broadcast
 no ip route-cache
 no ip mroute-cache
 shutdown
!
ip default-gateway 192.168.254.2
ip classless
ip route 0.0.0.0 0.0.0.0 192.168.254.2
!
!
```

```
!
line con 0
exec-timeout 0 0
 transport input none
line aux 0
line vty 0 4
password secret2
login
!
end
```

The beginning of the file identifies the major revision level of the IOS software being used. Also listed are any services running on the router. The next section shows logging options and privileged passwords. Note that the "secret" password is encrypted using MD5. The "enable password" is used for backwards compatibility. If you ever load an IOS version prior to 11.*x* (for example, during disaster recovery), this clear text-password will be used to gain access to privilege mode. During normal router operations, however, the encrypted password is used.

After that, we have some global configuration options. This file has a few host names listed, as well as the domain in which the router is located. Also identified is the local DNS server and the time zone where the router is located.

Next you can see configuration information for each of the router's interfaces. Note that this router (a Cisco 2501) has one Ethernet interface and two serial interfaces. The second serial interface (S1) is configured as shutdown, which means it has been administratively disabled.

After the interface information, we have route table entries as well as instructions on how to deal with IP subnet classes. Finally, you can see configuration information for console (con 0) and Telnet (vty) sessions.

NOTE This file does not contain all possible configuration options. The only configuration options listed are the ones that deviate from the default setup. For example, this router has Finger services listening on the router even though Finger does not show up in the configuration file. The reason there is no entry in the configuration files is that IOS enables Finger services by default. You would not get an entry in the configuration file unless you disabled Finger services, because having the service disabled is a deviation from the default setup.

The configuration file only shows you deviations from the base configuration. This can actually be pretty useful if you want to return a setting to its default value but do not remember what that default value may be. If the change shows up in the configuration file, you know you have deviated from the base setup.

Table 7.4 shows a list of commands you can use when working with configuration files. Note that these commands were introduced with IOS 11.*x*. Equivalent commands for earlier versions of IOS are also listed. Don't worry too much about the TFTP commands for right now. We will cover using TFTP in greater detail in the next chapter.

TABLE 7.4: COMMANDS TO USE WHEN MANIPULATING CONFIGURATION FILES

Command	Before 11.*x*	Usage
show startup-config	show config	View config used at startup
show running-config	write term	View running configuration
copy running startup	write	Save running config to startup config
copy startup running	config mem	Overwrite running config with startup config
copy running tftp	write tftp	Save config to a remote TFTP server
erase startup-config	write erase	Delete startup config file

 TIP When working with a Cisco router, get used to issuing the `copy running startup` command before you make changes. If you need to reboot to recover, this command insures that you will not lose and changes made prior to the current session.

Setting the Router's Date and Time

Maintaining an accurate system time is important when reviewing log entries. For example, if you will be logging access-list traffic and want to be able to compare these log entries to those generated by other systems, an accurate system clock is a must.

To set the date and time on the system, enter privilege mode (*not* global configuration mode) and enter this command:

```
router#clock set HH:MM:SS month day year
```

If you then enter the show clock command, you should see the current time and date displayed in a similar format:

```
router#show clock
08:39:56.811 EST Mon Nov 29 1999
```

 NOTE While manually setting the clock will get the system time in the same ballpark as your other systems, it will not match up exactly. Like any system with its own internal clock, the clock in a Cisco router will drift over time.

To insure that the clock stays accurate, you may wish to configure the router to check its time against an authoritative time source, such as a system that uses an atomic clock. This is done using the *Network Time Protocol* (NTP). A Cisco router can use NTP to retrieve time checks over the network. To configure NTP services, enter global configuration mode and type the following command:

```
ntp server <server name or IP address>
```

Working with Multiple Telnet Sessions

In our discussion of Figure 7.1, we touched upon being able to telnet from one router to another. Sometimes, however, you need to return to the command session on the first router in order to verify any changes you made to the second. For example, you could be making route changes to the second router and want to return to the command session on the first router in order to verify these changes.

You could use the exit command to tear down your session with the second router, but doing so would mean going back through the full authentication process if you need to return to privilege mode in order to make additional changes.

To simplify this process, Cisco routers allow you to suspend the session to the second router in order to work with the first router. Once you've finished working with the first router, you can reactivate the suspended session in order to continue working with the second router.

For example, let's say you use Telnet to connect to a router named Shelby. Next, you use the enable command to enter privilege mode.

Now you'd like to use Telnet from Shelby's command line in order to connect to a router named Loki. The session would look something like this:

```
Trying 192.168.0.254 (Shelby) ...
Connected to 192.168.0.254
```

```
User Access Verification

Password:
shelby>enable
Password:
shelby#telnet Loki
Trying Loki (192.168.50.1)... Open


User Access Verification

Password:
loki> enable
Password:
loki#
```

You can now enter global configuration mode on Loki and begin making your changes. Let's assume your changes are complete and you want to switch back to the command line on Shelby. Instead of killing your session with Loki, you could enter this command:

```
CTRL-^ x
```

In other words, press Ctrl+Shift+6, then press the X key. Your prompt changes to this:

```
loki#
shelby#
```

You can now enter any commands you need to on the first router (Shelby). If you perform your testing and decide that you need to return to the second router (Loki) to make additional changes, you can do so by simply pressing the Enter key while in privilege mode on the first router (Shelby). This will restore your connection to the second router, as shown here:

```
shelby#
[Resuming connection 1 to loki ... ]


loki#
```

This method can be a real time saver if you need to switch back and forth between two routers. In fact, you can even use it to create multiple sessions with multiple routers. Just make sure you do not inadvertently create so many sessions that you lose track of where you are.

System Names and Address Resolution

As carbon-based life forms, most of us find it far easier to work with names than with network addressing. For example, it's much easier to remember that the corporate router is "corp-router" than to try to remember the IP addresses associated with the device. With this in mind, Cisco IOS provides a number of options for using name resolution when working with your routers.

 TIP   Device names should be somewhat descriptive. It is far easier to remember that the router located in the Tampa field office is named "tampa-router" than to try and remember whether it is Voyager, Enterprise, or Defiant. While it is acceptable to take some poetic liberty when naming your routers, remember that a structured naming convention will scale much better and make troubleshooting easier.

Host Name

As I mentioned earlier in this chapter, Cisco IOS allows you to assign a host name to your router. This name is then used as part of the command prompt. This can be extremely valuable if you are working with a large environment.

For example, when we were troubleshooting connectivity problems in the network shown in Figure 7.1, we used Telnet to connect to the first router. Once we had gathered some additional information, we used Telnet again to connect to the second router directly from the CLI of the first router. Without a prompt identifying the name of the router you are currently working with, it's very easy to get confused about which router's interface you are looking at. So assigning a descriptive host name can be a real time saver when troubleshooting large environments.

To change the host name of a router, enter global configuration mode and type

```
router(config)#hostname springfield
springfield(config)#
```

replacing *springfield* with whatever descriptive name you would like to call your router. Note that the change takes place immediately. When the prompt is returned, the router name has already been changed.

Host File

Cisco routers have the ability to generate a local host file. Just like its operating-system counterpart, a host file can be used to map system names to their assigned IP addresses. This is useful if you are dealing with a small environment or if no domain name servers are present on your network. The addition of host file entries can make using tools such as Ping and Telnet much easier.

To add names to the local host file, enter global configuration mode and enter this command:

```
router(config)#ip host (host name) (IP address)
```

For example, a host entry for the system named Shelby could look like this:

```
router(config)#ip host shelby 192.168.50.113
```

DNS Resolution

The simplest way to use name resolution on your router is to enable DNS. This will allow the router to query the local DNS server when attempting to resolve host names to their IP addresses. Enabling DNS resolution is a two-step process:

1. Assign a domain name.

2. Add a name server entry for each domain name server.

We'll start by assigning a domain name. This allows you to resolve hosts through DNS without having to type in the fully qualified domain name. If you manage a small environment, a single domain name will usually suffice. To configure the router with the local domain name, enter global configuration mode and enter

```
router(config)#ip domain-name fubar.com
```

replacing *fubar.com* with the name of your domain. Now, when you enter the host name **nynt1**, the system appends the domain name to the end, resulting in the fully qualified domain name nynt1.fubar.com.

For large environments, you may wish to list multiple domain names for the router to try when resolving a fully qualified domain name. For example, let's say that your network uses the domain names fubar.com, foobar.com, and bohica.com. Each host in your domain may be associated with any one of these domain names. To simplify name resolution, you could create a domain name list. This would cause the router to append each domain name, in order, until the host resolves correctly.

So when you tell the router you wish to ping the host nynt1, the router would attempt to resolve the following:

- nynt1.fubar.com
- nynt1.foobar.com
- nynt1.bohica.com

NOTE The first time the name resolves to an IP address, that address will be used to connect to the remote system. If none of the names resolves properly, a name resolution error is returned.

To add these domain names to your domain list, you would enter the following from global configuration mode:

```
router(config)#ip domain-list fubar.com
router(config)#ip domain-list foobar.com
router(config)#ip domain-list bohica.com
```

Once you have your domain names straightened away, you are ready to point your router at the local domain name servers. To do so, enter the following in global configuration mode:

```
router(config)#ip name-server (DNS1) (DNS2) (DNS3)
```

where *DNS1*, *DNS2*, and *DNS3* would be replaced with the IP address of each of your local domain name servers. Up to six domain name servers can be listed in this fashion, so your entry may look something like this:

```
router(config)#ip name-server 192.168.1.10 192.168.1.11
```

Management via HTTP

The HTTP server allows you to both manage and monitor a Cisco router through an HTML interface. Figure 7.2 shows a screen shot of the configuration menu screen. You have the option of configuring the router by clicking HTML links or by entering the required command in the box at the top of the screen.

The HTML interface can be extremely useful if you are just starting to get used to the IOS command line interface. While seasoned professionals may find the HTML interface slow and cumbersome, administrators who are just starting to get the hang of working with a Cisco router may find it far easier to work with. It's nice to know there is a GUI if you need to fall back on it.

Along with configuring the system, you can also use the interface to monitor the router's status and diagnostic log. For example, Figure 7.3 shows a view of the statistics for interface Ethernet0. This is the equivalent of entering privilege mode and typing **show interface eth0**. Navigating the HTML interface is identical to working from the command line. Click the Show command, then Interface, then Ethernet, then enter the number **0**.

FIGURE 7.2

The configuration
menu of the HTML
interface

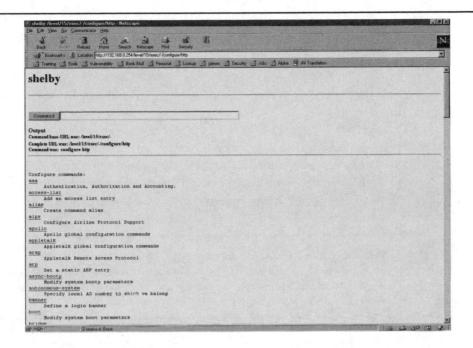

FIGURE 7.3

Statistics for
interface eth0

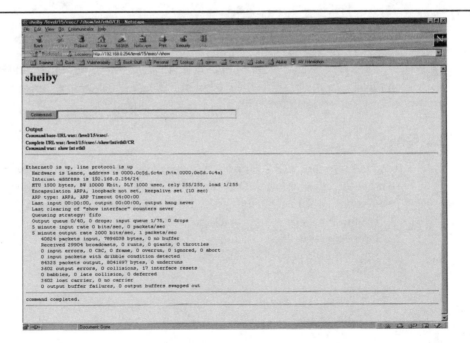

There are a couple of caveats about using the HTML interface. First, it is not enabled by default. You must run a Telnet or console session and enter the following command from global configuration mode:

```
ip http server
```

This means that you cannot completely get away from using the command line interface.

Also, when you authenticate to the router, you must log on as "admin" and use the privilege-level password. Once on the system, you can select to operate at a lower level of access, but the initial authentication requires that the user know the privilege-level password. This means you must have absolute trust in anyone you allow to use the HTML interface, as they will have access to all system commands.

 NOTE Since the command structures of the command line interface and the HTML interface are identical, I will not distinguish between them for the rest of this book. While the examples will assume you are working at the command line, you could just as easily enter the commands through the HTML interface.

Understanding Cisco Memory

Just like a computer, a Cisco router utilizes several different types of memory. Each type serves a specific purpose in helping the router to function. While this book is primarily about router software, it is worth taking a quick look at how memory is used, in order to better understand how the router operates.

ROM

Read-only memory (ROM) chips in a Cisco router perform a similar function to the ROM chips in a computer. They are used to save program code required to initialize the system. This includes the system boot strap code and power-on diagnostics.

In addition, ROM stores a backup operating system in case the original operating system becomes deleted or damaged. Typically, this operating system is a few revisions behind the current release level but is sufficient to get the router booted up and functional.

NOTE When you power up a Cisco router for the first time, you boot using the operating system stored in ROM memory.

As the name implies, ROM is read-only. You cannot modify any of the problem code stored in ROM. If you need to perform an upgrade, you must replace the ROM chips themselves.

Flash

Flash is read/write memory storage which retains data after the system is rebooted or powered off. This is the location where the current operating system is stored. In fact, if you have enough flash storage, you can even save multiple operating system copies. This is useful if you are in the process of upgrading to a newer version of IOS but are unsure of the new version's stability. By retaining both the new and the old versions of IOS, you give yourself a quick method of reverting back to the old version if problems arise.

How the operating system code is retrieved from flash depends on the router type. For example, Cisco 2500 series routers are referred to as *run-from-flash* devices. This means that code is retrieved from flash only as it is needed. Other routers, such as the Cisco 4000 series, are referred to as *run-from-RAM* devices. This is because the entire operating system is loaded into RAM before execution.

NOTE The only problem with flash is that it tends to be slow compared to other memory types like RAM. This is why run-from-flash routers tend to be slower than their run-from-RAM counterparts.

NVRAM

Nonvolatile RAM (NVRAM) is also read/write storage that retains data through reboots and power cycles. The sole purpose of NVRAM is to store the startup configuration file. NVRAM is fast but expensive. Since it only needs to hold a copy of the config file, the average router only has 32KB–128KB of NVRAM.

RAM

Random access memory (RAM) is read/write storage that gets cleared when the router is rebooted or powered off. Just like the RAM in a computer, RAM in a Cisco router is temporary storage for the operating system and data during execution so that the router's processor can access this information quickly. RAM storage is faster than any other storage method used on a Cisco router.

During operation, RAM contains routing table entries, ARP cache entries, log entries, and packets being queued prior to delivery. RAM will also contain the running configuration and any program code being executed.

As mentioned, any router which is a run-from-RAM device will also contain a complete copy of the operating system. This means that you must insure that devices have enough memory for the operating system and all of the temporary data just mentioned.

NOTE It is not uncommon for run-from-RAM devices to require 32MB or more of RAM storage.

Determining Memory Requirements

When selecting a Cisco router, you will need to specify how much memory you would like to have included with the device. While all products come with a minimal amount of memory installed, you may need to adjust these quantities, depending on your needs.

NOTE Cisco routers ship with a fixed amount of ROM and NVRAM. These are sufficient for whatever product model you are purchasing, and you shouldn't have to adjust them. The only kinds of memory you need to consider are flash and RAM.

How Much Flash?

The amount of flash required will depend on which version and release level of IOS you plan to install. For example, IOS 11.3 requires less flash storage than IOS 12.07. The features you choose to purchase will also affect flash memory requirements. Table 7.5 shows the storage requirements of a number of different feature sets for IOS version 12.07 for the 2500 series of routers. Note that memory is sold in 8MB chips, so you would need 8MB for either the base IP feature set or the IP-Plus 40. If you wish to use one of the Enterprise feature sets, you would need 16MB of flash.

TABLE 7.5: MEMORY REQUIREMENTS FOR DIFFERENT 12.07 FEATURE SETS	
Features	**Required Flash Memory**
IP pack	5.8MB
IP Firewall	6.1MB
IP/IPX/AT	6.9MB
IP Plus 40	7.7MB
Enterprise	10MB
Enterprise IPSec 56	11.2MB

NOTE Table 7.5 assumes that you will only be retaining one copy of the IOS operating system. If you want to retain two copies while performing an upgrade, adjust your memory requirements accordingly.

How Much RAM?

The amount of RAM you need will vary greatly, depending on the router model and the load you expect the router to handle. The following list of items will help guide you in selecting the amount of RAM you will require for your router:

- Run-from-RAM routers require more RAM than run-from-flash routers.
- More features on a run-from-RAM router will increase RAM requirements.
- Dynamic routing uses more RAM than static routing.
- Link state routing uses more RAM than distance vector.
- More local hosts will increase the size of the ARP cache and thus the memory requirements to save it.
- Heavy network loads will require more RAM for packet queuing.

For example, the RAM requirement for a 2500-series router running the Enterprise feature set is 4MB. The same feature set on a 3600-series router, which is a run-from-RAM device, is 32MB.

Be sure to look at the router model, as well as your infrastructure requirements, before selecting a quantity of RAM. Remember that it is better to have too much RAM than too little, so when in doubt, err on the side of caution.

Summary

In this chapter, we looked at the basics of using Cisco IOS. We covered the different modes of operation and learned some helpful tips for navigating the command line interface. We also looked at the HTML interface and discussed how to determine a router's memory requirements.

In the next chapter, we will discuss how to load the Cisco IOS. We'll also dig a little deeper into configuring a Cisco router.

CHAPTER **8**

Installing Cisco IOS

We spent some time in Chapter 7 getting familiar with the Cisco IOS interface. In this chapter, we will discuss the different IOS feature packs, as well as how to load an IOS image onto your router. Since a Cisco router does not have a floppy, ZIP, or CD-ROM drive, all installation methods rely on network connectivity to load the image from another local host.

Selecting a Feature Set

When ordering a Cisco router, you will typically want to purchase the latest production version of IOS. At the time of this writing, the latest version is 12.07. Along with selecting the version of IOS you wish to run, you will also need to select a *feature set*.

A feature set identifies the options to be enabled on your router. For example, if you are purchasing a router that will border the Internet, it is sufficient to order it with IP support only. There is no need to pay for IPX support, because you will never use it.

One step in ordering a Cisco router that may be confusing is determining exactly which IOS feature set you need. The actual hardware selection is pretty straightforward. For example, if you need to support 12 Ethernet ports, you know you are looking at a 3600-series or higher router. A 2500 simply will not provide enough ports. When selecting a feature set, however, the options become a bit more cloudy.

The confusion stems from the fact that feature sets are not consistent from router model to router model. For example, Quality of Service (QoS) and support for the Resource Reservation Protocol (RSVP) are included in the base IP package on the 3600 series of routers. If you order a 1600-series, however, you need to order the IP Plus feature set in order to get QoS and RSVP.

So you need to check the Cisco product catalog to make sure that all your required features are included in whatever feature pack you are considering. Table 8.1 shows some general guidelines you can use when selecting a feature set. Before submitting that PO, however, it's best to verify your order against the product catalog.

TABLE 8.1: FEATURE SET KEYWORDS AND THEIR MEANINGS

Keyword	Description
IP	Provides basic IP routing connectivity
Plus	Supports additional feature set commands
Desktop	Includes support for IP, IPX, and AT

Continued ▶

TABLE 8.1: FEATURE SET KEYWORDS AND THEIR MEANINGS (CONTINUED)	
Keyword	**Description**
Enterprise	Includes all LAN and WAN options for a specific router model
FW	Supports the firewall feature set
40/56	Includes encryption support to the number of bits indicated
IPSec56	Supports IPSec encryption to the number of bits indicated

These keywords can be mixed and matched to identify the complete feature set. For example, Desktop Plus would support extended features when working with IP, IPX, and AT. Enterprise 40 is the Enterprise feature set with 40-bit encryption included. Depending on the router model, you might see other keywords, as well. For example, Desktop IBM is the Desktop feature set with additional features to support the SNA protocol used to communicate to IBM mini and mainframe systems.

The Router Software Loader

The *Router Software Loader* (RSL) is a Windows-based GUI that greatly simplifies the process of installing an IOS image on a Cisco router. With the software loader, you do not even need to understand Cisco IOS; simply point and click your way through the installation.

 NOTE   The Router Software Loader is included on the same CD that contains your IOS image file.

Getting Started

RSL must run on a Windows-compatible system. This system should also have a copy of the IOS image you plan to load on the router. You can always retrieve the latest version of Cisco IOS from the following URL:

```
http://www.cisco.com/cgi-bin/Software/Iosplanner/Planner-tool/
iosplanner.cgi?majorRel=12.0
```

NOTE   This area is password protected. You need a Cisco support contract in order to gain access to free upgrades.

Once you have the required software, you will need to physically wire the router to the computer. Two connections are required:

1. Connect COM1 on the PC to the router's console port using the included terminal cable.

2. Connect the router's LAN interface to the PC's network card. If you are using Ethernet, this can be done using a cross cable, hub, or switch.

 TIP   While the router and the PC can be connected to your main network during the installation, it is best to isolate them if possible.

When you install the IOS image file, the serial connection is used to create a console session with the router. This is the connection that the Router Software Loader will use to transmit any required commands. The network connection is used to transmit the actual image file.

Running Router Software Loader

Launch RSL by executing the file cpswinst.exe. This produces the Connect Wizard screen shown in Figure 8.1. Notice the reminder that the software needs a serial and network connection to the router in order to install the image. The Wizard also prompts you to define the topology you will be using to communicate with the router.

Click the Next button, and you will be asked to indicate whether the router has an existing configuration. You can see this screen in Figure 8.2. If this is a new router with no configuration, you can click Finish to begin the image installation. If the router has an existing configuration, you need to identify both the non-privilege (console) and the privilege (enable) passwords. Selecting this option will also insure that your current configuration is backed up before the image installation.

FIGURE 8.1

The Connect Wizard window

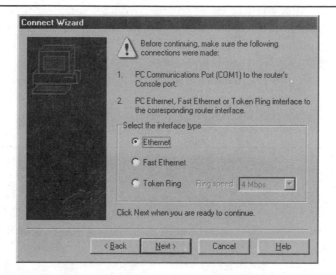

FIGURE 8.2

Password information is required for existing configurations.

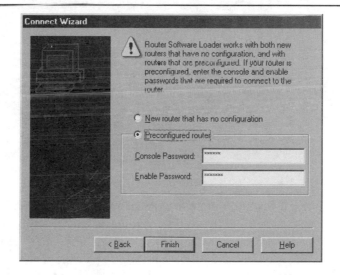

After you've entered any required password information and clicked the Finish button, RSL will establish a terminal session with the router. If it finds an existing configuration file, this file is backed up and then changed to facilitate the image installation. The program will also attempt to detect the computer's local IP address before communicating with the router over the network.

Once a communication session is established, the RSL main window appears. You can see this window in Figure 8.3.

FIGURE 8.3

The Router Software Loader main window

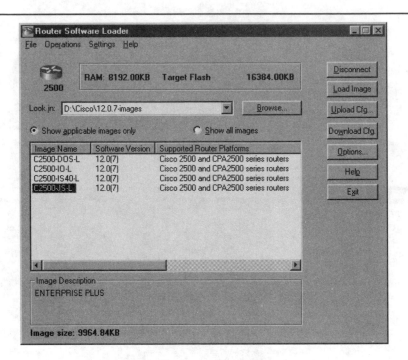

Just below the main menu, RSL reports the status of the connected router. Notice that RSL identifies the connected router as a 2500 series. Also reported is the amount of RAM (in this case 8MB) and the total amount of flash installed on the device (16MB).

Below the router status is a listing of all image files in the currently selected directory that can be used with this device. The file name, IOS version, and the supported platforms are identified.

NOTE If you highlight a filename, the Image Description box at the bottom of the page will tell you which features are included in the image, as well as how much flash is required for storage.

Take a look at the buttons on the right-hand side of the screen:

Disconnect   This button restores any preexisting configuration and kills the current session with the connected router.

Load Image   This button begins the process of loading whatever image file you have highlighted from the list of valid image files.

Upload Cfg   This button allows you to retrieve a copy of the router's startup or running configuration. This file can be saved to disk or loaded in a viewer for your review. Note that if you have run the Wizard, this will not be the original configuration but the configuration being used to load the IOS image. This may mean that some parameters, such as the subnet mask on the LAN interface, have been changed.

Download Cfg   This button allows you to take a local configuration file and load it on the router. Be careful not to load a configuration that might interfere with the image-loading process. Unless you are troubleshooting a problem, it is best to leave the router's configuration alone until the IOS image loading process is complete.

Options   This button allows you to customize RSL. For example, you can change the COM port used for the terminal session or even disable the Wizard from running whenever RSL is loaded.

The Help and Exit buttons are self-explanatory.

Installing the Image

Now that you are familiar with the RSL interface, let's load an image file. When you click the Load Image button, you will be presented with the screen shown in Figure 8.4. If an IOS image is already stored in flash, RSL will identify the image and present you with a number of options.

 NOTE You can choose to erase the existing image or leave it in flash along with the image you wish to download. This is fine as long as you have enough flash storage to hold both images.

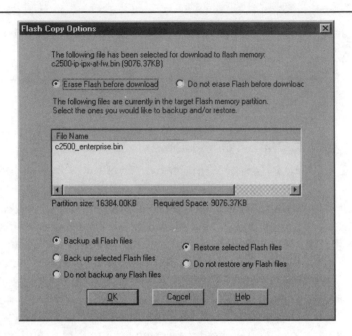

If you need to erase the existing image prior to download, you have the option of backing it up first. This stores a local copy of the existing image in case you run into trouble and need to revert to the earlier version. While performing the backup makes the installation process take longer, it offers cheap insurance in case you run into a problem.

Once you have set your load options, click OK to continue. RSL will now back up any existing image (if you told it to) and transfer the new IOS image file to the router. Once the new image has been loaded, RSL will reboot the target router.

When the reboot process is complete, the router will be using your new IOS image. It will still be using the temporary configuration, however. The original configuration files are not restored until you attempt to disconnect from the target router. This means that you must exit RSL or click the Disconnect button before you perform connectivity testing.

RSL Limitations

While RSL is very easy to use, it does require that the computer holding the image file be connected to the terminal port. This may be impractical—or even impossible—in large environments. For example, if the router is located in a field office on the other side of the country, you do not want to have to fly over there just to perform an IOS upgrade.

 NOTE When you need to perform an IOS upgrade but cannot gain physical access to the router, you must use TFTP. TFTP is explained in greater detail later in this chapter.

Cisco ConfigMaker

If you are going to use a GUI to load your image file, why not use a GUI to set your initial configuration? Cisco ConfigMaker is like Visio on steroids. You simply draw a picture of your network using drag-and-drop objects, and ConfigMaker uses this drawing to generate configuration files for each of your routers. ConfigMaker can even upload these configuration files to each router on your network. What could be easier?

Drawing Your Network with ConfigMaker

Figure 8.5 shows the ConfigMaker main screen. The Devices box at the upper left contains a series of network objects. Use these to create the hardware objects on your network. Clicking a product series will produce a drop-down list of all specific product models. If you click Cisco 2600 Series, for example, you will get a drop-down list showing the models 2610, 2611, 2620, and 2621. You can then drag and drop these objects into the blank Network Diagram section of the screen.

The Connections box at the left contains a list of possible network connections. Use objects in this box to define the circuits connecting each of your routers. Simply drag the object into the Network Diagram window and stretch the object to connect your routers.

Online help is on the right-hand side of the screen. Here you will find a list of simple instructions and links to tutorials and Wizards. The Help button at the bottom of the window provides detailed help files and a searchable index. The bottom of the screen is a legend describing what each potential object color means.

FIGURE 8.5

Cisco ConfigMaker

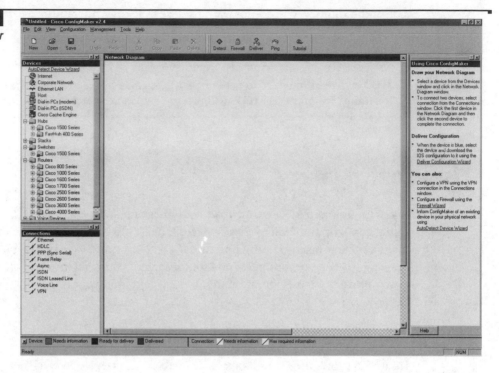

Across the top of the screen is the toolbar. The toolbar has the typical Windows icons, as well as a number of Cisco-specific goodies:

Detect   This button allows you to detect hardware and configuration information from devices on your network. Simply identify the device's IP address and any password information, and the device will be identified for you.

Firewall   This button allows you to configure the firewall feature set if it is present on the device.

Deliver   This button lets you upload the configuration to the router.

Ping   This button lets you test connectivity.

Setting up an Internet Border Router

The best way to learn how to use ConfigMaker is to jump in and start using it. Let's assume that you need to configure a Cisco 2501. This router will terminate your end of the WAN connection that leads to your ISP. Let's further assume that you have already used RSL to load the Cisco IOS image file.

Drag and Drop the Objects

The first thing you need to do is select a Cisco 2501 router from the Devices window. Simply click the Cisco 2500 Series object to get a drop-down list of the 2500 product series. Then click and drag the Cisco 2501 object to the middle of the Network Diagram window.

When you release the mouse click to drop the object, the Device Wizard initializes, as shown in Figure 8.6. The first thing you are asked to do is name your router. The default router name is the word *Cisco*, followed by the model number. Obviously, you will want to change this to something more descriptive. Once you have named the router, click the Next button.

FIGURE 8.6

ConfigMaker prompting for a device name

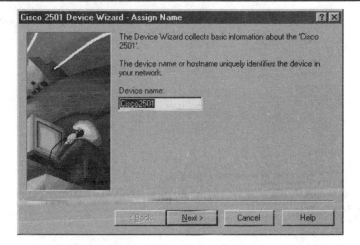

The next Device Wizard screen prompts you for the login and privilege mode (enable) passwords. You are prompted twice for both passwords to insure you have typed them correctly. If you are working with a router that already has a configuration, you should use the passwords that are currently programmed into the device. Once you have entered the passwords, click the Next button.

The next step is to identify which protocols you plan to use, as in Figure 8.7.

NOTE   You have not yet identified which feature set you are using. This means that ConfigMaker has no idea whether your router will even support all the listed protocols. This is a generic prompt and is not based on the capabilities of the router you are configuring. If you select a protocol that is not supported by your feature set, you will receive an error message when you try to deliver the configuration.

FIGURE 8.7

*ConfigMaker prompt-
ing for protocols*

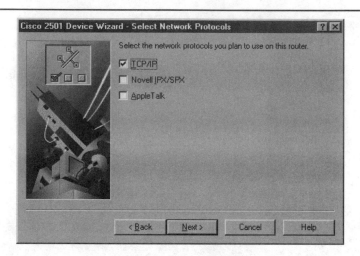

Since this router will be bordering the Internet, the only protocol you will need is TCP/IP. Since this option is selected by default, click Next to proceed.

The final Device Wizard screen tells you that your initial router configuration is complete and that you now need to create connections to the device using objects from the Connections window. You are also informed that you can review the configuration created for your router at any time by double-clicking it. Click the Finish button to close the Device Wizard.

After you have closed the Device Wizard, your router will appear in the middle of the Network Diagram window. You now need to add a few more objects. Once you do, it will be time to connect them all together.

Since this router will be connecting your local network to the Internet, you must add these objects, as well. Returning to the Devices window, drag and drop the Internet object and the Ethernet LAN object. Once you've done this, your Network Diagram window should look like Figure 8.8. Notice that the router is gray. According to the legend at the bottom of the screen, this means that you still need to supply additional configuration information before you can push out your configuration file to the router. This additional information will be generated when you create connections between the network objects.

FIGURE 8.8

Objects required for
the Internet connection

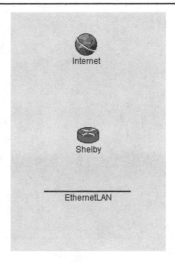

Creating Network Connections

The first connection you should create is to your Ethernet network. Click the Ethernet object within the Connections window. Note that you are not required to drag and drop the object. Your mouse pointer should now include a little lightning bolt on it. This lets you know that ConfigMaker is ready to draw in your Ethernet connections.

Move your mouse pointer over the router object within the Network Diagram window and notice that the connection points show up on the router. Simply click once on one of these connection points, then move the mouse cursor toward the Ethernet LAN object. As you do, you will see a connection line growing from the router to the Ethernet segment. Click once on the Ethernet LAN object to terminate the connection. The Ethernet Wizard will initialize so that you can configure the Ethernet interface of the router.

First, the Ethernet Wizard will ask you to enter the IP address for the Ethernet interface of the router. This is shown in Figure 8.9.

 NOTE You can identify the subnet mask in decimal format of by the number of network bits. While you can subnet addresses from this interface, you cannot supernet them (apply a lower mask value than the address' class specifies). For example, if you enter an IP address of 192.168.1.1, you will be forced to use 24 or more network bits. If you need to do supernetting (subnet using 23 bits or less), you must set the mask from the command line interface.

FIGURE 8.9

The Ethernet Wizard prompting for the router's IP address

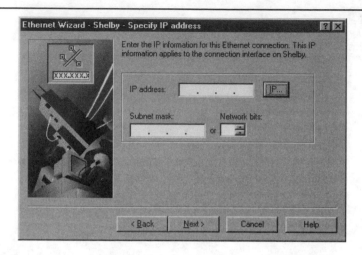

Just to the right of the IP address field is a button labeled IP. Clicking this button pulls up a Subnet Calculator that will report additional information on the IP address/ subnet mask combination you have selected. For example, the calculator will tell you what the network and broadcast addresses would be for the Ethernet segment to which the router is attached. You can even adjust the mask value to view the impact on the number of supported hosts, as well as valid IP addresses for this network.

Once you have entered an IP address, you can click the Next button to go on to the final Ethernet Wizard screen. This screen tells you that you have successfully configured the Ethernet interface. Click the Finish button to close the Ethernet Wizard. When you return to the Network Diagram window, you can see that the Wizard has labeled the Ethernet interface on the router as e0 and has drawn in the IP address you have entered.

Next, follow a similar process for configuring the serial interface. Before you can set this interface, you need to know whether you have a Frame Relay or a point-to-point connection to your Internet Service Provider. If the connection is point to point, you also need to know which WAN protocol your ISP is using. If your service provider is using Cisco gear, it's probably using the HDLC protocol. If it's using routers from any other manufacturer, you will need to use PPP.

For the sake of our example, let's assume you will be using HDLC. Click this object within the Connections window, adding a lightning bolt to your mouse pointer. Click the router object and then the Internet object in order to create a connection between them. This produces the HDLC Wizard, as shown in Figure 8.10.

FIGURE 8.10

The HDLC Wizard prompting for the serial interface

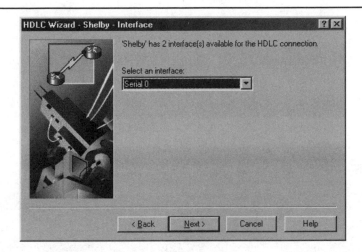

 NOTE This time around, you are asked to identify which interface will be used for this connection. This is because a Cisco 2501 router has two serial ports but only one Ethernet port. The software knows that you need to use a serial connection to communicate via HDLC; it just wants to know which of the serial ports you wish to use. Since the device only has one Ethernet port, there was only a single option for creating the Ethernet connection to the Ethernet network.

After identifying which interface to use and clicking the Next button, you are prompted to assign this interface an IP address. One additional option available on this interface, but not under Ethernet, is *IP Unnumbered*.

IP Unnumbered allows the interface to share an IP address with a LAN interface on the same router. This means that the serial and Ethernet ports could share the same IP address. The benefit here is that it saves on address space. You do not need to create a unique subnet off the serial port. The drawback to IP Unnumbered is that it can make troubleshooting and packet filtering more difficult. If you are short on address space, IP Unnumbered is a valuable tool. If addresses are plentiful, you may be better off assigning the interface its own unique IP address.

Once you've assigned an IP address, click the Next button, and you will be prompted to indicate whether network address translation (NAT) should be used. This screen is shown in Figure 8.11. As you saw in Chapter 3, NAT lets you hide multiple private addresses behind a small number of legal ones. For example, the option selected in 8.11 will translate all outbound traffic so that it appears to originate from this serial interface. As long as this interface has a legal IP address, all of your Ethernet systems can use private addressing and still access resources on the Internet.

 TIP If your firewall performs NAT, you do not need to perform NAT on your router, as well.

FIGURE 8.11

NAT options for this serial interface

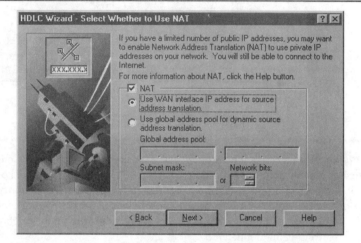

Your other NAT option is to define a pool of legal addresses that internal systems can use when they access the Internet. While certain game and groupware software packages require this method of NAT in order to work, it is less efficient than using the WAN interface for all NAT traffic. Use the WAN interface method unless you are having trouble getting your collaboration software to work. When you have selected any required NAT options, click Next to go on to the final HDLC Wizard screen.

This screen tells you that you have successfully configured the HDLC connection. Click the Finish button to close the HDLC Wizard. When you return to the Network Diagram window, you can see that the Wizard has labeled the serial interface and assigned an IP address. Your drawing should now look similar to the one shown in Figure 8.12.

Notice that your router now appears in blue. The legend at the bottom of the screen explains that this means that you have generated enough information to push the configuration down to the router. With just a few simple clicks, you have created enough information to produce a functional router. Fancy that.

FIGURE 8.12

*Network connections
are now complete.*

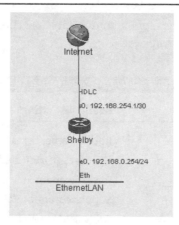

Final Configuration Settings

You can set additional parameters by double-clicking the router object. This produces the router Properties screen shown in Figure 8.13. Notice that in the status window on the right, you are being told that the configuration is ready to be loaded on the router and to do so you should click the Deliver button on the toolbar.

FIGURE 8.13

*Double-click the
router object to pro-
duce the Properties
screen.*

Shelby Properties

General | Connections | Passwords | Protocols | Firewall Configuration | SNMP | IP Services | IOS Configurati

Device
Model: Cisco 2501
Name: Shelby
Location:

Status:
Device is ready for delivery.

Action:
Deliver the configuration to the physical device by selecting this device and then clicking on the Deliver button in the toolbar.

Contact
Contact name:
Telephone #:
Email address:

MOTD Banner...   The Message Of The Day (MOTD) banner appears when you log into the router.

OK   Cancel   Apply   Help

The Properties screen has a number of tabs which allow you to configure additional parameters for the router. Table 8.2 shows these tabs and the options that can be configured under each.

TABLE 8.2: CONFIGURATION OPTIONS UNDER THE PROPERTIES TABS

Tab Name	Available Settings
General	Router name, contact information, logon banner
Connections	IP address, DHCP settings, NAT, Quality of Service
Passwords	Privilege and non-privilege passwords, password encryption
Protocols	Supported protocols
Firewall Configuration	Firewall IOS options
SNMP	SNMP parameters
IP Services	Domain name server, enable HTTP interface
IOS Configuration	Edit the startup-config file
Hardware Configuration	Display interfaces

Limitations of ConfigMaker

Although ConfigMaker feels this configuration is ready for delivery, you have probably noticed some glaring omissions. For example, you haven't selected a routing protocol or even defined a default route. And you were not allowed to set the system date and time, define access lists, or even disable unneeded services such as Finger. Clearly, the puzzle still has a few missing pieces.

Figure 8.14 answers the question, "What about routing?" Note that the system automatically created a default route entry that points to the serial interface. While this may seem a little odd, it is functional. Since you never defined the IP address on the other side of the WAN leading to the Internet, ConfigMaker has defaulted to routing all traffic going to an unknown destination to the serial interface. What is implied here is that the serial interface will forward all traffic to whatever IP address is located on the other end of the WAN link.

FIGURE 8.14

ConfigMaker will
automatically generate
a default route
statement.

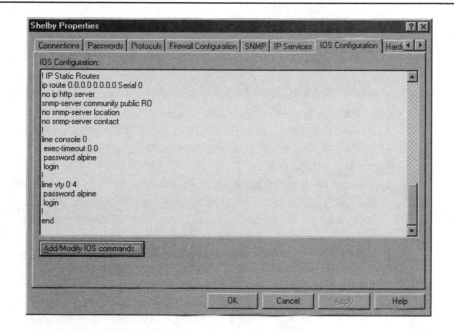

```
Shelby Properties                                                    ? X

Connections | Passwords | Protocols | Firewall Configuration | SNMP | IP Services | IOS Configuration | Hard ◄ ►

IOS Configuration:

! IP Static Routes
ip route 0.0.0.0 0.0.0.0 Serial 0
no ip http server
snmp-server community public RO
no snmp-server location
no snmp-server contact
!
line console 0
 exec-timeout 0 0
 password alpine
 login
!
line vty 0 4
 password alpine
 login
!
end

Add/Modify IOS commands...

                          OK      Cancel    Apply    Help
```

So, ConfigMaker has set a valid default route setting. What about the other parameters you could not set? Unfortunately, ConfigMaker is still a work in progress and is only designed to get an initial configuration up and running. If you need to set additional parameters, you have two choices:

- Enter the commands at the IOS Configuration screen shown in Figure 8.14. The problem here is that you must know the exact syntax of the commands you wish to enter, as there is no online help.

- Deliver this partial configuration, and then use either the command line or the HTML interface to make your remaining changes.

 NOTE You will find that some options cannot even be set from the IOS Configuration screen. For example, even if you know all the commands required to initialize OSPF routing, ConfigMaker will choke on them because it does not yet support OSPF. In this case, you have no option but to use the command line or HTML interface.

While ConfigMaker is a very useful tool, it is not "all that" just yet. The product is evolving quickly, however, so it may be only a few years before you can push out a complete configuration using the ConfigMaker utility. Until then, it still pays to know how to work with a Cisco router from the command line.

Delivering the Configuration

You have configured your router as much as possible using the ConfigMaker utility. It is now time to push out this configuration and load it on your router. To do so, click the router object once within the Network Diagram window, then click the Deliver button on the toolbar.

When you click the Deliver button, the Deliver Configuration Wizard starts automatically. This is shown in Figure 8.15. In the Device List, you will see a list of all the routers you have selected, as well as the method of delivering the configuration. The default delivery method is via a console cable connected to COM1. To change the delivery method, double-click the router's name.

FIGURE 8.15

The Deliver Configuration Wizard

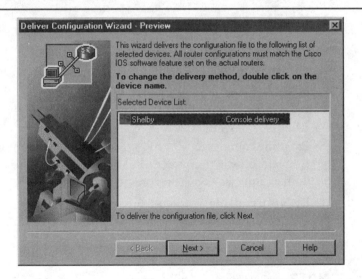

Let's assume you want to deliver this configuration over the network. Double-click the router's name to produce the router Delivery Method dialog box. From here, you can select whether to transmit the configuration via a terminal connection to a local COM port or to deliver the configuration file over the network. Select the Network Delivery radio button, then click OK to return to the list of routers. You should now see that the delivery method in Figure 8.15 has been changed to Network delivery.

The next screen is informational, reminding you which router you are about to configure. This is your last chance to verify that you are configuring the correct router before committing your changes. If the wrong router is displayed, click Cancel and no harm is done. If everything appears to be correct, click Next to continue with the configuration load.

Once you've clicked the Next button, ConfigMaker begins to deliver your new configuration file. This is shown in Figure 8.16. The Status box keeps you informed of ConfigMaker's progress. First, ConfigMaker establishes a connection with the router. Notice that the graphic above the status box is generic. You are actually connected to the router over the network, despite the image's claim that you are using a COM port.

FIGURE 8.16

ConfigMaker delivering the configuration file

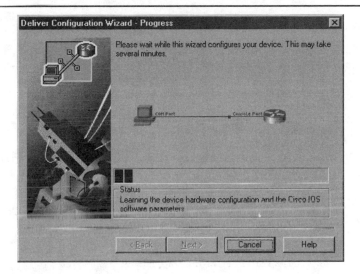

Once a connection is established, ConfigMaker will check the router's current configuration and IOS version to insure that all the options you have selected are supported by your router. For example, if you have selected NAT but the router is running IOS version 10.2, you will receive an error message because NAT was not yet supported in that version. Once the verification is done, the configuration is delivered and the router is rebooted. If all has gone well, you should see a Summary screen similar to the one shown in Figure 8.17. Notice that, in the Result column, ConfigMaker is reporting that the configuration was delivered successfully.

FIGURE 8.17

The Delivery
Configuration Wizard
Summary screen

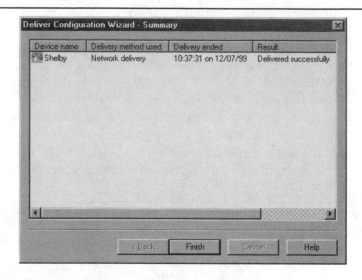

Why Use ConfigMaker?

I'm sure that some seasoned professionals out there are thinking, "The GUI is a pain; I can do this four times faster from the command line." This is absolutely true. Once you are proficient with the router's command line interface, configuration tasks go much faster than when you try to use a GUI. The fact is, however, that ConfigMaker can still work out to be a time saver.

One common task for all network administrators is keeping network diagrams up to date. This is required for troubleshooting, as well as for keeping upper management happy. If you must generate drawings of your network anyway, why not use a tool that can actually push this configuration out to your network devices? Another bonus of ConfigMaker is its ability to store additional information regarding your network devices. For example, in Figure 8.14 you saw that ConfigMaker retains a full copy of the device's startup-config file. This can be very useful information when you are troubleshooting a problem.

Even though using a GUI interface can be a bit slow at times, using ConfigMaker can still save you time in the long run. Just remember that ConfigMaker is still a work in progress and may not be up to the task of handling your environment's particular configuration. The only way to find out for sure is to run the AutoDetect feature and see whether ConfigMaker can parse the configuration on your network devices.

TFTP

The Trivial File Transfer Protocol (TFTP) has long been the mechanism used to transfer IOS image and configuration files to and from a Cisco router. It is a simple, yet efficient protocol that facilitates the transfer of files without requiring password authentication. In this sense, you can consider TFTP a stripped-down version of FTP.

 NOTE The TFTP protocol was discussed in detail in Chapter 3.

While TFTP may seem a bit antiquated compared to the snazzy GUI utilities we've covered so far, it is far from having outlived its usefulness. One of the benefits of TFTP is that you can do everything over the network. You do not need to wire a console session to load an image or create a configuration. Also, TFTP lends itself to being an efficient backup server. By saving your configuration to a TFTP server whenever you make changes, you are assured a quick recovery in case of a failure.

Preparing to Use TFTP

In order to install IOS using TFTP, the router must have a valid IP address. This means that before you load your image, the router must have a minimal configuration. Of course, this presents an interesting catch-22. You can't load the IOS without an IP address, but how do you assign an IP address if IOS has not been loaded yet?

You may recall that the router's ROM stores an emergency image of IOS. When no other IOS image exists, the router will boot using this file. While the IOS version stored in ROM is typically outdated by one or two major revisions, it is sufficient for getting the router into an operational state and providing IP connectivity.

When you first boot the router, it will initialize using this older image file. The router will also be missing a configuration file. When this occurs, the router will launch the setup script as part of the boot process. This is shown in Figure 8.18. Notice that you are being prompted to identify an initial configuration.

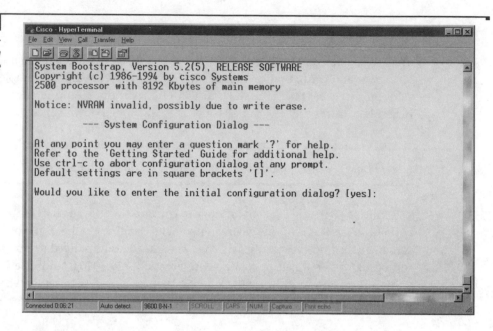

```
System Bootstrap, Version 5.2(5), RELEASE SOFTWARE
Copyright (c) 1986-1994 by cisco Systems
2500 processor with 8192 Kbytes of main memory

Notice: NVRAM invalid, possibly due to write erase.

          --- System Configuration Dialog ---

At any point you may enter a question mark '?' for help.
Refer to the 'Getting Started' Guide for additional help.
Use ctrl-c to abort configuration dialog at any prompt.
Default settings are in square brackets '[]'.

Would you like to enter the initial configuration dialog? [yes]:
```

You have two choices when running the setup script:

- Enter just enough information to connect to your TFTP server, then go back and finish the configuration later.
- Answer all of the setup script prompts and configure the system as much as possible.

The choice really depends on how you plan to configure the router.

If you will be configuring the router manually, you might as well configure it as much as possible now. If, however, you already have a configuration file that you plan to copy over from the TFTP server, it's better to configure just enough information to enable you to communicate with the TFTP server, because you will end up overwriting the configuration, anyway. In either case, answer yes to the prompt that asks whether you want to enter the initial configuration.

The next prompt will ask you if you would like to see a current interface summary. The summary will show you the status of each of the router's interfaces, as well as any assigned addressing. Since this is a new configuration, most of this information will be missing. Figure 8.19 shows the summary for a newly booted 2501 router. Notice that both serial interfaces are currently down. The Ethernet interface is active (it is physically plugged in), but it does not yet have an IP address assigned.

FIGURE 8.19

*The setup script show-
ing an interface sum-
mary status*

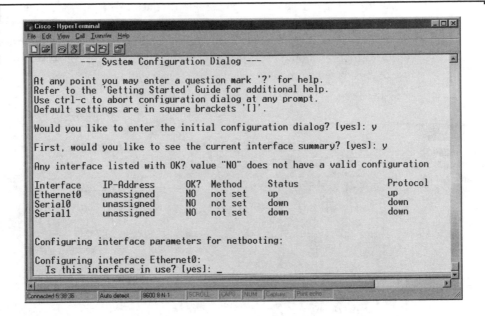

You are now ready to start configuring your router. Notice the prompt at the bottom of Figure 8.19 that asks whether you will be using the Ethernet interface. If you answer yes, you will then be asked whether you will be using IP. If you answer yes again, you are asked to assign this interface an IP address and subnet mask value.

NOTE If you are running the Desktop or Enterprise feature set and have loaded IOS before running the setup script, you will also be prompted to configure IPX and AT on each interface.

Once you have assigned an IP address to the Ethernet interface, you will receive the same set of prompts for any remaining interfaces on the router. For example, in the case of the 2501 router, you would also be asked whether you want to configure Serial0 and Serial1. Again, what to configure depends on your situation:

- If you will be configuring the router via TFTP, simply answer no to each of these prompts.
- If you will be configuring the device manually, you can take this opportunity to assign each interface an IP address.

After you have configured each of your interfaces, you will see the newly created configuration file. This is shown in Figure 8.20. Notice that only a minimal configuration has been created. As long as your TFTP server is located on the local Ethernet segment, this information should be sufficient to load your IOS image. You can now answer yes (to use the displayed configuration) or no (to go back and make changes). If you say yes, the configuration is saved as the startup-config file and the router is rebooted.

FIGURE 8.20

The basic configuration created with the setup script

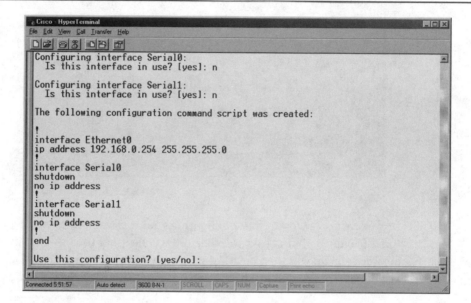

Loading the IOS Image

Once the router comes back up, it will be configured using the parameters you entered into the setup script. Note that you can enter privilege mode by typing **enable**, but you are not prompted for a password. This is because you have not yet assigned a privilege-level password to the system. Also note that the command prompt appears as follows:

```
Router(boot)#
```

The boot keyword indicates that you are still booting the router from the IOS stored in ROM.

TIP If the IOS version stored in ROM is 10.2 or earlier, you may need to use the command `write term` instead of `show running` to view the current running configuration.

The first things you should check are that your TFTP server is up and running and that the TFTP server directory has a valid image you can load onto your router.

 TIP If you do not have a TFTP server, check the IOS CD. Cisco includes its own TFTP server as part of the IOS distribution.

If you are connected to the router console, see whether any of the following messages appears every few minutes:

```
Loading network-confg … [timed out]
Loading router-confg … [timed out]
%Error opening TFTP://255.255.255.255/network-config
%Error opening TFTP://255.255.255.255/router-config
```

These messages indicate that the router is attempting to automatically retrieve a configuration from a local TFTP server. While the messages are not a problem, they can be annoying. To stop them from occurring, enter global configuration mode and enter this command:

```
no service config
```

Your next check should be to make sure that the router has connectivity to the TFTP server. You can do this by pinging from the router. If you receive a 100-percent success rate, you are ready to load the IOS image.

To retrieve a copy of the IOS, use a simple copy command. The syntax is

```
copy <source> <destination>
```

Since your IOS image is located on the TFTP server, use this as the source. Because the IOS image gets stored in flash memory, use flash as the destination. Including the command line, your copy command should look like this:

```
Router(boot)#copy tftp flash
```

When you execute this command, you are prompted for the IP address of the TFTP server. Next, you must identify the name of the file you want to retrieve. You also have the option to rename the file when it is saved to flash.

After a final confirmation, the file transfer is initialized. The entire session looks something like this:

```
Router(boot)>en
Router(boot)#copy tftp flash
System flash directory:
No files in System flash
[0 bytes used, 8388608 available, 8388608 total]
Address of remote host [255.255.255.255]?192.168.0.28
Source file name? c2500-ip-fw.bin
Destination file name [c2500-ip-fw.bin]?
Accessing file 'c2500-ip-fw.bin' on 192.168.0.28...
Loading c2500-ip-fw.bin from 192.168.0.28 (via Ethernet0): ! [OK]

Device needs erasure before copying new file
Erase flash device before writing? [confirm]y

Copy 'c2500-ip-fw.bin' from server
 as 'c2500-ip-fw.bin' into Flash WITH erase? [yes/no]y
Erasing device... eeeeeeeeeeeeeeeeeeeeeeeeeeeeeeeee erased
Loading c2500-ip-fw.bin from 192.168.0.28 (via Ethernet0):
!!!!!!!!!!!!!!!!!!!!!!!!!!!!!!!!!!!!!!!!!!!!!!!!!!!!!!!!!!!
!!!!!!!!!!!!!!!!!!!!!!!!!!!!!!!!!!!!!!!!!!!!!!!!!!!!!!!!!!!
[OK - 6231928/8388608 bytes]

Verifying checksum........ OK (0x8001)
Flash copy took 0:03:32 [hh:mm:ss]
Router(boot)#
```

If the checksum has verified properly, your image file has been properly loaded. You can now reboot the router using the reload command. When the router initializes, it will use this new image file. You can verify that you are running off this new image by entering this command:

```
show version
```

Configuring with TFTP

In the same way that you used TFTP to load your IOS image, you can also use TFTP to load a router configuration. Remember that the configuration file is just a text file. This means that you are free to load commands by placing them in a text file and using TFTP to transfer them to the router. The output below is a sample of a router's configuration file:

```
!
version 12.0
service timestamps debug uptime
service timestamps log uptime
no service password-encryption
!
hostname shelby
!
no logging console
enable secret 5 $1$NFrn$4m6BGqPue2ScpJaoR2npU0
enable password alpine
!
ip subnet-zero
ip host gwen 192.168.0.28
ip domain-name fubar.com
ip name-server 192.168.0.1
!
!
!
interface Ethernet0
 ip address 192.168.0.254 255.255.255.0
 no ip directed-broadcast
 no ip route-cache
 no ip mroute-cache
!
interface Serial0
 ip address 192.168.10.9 255.255.255.252
 no ip directed-broadcast
 encapsulation frame-relay
 no ip route-cache
 no ip mroute-cache
 frame-relay interface-dlci 132
!
interface Serial1
 ip address 192.168.10.1 255.255.255.252
 no ip directed-broadcast
```

```
  encapsulation ppp
  no ip route-cache
  no ip mroute-cache
 !
ip default-gateway 192.168.0.1
ip classless
ip route 172.16.0.0 255.240.0.0 192.168.10.2
ip route 192.168.20.0 255.255.254.0 192.168.10.10
 !
 !
line con 0
 exec-timeout 0 0
 transport input none
line aux 0
line vty 0 4
 password alpine
 login
 !
end
```

As you can see, except for the encrypted password information, this file would be pretty easy to generate. If you manage multiple routers, you could even create a template file and customize it whenever you need to bring a new router online. By using the template file, you are assured that all of your routers are running a consistent configuration.

To configure the router using the previous file, enter this command:

```
Router#copy tftp running
```

You will then be prompted for the IP address or host name of the TFTP server, as well as the name of the file you want to transfer. The file is then transferred to NVRAM and loaded as the running configuration. If you want to make sure that this configuration is used whenever the router is booted, enter the following command:

```
Shelby#copy running startup
```

This will overwrite the startup configuration file and insure that your settings remain in place the next time you reboot the router.

Even if you do not wish to load your entire configuration via TFTP, you may find it easier to load portions of your configuration this way. For example, you could use your favorite text editor to create multiple static-route or access-list entries. By using an editor you are familiar with, you should find that the task goes a whole lot faster. You can then use TFTP to transfer just these commands. When you enter the command

```
Router#copy tftp running
```

your Cisco router reads in the additional commands and adds them to the current configuration. In other words, the only change would be your route or access-list entries. If you don't specify interface commands, these parameters are not changed.

Summary

In this chapter, we examined the methods available for loading IOS onto a router and generating an initial configuration, covering the Router Software Loader, Config-Maker, and TFTP. We also discussed when it is better to use one tool rather than another.

In the next chapter, we will look at access lists and how to use them. Access lists are a great way to selectively control which packets you allow across your router.

CHAPTER <u>9</u>

Access Lists

isco *access lists* are used to selectively pass or block traffic received by a Cisco router. They are a useful way to control traffic attempting to pass your network perimeter. Since a router is typically used to segregate or partition network segments, anyway (for example, to separate your network from a business partner or the Internet), routers are a natural fit for implementing some form of perimeter security.

Available Options

Cisco routers provide a couple of methods for filtering traffic. The simplest is the *standard access list*, which lets you filter all traffic from a specific address or subnet range. Use *extended access lists* for advanced filtering. Extended access lists allow you to filter on source address, destination address, or service. You can even choose between static or dynamic packet filtering.

Once you've created an access list, it is applied to a specific interface on the router. The access list is told to screen either inbound network traffic (traffic coming from the attached network to the interface) or outbound network traffic (traffic leaving the router and headed towards the attached network). This ability to filter either "in" or "out" traffic can be a real time saver in complex configurations.

Cisco access lists perform static packet filtering by default. As just mentioned, you have the additional option of performing dynamic packet filtering. Before we discuss the actual implementation of access lists, let's explore the theory behind static and dynamic filtering.

Static Packet Filtering

Static packet filtering controls traffic by using information stored within the packet headers. As the filtering device receives packets, the device compares the attributes of the data stored within the packet headers against the access control list (ACL). Depending on how this header information compares to the ACL, the traffic is either allowed to pass or dropped.

In general, a static packet filter can use the following information when regulating traffic flow:

- Destination IP address or subnet
- Source IP address or subnet
- Destination service port
- Source service port
- Flags (TCP only)

The TCP Flag Field

When the TCP transport is used, static packet filtering can use the Flag field in the TCP header when making traffic control decisions. Figure 9.1 shows a packet decode of a TCP/IP packet. The Control Bits field identifies which flags have been set. Flags can be either turned on (binary value of 1) or turned off (binary value of 0).

FIGURE 9.1

A TCP/IP packet decode

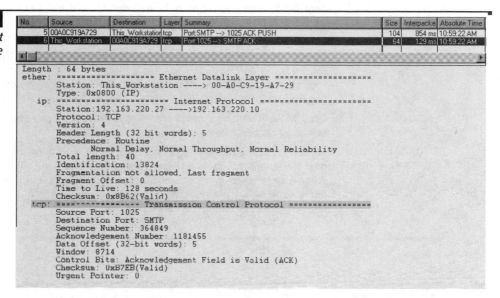

What does the Flag field tell us? You may remember from our discussion of the TCP three-packet handshake that different flag values identify different aspects of a communication session. The Flag field gives the recipient hosts some additional information regarding the data the packet is carrying. Table 9.1 lists the valid flags and their uses.

TABLE 9.1: VALID TCP/IP FLAGS

TCP Flag	Flag Description
ACK	Indicates that this data is a response to a data request and that there is useful information within the acknowledgment number field.
FIN	Indicates that the transmitting system wishes to terminate the current session. Typically, each system in a communication session issues a FIN before the connection is actually considered closed.

Continued

TCP Flag	Flag Description
TABLE 9.1: VALID TCP/IP FLAGS (CONTINUED)	
PSH	Used to prevent the transmitting system from queuing data before transmission. In many cases, it is more efficient to let a transmitting system queue small chunks of data before transmission so that fewer packets are created. On the receiving side, the push flag tells the remote system not to queue the data, but to immediately push the information to the upper protocol levels.
RST	Resets the state of a current communication session. Reset is used when a non-recoverable transmission failure occurs. It's a transmitting system's way of saying, "Were you listening to me? Do I have to say it again?" This is typically caused by a non-responsive host (or a spouse enthralled by an afternoon sporting event). When an RST is issued, the communication session must begin again from scratch.
SYN	Used while initializing a communication session. It should not be set during any other portion of the communication process.
URG	Indicates that the transmitting system has some high-priority information to pass along and that there is useful information within the Urgent Pointer field. When a system receives a packet with the urgent flag set, it processes the information before any other data that may be waiting in queue. This is referred to as processing the data *out-of-band*.

NOTE The Flag field plays an important part in helping a static packet filter regulate traffic. This is because a firewall is rarely told to block all traffic originating from a specific port or going to a particular host.

Using Flags to Filter Connection Requests

Consider this example: You have an access control policy that states, "Our internal users can access any service on the Internet, but all Internet traffic headed to the internal network should be blocked." While this sounds like the ACL should be blocking all traffic coming from the Internet, this, in fact, is not the case.

Remember that all communications involve a two-step process:

1. When you access a Web site, you make a data request.

2. The Web site replies by returning the data you requested.

During step 2, you are expecting data to be returned from the Internet-based host to the internal system. If the second half of your access control policy were taken verbatim (all Internet traffic headed to the internal network should be blocked), your replies would never make it back to the requesting host. This represents the "wire cutters as an effective security device" model, because your firewall would not allow a complete communication session.

This is where the Flag field comes into play. As you've seen, during the TCP three-packet handshake the originating system issues a packet with SYN=1 and all other flags equal to 0. The only time this sequence should be true is when one system wishes to establish a connection to another. A packet filter will use this unique flag setting to control TCP sessions. By blocking the initial connection request, a data session between the two systems cannot be established.

If you were to rewrite this access control policy to be more technically correct, you would state, "All Internet traffic headed to the internal network with SYN=1 and all other flags equal to 0 should be blocked." This means that any other flag sequence is assumed to be part of a previously established connection and allowed to pass through.

Playing with the Flags

As you can imagine, assuming that any packet without SYN=1 is part of a previously established session is not the most secure method of locking down your network perimeter. By playing with the flag values, a would-be attacker can fool a static packet filter into allowing malicious traffic through. This allows these predators to stay one step ahead of these security devices.

For example, there are software programs called *port scanners* that can probe a destination host to see whether any service ports are open. Port scanners do this by sending a connection request (SYN=1) to all the service ports within a specified range. If any of these connection requests causes the destination host to return a connection request acknowledgment (SYN=1, ACK=1), the software knows that there is a service monitoring that port.

Because a simple packet filter is capable of blocking this kind of scan, some people decided to become creative. The simple port scanner eventually evolved into the *FIN scanner*. A FIN scanner operates under a similar principle to the port scanner, except that the transmitted packets have FIN=1, ACK=1 and all other flags set to 0.

Continued

CONTINUED

Now, since your packet filter is only looking to block packets with SYN=1 and all other flags set to 0, these packets are happily passed along. The result is that an attacker can analyze the returning data stream to determine which hosts are offering which services. This means that our static packet filter cannot deter these scanning probes.

Packet Filtering UDP Traffic

As if TCP traffic were not hard enough to control, UDP traffic is actually worse. This is because UDP provides even less information regarding a connection's state than TCP does. Figure 9.2 is a packet decode of a UDP header.

FIGURE 9.2

A UDP header decode

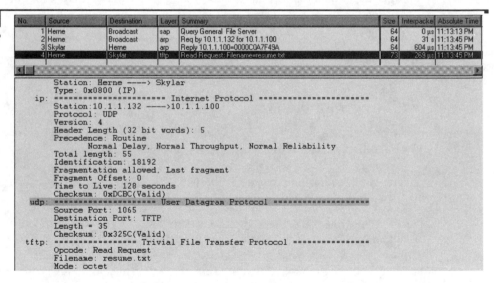

Notice that the UDP header does not use flags to indicate a session's state. This means that there is no way to determine whether a packet is a data request or a reply to a previous request. The only information that can be used to regulate traffic is the source and destination port number. Even this information is of little use in many situations, because some services use the same source and destination port number.

For example, when two Domain Name Servers (DNS) are exchanging information, they use a source and destination port number of 53. They do not use a reply port of greater than 1023, like many other services. This means that a static packet filter has no effective way to limit DNS traffic to only a single direction. You cannot block inbound traffic to port 53, because that would block data replies as well as data requests.

This is why the only effective means of controlling UDP traffic with a static packet filter is to block everything—or let it through and hope for the best. Needless to say, most people tend to stick with the former solution unless they have an extremely pressing need to allow through UDP traffic (such as running networked Quake games, which use UDP port 26000).

Packet Filtering ICMP

The *Internet Control Message Protocol* (ICMP) provides background support for the IP protocol. It is not used to transmit user data; rather, ICMP is used for maintenance duty to insure that all is running smoothly. For example, Ping uses ICMP to insure that there is connectivity between two hosts. Figure 9.3 is a packet decode of an ICMP header.

No.	Source	Destination	Layer	Summary	Size	Interpacket	Absolute Time
7	Herne	Skylar	tftp	Read Request; Filename=resume.txt	73	288 µs	12:07:45 AM
8	Skylar	Herne	icmp	Type=Destination Unreachable	74	2 ms	12:07:45 AM

```
ip:  ===================== Internet Protocol =====================
     Station:10.1.1.100 ---->10.1.1.132
     Protocol: ICMP
     Version: 4
     Header Length (32 bit words): 5
     Precedence: Routine
               Normal Delay, Normal Throughput, Normal Reliability
     Total length: 56
     Identification: 60026
     Fragmentation allowed, Last fragment
     Fragment Offset: 0
     Time to Live: 128 seconds
     Checksum: 0x3641(Valid)
icmp:  ================ Internet Control Message Protocol ================
     Type: Destination Unreachable
     Checksum: 0xC60F(Valid)
     Code: Protocol Unreachable
               Host Unreachable
ORIGINAL IP PACKET HEADER
     ip:  ===================== Internet Protocol =====================
     Station:10.1.1.132 ---->10.1.1.100
     Protocol: UDP
     Version: 4
     Header Length (32 bit words): 5
     Precedence: Routine
               Normal Delay, Normal Throughput, Normal Reliability
     Total length: 55
     Identification: 50202
     Fragmentation allowed, Last fragment
     Fragment Offset: 0
```

NOTE ICMP does not use service ports. There is a Type field to identify the ICMP packet type and a Code field to provide even more granular information about the current session.

The Code field can be a bit confusing. For example, in Figure 9.3 the code states, "Protocol Unreachable; Host Unreachable." This might lead you to think that the destination system is not responding. If you compare the source IP address for this ICMP packet to the destination IP address in the section after Original IP Packet Header, you will note that they are the same (10.1.1.100). If the destination is in fact "unreachable," how could it have possibly sent this reply?

The combination of these two codes actually means that the requested service was not available. If you look at the top of Figure 9.3, you will see that the transmission that prompted this reply was a Trivial File Transfer Protocol (TFTP) request for resume.txt. Only a destination host will generate a "protocol unreachable" error.

 NOTE Remember that UDP does not use a Flag field. This makes UDP incapable of letting the transmitting system know that a service is not available. To rectify this problem, ICMP is used to notify the transmitting system.

Table 9.2 identifies the different types of ICMP packets.

TABLE 9.2: ICMP TYPE FIELD VALUES

Type	Name	Description
0	Echo Reply	Is a response to an echo request.
3	Destination Unreachable	Indicates that the destination subnet, host, or service cannot be reached.
4	Source Quench	Indicates that the transmitting system or a routing device along the route is having trouble keeping up with the inbound data flow. Hosts that receive a source quench are required to reduce their transmission rate. This is to insure that the transmitting system will not begin to discard data due to an overload inbound queue.

Continued ▶

TABLE 9.2: ICMP TYPE FIELD VALUES (CONTINUED)		
Type	Name	Description
5	Redirect	Informs a local host that there is another router or gateway device that is better able to forward the data the host is transmitting. A redirect is sent by local routers.
8	Echo	Requests that the target system return an echo reply. Echo is used to verify end-to-end connectivity and measure response time.
9	Router Advertisement	Used by routers to identify themselves on a subnet. This is not a true routing protocol because no route information is conveyed. It is simply used to let hosts on the subnet know the IP addresses of their local routers.
10	Router Selection	Allows a host to query for router advertisements without having to wait for the next periodic update. Also referred to as a *router solicitation*.
11	Time Exceeded	Informs the transmitting systems that the time to live (TTL) value within the packet header has expired and the information never reached its intended host.
12	Parameter Problem	Is a catchall response returned to a transmitting systems when a problem occurs that is not identified by one of the other ICMP types.
13	Timestamp	Used when you are looking to quantify link speed more than system responsiveness. Timestamp is similar to an echo request, except that a quick reply to a timestamp request is considered more critical.
14	Timestamp Reply	Is a response to a timestamp request.
15	Information Request	Has been superseded by the use of bootp and DHCP. This request was originally used by self-configuring systems in order to discover their IP address.
16	Information Reply	Is a response to an information request.
17	Address Mask Request	Allows a system to dynamically query the local subnet about the proper subnet mask to be used. If no response is received, a host should assume a subnet mask appropriate to its address class.
18	Address Mask Reply	Is a response to an address mask request.
30	Traceroute	Provides a more efficient means of tracing a route from one IP host to another than using the legacy traceroute command. This option can only be used when all intermediary routers have been programmed to recognize this ICMP type. Implementation is via a switch setting using Ping.

Table 9.3 identifies valid codes that may be used when the ICMP type is Destination Unreachable (Type=3).

Code	Name	Description
TABLE 9.3: ICMP TYPE 3 CODE FIELD VALUES		
0	Net Unreachable	The destination network cannot be reached due to a routing error (such as no route information) or an insufficient TTL value.
1	Host Unreachable	The destination host cannot be reached due to a routing error (such as no route information) or an insufficient TTL value.
2	Protocol Unreachable	The destination host you contacted does not offer the service you requested. This code is typically returned from a host, while all others are returned from routers along the path.
4	Fragmentation Needed and Don't Fragment was Set	The data you are attempting to deliver needs to cross a network that uses a smaller packet size, but the `don't fragment` bit is set.
5	Source Route Failed	The transmitted packet specified the route that should be followed to the destination host, but the routing information was incorrect.

Table 9.4 identifies valid codes that may be used when the ICMP type is redirect (Type=5).

Code	Name	Description
TABLE 9.4: ICMP TYPE 5 CODE FIELD VALUES		
0	Redirect Datagram for the Network (or Subnet)	Indicates that another router on the local subnet has a better route to the destination network or subnet. If source routing is used, these updates are not sent.
1	Redirect Datagram for the Host	Indicates that another router on the local subnet has a better route to the destination host. If source routing is used, these updates are not sent.

By filtering on the values of the Type and Code fields, you gain a bit more granular control than by simply looking at source and destination IP address. Not all packet filters are capable of filtering on all types and codes. For example, many will filter out Type=3, which is Destination Unreachable, without regard to the code value. This limitation can cause some serious communication problems. Cisco routers, on the other hand, allow you to filter on both type and code information.

Static Packet Filtering Summary

Static packet filters are non-intelligent filtering devices. These filters offer only nominal protection against advanced attacks. They look at a minimal amount of information in order to determine which traffic should be allowed to pass and which traffic should be blocked.

If static packet filtering is so poor, why bother to use it? Although it does have its limitations, static packet filtering can be used to enhance the security posture of an existing security device (such as a firewall) or to implement security when the risk of exposure is minimal.

For example, maybe your firewall is providing the bulk of your perimeter security, but what if the software code contains a bug that would allow an attacker to punch through it? If you are relying on your firewall alone, the attacker may be able to wreak havoc on your network. If your security posture has been augmented by static packet filtering on your border router, you might be able to foil the attacker's attempt.

Static filtering should not be considered the last word in perimeter security. Used correctly, however, it can be a very effective security tool.

Dynamic Packet Filtering

Dynamic packet filtering takes static packet filtering one step further, in that it maintains a connection table in order to monitor the state of a communication session. It does not simply rely on the flag settings. This is a powerful feature which can be used to better control traffic flow.

For example, let's assume that an attacker sends a system a packet of data which has a payload designed to crash the system. The attacker may perform some packet trickery in order to make this packet look like a reply to information requested by the internal system. A regular packet filter would analyze this packet, see that the ACK bit is set, and be fooled into thinking that this was a reply to a data request. It would then happily pass the information along to the internal system.

A dynamic packet filter would not be so easily fooled, however. When the dynamic packet filter received the information, it would refer to its connection table (sometimes called a *state table*). When reviewing the table entries, the filter would realize that the internal system had never actually connected to this external system in order to place a data request. Since this information had not been explicitly requested, the dynamic packet filter would throw the packet into the bit bucket.

Dynamic Packet Filtering in Action

Let's take a look at how dynamic packet filtering works in order to get a better idea of the increased security it can provide. In Figure 9.4, you can see two separate network configurations: one in which the internal host is protected by a static packet filter and the other in which a dynamic packet filter is used.

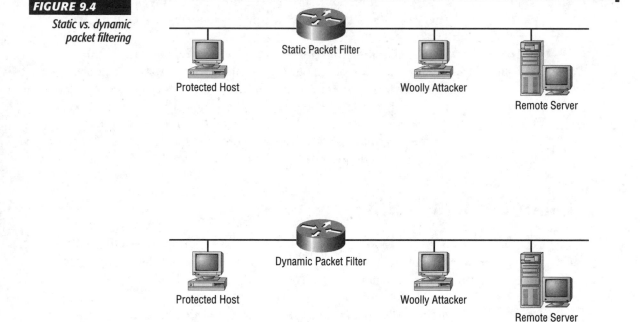

FIGURE 9.4

Static vs. dynamic packet filtering

Now, let's look at some access rules to see how each of these two filtering devices would handle traffic control. The ACL on both firewalls might look something like this:

- Allow the protected host to establish any service sessions with the remote server.
- Allow any session that has already been established to pass.
- Drop all other traffic.

The first rule allows the protected host to establish connections to the remote server. This means that the only time a packet with the SYN bit set is allowed to pass is if the source address is from the protected host and the destination is the remote server. When this is true, any service on the remote server may be accessed.

The second rule is a catchall. Basically, it says, "If the traffic appears to be part of a previously established connection, let it pass." In other words, all traffic is OK, provided that the SYN bit is not set and all other bits are off.

The final rule states that any traffic not fitting neatly into one of the first two rules should be dropped, just to be safe.

So both filtering devices are using the same ACL. The difference is in the amount of information each has available in order to control traffic. Let's transmit some traffic to see what happens.

In Figure 9.5, our internal system tries to set up a communication session with the remote server. Since all passing traffic passes the criteria set up in the access control lists, both filters allow this traffic to pass.

FIGURE 9.5

Connection establishment from the protected host

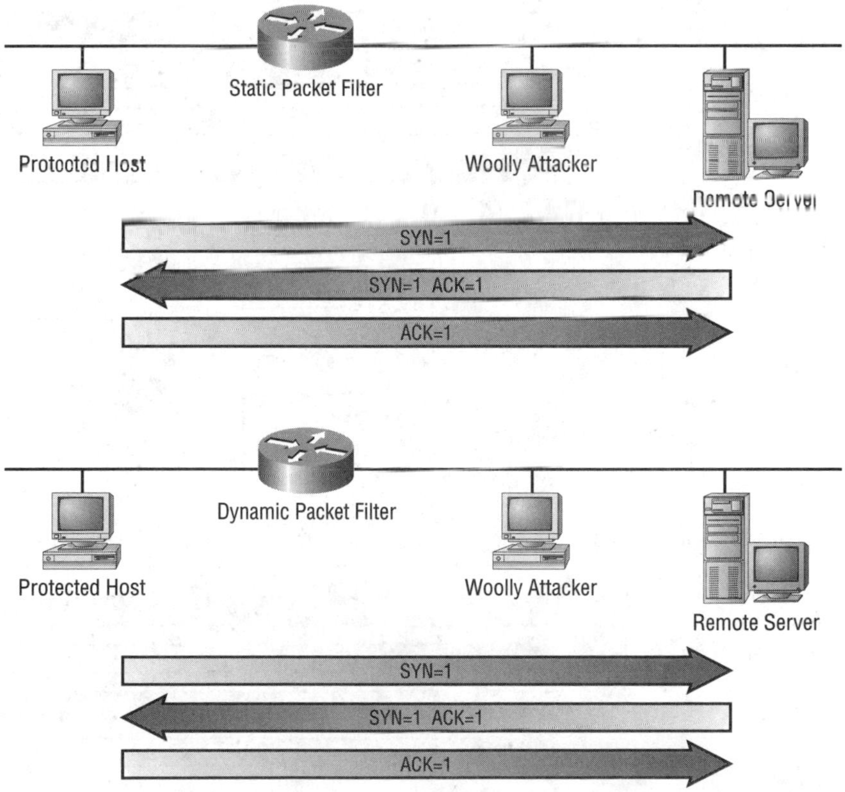

Once the handshake is complete, our protected host makes a data request. This packet will have the ACK bit set and also possibly the PSH bit. When the remote server receives this request, it will also respond with the ACK bit set and possibly the PSH bit. Once the data transfer is complete, the session is closed by having each system transmit a packet with the FIN bit set.

Figure 9.6 shows this established session passing data. Note that there are no problems passing the firewall devices because of the second rule, which states, "Allow any session that has already been established to pass." Each firewall is making this determination in a slightly different way, however.

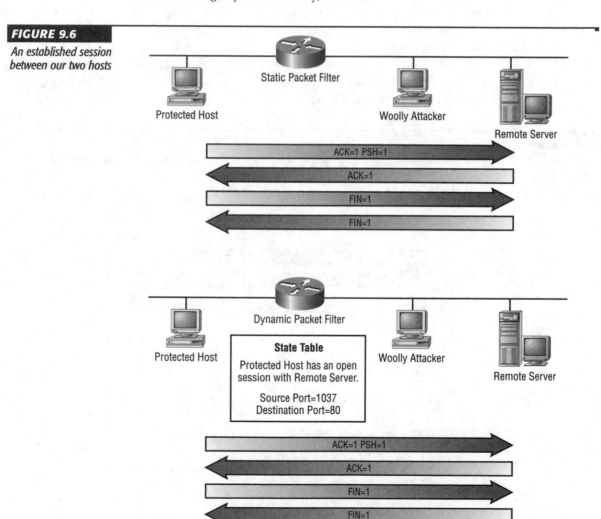

FIGURE 9.6

An established session between our two hosts

The static packet filter is simply looking at the Flag field to see whether the SYN bit is the only bit set. Since this is not true, the static packet filter assumes that this data is part of an established session and lets it pass through.

The dynamic packet filter is doing the same check, but it also created a state table when the connection was first established. Every time the remote server tries to respond to the protected host, the state table is referenced to insure the following:

- The protected host actually made a data request.

- The source port information is correct.

- The destination port information is correct.

Since all this data is correct, as well, the dynamic packet filter also allows the packets to pass. After each system has sent the FIN packet, the state table entry will be removed. Additionally, if no reply is received for a period of time (anywhere from one minute to one hour, depending on the configuration), the dynamic packet filter will assume that the remote server is no longer responding and will again delete the state table entry. This insures that the state table remains current.

Static vs. Dynamic Filtering

Now let's say that Woolly Attacker notices this data stream and decides to try to attack the protected host. The first thing he tries is a port scan on the protected system to see if it has any listening services. As shown in Figure 9.7, this scan is blocked by both firewall devices as the initial scanning packets have the SYN bit set and all other bits turned off.

Not to be put off, Woolly attempts to perform a FIN scan by transmitting packets with the ACK and FIN bits set to 1. Now, the results are a bit different, as you can see in Figure 9.8. Since the static packet filter is simply watching out for the SYN bit to be set to 1, it happily passes this traffic along because this condition has not been met.

The dynamic packet filter is a bit fussier, however. It recognizes that the SYN bit is not set, then compares this traffic to its state table. At this point, the filter realizes that the protected host has never set up a communication session with Woolly Attacker. There is no legitimate reason for Woolly Attacker to try to end a session if the protected host never created one in the first place. For this reason, the traffic would be blocked.

FIGURE 9.7

Each filtering method can block a port scan.

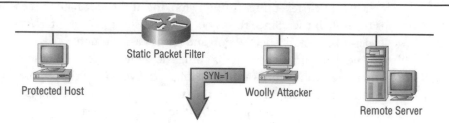

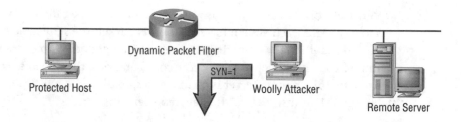

FIGURE 9.8

The effects of performing a FIN scan

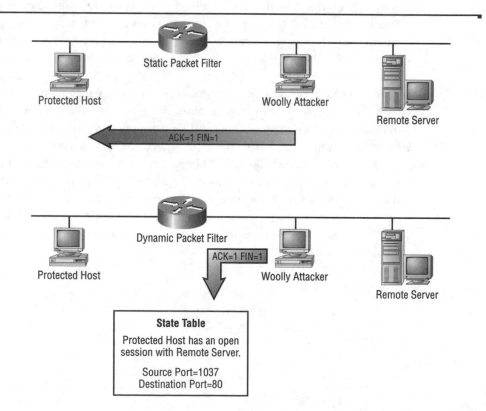

Dynamic Packet Filter Summary

Dynamic packet filters are intelligent devices that make traffic-control decisions based on packet attributes and state tables. State tables allow the router to "remember" previous communication packet exchanges and make judgments based on this additional information.

Access List Basics

Now that you've seen the differences between static and dynamic packet filtering, let's look at how each of these filtering methods is implemented on a Cisco router. All filtering on a Cisco router is deployed using access lists. While many people find access lists confusing, they are actually quite easy to deploy once you understand the basics.

Working with Access Lists

Access lists are generated by creating a number of test conditions that become associated with a list identifier number. You create access lists while in global configuration mode, using the following syntax:

```
access-list {list #} permit/deny {test condition}
```

Repeat this command for every test condition you wish to use in order to screen traffic (such as allow SMTP, deny HTTP, and so on). The list number you use identifies the protocol to which you want to apply these rules. Table 9.5 shows some of the protocols that can be filtered, along with the list numbers associated with them.

TABLE 9.5: CISCO ACCESS LIST NUMBERING

Protocol	List Type	Range/Identifier
IP	Standard	1–99
IP	Extended	100–199
Ethernet Type codes	N/A	200–299
AppleTalk	N/A	600–699
Ethernet Addresses	N/A	700–799
IPX	Standard	800–899
IPX	Extended	1000–1099

NOTE Only one type of filtering is supported for certain protocols. As of Cisco IOS 11.2 and higher, the range identifiers used by IP can be replaced by an alphanumeric name. This name can be up to 64 characters long but must start with an alphabetic character. The name must be unique and each name can only describe a single set of standard or extended filters. You cannot combine the two.

The syntax for creating an access list name is

```
IP access-list standard/extended {name}
```

Using names instead of access list numbers can be extremely beneficial. Doing so extends the number of unique lists that you can create and allows you to associate a descriptive name with a particular set of filters (such as "spoofing"). Also, reflexive filters (used for dynamic packet filtering) can only be associated with an access list name. You cannot use an access list identifier number.

Processing Access Lists

Access lists will be processed in the order you create them: If you create five filter conditions and place them in the same access list, the router will evaluate each condition in the order you created it until it finds the first match.

NOTE Conditions are processed as "first fit," not "best fit," so it is important to pay close attention to the order you use.

For example, let's say you have an access list that states the following:

• Allow all internal systems full IP access to the Internet.

• Do not let any internal systems telnet to hosts on the Internet.

Since the first rule states that all outbound traffic is OK, you would never actually make it to the second rule. This means that your internal users would still be able to use Telnet.

TIP When an access list is applied to an interface, it includes a hidden, implicit Deny command as the last rule. This means that the router adds a final command which states, "Any traffic that was not explicitly permitted by an earlier filter should be dropped." This insures that you do not accidentally permit traffic to pass through your router that you did not intend to let through. For example, if your access list states, "Traffic from the subnet 192.168.1.0 is OK to let through," the router will assume that it should block traffic from all subnets except 192.168.1.0.

Adding and Removing Access Lists

Once you have created an access list that you wish to apply to your router, enter configuration mode for a specific interface and enter the command

```
{protocol} access-group {list # or name} in/out
```

To remove an access list from an interface (always a good thing to know how to do if you are testing a new filter), simply precede the command with the word "no" as follows:

```
no {protocol} access-group {list # or name} in/out
```

Likewise, to delete an entire access list, enter this command:

```
no access-list {list # or name}
```

Keep in mind that this will delete all filter conditions associated with a particular access list number or name. One of the biggest drawbacks to access lists is that you cannot edit entries. This can make their data entry a bit tedious. For example, if you have created 15 access list entries and realize that you actually want entry 11 processed after entry 13, you must delete the entire list and recreate it from scratch.

 TIP Create your access lists offline in a text editor. Once you have the filters in the correct order, simply copy the rules to the Windows Clipboard and use the Paste ability of your terminal emulator. This also allows you to keep a local backup of all your filter conditions.

Standard Access Lists

Standard access lists allow you to filter on source IP address. This is useful when you wish to block all traffic from a specific subnet or host. Standard access lists do not look at the destination IP address or even at the service; these access lists base their filtering determination solely on the source address of the transmitting system.

While this sounds a bit limiting, it can actually be quite useful. Examine Figure 9.9, which shows a very simple network design. There is only one way in and out of this network: through the router. The internal network segment uses an IP subnet address of 206.121.73.0.

FIGURE 9.9

Using standard access lists

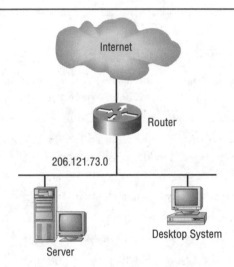

In this environment, it should be true that the router never sees any traffic originating from the Internet that appears to have originated from the IP subnet 206.121.73.0. This is because that segment is directly connected to the Ethernet port of the router. While the router will see traffic originating from this subnet on its Ethernet port, the router should never be detected off the serial (WAN) port.

IP Spoofing and Spoofing Filters

IP spoofing is a process in which an attacker pretends to be a system on your local network transmitting information, even though the attacker is off at some remote location. IP spoofing can be used effectively to exploit certain system vulnerabilities. For example, Microsoft Windows used to be vulnerable to a kind of attack known as *Land*. A Land attack packet has the following attributes:

- Source IP: The IP address of the system under attack
- Destination IP: The IP address of the system under attack
- Transport: TCP

- Source port: 135

- Destination port: 135

- Flag setting: SYN=1

Other ports and settings can be used, but this should give you the general idea. The attack fools the system into thinking that it is talking to itself. This will produce a race condition which will cause the system to eventually hang or lock up.

You may be thinking, "No problem, I plan to block all inbound connection requests. This packet would never get through because the SYN flag is set high." Not true, Grasshopper; look at the source address. When the router evaluates this packet, it might very well think that this packet originated from the internal network.

While later versions of Cisco IOS do not have this problem (they maintain the association of the packet with the interface on which it was received), many earlier versions of IOS do. If your access rules state, "Port 135 from the internal network is OK to let through," the router will approve the packet of data and pass the information along to the routing process, which would in turn pass the traffic along to the Ethernet segment.

How can you solve this problem? Since you will never see legitimate traffic originating from the Internet which uses your internal subnet address, there will be no loss in connectivity if you filter out this traffic in case it is received. Such *spoofing filters* insure that no traffic trying to spoof your internal address is allowed to pass.

It is also a good idea to place an inbound filter on the Ethernet port which states, "Only accept traffic from the 206.121.73.0 subnet." This is called *egress filtering*, and it helps to insure that none of your internal users attempt a spoofing attack on some other network. As administrator, it is your job to not only protect your own environment, but to make sure you do not inadvertently make someone else's life miserable, as well.

You can create these spoofing filters using standard access lists. The syntax for a standard access list entry is

```
access-list {list # or name} permit/deny {source} {mask}
```

So you could create the following access list entries in global configuration mode on the router in Figure 9.9.

```
access-list 1 deny 206.121.73.0 0.0.0.255
access-list 2 permit 206.121.73.0 0.0.0.255
```

Access list 1 would be applied by entering configuration mode for the WAN interface and entering the command

```
ip access-group 1 in
```

Likewise, access list 2 would be applied by entering configuration mode for the Ethernet interface and entering the command

```
ip access-group 2 in
```

Pattern Matching

You may notice that the mask value looks a little strange. This is because this value is a pattern match, not a subnet mask. A pattern match uses the following criteria when evaluating a test condition:

- 0: The corresponding byte in the defined address must match the test condition exactly.

- 1: Wildcard character, any value in this byte is considered a match.

In the previous example, our pattern match effectively says, "Any IP address that contains the byte values 206.121.73 is OK." As long as the first three bytes match the source IP address, the access list test condition considers it a match.

To match all network traffic, the following address and mask are used:

```
0.0.0.0 255.255.255.255
```

This tells the Cisco router that all traffic is to be considered a match. When you write your access rules, this address and mask can simply be replaced by the word "any." This is not very useful for standard access lists (if you do not want to accept any traffic, it's easier to just pull the plug), but it will come in handy when we get into extended access lists in the next section.

Pattern Matching VLSM Networks

If you think of the pattern match value as an "anti-subnet mask," you'll be in pretty good shape. The pattern match will always be the exact opposite of what you would use for a subnet mask. This is pretty easy to follow if you are filtering full subnet classes, but it can get a bit confusing if you are working with variable-length subnetting.

For example, let's say that instead of a full class C network, you are only using a portion of this class C address space. Let's assume that the network address is 206.121.73.64 and the subnet mask is 255.255.255.224. In this case, what would you use for a pattern match to insure that you are only filtering on your network space?

As you may recall from our discussion of TCP/IP, all address space is actually created using a binary number system. We use decimal simply because it is easier for human consumption. In order to determine the pattern match that you will use, you must first convert the last byte of the subnet mask to binary:

```
224 = 128 + 64 + 32 = 11100000
```

In the last byte, three bits are used for networking and five bits to identify each unique host. In order to ignore any host on the network, you would use a pattern match that has all the host bits set high, like this:

```
00011111 = 16 + 8 + 4 + 2 + 1 = 31
```

In order to accommodate your new network address and subnet mask, you would need to change your access list to the following:

```
access-list 1 deny 206.121.73.64 0.0.0.31
access-list 2 permit 206.121.73.64 0.0.0.31
```

In effect, what you have told your access list is this: "Filter the packet when you see an address space value 206.121.73.64 - 206.121.73.95 (64 + 31)." This will let you screen for your small chunk of this class C address space without having to filter or allow more than you must.

Other Uses for Standard Access Lists

Besides spoofing rules, for what other purpose might you wish to use standard access lists? Standard access lists are extremely effective at blocking access from any remote site from which you do not want to receive traffic. This could be known attackers, mail spammers, or even competitors.

Remember that this connection is yours to manage as you see fit. Nothing dictates that you must accept traffic from all sources once you are connected to the Internet. While doing so may be considered the polite thing, it may not always make the most business sense.

For example, some mailing lists and organizations have dedicated resources to identifying spam sites. Spam, or unsolicited advertising through e-mail, can be a waste of organizational resources at best or cause a denial of service at the worst. Many administrators have begun filtering traffic from sites that are known to support (or at the very least fail to prevent) spammers and their activities. All traffic is filtered because a site that does not control outbound spam mail typically will make little or no effort to prevent other types of attacks launched against your network.

 TIP A Cisco interface can only accept one access list per port, per direction. This means that you should only apply a standard access list when you will not need an extended access list. If you require the increased flexibility of an extended access list, simply incorporate your filters into a single list.

Extended Access Lists

Extended access lists take the concept of standard access lists one step further. Instead of simply filtering on source IP address, extended access lists can also filter on the following:

- Destination IP address
- Transport (IP, TCP, UDP, ICMP, GRE, IGRP)
- Destination port number
- Packet type or code (in the case of ICMP)
- Flag fields (verify whether or not SYN=1)

Clearly, this can give you a much more granular level of control over your perimeter traffic. Extended access lists are created in global configuration mode using the following syntax:

```
access-list {list # or name} permit/deny {protocol} {source} {mask}
{destination} {mask} {operator} {port} est (short for establish if
applicable)
```

Valid operators are

- lt: Less than
- gt: Greater than
- eq: Equal to
- neq: Not equal to

As an example, let's say you wish to create a set of extended access rules that allows open access to HTTP on the host 206.121.73.10. These extended access rules will also allow Telnet access, but only from hosts on the subnet 199.52.24.0. These rules would look similar to the following:

```
access-list 101 permit any 206.121.73.10 0.0.0.0 eq 80
access-list 101 permit 199.52.24.0 0.0.0.255 206.121.73.10 0.0.0.0 eq 23
```

You would then install these rules on the serial port by entering configuration mode for that interface and entering the command

```
ip access-group 101 in
```

Permitting Established Connections

So far, we have talked about the first half of the communication session, how to let through requests. For example, if you wish to let all internal users browse the Web, you could create an outbound filtering rule that looks similar to the following:

```
access-list 101 permit tcp 206.121.73.0 0.0.0.255 eq 80
```

What we have not discussed is the proper method for letting the replies to these requests back in. Since the communication process is two-sided (requests go out, replies come back), you must allow the acknowledgments to the above data requests back into the network. Remember that this is not an easy process because replies can be returned on any port above 1023.

This is where the establish switch comes into play. The est parameter effectively states, "As long as SYN=0, accept the traffic." In other words, the router should let through any traffic that is not trying to establish a new connection. So instead of having to allow in all traffic above 1023, you can filter out any traffic that is attempting to create a new connection.

The complement to the previous rule allowing internal users to browse the Web would be this:

```
access-list 102 permit tcp any 206.121.73.0 0.0.0.255 gt 1023 est
```

This rule would be installed inbound on the external interface in order to evaluate inbound traffic. In short, it directs, "Let through any TCP traffic to the internal network which does not have SYN=1." This allows your data replies back in to the internal network.

As you saw in the section on static packet filtering, blindly allowing in all traffic without SYN=1 can expose your network to a host of attack patterns, including FIN scans. Since state is not maintained, there is no guarantee that what you are allowing into the network is in fact legitimate data replies. Reflexive filters plug this hole by maintaining state on all outbound connections.

Reflexive Access Lists

As of IOS 11.3, Cisco routers support *reflexive access lists*. Reflexive access lists replace the static establish command. One of the benefits of reflexive filtering is that (as of IOS 12.0) it will work with any IP transport, not just TCP. When you use reflexive access lists, the router creates a dynamic state table of all active sessions. This provides traffic control that is far superior to static filters.

NOTE In order to use reflexive access lists, you must use access list names, not range identifier numbers. Using a name allows you to be far more descriptive in labeling your access lists.

Here's the syntax for creating a named access filter:

```
Ip access-list extended {name}
```

You would then define each of the filter rules that would be included in this named access list.

For example, let's say that you want to give anyone on your internal network the ability to establish a UDP-based session to hosts located on the Internet. You also want to block all inbound UDP traffic except for packets replying to earlier queries.

This implementation would be a two-step process:

1. Create a rule allowing the UDP traffic out, but also telling the router to make a state table entry for the packet.

2. Create an inbound filter that matches incoming UDP traffic against these state entries.

Entries that match are allowed onto the internal network. Entries that do not are dropped into the bit bucket.

Let's plug in some names and numbers to see how you would configure the above filtering. Let's assume that your internal network is the subnet 206.121.73.0. Let's further assume that you will be creating two filters: filterin, which will be applied inbound on serial0, which is the router's external interface, and filterout, which will be applied outbound on serial0.

Here is the syntax for creating a reflexive access list:

```
permit {protocol} {source} {mask} {destination} {mask} reflect {name}
```

By plugging in the values for the outbound filter, you get

```
ip access-list extended filterout
permit UDP 206.121.73.0 0.0.0.255 any reflect udpfilter
```

The first line creates an extended access filter named filterout. The second line allows all outbound UDP traffic. The reflect udpfilter portion of the command tells the router that it should make a state table entry in the table named udpfilter. This is where the router will keep track of all outbound UDP connections. You would then apply this filter outbound on the external interface by entering configuration mode for serial0 and typing the command

```
ip access-group filterout out
```

Returning to global configuration mode, you can now create your inbound filter. Do this by entering the following commands:

```
ip access-list extended filterin
evaluate udpfilter
```

The first line creates a new extended access list named `filterin`. The second line states, "Check the state table named `udpfilter`. If this is a reply to an entry from this table, allow the traffic to pass." You would then apply this filter inbound on the external interface by entering configuration mode for serial0 and typing the command

```
ip access-group filterin in
```

Once this change is complete, the only UDP traffic that should be allowed in to the internal network is replies to earlier queries. Note that you could just as easily make all IP traffic stateful by changing the outbound filter to read

```
ip access-list extended filterout
permit IP 206.121.73.0 0.0.0.255 any reflect filterall
```

NOTE The ability to generate a state table pushes the Cisco router into the realm of a true firewall. By monitoring state, the router is in a far better position to make filter determinations than equivalent devices that only support static filtering.

The only caveat about reflexive access lists is that entries are purged from the table after 300 seconds of inactivity. While this is not a problem for most protocols, the FTP control session (port 21) can sit idle for a far longer period of time during a file transfer. You can increase this time-out value using the following command:

```
ip reflexive-list timeout {timeout in seconds}
```

TIP Once you have applied your reflexive access lists, you can use the `show access-lists` command to view the entries stored in the state table.

Problems with FTP

As you read in the section on FTP, this protocol can be a real pain to support through a firewall. This is because the protocol actually uses two ports while transferring files. To summarize, we are stuck with the following:

- Active FTP: All inbound service ports above 1023 must be left open to support data connection.

- Passive FTP: All outbound service ports above 1023 must be left open to support data connection.

In a world of the lesser of two evils, it is usually better to support only passive FTP. This is supported by all Web browsers and most graphic FTP programs. It is typically not supported by command line FTP programs.

In order to support passive FTP, you must allow all internal hosts to access any TCP ports above 1023 on systems located out on the Internet. Not the best security stance, but it is certainly far better than the standard FTP alternative.

If there are specific services you wish to block, you could create these access list entries before the entry that opens all outbound ports. Since the rules are processed in order, the Deny rules would be processed first and the traffic would be dropped. For example, let's say you wish to block access to X11 and Open Windows servers, but you want to open the remaining upper ports for passive FTP use. In that case, you would create the following rules:

```
access-list 101 deny any any eq 2001
access-list 101 deny any any eq 2002
access-list 101 deny any any eq 6001
access-list 101 deny any any eq 6002
access-list 101 permit 199.52.24.75.0 0.0.0.255 any gt 1023
```

The only problem here is that you would receive random FTP file transfer failures when the client attempted to use ports 2001, 2002, 6001, or 6002. This would probably not happen often, but intermittent failures are usually the most annoying.

Logging Traffic

While it is great to be able to filter traffic, sometimes it is just as important to be able to see whether the bad guys are doing any knob-twisting. The best way to tell whether your filter rules are working is to log the traffic and see which filter rules are getting hit.

As of Cisco IOS 11.*x* and higher, you can selectively choose to log traffic that matches any of your filtering rules. Logged traffic can be reported to the console or sent to a syslog server. Simply add the log switch to the end of your access rule. For example, if you wish to log all inbound traffic coming from the 10.0.0.0 network, create your access list entry like this:

```
access-list 105 deny ip 10.0.0.0 0.255.255.255 any log
```

Once this filter is applied, any traffic hitting the router with a source IP address of 10.*x*.*x*.*x* would be dropped, and a log entry would be generated. Generating log entries with your router is also a great way to double-check the logging ability of your firewall. If you see traffic passing by your border router that does not appear in your firewall log, you know you have a problem.

TIP   Using a syslog server to record router log entries is covered in Chapter 12.

If you need additional information about a transmitting host, try using the switch `log-input` instead of `log`. This will record which interface received the traffic, as well as the MAC address of the transmitting host. If you are attempting to identify a host that is transmitting spoofed packets, you will need the MAC address in order to properly identify where the spoofed traffic is originating. The following is an example of an access list using the `log-input` switch:

```
access-list 105 deny ip 10.0.0.0 0.255.255.255 any log-input
```

 TIP   Need to monitor network traffic but don't have a sniffer handy? Simply use your Cisco router! Applying a filter rule of `access-list 101 permit ip any any log` will generate a log entry for all traffic passing through the router. You'll need to create two access lists, applying one inbound and the other outbound, in order to see both data requests and data replies.

Creating a Set of IP Access Lists

If you feel a little confused at this point, not to worry. Access lists make a lot more sense once you start applying them to an actual network setup. Let's go through a couple of examples to see how this would all pull together.

Layered Perimeter

Let's assume that you have a network configuration similar to the one shown in Figure 9.10. The firewall will be providing the brunt of perimeter security, but you would like to do a bit of filtering on the router, as well, in order to enhance your security posture.

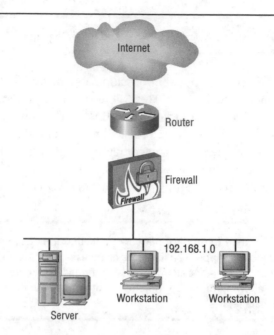

So, the question is, "What additional filtering should we perform?" Here are some useful choices:

- Spoofing filters
- Private address space
- Any traffic that can be used to probe the network
- Any critical ports you absolutely want to make sure do not become exposed
- Control sessions aimed at the router itself

The first two items simply block all traffic that the router should never see headed inbound unless someone is performing some packet trickery. You also want to block probing because doing so will make an attacker's life more difficult. For example, if you block the attacker's ability to traceroute to the router itself and beyond, mapping the network becomes more difficult. You also want to reinforce critical services, in case your firewall has a vulnerability that you do not know about. Better safe than sorry. Finally, you want to take steps to protect the router itself.

Filtering Packet Trickery

The first two items on the preceding bulleted list can be combined, because you are using private address space on the internal network. In short, you want to block all inbound traffic that is obviously bogus. Your filters would look like this:

```
access-list 101 deny ip 10.0.0.0 0.255.255.255 any
access-list 101 deny ip 192.168.0.0 0.0.255.255 any
access-list 101 deny ip 172.16.0.0 0.15.255.255 any
access-list 101 deny ip 127.0.0.0 0.255.255.255 any
access-list 101 deny ip 224.0.0.0 7.255.255.255 any
access-list 101 deny ip host 0.0.0.0 any
```

The first three lines block all traffic with a source IP address of a private network. The fourth line blocks all traffic with a source IP address of the loopback address. Since loopback is only used when a system is talking to itself, you should never see these crossing the wire. Line 5 blocks all multicast traffic. If you are using multicast, you would want to remove this line, but in most cases it's safe to leave it in. The file filter blocks all traffic that does not have a source IP address listed. Apply all of these filters inbound on the external interface.

Blocking Probes

Next, you want to block inbound probes. The two most common are Ping and Traceroute. Ping is pretty easy; it sends an ICMP echo request to the host being probed and expects an echo reply to be returned. If you block either one of these packets, you can stop Ping from being used to probe your network. With this in mind, your filter would look like this:

```
access-list 101 deny icmp any any echo
```

Traceroute is a bit more difficult. When the command is used on UNIX-based systems, it transmits UDP packets when performing a probe. The Tracert counterpart, which runs under Windows, transmits ICMP. Luckily, both implementations expect to see the same type of reply: a series of ICMP time-exceeded messages. This means that the easiest way to prevent people from mapping your network using Traceroute or Tracert is simply to block these returning messages. This can be done with the following filter:

```
access-list 102 deny ICMP any any time-exceeded
```

NOTE This filter should be applied outbound on the external interface. This is because you are blocking the replies on the way out. You are not trying to block the probes on their way in.

Critical Ports

The next task is to block critical ports. These can be ports used on internal systems or perhaps ports exposed on the firewall itself. For example, a Check Point FireWall-1 installation left at its default settings exposes approximately 10 ports, which can make the device vulnerable to attack. You could use your access lists to help plug these holes.

Let's assume that there are no known problems with your firewall. You run a straight Windows environment and simply wish to protect the ports used for file and print sharing. With this in mind, your inbound filters would appear as follows:

```
access-list 101 deny tcp any any eq 135
access-list 101 deny tcp any any eq 137
access-list 101 deny tcp any any eq 138
access-list 101 deny tcp any any eq 139
access-list 101 deny udp any any eq 135
access-list 101 deny udp any any eq 137
access-list 101 deny udp any any eq 138
access-list 101 deny udp any any eq 139
```

Table 9.6 lists a number of ports that, in some environments, may be considered critical. If you want to make absolutely sure that an attacker cannot get in using these ports, consider closing them on both your border router and your firewall. In most cases, organizations do not use any of the ports listed for Internet communications.

TABLE 9.6: CRITICAL SERVICES AND THE PORTS THEY USE

Service Name	Transport	Port Number	Description
Tcpmux	TCP	1	Potential point of intrusion on SGI Irix
Echo	TCP/UDP	7	Used for DoS attacks
Systat	TCP	11	Used for collecting attack info
Chargen	TCP/UDP	19	Used for DoS attacks
Finger	TCP	79	Used for collecting attack info

Continued ▐▶

TABLE 9.6: CRITICAL SERVICES AND THE PORTS THEY USE (CONTINUED)

Service Name	Transport	Port Number	Description
Linuxconf	TCP	98	Potential point of attack
Sunrpc/Portmap	TCP/UDP	111	Potential point of attack
Auth	TCP	113	Used for collecting attack info
MSrpc	TCP	135	Potential point of attack
NetBIOS	TCP/UDP	137–139	Potential point of attack
SNMP	UDP	161–162	Used for collecting info & DoS attacks
Login	TCP	513	Potential point of attack
Shell	TCP	514	Potential point of attack
Mountd	TCP/UDP	635	Potential point of attack on Linux
Mountd	TCP/UDP	2049	Potential point of attack on Solaris
SOCKS	TCP	1080	Potential point of attack
Sunrpc	TCP/UDP	32772	Potential point of attack on Solaris

In addition, Table 9.7 lists a number of Trojans which have been found in the wild and the default port numbers they use. Keep in mind that most modern Trojans can be configured to use any port number. The port numbers listed here are simply the defaults. Most lame attackers do not bother to change these default settings, however, so blocking them can afford some extra protection.

TABLE 9.7: COMMON TROJANS AND THEIR LISTENING PORTS

Trojan	Transport	Port(s) Used
Sub-7	TCP/UDP	1243, 6711–6713, 6776, 27374, 27573
Netbus	UDP	12345, 12346, 12356, 20034
NetSphere	TCP	30100–30102
Portal of Doom	UDP	10067, 10167
Back Orifice	UDP	31337, 31338
Hack-a-Tack	UDP	31785–31791
Back Orifice 2000	UDP	54320, 54321
RingZero	UDP	3028, 3128, 8080
Deep Throat	TCP/UDP	41, 999, 2140, 3150, 6670, 6671, 60000
Trin00	UDP	27444, 31335, 34555

Protecting the Router

Finally, you need to take steps to protect the router itself. Let's assume that the router can be accessed via Telnet and SNMP. You wish to insure that no one on the Internet can use these protocols to compromise your router. With this in mind, you would simply create an inbound filter that blocks these services. Assume the WAN interface of the router is IP address 200.200.200.1, while the internal interface is 200.200.100.1.

```
access-list 101 deny TCP any 200.200.200.1 0.0.0.0 eq 23
access-list 101 deny TCP any 200.200.100.1 0.0.0.0 eq 23
access-list 101 deny UDP any 200.200.200.1 0.0.0.0 eq 161
access-list 101 deny UDP any 200.200.100.1 0.0.0.0 eq 161
```

 NOTE You are filtering on both the external and the internal IP addresses. This is because any router interface can be used to establish a connection, not just the interface facing the connecting system.

The steps we've just gone over cover all the bullet items in the list at the beginning of this section. You could then enter configuration mode for the external interface and perform the following:

```
ip access-group 101 in
ip access-group 102 out
```

Upon doing so, you would find that you are no longer able to communicate with the Internet and that possibly your Telnet session to the router has just died as, well. Two questions immediately come to mind: "What went wrong?" and "How do I fix it?"

Implicit Deny

What went wrong is that you got caught by the implicit deny rule. There are lots of rules denying traffic, but none to let the remaining traffic through. Luckily, since you did not write the filters to memory, you can simply reboot the router to restore the original configuration, which does not include the filters. The other option would be to connect to the router's console port, enter configuration mode for the external interface and type

```
no ip access-group 101 in
no ip access-group 102 out
```

TIP When making changes to your router, do not save the new configuration right away. Perform your testing with the changes in active memory only. This way, if you have inadvertently locked yourself out of the device, you can simply power cycle it to return to the last saved configuration. Just don't forget to save just before making changes (in case the last changes you made were not saved) once you know the changes are acceptable!

These commands will remove the filters and give you a chance to fix them before applying them again. To fix the filters, simply add the following commands:

```
access-list 101 permit ip any any
access-list 102 permit ip any any
```

This will permit all traffic not explicitly denied by an earlier rule. If you wanted to monitor any one of your filters to see whether it is effective, you could have created the access list filter using the log switch parameter at the end of the command. This would allow you to see traffic which was being dropped by the rule.

 WARNING Changing the implicit deny to an implicit permit is a dangerous stance to take, unless you have implemented a layered security perimeter.

Single Line of Defense

For our next example, let's assume that you have very limited funds and will be using your Cisco router as your only method of perimeter security. You need to allow HTTP access to a Web server and SMTP access to a mail server. The mail server also runs the local DNS process. Additionally, you would like to provide unrestricted access to all TCP services for all your internal hosts, except for the ports used for NetBIOS/IP file and printer sharing. A network drawing is shown in Figure 9.11.

FIGURE 9.11

*Using access lists as a
sole line of defense*

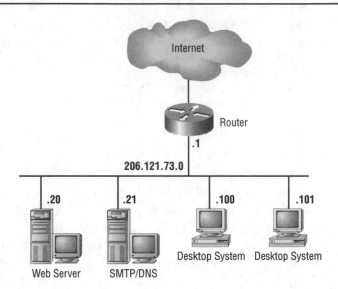

Breaking It Down

To determine what access rules to create, start by looking at the communication requirements. First, list all the traffic patterns you wish to support. These would include the following:

- Inbound connection requests from external users going to the Web server
- Outbound replies from the Web server to external users
- Inbound connection requests from external SMTP servers going to the internal mail server
- Outbound replies from the internal mail server to external SMTP servers
- Outbound DNS queries from the mail server
- Inbound DNS replies going to the mail server
- Outbound TCP connections (except for NetBIOS/IP) from any internal host
- Inbound TCP replies returning to the requesting host

After making this list of all the traffic to support, your access list requirements should be a bit clearer. All sessions identified as inbound should be applied in on the external interface of the router. All sessions identified as being outbound can be applied out on the external interface of the router. You could optionally apply the outbound filters in on the internal interface, but let's stick with the external interface for consistency.

Building the Filters

Since this will be your only line of defense, it would be prudent to use dynamic packet filtering via reflexive filters. While this will chew up a bit more memory and processing time on the router, it will provide a much stronger security perimeter.

In order to use reflexive access lists, you must use list names instead of numbers. Let's use the name filterin to include all rules that will apply to inbound traffic and the name filterout to include all rules that will apply to outbound traffic.

The first requirement is to provide access from the Internet to the Web server. With this in mind, your first set of commands would look like this:

```
ip access-list extended filterin
permit tcp any 206.121.73.20 0.0.0.0 eq 80 reflect httpfilter
```

The first line creates an extended access list and names it filterin. The second line creates a rule which states, "Allow anyone on the Internet to establish a connection to TCP port 80 on IP address 206.121.73.20. Record this connection in the state table named httpfilter."

Your connection requests will be allowed in; you now need a complementary rule to allow replies back out. This will be done within the filterout access list:

```
ip access-list extended filterout
evaluate httpfilter
```

This tells the router to allow outbound replies, provided that a state table entry exists for the connection within the httpfilter state table. Now connection requests will be allowed in, and responses to these connection requests will be allowed back out.

Create the filter rules for the SMTP server in a similar fashion. If you add the requirements for the SMTP server, you'll get

```
ip access-list extended filterin
permit tcp any 206.121.73.20 0.0.0.0 eq 80 reflect httpfilter
permit tcp any 206.121.73.21 0.0.0.0 eq 25 reflect smtpfilter

ip access-list extended filterout
evaluate httpfilter
evaluate smtpfilter
```

Next, the mail server must be able to send DNS queries to hosts out on the Internet. Create this rule in a similar fashion, except the rule permitting the traffic will appear in the `filterout` access list, while the `filterin` access list will be responsible for evaluating replies against state table entries. When you add the DNS requirement, your filters look like this:

```
ip access-list extended filterin
permit tcp any 206.121.73.20 0.0.0.0 eq 80 reflect httpfilter
permit tcp any 206.121.73.21 0.0.0.0 eq 25 reflect smtpfilter
evaluate dnsfilter


ip access-list extended filterout
permit udp 206.121.73.21 0.0.0.0 any eq 53 reflect dnsfilter
evaluate httpfilter
evaluate smtpfilter
```

Finally, you need to add the requirement that allows internal hosts to connect to any Internet host running TCP services, provided that the service is not NetBIOS/IP. Just like the DNS rule, you will put the filters in `filterout` while evaluating replies in `filterin`. The difference is that you will be providing access to an entire subnet, not just to a specific host:

```
ip access-list extended filterin
permit tcp any 206.121.73.20 0.0.0.0 eq 80 reflect httpfilter
permit tcp any 206.121.73.21 0.0.0.0 eq 25 reflect smtpfilter
evaluate tcpfilter
evaluate dnsfilter


ip access-list extended filterout
deny tcp any any eq 135
deny tcp any any eq 137
deny tcp any any eq 138
deny tcp any any eq 139
permit TCP 206.121.73.0 0.0.0.255 any reflect tcpfilter
permit udp 206.121.73.21 0.0.0.0 any eq 53 reflect dnsfilter
evaluate httpfilter
evaluate smtpfilter
```

The order of these rules is important. Remember that access lists are processed in "first fit," not "best fit," order. This means that if an internal workstation attempts to create an outbound NetBIOS/IP session, the router will evaluate traffic against the deny statements before it hits the `permit` TCP statement. If the `permit` statement had been entered first, the router would never make it down to the deny statements and would thus allow the traffic through.

Evaluating Your Filters

When you are working through a command interface, it can be very easy to generate a typo or perhaps miss an important part of a communication session when designing your access rules. For example, consider the following points with regard to the rules we've been discussing:

- There is no explicit rule allowing SMTP out from the mail server.
- There is no explicit rule allowing TCP-based DNS queries out from the mail server.
- What if someone tries to probe the network?
- What if someone tries to telnet to the router?
- What about spoofing?

While the requirements seemed pretty simple on the surface, they become far more complex when you take into account all of the "what if" scenarios that can occur while communicating on the Internet. Let's address each of these issues in turn.

It is true that you do not have an explicit rule allowing SMTP or TCP-based DNS out, but if you check the rules carefully you'll see that you don't need one. The `fil-terout` access list contains a rule permitting all outbound TCP sessions for the entire `206.121.73.0` subnet, provided that the service in question is not NetBIOS/IP. This means that this single rule will cover the requirement of letting out SMTP and DNS sessions from the mail server.

If you remember the access list you created in the "Layered Perimeter" example, you specifically blocked inbound echo requests and outbound time-exceeded packets in order to stop attackers from using these packets to probe your network. So why not do the same here?

The answer is the implicit deny rule. As I mentioned earlier, the last rule in a Cisco access list is always this: "Deny everything that is not expressly allowed." If you check the preceding rules, you'll see that ICMP traffic has not been enabled through your router. This means that the echo-request and time-exceeded packets will be blocked because of the implicit deny rule.

Of course, this may not exactly be a good thing. Remember that ICMP is the maintenance protocol of the Internet and as such it may provide some useful services to your internal hosts. For example, it would be nice if your internal hosts could use Ping to test connectivity. It might also be useful to allow in ICMP messages, such as host or network unreachable, time exceeded, source quench, and so on. Without allowing in these packet types, your internal systems may have difficulty communicating with some hosts on the Internet or may be slow to respond when a host is offline.

Table 9.8 shows a list of ICMP messages that can be manipulated using access list filters. You can create filters using the name of the message or the message type and code number. This means that each of the following two filters would perform exactly the same function:

```
access-list 105 permit icmp any any 3 1
access-list 105 permit icmp any any host-unreachable
```

TABLE 9.8: AVAILABLE ICMP SWITCHES

Switch	Usage
administratively-prohibited	Administratively prohibited
alternate-address	Alternate address
conversion-error	Datagram conversion
dod-host-prohibited	Host prohibited
dod-net-prohibited	Net prohibited
Echo	Echo (Ping)
echo-reply	Echo reply
general-parameter-problem	Parameter problem
host-isolated	Host isolated
host-precedence-unreachable	Host unreachable for precedence
host-redirect	Host redirect
host-tos-redirect	Host redirect for TOS
host-tos-unreachable	Host unreachable for TOS
host-unknown	Host unknown
host-unreachable	Host unreachable
information-reply	Information replies
information-request	Information requests
mask-reply	Mask replies
mask-request	Mask requests
mobile-redirect	Mobile host redirect
net-redirect	Network redirect
net-tos-redirect	Net redirect for TOS
net-tos-unreachable	Network unreachable for TOS
net-unreachable	Net unreachable
network-unknown	Network unknown

Continued

TABLE 9.8: AVAILABLE ICMP SWITCHES (CONTINUED)	
Switch	**Usage**
no-room-for-option	Parameter required but no room
option-missing	Parameter required but not present
packet-too-big	Fragmentation needed and DF set
parameter-problem	All parameter problems
port-unreachable	Port unreachable
precedence	Match packets with given precedence value
precedence-unreachable	Precedence cutoff
protocol-unreachable	Protocol unreachable
reassembly-timeout	Reassembly timeout
redirect	All redirects
router-advertisement	Router discovery advertisements
router-solicitation	Router discovery solicitations
source-quench	Source quenches
source-route-failed	Source route failed
time-exceeded	All time exceededs
timestamp-reply	Timestamp replies
timestamp-request	Timestamp requests
tos	Match packets with given TOS value
traceroute	Traceroute
ttl-exceeded	TTL exceeded
unreachable	All unreachables

At a minimum, you may wish to allow out echo. You may also wish to allow in echo reply, time, and TTL exceeded, as well as unreachable messages. This is simply a suggestion. Your mileage may vary, depending on your security policy. For the purpose of our example, let's assume that you wish to permit this traffic through your router.

Your next concern was whether people could telnet to the router itself. Based on the access list rules, this would only be permitted from the internal network. You could choose to tighten this up further or leave it as is.

The final point was the absence of spoofing filters. This is a valid concern, and you should add an appropriate set of spoofing filters. With this in mind, your new ruleset would appear as follows:

```
! Setup inbound filters
ip access-list extended filterin
!
! Block all spoofed traffic
deny ip 206.121.73.20 0.0.0.255 any
!
! Block packet trickry
deny ip 10.0.0.0 0.255.255.255 any
deny ip 192.168.0.0 0.0.255.255 any
deny ip 172.16.0.0 0.15.255.255 any
deny ip 127.0.0.0 0.255.255.255 any
deny ip 224.0.0.0 7.255.255.255 any
deny ip host 0.0.0.0 any
! Allow in HTTP to Web server and SMTP to mail server
permit tcp any 206.121.73.20 0.0.0.0 eq 80 reflect httpfilter
permit tcp any 206.121.73.21 0.0.0.0 eq 25 reflect smtpfilter
!
! Allow in only certain ICMP message types
permit icmp any 206.121.73.0 0.0.0.255 echo-reply
permit icmp any 206.121.73.0 0.0.0.255 time-exceeded
permit icmp any 206.121.73.0 0.0.0.255 ttl-exceeded
permit icmp any 206.121.73.0 0.0.0.255 unreachable
!
! Allow back in replies for TCP & DNS queries
evaluate tcpfilter
evaluate dnsfilter
!
! Setup Outbound Filters
ip access-list extended filterout
!
! Allow out echo-request
permit icmp 206.121.73.0 0.0.0.255 any echo
!
! Block NetBIOS/IP outbound
deny tcp any any eq 135
```

```
deny tcp any any eq 137
deny tcp any any eq 138
deny tcp any any eq 139
! Let all internal systems run any TCP based service
permit TCP 206.121.73.0 0.0.0.255 any reflect tcpfilter
!
! Allow mail system to send UDP based DNS queries
permit udp 206.121.73.21 0.0.0.0 any eq 53 reflect dnsfilter
!
! Allow out replies for inbound HTTP and SMTP traffic
evaluate httpfilter
evaluate smtpfilter
```

 NOTE You probably noticed that some of the lines in these rules start with an exclamation point (!). As your rules become more complex, it is a good idea to add comments describing the rationale behind including each filter in your access lists. This can be extremely beneficial if someone else needs to make sense of your rules or if you do not work with access lists on a regular basis. When a line begins with an exclamation point, the Cisco router will interpret the line as information rather than as a command.

Non-IP Access Lists

As you saw earlier in this chapter, access lists can be used to filter more than just IP traffic. While IP is by far the most widely used protocol, many environments still run IPX and AppleTalk, as well. In this section, we will look at a few examples of how to filter these other protocols.

IPX Access Lists

Much of the functionality that is included in IP access lists has been incorporated into IPX access lists, as well. Both standard and extended IPX access lists are supported. As with IP access lists, you are allowed to assign unique names instead of numbers to your IPX access lists. About the only major feature that's missing is that you cannot do dynamic filtering of IPX traffic. Only static packet filtering is supported.

WARNING Be very careful when filtering an IPX environment. Typically, NetWare servers must be able to stay in constant communication with each other. You should never filter communications between two NetWare servers that are part of the same NDS tree and that need to exchange replica information.

A Standard Access List Example

IPX access lists allow you to filter on both source and destination network addresses. This can be useful when you need to configure communications between two NetWare networks, but you only want connections to be established in a single direction. The only caveat is that standard filters must be applied in an outbound direction. You cannot filter inbound or outbound, as we did with IP.

For an example of how standard access lists can be applied, refer to Figure 9.12. This drawing shows a large firm that has just set up connectivity with two recent acquisitions. The firm, located on IPX network ba5eba11, wishes to gain access to NetWare resources on the two remote networks but does not want to grant these two new subsidiaries access to the corporate network. It is permissible, however, to let these two organizations exchange information with each other.

Because you are looking to block all access between specific networks, you can control traffic flow using standard IPX access lists. You can also satisfy all your filtering needs with a single access list on Router A. To configure Router A, enter global configuration mode and type the following commands:

```
ipx access-list standard corporate
deny abe1 ba5eba11
deny feed ba5eba11
permit -1 -1
exit
int eth0
ipx access-group corporate
```

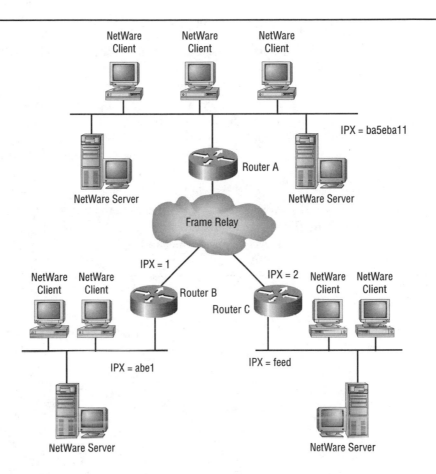

FIGURE 9.12

A large firm connected to two recent acquisitions

The first command tells the router that you wish to create a standard IPX access list named corporate. The next two lines define the networks you wish to block as part of this access list. The fourth line permits all IPX networks to communicate which were not explicitly blocked by the previous two rules. The –1 value is a wildcard for IPX networks. This setting will match any valid IPX network value.

In the last three commands, you leave access list configuration mode, enter interface configuration mode for the Ethernet interface, and apply your access rules. Remember that standard access lists can only be applied outbound. This is why you apply your filter to the Ethernet interface instead of the serial interface.

An Extended Access List Example

Extended access lists provide a bit more flexibility than standard access lists. Besides filtering on source and destination network addresses, you can also filter out specific IPX packet types and service advertisements from one or more servers. This is a powerful feature that provides a higher level of granularity in controlling traffic. Additionally, you can even specify filtering direction, which means traffic can be blocked inbound or outbound on any specified port.

For example, examine the network shown in Figure 9.13. In this environment, network AAA is the corporate network and network BBB is engineering. Only engineers need access to the test server. In fact, it would be extremely beneficial from both a security and a network-resource perspective if the test server were completely invisible to hosts on the AAA network. Hosts on the AAA network do need, however, access to the production server located on network BBB.

FIGURE 9.13

We need to filter out all SAPs originating from the test server.

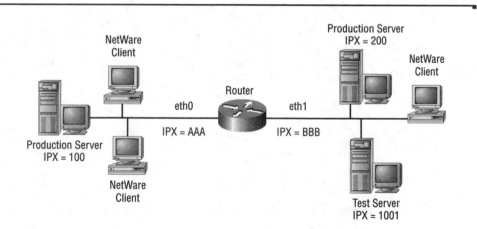

Obviously, in this situation you cannot use standard access lists. Blocking all connectivity from network AAA to BBB would break communications with the production server on BBB. Clearly, you need a way to single out a particular server so that you can deny access to the test server while providing access to the other production server.

An interesting feature of NetWare servers is that all SAP packets originate from the server's internal IPX number. By blocking all the SAPs that originate from the 1001 network, you can prevent the test server from being accessed from the AAA network. To set up your filters, enter global configuration mode and enter the following commands:

```
ipx access list extended filtertest
deny 1001
permit -1
exit
int eth1
ipx input-sap-filter filtertest
```

 NOTE In commands two and three, you did not need to specify a destination. When the destination is left blank, a wildcard entry is assumed. Also, notice that the last command specifies that SAP traffic is filtered in an inbound direction.

AppleTalk Access Lists

AppleTalk access lists are not quite as flexible as their IP and IPX counterparts. You cannot name AppleTalk access lists, which means you must always refer to them by access list numbers within the range 600–699. Also, only standard access lists are supported, meaning you can only filter on source identifier. You cannot define a destination test condition on which to filter traffic.

When creating AppleTalk access lists, you have the option of filtering on either source network address or zone name. If network address is specified, you can use a number of switches to help you identify which network you wish to filter. These switches follow:

Network   This switch affects only the specified network.

Cable-range   This switch affects only the specifically defined network range.

Within   This switch affects all networks that fall completely within the specified range.

Includes   This switch affects all networks that overlap any part of the specified range.

The first two switches are pretty straightforward. You must define the exact network numbers you wish to filter. The last two switches can cause some confusion and are best described through example. Let's assume you wish to filter out the AppleTalk network range 110–120.

In order to use the `within` switch, the 110–120 network range would have to fall within the filter values you specify. The following access list entries using the `within` switch would successfully filter out this network range:

```
access-list 601 deny within 100-125
access-list 601 deny within 1-1000
```

The following access lists using the `within` switch would not be acted upon, because the 110–120 range does not fall within the values they specify:

```
access-list 602 deny within 111-119
access-list 602 deny within 115-125
access-list 602 deny within 150-175
```

The `include` switch states that only a portion of the specified range needs to be identified in order for the filter to act on the entire network range. So, along with the two 601 access lists, using the `include` switch would also be valid for these access lists:

```
access-list 602 deny include 111-119
access-list 602 deny include 115-125
```

 NOTE Even though these access lists identify only a portion of the 110–120 network range, the entire 110–120 network range would be subject to the access list rule.

As mentioned, you can also filter on AppleTalk zone names. This is useful if you wish to allow information for one zone to be propagated but not for another. For example, if you only wanted the zone Accounting to be visible on the other side of a router, you could use an access list entry similar to the following:

```
access-list 608 permit zone Accounting
```

Filtering on Ethernet MAC Address

The ability to filter on the MAC address of a particular system can be extremely useful when you must block all communications regardless of a system's network address or even the protocols it is using to communicate. MAC address filters must be specified within the access list range 700–799 and can only be applied inbound on an Ethernet interface.

Let's look at an example of when this feature may be useful. When discussing IP access lists, I mentioned the concept of egress filtering. Egress filters are used to prevent your internal hosts from spoofing their source IP address when communicating with hosts on the Internet. Let's assume that you are reviewing your router logs and you identify an internal system that appears to be attempting to spoof traffic from multiple IP addresses. Your log entry may look similar to the following:

```
Feb 27 04:21:17 10.26.103.110 194169: %SEC-6-IPACCESSLOGP: list 100 denied
tcp 172.27.153.66(0) (Ethernet0 0020.afe7.33c8) -> 12.126.103.200(0), 1
packet
Feb 27 04:21:17 172.1.52.8 194170: %SEC-6-IPACCESSLOGP: list 100 denied tcp
172.27.153.101(0) (Ethernet0 0020.afe7.33c8) -> 12.126.103.200(0), 1 packets
Feb 27 04:21:17 192.168.10.11 194171: %SEC-6-IPACCESSLOGP: list 100 denied
tcp 172.27.153.66(0) (Ethernet0 0020.afe7.33c8) -> 12.126.103.200(0), 1
packet
```

In this log, you can see three different IP addresses attempting to contact 12.126.103.200 within a one-second period. The problem is that none of these source IP addresses is valid for the internal network. If you look at the log closely, you will see that the router is reporting that it received all three packets from the same MAC address: 0020.afe7.33c8. This leaves you with three possibilities:

- This is a router leading to a remote network.
- This is a host that has been compromised.
- You have a computer user who needs a refresher course in Internet ethics.

If the source is a host, it may be a good idea to block Internet access completely for this system until you know what's going on. The host may eventually start launching attacks using its real IP address or at least a legitimate address within your network.

Of course, this leaves you with a small problem. If the system is varying its source IP address, how do you filter it? The answer is to use MAC address filtering. No matter what source IP address the system uses, the MAC remains constant. To filter this system by MAC address, you would create the following access list:

```
access-list 701 deny 0020.afe7.33c8
access-list 701 permit any
```

and apply it to Ethernet 0. The router would now block all traffic originating from this host, giving you time to figure out what's causing the problem.

Filtering out Multiple Protocols

MAC address filtering can also be useful if you need to filter out multiple protocols. For example, let's say you have router A, which passes IP, IPX, and AppleTalk traffic between you and a client. You also have router B, which communicates with a different client using IP, IPX, and AppleTalk.

In order to block communications between these two sites, you have two options:

- Create a unique set of access lists for each protocol
- Simply filter on MAC address

By creating an access list on router A that filters out all traffic originating from router B's MAC address, for example, you can effectively block all protocol communications between these two clients.

Installing Your Access Rules

Typing commands at the command prompt is not your only option when it comes to installing your access lists. While this method is fine when you are working with only a few rules, manual entry can become tedious at best when you start creating large rulesets. Creating your rules offline allows you to use your favorite text editor, such as VI or Notepad. This way, you can use advanced editing functions like Copy and Paste.

Developing your rules offline also allows you to double-check them for accuracy and proper order before applying them to your router. Being able to review your ruleset in its entirety before making any router changes may help to prevent connectivity problems later. There are two methods for automating your rule installation:

- Pasting the rules through a console session
- TFTP

Pasting Rules From the Console

Most Telnet or terminal emulator programs allow you to paste in text from memory. This means that you could create your ruleset in Notepad, copy the rules to memory, then paste them to the router while connected via Telnet. While you can paste in rules during a console or Telnet session, you need to be mindful of the prompt created when each command executes.

For example, you should be in global configuration mode when you create a new access list by name. As soon as you do, however, the router changes from global config mode to a configuration mode for this specific access list. This will be obvious if you watch the change in prompts:

```
shelby(config)#ip access-list extended filterin
shelby(config-ext-nacl)#
```

NOTE After we created the access list named `filterin`, we left global configuration mode in order to enter the rules that will make up this list. If we then tried to create the access list `filterout` we would still be in access list configuration mode for `filterin`, leading to an `Invalid input detected` error message.

How do you get around this problem? When creating rules in your text editor, simply include the commands required to navigate between each of the prompts. For example, when you are done setting up `filterin` and need to return to global configuration mode in order to create `filterout`, simply issue the `exit` command. This will move you back one level and allow you to create the new list.

Assuming that you will navigate the system manually to reach global configuration mode, your final set of access list rules would look like this:

```
! Remove any existing filter rules
no ip access-list extended filterin
no ip access-list extended filterout
!
! Setup inbound filters
ip access-list extended filterin
!
! Block all spoofed traffic
deny ip 206.121.73.20 0.0.0.255 any
!
! Block packet trickry
deny ip 10.0.0.0 0.255.255.255 any
deny ip 192.168.0.0 0.0.255.255 any
deny ip 172.16.0.0 0.15.255.255 any
deny ip 127.0.0.0 0.255.255.255 any
deny ip 224.0.0.0 7.255.255.255 any
deny ip host 0.0.0.0 any
! Allow in HTTP to Web server and SMTP to mail server
permit tcp any 206.121.73.20 0.0.0.0 eq 80 reflect httpfilter
permit tcp any 206.121.73.21 0.0.0.0 eq 25 reflect smtpfilter
!
! Allow in only certain ICMP message types
permit icmp any 206.121.73.0 0.0.0.255 echo-reply
permit icmp any 206.121.73.0 0.0.0.255 time-exceeded
permit icmp any 206.121.73.0 0.0.0.255 ttl-exceeded
```

```
permit icmp any 206.121.73.0 0.0.0.255 unreachable
!
! Allow back in replies for TCP & DNS queries
evaluate tcpfilter
evaluate dnsfilter
!
! return to global config mode
exit
! Setup Outbound Filters
ip access-list extended filterout
!
! Allow out echo-request
permit icmp 206.121.73.0 0.0.0.255 any echo
!
! Block NetBIOS/IP outbound
deny tcp any any eq 135
deny tcp any any eq 137
deny tcp any any eq 138
deny tcp any any eq 139
! Let all internal systems run any TCP based service
permit TCP 206.121.73.0 0.0.0.255 any reflect tcpfilter
!
! Allow mail system to send UDP based DNS queries
permit udp 206.121.73.21 0.0.0.0 any eq 53 reflect dnsfilter
!
! Allow out replies for inbound HTTP and SMTP traffic
evaluate httpfilter
evaluate smtpfilter
!
! Return to global config mode
exit
!
! Configure Serial0
interface s0
ip access-group filterin in
ip access-group filterout out
exit
exit
show running
```

Pasting in these rules would clear any existing `filterin` or `filterout` access lists that may exist. This insures that you are starting with a clean slate. Then, create your filter rules, apply them to the appropriate interface, and return to enable mode. Finish up by executing the `show running` command. This will allow you to review the configuration running in memory in order to determine whether your rules were properly applied.

 NOTE When you view the configuration, all comment lines will be removed.

Using TFTP to Apply Access Lists

Pasting from a terminal session is by far the easiest way to apply your access rules, but it is not your only option. You can also use TFTP to install your filters. The benefit of using TFTP is that you can retain a full backup of your router's configuration including all IP addressing and configuration parameters. If you ever need to swap in a new router, simply install the OS and copy over your backup configuration.

TFTP is covered in greater detail in Chapters 8 and 12, so we will only touch on the steps here. The first thing you should do is save your current configuration in case the worst happens and you need to reboot the router to recover:

```
copy running startup
```

Next, copy your running config over to your TFTP server so that you can add your access lists:

```
copy running tftp
```

Enter in the IP address of your TFTP server and give the configuration file a descriptive name. Once the transfer is complete, you can open the file with a text editor and add your access list rules. As an example, let's assume that your current config appears as follows:

```
!
version 12.0
service timestamps debug uptime
service timestamps log uptime
no service password-encryption
!
hostname shelby
```

```
!
enable secret 5 $1$NFrn$4m6BGqPue2ScpJaoR2npU0
enable password 2$ecret4u
!
interface Ethernet0
 ip address 206.121.73.1 255.255.255.0
 no ip directed-broadcast
!
interface Serial0
 ip address 200.200.200.2 255.255.255.252
 no ip directed-broadcast
!
interface Serial1
 no ip address
 no ip directed-broadcast
 shutdown
!
ip classless
!
!
line con 0
 exec-timeout 0 0
 transport input none
line aux 0
line vty 0 4
 password 2$ecret4me
 login
!
end
```

You can now edit this text file to add your access lists. Under the configuration information for s0, you would apply your filters to the interface. Add your access list rules anywhere after the configuration information for each of the interfaces.

 TIP   Never work with the original file in case you have to restore it. Create a backup, then modify the backup file in order to add your access lists.

Assuming that you added your access list rules directly after the `ip classless` statement, your new file would look like this:

```
!
version 12.0
service timestamps debug uptime
service timestamps log uptime
no service password-encryption
!
hostname shelby
!
enable secret 5 $1$NFrn$4m6BGqPue2ScpJaoR2npU0
enable password 2$ecret4u
!
interface Ethernet0
 ip address 206.121.73.1 255.255.255.0
 no ip directed-broadcast
!
interface Serial0
 ip address 200.200.200.2 255.255.255.252
 no ip directed-broadcast
 ip access-group filterin in
 ip access-group filterout out
!
interface Serial1
 no ip address
 no ip directed-broadcast
 shutdown
!
ip classless
!
ip access-list extended filterin
deny ip 10.0.0.0 0.255.255.255 any
deny ip 192.168.0.0 0.0.255.255 any
deny ip 172.16.0.0 0.15.255.255 any
deny ip 127.0.0.0 0.255.255.255 any
deny ip 224.0.0.0 7.255.255.255 any
deny ip host 0.0.0.0 any
permit tcp any 206.121.73.20 0.0.0.0 eq 80 reflect httpfilter
```

```
      permit tcp any 206.121.73.21 0.0.0.0 eq 25 reflect smtpfilter
      permit icmp any 206.121.73.0 0.0.0.255 echo-reply
      permit icmp any 206.121.73.0 0.0.0.255 time-exceeded
      permit icmp any 206.121.73.0 0.0.0.255 ttl-exceeded
      permit icmp any 206.121.73.0 0.0.0.255 unreachable
      evaluate tcpfilter
      evaluate dnsfilter
      !
      ip access-list extended filterout
      permit icmp 206.121.73.0 0.0.0.255 any echo
      deny tcp any any eq 135
      deny tcp any any eq 137
      deny tcp any any eq 138
      deny tcp any any eq 139
      permit TCP 206.121.73.0 0.0.0.255 any reflect tcpfilter
      permit udp 206.121.73.21 0.0.0.0 any eq 53 reflect dnsfilter
      evaluate httpfilter
      evaluate smtpfilter
      !
      !
      line con 0
       exec-timeout 0 0
       transport input none
      line aux 0
      line vty 0 4
       password 2$ecret4me
       login
      !
      end
```

You can now save the file and transfer it to the router. Do this from the router interface using the command

```
copy tftp running
```

As you did before, simply identify the IP address of your TFTP server and the name of the file you wish to transfer. When the transfer is complete, check the console for error messages. If no error messages are reported, you should check the running configuration to insure that the configuration looks correct.

At this point, it is time to check connectivity. Make sure that all your hosts can communicate as planned. If this checks out OK, grab a copy of your favorite port scanning program and verify that any traffic you wish to block (both inbound and outbound) is not making it through. If you run into trouble, try using the log switch at the end of your filter rules to see where things are going wrong. This may help you to identify an incorrect or missing rule. If you think it's the implicit deny rule catching you up, go ahead and create a final rule that states:

```
deny ip any any log
```

This will allow you to continue dropping all traffic that was not expressly allowed, but will log it when this traffic is dropped.

Summary

In this chapter, we covered the theory behind static and dynamic packet filtering. We also looked at how Cisco access lists use packet filtering to control traffic flow across your router. We discussed both standard and extended access lists, as well as examples of each.

In the next chapter, we will discuss how to turn a Cisco router into a bastion host. Since routers tend to be on the outskirts of a network's perimeter, it is prudent to lock them down in order to insure they are not vulnerable to attack.

CHAPTER <u>10</u>

Creating a Bastion Router

Because of the functionality routers provide, it is not uncommon to have one or more routers on the outside border of your network perimeter. This means that your router may be exposed to attacks from would-be assailants. With this in mind, it is good security practice to lock down your routers as much as possible.

What Is a Bastion Host?

A *bastion host* is any networked system that has been "hardened" against attack. This hardening process may include disabling any unneeded services, using a strong password policy, or even limiting the networks allowed to communicate with the device. The primary goal is to make the system as resilient as possible in resisting attacks. You should take extra care to secure a bastion host, because these devices will typically be placed outside a network's security perimeter.

A *bastion router* is simply an extension of the bastion host classification; the same principles apply. The perimeter of an organization's network typically borders WAN connections to the Internet and possibly one or more business partners. If your network uses a firewall for perimeter security, you will still have one or more routers sitting outside this security perimeter in order to provide WAN connectivity. These routers are most vulnerable to attack.

Security Check

The first step in securing your router is to evaluate your current security posture. You need to identify any services running on the router that could provide potential entry points for an attacker. You also need to determine whether there are any known vulnerabilities with the version of Cisco IOS you are running.

Running Services

Start by checking running services. It may surprise you to find out that your router does double duty as a server. This is required to provide additional functionality. For example, in order for you to connect to the router via a Telnet session, there must be a Telnet daemon running which will listen for and accept inbound Telnet connections. Without this functionality, all management would have to be performed at the console.

One would think that the best way to check and see what services are running is to review the running configuration. Unfortunately, this is not always the case. The running configuration only shows settings that deviate from the default values. Unless you know all the default values off the top of your head, you may miss some critical information.

Port Scanning the Router

To illustrate why you need to check more than the running configuration file, consider the following two port scans against a Cisco router. The first was performed with the router running IOS 10.2. The second was performed using IOS 12.07. In both cases, the running configuration files were identical.

Here is the port scan of 10.2:

```
Parameters
***********
Host: 192.168.0.250
Start Port: 1
End Port: 200
Scan Type: TCP and UDP
TCP Timeout: 500
UDP Timeout: 1000


Results
Port      Short Name      TCP test;     UDP test
*********************************************************

7         echo            4             ;
9         discard         3             ;
19        chargen         3             ;
23        telnet          4             ;
79        finger          4             ;
```

And here is the port scan of 12.07:

```
Parameters
***********
Host: 192.168.0.250
Start Port: 1
End Port: 200
Scan Type: TCP and UDP
TCP Timeout: 500
UDP Timeout: 1000
```

```
Results
Port        Short Name      TCP test;    UDP test
****************************************************
23          telnet          4            ;
79          finger          5            ;
```

Notice that IOS 10.2 has a lot more open ports. You may be wondering how this is possible if the running configuration files were identical. The reason is that IOS 10.2 enables more services than IOS 12.07 by default. The running and startup configuration file only lists variations of the default settings. Since these services were the "default" on IOS 10.2, they are enabled unless you specifically shut them off.

 TIP When creating a bastion router, it is prudent to perform a port scan against the device in order to verify which service ports are open. This is the best way to determine what an attacker who decides to target your router would see. You should make a note of any open ports you see on your router. Later in this chapter, we will discuss how to remove all of these potential entry points.

Check Running Processes

If you are unable to perform a port scan against your router, you can still check to see what services are running by reviewing a list of processes being executed by the CPU. For example, review the output below:

```
shelby#show processes cpu

CPU utilization for one minute: 8%; five minutes: 9%
 PID  5Sec  1Min  5Min TTY Process
   1 0.00% 0.00% 0.00%  0 Load Meter
   2 0.00% 0.00% 0.00%  0 Exec
   3 1.22% 0.26% 0.20%  0 Check heaps
   4 0.00% 0.00% 0.00%  0 Pool Manager
   5 0.00% 0.00% 0.00%  0 Timers
   6 0.00% 0.00% 0.00%  0 Serial Backgroun
   7 0.00% 0.00% 0.00%  0 ARP Input
   8 0.00% 0.00% 0.00%  0 DDR Timers
   9 0.00% 0.00% 0.00%  0 Entity MIB API
  10 0.00% 0.00% 0.00%  0 SERIAL A'detect
```

```
11  1.04% 0.44% 0.14%  0 IP Input
12  0.00% 0.00% 0.00%  0 CDP Protocol
13  0.00% 0.00% 0.00%  0 PPP IP Add Route
14  0.00% 3.53% 2.23%  2 Virtual Exec
15  0.00% 0.00% 0.00%  0 X.25 Encaps Mana
16  0.00% 0.01% 0.00%  0 IP Background
17  0.00% 0.00% 0.00%  0 TCP Timer
18  0.32% 0.04% 0.01%  0 TCP Protocols
19  0.00% 0.00% 0.00%  0 Probe Input
20  0.00% 0.00% 0.00%  0 RARP Input
21  0.00% 0.00% 0.00%  0 BOOTP Server
22  0.00% 0.00% 0.00%  0 IP Cache Ager
23  0.00% 0.00% 0.00%  0 PAD InCall
24  0.00% 0.00% 0.00%  0 X.25 Background
25  0.00% 0.00% 0.00%  0 Socket Timers
26  0.00% 0.00% 0.00%  0 TCP Intercept Ti
27  0.00% 0.00% 0.00%  0 SPX Input
28  0.00% 0.00% 0.00%  0 ISDN Timer
29  0.00% 0.00% 0.00%  0 TCP Echo
30  0.00% 0.00% 0.00%  0 CallMIB Backgrou
31  0.00% 0.00% 0.00%  0 ISDNMIB Backgrou
32  0.00% 0.00% 0.00%  0 SNMP ConfCopyPro
33  0.00% 0.00% 0.00%  0 Syslog Traps
34  0.00% 0.00% 0.00%  0 Critical Bkgnd
35  0.00% 0.00% 0.00%  0 Net Background
36  0.00% 0.00% 0.00%  0 Logger
37  0.00% 0.00% 0.00%  0 TTY Background
38  0.00% 0.00% 0.00%  0 Per-Second Jobs
39  0.00% 0.00% 0.00%  0 Net Input
40  0.00% 0.00% 0.00%  0 Compute load avg
41  0.00% 0.13% 0.12%  0 Per-minute Jobs
42  0.00% 0.00% 0.00%  0 TCP Discard
43  0.00% 0.00% 0.00%  0 TCP Echo
44  0.00% 0.00% 0.00%  0 TCP Discard
```

Notice that Process IDs (PID) 29 and 43 identify that the TCP Echo service is running. Also note that PIDs 42 and 44 reference the TCP Discard service. This is an indication that `tcp-small-servers` has been enabled on the router. For older IOS versions (some 11.*x* and earlier), this was the default setting. For newer versions of IOS

CHAPTER 10 • CREATING A BASTION ROUTER

(some 11.*x* and later), the command was disabled by default and must be manually activated.

While a port scan is the quickest way to determine which ports are open on your router, it is possible to gather this information based on the processes being executed by the CPU.

Checking for Known Exploits

Along with disabling unneeded services, you should also insure that there are no known exploits or vulnerabilities against the version of IOS that you are running on your router. Cisco is extremely diligent in fixing security problems as soon as they surface. Unfortunately, you cannot simply patch Cisco IOS; you must perform a full upgrade to a later version. Luckily, Cisco makes these upgrades available for free.

Cisco maintains a list of security advisories at this Web page:

`http://www.cisco.com/warp/public/707/advisory.html`

You can use this page as a reference in determining whether there are any worrisome security-related bugs in your version of IOS. The page lists all Cisco security advisories and includes a description of the problem, as well as the affected IOS versions. If you find a problem that affects your version of IOS, simply contact Cisco for a free upgrade. Then all you have to do is replace your current version of IOS with the newly patched version.

 NOTE This page also includes links to a number of useful security papers. For example, there are tips on minimizing the effects of TCP SYN and Smurf attacks. There are even tips for tracking down attackers who use spoofed source IP addresses.

Disabling Unneeded Services

Now that you know how to determine what services are running on your Cisco router, let's look at how to disable the ones you do not need. Most services are provided for either administration or diagnostic purposes. If you can do without these services, it is best to disable them or at the very least limit their use.

Cisco Discovery Protocol

The *Cisco Discovery Protocol* (CDP) can be used by a Cisco router to identify other Cisco devices running on the same network segment. CDP reports device type (router, switch, and so on), as well as the device's make and model. It will also report which of the device's interfaces are connected to the local network segment.

CDP is not propagated across networks. In order to exploit the CDP protocol, an attacker would need access to the local network segment. Still, this could very easily be your ISP's or business partner's router on the other end of the WAN connection. If the remote router were compromised, CDP could provide a would-be attacker with critical information about your network's perimeter. For routers that are exposed to external networks, it is best to disable CDP. You can do this by entering the following command in global configuration mode:

```
no cdp run
```

Finger

Finger is an information-gathering tool. It ships with most UNIX operating systems and is included in many Windows IP-based diagnostic tools, such as Sam Spade. Typically, Finger is used to retrieve information regarding a specific user account on a system. For example, you could finger the root account on a UNIX system in order to determine when was the last time root logged on to the system, from which location it logged on, and whether the root account has any unread mail. Needless to say, this may be more information than you wish to hand out to just anyone.

With a Cisco router, you finger not specific accounts but the router itself. This activity is shown in the following session:

```
finger @192.168.0.254 ...

Line      User     Host(s)   Idle        Location
0 con 0            idle      40:08:36
2 vty 0            idle      01:01:01    192.168.0.196
```

You may notice that Finger has produced some very useful information to a would-be attacker. The line con 0 tells you that someone is plugged directly into the console port and is logged on to the router. The idle time tells you that this session has been active for more than 40 hours. This means that a logged-on console session is just waiting for any attacker who can gain physical access to the router.

The last line provides some interesting information, as well. This line tells you that someone has established a network-based session (vty) with the router from IP address

192.168.0.196. This is probably a Telnet session, but it could be any other command session, such as HTTP. If I cannot connect to any of the command ports from my current IP address, I know I can connect from 192.168.0.196 if I can compromise that system or find a way to spoof its IP address.

So Finger can produce a lot more information about the terminal sessions with this router than you would like to make available to the general public. To disable Finger, enter configuration mode and enter this command:

```
no ip finger
```

This will prevent the router from servicing Finger requests on TCP/79. You should also see this command appear toward the beginning of your running configuration file.

Finger and Timeout Values

The Finger output also provides clues to another problem. By default, a Cisco router will close inactive vty sessions after 10 minutes. The fact that the listed vty session has been idle for over an hour tells you that someone has changed this timeout value. To verify this, check the vty section of the running configuration for the instance of

```
session-timeout xxxx
```

where *xxxx* is the new timeout value in minutes.

In order to insure that network-based sessions are not left unattended for long periods of time, you can either leave the timeout at its default value of 10 minutes or change it to something else by typing the following from configuration mode:

```
router(config)# line vty 0 197
router(config-line)# session-timeout xxxx
```

where *xxxx* is the number of minutes you wish to let pass before disconnecting inactive network-based sessions.

To change the timeout value for the system console, enter the following:

```
router(config)# line console 0
router(config-line)# session-time xxxx
```

HTTP Server

The *HTTP server* allows you to perform most of the Cisco management and monitoring functions through an HTML interface. Figure 10.1 shows the configuration menu screen. Notice that it is nearly identical to creating a terminal session with the router and entering configuration mode.

NOTE While the HTTP server port is disabled by default, it is worth covering in case you happen to find it enabled.

FIGURE 10.1

The configuration menu of the HTML interface

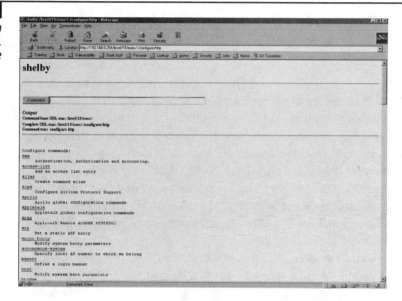

Since this interface allows you to control the functionality of your router from a remote location, you should guard its use just as closely as you would guard the ability to connect to the router via Telnet session. To see whether the HTTP server is running, review the running configuration and look for the following entries:

```
ip http server
ip http port 10000
```

The first line enables the HTTP server. As of the time of this writing, HTTP is disabled by default in all versions of IOS. This means that if it is running, it will appear in the running configuration output. The second line assigns a listening port for the HTTP server. If a port is not specified, TCP/80 is used by default.

NOTE HTTP can be listening on any TCP port, so you may not detect the running service by performing a port scan of TCP/80. It could be listening on any port up to TCP/65535.

SNMP Support

Simple Network Management Protocol (SNMP) can be used to collect statistics and to make configuration changes to a Cisco router. This is done through the use of *community strings*. In brief, a community string is a password system that identifies a specific level of access for a device (either read-only or read-write). For example, most devices come preconfigured to use a community string of public for read-only access to the device. Anyone who accesses the router via SNMP using this community string is automatically granted access.

Besides poor authentication, SNMP has another major security flaw: It transmits all information in clear text. This means that anyone monitoring the network can grab the community name from passing traffic. SNMP also uses UDP as a transport. As we discussed in Chapter 9, UDP can be extremely difficult to filter due to its connectionless state.

For these reasons, you should avoid using SNMP on any bastion routers. While the manageability can be a real bonus in a large environment, this back-door access to your router can be a serious security concern. If you must use SNMP, use SNMPv2. The latest version supports MD5 authentication to improve security. While this security is not foolproof, it is far better than the original SNMP specification.

 NOTE Cisco routers versions 10.3 and up support SNMPv2.

All versions of IOS ship with SNMP disabled by default. If you have it running on a router and you need to shut it off, type the following while in global configuration mode:

```
no snmp
```

tcp-small-servers

The `tcp-small-servers` command enables a number of diagnostic services. These include Echo (port 7), Discard (port 9), and Chargen (port 19). All of these services can be used for diagnosing connectivity or throughput problems.

Echo and Chargen can be used by an attacker to launch a denial of service (DoS) attack. Whenever a connection is made to the Chargen port, a complete set of ASCII characters is transmitted to the connecting host. The Echo port reflects back any ASCII characters sent to it. An effective DoS can be performed by spoofing traffic to tie the Echo port on one system to the Chargen port on another. Every time Echo returns a character, Chargen responds with a full set of ASCII characters. The result is that so much traffic flows between these two systems that network performance grinds to a halt. With this in mind, it is a good idea to disable these services on all your exposed routers. To disable all three services, enter global configuration mode and type this command:

```
no service tcp-small-servers
```

udp-small-servers

Identical to its `tcp-small-servers` counterpart, this command enables the UDP ports for Echo, Discard, and Chargen. It can also be used as a diagnostic tool if you are attempting to troubleshoot UDP-specific problems. The command to disable these services is

```
no service udp-small-servers
```

Password Security

Password security is your best line of defense when locking down your router. The importance of a strong authentication policy cannot be stressed enough. Passwords should be a mixture of upper- and lower-case letters, as well as numbers. The longer the password string, the more difficult it will be to break during a brute force attack.

Changing the Terminal Password

A Cisco router can support up to five concurrent Telnet sessions. These sessions are labeled vty 0–4 (vty means *virtual terminal*). It is a good idea to change these passwords on a regular basis to help insure that the device is not compromised. You can change these passwords by entering global configuration mode and entering the following commands:

```
line vty 0 4
password 2SeCret4U
```

 NOTE Remember that Cisco passwords are case-sensitive, so use a combination of cases to make the password harder to guess.

Since you cannot select which vty you wish to use when connecting remotely, Cisco recommends that you set all vty passwords to the same character string. Depending on your organization's configuration, you may wish to reconsider this philosophy. As mentioned, the router will only support five virtual sessions. If you run a large WAN environment, where it is conceivable that a number of people may be logged in to the device at the same time, you could become locked out if all five sessions are in use.

 TIP You may wish to leave yourself an administrative back door by configuring vty 0-3 to use one password and vty4 to use another. This will prevent anyone else from using this last session, thus insuring that you can gain access to the device when you need it.

Changing the Enable Password

Access to the enable password in the Cisco world is the equivalent to Administrator under NT or root under UNIX. A person who has a Cisco router's enable password has free rein on the system. With this in mind, it's a good idea to guard this password and change its value frequently. To change the enable password, enter global configuration mode and type the command

```
enable secret (new_password)
```

where *new_password* is the new, case-sensitive password you wish to assign.

Note that

```
enable password (new_password)
```

will work, as well, but uses a weaker encryption algorithm when writing the password to memory.

NOTE Unless you have an older version of IOS, you should always use the secret switch when generating a new enable password.

Creating User Accounts

The problem with having all router administrators use the same enable password is that there is no accountability when changes are made. For example, if the router's configuration suddenly changes and no one wants to own up to making the change, there is no audit trail to identify who was on the system and when.

It is possible to create user-level accounts on a Cisco router. If the router is logging to an external resource such as a syslog server, user-level accounts can be a great way to keep track of who is making system changes.

To create a user account, enter global configuration mode and type these commands:

```
username (user) password (new_password)
username (user) privilege (1-15)
```

The first command creates the user account and assigns it a password. The second command assigns a privilege level to the account. On a Cisco router, a privilege level of 1 signifies a minimal access account. This is the privilege level used when a user establishes a session with a router but has not yet issued the enable command. Level 15 is the level of access provided when a user issues the enable command. Levels in between provide mid-level access. For example, a user who has been granted privilege level 3 may be able to run debug commands but not to erase the contents of flash.

The greatest strength in creating user accounts is accountability. As long as your router is sending log information to an external host, you will be able to track who has made configuration changes to the system.

TACACS

Cisco routers have the capability to use external authentication. *Terminal Access Controller Access Control System* (TACACS) provides a way to validate every user on an individual basis before any user can gain access to the router. When a user attempts to authenticate to the router (either for a terminal session or for privilege-level access), the user is prompted for a logon name and server. This information is then sent to a remote TACACS server for verification. If the authentication is correct, the user is granted access.

There are a number of TACACS servers available within the public domain for a variety of UNIX platforms. You can find samples on the Cisco FTP site. One of the more powerful features of TACACS is the ability to support *token cards*.

Token Cards

Token cards provide a one-time password authentication scheme. This means that a user's password changes periodically (usually once per minute). If an attacker is looking over an administrator's shoulder when the administrator accesses the router, the password used is only good for a very short period of time. This insures that any user password grabbed by an attacker will probably be of little use.

The only drawback to TACACS is that the router must be able to communicate with the TACACS server. Since we are talking about bastion routers, this may mean punching holes in a firewall so that the router can relay authentication information to a server located within the security perimeter.

Guarding Your Configuration File

The configuration of a Cisco router can be displayed by entering the command

```
write term
```

or

```
show running-config
```

The configuration can even be backed up to a remote server using the TFTP protocol. A sample header from a Cisco router configuration file is shown below:

```
! Cisco router configuration file
hostname lizzybell
enable secret 5 $1$722$CE
enable password SuperSecret
line vty 04
password SortaSecret
!
```

The privilege mode (enable) password is encrypted using a one-way encryption algorithm. This way, anyone who might see your configuration file will not immediately become privy to this password. The `enable password` string is simply used for backwards compatibility. If this configuration file were mistakenly loaded on an older revision router which does not support encrypted passwords, this password would be used instead of the encrypted one.

The Telnet and user passwords are in clear text, however, so you should guard this file as closely as possible. To better safeguard this information, you can encrypt all passwords by typing the following command in global configuration mode:

```
service password-encryption
```

This will encrypt the memory copy of all password strings. In order to make this permanent, you need to save these changes by typing

```
write term
```

or

```
copy running-config startup-config
```

NOTE Even though all your password strings are now encrypted, you should still take precautions to safeguard the configuration file. Cracker programs exist that attempt to guess a password's value by comparing the encrypted string to entries in a dictionary file. If a match is found, the clear-text equivalent of the password is returned. The only way to prevent this type of attack is to insure that even your encrypted password strings do not fall into the wrong hands.

Additional Security Precautions

So far, we have covered patching the Cisco IOS, disabling services, and implementing a strong password policy. There are a few more tricks you can perform in order to lock down your router a bit more tightly. Some are designed to protect the router itself, while others help to secure the internal network sitting inside your network perimeter.

Enable Logging

We have covered a few instances in which logging would be useful. These include

- System access
- Error messages
- Any access lists created using the log switch

To insure that your log does not become compromised, your best bet is to send log messages to an external system.

Sending Log Messages to an External System

Redirecting log output to an external host is actually quite simple. First, you need a host that will accept the log entries. Any system which has a syslog-compliant service running on it will do.

 NOTE Syslog is included with most UNIX operating systems and is available as third-party software for Windows platforms.

The first thing you need to do is set your logging level. Enter global configuration mode and type the following command:

```
logging trap (0-7)
```

where the values 0–7 correspond to each of the logging levels shown in Table 10.1.

TABLE 10.1: AVAILABLE LOGGING LEVELS

Log Level	Name	Description
0	Emergencies	System is unusable
1	Alerts	Immediate action needed
2	Critical	Critical conditions
3	Errors	Error conditions
4	Warnings	Warning conditions
5	Notifications	Normal but significant conditions
6	Informational	Informational messages
7	Debugging	Debugging messages

Once you have identified the logging level you wish to use, you can specify where to send the logging information. Do this by entering the following command:

```
logging (IP address or host name of syslog server)
```

 NOTE You can even enter the command multiple times to list multiple systems if you wish to record more than one copy of your log. If the syslog server is located inside the firewall perimeter, UDP/514 must be opened from the router to the server.

Controlling Telnet Access via Access Lists

Using access lists to control which IP addresses may create a Telnet session to your router was discussed in detail in Chapter 9. It is worth mentioning again here simply because access lists are such an effective deterrent against network-based attacks. An attacker who cannot connect to your router cannot use a brute force attack to crack your passwords. The more layers of security you have employed, the better.

Changing the Logon Banner

It's a good idea to change the logon screen banner to display a customized message. The last thing you want a potential attacker to see is a welcome message. Your message should reflect your organization's stance on unauthorized access to network hardware. Change the banner in global configuration mode with the following command:

```
banner incoming # message #
```

where # can actually be any ASCII-delimited character. This character cannot be used in the message and is simply used to let the command know where the message ends— you can place your message over multiple lines in order to change its appearance.

An example of this command would be

```
banner incoming # Unauthorized access prohibited #
```

Source Routing

Typically, IP packets contain no routing information. It is the job of the routers located along the network to select the best route for the IP packets to follow. It is possible, however, to add to the header information the route you wish to take when accessing a remote system. This is called *source routing*.

When a router receives a source routed packet, it forwards the information along to the next hop defined in the header. Even if the router is sure that it knows a better path for reaching the remote system, it will comply with the path specifications within the packet header. Typically, when a remote system receives a source route packet, it replies to the request along the same specified path.

Why Source Routing Is Evil

Source routing can be used by an attacker to exploit potential back doors within your network. For example, let's say that your company has invested a lot of time and money in a proper firewall solution. You have taken every effort to lock down your Internet connection as tightly as possible.

Let's also assume that you have a WAN link to a remote business partner which connects to your network behind the firewall. This organization also has an Internet connection but, unlike yours, it is composed of very trusting souls who think all the security hype is a marketing ploy by firewall vendors. For this reason, this organization has zero protection at its network perimeter.

Using source routed packets, a potential attacker could send traffic to your remote business partner, then have the traffic sent over the WAN link to your network. Despite all your security efforts, Woolly Attacker has found an easy entrance to your networking environment. The only thing missing is valet parking.

Source routing can be a bad thing and should be disabled at all your network perimeters. The only legitimate reason for allowing source routed packets is if you need to do connectivity diagnostics across specific links on the Internet. Since this is not an activity many of us must do, it is best to leave the feature disabled.

To disable source routing, enter global configuration mode and enter the command

```
no ip source-route
```

Dealing with Smurf

Along with all the countermeasures we have looked at so far, one more is worth adding to the list. Our final task is to help prevent *Smurf attacks*. Named after the original program that would launch this attack, Smurf uses a combination of IP spoofing and ICMP replies to saturate a host with traffic and cause a denial of service.

The attack goes like this: Woolly Attacker sends a spoofed Ping packet (echo request) to the broadcast address of a network with a large number of hosts and a high-bandwidth Internet connection. The spoofed Ping packet has a source address of the system Woolly wishes to attack.

The premise of the attack is that when a router receives a packet sent to an IP broadcast address (such as 206.121.73.255), it recognizes this as a network broadcast and will map the address to an Ethernet broadcast address of FF:FF:FF:FF:FF:FF. So when your router receives this packet from the Internet, it will broadcast it to all hosts on the local segment.

I'm sure you can see what happens next. All the hosts on that segment respond with an echo-reply to the spoofed IP address. If this is a large Ethernet segment, there may be 500 or more hosts responding to each echo request they receive.

Since most systems try to handle ICMP traffic as quickly as possible, the target system whose address the Woolly Attacker spoofed quickly becomes saturated with echo replies. This can easily prevent the system from being able to handle any other traffic, thus causing a denial of service.

This affects not only the target system, but the organization's Internet link, as well. If the bounce site has a T3 link (45Mbps), but the target system's organization is hooked up to a leased line (56Kbps), all communication to and from your organization will grind to a halt.

How can you prevent this type of attack? You can take steps at the source site, the bounce site, and the target site to help limit the effects of a Smurf attack.

Blocking Smurf at the Source

Smurf relies on the attacker's ability to transmit an echo request with a spoofed source address. You can stop this attack at its source by using the standard access list described earlier in this chapter. This will help to insure that all traffic originating from your network does in fact have a proper source address.

Blocking Smurf at the Bounce Site

In order to block Smurf at the bounce site, you have two options. The first is to simply block all inbound echo requests. This will prevent these packets from ever reaching your network.

If blocking all inbound echo requests is not an option, you need to stop your routers from mapping traffic destined for the network broadcast address to the LAN broadcast address. When you prevent this mapping, your systems will no longer receive these echo requests.

To prevent a Cisco router from mapping network broadcasts to LAN broadcasts, enter configuration mode for the LAN interface and enter the command

```
no ip directed-broadcast
```

You must do this on every LAN interface on every router in order for it to be effective. This command will not be effective if it is performed only on your perimeter router.

Blocking Smurf at the Target Site

Unless your ISP is willing to help you out, there is little you can do to prevent the effects of Smurf on your WAN link. While you can block this traffic at the network perimeter, this is too late to prevent the attack from eating up all your WAN bandwidth.

You can, however, minimize the effects of Smurf by at least blocking it at the perimeter. By using reflexive access lists or some other firewalling device that can maintain state, you can prevent these packets from entering. Since your state table would be aware that the attack session did not originate on the local network (it would not have a table entry showing the original echo request), this attack would be handled like any other spoof attack and promptly dropped.

Summary

By now you should know how to turn a Cisco router into a bastion host and why it is important to protect routers exposed to potentially hostile networks. We covered locking down the router itself, as well as additional steps that you can take to reinforce your security perimeter.

In the next chapter, we will look at using Cisco routers to create virtual private networks. Just as border routers are a natural choice for implementing perimeter security, they are also a good choice for extending your networks with VPN technology.

CHAPTER <u>11</u>

Virtual Private Networking

Not since the introduction of the Internet has a single technology brought with it so much promise—or so much controversy. *Virtual private networking* (VPN) has been touted as the cure-all for escalating WAN expenses, and feared as the Achilles' heel in perimeter security. Obviously, the true classification of VPN technology lies somewhere in between these extremes.

Interestingly, it has been financial institutions, trading companies, and other organizations at high risk of attack that have spearheaded the deployment of VPN technology. Financial and economic organizations have embraced VPNs in order to extend their network perimeters.

VPNs rely heavily on two technologies:

- Authentication
- Encryption

Before jumping into how a VPN works, we'll see how these two technologies can be combined to secure your data.

Authentication and Encryption

Authentication and encryption are two intertwined technologies that help to insure that your data remains secure. *Authentication* insures that each end of a connection is in fact who it says it is. This not only applies to the entity trying to access a service (such as an end user) but to the entity providing the service, as well (such as a file server). *Encryption* helps to insure that the information within a session is not compromised. This includes not only reading the information within a data stream, but altering it, as well.

While each of these technologies has its own responsibilities in securing a communication session, you can only achieve maximum protection by combining them. For this reason, a VPN includes both authentication and encryption.

The Need for Improved Security

When IP version 4, the version currently in use on the Internet, was created back in the '70s, network security was not a major concern. While system security was important, little attention was paid to the transport used when exchanging information. For this reason, when IP was first introduced that it contained no inherent security standards. The specifications for IP do not take into account that you may wish to protect the data that IP is transporting. This will change with IP version 6, but it appears that wide acceptance of this new specification is still many years away.

Clear-Text Transmissions

IP currently transmits all data as clear text, which is commonly referred to as *transmitting in the clear*. This means that the data is not scrambled or rearranged; it is simply transmitted in its raw form. This includes data and authentication information. To see how this appears, take a look at Figure 11.1.

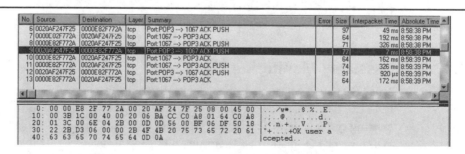

FIGURE 11.1

A packet decode of an authentication session initializing

Figure 11.1 shows a network analyzer's view of a communication session. It shows a user who is in the process of retrieving mail with a POP3 mail client. Packets 3–5 are the TCP three-packet handshake used to initialize the connection. Packets 6 and 7 are the POP3 mail server informing the client that it is online and ready. In Packet 8, we start finding some very interesting information. If you look toward the bottom of Figure 11.1, you will see the decoded contents of the data field within Packet 8. The command USER is used by a POP3 client to pass the logon name to a POP3 server. Any text following the USER command is the name of the person attempting to authenticate with the system.

Figure 11.2 shows the POP3 server's response to this logon name. If you look at the decode for Packet 9, you can see that the logon name was accepted. This tells you that the logon name you captured in Figure 11.1 is in fact legitimate. If you can discover this user's password, you will have enough information to gain access to the system.

FIGURE 11.2

The POP3 server accepting the logon name

Figure 11.3 shows a decode of Packet 11. This is the next set of commands sent by the POP3 mail client to the server. The command PASS is used by the client to send the password string. Any text that follows this command is the password for the user attempting to authenticate with the system. As you can see, the password is plainly visible.

FIGURE 11.3

The POP3 client sending the user's password

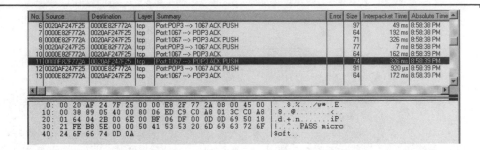

In Figure 11.4 you can see a decode of Packet 12. This is the server's response to the authentication attempt. Notice that the server has accepted the logon name and password combination. We now know that this was a valid authentication session and that we have a legitimate logon name and password combination in order to gain access to the system. In fact, if we decoded further packets, we would be able to view every e-mail message downloaded by this user.

FIGURE 11.4

The POP3 server accepting the authentication attempt

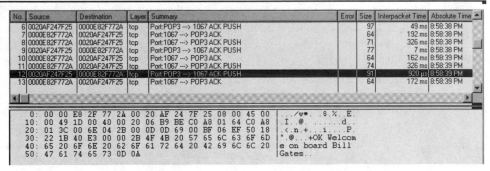

Passively Monitoring Clear Text

This POP3 authentication session was captured using a *network analyzer*. A network analyzer can be either a dedicated hardware tool or a software program that runs on an existing system. Network analyzer software can be purchased for less than $1,000 for Windows or Mac platforms. There are also freeware versions available for UNIX.

Network analyzers operate as truly passive devices, meaning that they do not need to transmit any data to the network in order to monitor traffic. While some analyzers do transmit traffic (usually in an effort to locate a management station), it is not a requirement. In fact, an analyzer does not even need a valid network address. This means that a network analyzer could be monitoring your network and you would have no means of detecting its presence without tracing cables and counting hub and switch ports.

It is also possible for an attacker to load network analyzer software onto a compromised system. This means that an attacker does not need physical access to your facility in order to monitor traffic. She can simply use one of your existing systems to capture the traffic for her. This is why it is so important to perform regular audits on your systems. You clearly do not want a passively monitoring attack to go unnoticed.

Clear Text Protocols

POP3 is not the only IP service that communicates via clear text. Nearly every non-proprietary IP service not specifically designed to provide authentication and encryption services transmits data as clear text. A partial list of clear text services includes

- FTP: Authentication is clear text.
- Telnet: Authentication is clear text.
- SMTP: Contents of mail messages are delivered as clear text.
- HTTP: Page content and the contents of fields within forms are sent as clear text.
- IMAP: Authentication is clear text.
- SNMPv1: Authentication is clear text.

NOTE The fact that SNMPv1 uses clear text is particularly nasty. SNMP is used to manage and query network devices. This includes switches and routers, as well as servers and even firewalls. If the SNMP password is compromised, an attacker can wreak havoc on your network. SNMPv2 and SNMPv3 include a message algorithm similar to the one used with Open Shortest Path First (OSPF). This provides a much higher level of security and data integrity than the original SNMP specification.

Good Authentication Required

The need for good authentication should by now be obvious. A service that passes logon information as clear text is far too easy to monitor. Easily snooped logons can be an even bigger problem in environments that do not require frequent password changes. This gives an attacker plenty of time to launch an attack using the compromised account. Also of concern is that most users try to maintain the same logon name and password for all accounts. This means that if an attacker can capture the authentication credentials from an insecure service (such as POP3), the attacker may now have a valid logon name and password to other systems on the network, such as NT and NetWare servers.

Good authentication goes beyond validating the source attempting to access a service during initial logon. You should also validate that the source has not been replaced by an attacking host in the course of the communication session. This type of attack is commonly called *session hijacking*.

Session Hijacking

Consider the simple network drawing in Figure 11.5. A client is communicating with a server over an insecure network connection. The client has already authenticated with the server and has been granted access. Let's make this a fun example and assume that the client has administrator-level privileges. Woolly Attacker is sitting on a network segment between the client and the server and has been quietly monitoring the session. This has given the attacker time to learn what port and sequence numbers are being used to carry on the conversation.

FIGURE 11.5

An example of a man-in-the-middle attack

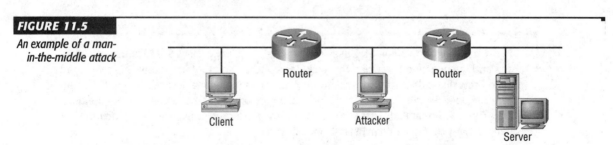

Now let's assume that Woolly Attacker wishes to hijack the administrator's session in order to create a new account with administrator-level privileges. The first thing he does is force the client into a state where it can no longer communicate with the server. This can be done by leveraging some exploit to crash the client, or by launching an attack such as an ICMP flood. No matter what type of attack Woolly launches, the goal is to insure that the client cannot respond to traffic sent by the server.

NOTE When an ICMP flood is launched against a target, the target spends so much time processing ICMP requests it does not have enough time to respond to any other communications.

Now that the client is out of the way, Woolly Attacker is free to communicate with the server as if he were the client. He can do this by capturing the server's replies as they head back to the client in order to formulate a proper response. If Woolly has an intimate knowledge of IP, he may even be able to completely ignore the server's replies and transmit port and sequence numbers based on what the expected responses from the server will be. In either case, Woolly Attacker is now communicating with the server—except that the server thinks it is still communicating with the original client.

 NOTE Good authentication should verify that the source remains constant and has not been replaced by another system. You can do this by having the two systems exchange a secret during the course of the communication session. A secret can be exchanged with each packet transmitted or at random intervals during the course of the session. Obviously, verifying the source of every packet is far more secure then verifying the source at random intervals. The communication session would be even more secure if you could vary the secret with each packet exchange. This would help to insure that your session would not be vulnerable to session hijacking.

Verifying the Destination

It's easy to see the need to authenticate the source both before and during a communication session. What may not be apparent is the need to verify the server. Many people take for granted that they will either connect to the intended server or that they will receive some form of "host unreachable" message. It may not dawn on them that what they assume to be the server may actually be an attacker attempting to compromise the network.

C2MYAZZ

The *C2MYAZZ* utility is an excellent example of a server spoofing attack. When Windows 95 was originally introduced, it included two methods of authenticating with a session message block (SMB) system. The default was to authenticate using an encrypted password. This was the preferred method for authenticating with a Windows NT domain. LANMAN authentication was also included, however, for backwards compatibility with an SMB LANMAN server. LANMAN authentication requires that the logon name and password be sent in the clear.

When C2MYAZZ is run, it passively waits for a client to authenticate to the NT server. When it detects a logon, C2MYAZZ transmits a single packet back to the client requesting that LANMAN authentication be used instead. The client, trusting the server is sending this request, happily obliges and retransmits the credentials in the clear. The C2MYAZZ utility would then capture and display the logon name and password combination. C2MYAZZ causes no disruption in the client's session; the user will still be able to logon and gain system access.

What makes this utility even more frightening is that it can be run from a single bootable floppy disk. An attacker only needs to place this disk into the floppy drive of a system, power the system on, and come back later to collect the captured credentials.

NOTE Microsoft did release a patch for this vulnerability, but you need to install it on every Windows 95 workstation.

DNS Poisoning

Another exploit that displays the need for authentication is *DNS poisoning*. DNS poisoning, also known as *cache poisoning*, is the process of handing out incorrect IP address information for a specific host with the intent to divert traffic from its true destination. Eugene Kashpureff proved this was possible in the summer of 1997 when he diverted requests for InterNIC hosts to his alternate domain name registry site called AlterNIC. He diverted these requests by exploiting a known vulnerability in DNS services.

When a name server receives a reply to a DNS query, it does not validate the source of the reply or ignore information not specifically requested. Kashpureff capitalized on these vulnerabilities by hiding bogus DNS information inside valid replies. The name server receiving the reply would cache the valid information, as well as the bogus information. The result was that if a user tried to resolve a host within the InterNIC's domain (for example, `rs.internic.net`, which is used for `whois` queries), she would receive an IP address within AlterNIC's domain and be diverted to a system on the AlterNIC network.

While Kashpureff's attack can be considered little more than a prank, it does open the door to some far nastier possibilities. In an age when online banking is the norm, consider the ramifications if someone diverted traffic from a bank's Web site. An attacker, using cache poisoning to divert bank traffic to an alternate server, could configure the phony server to appear identical to the bank's legitimate server.

When a bank client attempted to authenticate to the bank's Web server in order to manage his bank account, an attacker could capture the authentication information and simply present the user with a banner screen stating that the system is currently offline. Unless the user took the time to check the server's digital certificate, he would have no way of knowing he'd been diverted to another site unless he happened to notice the discrepancy in IP addresses.

 NOTE Digital certificates are used as a method of authenticating a system's identity.

It is just as important that you verify the server you are attempting to authenticate with as it is to verify the client's credentials or the integrity of the session. All three points in the communication process are vulnerable to attack.

Encryption 101

Cryptography is a set of techniques used to transform information into an alternate format which can later be reversed. This alternate format is referred to as the *ciphertext* and is typically created using a crypto algorithm and a crypto key. The *crypto algorithm* is simply a mathematical formula which is applied to the information you wish to encrypt. The *crypto key*, also called the *cipher key*, is an additional variable injected into the algorithm to insure that the ciphertext is not derived using the same computational operation each time the algorithm processes information.

How Encryption Works

Let's say the number 42 is extremely important to you and you wish to guard this value from peering eyes. You could create the following crypto algorithm in order to encrypt this data:

```
data / crypto key + (2 × crypto key)
```

This process relies on two important pieces:

- The crypto algorithm itself
- The cipher key

Both are used to create the ciphertext, which would be a new numeric value. In order to reverse the ciphertext and produce an answer of 42, you need to know both the algorithm and the key. There are less secure crypto algorithms known as *Caesar ciphers* which do not use keys, but these are typically not used because they do not have the additional security of a crypto key. You only need to know the algorithm for a Caesar cipher in order to decrypt the ciphertext.

 NOTE Julius Caesar is credited as being one of the first people to use encryption. It is believed that he used a simple form of encryption to send messages to his troops.

Since encryption uses mathematical formulas, there is a symbiotic relationship between

- The algorithm
- The key
- The original data
- The cipher text

This means that knowing any three of these pieces will allow you to derive the fourth. The exception is knowing the combination of the original data and the cipher text. If you have multiple examples of both, you may be able to discover the algorithm and the key.

Methods of Encryption

The two methods of producing ciphertext are

- The stream cipher
- The block cipher

These two methods are similar except for the amount of data each encrypts on each pass. Most modern encryption schemes use some form of a block cipher.

Stream Cipher

The *stream cipher* is one of the simplest methods of encrypting data. When a stream cipher is employed, each bit of the data is sequentially encrypted using one bit of the key. A classic example of a stream cipher was the Vernam cipher used to encrypt teletype traffic. The cipher key for the Vernam cipher was stored on a loop of paper. As the teletype message was fed through the machine, one bit of the data would be combined with one bit of the key in order to produce the ciphertext. The recipient of the ciphertext would then reverse the process, using an identical loop of paper to decode the original message.

The Vernam cipher used a fixed-length key, which can actually be pretty easy to deduce if you compare the ciphertext from multiple messages. In order to make a stream cipher more difficult to crack, you could use a cipher key that varies in length. This would help to mask any discernible patterns in the resulting ciphertext. In fact, by randomly changing the cipher key used on each bit of data, you can produce ciphertext that is mathematically impossible to crack. Using different random keys would not generate the repeating patterns that can give a cracker the clues required to break the cipher key. The process of continually varying the encryption key is known as a *one-time pad*.

Block Cipher

Unlike stream ciphers, which encrypt every single bit, *block ciphers* are designed to encrypt data in chunks of a specific size. A block cipher specification will identify how much data should be encrypted on each pass (called a *block*), as well as what size key should be applied to each block. For example, the Data Encryption Standard (DES) specifies that DES-encrypted data should be processed in 64-bit blocks using a 56-bit key.

There are a number of different algorithms you can use when processing block cipher encryption. The most basic is to simply take the data and break it into blocks while applying the key to each. While this method is efficient, it can produce repetitive ciphertext. If two blocks of data contain exactly the same information, the two resulting blocks of ciphertext will be identical, as well. As mentioned earlier, a cracker can use ciphertext which repeats in a nonrandom fashion to break the cipher key.

A better solution is to use earlier resultants from the algorithm and combine them with later keys. Figure 11.6 shows one possible variation. The data you wish to encrypt is broken up into data blocks labeled DB1–DB4. An Initialization Vector (IV) is added to the beginning of the data to insure that all blocks can be properly ciphered. The IV is simply a random character string to insure that two identical messages will not create the same cipher text. To create your first block of ciphertext (CT1), you mathematically combine the cipher key, the first block of data (DB1), and the initialization vector (IV).

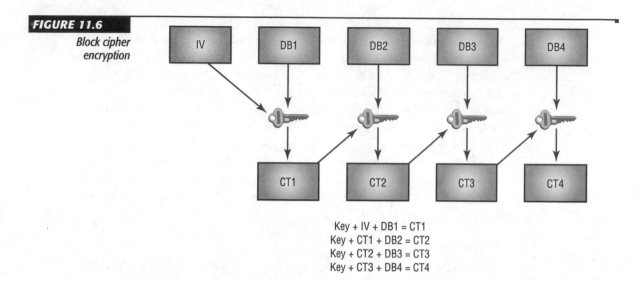

FIGURE 11.6

Block cipher
encryption

Key + IV + DB1 = CT1
Key + CT1 + DB2 = CT2
Key + CT2 + DB3 = CT3
Key + CT3 + DB4 = CT4

When you create the second block of ciphertext (CT2), you mathematically combine the cipher key, the first block of ciphertext (CT1), and the second block of data (DB2). Because the variables in your algorithm have changed, DB1 and DB2 could be identical, but the resulting ciphertext (CT1 and CT2) will contain different values. This helps to insure that the resulting ciphertext is sufficiently scrambled so that it appears completely random. This process of using resulting ciphertext in order to encrypt additional blocks of data will continue until all the data blocks have been processed.

There are a number of different variations on how to mathematically combine the cipher key, the initialization vector, and previously created ciphertext. All these methods share the same goal, which is to create a seemingly random character string of ciphertext.

Public/Private Cipher Keys

So far, all the encryption techniques we have discussed use *secret key algorithms*. A secret key algorithm relies on the same key to encrypt and to decrypt the ciphertext. This means that the cipher key must remain secret in order to insure the confidentiality of the ciphertext. An attacker who learns your secret key can unlock all encrypted messages. This creates an interesting catch-22, because you now need a secure method of exchanging the secret key in order to use the secret key to create a secure method of exchanging information!

In 1976, Whitfield Diffie and Martin Hellman introduced the concept of public cipher keys in their paper "New Directions in Cryptography." Not only did this paper revolutionize the cryptography industry, the process of generating public keys is now known as Diffie-Hellman.

In layman's terms, a *public key* is a cipher key that has been mathematically derived from a private or secret cipher key. Information encrypted with the public key can only be decrypted with the private key; however, information encrypted with the private key cannot be decrypted with the public key. In other words, the keys are not symmetrical. They are specifically designed so that the public key is used to encrypt data, while the private key is used to decrypt ciphertext.

This eliminates the catch-22 of the symmetrical secret key, because a secure channel is not required in order to exchange key information. Public keys can be exchanged over insecure channels while still maintaining the secrecy of the messages they encrypted. If your friend Fred Tuttle wants to send you a private message, all Fred has to do is encrypt it using your public key. The resulting ciphertext can then only be decrypted using your private key.

 NOTE Since the public and private keys are mathematically related, it is theoretically possible to use the public key in order to derive the value of the private key. Typically, however, large key lengths are used to make this nearly impossible in practice. We will discuss key lengths and why they are important in the next section.

Diffie-Hellman can even be used to provide authentication. This is performed by *signing* a message with your private key before encrypting it with the recipient's public key. Signing is simply a mathematical algorithm which processes your private key and the contents of the message. This creates a unique digital signature, which is appended to the end of the message. Since the contents of the message are used to create the signature, your digital signature will be different on every message you send.

For example, let's assume that you wish to send Fred a private message. You first create a digital signature using your private key and then encrypt the message using Fred's public key. When Fred receives the message, he first decrypts the ciphertext using his private key and then checks the digital signature using your public key. If the signature matches, Fred knows that the message is authentic and has not been altered in transit. If the signature does not match, Fred knows that either the message was not signed by your private key or that the ciphertext was altered in transit. In either event, the recipient knows that he should be suspicious of the contents of the message.

All these keys can get a little confusing. In short, these are the points to remember:

- Authentication: You sign using your private key, the recipient checks the signature with your public key.
- Encryption: You encrypt using the recipient's public key, the recipient decrypts using his private key.

Encryption Weaknesses

Encryption weaknesses fall into one of three categories:

- Mishandling or human error
- Deficiencies in the cipher itself
- Brute force attacks

When deciding which encryption method best suits your needs, make sure you are aware of the weaknesses of your choice.

Mishandling or Human Error

While the stupid-user syndrome may be an odd topic to bring up when discussing encryption methods, it does play a critical role in insuring that your data remains secure. Some methods of encryption lend themselves better to poor key management practices than others. When selecting a method of encryption, make sure you have the correct infrastructure required to administer the cipher keys in an appropriate manner.

Proper Key Management Is Key

Back in the 1940s, the Soviet Union was using a one-time pad in order to encrypt its most sensitive data. As you saw in the section on stream ciphers, it is mathematically impossible to break encryption using a one-time pad. This, of course, assumes that the user understands the definition of "one-time." Apparently, the Soviet Union did not.

Since cipher keys were in short supply, the Soviet Union began reusing some of its existing one-time pad keys by rotating them through different field offices. The assumption was that as long as the same office did not use the same key more than once, the resulting ciphertext would be sufficiently secure. (How many of you can see your pointy-haired boss making a similar management decision?)

Continued

Apparently, this assumption was off base: The United States was able to identify the duplicate key patterns and decrypt the actual messages within the ciphertext. For more than five years, the United States was able to track Soviet spying activity within the United States. This continued until information regarding the cracking activity was relayed to a double agent.

While a one-time pad may be the most secure cipher to use, you must be able to generate enough unique keys to keep up with your data encryption needs. Even if a regular secret key cipher is to be used, you must make sure that you have a secure method of exchanging key information between hosts. It does little good to encrypt your data if you are simply going to transmit your secret key over the same insecure channel.

Simple key management is one of the reasons that public/private cipher keys have become so popular. The ability to exchange key information over the same insecure channel that you wish to use for your data has great appeal. This greatly simplifies management: You can keep your private key locked up and secure while transmitting your public key using any method you choose.

 WARNING You must make sure that the public keys you use to encrypt data have been received from the legitimate source and not from an attacker who swapped in a public key of her own. The validity of a public key can easily be authenticated through a phone call or some other means.

Cipher Deficiencies

Determining whether there are any deficiencies in the cipher algorithm of a specific type of encryption is probably the hardest task a non-cryptographer can attempt to perform. There are, however, a few things you can look for to insure that the encryption is secure:

- The mathematical formula which makes up the encryption algorithm should be public knowledge. Algorithms which rely on secrecy may very well have flaws that can be extorted in order to expedite cracking.

- The encryption algorithm should have undergone open public scrutiny. Anyone should be able to evaluate the algorithm and be free to discuss their findings. This means that analysis of the algorithm cannot be restricted by confidentiality agreements or contingent on the cryptographer's signing a nondisclosure agreement.

- The encryption algorithm should have been publicly available for a reasonable amount of time in order to insure that a proper analysis has been performed. An encryption algorithm with no known flaws that has only been publicly available for a few months has not stood the test of time. One of the reasons that many people trust DES encryption is that it has been around for nearly 15 years.

- Public analysis should have produced no useful weaknesses in the algorithm. This can be a gray area because nearly all encryption algorithms have some form of minor flaw. As a rule of thumb, the flaws found within an algorithm should not dramatically reduce the amount of time needed to crack a key beyond what could be achieved by trying all possible key combinations.

By following these simple guidelines, you should be able to make an educated estimate about the relative security of an encryption algorithm.

Brute Force Attacks

A *brute force attack* is simply an attempt to try all possible key combinations in order to find the one which unlocks the ciphertext. This is why this attack is also known as an *exhaustive key search*. The cracker makes no attempt to actually crack the key but relies on the ability to try all possible key combinations in a reasonable amount of time. All encryption algorithms are vulnerable to brute force attacks.

There are a couple of key terms in the preceding paragraph. The first is "reasonable." An attacker must feel that launching a brute force attack is worth the time. If an exhaustive key search will produce your VISA platinum card number in a few hours, the attack may be worth the effort. If, however, four weeks of work may be required in order to decrypt your father-in-law's chili recipe, a brute force attack may not be worth the attacker's effort.

The other operative word is "vulnerable." While all encryption algorithms are susceptible to a brute force attack, some may take so long to try all possible key combinations that the amount of time spent cannot be considered reasonable. For example, encryption using a one-time pad can be broken using a brute force attack, but the attacker had better plan on having many of his descendants carry on his work long after he is gone. To date, the earth has not existed long enough for an attacker to be able to break a proper one-time pad encryption scheme using existing computing power.

So the amount of time required to perform a brute force attack is contingent on two factors:

- How long it takes to try a specific key
- How many possible key combinations there are

The amount of time required to try each key is dependent on the device providing the processing power.

As for the number of possible key combinations, this is directly proportional to the size of the cipher key. Size does matter in cryptography: The larger the cipher key the more possible key combinations exist. Table 11.1 shows some common methods of encryption, along with their associated key size. Notice that as the size of the key increases, the number of possible key combinations increases exponentially.

TABLE 11.1: METHODS OF ENCRYPTION AND THEIR ASSOCIATED KEYS		
Encryption	**Bits in Key**	**Number of Possible Keys**
Netscape	40	1.1×10^{12}
DES	56	7.2×10^{16}
Triple DES (2 keys)	112	5.2×10^{33}
RC4/128	128	3.4×10^{38}
Triple DES (3 keys)	168	3.7×10^{50}
Future standard?	256	1.2×10^{77}

Of course, all this leads to the question "How long does it take to exhaustive key search a particular encryption algorithm?" The answer should scare you. DES encryption (discussed in the DES section of this chapter) has become something of an industry standard. Over the past few years, RAS Laboratories has staged a DES challenge in order to see how long it would take for someone to crack a string of ciphertext encrypted using 56-bit DES encryption and discover the message hidden inside.

In 1997, the challenge was completed in approximately five months. In January, 1998, the challenge was completed in 39 days. In July 1998, the Electronic Frontier Foundation (EFF) was able to complete the challenge in just under three days. The last challenge was staged on January 18, 1999, and the EFF was able to crack a 56-bit DES encrypted message in just 22 hours.

The EFF accomplished this task through a device designed specifically for brute forcing DES encryption. The cost of the device was approximately $250,000—well within the price range of organized crime, big business, and your average government. Just after the challenge, the EFF published a book entitled *Cracking DES* (O'Reilly and Associates), which completely documents the design of the device they used. Obviously, this has put a whole new spin on what key lengths are considered secure.

Good Encryption Required

If you are properly verifying your authentication session, why do you even need encryption? Encryption serves two purposes:

- To protect the data from snooping
- To protect the data from being altered

In the section on clear-text transmissions earlier in this chapter, you saw how most IP services transmit all information in the clear. This should be sufficient justification for why you need encryption to shield your data from peering eyes.

Encryption can also help to insure that your data is not altered during transmission. This is commonly referred to as a *man-in-the-middle attack*, because it relies on the attacker's ability to disrupt the data transfer. Let's assume that you have a Web server configured to accept online catalog orders. Your customer fills out an online form, which is then saved on the Web server in a plain-text format. At regular intervals, these files are transferred to another system via FTP or SMTP.

An attacker who can gain access to the Web server's file system would be able to modify these text files prior to processing. A malicious attacker could then change quantities or product numbers to introduce inaccuracies. The result is a very unhappy client when the wrong order is received. While this example assumes that the attacker has gained access to a file system, it is possible to launch a man-in-the-middle attack while information is in transit on the network, as well.

The attacker has not actually stolen anything but has altered the data—and disrupted your business. Had this information been saved using a good encryption algorithm, this attack would have been far more difficult to stage because the attacker would not know which values within the encrypted file to change. Even if the attacker were a good guesser, the algorithm decrypting the cipher would detect the change in data.

VPN Basics

A virtual private network session is an authenticated and encrypted communication channel across some form of public network, such as the Internet. Since the network is considered insecure, encryption and authentication are used to protect the data while it is in transit. Typically, a VPN is service independent, meaning that all information exchanged between the two hosts (Web, FTP, SMTP, and so on) is transmitted along this encrypted channel.

Figure 11.7 illustrates a typical example of a VPN configuration. The figure shows two different networks that are both connected to the Internet. These two networks wish to exchange information, but they want to do so in a secure manner, as some of the data they will be exchanging is private. To safeguard this information, the border routers are used to set up a VPN between the two sites.

FIGURE 11.7

A sample VPN between two Internet sites

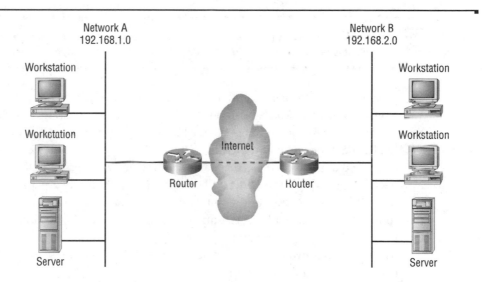

VPNs require a bit of advance planning. *Before* establishing a VPN, the two networks must do the following:

- Each site must set up a VPN-capable device on the network perimeter. In the case of a Cisco router, make sure you have a flavor of IOS that supports VPNs. Typically this will be a feature pack which is identified as IPSec56.

- Each site must know the IP subnet addresses used by the other site.
- Both sites must agree on a method of encryption and exchange encryption keys as required. Cisco IOS only supports IPSec, so whatever device is sitting on the other end must support IPSec, as well. Of course, if the other device is a Cisco router, as well, you are all set.

In Figure 11.7, the router on Network A must be configured so that all outbound traffic headed for the 192.168.2.0 subnet is encrypted. This is known as the remote *encryption domain*. Conversely, the router on Network A also must know that any data received from the router on Network B will require decryption. The router on Network B would be configured in a similar fashion, encrypting all traffic headed for the subnet 192.168.1.0 while decrypting any replies received from the router on Network A. Data sent to all other hosts on the Internet is transmitted in the clear. Only communications between these two subnets will be encrypted.

NOTE A VPN only protects communications sessions between the two encryption domains. While it is possible to set up multiple VPNs, you must define multiple encryption domains.

With some VPN configurations, a network analyzer placed between the two routers would display all packets using a source and destination IP address of the interfaces of the two routers. You do not get to see the IP address of the host that actually transmitted the data, nor do you see the IP address of the destination host. This information is encrypted along with the actual data within the original packet. Once the original packet is encrypted, the router will encapsulate this ciphertext within a new IP packet using its own IP address as the source and a destination IP address of the remote router. This is called *tunneling*. Tunneling helps to insure that a snooping attacker will not be able to guess which traffic crossing the VPN is worth trying to crack, since all packets use the two routers' IP addresses. Not all VPN methods support this feature, but it is nice to use when it is available.

Since you have a virtual tunnel running between the two routers, you have the added benefit of being able to use private address space across the Internet. For example, a host on Network A would be able to transmit data to a host on the 192.168.2.0 network without requiring network address translation. This is because the routers encapsulate this header information as the data is delivered along the tunnel. When the router on Network B receives the packet, it simply strips off the encapsulating packet, decrypts the original packet, and delivers the data to the destination host.

Your VPN also has the benefit of being platform- and service-independent. In order to carry on secure communications, your workstations do not have to use software that supports encryption. This is done automatically as the traffic passes between the two routers. This means that services such as SMTP, which are transmitted in the clear, can be used in a secure fashion—provided the destination host is on the remote encryption domain.

VPN Usage

Although VPNs are beginning to enjoy a wide deployment, there are only two specific applications for which they are being used. These are

- Replacement for dial-in modem pools
- Replacement for dedicated WAN links

A VPN can completely replace the listed technology or only in specific situations. The limited application is greatly due to the amount of manual configuration that is required in order to configure a VPN. As technology evolves, you may see this process become more dynamic. For example, two IPSec-compatible routers may dynamically handshake and exchange keys before passing SMTP traffic. When the delivery process is complete, the VPN could be torn down. While this technology is currently not on the horizon, it is certainly possible.

Modem Pool Replacement

Modem pools have always been the scourge of the network administrator. While stable solutions are available, these are usually priced beyond the budget of a small to mid-sized organization. Most of us end up dealing with modems that go off auto-answer, below-grade wiring, incorrectly configured hunt groups, and the salesperson who is having trouble dialing in because little Timmy deleted some files to make room for another game. For anyone who has been responsible for administering a modem pool, the prospect of getting rid of such headaches can bring tears of joy.

A VPN solution for remote users can dramatically reduce support costs. There are no more phone lines to maintain or 800 numbers to pay for. You are not required to upgrade your hardware every time a new modem standard is released or to upgrade your phone lines to support new technology, such as ISDN. All inbound access is managed through your Internet connection, a connection your company already maintains in order to do business on the Internet.

Access costs can be cheaper, as well. For example, many organizations maintain an 800 number in order to allow employees remote access to the network free of charge. This can place a large cost burden on the organization, as the per-minute charge for using an 800 number can be double the cost of calling direct. Most ISPs charge $20 per month or less for unlimited access. Large ISPs, such as CompuServe, can even provide local dial-up numbers internationally. For heavy remote access users, it may be far more cost effective for an organization to reimburse the employee for an ISP account than it would be to pay 800-number charges.

Besides reducing infrastructure costs, you can reduce end-user support costs, as well. The most common remote access helpdesk problem is helping the end user configure network settings and connect to the network. If the user first needs to dial in to an ISP, this support can be given by the ISP providing access. Your organization's helpdesk only needs to get involved when the user can access resources out on the Internet but is having problems connecting to internal resources. This greatly limits the scope of required support.

 TIP When selecting a firewall solution, consider whether you will be providing end users with remote VPN access. Most firewall packages provide special client software so that an end user can create a VPN to the firewall.

There are a few drawbacks to consider when you are deciding whether to provide end users with remote VPN access. The first is the integrity of the remote workstation. With penetration tools such as the L0pht's Netcat and the Cult of the Dead Cow's Back Orifice freely available on the Internet, it is entirely possible that the remote workstation can become compromised. Most ISPs do not provide any type of firewall for dial-in users. This means that dialed-in systems are wide open to attack. The remote client could be infiltrated by an attacker, who could then use the VPN tunnel to attack internal resources.

If you will be providing client VPN access to your network, keep a sharp eye on system capacity. Here are some questions you should ask yourself:

- How many concurrent users will there be? More users means more capacity will be required.

- When will VPN clients be remotely connecting to my network? If most remote VPN access will take place during normal business hours, a faster Internet link and faster hardware may be required.

- What services will the clients be accessing? If remote VPN access will be for bandwidth-intensive applications such as file sharing, a faster Internet link and faster hardware may be required, as well.

Dedicated WAN Link Replacement

As you saw in Figure 11.7, a VPN can be used to connect two geographically separate networks over the Internet. This is most advantageous when the two sites are separated by large distances, such as when your organization has one office in Germany and another in New York. Instead of having to pay for a dedicated circuit halfway around the world, each site would only be required to connect to a local ISP. The Internet could then be used as a backbone to connect these two networks.

A VPN connection may even be advantageous when two sites are relatively close to one another. For example, if you have a business partner that you wish to exchange information with but the expected bandwidth does not justify a dedicated connection, a VPN tunnel across an already existing Internet connection may be just the ticket. In fact, it may even make life a bit easier.

Consider the network drawing in Figure 11.8. There is an internal network protected by a firewall. There is also a DMZ segment which holds your Web server and SMTP relay. Additionally, you have an extra network card in the firewall for managing security to a number of dedicated T1 lines. The T1 circuits connect you to multiple business partners and are used so that sensitive information does not cross the Internet. This sensitive information may be transmitted via e-mail or by FTP.

While this setup may appear pretty straightforward on the surface, it could potentially run into a number of problems. The first is routing. Your firewall would need to be programmed with the routing information for each of these remote networks. Otherwise, your firewall would simply refer to its default route setting and send this traffic out to the Internet. While these routing entries can be set in advance, how will you be updated if one of the remote networks makes a routing or subnet change? While you could use RIP, you have already seen in Chapter 5 that this is a very insecure routing protocol. Open Shortest Path First (OSPF) would be a better choice, but depending on the equipment at the other end of the link, you may not have the option of running OSPF.

FIGURE 11.8

*A network using dedi-
cated links to safe-
guard sensitive
information*

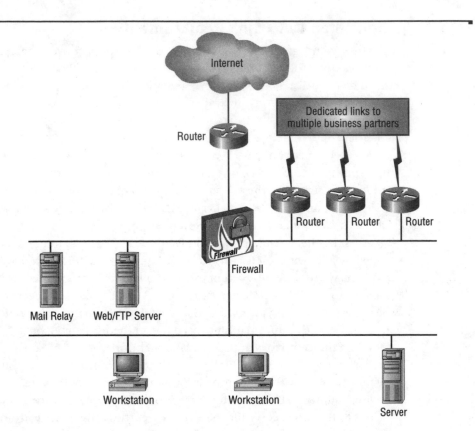

You may also run into IP address issues. What if one of the remote networks is using NAT with private address space? If you perform a DNS lookup on one of these systems, you will receive the public IP address, not the private. This means that you may have additional routing issues or you may be required to run DNS entries for these systems locally. Also, what if two or more of the remote networks are using the same private address space? You now may be forced to run NAT on the router at your end of the connection just so your hosts can distinguish between the two networks.

There is also a liability issue here. What if an attacker located at one of your remote business partners launches an attack against one of the other remote business partners? You have now provided the medium required for this attack to take place. Even if you can legally defend yourself, this would certainly cause a lot of embarrassment and strain your business relationships.

Replacing your dedicated business partner connections with VPNs would resolve each of these problems. As long as you can insure the integrity of the data stream, administering multiple VPNs would be far simpler than managing multiple dedicated circuits.

Standards Used by Cisco

When creating a VPN connection, Cisco routers rely on a number of industry standard protocols. Each of these protocols plays a part in establishing and maintaining a VPN connection between two routers. These standards are IP Security (IPSec), the Internet Key Exchange (IKE), and the Data Encryption Standard (DES).

IP Security (IPSec)

IPSec, as specified in Request for Comments (RFC) 2401, is an attempt to bring order to the chaotic world of VPN connectivity. When VPN technology was in its infancy, implementations were vendor-specific. In other words, a VPN product from one vendor would rarely communicate with a VPN product from another vendor. This means that if you wanted to create a VPN using Check Point FireWall-1 at one end of the circuit, you would need to have FireWall-1 at the other end, as well.

IPSec is not so much a new specification as a collection of open standards. For example, IPSec does not try to specify how or when encryption keys will be exchanged. IPSec simply defines the VPN framework and points to other specifications, such as the Internet Key Exchange, to fill in the blanks. This allows IPSec to be modular, permitting portions of the communication process to be improved when technology advances—without requiring a rewrite of the IPSec protocol itself.

 TIP   RFC 2411 is a listing of all the protocols used to formulate IPSec along with their reference RFC numbers.

Packet Authentication

For authentication, IPSec uses the Authentication Header (AH) protocol as specified in RFC 2402. The AH provides a method of authenticating each packet received by the target system. AH verifies that the transmitting system is in fact who it claims to be and that the data has not been altered in transit. AH helps to insure that an attacker cannot attempt to launch a spoofing or man-in-the-middle attack.

Encapsulation Support

IPSec also includes support for the IP Encapsulating Security Payload (ESP) protocol as defined in RFC 2406. ESP can provide an additional layer of authentication, but its real strength lies in its ability to encapsulate or tunnel all traffic flowing between two end points of a VPN. This allows private address space to be used by both networks connecting through the tunnel. It also masks the true source and destination IP address of all traffic passing through the VPN.

Why Is Encapsulation Important?

Let's review each of these features one at a time to see how they work. In Figure 11.9, you see two networks using a VPN to communicate over the Internet. Let's assume that a user at IP address 192.168.1.25 needs to retrieve data from the server located at IP address 192.168.2.10. Let's also assume that tunneling is not being used initially.

FIGURE 11.9

Two networks communicating via a VPN

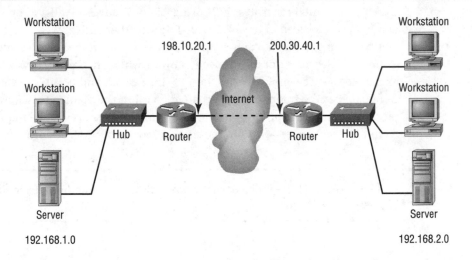

The user's system would first formulate a data request. This would be passed down the protocol stack and identified as having a destination IP address of 192.168.2.10. Since this address is not on the local network, the desktop system would forward the request to the router leading to the Internet.

The Internet router would look at the destination IP address and note that the address is not local. It would then realize that the packet is destined for the other end of the VPN. At this point, the router would encrypt the payload of the packet and include any required authentication information. The router would then forward the packet to its default route entry, which would be the ISP's router on the other side of the WAN link. At this point, the packet of data has been successfully encrypted and has left the local network.

A funny thing happens to this packet on its way to the 192.168.2.0 network, however. Since this address space is considered private, there is no routing information on the Internet that will allow this packet to reach its intended destination. The packet may traverse one or two additional routers before it is rejected with a "network unreachable" error. In fact, this error message will get dropped, as well; there is no route information leading back to the 192.168.1.0 network because this is also private address space.

It is quite possible we have a fully functional VPN. We just can't pass traffic across it because all of the systems using the VPN have been addressed using private address space. While we could use NAT, this may not be possible in all cases. NAT breaks many applications that like to include address information in the payload of the packets. Some good examples are Microsoft file sharing, NetMeeting, and Exchange. When the IP address in the header of these packets gets translated to a legal IP address during the NAT process, it no longer matches the IP address hidden in the payload of the packet. This causes the communication process to fail.

 WARNING If NAT is used with IPSec, you cannot use the per-packet authentication feature of AH.

Now let's look at the same example, but this time we will assume that the router supports ESP so that data encapsulation is being performed. Just like last time, the local workstation passes the data request down the protocol stack and identifies it as having a destination IP address of 192.168.2.10. Again, since this address is not on the local network, the desktop system would forward the request to the router leading to the Internet.

This time, however, when the router realizes that the packet is destined for the other end of the VPN, it realizes that the data must be encapsulated. Instead of encrypting just the payload of the packet, the router will encrypt the packet in its entirety. The router will then wrap a new packet around the encrypted one, using a source IP address of 198.10.20.1 and a destination IP address of 200.30.40.1.

Since this new outer packet has a legal source and destination IP address, the packet will have no problem being delivered to its final destination. When the router at 200.30.40.1 receives the packet, it can then remove the wrapping, decrypt the internal packet (which is using private addressing), and deliver the packet to its final destination. By encapsulating or tunneling our traffic, we remove the communication problems that arise when both ends of the VPN use private addressing.

As mentioned above, tunneling provides the additional feature of masking the true source and destination IP addresses. Let's assume that our example network in Figure 11.9 is using legal instead of private addressing on both networks. In this case, we do not need to use ESP, but it may still be a good idea—just for the added security.

For example, let's assume Woolly Attacker has heard through the grapevine that these two networks perform an FTP transfer once a week that includes a list of customers, each customer's Social Security number, and each customer's credit card number. Let's further assume that Woolly has been able to figure out the IP address of the FTP server used to transfer this data.

Given these conditions, Woolly could attempt to capture all traffic crossing the VPN that is headed for the FTP server's IP address. While it is true this traffic will be encrypted, Woolly could attempt to perform a brute force attack against the encryption used to scramble the data. If a small key size was used and only a few packets need to be deciphered, Woolly may be able to successfully steal this customer information.

When you use ESP, all packets are encapsulated. This means that the only IP addresses visible from the Internet are the IP addresses assigned to the serial interface of each router (in this case, 198.10.20.1 and 200.30.40.1). With ESP, knowing the real IP address of the FTP server does not do Woolly any good, because he would never be able to spot the address in the data stream. Woolly would be forced to decrypt all traffic crossing the VPN and hope that he gets lucky in finding the FTP transfer. While this is more "security through obscurity" than a legitimate security solution, it does make Woolly's task far more difficult.

The Security Association

As mentioned earlier in this section, IPSec is designed to be modular. While this adds to IPSec's flexibility, it can also introduce interoperability problems. My VPN device needs some method of establishing the communication ground rules with the system on the remote end of the VPN. The two systems need to be able to negotiate such parameters as what type of authentication to use, what type of encryption to use, and how often the keys should be exchanged. Without a method for exchanging this information, IPSec's flexibility can quickly become its biggest problem.

To resolve these issues, the concept of the *Security Association* (SA) was created. The SA is the mechanism used by IPSec to keep track of all the settings required to build and maintain a VPN connection. The SA specifies everything from the protocols used to perform authentication and encryption to the settings used with each of these protocols. The SA even specifies how long the current SA entry is to be considered valid. Think of the SA as your VPN security database, and you'll get the idea. The SA is responsible for cataloguing all communication parameters for each individual IPSec VPN connection.

Security Parameter Index

We have drawn a parallel between IPSec's SA and a security database. Just like a database, IPSec needs some method to uniquely identify each of the records contained within the SA. Remember that IPSec allows you to create multiple VPNs to many other networks across the Internet. This means that the SA could have entries for many different VPN connections.

To identify each of these unique VPN sessions, IPSec uses a value called the *Security Parameter Index* (SPI). The SPI is a 32-bit number used to uniquely identify each VPN session. When communicating via IPSec, the SPI identifies which negotiated settings should be applied to the incoming traffic.

The best way to demonstrate how the SPI works is to go through an example. If you examine Figure 11.10, you will see that the Corporate network has two VPNs in place, one leading to the Boston office and the other leading to New York. The SA on each router has created an entry specifying the parameters of each VPN and identified the connection with a unique SPI. The information in each SA record has been abbreviated in order to conserve space. What is important is the SPI value associated with each record. As part of the IPSec negotiation, SPI values are exchanged with the router on the other end of the VPN.

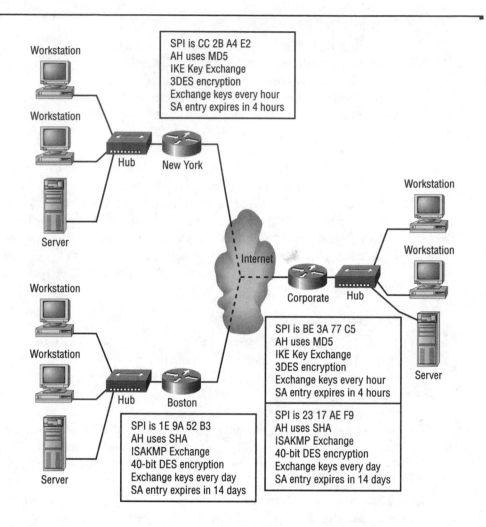

FIGURE 11.10

The SA entries generated by three routers while creating VPN connections

SPI is CC 2B A4 E2
AH uses MD5
IKE Key Exchange
3DES encryption
Exchange keys every hour
SA entry expires in 4 hours

Workstation

Workstation

Server

Hub New York

Internet

Corporate Hub

Workstation

Workstation

Server

SPI is BE 3A 77 C5
AH uses MD5
IKE Key Exchange
3DES encryption
Exchange keys every hour
SA entry expires in 4 hours

Workstation

Workstation

Hub Boston

Server

SPI is 1E 9A 52 B3
AH uses SHA
ISAKMP Exchange
40-bit DES encryption
Exchange keys every day
SA entry expires in 14 days

SPI is 23 17 AE F9
AH uses SHA
ISAKMP Exchange
40-bit DES encryption
Exchange keys every day
SA entry expires in 14 days

Let's assume that a user on the Boston network needs to make a data request to a server on the Corporate network. When the traffic reaches the Boston router, the Boston router must encrypt the traffic before transmitting it over the Internet. It does so using the parameters stored in the SA. Since the Boston router needs a way of uniquely identifying this session, it tags the packet with the SPI value generated by the Corporate router. In other words, the Boston router will record an SPI value of 23 17 AE F9 because this is the SPI value that was generated by the Corporate router during negotiation.

When the packet arrives at the Corporate router, the router simply reads the 23 17 AE F9 SPI value and checks its local SA. When it finds a match, it now has all the information it needs to authenticate and decrypt the packet.

Assume that delivery to the local server on the Corporate network was successful and the server returns a reply to the user on the Boston network. When the packet reaches the Corporate router, the packet is encrypted using the settings stored in the SA. The packet is then tagged using the SPI generated by the Boston router (1E 9A 52 B3), so that the Boston router will know how to authenticate and decrypt the packet once it arrives.

The SPI in use by the destination network gets recorded in the packet. This means that the SA actually contains two sets of records:

- One recording the SPIs generated locally
- One for the SPI generated by the remote VPN device

The reason the local SPI is not recorded in the packet is to eliminate the chance of duplicates. For example, it is statistically possible for the New York and the Boston routers to generate the same SPI value. If the Corporate router received a packet tagged with this duplicate SPI, that router may become confused about how to handle it.

 WARNING While many VPN products support IPSec, not all IPSec implementations are compatible. This means that you might have difficulty establishing a VPN connection between the products of two different vendors. An excellent reference for interoperability problems, as well as VPN information in general, is Tina Bird's Web site: http://kubarb .phsx.ukans.edu/~tbird/vpn.html.

Internet Key Exchange

The *Internet Key Exchange* (IKE) is actually a combination of two earlier specifications:

- The Internet Security Association and Key Management Protocol (ISAKMP)
- Portions of the Oakley key exchange

IKE has the following responsibilities during an IPSec session:

- Insure that the target system is who it claims to be
- Perform the actual process of negotiating keys and protocols
- Provide management for the key information stored in the SA

When a connection is under negotiation, IKE is first responsible for authenticating the remote system and establishing a secure channel of communication. Initial authentication is typically performed by using a shared secret: a key word or phrase known only to the VPN administrators. This password is established before you attempt to set up the VPN and is used for initial authentication only.

Once the initial authentication is complete, IKE performs a Diffie-Hellman key exchange. As we discussed in the "Public/Private Cipher Keys" section of this chapter, Diffie-Hellman can be used safely over insecure channels such as the Internet because only public key information is exchanged. Once the public key exchange is complete, we now have a method of protecting information as it is exchanged between the two VPN endpoints.

The only problem with using Diffie-Hellman for all of your VPN traffic is that it is very slow compared to secret-key algorithms such as DES. Since performance is a key factor in VPN functionality, Diffie-Hellman is only used to establish a secure connection. This connection can then be used to exchange secret keys. Once the secret keys are exchanged, they are used to encrypt all traffic crossing the VPN. Diffie-Hellman is not used again until the secure keys expire and a new set of keys must be exchanged.

Data Encryption Standard (DES)

DES is the encryption standard used by the United States government for protecting sensitive, but not classified, data. The American National Standards Institute (ANSI) and the Internet Engineering Task Force (IETF) have also incorporated DES into security standards. DES is by far the most popular secret-key algorithm in use today.

The original standard of DES uses a 40-bit (for export) or 56-bit key for encrypting data. The latest standard, known as *Triple DES*, encrypts the plain text three times using two or three different 56-bit keys. This produces ciphertext which is scrambled to the equivalent of a 112-bit or 168-bit key, while still maintaining backwards compatibility.

DES is designed so that even if someone knows some of the plain text data and the corresponding ciphertext, that person has no way to determine the key without trying all possible keys. The strength of DES security rests on the size of the key and on properly protecting the key. While the original DES standard has been broken in brute force attacks of less than one day, the new Triple DES standard should remain secure for many years to come.

Once IKE has set up a secure communication channel between the two end points of the VPN, a DES secret key is negotiated. This secret key is then used to encrypt all passing traffic. At an administrator-specified period of time, the DES keys expire, causing a new set of keys to be negotiated. This changing of keys helps to insure that if a key is cracked, the amount of data which can be deciphered is limited.

Besides changing the value of the keys, you want to make sure that each key you use has no direct relationship to any previously generated key. For example, if you change key values once per minute but each new key value is simply the old key value plus one, it is not going to take a cracker long to figure out this pattern and compromise the entire session. When you use DES with IPSec, you have the option of enabling *perfect forward secrecy*. This setting tells each of the systems establishing the VPN that key values should be random. There should be no mathematical relationship between one key and the next. While this results in a slight performance hit, perfect forward secrecy helps to make a cracker's life a bit more difficult.

VPN Deployment

A big part of deploying a VPN is determining where it should terminate with reference to your perimeter security. There are four possible placements for your VPN hardware:

- Outside your firewall on the DMZ
- Off a third NIC on the firewall (service network)
- Inside the protective perimeter of the firewall
- Integrated with the firewall itself

Each method of deployment has its strengths and weakness. Let's evaluate each so that we can determine the benefits and drawbacks to each possible design.

VPN outside the Firewall

Figure 11.11 shows a VPN solution deployed using the perimeter routers on two Internet sites. In this example, all VPN activity is invisible to the firewall and the inside network. Traffic through the firewall is routed in the same way as any traffic headed for the Internet. The difference is that when the border router determines that the traffic is headed for the remote encryption domain, the traffic gets encrypted and tunneled to the border router sitting on the other end of the VPN.

FIGURE 11.11

VPN terminating outside the firewall

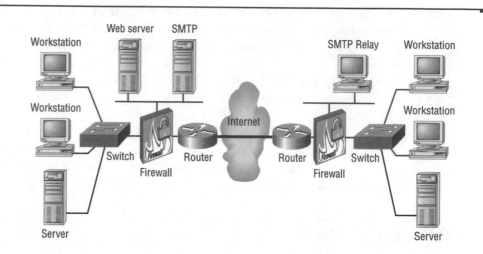

External Deployment Benefits

There are a number of benefits to this method of deployment. First, no routing changes are required. Some of the other deployment methods require you to make changes to the routing table in order to get VPN traffic to flow properly. Since this model sends all outbound traffic to the perimeter router, you don't have to make any routing changes.

Another benefit to this design is that it uses existing hardware. You are going to need a router to connect your site to the Internet. It's nice to be able to leverage this investment and not have to buy additional hardware and software. Purchasing less hardware and software can help reduce initial startup costs and could make the difference between high-level approval for a VPN project and rejection due to excessive expenditure.

Another nice feature of an externally terminated VPN is that all traffic passes through your firewall after it has been decrypted. This means that you can use your firewall to enforce access control between the two sites. For example, if the remote site attempts to telnet to one of your internal hosts and this is not considered acceptable policy, you could drop and log the session request at the firewall.

External Deployment Drawbacks

Unfortunately, terminating your VPN externally also has a number of drawbacks. First, your perimeter router is exposed to the woolly Internet with nothing to protect it but its own access lists. While it is true that you could use the tips outlined in Chapter 10 to help lock down your perimeter router, there is always a possibility that there is some yet-to-be-found vulnerability that someone could use to compromise the router. If this occurred, all configuration information could be exposed. While the chances of an intrusion occurring are minimal—as long as you are diligent in your security practices—it is statistically possible.

Another possible problem could be network address translation (NAT). If your firewall is translating all outbound traffic from private to legal addresses, it is possible that some IP-based services will not work. For example, applications based on the Distributed Component Object Model (DCOM) pass IP address and port information within the payload portion of a packet. On many firewalls, the NAT implementation can only translate the IP address and port information within the packet header. This means that if your firewall breaks DCOM-based applications (such as Exchange and NetMeeting), these applications will not work when communicating with hosts on the Internet, including hosts on the other side of your VPN.

With some firewalls, like Check Point FireWall-1, it is possible to manually edit your NAT rules in order to prevent network address translation from taking place under certain conditions. For example, if you know that the IP address for the network on the other end of the VPN is 192.168.3.0, you could create a manual NAT rule telling the firewall not to translate traffic headed to and from this subnet. Unfortunately, not all firewalls have this feature, so if you go with this method of deployment you could end up with some applications that do not work.

VPN on the Service Network

Another option is to place your VPN hardware on the service network. This is shown in Figure 11.12. In this example, all traffic headed to the remote network is forwarded to the VPN hardware on the service network. The traffic is then encrypted and encapsulated and sent out through the firewall. When the traffic is received on the other end, the remote firewall forwards it to the local VPN hardware, where the packets are decrypted and forwarded to the local network.

FIGURE 11.12

VPN terminating on the service network

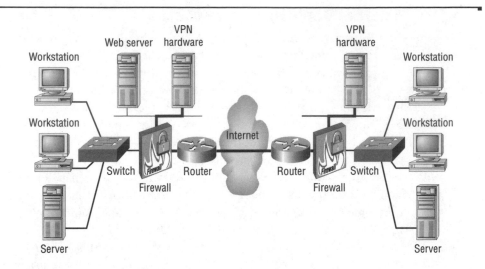

Since your VPN hardware must be a single-interface device, a Cisco router is not intended for this application. We will, however, cover some of the benefits and drawbacks for completeness.

Service Network Benefits

One of the biggest benefits to terminating your VPN connection on the service network is that the VPN device gains the benefit of being protected by the firewall. The firewall can be used to restrict which IP addresses are even allowed to connect to the box, thus helping to protect it from outside attack. Since decrypted traffic must flow back through the firewall in order to reach the internal network, you have the additional benefit of using your firewall for VPN access control.

Service Network Drawbacks

One of the biggest drawbacks to a service network VPN is that it leaves a potential hole in your network perimeter. For example, let's assume that an attacker has found a way to gain control of your Web server. Let's further assume that the attacker is able to use the Web server for capturing traffic going to and from the VPN server. If this happens, the safety of the VPN traffic is compromised—the attacker can now capture unencrypted traffic. Even worse, the attacker may be able to pretend to be a remote VPN user by spoofing traffic, thereby finding a way to gain access to internal resources.

VPN inside the Firewall

Your VPN can also be terminated inside the firewall perimeter, as you can see in Figure 11.13. In this example, all traffic is encrypted and decrypted within the protected area of the network.

FIGURE 11.13

A VPN terminating inside the firewall

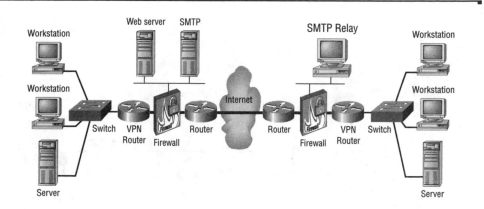

Internal Deployment Benefits

Terminating your VPN within the confines of your perimeter security may be your safest option. In this case, the firewall can be used to regulate which hosts on the Internet can attempt to create a VPN connection to your network. This provides additional security beyond the authentication provided by the VPN itself. Also, a breech in security either outside the firewall or on the service network will not allow an attacker to capture decrypted traffic.

Internal Deployment Drawbacks

The first drawback to an internal solution is that you can no longer use your firewall to regulate traffic exiting the VPN and headed for the local network. While you can implement access control directly on the VPN router, this will create an additional set of logs to review when you are checking activity. Not a big deal, but this does add to the network administrator's workload.

The biggest drawback to internal deployment is the need for additional legal address space. The subnet between the VPN router and the firewall should use legal addressing in order to insure that no NAT problems are experienced. If your ISP is only willing to give you a small pool of legal addresses, you may not have sufficient address space left over after assigning addresses to your public servers, such as your

Web and SMTP servers. While you may be able to negotiate additional address space from your ISP, its important to plan ahead before deployment.

Integrated with the Firewall

Figure 11.14 shows the final deployment option. In this case, the router acts both as a firewall and as the termination for your VPN.

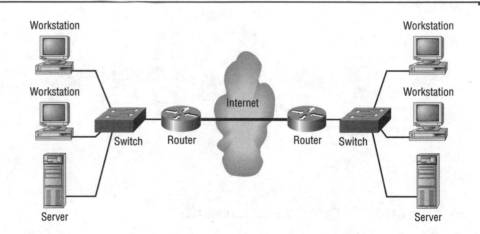

FIGURE 11.14

Integrating firewall and VPN functions

Integrated Deployment Benefits

The greatest benefit to an integrated solution is cost savings. Since everything is being done with a single device, your hardware and software expenditure is far less than any of the other solutions. For a small shop on a tight budget, an integrated solution may be the only option.

Integrated Deployment Drawbacks

The drawbacks to an integrated solution are many. First, you have a single point of failure with regard to security: If this one router is compromised, the entire site is at risk. Clearly, this is the least secure option of the group.

Another potential problem is performance. By making a single router wear so many hats, communication speed may degrade. For a small shop with limited needs, however, there may not be enough traffic for performance to ever be an issue.

Mixing and Matching

Your entire VPN does not have to be built on a single type of deployment. For example, let's assume you have a corporate office that needs to have VPN activity with three or four small field offices. In this case, the best fit may be to terminate the VPN internally at the corporate office, while going with an integrated solution at each field office. Every situation is unique, so your best bet is to evaluate the needs of each network and deploy a best-fit solution for each.

Configuring VPN Access

The process for setting up a VPN between two sites is relatively simple. Just follow these steps:

1. Determine a pre-shared key (secret password).

2. Configure IKE for SA negotiation.

3. Configure IPSec.

For the purpose of our example, we will assume that you are setting up a VPN between the two networks shown in Figure 11.15.

FIGURE 11.15

Sample VPN built on Cisco routers

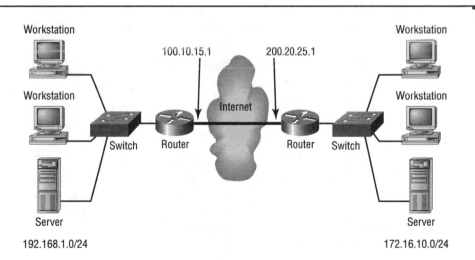

NOTE This example assumes you have a version of Cisco IOS which supports IPSec.

Determining a Pre-shared Key

In order to authenticate initially, your routers need some way to prove who they are. One method is to use a certificate authority and validate as required. The problem here is that you would need to maintain a valid copy of your public key with some registered authority or maintain your own certificate server.

A much simpler method is to use a secret code or password. When the two routers begin negotiating a VPN connection, this code word can then be used to authenticate each router. If the passwords do not match, the VPN will fail to initialize.

This password can be any value you wish to assign. What's important is that each router on each end of the VPN is programmed with the same password. This value is case sensitive, so make sure it matches exactly on both routers. Numbers, letters, and special characters are acceptable. For the purpose of this example, we will use the password noIP4u.

Configuring IKE

You need to configure IKE so that key information can be exchanged. Do this by identifying the policy number for this connection and the security parameters you wish to use.

From global configuration mode, enter the following command:

```
Shelby(config)#crypto isakmp policy 1
```

This tells the router that all configuration information you are about to enter is to be associated with policy number 1. If you wished to create a second VPN connection to yet another router on the Internet, you would assign a different policy number (such as policy 2). This lets you establish multiple VPNs and use different configuration options for each.

Next, you must define the size of the public/private key you wish to use. Do this by using the group command. The group command has two valid values: 1 and 2. A group value of 1 tells the router to use a 768-bit key for the public/private pair, while a value of 2 indicates a 1024-bit key. While group 2 provides an additional level of security, it also increases the amount of CPU time required for encryption and decryption. To specify group 1, enter this command:

```
Shelby(config-isakmp)#group 1
```

TIP Unless you have purchased a high-end router or you expect to see little VPN traffic, your best bet is to go with group 1.

Next, you need to tell the router that you will be using a pre-shared key. To do this, use the following command:

```
Shelby(config-isakmp)#authentication pre-share
```

Optionally, you can also choose to adjust the frequency at which a new SA must be generated. This value is expressed in seconds and defaults to 86400, or one day. For example, if you wanted to generate a new SA every hour, you would enter the command

```
Shelby(config-isakmp)#lifetime 3600
```

 TIP Make sure that both routers are set to the same SA lifetime. Otherwise, your VPN may initialize but then break after the shorter of the two time intervals.

Finally, return to global configuration mode and identify the pre-shared key you wish to use. Along with the key, you also need to identify the IP address of the router on the other end of the VPN. Refer back to Figure 11.15; you would enter the following command on the router at IP address 100.10.15.1:

```
Shelby(config)#crypto isakmp key noIP4u address 200.20.25.1
```

Conversely, you would enter the following command on the router at IP address 200.20.25.1:

```
Skylar(config)#crypto isakmp key noIP4u address 100.10.15.1
```

Once you've done this, the IKE portion of your configuration is complete.

Configuring IPSec

The first thing you must determine is the type of traffic you will allow across your VPN. Access control is done using access lists, just as we discussed in Chapter 9. While "permit" usually means to allow through all traffic meeting the specified criteria, when the permit statement is associated with a VPN it actually means that all traffic meeting the specified criteria should be encrypted.

For example, to create an access list for the left-hand router that will encrypt all traffic headed for the remote network, issue this command:

```
Shelby(config)#access-list 130 permit ip 192.168.1.0 0.0.0.255 172.16.10.0
0.0.0.255
```

NOTE The access list number you use cannot be the same as any of your filtering access lists. Use a unique access list number to identify your VPN rules.

Next, you need to define which IPSec parameters you wish to use. For additional security, enable the authentication header. You should also use the security encapsulation protocol because both networks are using private addressing and will need to have their traffic tunneled. Finally, you will define DES as your secret-key encryption. The following command will enable all of these options:

```
Shelby(config)#crypto ipsec transform-set vpn1 ah-md5-hmac esp-des esp-md5-
hmac
```

NOTE This command must match exactly on both routers. The only exception is the vpn1 parameter, which is simply a name we have defined for this particular combination of options. This name can be the same or different on each of the two routers.

Next, define how often a new secret key should be generated. Remember that an attacker who breaks a secret key can decrypt all traffic encrypted while this session key was active. With this in mind, you want to set a short time period for key renewal. For example, to generate a new key once per minute, enter the command

```
Shelby(config)#crypto map shortsec 60 ipsec-isakmp
```

Again, this command must match on both ends of the VPN. The parameter shortsec is actually a name we have assigned to this configuration so that it may be associated later with the router's external interface.

In your next command, identify the legal IP address for the peer router. This is similar to the way you had to declare the pre-shared key under the IKE portion of the configuration. On the router at IP address 100.10.15.1, issue the command

```
Shelby(config-crypto-map)#set peer 200.20.25.1
```

Do the same on the remote router, except you would set the peer to be 100.10.15.1.

Finally, identify the transform set and access list you wish to use for this connection:

```
Shelby(config-crypto-map)#set transform-set vpn1
Shelby(config-crypto-map)#match address 130
```

Your VPN setup is almost complete. The only step left is to assign the crypto map you just defined to the external interface of the router. To do so, enter the following commands from global configuration mode:

```
Shelby(config)#interface s0
Shelby(config-if)crypto map shortsec
```

You can now test your VPN connectivity and insure that traffic is flowing as expected.

 TIP   Once you've finished testing, don't forget to save the running configuration so that the new setup is available if the router is rebooted.

Summary

In this chapter, we discussed authentication and encryption and how these apply to virtual private networking. We looked at different VPN deployment methods and covered how to configure two Cisco routers to communicate via an encrypted channel.

Chapter 12 will show how to maintain and manage Cisco routers in a large enterprise environment.

CHAPTER <u>12</u>

Managing Cisco Routers

O nce you have your Cisco routers configured, you will want to make sure they continue to function properly. While I have seen Cisco routers operate for many years with zero intervention, it is prudent to take a proactive approach and keep tabs on how things are running. Many tools are available that can aid you in monitoring the health and status of your Cisco routers. In this chapter, we will take a look at some of these tools and how to deploy them.

Logging to Syslog

Syslog is a logging facility that runs under UNIX. One of syslog's useful features is that it will accept log entries from remote systems. This can be extremely valuable because syslog allows you to view a single log that includes entries from multiple systems. Instead of having to connect to multiple systems, you can view all entries in one location.

 TIP By modifying `syslogd.conf`, you can tell syslog to create a separate log file for each of your routers.

A side benefit of syslog is that it can help to augment security. The first thing an attacker who compromises a system will try to do is sanitize the logs. If the log entries are being sent off to another system, the attacker's job of covering his tracks has become much more difficult.

In the Cisco world, syslog is a requirement if you want to be able to log activity over an extended period of time. A Cisco router keeps a small buffer of log entries (4KB by default), which can be viewed with the `show log` command, but the lifecycle of these entries on a busy router is a few minutes at best. The buffer processes log entries in a "first in, first out" fashion; the earliest entries are overwritten as new log entries are created.

 NOTE Remember that a Cisco router does not have a hard drive. It has no capacity for archiving log files locally.

Sending Router Log Entries to Syslog

Configuring a Cisco router to forward log entries to a syslog server is easy. From global configuration mode, enter the following two commands:

```
logging on
logging 192.168.1.10
```

replacing 192.168.1.10 with the IP address of your syslog server. If you wish to send log entries to multiple syslog servers, simply repeat the second command with the additional IP addresses. Up to five syslog servers may be specified.

Once you exit global configuration mode, your router should begin forwarding log entries. Now it is a matter of setting up your syslog server to accept these entries.

Running Syslog under UNIX

Most UNIX systems ship with syslog configured and running. These are the major components:

- The `syslogd` binary
- The `syslog.conf` file
- The `services` file
- The startup script, which initializes syslog

The *syslogd* Binary

The syslogd binary is normally stored in either the /sbin or the /usr/sbin directory. To check and see what version of syslog you are running, you can enter the syslogd -v command while logged on as root.

TIP It's a good idea to make sure you are running the latest version of syslog, because some security vulnerabilities have been found in the past.

NOTE Syslogd is short for Syslog Daemon.

Besides the -v switch used for printing version information, syslogd supports a number of other useful switches, as well. The -d switch will allow syslogd to run as a foreground application and direct debug information to the current terminal session.

This is useful if you are attempting to collect log entries from a remote host but the entries are not appearing on the local system.

 NOTE Unless you are testing or troubleshooting, syslogd should not be run with the −d switch.

By default, syslogd reads its logging parameters from the file /etc/syslogd.conf. You can use the −f switch if you want to change this behavior. This is useful if you wish to set up a new set of logging parameters, but you do not want to change the original syslogd.conf file until you know everything is working properly. For example, you could put your changes in the file /etc/syslogd.alt and execute syslogd by entering the command

```
syslogd -f /etc/syslogd.alt
```

When you are happy with your changes, simply overwrite the original syslogd.conf file and start syslogd normally.

Older versions of syslog would accept log entries from remote systems by default. Newer versions, however, must be specifically told to accept remote log entries. Do this using the −r switch. When the −r switch is included during syslogd initialization, the local system will accept all syslog-compliant messages sent to it.

 TIP If you will be using the latest version of syslog to accept log entries from your Cisco routers, you will need to start syslogd using the −r switch.

The syslog.conf File

The syslog.conf file is used to define where log entries should be stored. Unfortunately, you cannot break out local log entries from remote log entries. For example, if you specify that informational messages get stored to /var/log/messages, then all information messages (both local and remote) will be recorded to this file.

The following is a sample syslog.conf file from a Linux system. Notice that all Cisco messages will get logged to /var/log/messages.

```
# Log all kernel messages to the console.
# Logging much else clutters up the screen.
#kern.*                              /dev/console
```

```
# Log anything (except mail) of level info or higher.
# Don't log private authentication messages!
*.info;mail.none;authpriv.none    /var/log/messages

# The authpriv file has restricted access.
authpriv.*                              /var/log/secure

# Log all the mail messages in one place.
mail.*                                  /var/log/maillog

# Everybody gets emergency messages
*.emerg                 *

# Save mail and news errors of level err and higher in a
# special file.
uucp,news.crit          /var/log/spooler
```

The *services* File

The services file identifies known IP services and associates them with the transport and port numbers that they use for communications. This allows the local system to identify port queries by service name. For example, the entry

```
telnet    23/tcp
```

would tell the local system that all communications using TCP as a transport and a destination port of 23 should be identified as Telnet sessions.

By default, syslog uses UDP as a transport and a destination port of 514. This means that its services entry would appear similar to the following:

```
syslog    514/udp
```

Without this entry in the services file, syslog will be unable to send or receive logging messages.

 NOTE If your router is located on the other side of a firewall from the syslog server, you need to open port 514/UDP.

Initializing Syslog

You will want to have syslog automatically started during system initialization. This way, no manual intervention is required in order to accept log entries. The following is the script supplied with Red Hat Linux in order to initialize and cleanly shut down syslog. The only modification made to this file is that syslog is being initialized with the −r switch so that it will accept log entries from remote hosts (the default is to initialize syslog without the −r switch).

```
# description: Syslog is the facility by which many daemons use to log \
# messages to various system log files. It is a good idea to always \
# run syslog.

# Source function library.
. /etc/rc.d/init.d/functions

[ -f /usr/sbin/syslogd ] || exit 0
[ -f /usr/sbin/klogd ] || exit 0

# See how we were called.
case "$1" in
 start)
    echo -n "Starting system loggers: "
    daemon syslogd -r
    daemon klogd
    echo
    touch /var/lock/subsys/syslog
    ;;
 stop)
    echo -n "Shutting down system loggers: "
    killproc syslogd
    killproc klogd
    echo
    rm -f /var/lock/subsys/syslog
    ;;
 status)
status syslogd
    status klogd
    ;;
 restart)
```

```
    $0 stop
    $0 start
    ;;
 *)
    echo "Usage: syslog {start|stop|status|restart}"
    exit 1
esac


exit 0
```

Insuring Syslog Is Running

Once syslog is configured, you will want to make sure that it has initialized correctly and is waiting for inbound connections. This can be done using the ps command, as shown in the following example:

```
[root@gakar /etc]# ps ax |grep syslogd
 200 ? S 347:18 syslogd -r
14467 p0 S  0:00 grep syslogd
[root@gakar /etc]#
```

In this example, we have run ps using the switches a and x. This will give us detailed output on all the processes running on this machine. Additionally, we are piping the output through the grep command so that we can search for the text string *syslogd*. This way, we do not have to see all the processes. We are only shown the processes that contain the text string *syslogd*.

Notice that the output shows two processes that contain the text string *syslogd*. The second listed process is our search using Grep and can be ignored. The first is the actual process we are interested in. This output shows that syslog has successfully loaded on the system. The output also shows that the –r switch is used so that syslog will accept log entries from remote systems.

Our last verification would be to insure that syslog is in fact listening for remote log entries. While this is implied because the –r switch was used, it does not hurt to check the system before assuming that all is functioning properly. To verify that syslog is listening, we can use the netstat command with the –a switch, as shown in the following example:

```
[root@gafar /etc]# netstat -a
Active Internet connections (including servers)
Proto Recv-Q Send-Q Local Address  Foreign Address State
tcp   0    0 *:smtp     *:*      LISTEN
tcp   0    0 *:telnet    *:*      LISTEN
```

```
tcp   0   0 *:ftp      *:*      LISTEN
udp   0   0 *:tftp     *:*
udp   0   0 *:syslog   *:*
raw   0   0 *:1        *:*
[root@gafar /etc]#
```

In this output, you can see all of the open ports on this machine that are capable of accepting inbound connections. Since syslog is listed, you can assume that this system will be able to accept log entries from remote systems. Notice that the UDP services are not listed as listening; this is because UDP is connectionless and does not maintain state.

Running Syslog under NT

Unfortunately, NT does not accept syslog-compliant log entries. If you wish to use an NT platform for accepting log entries from your routers, you will have to use third-party software. The following link contains both free and commercial syslog packages that will run on NT Server:

```
http://www.winsite.com/info/pc/win3/winsock/syslogd.zip/
http://www.netal.com/
```

Each package has a fairly straightforward installation. Simply run the included setup program and the syslog program will install as a service. You may need to reboot the system to activate your changes.

Testing Syslog

Once you have enabled remote logging on your router and you have your syslog server up and running, it's time to check that log entries are being properly recorded. You can do this by performing an event on the router that should generate a log entry on the syslog server. If the entry makes it to the syslog server, you know you are in business.

The first thing you should do is clear the local logging buffer on the Cisco router. If your log entry does not make it to the syslog server, you will want to verify that the router did, in fact, log the event. If you clear the buffer now, you'll know that any entries generated going forward should be recorded in the local buffer, as well as forwarded to the syslog server. To clear the buffer, enter the command clear log from privilege mode (not global configuration mode):

```
shelby#clear log
Clear logging buffer [confirm]y
```

```
shelby#show log
Syslog logging: enabled (0 messages dropped, 0 flushes, 0 overruns)
  Console logging: disabled
  Monitor logging: level debugging, 0 messages logged
  Buffer logging: level debugging, 1799 messages logged
  Trap logging: level informational, 1803 message lines logged

Log Buffer (4096 bytes):
shelby#
```

Note that no log entries are displayed. This tells you that the log buffer was in fact cleared properly.

Now you need to generate a log entry in order to insure that it gets recorded. Whenever you make a configuration change to your router, the event gets logged. The actual change does not get recorded; rather, the router will log an entry telling you that someone has been working with the router in global configuration mode. This means that if you simply enter global configuration mode and then leave, a log entry should be generated.

```
shelby#config t
Enter configuration commands, one per line. End with CNTL/Z.
shelby(config)#^Z
shelby#
```

These commands moved us from privilege mode to global configuration mode and back to privilege mode again. We can now check the local log buffer to see if a log entry was generated.

```
shelby#show log
Syslog logging: enabled (0 messages dropped, 0 flushes, 0 overruns)
  Console logging: disabled
  Monitor logging: level debugging, 0 messages logged
  Buffer logging: level debugging, 1800 messages logged
  Trap logging: level informational, 1804 message lines logged

Log Buffer (4096 bytes):

1w0d: %SYS-5-CONFIG_I: Configured from console by vty0 (192.168.0.28)
shelby#
```

We now have a log buffer entry telling us that the router was configured via the Telnet session vty0. We have successfully performed a task that was recorded in our log. The next step is to check the syslog server and verify that this entry was logged there, as well.

```
[root@gakar log]# tail messages
Feb 7 17:56:21 192.168.0.254 1800: %SYS-5-CONFIG_I: Configured from console
by vty0 (192.168.0.28)
[root@gakar log]#
```

Part of this log entry includes the IP address 192.168.0.254, which was not shown in the router's buffer output. This is the IP address of the router and is used by syslog to identify the source of the log entry. If you have multiple routers logging to the same syslog server, you will be able to distinguish the entries by the recorded IP address.

 WARNING Syslog does not perform authentication, so it is very easy to spoof the source IP address. This means that an attacker could easily send fraudulent log entries to the server. Make sure that you use packet filtering or some other form of protection to keep bogus entries out of your log.

Reading Syslog Entries

Once you start logging information to your syslog server, you must be able to interpret the log entries. Reading Cisco log entries is actually pretty straightforward once you get the hang of it. The best way to learn is to look at a few examples.

Configuration Changes

When we were testing our syslog server, we did so by entering global configuration mode and seeing whether this activity was logged to the server. Although I showed the generated log entry, we did not discuss how we knew that this was a configuration change. Let's look at each portion of the log entry to see what information is being conveyed to us.

```
Feb 7 17:56:21 192.168.0.254 1800: %SYS-5-CONFIG_I: Configured from console
by vty0 (192.168.0.28)
```

The first few pieces of information are pretty straightforward. The log entry includes the date and time that the entry was created. This is in reference to the clock on the syslog server itself. The time setting on the router is ignored for the purpose of creating the log entry. Stamping log entries using the syslog system's clock is useful because it provides a single time reference. You don't have to check each router's clock to see if all are synchronized.

The next two pieces of information are the IP address of the host which submitted the log entry and the log ID number. Cisco routers increment the log ID number by one for each log entry submitted. For example, the next log entry submitted by this router should have a log ID of 1801. This ID number is useful if you wish to index all of the entries received by a single router. To do this, simply sort them by ID number.

 TIP To extract all log entries for a particular host, use the `grep` command. For example, if you wish to create a file named `router.txt` which only contains log entries for the router at `192.168.1.1`, you would type the following command at the UNIX prompt: **grep '192.168.1.1' messages > router.txt**. NT does not include a `grep` command, but there are third-party tools that will perform the same functionality.

The next piece of information is `%SYS-5-CONFIG_I`. The `SYS-5` portion of the entry tells us that this message is a severity 5, or notification, log entry. Logging levels were discussed in the "Enable Logging" section of Chapter 10; however, a quick review would be useful.

Table 12.1 shows the different severity levels associated with each log level. The log levels allow you to customize which messages actually get sent to the syslog server. The higher the logging level, the more information is sent to the syslog server.

TABLE 12.1: AVAILABLE LOGGING LEVELS

Log Level	Name	Description
0	Emergencies	System is unusable
1	Alerts	Immediate action needed
2	Critical	Critical conditions
3	Errors	Error conditions
4	Warnings	Warning conditions
5	Notifications	Normal but significant conditions
6	Informational	Informational messages
7	Debugging	Debugging messages

For example, let's say that you set the logging level to 2 (critical). The only messages that would be sent to your syslog server would be messages that are considered to be critical: alerts or emergencies. You would not see messages for any of the other logging levels. In fact, the configuration change entry we are discussing would not get logged because it is a log level 5 (notifications).

 TIP You can set the log level of messages sent to your syslog server by entering the command **logg trap #** where # is the log level of the messages you wish to record.

We now know the log level of this message. The CONFIG portion tells us that this log entry is recording a configuration change. The remaining information tells us how the change was made (via a vty or Telnet session) and from what location (192.168.0.28).

Access List Log Entries

If you will be filtering packets with your Cisco router, a majority of the log entries will probably be due to your access lists. Let's look at a sample entry to see if we can determine what's going on:

```
Feb 13 04:05:49 200.2.2.110 100911: %SEC-6-IPACCESSLOGP: list 100 denied tcp
172.27.153.101(0) (Ethernet0 0800.20e0.f0ec) -> 208.218.3.6(0), 10 packets
```

The first portion of the log entry is similar to our last example. We have the date and time the log entry was recorded, as well as the IP address of the router. We also know the log ID number (100911) for this entry.

The next portion of information is SEC-6; this tells us that this is a security log entry of severity 6 (informational). The IPACCESSLOGP portion tells us that the message was generated due to a match in one of our access lists. The entry list 100 denied tells us which access list generated the entry and what action was taken against the packet.

The remaining details are further information about the traffic that was denied. The packets in question were using the TCP protocol and originated from the IP address 172.27.153.101. The log entry then goes on to say that the packet was received by the port Ethernet 0 and the system that transmitted the packet has a MAC address of 0800.20e0.f0ec. Finally, the packet was headed to the IP address 208.218.3.6, and a total of 10 packets were transmitted.

NOTE We know what packet was blocked, but we don't really know why it was blocked beyond the fact that it was not permitted by ACL 100. To determine why the router did not pass this packet, we must look at a network diagram and the rules specified in access list 100.

Figure 12.1 shows the network drawing for the router which reported this log entry. Notice that Ethernet 0 is the interface facing the internal network. Access list 100 contains the following rules, which have been applied inbound on Ethernet 0:

```
access-list 100 permit ip 200.2.2.0 0.0.0.255 any
access-list 100 deny ip any any log-input
```

FIGURE 12.1

A network drawing showing the router that is dropping packets

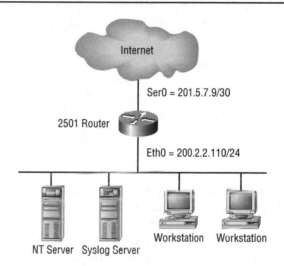

The first access list rule states that any host coming from an IP address on the 200.2.2.0/24 network will be allowed to pass through to the Internet. This makes sense because the internal network is using this address space. We would expect all internal hosts to be using an address from the 200.2.2.0/24 subnet range. The second rule states that all other traffic should be dropped and logged. The combination of the two rules insures that no one on the internal network can spoof the source IP address of traffic headed to the Internet.

We now have an interesting puzzle. Why would one of the hosts on the internal network claim its source IP address is 172.27.153.101 when that address space is not in use on the network? Clearly, we either have a misconfigured system or someone is attempting to spoof their IP address. Luckily, the log entry includes the MAC address of the transmitting system. The log claims that the packet originated from the host, using MAC address 0800.20e0.f0ec. If we check the vendor code portion of this address (080020), we find out that this is a Sun system. We would now want to track down this host to determine why it is transmitting spoofed packets.

 NOTE If you see a vendor code of 0000c0, this is another Cisco device. This implies that the traffic originated from a remote subnet. You would have to check the logs for this other Cisco device, as well, in order to trace the packets back to the true source.

Monitoring Link Status

Along with ACL traffic logging, syslog will keep track of when circuit errors take place. For example, review the two following log entries:

```
Feb 11 11:20:51 10.1.1.1 832: %LINK-3-UPDOWN: Interface Serial2, changed
state to down
Feb 11 11:20:52 10.1.1.1 833: %LINEPROTO-5-UPDOWN: Line protocol on
Interface Serial2, changed state to down
```

The first log entry tells you that Serial 2 on the router located at 10.1.1.1 experienced a connectivity problem. The error code LINK-3-UPDOWN tells you that the physical link off of Serial 2 encountered an error level (level 3) condition, which resulted in a change in connectivity state. The detail information in this log entry tells you that the state was changed to down. In other words, there is a break in connectivity somewhere off Serial 2. This could be a DSU failure, a problem with the line, or even a problem with the CO. While we do not know the exact cause of failure, we do know that there is a problem with the circuit.

It is normal to see the second log entry generated when you experience a link failure. This entry tells you that communication is broken at a protocol level off Serial 2. This makes sense, because if there is a physical circuit problem off Serial 2 (as indicated in the first log entry), any protocol communications along this circuit will fail. So, this second entry is not an indication of a separate problem; it is simply a symptom of the link failure recorded in the first log entry.

Syslog Server Placement

You have decided to set up a syslog server in order to capture log entries from your routers. You are now faced with deciding where to put the device. While this may seem like a straightforward decision, there are actually some functionality problems you need to address if you wish to capture log entries from routers outside your firewall. Since your border router is exposed to the wild Internet, it only makes sense that this is one of the routers you will want to watch most closely.

Our Sample Network

To walk through the possible options of where to place your syslog server, we will use the sample network shown in Figure 12.2. This network has a full-time connection to the Internet, so there is a border router that will need to be monitored. There is also a router with multiple T1 connections leading to different business partners. Finally, you have three routers creating a wide area network between this site and two field offices. You will want to capture information from all three of these routers. In total, you have five routers from which you will capture data. In fact, you may even wish to log information from your backbone switch.

 TIP Cisco routers and switches use an identical command set for telling the device to forward log entries to a syslog server.

FIGURE 12.2

Our sample network that requires a syslog server

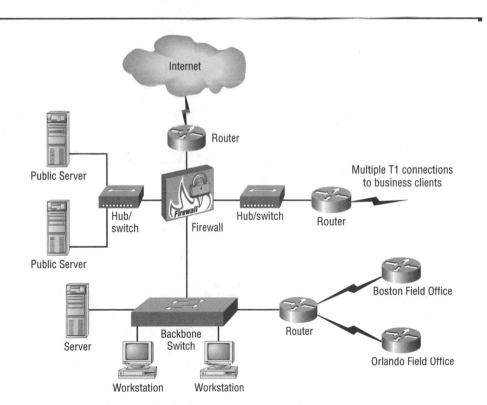

There are three basic placement options for installing your syslog server:

- Outside your firewall
- On the internal network itself
- On one of the special service networks

All three deployments have their strengths and weaknesses. We will discuss each option here so that you will be able to make the right choice for your specific environment.

Syslog outside the Firewall

The first option is to place the syslog server outside the firewall. This is shown in Figure 12.3. In this example, your syslog server is sitting outside the protective ring of your firewall. Its only protection is the hardening of the host itself, as well as any access-list filtering you may choose to deploy.

FIGURE 12.3

A syslog server located outside the firewall

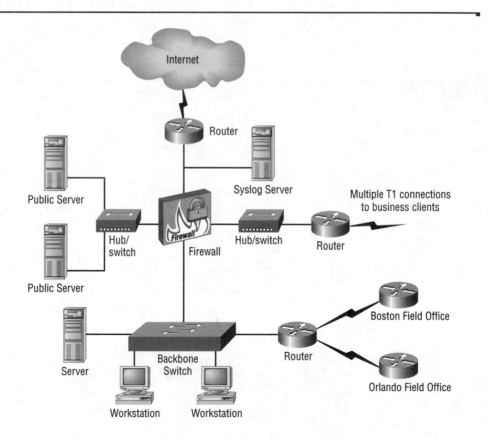

One strength of this design is that you do not have to poke any inbound holes through the firewall. If the syslog server were located on the internal network, you would need to open a hole through your firewall from the border router to the syslog server on UDP/514. This is required so that the router can transmit the log entries to the server. Poking an inbound hole through the firewall could be considered a potential security risk. By locating the server outside of the firewall, this potential risk is eliminated.

There are, however, a number of functional and security-related problems with this design. The first involves the method used by syslog to record which device sent it a particular log entry. When a log entry is submitted, syslog records the IP address of the transmitting system and associates it with the log entry. This provides a minimal level of authentication as to which host generates each entry.

The problem here is that you want to pass syslog traffic through the firewall. Most networks utilize some level of network address translation (NAT) when communicating with hosts on the Internet. This allows multiple internal systems to be assigned a private IP address but to be translated to a legal IP address when they communicate with hosts on the Internet. The result is that when traffic generated by these hosts leaves the firewall, the IP address used in the packet header is not the real IP address that was assigned to the transmitting system.

So, if all your internal hosts are translated to the external IP address of the firewall when they leave the network, you're going to have an accountability problem. Except for the border router, all recorded traffic is going to be logged as originating from the firewall. This means that if you see a log entry stating that one of your WAN links went down, you will have no way to determine whether the failure occurred on a circuit leading to a customer site or to one of your field offices.

Many firewalls will in fact do one-to-one NAT, which allows you to associate one legal IP address with one private address. Using this method, you could assign one legal address to each of your four internal routers (you would use five addresses if you're monitoring the switch, as well). While this would fix the logging problem, it wastes a number of legal addresses on hosts that will never actually communicate with hosts outside the border router.

In fact, this strategy may put a chink in your security armor. If a device is only accessible via a private address, communicating with that device across the Internet is an extremely difficult task. This is because the attacker cannot rely on normal routing to transmit traffic to your network. If, however, there is a legal address associated with the device, sending it traffic is just a matter of sneaking the attacker's nasty traffic past the firewall.

Another security issue is what could happen if the syslog server were ever to become compromised. Because of its location, an attacker could use the device to sniff all passing traffic. This could yield possible logon names and passwords as users authenticate with remote servers—or even sensitive company information by checking passing e-mail.

Placing a syslog server outside of your firewall includes a number of functionality and security problems. Make sure you have a plan to deal with each of these issues before selecting this method of placement.

Syslog on the Internal Network

Another option is to simply place the syslog server on the internal network. This design is shown in Figure 12.4. Since the server is now within the protective ring of the firewall, many of the security problems mentioned in the last section are no longer an issue. The firewall helps to insure that an attacker does not gain access to your log information.

FIGURE 12.4

A syslog server located on the internal network

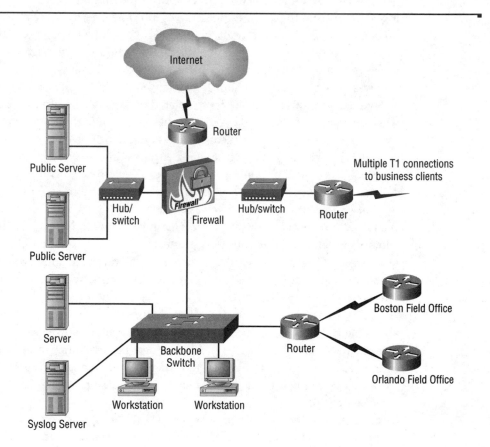

Another benefit of this design is that all of the NAT problems go away. The syslog server would have a private address, just like the rest of your internal systems, which means you do not need to use NAT. This design keeps the server from being directly addressable across the Internet and conserves the limited pool of legal addresses.

 NOTE The only caveat to this design is that your border router will need a route entry telling it how to reach the internal network. For example, if you have used the address space 172.30.1.0 for the internal network, the router will need to know that traffic headed for this network must be forwarded to the firewall, not the default route entry that leads out to the Internet.

One drawback to this design is that you will need to punch a few holes in the firewall in order to allow log traffic through. This could potentially give an attacker the conduit to internal resources. For example, an attacker who could spoof traffic pretending to be the border router might be able to sneak in a payload that could cause a buffer overrun on the syslog server. If the syslog server is compromised, the attacker would now have a jump point leading to all internal systems. While this attack is theoretically possible, I have never heard of an attacker successfully using it to gain access to a network. Also, note that this method of attack could easily be prevented by installing spoofing filters on the border router.

Although locating the syslog server on the internal network poses a number of risks, the threat level of these risks is minimal.

Syslog on a Service Network

The final option is to locate the syslog server on a service network. This is shown in Figure 12.5. In this example, the syslog server is located on the same service network as the WAN connections leading to your business partners. The router leading to your business partners could be outfitted with a proper set of access control lists to provide protection from any potential attacks originating along one of these circuits.

Locating the syslog server on the service network shares a number of strengths with each of the placement methods we have already discussed. To start, you do not need to punch any holes through the firewall leading to the main network. While you will still need a hole leading from the Internet border router to the syslog server, you do not need to open any conduits to the internal network. This means that the theoretical attack we discussed with the syslog server located on the internal network is not even an option with the service network model.

FIGURE 12.5

A syslog server located on a service network

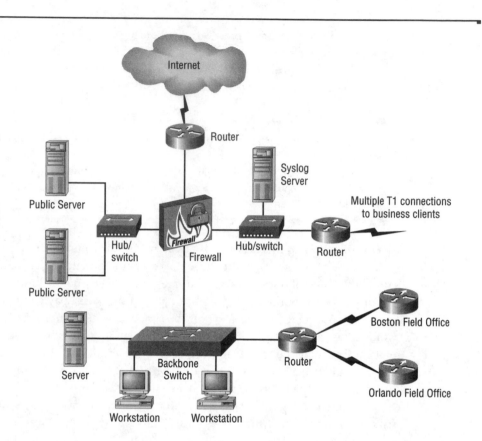

You also do not have any NAT issues to worry about. Since the syslog server is not outside the firewall, your internal routers will not be translated to the firewall's external IP address when they send log entries to the server. This means that you will not end up with multiple systems submitting log entries with the same source IP address.

The only real weakness of this design is that a compromised syslog server may allow an attacker to capture traffic headed to and from your business partners. This risk is below minimal, however, because the server is protected by the firewall and the Internet border router on one side and by the ACLs installed on the business client router on the other. Provided that the syslog server has been hardened against attack, the threat level to this system would be miniscule.

NOTE You could have decided to locate the syslog server on the other service network. This is not as secure an option because the other segment contains servers that are accessible from the Internet. This opens the possibility that a compromised server could allow an attacker to monitor log entries or even break into the syslog server itself.

Finding Your Best Solution

Obviously, with this particular network example, the best option is to place the syslog server on the service network leading to the business client WAN. All of the other options had some security or functionality issues that made them less appealing. Of course, the problem with applying this model to your environment may be that you do not have a service network to provide connectivity to your business partners.

One option not covered would be to add an additional NIC to the firewall and set up a special management network. The sole device on this network could be your syslog server. While this configuration requires a greater amount of time and resources to configure, it may be your best option if the only service network you currently have contains publicly accessible servers.

Backup and Management via TFTP

In Chapter 8, you read about using TFTP to configure your router. Chapter 8 focused on setting up your router for the first time, but you can use TFTP as a means of performing regular backups and maintenance. Having current backups insures that you can recover quickly from a catastrophic failure. A Cisco router has no facilities for being backed up by tape. This means that your only option for backups is to use TFTP.

Both the running configuration file and the Cisco IOS can be backed up to a TFTP server. By archiving both the configuration and the operating system, you have all the pieces you need to get a replacement router back online quickly. Since we already covered the IOS TFTP commands in Chapter 8, in this section we will focus on the best ways to deploy and integrate a TFTP server into your environment.

Running TFTP under UNIX

Just like syslog, most UNIX operating systems ship with a TFTP server. This means that all you should need to do is define a directory location to be used for sending and receiving files and enable the service. These are the files used by the TFTP server:

- `in.tftpd`: Executes TFTP server process
- `inetd.conf`: Used to initialize `in.tftpd`
- `services`: Defines the port on which `in.tftpd` should listen

The file `in.tftpd` is normally stored in the /usr/sbin directory. Both `inetd.conf` and `services` are stored in the /etc directory.

Setting up a TFTP Directory

By default, the TFTP server will use the /tftpboot directory to send and receive files. You can, however, specify any directory location you wish to use within inetd.conf file. Many network administrators like to use /home/tftp, but obviously you can choose any location that you want.

The first thing you need to do is create the directory. You also need to set the directory permission so that everyone is able to read and write to this directory. This is done by using the chmod command as follows:

```
Chmod 666 /home/tftp
```

This command tells the system to make the directory at the location /home/tftp read/write by all users.

 TIP Even though you have just enabled write access for all users, the TFTP server will not allow new files to be created in this directory. This is done for security reasons. You can only TFTP files into this directory if a file of the same name already exists. In other words, you can overwrite existing files with TFTP, but you cannot create new ones. If you need to create a new file in this directory, connect to the server via a command session and use the touch command. You can then use TFTP to overwrite this file with the information you need to save.

Starting the TFTP Server

In order to have the TFTP server initialize at startup, you will need to edit two files. The first is the /etc/services file. As you saw earlier in this chapter, the services file identifies which ports are used by a particular service. Make sure that you have an entry similar to the following so that the TFTP server knows which port to listen on:

```
tftp              69/udp
```

Next, you need to edit the inetd.conf file in order to allow inetd to initialize the TFTP server when it is needed. Here is the syntax to use:

```
tftp dgram udp wait root in.tftpd /home/tftp
```

Once these two files have been updated, you need to reinitialize inetd. Now, whenever a connection request comes in to UDP port 69, the system knows to pass the request to in.tftpd.

If you have Wrapper on the system, you can increase security by passing all connection requests through tcpd. In this case, you would edit inetd.conf as follows:

```
tftp dgram udp wait root /usr/sbin/tcpd in.tftpd /home/tftp
```

With Wrapper controlling inbound connection requests, you can now use host.allow and host.deny to specify which IP addresses can create a connection with your TFTP server. This lets you control inbound access so that only your routers can access the TFTP server.

 NOTE   Wrapper is a UNIX utility that lets you define which IP addresses can access specific services. To find out more about Wrapper, consult your man pages. Typically, the command man hosts_access will access the online help files.

Running TFTP under NT

Unfortunately, Windows 98, NT, and 2000 do not include a TFTP server. Luckily, your Cisco IOS CD includes a version of a TFTP server that will run under all of these Windows operating systems. Simply run the Tftpserv.exe file to start the installation process. The only option during the installation process is where to store the TFTP server files. The setup process will automatically create icons for launching the server.

To start the server, simply double-click the Cisco TFTP Server icon. This produces the Cisco TFTP Server window shown in Figure 12.6. The top bar of the window will identify the local system's IP address, as well as the default directory for sending and receiving files.

FIGURE 12.6

Cisco's Windows-compatible TFTP Server

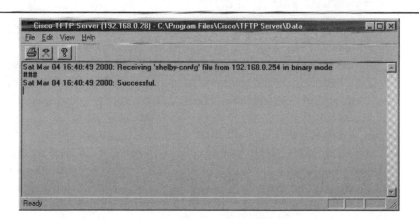

The bottom panel of this window is used for displaying any recent server activity. Note that a device at IP address 192.168.0.254 attempted to write a file named shelby-config. The second log entry tells us this write command was successful.

The Cisco TFTP server is pretty bare bones, having very few features. By selecting View ➣ Options, you can enable or disable logging, as well as change the directory location for sending and receiving files. Beyond these two settings, there are not many options available.

TFTP Functionality

There are a couple of functionality issues with the Cisco TFTP server that you know about. To start, it does not run as a service. This means that someone must log on to the system in order to launch the TFTP server; you cannot have the TFTP server initialize at boot time.

Another problem is that a stock Windows system is unable to restrict access to the TFTP server based on IP address. This means that any user with network access to the system could potentially read and write files. This is compounded by the fact that Cisco's TFTP server implementation does not prevent file creations like its UNIX counterpart. While the TFTP server is functional, you have to be very careful in deploying it.

There are a number of third-party TFTP solutions that bring some additional functionality to the table. For example, Walusoft's TFTP Pro has the ability to run as a service and adds some security features. An evaluation copy of the software can be obtained from this Web site:

```
http://www.walusoft.co.uk/
```

TFTP Server Placement

Many of the functionality and security issues that apply in deploying a syslog server also apply when deploying a TFTP server. In fact, you may even wish to combine these two services on the same machine. This would give you a single system for all router administration. Rather than going back through all your possible server placement options, we will simply cover a few points that show where the two deployments differ.

To start, NAT does not cause problems with TFTP as it does with syslog. When deploying our syslog server, we discussed that NAT would cause problems when log entries are associated with their source IP address because all internal routers would appear to come from the firewall's external IP address. Since TFTP is simply transferring files, an accurate record of source address is not required. The fact that the transfer appears to come from the firewall would not be a problem.

Another difference is that TFTP's security risks are higher than syslog's. This is because some of the files that you store on the TFTP server will completely document the configuration of your routers. While it can be argued that log entries are sensitive, as well, an attacker can do far more damage with a copy of the router's configuration.

Finally, by its very nature TFTP is less secure than syslog. This is because TFTP allows anonymous users to both read and write files, while syslog only allows remote hosts to append to log entries. The fact that TFTP allows information to be read creates the possibility that a remote attacker with network access to the server may be able to guess the names used for your configuration files and retrieve a copy for review.

The bottom line: Keep security in mind when deciding where to place your TFTP server. Understand the risks involved before you connect the system up to the wire.

Management via SNMP

As you saw in Chapter 3, the Simple Network Management Protocol (SNMP) is used to manage and monitor network devices remotely. SNMP is an extremely powerful tool that can provide you with great insight and control over your infrastructure. This section offers only an overview of what you can do with SNMP. For an extensive reference of SNMP's functionality, see William Stallings' excellent book, *Snmp, Snmpv2, and Rmon: Practical Network Management*, published by Addison-Wesley.

There are three common uses for SNMP:

- To monitor the status of a network device
- To collect data in order to report performance characteristics
- To make configuration changes

Each of these functions has its place in making sure that your network runs smoothly.

Monitoring Status

Even the most stable networks experience a failure from time to time. How long it takes you to recover from the failure depends on how long it takes you to find out that a problem exists and then to discover the root cause of what went wrong. Obviously, it helps to have a good understanding of what has failed before your phone starts ringing off the hook from disgruntled users.

SNMP can be used to monitor the status of devices on the network. Along with device availability, SNMP can report on the condition of each of a device's network interfaces. This additional information can help you drill down to the root cause of a problem.

For example, examine Figure 12.7. This is a screen capture from a freeware utility called SNMP Trap Watcher. Trap Watcher can be configured to accept trap messages from SNMP devices. With a bit of scripting, the information collected by this tool can notify you of a potential problem. For example, you could set up a script to transmit the summary trap information to your pager.

FIGURE 12.7

SNMP Trap Watcher can be used to collect SNMP trap errors.

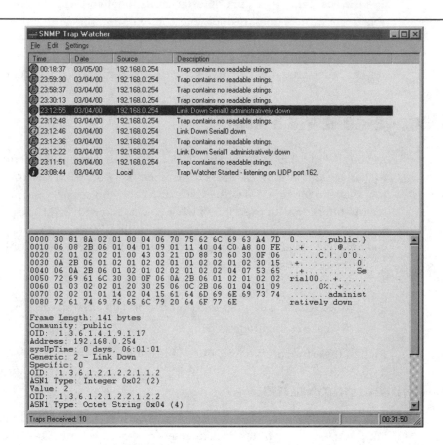

With a tool like Trap Watcher, you could make sure that you are alerted whenever a problem occurs on one of your SNMP-enabled devices. This can help you to formulate a proper response for the reported error condition. For example, if you're paged with the highlighted entry in Figure 12.7 and you know that the link connected to this serial interface is a critical part of your infrastructure, it's time to hop in the car and get to your data center ASAP. If you know that this link is only used once a week, you can stay home in your fuzzy slippers and address the problem in the morning.

There is a plethora of tools capable of capturing SNMP trap information. For example, one of the more popular packages for large-scale networks is HP OpenView, which is shown in Figure 12.8. Notice that OpenView provides a nice graphical representation of all our network objects. We can even see how all of these objects are connected.

FIGURE 12.8

An HP OpenView network map

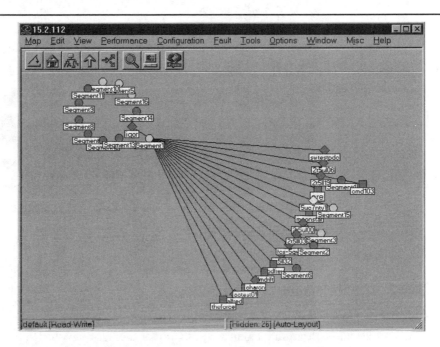

One of the nice things about OpenView is that the network objects are color coded. When a device is green, it is functioning normally. If it is yellow, there is some form of non-critical error. Red means that the device has dropped offline, and black means that it has been offline for an extended period of time.

If a problem is indicated, you can zoom in on this portion of the network to get a better look at what's going on. This is shown in Figure 12.9. Notice that we are still looking at the same network; we have just zoomed in on a specific part of it. You could now click the Segment3 object to obtain a list of the errors that have been reported with this device.

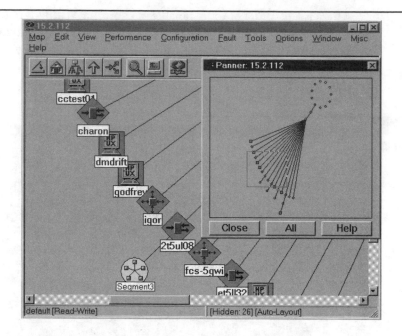

Although both Trap Watcher and OpenView use the same SNMP information to tell you the status of your network devices, OpenView has a much slicker interface for reporting this information. You also have the option to pick up a number of plug-ins for OpenView, expanding its abilities to include inventory control and data analysis. Of course, all this functionality comes at a price: An enterprise copy of OpenView costs a few thousand dollars without any of the optional plug-ins.

 NOTE Cisco makes a similar product to HP OpenView called Cisco Works. The two products are comparable in features and price.

Configuring SNMP Traps

No matter what product you use to monitor the status of your routers, you will need to configure these devices to forward trap messages to the SNMP management console. This configuration is similar to the configuration you did for sending log entries to a syslog server. You first need to determine which system should receive SNMP trap messages. Then, identify the level of detail you wish to have sent to the SNMP management console.

From global configuration mode, the syntax for identifying which system should receive SNMP traps is

```
snmp host <target IP or host name> traps <community string>
```

If you wished to send all log entries to IP address 192.168.1.10, and that server required a community string of 4fu2, here is the command you would use:

```
snmp host 192.168.1.10 traps 4fu2
```

You also need to specify the level of detail you wish to send to the management console. Do this by specifying the trap level for entries to be forwarded. For example, issuing the commands

```
snmp-server enable traps snmp
snmp-server enable traps config
```

would transmit all regular SNMP traps, along with configuration-related traps, to the host specified in the previous command.

 TIP You can find out what SNMP information is being forwarded and to which target address by using the show snmp command.

Performance Reporting

It is absolutely amazing how much information you can collect from a Cisco router using SNMP. Every possible performance parameter, from CPU utilization to how many ICMP packets have been received on a specific interface, can be retrieved. Figure 12.10 shows a screen capture of Network Data Viewer, a tool that is part of Alpine Computer's ProVision package. This tool is used to produce reports based on the SNMP data collected by ProVision. Notice that you can generate reports on any aspect of your router's functionality.

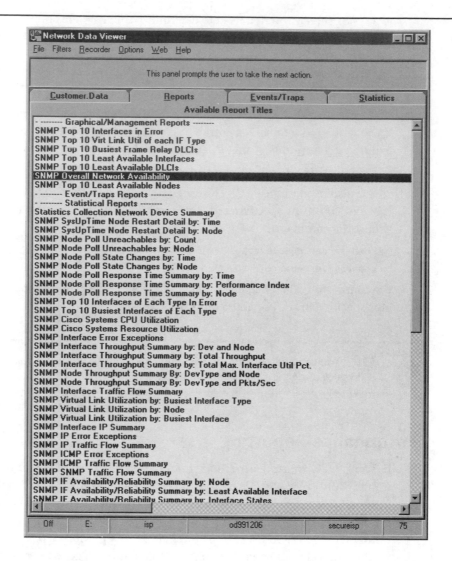

The real strength is in collecting this data over a long period of time. This helps you to identify patterns and analyze trends. For example, check out the graph in Figure 12.11. This graph was produced using the data collected by ProVision over a week. The solid blue line shows the average utilization level for traffic passing through this router interface. The upper and lower dashed lines represent minimum and maximum peaks.

FIGURE 12.11

*Long-term data collec-
tion lets you analyze
overall performance.*

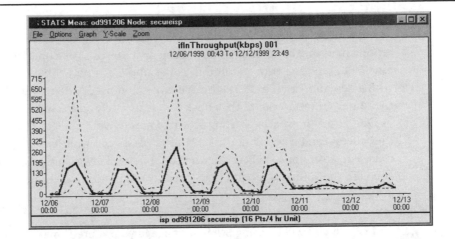

Trend reports like the one shown in Figure 12.11 can be extremely valuable if you
are planning for future infrastructure growth. For example, if this interface is a full T1
circuit capable of 1544Kbps, you know that you are nowhere near pushing this circuit
speed to the limit. If you wanted to see how well the router itself was holding up, you
could run a similar report on CPU and resource usage. The results of these reports
would give you an indication of how long you have before you will need to upgrade
the router.

TIP   Red Hat Linux includes a set of tools called the SNMP Commands. These tools
allow you to collect all of the same raw data as high-end tools like ProVision. You can even
collect SNMP trap information.

To allow a Cisco router to be SNMP-queried by a remote management station,
enter the following command in global configuration mode:

```
snmp community <community string> ro
```

The community string is the "password" the management station must use to gain
access to the router's SNMP information. The ro switch limits the level of access to
read only. So, if we were still using the community string 4fu2, the command would
look like this:

```
snmp community 4fu2 ro
```

Making Configuration Changes

Along with its ability to query information, SNMP can also be used to make configuration changes. This allows the management station console operator to respond quickly to reported error conditions. For example, if a network is currently being hit with a denial-of-service attack, the operator could use SNMP to quickly disable one of the router's interfaces until the attack can be properly addressed.

One of the drawbacks to using SNMP to modify your router's configuration is that the process can be fairly high risk. SNMPv1 passes community string information as clear text, so anyone sniffing the wire could potentially grab the community string and gain the ability to modify the router's configuration at leisure.

 TIP   If you will be using SNMP to manage your routers, make sure you are using SNMPv2 or higher.

To configure your router to accept changes via SNMP, enter the following command from global configuration mode:

```
snmp community <community string> rw
```

Notice the similarities with the command we used to allow queries to be performed. The only difference is that we have set the access level to read/write instead of read only. Since we are specifying a different level of access than we did in the first command, we need to make sure that we use a different community string. Here's an example:

```
snmp community 2secret rw
```

Once this command has been entered, anyone passing the community string 2secret would be granted read/write privileges. Systems using a community string of 4fu2 would continue to receive read-only access.

As an additional precaution in guarding who can manage your router, you may wish to apply a set of access lists. With access lists, you cannot distinguish between someone with read/write access and someone with read only. You can simply limit the hosts that are allowed to connect to the router via SNMP.

Summary

In this chapter, we looked at a number of the tools available for helping you to manage your Cisco routers. We discussed collecting log entries using syslog, file management and backups using TFTP, and overall monitoring with SNMP.

In the next chapter, we will see how to go about designing a network using Cisco routers. We will start by evaluating the environment's networking needs and then focus on deploying an appropriate solution.

CHAPTER 13

Network Case Studies

I t's time to take the plunge into real network design. In Chapters 4 and 5, we got our toes wet by looking at some basic design examples. In the next two chapters, we will follow the design process from start to finish by evaluating a number of case studies. Each case study will begin by analyzing a business need, then follow the process all the way through to the actual configuration of the network hardware. We'll even include sample configuration files.

 TIP If you are reading this book, you are probably looking for help with developing your own network design. For this reason, we've tried to include samples that cover a wide range of business needs. Please feel free to find a sample that best matches your specific need and use the included configuration files as a template for your own environment.

Case Study 1: A Subnet Masking Puzzle

The first case study is more of a puzzle problem to get you warmed up. You have been brought in as a consultant for the network shown in Figure 13.1. The Internet connection has not yet been hooked up but is due to come online very soon. The organization is a publicity company and plans to make heavy use of multimedia, including both audio and video conferencing, as well as a number of collaboration products. The problem is that these products require each workstation to be assigned a legal Internet address. Unfortunately, this organization's ISP would allocate no more than a single class C of legal IP addresses.

 NOTE Many collaboration or conferencing products break when NAT is used. If you have multiple systems hiding behind a single IP address, the NAT device has no way of knowing which internal host an inbound connection is trying to connect to. This is why each host that will be accepting inbound conferencing sessions must be identified by a unique legal IP address.

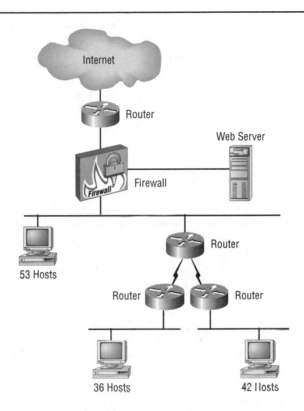

Take a moment to examine the figure to see whether it is possible to address this network using only a single class C address. Obviously, we are going to need to use variable-length subnet masking (VLSM), since we have more than one logical network. For the purpose of example, assume that the assigned address space was 200.200.200.0/24.

Breaking It Down

If you are going to solve this puzzle, you need a place to start. Begin by taking an inventory of the number of subnets you need to address, as well as the number of hosts located on each. This is shown in Table 13.1. Each line represents a unique subnet. The table defines the number of hosts you will need to address on each of these subnets.

TABLE 13.1: AN INVENTORY OF THE NUMBER OF HOSTS TO ADDRESS	
Subnet	**Number of Hosts**
Local network	53 hosts
First field office	36 hosts
Second field office	42 hosts
WAN to first field office	2 hosts
WAN to second field office	2 hosts
Service network	2 hosts
Firewall/router segment	2 hosts

As you can see, you have three subnets that will require legal IP addresses for a large number of hosts and four subnets that require legal addresses for only two hosts. In total, you have seven networks that need to be addressed.

 TIP You could ignore the two WAN segments because the routers will not need to communicate directly with the Internet. It's a good idea to include them, however, because assigning them legal addresses will allow you to test Internet connectivity from different points on your WAN.

Finding a Proper Fit

Clearly, you will need to use VLSM in order to break up your legal class C address into smaller chunks. First, determine what subnet mask to use in breaking up your network. If you refer back to Table 3.9, you can see that you have a bit of a problem: If you use a mask that accommodates your largest subnet (53 hosts), you do not have enough networks to work with. For example, a mask of 255.255.255.192 will address 62 hosts but will provide support for only four different networks. If you use a mask that accommodates the number of networks you need to address (seven), you can only address 30 hosts on each. This leaves you short on all of your LAN segments.

As was shown in Figure 3.9, you will need to use a mixture of subnet mask values in order to address all of your hosts. The trick is finding the right combination of mask values to satisfy your addressing needs.

Determining the Correct Mask Values

When working with VLSM, you should start by finding a mask value that accommodates your largest subnet. You can then work through your networks one by one, finding an appropriate mask value for each. For example, the largest network in our case study is 53 hosts. The subnet mask value that most closely matches this host count is 255.255.255.192, which will address 62 hosts. This gives you enough address space to handle your 53 systems, while still leaving enough room for growth.

Next, move on to your next-largest network, which is 42 hosts. The next smallest mask value after 255.255.255.192 is 255.255.255.224. This mask is capable of supporting 30 unique hosts. Since 30 hosts would be insufficient for your needs, you would again use the 255.255.255.192 mask value. This would also be true for your remaining LAN, since it needs to be able to support 36 hosts.

The remaining four networks only require two hosts on each. With this in mind, you could use a 255.255.255.252 on all these segments. This is fine for the WAN links because you will never have more than two hosts. The same could be said for the link between the firewall and the router, because you will probably never want to locate a host outside the protected ring of your firewall. With the service network, however, you may want to leave a little room for growth. While the requirement today is to address only two hosts, this organization might want to place additional systems on the service network at a later time. Planning for that growth now may help to prevent having to make major address scheme changes later. If you use a mask value of 255.255.255.248 for the service network, you could support the current requirements plus four additional systems.

TIP Very rarely will a customer requirement state that it needs to include planning for future growth. Your job as a network designer is to always keep this thought in the back of your mind.

Laying out the Address Space

We have calculated the mask value you need to use on each of your network segments. You should now apply these mask values to the address space you have been assigned in order to figure out the addressing for the network. This is shown in Table 13.2. Notice that the table begins with the largest segments and works toward the smaller networks.

TABLE 13.2: VLSM USED TO SUBNET THE NETWORK			
Subnet	Number of Hosts	Network Address	Mask
Local network	53 hosts	200.200.200.0	255.255.255.192
First field office	36 hosts	200.200.200.64	255.255.255.192
Second field office	42 hosts	200.200.200.128	255.255.255.192
Service network	2 hosts and 4 spares	200.200.200.192	255.255.255.248
WAN to first field office	2 hosts	200.200.200.200	255.255.255.252
WAN to second field office	2 hosts	200.200.200.204	255.255.255.252
Firewall/router segment	2 hosts	200.200.200.208	255.255.255.252

This network, with the addressing shown in Table 13.2, is shown in Figure 13.2. As you can see, we were successful in chopping up a single class C address in order to provide enough addressing for the entire network. In fact, we did not use the addresses 200.200.200.212–200.200.200.255. If a new segment is added at a later date, you could dip into this remaining pool in order to assign addresses to it, as well.

FIGURE 13.2

Network addressing assigned to each subnet

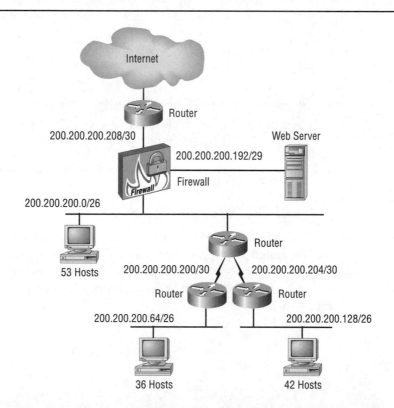

Case Study 1: Implementing the Solution

Now that you know which portions of the address space will be used on each of your segments, all you need to do is assign IP addresses to each of your routers and build the appropriate routing table. Since this is a small network with no redundant routes, static routing will suffice.

 NOTE   Remember that even if you had decided to use dynamic routing, you could not use RIP because RIP does not support VLSM.

Another thing to keep in mind is that you will be using subnet zero. You may recall from Chapter 3 that subnet zero is the first and last subnet created when you subnet a network. Since one of your LANs will be using 200.200.200.0 as its network address, you will need to enable support for subnet zero on all of your routers. This is done by entering the following command in global configuration mode:

```
ip subnet-zero
```

First Field Office

Let's start by looking at the configuration file for the router located at the first field office. This is the office with a total of 36 hosts. First, you could configure the Ethernet interface with the first available address out of the subnet you allocated. This means that you would assign an IP address of 200.200.200.65 with a subnet mask of 255.255.255.192. Doing the same to the serial interface, you would assign an address of 200.200.200.201 with a subnet mask of 255.255.255.252.

You also need to configure routing. Since the router is directly attached to 200.200.200.64 and 200.200.200.200, you do not need to tell it how to reach these networks. What you do need to tell the router is how to reach all the other subnets on your network. Since all other networks are located on the other side of the corporate router, you can get away with a single route entry that identifies the default route. Assuming that you will assign the IP address 200.200.200.202 to the remote side of the WAN link, you would enter the following command from global configuration mode:

```
ip route 0.0.0.0 0.0.0.0 200.200.200.202 1
```

Once complete, the router configuration file would look similar to the following:

```
!
version 12.0
!
hostname field1
!
enable secret 5 $1$NFrn$4m6BGqPue2ScpJaoR2npU0
enable password 2secret4u
!
ip subnet-zero
!
interface Ethernet0
 ip address 200.200.200.65 255.255.255.192
 no ip directed-broadcast
!
interface Serial0
 ip address 200.200.200.201 255.255.255.252
 encapsulation ppp
!
interface Serial1
 no ip address
 shutdown
!
ip route 0.0.0.0 0.0.0.0 200.200.200.202
!
!
line con 0
 exec-timeout 0 0
 transport input none
line aux 0
line vty 0 4
 password 99beers
 login
!
end
```

This completes all the necessary steps for your first router. You now need to configure the rest of your routers in order to complete connectivity.

Second Field Office

The router at the second field office would be configured in an identical manner to the router in the first field office. The only differences would be the addresses you assign to each interface and the IP address you use to configure the default route. With this in mind, your second configuration file would appear as follows:

```
!
version 12.0
!
hostname field2
!
enable secret 5 $1$NFrn$4m6BGqPue2ScpJaoR2npU0
enable password 2secret4u
!
ip subnet-zero
!
interface Ethernet0
 ip address 200.200.200.129 255.255.255.192
 no ip directed-broadcast
!
interface Serial0
 ip address 200.200.200.205 255.255.255.252
 encapsulation ppp
!
interface Serial1
 no ip address
 shutdown
!
ip route 0.0.0.0 0.0.0.0 200.200.200.206
!
!
line con 0
 exec-timeout 0 0
 transport input none
line aux 0
line vty 0 4
 password 99beers
 login
!
end
```

Corporate Router

The corporate router on your main network would be configured in a slightly different manner. While you still need to assign IP addresses to each of the interfaces, you cannot get away with configuring a single route entry. The default route entry on the corporate router will point at the firewall's internal interface. This is the next hop in reaching all other networks, except 200.200.200.64 and 200.200.200.128. Since these two networks are an exception to the default route entry, you must provide specific route entries to identify how to reach each of these two networks.

In order to create your routing table, execute the following commands from global configuration mode:

```
ip route 0.0.0.0 0.0.0.0 200.200.200.1 1
ip route 200.200.200.64 255.255.255.192 200.200.200.201 1
ip route 200.200.200.128 255.255.255.192 200.200.200.205 1
```

The first command is the router's default route entry. The second command tells the router that any traffic headed to the network 200.200.200.64 needs to be sent to the router field1. The last entry tells the router that all traffic going to 200.200.200.128 needs to be forwarded to the router field2. Once complete, your configuration file would look similar to the following:

```
!
version 12.0
!
hostname corporate
!
enable secret 5 $1$NFrn$4m6BGqPue2ScpJaoR2npU0
enable password 2secret4u
!
ip subnet-zero
!
interface Ethernet0
 ip address 200.200.200.2 255.255.255.192
 no ip directed-broadcast
!
interface Serial0
 ip address 200.200.200.202 255.255.255.252
 encapsulation ppp
!
interface Serial1
```

```
  ip address 200.200.200.206 255.255.255.252
  encapsulation ppp
!
ip route 0.0.0.0 0.0.0.0 200.200.200.1
ip route 200.200.200.64 255.255.255.192 200.200.200.201
ip route 200.200.200.128 255.255.255.192 200.200.200.205
!
!
line con 0
 exec-timeout 0 0
 transport input none
line aux 0
line vty 0 4
 password 99beers
 login
!
end
```

Conclusion

You should now have a good understanding of how to deploy VLSM. As you can see from the configuration files, the setup is very straightforward. The only caveats are

- Insure that you enable the use of subnet zero
- Configure the proper mask values when assigning IP addresses or building your routing table

Case Study 2: Router Table Efficiency

Case study 2 is an exercise in efficiency. You have just been hired as the senior network administrator for the environment shown in Figure 13.3. This network has grown quickly in a short period of time, causing it to be constructed haphazardly. The routing tables have become huge as new networks are being added on a monthly basis. The network only uses TCP/IP, and all networks use private addressing.

Each field office has its own administrator who is responsible for the local network. One common problem has been that these administrators will allocate address space that conflicts with some other network. Since RIP is being used to dynamically update the routing table, the conflicting addresses result in routing loops and loss of connectivity. Your job, if you choose to accept it, is to produce order out of chaos. Your only weapon is high-level management approval to assign new IP addressing to the entire network.

FIGURE 13.3

A large environment suffering from accelerated growth

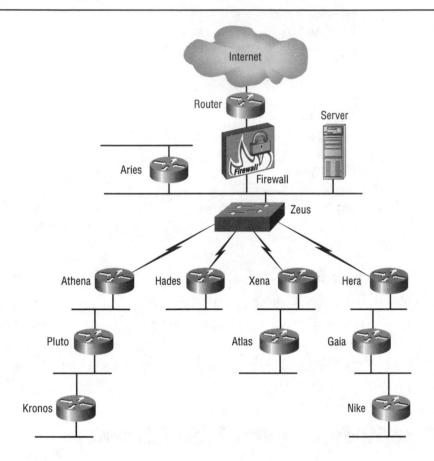

Breaking It Down

Before you resubmit your résumé to monster.com, let's see if we can break down the description into a list of business requirements:

- You need an orderly method of assigning IP addresses that will allow you to block out chunks of numbers for each field office.
- You should be able to consolidate these blocks in order to reduce the size of the routing table.

- You need to be able to make sure that if Renegade Bob decides to assign "any old block of addresses" to a particular subnet, this does not affect connectivity throughout the rest of the network.

The third action item is the most critical. Since the field office administrators have a history of not following approved address schemes, you need to make your network resistant to improper addressing. This means that you can rule out any kind of dynamic routing, because using a routing protocol that automatically updates the routing table could potentially break connectivity if someone assigns a conflicting network address.

Selecting a Routing Protocol

Your only option is to build your routing table using static routing. If an administrator assigns an improper network address to one of her subnets, static routing will insure that the routing table remains stable and connectivity is not broken in some other area of the network. A side benefit of static routing is that you can gently guide an administrator into making the right addressing decision. Administrators who do not use addresses out of their assigned block of numbers will not have connectivity to the corporate network.

Of course, the problem with static routing is that it can be a bear to maintain. This falls back to the first and second action items on the list. You need to design your address scheme so that the routing tables remain small and manageable. You also want to insure that you will not have to modify the routing table on each of your routers every time a new subnet is added.

 NOTE As an exercise, stop here for a moment and calculate how many static route entries you would have to make on each of these routers in order to provide connectivity throughout the network. Don't peek at the remaining text until you have finished!

Designing an Address Scheme

The key to using static routing efficiently is to route networks in large blocks of numbers. This lets you use a single route entry to forward traffic for multiple subnets. For example, consider the following route entry:

```
ip route 172.30.0.0 255.255.0.0 192.168.1.1
```

This entry says, "Forward all traffic with a destination IP address of 172.30.x.x to the router at IP address 192.168.1.1." While this looks like there is a single class B network sitting behind 192.168.1.1, you may in fact have 255 networks using the subnet mask 255.255.255.0. Your router doesn't care how the remote network is subnetted; all it knows is that whenever it sees a destination IP address that starts with 172.30, that traffic should be forwarded 192.168.1.1.

So, by adjusting the mask value, you can use a single route entry to express route information to multiple subnets. By wisely laying out your address space, you can make sure that you leverage this feature in order to reduce the size of your routing tables.

Another routing feature that may come in handy is the fact that routers forward traffic based on "best fit, not first fit" criteria. For example, think of how to apply a default route entry. The syntax used is

```
ip route 0.0.0.0 0.0.0.0 next_gateway 1
```

In effect, this entry says, "Forward all IP traffic that does not have an explicit route entry to next_gateway." When forwarding traffic, a router will compare the target address to the routing table and select the most specific mask value to determine the next hop. This is why the default route is always used as a last resort; 0.0.0.0 is a global pattern match, which is as non-specific as you can get. Let's look at an example to show you what I mean. Evaluate the following router table and determine which next-hop router would receive a packet headed for 192.168.2.5:

```
ip route 0.0.0.0 0.0.0.0 192.168.1.1
ip route 192.168.2.0 255.255.255.0 192.168.1.2
ip route 192.168.2.0 255.255.255.192 192.168.1.3
ip route 192.168.2.5 255.255.255.255 192.168.1.4
```

All of these route entries could be used to determine where to send 192.168.2.5. The last entry is the most specific, however, because the mask states that this route entry applies only to 192.168.2.5. Since this entry is the most specific, the packet would be forwarded to 192.168.1.4.

 TIP Along with reducing the number of route entries by routing in blocks of numbers, you may be able to reduce the size of the routing table even further by leveraging this best-fit feature.

Choosing Subnet Addresses

A focal point of laying out your address space should be planning for growth. With a network that is growing as quickly as this one, you do not want to have to revisit this problem again in the near future. With this in mind, you should plan to allocate large blocks of addresses to each of your field offices, as well as the corporate network. An obvious choice would be to work with the private address space 10.0.0.0–10.255.255.255.

A possible layout is shown in Figure 13.4. In this design, a class B worth of addresses is allocated to each office. This allows each office to support 255 networks, with 254 hosts located on each. This also simplifies address allocation: You can tell the administrator responsible for the network behind Athena that he can allocate any address space within the 10.1.x.x range. This gives him a large chunk of numbers to use as he sees fit.

FIGURE 13.4

Allocating large address pools to each LAN to accommodate future growth

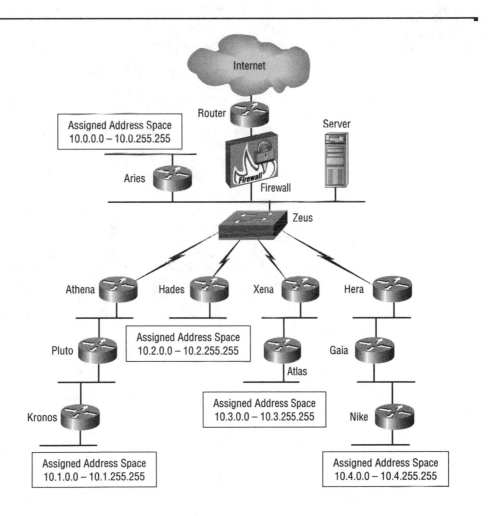

Case Study 2: Implementing the Solution

We have blocked out address space for each of your field offices. Now, it's just a matter of assigning specific addresses to each subnet and generating the required configuration files. The address layout is shown in Figure 13.5. Note that 10.x.0.x is consistently used for the WAN links. All LAN segments use 10.x.1.x and higher. While you could have used a 255.255.255.252 subnet mask on the WAN in order to conserve addresses, we have used a class C mask for consistency. The address pool is large enough that the loss of one full class C should have no long-term impact.

FIGURE 13.5

Subnet addressing assigned to each link

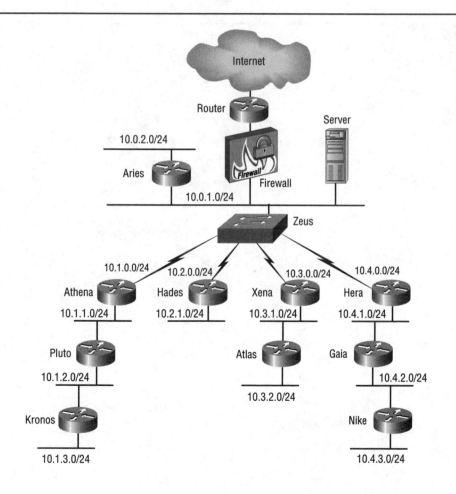

Zeus's Configuration File

Let's jump right in with the router that will be responsible for the most complex configuration file. This would be Zeus, which is responsible for providing WAN connectivity to all your field offices. Zeus is a Cisco 4500-series router, which is configured in a slightly different manner from the routers we have covered so far.

Configuring Routers with Card Slots

Until now, all the interfaces we have used have been identified with a single designation. For example, if you are in global configuration mode and need to configure the first serial port, you would enter this command:

```
interface s0
```

On larger routers, however, the convention is a bit different. From the Cisco 3600 series on up, the router has the ability to accept multiple card slots. This is useful because it allows you to pick and choose the options you need. For example, if you need six Ethernet ports, simply purchase the required number of cards (the number of cards varies because port density per card is different from model to model). Later, if you need serial ports instead of Ethernet ports, simply swap a card. This way, you do not have to replace the whole router; just add or replace a single card.

When configuring an interface on one of these larger routers, you need to specify both the card slot and the port. For example, if you wish to configure serial0 on card slot 2, you would enter the following command from global configuration mode:

```
interface serial2/0
```

 NOTE Specify the slot number first, then the interface you wish to configure. When you review a configuration file, use the same syntax to describe the settings for each port.

Assigning IP Addresses

As you configure Zeus, you will need to use the slot/port convention to configure each of the interfaces. The first thing you should do is assign IP addresses. For simplicity's sake, assign each interface a .1 address from its respective subnet range. If you started from global configuration mode, the sequence of commands would look something like this:

```
interface eth0/0
ip address 10.0.1.1 255.255.255.0
exit
```

```
interface ser1/0
ip address 10.1.0.1 255.255.255.0
exit
interface ser1/1
ip address 10.2.0.1 255.255.255.0
exit
interface ser2/0
ip address 10.3.0.1 255.255.255.0
exit
interface ser2/1
ip address 10.4.0.1 255.255.255.0
```

The first command tells the router that you wish to address the first Ethernet port in the first card slot. You then assign this port an IP address. When you type **exit**, you return to global configuration mode, so you can now choose to configure the first serial port in the second card slot. This pattern continues until all of your interfaces are configured.

Classless vs. Classful Routing

You are now ready to configure routing. The first thing you must do is tell the router how to handle address classes. By default, a Cisco router will perform what is referred to as *classful routing*. With classful routing, the next hop is selected based on the address class and any associated route entries. For example, consider the following route table:

```
ip route 0.0.0.0 0.0.0.0 10.1.1.1
ip route 10.2.2.0 255.255.255.0 10.1.1.2
```

While you would expect a packet headed to 10.100.5.0 to be forwarded to 10.1.1.1, by default a Cisco router would actually forward the packet to 10.1.1.2. This is because the 10.2.2.0 entry is part of the same class A 10.x.x.x subnet. Even though you may be using a 255.255.255.0 subnet mask, the router assumes a class A mask and forwards all traffic accordingly.

Classful routing was useful when networks adhered strictly to the subnet class model. In an environment such as our case study, where different portions of the class A address will be located off different router interfaces, classful routing would force us to create specific route entries for every single network. Needless to say, this is a bad thing because the point of the exercise is to keep the routing table as small as possible. With this in mind, you should use *classless routing*.

Classless routing ignores the assumed mask value and makes forwarding decisions based strictly on the routing table. For example, with classless routing the packet headed to 10.100.5.0 would in fact be forwarded to 10.1.1.1. To enable classless routing, enter the following command from global configuration mode:

```
ip classless
```

Building Your Routing Table

It is now time to start defining static route entries. First, configure a default route and a route entry for 10.0.2.0. Assuming that Aries is at 10.0.1.2 and the firewall is 10.0.1.3, you would enter the following commands from global configuration mode:

```
ip route 0.0.0.0 0.0.0.0 10.0.1.3
ip route 10.0.2.0 255.255.255.0 10.0.1.2
```

You also need to define route entries for each of the field offices. As we discussed in the section "Designing an Address Scheme" earlier in this chapter, you can represent each field office with a single route statement. For example, the only route entry you would need on Zeus for the 10.1.0.0 network would be

```
ip route 10.1.0.0 255.255.0.0 10.1.0.2 1
```

Remember that your router will automatically add any directly connected networks. Since Serial1/0 is directly connected to 10.1.0.0/24, your route table will actually look like this:

```
ip route 10.1.0.0 255.255.255.0 direct
ip route 10.1.0.0 255.255.0.0 10.1.0.2 1
```

Since the router goes by best fit, any traffic headed to 10.1.0.0/24 would match the directly connected entry. All other 10.1.x.x packets would be forwarded to the next hop address of 10.1.0.2.

The beauty of this design is that you can provide connectivity to all of your field offices by creating a single route entry per WAN segment. Since you have grouped your addresses at a class B level, the remote field office can have one network or 200; it does not matter. One route entry will suffice for providing connectivity.

You would create route entries for the remaining networks in a similar fashion. From global configuration mode, enter the following commands:

```
ip route 10.2.0.0 255.255.0.0 10.2.0.2 1
ip route 10.3.0.0 255.255.0.0 10.3.0.2 1
ip route 10.4.0.0 255.255.0.0 10.4.0.2 1
```

That's all you need to get Zeus online. Your completed configuration file would look similar to this:

```
!
version 12.0
```

```
!
hostname Zeus
!
enable secret 5 $1$NFrn$4m6BGqPue2ScpJaoR2npU0
enable password bobafat
!
ip subnet-zero
!
interface Ethernet0/0
 ip address 10.0.1.1 255.255.255.0
 no ip directed-broadcast
!
interface Serial1/0
 ip address 10.1.0.1 255.255.255.0
 encapsulation ppp
!
interface Serial1/1
 ip address 10.2.0.1 255.255.255.0
 encapsulation ppp
!
interface Serial2/0
 ip address 10.3.0.1 255.255.255.0
 encapsulation ppp
!
interface Serial2/1
 ip address 10.4.0.1 255.255.255.0
 encapsulation ppp
!
ip route 0.0.0.0 0.0.0.0 10.0.1.3
ip route 10.0.2.0 255.255.255.0 10.0.1.2
ip route 10.1.0.0 255.255.0.0 10.1.0.2
ip route 10.2.0.0 255.255.0.0 10.2.0.2
ip route 10.3.0.0 255.255.0.0 10.3.0.2
ip route 10.4.0.0 255.255.0.0 10.4.0.2
ip classless
!
!
line con 0
 exec-timeout 0 0
```

```
   transport input none
  line aux 0
  line vty 0 4
   password 2114zhu
   login
  !
  end
```

Athena's Configuration File

When you understand how to consolidate route entries, Athena's configuration is fairly straightforward. Athena will need a default route entry that points back to Zeus. You can also use the consolidation trick to point all 10.1.x.x subnets at Pluto. This route will only be used for 10.1.x.x traffic that is not headed to one of the 10.1.x.x networks directly connected to Athena.

Athena's configuration file would appear similar to the following:

```
!
version 12.0
!
hostname Athena
!
enable secret 5 $1$NFrn$4m6BGqPue2ScpJaoR2npU0
enable password bobafat
!
ip subnet-zero
!
interface Ethernet0
 ip address 10.1.1.1 255.255.255.0
 no ip directed-broadcast
!
interface Serial0
 ip address 10.1.0.2 255.255.255.0
 encapsulation ppp
!
ip route 0.0.0.0 0.0.0.0 10.1.0.1
ip route 10.1.0.0 255.255.0.0 10.1.1.2
ip classless
!
!
```

```
line con 0
 exec-timeout 0 0
 transport input none
line aux 0
line vty 0 4
 password 2114zhu
 login
!
end
```

Pluto's Configuration File

Once you get to Pluto, routing becomes a bit simpler. You can point to Athena with your default route entry, which will allow you to access a majority of the network. You will also need to create a specific entry for the 10.1.3.0/24 network, because this network lies behind Kronos. The remaining networks are directly connected and do not require a specific route entry.

Pluto's configuration file would appear as follows:

```
!
version 12.0
!
hostname Pluto
!
enable secret 5 $1$NFrn$4m6BGqPue2ScpJaoR2npU0
enable password bobafat
!
ip subnet-zero
!
interface Ethernet0
 ip address 10.1.1.2 255.255.255.0
 no ip directed-broadcast
!
interface Serial0
 ip address 10.1.2.1 255.255.255.0
 encapsulation ppp
!
ip route 0.0.0.0 0.0.0.0 10.1.1.1
ip route 10.1.3.0 255.255.0.0 10.1.2.2
ip classless
```

```
!
!
line con 0
 exec-timeout 0 0
 transport input none
line aux 0
line vty 0 4
 password 2114zhu
 login
!
end
```

Kronos's Configuration File

Kronos's configuration file is the simplest of all. The only route entry required is a default route entry that points at Pluto. The configuration file for Kronos would look like this:

```
!
version 12.0
!
hostname Kronos
!
enable secret 5 $1$NFrn$4m6BGqPue2ScpJaoR2npU0
enable password bobafat
!
ip subnet zero
!
interface Ethernet0
 ip address 10.1.2.2 255.255.255.0
 no ip directed-broadcast
!
interface Serial0
 ip address 10.1.3.1 255.255.255.0
 encapsulation ppp
!
ip route 0.0.0.0 0.0.0.0 10.1.2.1
ip classless
!
!
```

```
line con 0
 exec-timeout 0 0
 transport input none
line aux 0
line vty 0 4
 password 2114zhu
 login
!
end
```

Configuring the Remaining Routers

The remaining routers would be configured in an identical fashion to the routers we have covered so far. For this reason, we will not cover them in detail here. In order to generate configuration files for the remaining routers, you could simply borrow the configuration files we have already generated and modify the IP address and route values to match the remaining blocks of addresses.

Conclusion

This case study is an excellent example of why you do not always need to use dynamic routing on medium to large networks. With a bit of planning, static routing can be used to provide resilience to improper addressing and to make the routing table much easier to manage. Note that despite the size of this network, the largest routing table contained only six entries. In fact, this network could grow to hundreds of subnets and still be managed with a minimal number of route entries.

Case Study 3: Designing a New WAN

Our last case study is a new WAN design. You have an organization that includes a corporate office and two field offices. Until now, connectivity to the corporate office has been supplied via a dial-up modem pool of 15 modems. Over the last few months, the modem pool has become so active that it is now more cost effective to install permanent WAN links. Users have also been complaining that they receive frequent busy signals.

Each field office consists of about 30 users. While each field office has its own local server, users must connect to the corporate office on a frequent basis in order to update a number of central databases. One database resides on a legacy NetWare server, while the rest run off of UNIX. The protocols in use are TCP/IP and IPX.

Breaking It Down

This description contains a lot of good information you can use to develop your WAN design. Hitting on the high points, here's what you know:

- There are two field offices that must be tied in to the corporate network.
- Each site consists of 30 users.
- There is enough traffic headed back to the corporate site to tie up a pool of 15 modems.
- Your WAN must support both TCP/IP and IPX connectivity.

Calculating Required Bandwidth

Your first task is to get an idea of how much bandwidth will be required along each of the WAN links. Since a WAN does not exist today, you do not have absolute metrics to work with. All you know is that there is enough traffic to tie up 15 modems all day long.

If you assume that 33.6Kb modems are being used, you can calculate

$33.6 \times 15 = 504Kb$

Based on current usage, then, total bandwidth for your WAN should be at least 504Kb. Of course, one piece that's missing from the puzzle is the breakdown of the dial-in users. For example, is there an equal number of people calling in from each field office, or are there normally 12 users from the first office but only three users from the second? Without this information, you are a bit in the dark about how much bandwidth to assign on each link.

Also mentioned in the description is the fact that users frequently receive a busy signal. This means that you can expect to see more traffic passing across the WAN than was generated through the modem pool.

So, how much bandwidth do you allocate to each of your WAN links? This is where network administration becomes less of a science and more of a mystical art. You do not have enough data to arrive at an exact bandwidth figure. Much like Mr. Spock, you must make as accurate a guess as you possibly can.

Given the above information, you will probably be safe if you allocate 512Kb to each of your WAN links. This will at least get you in the ballpark of where you need to be—without taking the chance that the WAN will provide poorer performance than the modem pool. Once the circuits are in place, you can monitor utilization and adjust the amount of available bandwidth to better suit your requirements.

Selecting the WAN Circuits

Now that you know how much bandwidth you will need, you can go about determining the best way to wire your WAN. First, decide whether to use dedicated circuits or

Frame Relay. If your requirements had included supporting voice as well as data, you might be partial to a dedicated circuit because voice quality tends to be much higher. Since you will only be moving data, the deciding factor will be a matter of cost.

Your best bet would be to ask your local Telco provider for four different bids. You want to know the cost of using dedicated circuits versus Frame Relay on each of your two WAN connections. Typically, the metric that controls these costs is distance. The closer the remote site is to the corporate office, the more likely that a dedicated circuit will be more cost effective. If the remote site is far away, Frame Relay starts to become more attractive.

 TIP When choosing between dedicated circuits and Frame Relay, don't forget to factor in hardware costs. Each dedicated circuit will require its own serial port on a router. When using Frame Relay, multiple circuits can be connected to the same serial port. If you need to create many WAN links, going with Frame Relay may reduce your implementation costs by lowering your hardware requirements.

Let's assume that, based on the bids you have received, the most cost-effective method of deployment will be to connect one office via a dedicated circuit and the other via Frame Relay. This becomes an easy decision about how to wire your dedicated circuit, because your only option is a T1. A leased line circuit does not support enough bandwidth to fulfill your requirements.

For the Frame Relay circuit, however, you may have a few options. While the classic design is to use a T1 to wire each location to its local CO, you may be able to replace one or both of these connections with a DSL circuit. As mentioned in Chapter 2, DSL is far cheaper than a T1 and can be used as a replacement for connecting to a Frame Relay cloud. This may help to reduce your implementation costs even further.

There are two problems with going the DSL route:

- Availability
- Bandwidth

DSL is still not available in all areas. With this in mind, you may not even have the option of using a DSL circuit. Even if you can use DSL, the available bandwidth speeds tend to be limited. You may not be able to get a 512Kb connection—and even if you can, you may not be able to increase this bandwidth level later if you find that your WAN utilization demands it.

So DSL would probably look more attractive if you were talking slower WAN links. In order to insure that you do not design yourself into a corner, you would be better off using T1 circuits to connect to each point in the Frame Relay cloud.

Selecting Encapsulation Protocols

Now that you know what type of circuits you will be using to set up your WAN, you need to select encapsulation protocols. Remember that protocols such as IPX and IP only define network addressing. You still need to encapsulate these packets in some kind of a frame that includes hardware address information. When communicating on a LAN, topologies like Ethernet provide the hardware address information required to deliver information between networked systems. So, what you need is an Ethernet equivalent for communicating over a WAN.

The Frame Relay circuit is an easy decision because Frame Relay uses its own encapsulation protocol. All traffic passing through the Frame Relay cloud must be encapsulated in the Frame Relay protocol. When it comes to the dedicated circuit, you have two different methods of encapsulation to choose from:

- High-level Data Link Control (HDLC)
- Point-to-Point Protocol (PPP)

HDLC is the older of the two protocols and is the default method of encapsulation on a Cisco router. The problem with HDLC is that the specification is rather loose. This has led to interoperability problems between implementations that have been developed by different vendors. For example, if you were to place a Cisco router on one end of a dedicated circuit and a 3COM router on the other and try to get them to communicate via HDLC, the circuit would fail. Although HDLC is not a proprietary protocol, use it only when you have similar hardware on both ends of the circuit.

PPP has a much tighter specification and therefore solves many of the interoperability problems that exist with HDLC. In addition, PPP uses less overhead for error correction and can compress encapsulated traffic more efficiently before transmitting it across a WAN link. This means that PPP can produce more usable bandwidth than a similar circuit using HDLC. With this in mind, most dedicated circuits are set up using PPP.

You will end up running two encapsulation protocols across your WAN. Traffic passing through the Frame Relay circuit will be encapsulated using Frame Relay. Traffic passing across the dedicated circuit will be encapsulated using PPP.

Checking for Compatibility

Your final task before hooking up the hardware is making sure that there will not be any surprises when the networks are wired together. For example, if the corporate office and one of the remote field offices are both using 192.168.1.0/24 to subnet the local LAN, you must resolve this conflict before providing connectivity between the two networks. You also need to look at the IPX frame types being used. For example, you would need to define a standard if the corporate network is currently using 802.2 while the field offices are using 802.3.

TIP Take the time to map out your network and see how all the pieces will fit together. A little bit of planning can go a long way toward smoothing over the bumps experienced during an integration project.

Figure 13.6 shows an address map of how your network will look once the WAN links are in place. Notice that both IP and IPX network addresses have been designated for each network segment. Also, an IPX network number has been assigned to each router.

FIGURE 13.6

The network layout for case study 3

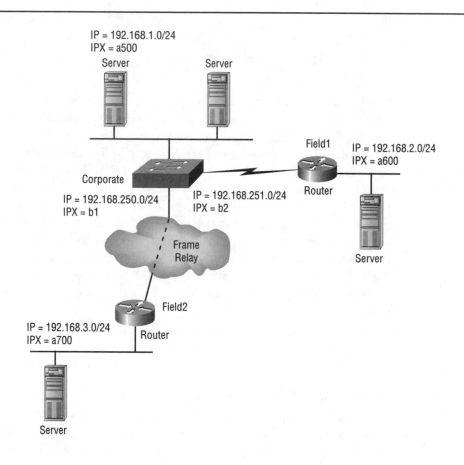

Case Study 3: Implementing the Solution

One last piece of missing information is the DLCI numbers for the Frame Relay cloud. You may recall from Chapter 2 that the DLCI numbers are the OSI layer 2 addresses used to transmit your packets across the Frame Relay network. The carrier responsible for the cloud will tell you which DLCI numbers to use on each end of the circuit. Sometimes the DLCI numbers will be the same for both circuits, and sometimes they will be different. This will vary depending on how the carrier has allocated DLCI numbers.

In either case, you simply associate the DLCI with the appropriate interface. For example, if Serial1 will be connected to DLCI 105, you would enter the following commands from global configuration mode:

```
interface serial1
frame-relay interface-dlci 105
```

Configuring Dynamic Routing

You also need to select which routing protocols to use. For the sake of simplicity, let's assume that you will be using IP RIP and IPX RIP to update your routing tables. Start by enabling IP RIP routing by entering the following commands from global configuration mode:

```
corporate(config)#router rip
corporate(config-router)#
```

Notice that after you enable RIP, you are placed in router configuration mode. From here, you need to identify each of the locally connected networks you wish to have added to the routing table. For example, if you are configuring the corporate router from Figure 13.6, you would now enter these commands:

```
network 192.168.1.0
network 192.168.250.0
network 192.168.251.0
```

This would tell RIP to propagate route information on all locally attached networks.

Configuring IPX RIP is much easier. From global configuration mode, enter the command

```
ipx routing
```

Issuing this command enables IPX RIP and assigns an internal IPX network address of the same value as the MAC address assigned to the first Ethernet interface.

NOTE Remember that IPX routers need to have an internal network address. Using one of the router's MAC addresses insures that the internal network address will always be unique from router to router; no two hosts should ever have the same MAC address.

Corporate's Configuration File

We have already discussed how to enable routing on the corporate router, so all you have left to do is assign network addressing to each of the corporate router's interfaces. Let's assume that, for the purpose of this example, your carrier has told you to use a DLCI value of 110 on this side of the Frame Relay circuit. With this in mind, your router configuration file would appear as follows:

```
!
version 12.0
!
hostname Corporate
!
enable secret 5 $1$NFrn$4m6BGqPue2ScpJaoR2npU0
enable password 2manypass
!
ipx routing 0000.0c3f.1e05
!
interface Ethernet0
 ip address 192.168.1.1 255.255.255.0
 ipx network a500
!
interface Serial0
 ip address 192.168.251.1 255.255.255.0
 ipx network b2
 encapsulation ppp
!
interface Serial1
 ip address 192.168.250.1 255.255.255.0
 ipx network b1
 frame-relay interface-dlci 110
!
router rip
 network 192.168.1.0
```

```
 network 192.168.250.0
 network 192.168.251.0
!
!
line con 0
 exec-timeout 0 0
 transport input none
line aux 0
line vty 0 4
 password hunt357
 login
!
end
```

Field1's Configuration File

Field1 will receive a similar configuration to the corporate router. The only difference is that you don't have to worry about the Frame Relay portion of the setup. Field1's configuration file would look like this:

```
!
version 12.0
!
hostname Field1
!
enable secret 5 $1$NFrn$4m6BGqPue2ScpJaoR2npU0
enable password 2manypass
!
ipx routing 0000.0ca3.d52b
!
interface Ethernet0
 ip address 192.168.2.1 255.255.255.0
 ipx network a600
!
interface Serial0
 ip address 192.168.251.1 255.255.255.0
 ipx network b2
 encapsulation ppp
!
router rip
```

```
 network 192.168.2.0
 network 192.168.251.0
!
!
line con 0
 exec-timeout 0 0
 transport input none
line aux 0
line vty 0 4
 password hunt357
 login
!
end
```

Field2's Configuration File

In Field2's configuration file, you need to define a DLCI number in order to terminate the remote end of the Frame Relay connection. Let's assume that your provider has told you to use 850 on this end of the circuit. With this in mind, your configuration file would appear as follows:

```
!
version 12.0
!
hostname Field2
!
enable secret 5 $1$NFrn$4m6BGqPue2ScpJaoR2npU0
enable password 2manypass
!
ipx routing 0000.0c22.7abb3
!
interface Ethernet0
 ip address 192.168.3.1 255.255.255.0
 ipx network a700
!
interface Serial0
 ip address 192.168.250.1 255.255.255.0
 ipx network b1
 frame-relay interface-dlci 850
!
```

```
router rip
 network 192.168.3.0
 network 192.168.250.0
!
!
line con 0
 exec-timeout 0 0
 transport input none
line aux 0
line vty 0 4
 password hunt357
 login
!
end
```

Conclusion

While this is a relatively simple case study, it highlights the differences between setting up a dedicated circuit and a Frame Relay circuit. You will need this foundation in the next chapter, when we move on to more advanced WAN designs. You also saw how to go about calculating the required amount of bandwidth for each circuit, even though we did not have enough data to make a precise decision.

Summary

This chapter focused on the initial process of identifying network requirements and using good problem-solving skills to develop an efficient design. You should now have a better idea of how to pull out the essential pieces from a specification and use them to guide you in developing a proper infrastructure solution.

In the next chapter, we will look at some more case studies, with a greater emphasis on the actual implementation. To provide a little diversity and a wider range of scope, the design process will be guided by a couple of guest authors.

CHAPTER **14**

Real-World Routing: Advice from the Field

They say that variety is the spice of life. Certainly, when it comes to network design, it doesn't hurt to get input from a number of qualified sources. This discipline is far too diverse for any one person to have all the answers. With this in mind, this chapter has been written by a couple of guest authors who have been gracious enough to share their knowledge and expertise in these pages.

The first three case studies were written by author, teacher, and consultant Gary Kessler. Gary is a true computing sage, working for such major Internet providers as BBN Technologies (now GTE) and principal training companies as Hill Associates. He has presented for such prestigious organizations as the International Communications Association (ICA) and the Institute of Electrical and Electronics Engineers (IEEE) and is also certified under the Cisco Certified Network Associate (CCNA) program. Gary has published an amazing number of books and articles on a diverse range of networking technologies, including e-commerce, networking, and security. Many of these publication are available online at http://www.garykessler.net.

The last three case studies were written by author and consultant Andrew Hamilton. I met Andy back when I was still consulting and working in the Boston area. He's young, works far too many hours, and devours technology like it was candy. On more than one occasion, I would catch him hanging around the NOC at midnight because he had thought up some method of streamlining the SNMP query process or found something in a log file that was bugging him enough to want to run a few simulations. As you will see in these pages, Andrew has come up with some amazing designs in his time and is a crack Cisco engineer. I consider Andrew's book *Cisco Routers 24seven* a must-read for anyone who is serious about bringing their Cisco skills up to the next level.

Case Study 1: Dedicated Internet Access

In the "old" days (say, back before 1995), routers were used in what seemed like only the largest of networks and only by hardcore network professionals. Much the same could have been said about the Internet; it was only used by techies at organizations with the money to afford a connection. Today, there is no industry untouched by the Internet, and even the smallest companies are getting connected.

Setting the Stage

Today, many companies connecting to the Internet forgo dial-up access and instead employ some sort of dedicated connection, either using an access technology such as Frame Relay or private lines such as Digital Data Service (DDS) or T1. Although a 56Kbps modem shared among several users may have once been sufficient, Parkinson's Law and the requirement for an ever-increasing amount of bandwidth have made even the 128Kbps available with ISDN insufficient for many users. The falling prices of digital services are encouraging this trend, with some fractional T1 (FT1) rates falling below the 56Kbps DDS rates of just a few years ago.

Another way in which relatively high-speed Internet access is becoming more affordable for the small business is by combining Internet access and access to telephone service on the same facility. Indeed, as more telephone companies have started to offer Internet services (and more ISPs to offer telephone services), falling rates for both can yield some great bargains. Figure 14.1 shows one such scenario. An organization needing Internet access has a private branch exchange (PBX) on its premises that is capable of interfacing with digital circuits. In this example, a T1 local loop is brought to the customer's premises from a local telephone company switch. Four of the T1 time slots (256Kbps) are allocated for Internet access, and the remaining 20 time slots (1.28Mbps) are used for telephone services via the PBX.

 NOTE   Working with NAT was discussed in Chapters 3 and 11.

FIGURE 14.1

Dedicated Internet access (with NAT)

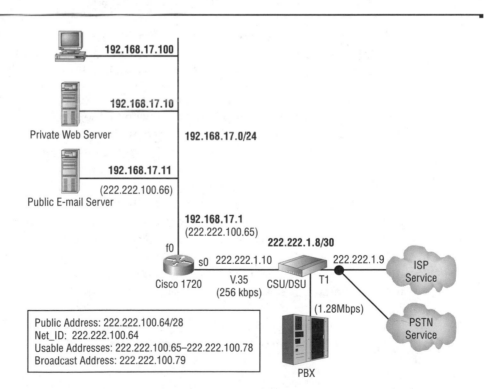

The Technology

Since the telephone/Internet Service Provider is bringing in a T1 loop that multiplexes multiple services, the carrier will usually place some sort of T1 multiplexer (MUX) on the premises. The T1 MUX will generally have a CSU/DSU to terminate the local loop and will be configured so that the proper time slots will be directed to the appropriate interconnect ports on the MUX. In this case, we only care about the four time slots (probably 1–4 or 21–24) for Internet access.

Because of the scarcity of IP addresses, most ISPs today will assign as few as possible to customers. Because most organizations actually have more hosts than their ISP will grant addresses, NAT is commonly employed. In this example, an organization has been assigned the address block 222.222.100.64–222.222.100.79 with the subnet mask 255.255.255.240 (or /28). In this block of 16 addresses, one (222.222.100.64) is reserved as the NET_ID and one (222.222.100.79) is reserved as the broadcast address. Most ISPs will want to be able to ping the LAN port of the router, so another address is usually assigned to the router, generally the .1 address in the block; in this case, that would be 222.222.100.65. Any other systems that need to be publicly advertised also need a public address, such as the e-mail server's 222.222.100.66. The remaining addresses can be shared by the hosts accessing the network.

 NOTE The 222.222.1.0 and 222.222.100.0 class C addresses are actually valid public addresses on the Internet. These addresses are used here for illustrative purposes only.

The 222.222.100.64/28 block is sufficiently limited so that the organization cannot assign a unique global IP address to every host. But the internal IP network cannot work unless every host has its own address. The organization, then, can choose any RFC 1918 private address for that purpose; in this case, we have selected the class C address 192.168.17.0. One good practice is to choose an IP address that is in the same address class that you need; for example, choosing a class C address makes sense here because the user is reasonably small. A class A or class B address could also have been used, but this strategy doesn't fit logically and is not as well suited to any potential future growth. In this scenario, 192.168.17.1 (the .1 address) is assigned to the router. It is up to the organization to decide how to assign the rest of the addresses; we have chosen here to start host addressing at .10 for servers and at .100 for other hosts.

This scenario employs a Cisco 1720 router. This router has an optimal match of low price, high performance, and flexible options. Its Fast Ethernet port is well suited to the speeds commonly seen on LANs today. It has a V.35 serial WAN interface and can easily support an FT1 line. It also has enough RAM that a good set of packet filters can be put in place; it is surprising how many organizations don't have the budget or feel the need to employ a stand-alone firewall. The 1720 also has enough CPU horsepower that packet filtering and even virtual private network (VPN) support is viable at this speed. The router is connected to the DSU (or other ISP termination equipment) via a V.35 cable.

On the WAN link, the ISP employs the common industry practice of assigning a /30 block. This address scheme employs a block of four addresses; after eliminating the two reserved addresses, two are left over for the two ends of the point-to-point link. In this example, the ISP has allocated the address block 222.222.1.8 with a subnet mask of 255.255.255.252 to the WAN link; 222.222.1.10 is assigned to the serial port of the router, and 222.222.1.9 is assigned to the ISP's end of the WAN link.

Configuration Issues

There are a number of things that we need to do to configure the router for this environment, building on the basic tasks that have been discussed in earlier chapters. First, let's set up NAT. We need to maintain a static, public (global) address for only two systems on the LAN:

- The router itself
- The e-mail server

The following lines will successfully accomplish this:

```
!
! Static NAT addresses (router, e-mail server)
!
ip nat inside source static 192.168.17.1 222.222.100.65
ip nat inside source static 192.168.17.11 222.222.100.66
!
! Set up NAT pool (with overload)
!
ip nat pool nat-pool 222.222.100.67 222.222.100.78 netmask 255.255.255.240
ip nat inside source list 1 pool nat-pool overload
!
access-list 1 permit 192.168.17.0 0.0.0.255
```

The NAT statements will result in all hosts (at least, the first 4,000 or so) sharing the IP address 222.222.100.67 using *port address translation* (PAT) because of the overload keyword. That is certainly OK, but PAT tables are necessarily larger than NAT tables and require slightly more processing cycles from the router.

 NOTE   PAT is a form of address translation that allows you to hide multiple private IP addresses behind a single legal IP address. With NAT, each private IP address is mapped to a public IP address; with PAT, each private IP address is mapped to different TCP/UDP port using the same public IP address.

If we remove the overload keyword above, we will use straight NAT, but we will then only be able to have 12 LAN hosts access the Internet simultaneously; the thirteenth host that tries to get outside will be blocked because no outside addresses are available.

A combination of NAT and PAT could be accomplished using the following commands:

```
!
! Static NAT addresses (router, e-mail server)
!
ip nat inside source static 192.168.17.1 222.222.100.65
ip nat inside source static 192.168.17.11 222.222.100.66
!
! Set up NAT and PAT pools
!
ip nat pool nat-pool 222.222.100.67 222.222.100.77 netmask 255.255.255.240
ip nat pool pat-pool 222.222.100.78 222.222.100.78 netmask 255.255.255.240
ip nat inside source list 1 pool nat-pool
ip nat inside source list 1 pool pat-pool overload
!
access-list 1 permit 192.168.17.0 0.0.0.255
```

In these configuration lines, we will use 11 host addresses for NAT and only revert to PAT when we've run out of available addresses. There are pros and cons to this approach, and it can be argued that mixing NAT and PAT only really makes sense when the number of internal hosts is roughly the same as the number of IP addresses in the NAT/PAT pool. One downside of this is that PAT does not work well with those applications that specify which TCP/UDP port to use, such as videoconferencing and some audio applications. In a PAT-only environment, these applications will consistently fail, which will make tracking down the problem easier; in a mixed NAT/PAT environment, the applications may sometimes work and sometimes fail.

The lines below provide information about the LAN interface:

```
interface fastethernet 0
 full-duplex
 ip address 192.168.17.1 255.255.255.0
 ip nat inside
 bandwidth 100000
```

Configuring the LAN

The LAN configuration is straightforward. Note that the interface is assigned an address from the private address range and that we turn NAT on indicating use of the inside, private address space. Assuming a Fast Ethernet connection to a hub, we set the interface to full-duplex mode. The bandwidth command is only relevant to routing protocols, of course, but it can be useful also for documentation purposes.

```
interface serial 0
 description Dedicated link to the Internet
 ip address 222.222.1.10 255.255.255.252
 ip nat outside
 encapsulation ppp
 bandwidth 256
```

Configuring the WAN

The WAN configuration is similarly straightforward. Note the use of the public address assigned by the ISP and that we turn NAT on indicating use of outside, public addresses. The description command is useful on WAN ports, particularly when there are many interfaces. Also note the use of the encapsulation command; PPP is the most commonly used encapsulation scheme on dedicated lines, but you do have to confirm this with the ISP. Many ISPs use Cisco routers on their periphery and will use Cisco's HDLC encapsulation if the customer is also using a Cisco router; HDLC can be invoked as an option on the encapsulation command and is also the default encapsulation method if another one is not specified.

This router is directly connected to the 222.222.100.64/28 and 222.222.1.8/30 networks and, therefore, knows how to route packets between them. Packets to all other networks are assumed to be destined for the Internet, so they should be forwarded there by setting the default gateway to the ISP's router address:

```
ip route 0.0.0.0 0.0.0.0 222.222.1.9
```

You can accomplish the same thing with this command:

```
ip route 0.0.0.0 0.0.0.0 serial0
```

TIP I prefer the first method because it provides better documentation. If I need to ping my ISP, for example, the address of the next hop is right there in front of me. The latter method is easier and certainly more generic, but I think you lose something in the generality.

In any case, note that static routing is employed. About the only time that you will use *any* routing protocol between your LAN and an ISP is if you have multiple physical connections and wish to employ the Border Gateway Protocol (BGP). Use of BGP must be done in close cooperation with your ISP(s).

Firewall Protection

Last but not least is some sort of firewall protection. For many organizations, the router is the only thing standing between their LAN and the Internet. While a stand-alone firewall such as a PIX, Raptor, FireWall-1, or GNATBox is ideal, recognize that the Internet access router is the first line of defense and, in some organizations, the *only* line of defense. The Cisco Secure Integrated Software (also known as the IOS Firewall) feature set may be the best way to lock down a router, but some organizations view this as a big budget item. And while reflexive packet filters, as discussed in Chapter 9, are an excellent tool, static packet filters place less of a burden on the processor.

 NOTE I am not trying to make excuses for static packet filtering! I am merely observing that all security implementations and policies require a tradeoff between cost, performance, and benefit. If an organization is trying to protect itself from pedestrian attackers, then static packet filters will usually work just fine, are available with standard IOS, and place a minimal burden on the router's performance. If an organization is trying to protect itself from a determined foe, then significantly more resources will be required. This is another reason that I selected the 1720 router for this scenario; it has enough processor power and RAM to accept relatively complex packet filtering rules.

The following paragraphs will describe one way of building packet filters for an organization's boundary router to the Internet. These packet filter rules are applied to the WAN interface. There are two sets of rules:

- One for inbound packets from the Internet
- One for outbound packets to the Internet

The rationale for two sets of filters is partially for better protection. Even more importantly, however, you must not only defend yourself from a potential incoming attack, you must also protect other sites from an attack launched from your site. This is consistent with the philosophy expounded in RFC 2267 that suggests that, as a community, we are obliged to protect ourselves and others.

In any case, the two access lists are numbered 101 (inbound) and 102 (outbound), and need to be applied to the s0 interface:

```
interface Serial0
 ip access-group 101 in
 ip access-group 102 out
```

Why were these filters selected? All too often at a site, the *de facto* security policy is whatever was implemented at the router and/or firewall. It should be the other way around; the organization's policies should dictate the implementation at the firewall! The following filters implement policies that are appropriate for this sample site and may be a useful baseline for other sites. In these filters, we allow the most common TCP application connections to go out (for example, FTP, Telnet, HTTP, SSL, SMTP, and POP3), while allowing only two incoming application connections (SMTP and POP3), which must be directed to the appropriate server. We also allow DNS and Time queries and responses, limit the types of allowable ICMP messages, and block obvious attempts at IP address spoofing. Again, these rules fit the policies chosen for this site; other sites will be different.

The first set of filters blocks any incoming packet with our organization's NET_ID (222.222.100.64/28) in the source address field (one type of address-spoofing attack), packets directed to our network's broadcast address, or packets ostensibly coming from the loopback address (127.0.0.0/8) or any RFC 1918 address.

```
access-list 101 deny   ip 222.222.100.64 0.0.0.15 any log
access-list 101 deny   ip any host 222.222.100.79 log
access-list 101 deny   ip 127.0.0.0 0.255.255.255 any log
access-list 101 deny   ip 10.0.0.0 0.255.255.255 any log
access-list 101 deny   ip 172.16.0.0 0.15.255.255 any log
access-list 101 deny   ip 192.168.0.0 0.0.255.255 any log
```

The next set of filters defines ICMP usage. We want to allow incoming Pings only to the router's LAN and WAN interfaces, but we will allow any host on our network to ping out. We will also accept some other ICMP message types, such as `ttl-exceeded` and `traceroute`, but block all others:

```
access-list 101 permit icmp any host 222.222.100.65 echo
access-list 101 permit icmp any host 222.222.1.10 echo
access-list 101 permit icmp any 222.222.100.64 0.0.0.15 echo-reply
access-list 101 permit icmp any 222.222.100.64 0.0.0.15 ttl-exceeded
```

```
access-list 101 permit icmp any 222.222.100.64 0.0.0.15 traceroute
access-list 101 permit icmp any 222.222.100.64 0.0.0.15 source-quench
access-list 101 permit icmp any 222.222.100.64 0.0.0.15 parameter-problem
access-list 101 permit icmp any 222.222.100.64 0.0.0.15 unreachable
access-list 101 permit icmp any 222.222.100.64 0.0.0.15 port-unreachable
access-list 101 deny  icmp any 222.222.100.64 0.0.0.15
```

Now we get into the protocols. Recall that for TCP filters, the established keyword refers to packets that are part of a completed logical connection. In the first filter that follows, then, we will accept any HTTP packet from any host that is addressed to any host on our own network, as long as the packet is part of an established connection. Other filters will allow our users to have established FTP, SMTP, POP3, Telnet, Gopher, Whois, SSL (443), WAIS (210), Finger, and NNTP connections. Two of the filters allow incoming SMTP and POP3 connections to be made to our e-mail server (222.222.100.66). DNS, Time, and Archie queries are also allowed. The final filter, allowing any TCP packets with both source and destination port above 1023, is needed for passive FTP.

```
access-list 101 permit tcp any eq www 222.222.100.64 0.0.0.15 gt 1023
established
access-list 101 permit udp any eq domain 222.222.100.64 0.0.0.15
access-list 101 permit tcp any eq ftp 222.222.100.64 0.0.0.15 gt 1023
established
access-list 101 permit tcp any eq ftp-data 222.222.100.64 0.0.0.15 gt 1023
access-list 101 permit tcp any gt 1023 host 222.222.100.66 eq smtp
access-list 101 permit tcp any eq smtp 222.222.100.64 0.0.0.15 gt 1023
established
access-list 101 permit tcp any gt 1023 host 222.222.100.66 eq pop3
access-list 101 permit tcp any eq pop3 222.222.100.64 0.0.0.15 gt 1023
established
access-list 101 permit tcp any eq telnet 222.222.100.64 0.0.0.15 gt 1023
established
access-list 101 permit tcp any eq gopher 222.222.100.64 0.0.0.15 gt 1023
established
access-list 101 permit tcp any eq whois 222.222.100.64 0.0.0.15 gt 1023
established
access-list 101 permit tcp any eq 443 222.222.100.64 0.0.0.15 gt 1023
established
access-list 101 permit tcp any eq 210 222.222.100.64 0.0.0.15 gt 1023
established
```

```
access-list 101 permit udp any eq time 222.222.100.64 0.0.0.15 gt 1023
access-list 101 permit udp any eq ntp 222.222.100.64 0.0.0.15 eq ntp
access-list 101 permit udp any eq 1525 222.222.100.64 0.0.0.15 gt 1023
access-list 101 permit tcp any eq finger 222.222.100.64 0.0.0.15 gt 1023
established
access-list 101 permit udp any gt 32768 222.222.100.64 0.0.0.15 gt 32768
access-list 101 permit tcp any eq nntp 222.222.100.64 0.0.0.15 gt 1023
established
access-list 101 permit tcp any gt 1023 222.222.100.64 0.0.0.15 gt 1023
established
```

The following packet filters are applied to outbound packets and are basically the reverse of the filters above. The first three filters block outbound packets with an RFC 1918 private address in the source address field to block outbound address spoofing:

```
access-list 102 deny   ip any 10.0.0.0 0.255.255.255 log
access-list 102 deny   ip any 172.16.0.0 0.15.255.255 log
access-list 102 deny   ip any 192.168.0.0 0.0.255.255 log
access-list 102 permit icmp host 222.222.100.65 any echo-reply
access-list 102 permit icmp host 222.222.1.10 any echo-reply
access-list 102 permit icmp 222.222.100.64 0.0.0.15 any echo
access-list 102 permit icmp 222.222.100.64 0.0.0.15 any ttl-exceeded
access-list 102 permit icmp 222.222.100.64 0.0.0.15 any traceroute
access-list 102 permit icmp 222.222.100.64 0.0.0.15 any source-quench
access-list 102 permit icmp 222.222.100.64 0.0.0.15 any parameter-problem
access-list 102 permit icmp 222.222.100.64 0.0.0.15 any unreachable
access-list 102 permit icmp 222.222.100.64 0.0.0.15 any port-unreachable
access-list 102 deny   icmp 222.222.100.64 0.0.0.15 any
access-list 102 permit tcp 222.222.100.64 0.0.0.15 gt 1023 any eq www
access-list 102 permit udp 222.222.100.64 0.0.0.15 any eq domain
access-list 102 permit tcp 222.222.100.64 0.0.0.15 gt 1023 any eq ftp
access-list 102 permit tcp 222.222.100.64 0.0.0.15 gt 1023 any eq ftp-data
established
access-list 102 permit tcp host 222.222.100.66 eq smtp any gt 1023
established
access-list 102 permit tcp 222.222.100.64 0.0.0.15 gt 1023 any eq smtp
access-list 102 permit tcp host 222.222.100.66 eq pop3 any gt 1023
established
access-list 102 permit tcp 222.222.100.64 0.0.0.15 gt 1023 any eq pop3
access-list 102 permit tcp 222.222.100.64 0.0.0.15 gt 1023 any eq telnet
```

```
access-list 102 permit tcp 222.222.100.64 0.0.0.15 gt 1023 any eq gopher
access-list 102 permit tcp 222.222.100.64 0.0.0.15 gt 1023 any eq whois
access-list 102 permit tcp 222.222.100.64 0.0.0.15 gt 1023 any eq 443
access-list 102 permit tcp 222.222.100.64 0.0.0.15 gt 1023 any eq 210
access-list 102 permit udp 222.222.100.64 0.0.0.15 gt 1023 any eq time
access-list 102 permit tcp 222.222.100.64 0.0.0.15 gt 1023 any eq 37
access-list 102 permit udp 222.222.100.64 0.0.0.15 gt 1023 any eq ntp
access-list 102 permit udp 222.222.100.64 0.0.0.15 eq ntp any eq ntp
access-list 102 permit udp 222.222.100.64 0.0.0.15 gt 1023 any eq 1525
access-list 102 permit tcp 222.222.100.64 0.0.0.15 gt 1023 any eq finger
access-list 102 permit udp 222.222.100.64 0.0.0.15 gt 32768 any gt 32768
access-list 102 permit tcp 222.222.100.64 0.0.0.15 gt 1023 any eq nntp
access-list 102 permit tcp 222.222.100.64 0.0.0.15 gt 1023 any gt 1023
```

Router Configuration File

The following is the final configuration file that was generated for this router:

```
! Router configuration for dedicated Internet access.
! Cisco 1720 (GCK)
!
version 12.0
!
hostname GCK
enable secret 5 $1$Mgs1$6qC6QfPue2ScpJaoS3lpUO
!
no service udp-small-servers
no service tcp-small-servers
service password-encryption
no ip source-route
ip classless
ip subnet-zero
no ip proxy-arp
no service finger
no ip bootp server
no ip http server
!
! Static NAT addresses (router, e-mail server)
!
ip nat inside source static 192.168.17.1 222.222.100.65
```

```
ip nat inside source static 192.168.17.11 222.222.100.66
!
! Set up NAT and PAT pools
!
ip nat pool nat-pool 222.222.100.67 222.222.100.78 netmask 255.255.255.240
ip nat inside source list 1 pool nat-pool overload
!
interface fastethernet0
 full-duplex
 ip address 192.168.17.1 255.255.255.0
 arp timeout 300
 bandwidth 100000
 ip nat inside
 no ip directed-broadcast
 ntp disable
 no ip redirects
 no ip unreachables
 no ip route-cache
 no ip mroute-cache
 no mop enabled
!
interface Serial0
 description Dedicated link to the Internet
 ip address 222.222.1.10 255.255.255.252
 ip access-group 101 in
 ip access-group 102 out
 encapsulation ppp
 bandwidth 256
 ip nat outside
 no ip directed-broadcast
 ntp disable
 no ip redirects
 no ip unreachables
 no ip route-cache
 no ip mroute-cache
 no mop enabled
!
ip route 0.0.0.0 0.0.0.0 222.222.1.9
!
```

```
access-list 1 permit 192.168.17.0 0.0.0.255
!
access-list 101 deny   ip 222.222.100.64 0.0.0.15 any log
access-list 101 deny   ip any host 222.222.100.79 log
access-list 101 deny   ip 127.0.0.0 0.255.255.255 any log
access-list 101 deny   ip 10.0.0.0 0.255.255.255 any log
access-list 101 deny   ip 172.16.0.0 0.15.255.255 any log
access-list 101 deny   ip 192.168.0.0 0.0.255.255 any log
access-list 101 permit icmp any host 222.222.100.65 echo
access-list 101 permit icmp any host 222.222.1.10 echo
access-list 101 permit icmp any 222.222.100.64 0.0.0.15 echo-reply
access-list 101 permit icmp any 222.222.100.64 0.0.0.15 ttl-exceeded
access-list 101 permit icmp any 222.222.100.64 0.0.0.15 traceroute
access-list 101 permit icmp any 222.222.100.64 0.0.0.15 source-quench
access-list 101 permit icmp any 222.222.100.64 0.0.0.15 parameter-problem
access-list 101 permit icmp any 222.222.100.64 0.0.0.15 unreachable
access-list 101 permit icmp any 222.222.100.64 0.0.0.15 port-unreachable
access-list 101 deny   icmp any 222.222.100.64 0.0.0.15
access-list 101 permit tcp any eq www 222.222.100.64 0.0.0.15 gt 1023
established
access-list 101 permit udp any eq domain 222.222.100.64 0.0.0.15
access-list 101 permit tcp any eq ftp 222.222.100.64 0.0.0.15 gt 1023
established
access-list 101 permit tcp any eq ftp-data 222.222.100.64 0.0.0.15 gt 1023
access-list 101 permit tcp any gt 1023 host 222.222.100.66 eq smtp
access-list 101 permit tcp any eq smtp 222.222.100.64 0.0.0.15 gt 1023
established
access-list 101 permit tcp any gt 1023 host 222.222.100.66 eq pop3
access-list 101 permit tcp any eq pop3 222.222.100.64 0.0.0.15 gt 1023
established
access-list 101 permit tcp any eq telnet 222.222.100.64 0.0.0.15 gt 1023
established
access-list 101 permit tcp any eq gopher 222.222.100.64 0.0.0.15 gt 1023
established
access-list 101 permit tcp any eq whois 222.222.100.64 0.0.0.15 gt 1023
established
access-list 101 permit tcp any eq 443 222.222.100.64 0.0.0.15 gt 1023
established
```

```
access-list 101 permit tcp any eq 210 222.222.100.64 0.0.0.15 gt 1023
established
access-list 101 permit udp any eq time 222.222.100.64 0.0.0.15 gt 1023
access-list 101 permit udp any eq ntp 222.222.100.64 0.0.0.15 eq ntp
access-list 101 permit udp any eq 1525 222.222.100.64 0.0.0.15 gt 1023
access-list 101 permit tcp any eq finger 222.222.100.64 0.0.0.15 gt 1023
established
access-list 101 permit udp any gt 32768 222.222.100.64 0.0.0.15 gt 32768
access-list 101 permit tcp any eq nntp 222.222.100.64 0.0.0.15 gt 1023
established
access-list 101 permit tcp any gt 1023 222.222.100.64 0.0.0.15 gt 1023
established
!
access-list 102 deny  ip any 10.0.0.0 0.255.255.255 log
access-list 102 deny  ip any 172.16.0.0 0.15.255.255 log
access-list 102 deny  ip any 192.168.0.0 0.0.255.255 log
access-list 102 permit icmp host 222.222.100.65 any echo-reply
access-list 102 permit icmp host 222.222.1.10 any echo-reply
access-list 102 permit icmp 222.222.100.64 0.0.0.15 any echo
access-list 102 permit icmp 222.222.100.64 0.0.0.15 any ttl-exceeded
access-list 102 permit icmp 222.222.100.64 0.0.0.15 any traceroute
access-list 102 permit icmp 222.222.100.64 0.0.0.15 any source-quench
access-list 102 permit icmp 222.222.100.64 0.0.0.15 any parameter-problem
access-list 102 permit icmp 222.222.100.64 0.0.0.15 any unreachable
access-list 102 permit icmp 222.222.100.64 0.0.0.15 any port-unreachable
access-list 102 deny  icmp 222.222.100.64 0.0.0.15 any
access-list 102 permit tcp 222.222.100.64 0.0.0.15 gt 1023 any eq www
access-list 102 permit udp 222.222.100.64 0.0.0.15 any eq domain
access-list 102 permit tcp 222.222.100.64 0.0.0.15 gt 1023 any eq ftp
access-list 102 permit tcp 222.222.100.64 0.0.0.15 gt 1023 any eq ftp-data
established
access-list 102 permit tcp host 222.222.100.66 eq smtp any gt 1023
established
access-list 102 permit tcp 222.222.100.64 0.0.0.15 gt 1023 any eq smtp
access-list 102 permit tcp host 222.222.100.66 eq pop3 any gt 1023
established
access-list 102 permit tcp 222.222.100.64 0.0.0.15 gt 1023 any eq pop3
access-list 102 permit tcp 222.222.100.64 0.0.0.15 gt 1023 any eq telnet
access-list 102 permit tcp 222.222.100.64 0.0.0.15 gt 1023 any eq gopher
```

```
access-list 102 permit tcp 222.222.100.64 0.0.0.15 gt 1023 any eq whois
access-list 102 permit tcp 222.222.100.64 0.0.0.15 gt 1023 any eq 443
access-list 102 permit tcp 222.222.100.64 0.0.0.15 gt 1023 any eq 210
access-list 102 permit udp 222.222.100.64 0.0.0.15 gt 1023 any eq time
access-list 102 permit tcp 222.222.100.64 0.0.0.15 gt 1023 any eq 37
access-list 102 permit udp 222.222.100.64 0.0.0.15 gt 1023 any eq ntp
access-list 102 permit udp 222.222.100.64 0.0.0.15 eq ntp any eq ntp
access-list 102 permit udp 222.222.100.64 0.0.0.15 gt 1023 any eq 1525
access-list 102 permit tcp 222.222.100.64 0.0.0.15 gt 1023 any eq finger
access-list 102 permit udp 222.222.100.64 0.0.0.15 gt 32768 any gt 32768
access-list 102 permit tcp 222.222.100.64 0.0.0.15 gt 1023 any eq nntp
access-list 102 permit tcp 222.222.100.64 0.0.0.15 gt 1023 any gt 1023
!
no scheduler allocate
banner exec #

You are accessing a private system.

If you are not explicitly authorized to use this system, please go away.

#
!
banner incoming #This is a private system. Unauthorized use is prohibited.#
!
line con 0
 transport input none
!
line aux 0!
line vty 0 4
 exec-timeout 0 0
 password 7 02563f90a7b2
 login
!
end
```

Conclusion

This scenario shows a very common type of implementation today. There are, of course, many variations on this theme; for example, you might use Frame Relay rather than a point-to-point connection. The actual protocol for access will depend upon the ISP, geographic location, service availability, and cost.

Case Study 2: Private WAN Using Dedicated Lines

In this scenario, we will consider a private WAN built by an organization to interconnect multiple sites that are geographically close to each other. A central site will be connected to two remote sites using dedicated 56Kbps DDS and T1 lines. We will also discuss the use of internal and external DSUs, as well as the creation of a private network addressing scheme.

Setting the Stage

An organization that needs to connect multiple locations for data networking and/or LAN interconnection has traditionally had just a few choices. Point-to-point circuits, such as DDS and T1, are billed based on speed and distance between the two sites. Data networking alternatives include X.25, SMDS, and Frame Relay. X.25, the grandparent of all packet-switching services and once widely available in the U.S., was generally limited in speed to about 56Kbps; it is also difficult to find new X.25 services today. SMDS, an excellent choice as a data network service (particularly for IP applications), has also passed its peak for wide availability. Frame Relay, in fact, has emerged as a major private-line replacement technology, but as prices of DDS and T1 lines continue to drop, some users are actually going back to private lines.

This scenario, illustrated in Figure 14.2, shows an organization with three sites located within a few miles of each other. For economic reasons, the company has decided to use private lines rather than a traditional data service. Because of the expected traffic volume and desired response times, the organization will employ a 56Kbps DDS line to Remote Site #1 and a 768Kbps FT1 to Remote Site #2.

FIGURE 14.2

*Private WAN using
dedicated lines*

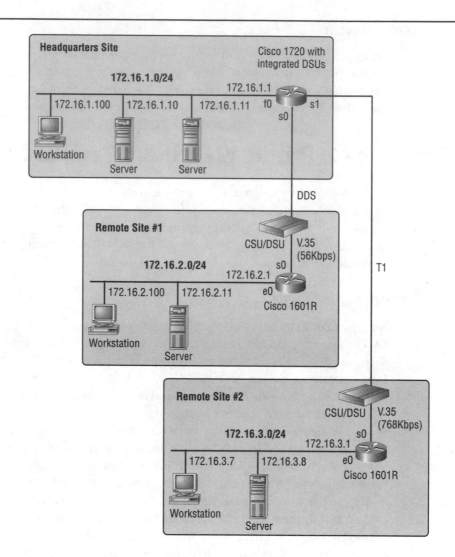

The Technology

This scenario requires three routers. We decided to use Cisco 1601R routers at the remote sites. In terms of configuration, the 1601R has an Ethernet port and V.35 serial port, which we will use to attach to an external DSU. From a processor viewpoint, the 1601R is quite adequate for the expected use.

The Headquarters location uses a Cisco 1720 router. One reason for this is rather contrived: It allows us to demonstrate the use of an internal DSU, and the 1600s don't have an internal T1 DSU option. From a more practical viewpoint, the 1720 is fine for this scenario but provides no potential for growth, such as the addition of a third remote site. A Cisco 3620 router, on the other hand, also supports internal DSUs and would allow at least a couple more WAN ports, but it is noticeably more expensive than a 1720. Always use what best fits the situation.

This scenario will employ an IP addressing scheme using the RFC 1918 private class B address 172.16.0.0. The use of a private address here is largely pragmatic; we may one day attach to the Internet and we won't have to worry about renumbering. We will use subnetting to provide the equivalent of a full class C address to each of the sites.

For demonstration purposes, we will employ the unnumbered IP capability on the point-to-point WAN links. Many sites use this feature because it saves on addressing (although there are plenty of addresses in the RFC 1918 space) and/or the hassle of creating /30 subnets. I like addressing the WAN links because the ability to ping every individual port of a router helps during troubleshooting, particularly on connections to the Internet. Nevertheless, many network administrators use unnumbered interfaces within the private network, and some ISPs even use this feature.

Finally, we will also employ static routing. The issues are simplicity, bandwidth conservation, and the fact that a routing protocol is just not necessary. We have here two point-to-point links interconnecting three networks and, in fact, there are no alternate routes, so a routing protocol offers little real benefit.

Configuration Issues

Although there are three routers here, the configuration is actually rather straightforward. Be sure that the routers sharing a WAN link use the same encapsulation scheme, and pay attention to configuring the internal DSUs. The sections that follow describe configuring the remote-site routers first, followed by the configuration of the central router.

Configuring the Remote Sites' Routers

Each remote site will employ a 1601R router with an external DSU. Since the router configurations are pretty simple and very similar, we will start with them. In fact, all we have to do at the remote sites is assign an IP address to the Ethernet port, set up IP unnumbered at the serial port, and provide routing information. The configuration for the router at Remote Site #1 would contain the following:

```
interface ethernet0
 ip address 172.16.2.1 255.255.255.0
```

```
!
interface Serial0
 ip unnumbered ethernet0
 encapsulation ppp
!
ip route 0.0.0.0 0.0.0.0 serial0
```

The only difference in the router configuration at Remote Site #2 would be to assign the IP address 172.16.3.1 to the e0 port. Note also that we selected PPP encapsulation. In fact, we could have left this line out completely and the routers would have defaulted to HDLC; we just have to be sure that the encapsulation method at the remote sites agrees with the encapsulation specified at the Headquarters site.

Despite the fact that the router configurations are essentially identical, the DSU configurations are very different. Remote Site #1 uses a DDS line to connect to the Headquarters site. We will need a 56Kbps DSU to terminate this connection. Most 56Kbps DSUs do not require any configuration.

T1 DSUs are another story entirely. Your T1 service provider will advise you how to configure such parameters as the framing format, line code, and time slots to use. We will see this again when we configure the internal DSU below.

 NOTE Although most DDS DSUs today support both 56 and 64Kbps, you cannot use a T1 DSU configured for a single time slot to terminate a DDS line. The line code, signaling, and frame format of T1 and DDS circuits are not the same.

Configuring the Headquarters Router

The configuration of the 1720 router at Headquarters is also pretty straightforward. The most complicated thing to do is to configure the serial ports with their integrated DSUs. Configuring the fa0 port is simple; it only needs an IP address:

```
interface fastethernet0
 ip address 172.16.1.1 255.255.255.0
```

Next, we need to configure the s0 port. You can usually take the defaults when configuring the internal 56Kbps DSU, and you might even be able get away with using no configuration statements at all. The three `service-module 56k` configuration lines that follow force the line timing to come from the network (rather than an internal clock), assume a point-to-point dedicated DDS line (rather than a switched digital connection), and employ normal data encoding (rather than inverse encoding). Note that we also employ unnumbered IP and PPP encapsulation:

```
interface Serial0
 description DDS link to Remote Site #1
 service-module 56k clock source line
 service-module 56k network-type dds
 service-module 56k data-coding normal
 ip unnumbered fastethernet0
 encapsulation ppp
 bandwidth 56
```

Next, we configure the s1 port. As above, you need to obtain the T1 line parameters from the service provider in order to configure the DSU. There are five common T1 parameters that can be set with the `service-module t1` configuration lines:

- Set the clock source; usually set to `line`.

- Specify the time slots to use for the data connection. In this example, we will use time slots 1–12 to form the 768Kbps data channel. Each time slot can be configured to operate at either 56 or 64Kbps; the latter is the usual setting.

- Specify the T1 framing format; Extended Superframe (ESF) format is most common.

- Specify the T1 line code; Binary 8 with Zero Substitution (B8ZS) is most common.

- Set the *line build-out* (LBO) level. This is information that you sometimes have to get from the service provider in real-time as you install the router; you may still have to experiment to select the correct value. The most common choices for this parameter are none and auto (auto detects the LBO level).

 NOTE Setting the LBO level is the most common sticking point in installing any T1 DSU, either internal or external.

The following lines configure the internal T1 DSU and set up unnumbered IP and PPP encapsulation:

```
interface Serial1
 description FT1 link to Remote Site #2
 service-module t1 clock source line
 service-module t1 time slots 1-12 speed 64
```

```
service-module t1 framing esf
service-module t1 linecode b8zs
service-module t1 lbo none
ip unnumbered fastethernet0
encapsulation ppp
bandwidth 768
```

Finally, we need to set up routing so that the Headquarters router can find the two remote routers:

```
ip route 172.16.2.0 255.255.255.0 s0
ip route 172.16.3.0 255.255.255.0 s1
```

Router Configuration File

The following is the final configuration file that was generated for the Headquarters router and the first remote site. Also listed are the configuration file differences between the two remote sites.

Headquarters Router

This is a complete configuration for the Headquarters router:

```
! Router configuration for private WAN w/ dedicated lines.
! Cisco 1720 (GCK)
!
version 12.0
hostname Headquarters
enable secret 5 $1$Mgs1$6qC6QfPue2ScpJaoS3lpUO
service password-encryption
!
interface fastethernet0
 full-duplex
 ip address 172.16.1.1 255.255.255.0
 arp timeout 300
 bandwidth 100000
!
interface Serial0
 description DDS link to Remote Site #1
 service-module 56k clock source line
 service-module 56k network-type dds
 service-module 56k data-coding normal
```

```
 ip unnumbered fastethernet0
 encapsulation ppp
 bandwidth 56
!
interface Serial1
 description FT1 link to Remote Site #2
 service-module t1 clock source internal
 service-module t1 time slots 1-12 speed 64
 service-module t1 framing esf
 service-module t1 linecode b8zs
 service-module t1 lbo none
 ip unnumbered fastethernet0
 encapsulation ppp
 bandwidth 768
!
ip route 172.16.2.0 255.255.255.0 s0
ip route 172.16.3.0 255.255.255.0 s1
!
line con 0
 transport input none
!
line aux 0!
line vty 0 4
 exec-timeout 0 0
 password 7 02563f90a7b2
 login
!
end
```

Remote Site Routers

This is a complete configuration for the Remote Site #1 router:

```
! Router configuration for private WAN w/ dedicated lines.
! Cisco 1601R. (GCK)
!
version 12.0
!
hostname Remote_1
enable secret 5 $1$Mgs1$6qC6QfPue2ScpJaoS3lpUO
```

```
service password-encryption
!
interface ethernet0
 ip address 172.16.2.1 255.255.255.0
 arp timeout 300
 bandwidth 10000
!
interface Serial0
 description DDS link to Headquarters
 ip unnumbered ethernet0
 encapsulation ppp
 bandwidth 56
!
ip route 0.0.0.0 0.0.0.0 serial0
!
line con 0
 transport input none
!
line aux 0!
line vty 0 4
 exec-timeout 0 0
 password 7 02563f90a7b2
 login
!
end
```

The following lines show the changes to the previous configuration for the Remote Site #2 router:

```
hostname Remote_2
!
interface ethernet0
 ip address 172.16.3.1 255.255.255.0
!
interface Serial0
 description T1 link to Headquarters
 bandwidth 768
```

Conclusion

This scenario shows a common implementation when interconnecting multiple sites that are geographically close. A minor variation of this configuration could have used Frame Relay instead; you'll see this in the next case study.

In some instances, the network administrator might want to allow traffic only between the remote sites and headquarters but not between the remote sites themselves. In that case, packet filters on the Headquarters router can control what traffic is allowed where.

This same general configuration can also be used in a cluster of buildings, such as a campus environment. On a campus, however, you are more likely to use a network backbone that provides alternative and/or multiple routes between buildings, such as the Fiber Distributed Data Interface (FDDI) or multiple physical lines. In this case, you would probably want to use a routing protocol.

Case Study 3: Private IP/IPX WAN Using Frame Relay

In this section, we will bring together several topics. Whereas the previous two WAN scenarios described small and medium-sized organizations, we will now address a somewhat more complex scenario. First, we will build a WAN using Frame Relay. Second, we will support both IPX and IP, and employ IPX routing. Finally, we will connect this WAN to the organization's LAN connection to the Internet.

Setting the Stage

In this scenario, we have an organization with a central site and multiple remote sites that are geographically distant. We are also running IP and NetWare's IPX. Because of the distances involved, we will employ Frame Relay for the WAN. See Figure 14.3 for an illustration of this scenario.

Because of the anticipated traffic levels, we want to provide access to the Frame Relay network at a rate of at least 512Kbps, which is the rate we will employ at each remote site. We will use a full T1 to access the Frame Relay network from the central site. Notice that the aggregate bandwidth of all of the remote sites (2.048Mbps) is greater than the bandwidth available at the central site (1.536Mbps). For Frame Relay, of course, this is not a problem because most Frame Relay service providers allow oversubscription.

FIGURE 14.3

Private IP/IPX WAN using Frame Relay

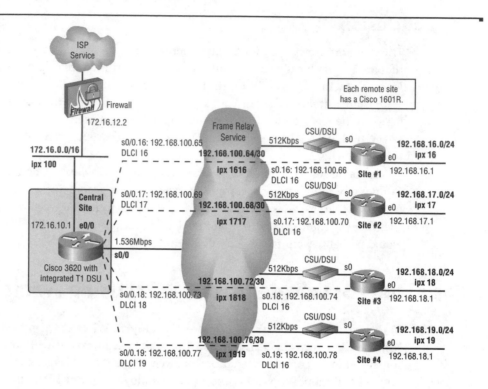

 TIP Using IPX over a WAN at speeds less than 256Kbps is generally unsatisfactory for users. But at any speed, be sure to employ NCP packet burst.

Although we won't discuss this in depth, we are also assuming that this organization has an Internet connection and a firewall. The WAN router at the central site is attached to the LAN with the firewall, so this router is the gateway between the remote sites and the Internet.

The Technology

Frame Relay is not only well suited to interconnecting geographically distant sites; it is also well suited for multiprotocol encapsulation. For this reason, we will have no problem transporting IP and IPX traffic over the WAN.

We will employ RFC 1918 class C addresses for the WAN. Each remote site will be allocated its own class C address, and another class C address (192.168.100.0) will be used to create /30 addresses for the WAN links. Note that the addresses all somehow reference the Data Link Connection Identifier (DLCI) as seen from the central site: The remote sites' IP address is 192.168.<DLCI>.0 and the IPX address is merely <DLCI>. The IP and IPX WAN addresses are also based on the DLCI. I often use a plan like this because it provides documentation, is easy to extend as PVCs are added, and makes it easy to keep track of which network site I am dealing with.

 NOTE The DLCI in Frame Relay is a 10-bit number that can take a value between 0 and 1023. The lowest DLCI value that can be assigned to end users is 16, which is the number that most providers start with. In this scenario, each of the remote sites is assigned DLCI 16, which refers the permanent virtual circuit (PVC) back to the central site. The central site terminates four PVCs, however, so they would be numbered 16–19, as shown. The IP and IPX address scheme that we use here is based on the DLCI value as seen from the central site.

We will reserve the "class B" space 192.168.0.0/16 for the WAN and remote LANs. At the central site, we will use the IP NET_ID 172.16.0.0/16 and IPX network number 100. Static routing will work fine on the WAN for IP, and we'll use RIP for the IPX traffic.

We've selected Cisco 1601R routers for the remote sites because they provide a LAN and WAN port, and they can handle the expected traffic level. A Cisco 3620 router was selected for the central site for a couple of reasons, even though a 1720 is another candidate:

- Although a 1720 can handle multiple V.35 WAN ports, the 3620 allows even more growth in case additional sites are added or additional services (such as dial-up access) are needed.
- The 3620 has more processing power than a 1720. This extra power might be useful if additional lines are connected to the central site router.
- The 3620 is better suited than a 1720 for some advanced IOS features, such as filtering protocol traffic based on load.

Configuration Issues

The router configurations here are not difficult, although we must keep track of Frame Relay, IP, and IPX numbering, as well as IP and IPX routing. The first section that follows describes configuring the central router; the next section describes what needs to be done at each remote site. Comments are also included about the network's firewall.

Configuring the Central Site's Router

Let's begin the configuration overview by looking at the central site's router. We'll start by turning on IPX RIP routing:

```
ipx routing
```

 NOTE This command is actually supposed to include the MAC address of the router, but IOS is smart enough to insert it for you.

The configuration of the e0/0 port is simple; we merely have to assign an IP address from the 172.16.0.0/16 space and assign an IPX network number:

```
interface Ethernet0/0
 ip address 172.16.10.1 255.255.0.0
 ipx network 100
```

Configuring the s0/0 interface is also straightforward, if a tad more complicated. In this scenario, the 3620 has an internal T1 DSU, so we have to provide appropriate configuration information; note that we use all 24 time slots of the T1 for this connection. No IP address is specifically assigned to s0/0; individual IP addresses will be assigned to the Frame Relay subinterfaces later.

We then have to specify Frame Relay as the encapsulation type. The IETF keyword is essential when connecting a Cisco router to a non-Cisco router in a Frame Relay environment; your Frame Relay service provider will have to tell you whether or not it uses Cisco equipment. The safest thing is to use the IETF keyword unless you are specifically told to use Cisco Frame Relay encapsulation. We can turn off Frame Relay's Inverse Address Resolution Protocol (InARP) because we don't need it; we statically associate the DLCIs and IP addresses. Finally, note that we do not specify the Frame Relay Local Management Interface (LMI) format because Cisco IOS can auto-detect the LMI type.

 NOTE LMI auto-detection takes a little time, so it may take a minute or more for the Frame Relay link to activate. On the other hand, auto-detection works and is accurate, and that may be worth the price of admission. I have been given incorrect LMI information several times by various Frame Relay service providers, once being told that all I had to do was to configure the two routers to use the same LMI type (this is incorrect; the LMI is a premises-to-network protocol, not end-to-end).

```
interface Serial0/0
 service-module t1 clock source line
 service-module t1 time slots 1-24 speed 64
 service-module t1 framing esf
 service-module t1 lbo none
 service-module t1 linecode b8zs
 !
 no ip address
 encapsulation frame-relay ietf
 no frame-relay inverse-arp
```

Each Frame Relay PVC is configured on a separate subinterface. To keep everything straight, I usually use a numbering scheme where the subinterface number matches the DLCI number. Here is where the WAN IP address, DLCI, and IPX network number are assigned to the subinterfaces:

```
interface Serial0/0.16 point-to-point
 Description FR PVC (DLCI 16) to Site #1
 ip address 192.168.10.65 255.255.255.252
 bandwidth 512
 frame-relay interface-dlci 16
 ipx network 1616
 !
interface Serial0/0.17 point-to-point
 Description FR PVC (DLCI 17) to Site #2
 ip address 192.168.10.69 255.255.255.252
 bandwidth 512
 frame-relay interface-dlci 17
 ipx network 1717
 !
interface Serial0/0.18 point-to-point
 Description FR PVC (DLCI 18) to Site #3
 ip address 192.168.10.73 255.255.255.252
 bandwidth 512
 frame-relay interface-dlci 18
 ipx network 1818
 !
interface Serial0/0.19 point-to-point
 Description FR PVC (DLCI 19) to Site #4
 ip address 192.168.10.77 255.255.255.252
```

```
bandwidth 512
frame-relay interface-dlci 19
ipx network 1919
```

Finally, we have to set up the static IP routes. The first four lines of the following commands direct traffic for the four remote LANs to the four serial subinterfaces' IP WAN address. The last line provides a default gateway; packets with unknown IP addresses are assumed to be going to the Internet and are forwarded to the firewall.

```
ip route 192.168.16.0 255.255.255.0 192.168.10.66
ip route 192.168.17.0 255.255.255.0 192.168.10.70
ip route 192.168.18.0 255.255.255.0 192.168.10.74
ip route 192.168.19.0 255.255.255.0 192.168.10.78
ip route 0.0.0.0 0.0.0.0 172.16.12.2
```

Configuring the Remote Routers

The remote routers have configurations similar to the central site's router, although simpler. As before, we start by turning on IPX RIP and configuring the Ethernet interface with an IP address and IPX network number:

```
ipx routing
!
interface Ethernet0
 ip address 192.168.16.1 255.255.255.0
 ipx network 16
```

Next, we configure the serial interface. As before, no IP address is assigned to the interface itself, and we have to specify Frame Relay encapsulation. The subinterface is assigned an IP address, IPX network number, and DLCI.

```
interface Serial0
 no ip address
 encapsulation frame-relay ietf
 no frame-relay inverse-arp
!
interface Serial0.16 point-to-point
 Description FR link to Central Site
 ip address 192.168.10.66 255.255.255.252
 bandwidth 512
 ipx network 1616
 frame-relay interface-dlci 16
```

Finally, we assign the default gateway using the IP address of the central site's side of the WAN link.

```
ip route 0.0.0.0 0.0.0.0 192.168.10.65
```

Each of the remote routers will be configured as before, with obvious differences:

- The appropriate IP addresses and IPX network numbers need to be assigned to the e0 interface and s0.16 subinterface.
- The appropriate IP address must be used for the default gateway.

Configuring the Firewall

A few words about the configuration of the firewall are also in order. The firewall, while connected to the same LAN as the central site router, must be able to recognize the WAN and remote sites' networks. Regardless of the type of firewall, there will be some way to configure its routing table as follows:

- The firewall's default gateway should be whatever IP address it is using to access the Internet.
- Packets to the 172.16.0.0/16 address space should just go out on the connected LAN.
- Packets to the 192.168.0.0/16 address space should be forwarded to 172.16.10.1. Making a simple routing table entry was the primary reason that the WAN links and remote LANs were given IP addresses within the same address space *and* one that was different than the central site's LAN address space.

Router Configuration Files

The following sections show completed configuration files from each of our routers.

Central Router

This is a complete configuration for the central site's router:

```
! Router configuration for private IP/IPX
! WAN using frame relay
! Cisco 3620 (GCK)
!
version 12.0
hostname CentralSite
enable secret 5 $1$Mgs1$6qC6QfPue2ScpJaoS3lpUO
service password-encryption
```

```
ip classless
ipx routing
!
interface Ethernet0/0
 ip address 172.16.10.1 255.255.0.0
 arp timeout 300
 bandwidth 10000
 ipx network 100
!
interface Serial0/0
 service-module t1 clock source line
 service-module t1 time slots 1-24 speed 64
 service-module t1 framing esf
 service-module t1 lbo none
 service-module t1 linecode b8zs
!
 no ip address
 encapsulation frame-relay ietf
 no frame-relay inverse-arp
!
interface Serial0/0.16 point-to-point
 Description FR PVC (DLCI 16) to Site #1
 ip address 192.168.10.65 255.255.255.252
 bandwidth 512
 frame-relay interface-dlci 16
 ipx network 1616
!
interface Serial0/0.17 point-to-point
 Description FR PVC (DLCI 17) to Site #2
 ip address 192.168.10.69 255.255.255.252
 bandwidth 512
 frame-relay interface-dlci 17
 ipx network 1717
!
interface Serial0/0.18 point-to-point
 Description FR PVC (DLCI 18) to Site #3
 ip address 192.168.10.73 255.255.255.252
 bandwidth 512
 frame-relay interface-dlci 18
```

```
 ipx network 1818
!
interface Serial0/0.19 point-to-point
 Description FR PVC (DLCI 19) to Site #4
 ip address 192.168.10.77 255.255.255.252
 bandwidth 512
 frame-relay interface-dlci 19
 ipx network 1919
!
ip route 192.168.16.0 255.255.255.0 192.168.10.66
ip route 192.168.17.0 255.255.255.0 192.168.10.70
ip route 192.168.18.0 255.255.255.0 192.168.10.74
ip route 192.168.19.0 255.255.255.0 192.168.10.78
ip route 0.0.0.0 0.0.0.0 172.16.12.2
!
line con 0
 transport input none
!
line aux 0!
line vty 0 4
 exec-timeout 0 0
 password 7 02563f90a7b2
 login
!
end
```

Remote Routers

This is a complete configuration for the site #1 router:

```
! Router configuration for private IP/IPX
! WAN using frame relay
! Cisco 1601R (GCK)
!
version 12.0
hostname Site_16
enable secret 5 $1$Mgs1$6qC6QfPue2ScpJaoS3lpUO
service password-encryption
ip classless
ipx routing
```

```
!
interface Ethernet0
 ip address 192.168.16.1 255.255.255.0
 arp timeout 300
 bandwidth 10000
 ipx network 16
!
interface Serial0
 no ip address
 encapsulation frame-relay ietf
 no frame-relay inverse-arp
!
interface Serial0.16 point-to-point
 Description FR link to Central Site
 ip address 192.168.10.66 255.255.255.252
 bandwidth 512
 ipx network 1616
 frame-relay interface-dlci 16
!
ip route 0.0.0.0 0.0.0.0 192.168.10.65
!
line con 0
 transport input none
!
line vty 0 4
 password 7 02563f90a7b2
 login
!
end
```

The lines that follow show the changes to the configuration above for the site #2 router:

```
hostname Site_17
!
interface Ethernet0
 ip address 192.168.17.1 255.255.255.0
 ipx network 17
!
interface Serial0.17 point-to-point
 ip address 192.168.10.70 255.255.255.252
```

```
 ipx network 1717
 frame-relay interface-dlci 17
!
ip route 0.0.0.0 0.0.0.0 192.168.10.69
```

The following lines show the changes to the previous configuration for the site #3 router:

```
hostname Site_18
!
interface Ethernet0
 ip address 192.168.18.1 255.255.255.0
 ipx network 18
!
interface Serial0.18 point-to-point
 ip address 192.168.10.74 255.255.255.252
 ipx network 1818
 frame-relay interface-dlci 18
!
ip route 0.0.0.0 0.0.0.0 192.168.10.73
```

The following lines show the changes to the configuration above for the site #4 router:

```
hostname Site_19
!
interface Ethernet0
 ip address 192.168.19.1 255.255.255.0
 ipx network 19
!
interface Serial0.19 point-to-point
 ip address 192.168.10.78 255.255.255.252
 ipx network 1818
 frame-relay interface-dlci 18
!
ip route 0.0.0.0 0.0.0.0 192.168.10.77
```

Conclusion

Many different variations on a theme could be implemented here. Instead of static IP routing, for example, we could employ a routing protocol and, in fact, almost enforce the Frame Relay committed information rate (CIR). If it made economical sense, we could mix and match dedicated lines and Frame Relay. If the aggregate Frame Relay rate were to grow beyond the capacity of the single T1 at the central site, we could employ multiple T1s to the Frame Relay service. The `rate-limit` command could be used to set different acceptable thresholds for different types of traffic, effectively establishing a prioritization. The list goes on and on.

 NOTE There are other views on routing IP. Although I am a proponent of using static routing when the network topology is simple and there are no alternate routes, do compare the ease of configuring IP with RIP routing versus IP with static routing.

Many other sets of router configurations can be found on Cisco's Web site at `http://www.cisco.com/warp/public/793/`.

Case Study 4: A Multipoint VPN

Monson Management is a relatively small company with an international presence. Monson has offices in the United Kingdom, Mexico, and the U.S. Currently, Monson does not have a wide area network to connect any of its offices. We have been asked to design a wide area network solution that will allow Monson to link its offices together.

Monson currently has offices in Reno, Nevada; Houston, Texas; Boston, Massachusetts; Mexico City, Mexico; Morelos, Mexico; and London, England. The solution needs to be cost effective. Cost is more of a concern than reliability since Monson currently does not have any WAN in place.

Identifying a Solution

The far-flung locations of Monson's offices make leased lines impractical due to the associated cost. Frame Relay is an option, but Monson would like to go ahead and attempt to use its existing Internet connections at each site to develop a VPN solution. The VPN will be used to connect the offices to achieve connectivity with minimal expense. The fact that we are going to use the Internet means that we must be very careful about security.

Since there is no existing network, we can start with whatever routers we choose. The Boston office is the main corporate office; because this office will have the most traffic, we will use a 3640 router. This is a good choice because we might want later to develop an internal LAN presence using this router. The 3640 offers a lot of room to grow. The other offices will each have a 2610 router. The 2610 gives us enough processing power to run the VPN encryption and route data into the Internet. All of the routers will run IOS 12.0 with the Firewall feature set. The proposed VPN network will look like Figure 14.4.

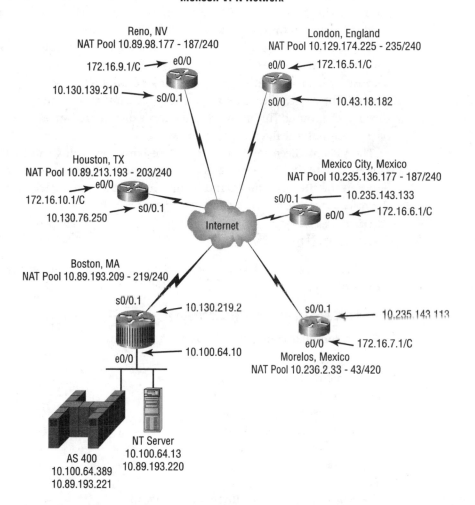

FIGURE 14.4

Monson VPN logical topology

Monson VPN Network

As you can see from Figure 14.4, Monson will be using NAT to allow users access to the Internet. Overload NAT translations will be used with a typical NAT pool of 10 addresses. This should be enough to support the users in each location. In fact, it is really more than enough, but it is usually better to err on the side of caution. Static translations will be set up for the NT server and AS400 in the Boston office so that users will have access these devices.

We will allow out-of-band management by configuring a modem on the AUX port of each router. This is important because if the VPN somehow gets messed up, there is no way to go in and fix anything without the modems. For security reasons, the modems will be left turned off until there is a problem. They will be turned on as needed by staff in the office that's experiencing the problem.

To enhance security on the routers, we'll use reflexive access lists to do dynamic packet filtering. Reflexive filters offer improved security over standard access lists because, when making decisions on whether on not to allow a specific packet through the router, these filters take into account the traffic that has previously gone through the router. This makes it much more difficult for an attacker to sneak a packet through the filters.

The VPN has been configured to use preshared keys using triple DES encryption and an MD5 hash algorithm. Additionally, static routes are used to define the routes between the sites. This makes it difficult for an attacker to hijack data by corrupting the routes that the router is using.

Sample Configurations

Registered IP addresses have been changed to private addresses in the following configurations.

Boston Router Configuration

This is a complete configuration for the Boston router:

```
!
version 12.0
service timestamps debug uptime
service timestamps log uptime
service password-encryption
!
hostname Boston
!
enable password 7 000D1D120149070701701D
!
!
!
!
```

```
!
ip subnet-zero
no ip domain-lookup
!
ip audit notify log
ip audit po max-events 100
ip reflexive-list timeout 900
!
!
crypto isakmp policy 1
 encr 3des
 hash md5
 authentication pre-share
!
crypto isakmp policy 2
 encr 3des
 hash md5
 authentication pre-share
!
crypto isakmp policy 3
 encr 3des
 hash md5
 authentication pre-share
!
crypto isakmp policy 4
 encr 3des
 hash md5
 authentication pre-share
!
crypto isakmp policy 5
 encr 3des
 hash md5
 authentication pre-share
crypto isakmp key orkleey address 10.235.143.113
crypto isakmp key orkleey address 10.235.143.133
crypto isakmp key orkleey address 10.43.18.182
crypto isakmp key orkleey address 10.130.139.210
crypto isakmp key orkleey address 10.130.76.250
!
```

```
!
crypto ipsec transform-set cm-transformset-1 ah-md5-hmac esp-3des
crypto ipsec transform-set cm-transformset-2 ah-md5-hmac esp-3des
crypto ipsec transform-set cm-transformset-3 ah-md5-hmac esp-3des
crypto ipsec transform-set cm-transformset-4 ah-md5-hmac esp-3des
crypto ipsec transform-set cm-transformset-5 ah-md5-hmac esp-3des
!
!
crypto map cm-cryptomap local-address Serial0/0.1
crypto map cm-cryptomap 1 ipsec-isakmp
 set peer 10.130.76.250
 set transform-set cm-transformset-1
 match address 100
crypto map cm-cryptomap 2 ipsec-isakmp
 set peer 10.130.139.210
 set transform-set cm-transformset-2
 match address 101
crypto map cm-cryptomap 3 ipsec-isakmp
 set peer 10.43.18.182
 set transform-set cm-transformset-3
 match address 102
crypto map cm-cryptomap 4 ipsec-isakmp
 set peer 10.235.143.133
 set transform-set cm-transformset-4
 match address 103
crypto map cm-cryptomap 5 ipsec-isakmp
 set peer 10.235.143.113
 set transform-set cm-transformset-5
 match address 104
!
!
interface Loopback0
 ip address 10.168.254.1 255.255.255.0
 no ip directed-broadcast
!
interface Ethernet0/0
 description connected to 10.100.64.0
 ip address 10.100.64.10 255.255.255.0
 no ip directed-broadcast
```

```
  ip nat inside
  no cdp enable
!
interface Serial0/0
 no ip address
 no ip directed-broadcast
 encapsulation frame-relay IETF
 no ip mroute-cache
 no fair-queue
 service-module t1 time slots 17-24
 service-module t1 remote-alarm-enable
 frame-relay lmi-type ansi
!
interface Serial0/0.1 point-to-point
 description connected to Internet
 ip address 10.130.219.2 255.255.255.252
 ip access-group filterin in
 ip access-group filterout out
 no ip directed-broadcast
 ip nat outside
 no ip mroute-cache
 no arp frame-relay
 no cdp enable
 frame-relay interface-dlci 157 IETF
 crypto map cm-cryptomap
!
ip nat pool boston-natpool-33 63.89.193.209 63.89.193.219 netmask
255.255.255.240
ip nat inside source list 109 pool boston-natpool-33 overload
ip nat inside source static 10.100.64.13 10.89.193.221
ip nat inside source static 10.100.64.3 10.89.193.220
ip classless
ip route 0.0.0.0 0.0.0.0 Serial0/0.1
no ip http server
!
!
ip access-list extended filterin
 deny   ip 127.0.0.0 0.255.255.255 any
 deny   ip 10.100.64.0 0.0.0.255 any
```

```
permit ip 172.16.0.0 0.0.255.255 10.100.64.0 0.0.0.255
permit icmp any 10.89.193.208 0.0.0.15 administratively-prohibited
permit icmp any 10.89.193.208 0.0.0.15 echo-reply
permit icmp any 10.89.193.208 0.0.0.15 packet-too-big
permit icmp any 10.89.193.208 0.0.0.15 time-exceeded
permit icmp any 10.89.193.208 0.0.0.15 unreachable
permit tcp any host 10.89.193.220 eq smtp reflect smtpfilter
permit tcp any host 10.89.193.221 eq smtp reflect smtpfilter
permit tcp any host 10.89.193.220 eq 1352 reflect notesfilter
permit tcp any host 10.89.193.221 eq 1352 reflect notesfilter
permit esp any any
permit ahp any any
permit udp any eq isakmp any
permit tcp 10.112.202.0 0.0.0.255 eq telnet any
evaluate ipfilter
permit ip 10.112.202.0 0.0.0.255 any
permit icmp host 10.39.203.213 host 10.130.219.2
permit icmp host 10.39.201.213 host 10.130.219.2
permit icmp host 10.39.203.154 host 10.130.219.2
permit icmp host 10.39.201.154 host 10.130.219.2
permit icmp host 10.39.129.30 host 10.130.219.2
permit icmp host 10.39.129.196 host 10.130.219.2
permit icmp host 10.39.57.196 host 10.130.219.2
permit icmp host 10.39.57.136 host 10.130.219.2
permit icmp host 10.39.129.230 host 10.130.219.2
permit icmp host 10.39.201.87 host 10.130.219.2
permit icmp host 10.39.203.87 host 10.130.219.2

ip access-list extended filterout
 permit ip 10.100.64.0 0.0.0.255 172.16.0.0 0.0.255.255
 permit ip 10.89.193.208 0.0.0.15 any reflect ipfilter
 evaluate smtpfilter
 evaluate notesfilter
 permit ip any 10.112.202.0 0.0.0.255
access-list 100 permit ip 10.100.64.0 0.0.0.255 172.16.10.0 0.0.0.255
access-list 101 permit ip 10.100.64.0 0.0.0.255 172.16.9.0 0.0.0.255
access-list 102 permit ip 10.100.64.0 0.0.0.255 172.16.5.0 0.0.0.255
access-list 103 permit ip 10.100.64.0 0.0.0.255 172.16.6.0 0.0.0.255
access-list 104 permit ip 10.100.64.0 0.0.0.255 172.16.7.0 0.0.0.255
```

```
access-list 109 deny   ip 10.100.64.0 0.0.0.255 172.16.0.0 0.0.255.255
access-list 109 permit ip 10.100.64.0 0.0.0.255 any
no cdp run
snmp-server engineID local 00000009020000505073468181
snmp-server community secret_squirrel RO
!
line con 0
 exec-timeout 15 0
 password 7 011A08105E190A0E2F1D
 login
 transport input pad v120 lapb-ta telnet rlogin udptn
line aux 0
 password 7 130C19060E1E082B2575
 login
 modem InOut
 modem autoconfigure type usr_courier
 transport input all
 speed 115200
 flowcontrol hardware
line vty 0 4
 exec-timeout 15 0
 password 7 141E1C1F0916262A2A79
 login
 transport input pad v120 lapb-ta telnet rlogin udptn
!
end
```

Reno Router Configuration

This is a complete configuration for the Reno router:

```
!
version 12.0
service timestamps debug uptime
service timestamps log uptime
service password-encryption
!
hostname RENO
!
enable password 7 011A08105E190A0E2F1F1D
```

```
!
!
memory-size iomem 10
ip subnet-zero
no ip domain-lookup
!
ip audit notify log
ip audit po max-events 100
ip reflexive-list timeout 900
!
!
crypto isakmp policy 1
 encr 3des
 hash md5
 authentication pre-share
!
crypto isakmp policy 2
 encr 3des
 hash md5
 authentication pre-share
!
crypto isakmp policy 3
 encr 3des
 hash md5
 authentication pre-share
!
crypto isakmp policy 4
 encr 3des
 hash md5
 authentication pre-share
!
crypto isakmp policy 5
 encr 3des
 hash md5
 authentication pre-share
crypto isakmp key orkleey address 10.130.219.2
crypto isakmp key orkleey address 10.130.76.250
crypto isakmp key orkleey address 10.43.18.182
crypto isakmp key orkleey address 10.235.143.133
```

```
crypto isakmp key orkleey address 10.235.143.113
!
!
crypto ipsec transform-set cm-transformset-1 ah-md5-hmac esp-3des
crypto ipsec transform-set cm-transformset-2 ah-md5-hmac esp-3des
crypto ipsec transform-set cm-transformset-3 ah-md5-hmac esp-3des
crypto ipsec transform-set cm-transformset-4 ah-md5-hmac esp-3des
crypto ipsec transform-set cm-transformset-5 ah-md5-hmac esp-3des
!
!
crypto map cm-cryptomap local-address Serial0/0.1
crypto map cm-cryptomap 1 ipsec-isakmp
 set peer 10.130.219.2
 set transform-set cm-transformset-1
 match address 100
crypto map cm-cryptomap 2 ipsec-isakmp
 set peer 10.130.76.250
 set transform-set cm-transformset-2
 match address 101
crypto map cm-cryptomap 3 ipsec-isakmp
 set peer 10.43.18.182
 set transform-set cm-transformset-3
 match address 102
crypto map cm-cryptomap 4 ipsec-isakmp
 set peer 10.235.143.133
 set transform-set cm-transformset-4
 match address 103
crypto map cm-cryptomap 5 ipsec-isakmp
 set peer 10.235.143.113
 set transform-set cm-transformset-5
 match address 104
!
!
interface Ethernet0/0
 description connected to 172.16.9.0
 ip address 172.16.9.1 255.255.255.0
 no ip directed-broadcast
 ip nat inside
 no cdp enable
```

```
!
interface Serial0/0
 no ip address
 no ip directed-broadcast
 encapsulation frame-relay
 no ip mroute-cache
 no fair-queue
 service-module t1 time slots 24
 service-module t1 remote-alarm-enable
 frame-relay lmi-type ansi
!
interface Serial0/0.1 point-to-point
 description connected to Internet
 ip address 10.130.139.210 255.255.255.252
 ip access-group filterin in
 ip access-group filterout out
 no ip directed-broadcast
 ip nat outside
 no ip mroute-cache
 no arp frame-relay
 no cdp enable
 frame-relay interface-dlci 155 IETF
 crypto map cm-cryptomap
!
ip nat pool Reno-natpool-33 10.88.98.177 10.88.98.187 netmask
255.255.255.240
ip nat inside source list 109 pool Reno-natpool-33 overload
ip classless
ip route 0.0.0.0 0.0.0.0 Serial0/0.1
no ip http server
!
!
ip access-list extended filterin
 deny   ip 127.0.0.0 0.255.255.255 any
 deny   ip 172.16.9.0 0.0.0.255 any
 permit ip 172.16.0.0 0.0.255.255 any
 permit ip 10.100.64.0 0.0.0.255 any
 permit icmp any 10.88.98.176 0.0.0.15 administratively-prohibited
 permit icmp any 10.88.98.176 0.0.0.15 echo-reply
```

```
  permit icmp any 10.88.98.176 0.0.0.15 packet-too-big
  permit icmp any 10.88.98.176 0.0.0.15 time-exceeded
  permit icmp any 10.88.98.176 0.0.0.15 unreachable
  permit esp any any
  permit ahp any any
  permit udp any eq isakmp any
  permit ip 10.112.202.0 0.0.0.255 any
  permit icmp host 10.39.203.213 host 10.130.139.210
  permit icmp host 10.39.201.213 host 10.130.139.210
  permit icmp host 10.39.203.154 host 10.130.139.210
  permit icmp host 10.39.201.154 host 10.130.139.210
  permit icmp host 10.39.129.30 host 10.130.139.210
  permit icmp host 10.39.129.196 host 10.130.139.210
  permit icmp host 10.39.57.196 host 10.130.139.210
  permit icmp host 10.39.57.136 host 10.130.139.210
  permit icmp host 10.39.129.230 host 10.130.139.210
  permit icmp host 10.39.201.87 host 10.130.139.210
  permit icmp host 10.39.203.87 host 10.130.139.210
  evaluate ipfilter
ip access-list extended filterout
  permit ip 172.16.9.0 0.0.0.255 any
  permit ip 10.88.98.176 0.0.0.15 any reflect ipfilter
access-list 100 permit ip 172.16.9.0 0.0.0.255 10.100.64.0 0.0.0.255
access-list 101 permit ip 172.16.9.0 0.0.0.255 172.16.10.0 0.0.0.255
access-list 102 permit ip 172.16.9.0 0.0.0.255 172.16.5.0 0.0.0.255
access-list 103 permit ip 172.16.9.0 0.0.0.255 172.16.6.0 0.0.0.255
access-list 104 permit ip 172.16.9.0 0.0.0.255 172.16.7.0 0.0.0.255
access-list 109 deny  ip any 172.16.0.0 0.0.255.255
access-list 109 deny  ip any 10.100.64.0 0.0.0.255
access-list 109 permit ip 172.16.9.0 0.0.0.255 any
no cdp run
snmp-server engineID local 00000009020000D0BAEB8001
snmp-server community secret_squirrel RO
!
line con 0
  exec-timeout 0 0
  password 7 130C19060E1E082B2577
  login
  transport input none
```

```
line aux 0
 password 7 141E1C1F0916262A2A7B
 login
 modem InOut
 modem autoconfigure type usr_courier
 transport input all
 flowcontrol hardware
line vty 0 4
 exec-timeout 15 0
 password 7 12100B03171900052478
 login
!
end
```

Houston Router Configuration

This is a complete configuration for the Houston router:

```
Current configuration:
!
version 12.0
service timestamps debug uptime
service timestamps log uptime
service password-encryption
!
hostname Houston
!
enable password 7 141E1C1F0916262A2A7A61
!
!
memory-size iomem 10
ip subnet-zero
no ip domain-lookup
!
ip audit notify log
ip audit po max-events 100
ip reflexive-list timeout 900
!
!
crypto isakmp policy 1
```

```
 encr 3des
 hash md5
 authentication pre-share
!
crypto isakmp policy 2
 encr 3des
 hash md5
 authentication pre-share
!
crypto isakmp policy 3
 encr 3des
 hash md5
 authentication pre-share
!
crypto isakmp policy 4
 encr 3des
 hash md5
 authentication pre-share
!
crypto isakmp policy 5
 encr 3des
 hash md5
 authentication pre-share
crypto isakmp key orkleey address 10.235.143.113
crypto isakmp key orkleey address 10.235.143.133
crypto isakmp key orkleey address 10.43.18.182
crypto isakmp key orkleey address 10.130.139.210
crypto isakmp key orkleey address 10.130.219.2
!
!
crypto ipsec transform-set cm-transformset-1 ah-md5-hmac esp-3des
crypto ipsec transform-set cm-transformset-2 ah-md5-hmac esp-3des
crypto ipsec transform-set cm-transformset-3 ah-md5-hmac esp-3des
crypto ipsec transform-set cm-transformset-4 ah-md5-hmac esp-3des
crypto ipsec transform-set cm-transformset-5 ah-md5-hmac esp-3des
!
!
crypto map cm-cryptomap local-address Serial0/0.1
crypto map cm-cryptomap 1 ipsec-isakmp
```

```
    set peer 10.130.219.2
    set transform-set cm-transformset-1
    match address 100
crypto map cm-cryptomap 2 ipsec-isakmp
    set peer 10.130.139.210
    set transform-set cm-transformset-2
    match address 101
crypto map cm-cryptomap 3 ipsec-isakmp
    set peer 10.43.18.182
    set transform-set cm-transformset-3
    match address 102
crypto map cm-cryptomap 4 ipsec-isakmp
    set peer 10.235.143.133
    set transform-set cm-transformset-4
    match address 103
crypto map cm-cryptomap 5 ipsec-isakmp
    set peer 10.235.143.113
    set transform-set cm-transformset-5
    match address 104
!
!
interface Ethernet0/0
    description connected to 172.16.10.0
    ip address 172.16.10.1 255.255.255.0
    no ip directed-broadcast
    ip nat inside
    no cdp enable
!
interface Serial0/0
    no ip address
    no ip directed-broadcast
    encapsulation frame-relay
    no ip mroute-cache
    no fair-queue
    service-module t1 time slots 23-24
    service-module t1 remote-alarm-enable
    frame-relay lmi-type ansi
!
interface Serial0/0.1 point-to-point
```

```
      description connected to Internet
      ip address 10.130.76.250 255.255.255.252
      ip access-group filterin in
      ip access-group filterout out
      no ip directed-broadcast
      ip nat outside
      no ip mroute-cache
      no arp frame-relay
      no cdp enable
      frame-relay interface-dlci 155 IETF
      crypto map cm-cryptomap
     !
     ip nat pool Houston-natpool-33 10.89.213.193 10.89.213.203 netmask
     255.255.255.240
     ip nat inside source list 109 pool Houston-natpool-33 overload
     ip classless
     ip route 0.0.0.0 0.0.0.0 Serial0/0.1
     no ip http server
     !
     !
     ip access-list extended filterin
      deny   ip 127.0.0.0 0.255.255.255 any
      deny   ip 172.16.10.0 0.0.0.255 any
      permit ip 172.16.0.0 0.0.255.255 any
      permit ip 10.100.64.0 0.0.0.255 any
      permit icmp any 10.89.213.192 0.0.0.15 administratively-prohibited
      permit icmp any 10.89.213.192 0.0.0.15 echo-reply
      permit icmp any 10.89.213.192 0.0.0.15 packet-too-big
      permit icmp any 10.89.213.192 0.0.0.15 time-exceeded
      permit icmp any 10.89.213.192 0.0.0.15 unreachable
      permit esp any any
      permit ahp any any
      permit udp any eq isakmp any
      permit ip 10.112.202.0 0.0.0.255 any
      permit icmp host 10.39.203.213 host 10.130.76.250
      permit icmp host 10.39.201.213 host 10.130.76.250
      permit icmp host 10.39.203.154 host 10.130.76.250
      permit icmp host 10.39.201.154 host 10.130.76.250
      permit icmp host 10.39.129.30 host 10.130.76.250
```

```
 permit icmp host 10.39.129.196 host 10.130.76.250
 permit icmp host 10.39.57.196 host 10.130.76.250
 permit icmp host 10.39.57.136 host 10.130.76.250
 permit icmp host 10.39.129.230 host 10.130.76.250
 permit icmp host 10.39.201.87 host 10.130.76.250
 permit icmp host 10.39.203.87 host 10.130.76.250
 evaluate ipfilter
ip access-list extended filterout
 permit ip 172.16.10.0 0.0.0.255 any
 permit ip 10.89.213.192 0.0.0.15 any reflect ipfilter
access-list 100 permit ip 172.16.10.0 0.0.0.255 10.100.64.0 0.0.0.255
access-list 101 permit ip 172.16.10.0 0.0.0.255 172.16.9.0 0.0.0.255
access-list 102 permit ip 172.16.10.0 0.0.0.255 172.16.5.0 0.0.0.255
access-list 103 permit ip 172.16.10.0 0.0.0.255 172.16.6.0 0.0.0.255
access-list 104 permit ip 172.16.10.0 0.0.0.255 172.16.7.0 0.0.0.255
access-list 109 deny  ip any 172.16.0.0 0.0.255.255
access-list 109 deny  ip any 10.100.64.0 0.0.0.255
access-list 109 permit ip 172.16.0.0 0.0.255.255 any
no cdp run
snmp-server engineID local 00000009020000D0BAEB8CA0
snmp-server community avox2268 RO
!
line con 0
 exec-timeout 0 0
 password 7 130C19060E1E082B2576
 login
 transport input none
line aux 0
 password 7 141E1C1F0916262A2A7A
 login
 modem InOut
 modem autoconfigure type usr_courier
 transport input all
 speed 300
 flowcontrol hardware
line vty 0 4
 exec-timeout 15 0
 password 7 12100B03171900052479
 login
```

```
!
no scheduler allocate
end
```

Conclusion

As VPN technology becomes more and more popular, networking designs incorporating VPNs will become more and more common. The biggest problem with VPNs is that you have no control over the network that carries the data—the Internet. You are subject to the delays caused by other users who run traffic through the Internet. As more companies begin to use VPN technology, the demands placed on the Internet will continue to increase. This means that Monson will have to keep a watchful eye on VPN response time to make sure that it does not degrade too much.

When implementing a VPN solution, security must be your first concern. You have no real control over where your data goes within the cloud that is the Internet. For this reason, you need to make sure that things are secure. At the moment, this implementation serves Monson well; in the future, Monson may need to move away from the VPN and toward a more traditional WAN solution. For right now, however, Monson is very happy with this configuration, which is a perfect fit for its current networking needs and budget.

Case Study 5: A Network Operations Center

Caird Computing is looking to provide a remote management and monitoring solution to augment its traditional business of consulting services. Caird is looking to use various management tools, such as HP OpenView, SNMP, and Transcend, to monitor the state of its clients' systems. Additionally, the company intends to gather statistical information about the health of their client's networks over time. This information will be compiled and used by Caird's network analyst team to provide clients with quarterly state-of-the-network reports.

In order for this model to be profitable, Caird has developed a centralized network operations center. From this operations center, Caird needs to be able to poll devices on its clients' networks. Once we have developed the design, the model must be scalable so that new clients can be added easily. The design should also be standardized so that there is minimal difference between client connections.

Caird computing currently has a corporate WAN with seven remote sites. This means that the company has experience maintaining a WAN environment.

Identifying a Solution

The fact that Caird has an existing WAN is irrelevant. We do not want to tie any of the managed networks to Caird's production environment. The most common client concern about this service is security. Caird's management center will basically be the hub, as shown in Figure 14.5. Notice that all client networks tie into the management center, but any existing Caird WAN links are kept completely separate.

FIGURE 14.5

Caird's network management center is a hub.

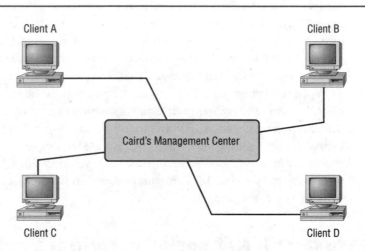

We must take care to prevent Client A from knowing anything about Client B, C, or D. A monitored client should never have any indication that Caird has other clients being monitored from the same network management center.

Since Caird will be responsible for knowing the status of remote client devices around the clock, we'll need a dedicated connection. The bandwidth requirements for management traffic, however, are relatively small. This means that we will not need T1 access speed to most clients. In fact, if we end up needing a T1 to pass management traffic to and from the client, we are definitely degrading the client's network performance—a very bad thing. The goal of network management is to be as unobtrusive as possible. There is no way to be completely unobtrusive, though. Remember the Heisenburg uncertainty principle: The closer you study something, the more you change its behavior through the tools you use to observe it.

Using Frame Relay

Careful analysis of the types and quantity of traffic needed to provide the necessary services to the clients has shown that normally a 56Kbps line will be adequate.

Because Caird is looking to establish a national clientele, Frame Relay is the most cost-effective solution. For locations that are geographically close to the management center, this may not always be the cheapest solution, so we will need to be able to support a few point-to-point connections. In addition to being cost effective over long distances, Frame Relay gives the added benefit of allowing one router interface to service multiple links through the frame cloud by using subinterfaces. This can significantly reduce the cost per client because a router port does not have to be allocated to each client.

When purchasing Frame Relay, you buy a committed information rate (CIR), which is the amount of data you are guaranteed to be able to pass through the frame at all times, and a *port speed*. The port speed limits the amount of data that can be sent in a burst. This is shown in Figure 14.6.

 NOTE Although we can configure our port speed to be higher than our CIR, any passing traffic that pushes the bandwidth above the CIR level could potentially be discarded within the Frame Relay cloud if the network is busy.

FIGURE 14.6

Frame Relay CIR

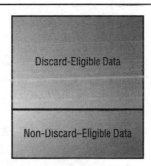

Data that falls below the CIR is treated normally. Data in excess of the CIR has the discard-eligible bit set. When a packet has the discard-eligible bit set, any Frame Relay device experiencing congestion is allowed to simply throw the packet away to try to ease the congestion. In the United States, however, CIR is almost never enforced, so if you order a circuit with a port speed of 56Kbps and a CIR of 16Kbps, you are virtually guaranteed to be able to pass 56Kbps of data all the time.

NOTE CIR is enforced on international links, and different frame carriers have different policies on CIR enforcement. While CIR may not be enforced today, it could be enforced tomorrow. For this reason, you should avoid getting a 0 CIR line (which is available) because it may stop working completely some day.

Using PVCs

You should recommend a Frame Relay circuit with a CIR of 16 and a port or access speed of 56Kbps for most of Caird Computing's customers. The port or access speed is really derived from the leased line used to get into the frame cloud. Generally, we will be going with 56K leased-line access into the frame cloud. 56Kbps access with a 16Kpbs CIR will be the base circuit configuration. It is possible that this will need to be bumped up if the client wants Caird to provide more services. For security reasons, we will have the frame carrier lay out permanent virtual circuits (PVCs) from each client to Caird. Figure 14.7 shows the layout of the connection from clients to Caird's management center.

FIGURE 14.7

Caird's management network logical layout

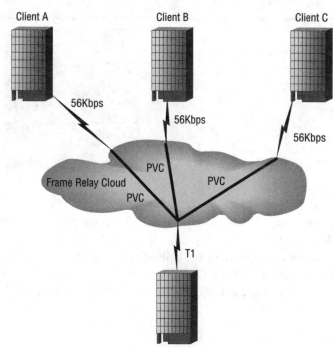

Notice that Caird has T1 access into the frame cloud. We have also upped the CIR for data coming from Caird into the frame cloud. We have chosen a CIR of 56Kbps. This is because Caird will be sending data and receiving data from multiple clients, so the Caird link into the frame cloud will have a greater traffic load. Since all PVCs terminate at Caird's router, we would expect this link to experience significantly more traffic than any other link.

The use of PVCs addresses some of the clients' security concerns, but not all. Careful use of access lists will also be needed to prevent data from going to unwanted places. Also, since the addition of this management connection gives Caird's staff direct access to its clients' networks, careful screening must be done for all individuals employed in the Caird management center.

Hardware Requirements

We have already decided on 56Kbps circuits as the standard for client access to the frame cloud. This means that we can use virtually any router we want, because the data demands will not be very high. We will need at least 16MB of flash to store the IOS and 8MB of RAM. For the most part, we will be running the IP/IPX/DEC IOS feature set.

We have decided to use a combination of 2501- and 2600-series routers. We'll use the 2600 series because we can get an imbedded CSU/DSU for them, which means we have to put less equipment on the client site and we can control it all from the router. We chose the 2501s because there are a lot of them sitting in the basement at Caird, and they can handle the job. Going forward, we will be purchasing 2600-series routers after we have placed all the old 2500s in service.

Now that we have the remote routers selected, we need a router for the connection at Caird. This needs to be able to handle the mainframe connection and some serial connections. For this reason, we have chosen a Cisco 3640. The 3640 offers a lot of processing power and a modular design, so we can change the configuration to support the growing network.

This gives us a configuration like the one shown in Figure 14.8.

FIGURE 14.8

*Caird Management
WAN hardware
perspective*

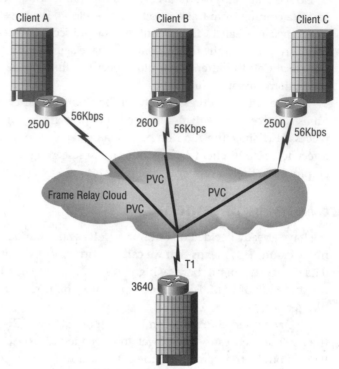

Caird's Computing Management Center

Configuration Issues

After we have settled on a topology and the hardware, it is time to build the configurations. The first thing we need to do is to decide on a routing protocol. Because we want to have as little impact on the clients' networks as possible and security is a concern, we will be using static routes throughout the environment for IP traffic. When we need to use IPX (which is not all that often), we will run IPX RIP and use SAP filters to limit the traffic. Using RIP for IPX is not an ideal solution, but because of the way most Novell servers and IPX clients work, it is the easiest to implement. Since we hope that IPX will not be needed very much, we should be able to support it running IPX RIP.

Addressing the Frame Links

For the Frame Relay links, we need to come up with an addressing scheme. Caird has been given a class C address for its management network. Let's call it 10.0.98.0/24. Since this is all done across a private network, we could use any address, but we decided to use a registered address for the management systems to prevent problems with duplicate IP addresses down the line. Knowing that Caird is using a registered address for the management center has also eased some of the clients' fears.

Now that we know the network address of the Caird network management center, we can select the frame link addresses. These don't matter at all, since they are in a private Frame Relay network that uses PVCs.

We have chosen to use the 172.31.1.x network for the frame connections. These are point-to-point links, so we only need two addresses for each connection; we will be using a 255.255.255.252 subnet mask. This addressing scheme gives us usable addresses like those shown in Table 14.1.

TABLE 14.1: IP ADDRESSING WITHIN THE WAN CLOUD

Network	Host Address	Host Address	Broadcast
172.31.4	172.31.1.5	172.31.1.6	172.31.1.7
172.31.8	172.31.1.9	172.31.1.10	172.31.1.11
172.31.12	172.31.1.13	172.31.1.14	172.31.1.15
172.31.16	172.31.1.17	172.31.1.18	172.31.1.19
172.31.20	172.31.1.21	172.31.1.22	172.31.1.23
172.31.24	172.31.1.25	172.31.1.26	172.31.1.27
172.31.28	172.31.1.29	172.31.1.30	172.31.1.31
Etc.	Etc.	Etc.	Etc.

We will suggest that the Caird side of the connection always use the lower, or odd, host address and the remote side use the higher, or even, host address. This sets a convention and makes understanding that network a little easier. On the remote routers, the serial 0 interface will be used to connect to the frame cloud. Caird's 3640 router will use Serial 1/1 as the master Frame Relay interface. Individual links will be created by defining subinterfaces on this serial port.

Caird will also use a registered IPX network number for its local management network. Random IPX network numbers will be used to address the frame links, but only when needed. The IPX network number and encapsulation configured on the Ethernet side of the client border routers will be defined by the existing LAN environment to which the border router connects. Most of the management functions that Caird wishes to perform can be done without the need to support IPX. This means that most of the time we will not be concerned with supporting IPX through the management frame network.

This configuration will give us a logical network that looks something like Figure 14.9.

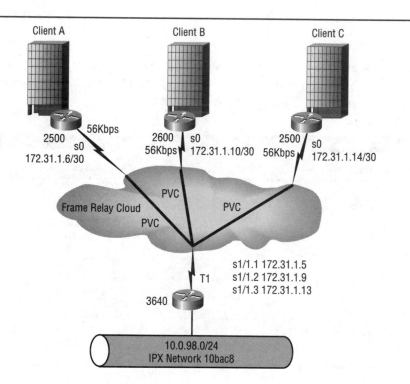

FIGURE 14.9.

Caird logical network with links addressed

Dealing with Routing Issues

Now all we need to do is add our static routes. The remote side is simple: Just add a static route back to the management network in the border router. What makes things complicated is that the client also must add this route into its network. Normally, this is not a problem if there is a default router that we can add the route to. Problems arise when the route we are advertising, 10.0.98.0/24, gets redistributed into a RIP environment. Because RIP does not carry subnet mask information, what really gets propagated is a route to the class A network 10.x.x.x, because the natural subnet mask for 10.x.x.x is 255.0.0.0. This can be a real problem; in a RIP environment, the only solution is to not allow the static route to be redistributed.

Another possible problem arises if we put a static route into the default router for the network and that router goes down: Caird will lose contact with all the devices on the client's network, not just with the default router.

Dealing with Security

Security is another major concern. To address this, we'll use extended access lists to protect the client. On the remote border routers inbound on the serial interfaces connecting to the frame cloud, these lists look something like the following:

```
access-list 101 permit udp any any gt 1023
access-list 101 permit udp any any eq snmp
access-list 101 permit udp any any eq snmptrap
access-list 101 permit icmp any any
```

As you can see, we are permitting SNMP and SNMP trap messages. Port numbers above 1023 are permitted in order to allow through reply traffic. Basically, we are allowing only a one-way communication setup, protecting the client from the world outside of the frame network.

The same access list filtering is done on the inbound serial connections to the Caird management center. In fact, in most cases when traffic filtering is required, the same access list can be used.

Dealing with Network Address Conflicts

On the surface, it seems like we've done all we need to do. In fact, this design was implemented and ran for a year. There is a problem, however. Due the lack of availability of legal IP address space, many of Caird's clients are using private address space in the 10.0.0.0–10.255.255.255, 192.168.0.0–192.168.255.255, or 172.16.0.0–172.31.255.255 areas. This is not a bad thing in itself. However, most clients are using the 192.168.x.x network, and Caird is seeing situations in which Client A and Client B have used the same IP address scheme. Obviously, this causes a problem. Figure 14.10 illustrates the problem.

FIGURE 14.10.

Duplicate IP addresses cause problems for Caird.

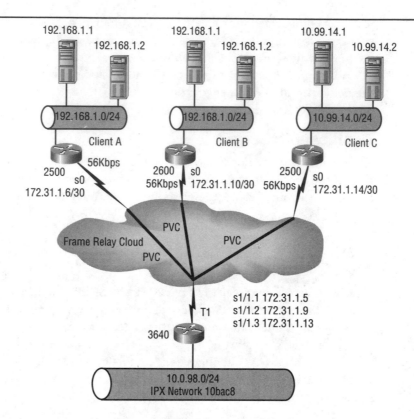

Examine Figure 14.10. How should Caird handle the problem that Client A and Client B have used the same IP addresses? There are several options:

- Caird could screen all potential clients' IP addresses for compatibility with the existing network. This is too limiting because Caird would end up turning away clients. How do you turn down a $500,000 deal because a $1,000 client already is using the $500,000 potential client's IP addresses?

- Caird could use one-to-one address translation. Because Caird is using SNMP as a management tool, however, this causes problems. The IP address of the sending system is stored in the SNMP datagrams, which causes a major problem with HP OpenView. Caird relies heavily on HP OpenView to monitor the status of client systems.

- Caird could deploy a completely separate network to handle those clients which have duplicates of existing client addresses. This is cost prohibitive, since Caird would need to duplicate the whole network every time there was a conflict.

To be honest, there is no really good answer. The best that we can do is to set up a separate management segment in the Caird building and duplicate the management stations that are being used. Duplicating can handle two clients with the same addresses, but not three. Three would require a third management segment at Caird. Obviously, there are serious routing issues with this solution. The Main_rtr router cannot choose between two different routers to 192.168.1.x. In order to do this, we need to trick the Main_rtr router.

The Main_rtr cannot know that there are any duplicate addresses out on the network. To prevent Main_rtr from seeing duplicate addresses, we need to add two additional routers: Router A and Router B. This is shown in Figure 14.11. Router A will use basically the same setup we had before there were any duplicates and will handle most of the management network. It will have one static route in it, sending all data to the Main_rtr, which will handle the route to what it thinks are unique addresses. Thus, if we assume that Client A signed on first, there would be a routing statement in the Main_rtr:

```
ip route 192.168.1.0 255.255.255.0 172.31.1.6
```

Great—now Caird can manage Client A. But how does it handle Client B? Obviously, we cannot add another route to 192.168.1.0 in the Main_rtr. Neither can Router B pass a packet to the Main_rtr with a destination address of 192.168.1.0, because the Main_rtr will send the packet to Client A.

What we need to do is somehow hide the actual IP addresses at Client B from the Main_rtr. The best way to do this is to create a tunnel. Creating a tunnel between Router B and Client B will hide the IP addresses from the Main_rtr. From the Main_rtr's perspective, the only IP address that it sees are the tunnel source and destination IP addresses. The real IP addresses are encapsulated while the data is in the tunnel. These tunnel addresses end up being interface addresses on the Client B router and Router B, which we can control. This will give you a network that looks like Figure 14.12.

FIGURE 14.11

Duplicating operations to handle network address conflicts

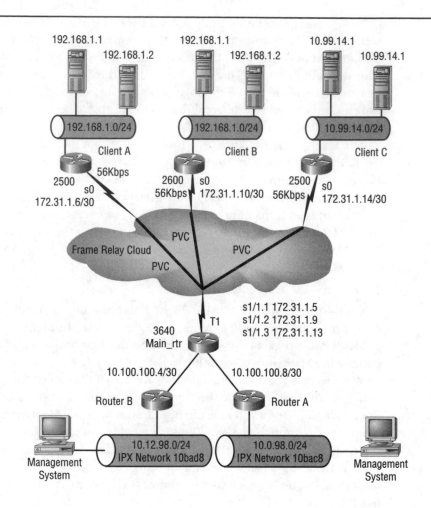

FIGURE 14.12

Using a tunnel to hide the duplicate IP addresses from the Main_rtr

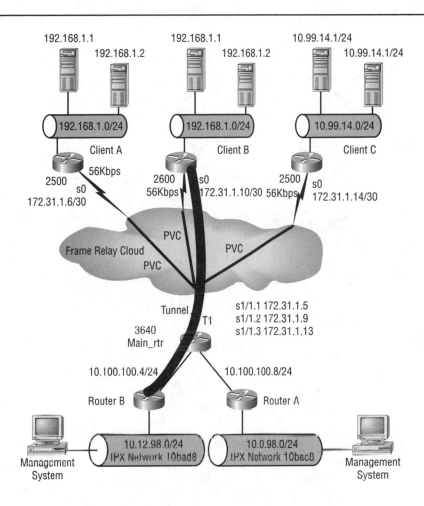

Because the data is encapsulated in the tunnel when it passes through the Main_rtr, the Main_rtr just sends it to the tunnel destination.

Setting up the tunnel between Router B and Client B's border router is pretty simple. For Router B, the commands would look like the following:

```
interface Tunnel0
 ip address 172.16.1.5 255.255.255.252
 tunnel source Ethernet1
 tunnel destination 172.31.1.10
ip route 172.31.1.8 255.255.255.252 10.100.100.6
ip route 192.168.1.0 255.255.255.0 Tunnel0
```

For Client B, the commands would look like this:

```
interface Tunnel0
 ip address 172.16.1.6 255.255.255.252
 tunnel source Serial0
 tunnel destination 10.100.100.5
ip route 10.12.98.0 255.255.255.0 Tunnel0
```

Router Configuration Files

Following are the completed configuration files we created in building our network operation center.

Border_rtr Configuration File

This is a complete configuration for the Border_rtr router:

```
!
version 11.2
service udp-small-servers
service tcp-small-servers
!
hostname Border_rtr
!
enable secret 5 $1$e3lx$4k/41E3fLJQbaZ432hmin0
enable password router_boy
!
ip telnet source-interface Ethernet0
ip name-server 172.30.254.10
ipx routing 00e0.1ea9.619a
ipx internal-network 10BADE5
!
interface Ethernet0
 ip address 192.168.144.13 255.255.255.0
 ipx network 10ABC90 encapsulation SAP
!
interface Serial0
 description frame-relay to Caird
 ip address 172.31.1.10 255.255.255.252
 ipx network 10BACE6
 ipx output-network-filter 801
 ipx output-sap-filter 1002
```

```
 frame-relay interface-dlci 900
!
!
no ip classless

ip route 10.0.98.0 255.255.255.0 Serial0
ip route 0.0.0.0 0.0.0.0 192.168.144.1
access-list 101 permit udp any any gt 1024
access-list 101 permit udp any any eq snmp
access-list 101 permit udp any any eq snmptrap
access-list 101 permit tcp any any gt 1024
access-list 101 permit tcp any any eq 162
access-list 101 permit tcp any any eq www
access-list 101 permit icmp any any
access-list 801 permit 10ABC80 FFFFFFFF
access-list 801 permit 10ABC83 FFFFFFFF
access-list 801 permit 10ABC85 FFFFFFFF
access-list 801 permit 10ABC86 FFFFFFFF
access-list 801 permit 10ABC87 FFFFFFFF
access-list 801 permit 10ABC88 FFFFFFFF
access-list 801 permit 10ABC84 FFFFFFFF
access-list 801 permit 10ABC8B FFFFFFFF
!
access-list 1002 permit 10ABC80 4 SERVER_1
access-list 1002 permit 10ABC86 4 KAH_SERVER
access-list 1002 permit 10ABC83 4 MO_SERVER
access-list 1002 permit 10ABC85 4
access-list 1002 permit 10ABC88 4
access-list 1002 permit 10ABC87 4
access-list 1002 permit 10ABC84 4
access-list 1002 permit 10ABC8B 4
access-list 1002 permit 10ABCA7 4
access-list 1002 permit 10ABCA3 4
!
!
snmp-server community public RO
snmp-server community 21smra RW
!
line con 0
```

```
   exec-timeout 0 0
   password mudd799
 line aux 0
   transport input all
 line vty 0 4
   password mudd799
   login
 !
 end
```

Main_rtr Configuration File

This is a complete configuration for the Main_rtr router:

```
!
version 12.0
service timestamps debug uptime
service timestamps log datetime msec
no service password-encryption
!
hostname CAIRDmain_RTR
!
logging buffered 4096 debugging
enable secret 5 $1$.MEz$QmwdiHGrVHAB/XaUTduGS.
enable password abraham
!
no ip subnet-zero
no ip domain-lookup

ipx routing 00d0.ba0e.2961
ipx internal-network 10BACE0
!
!
process-max-time 200
!
interface Ethernet0/0
 ip address 10.100.100.6 255.255.255.252
 no ip directed-broadcast
 ipx network 10BACFF
 ipx network 10BACFE encapsulation SAP secondary
```

```
!
interface Ethernet0/1
 ip address 10.100.100.10 255.255.255.252
 no ip directed-broadcast
 ipx network 10BACB4
 ipx network 10BACB3 encapsulation SAP secondary
!
interface Serial1/0
 description MCI Frame-Relay Master Interface
 no ip address
 no ip directed-broadcast
 encapsulation frame-relay
 no ip route-cache
 no ip mroute-cache
 frame-relay lmi-type ansi
!
!
interface Serial1/1
 description AT&T Master Frame Relay Circuit
 bandwidth 384
 no ip address
 no ip directed-broadcast
 encapsulation frame-relay
 no ip route-cache
 no ip mroute-cache
!
interface Serial1/1.1 point-to-point
 description Circuit to Client Y
 ip address 172.31.1.5 255.255.255.252
 ip access-group 101 in
 no ip route-cache
 no ip mroute-cache
 ipx network 10BACF0
 ipx output-network-filter 805
 frame-relay interface-dlci 955
!
interface Serial1/1.2 point-to-point
 description Circuit to Client W
 ip address 172.31.1.9 255.255.255.252
```

```
 ip access-group 101 in
 no ip directed-broadcast
 no ip route-cache
 no ip mroute-cache
 ipx network 10BACE6
 ipx output-network-filter 888
 ipx output-sap-filter 1001
 ipx rip-multiplier 60
 frame-relay interface-dlci 920
!
interface Serial1/1.3 point-to-point
 description Circuit to Client D
 ip address 172.31.1.13 255.255.255.252
 ip access-group 101 in
 no ip directed-broadcast
 no ip route-cache
 no ip mroute-cache
 frame-relay interface-dlci 995
!
interface Serial1/1.4 point-to-point
 description Circuit to Client F
 ip address 172.31.1.17 255.255.255.252
 ip access-group 101 in
 no ip directed-broadcast
 no ip route-cache
 no ip mroute-cache
 frame-relay interface-dlci 985
!
interface Serial1/2
 description world comm point to point link
 bandwidth 56
 ip address 172.29.1.5 255.255.255.252
 no ip directed-broadcast
 no ip route-cache
 no ip mroute-cache
 ipx network 10BAC8B
 ipx output-network-filter 802
 ipx output-sap-filter 1002
 no fair-queue
```

```
!
ip route 10.12.98.0 255.255.255.0 10.100.100.5
ip route 10.0.98.0 255.255.255.0 10.100.100.9
ip route 192.168.1.0 255.255.255.0 Serial1/1.1
ip route 10.0.75.0 255.255.255.0 Serial1/1.4
ip route 10.0.126.0 255.255.255.0 Serial1/1.4
ip route 10.5.0.0 255.255.0.0 Serial1/1.2
ip route 172.20.1.0 255.255.255.0 Serial1/1.2
ip route 172.20.3.0 255.255.255.0 Serial1/1.2
ip route 192.168.9.0 255.255.255.0 Serial1/1.4
!
access-list 101 permit udp any any gt 1024
access-list 101 permit udp any any eq snmp
access-list 101 permit udp any any eq snmptrap
access-list 101 permit tcp any any gt 1024
access-list 101 permit tcp any any eq 162
access-list 101 permit tcp any any eq 5631
access-list 101 permit tcp any any eq 5632
access-list 101 permit udp any any eq 5631
access-list 101 permit udp any any eq 5632
access-list 101 permit icmp any any
access-list 101 permit tcp any any eq telnet
access-list 802 permit 10BACAA FFFFFFF
access-list 802 permit 10BACAB FFFFFFF
access-list 805 permit BDE701 FFFFFFFF
access-list 805 permit 93B38CF FFFFFFFF
access-list 805 permit E8F432A FFFFFFFF
access-list 805 permit 14723226 FFFFFFFF
access-list 805 permit CB3E866 FFFFFFFF
access-list 805 permit 27272197 FFFFFFFF
access-list 805 permit 17272197 FFFFFFFF
access-list 805 permit 22491661 FFFFFFFF
access-list 805 permit 12491661 FFFFFFFF
access-list 805 permit 13245767 FFFFFFFF
access-list 805 permit 14741273 FFFFFFFF
access-list 805 permit 17437012 FFFFFFFF
access-list 805 permit 10BAC8D FFFFFFFF
access-list 805 permit 10BAC8C FFFFFFFF
access-list 805 permit 14369711 FFFFFFFF
```

```
access-list 805 permit 3FB921 FFFFFFFF
access-list 888 permit 10BAC8D
access-list 888 permit 10BAC8C
access-list 1001 permit 10BAC8C
access-list 1001 permit 10BAC8D
!
snmp-server community public RO
snmp-server community 21smra RW
snmp-server trap-source Ethernet0/0
snmp-server enable traps isdn call-information
snmp-server enable traps config
snmp-server enable traps frame-relay
snmp-server host 10.0.98.12 traps public
!
!
line con 0
 exec-timeout 0 0
 password mudd799
 transport input none
line aux 0
 session-timeout 30
 password service
 login
 modem Dialin
 speed 2400
line vty 0 4
 session-timeout 180
 exec-timeout 0 0
 password mudd799
 login
!
end
```

Remote Client Configuration File Using a Tunnel

This is a complete configuration for a router using tunneling to prevent IP address conflicts:

```
!
version 11.2
service udp-small-servers
```

```
service tcp-small-servers
!
hostname Border_tunnel_rtr
!
enable secret 5 $1$e3lx$4k/41E3fLJQbaZ432hmin0
enable password router_boy
!
ip telnet source-interface Ethernet0
ip name-server 172.30.254.10
ipx routing 00e0.1ea9.619a
ipx internal-network 10BADE5
!
interface Tunnel0
 ip address 172.16.1.6 255.255.255.252
 tunnel source Serial0
 tunnel destination 10.100.100.5
 ip access-group 101 in

interface Ethernet0
 ip address 192.168.144.13 255.255.255.0
 ipx network 10CBE90 encapsulation SAP
!
interface Serial0
 description frame-relay to Caird
 ip address 172.31.1.10 255.255.255.252
 frame-relay interface-dlci 900
!

!
no ip classless

ip route 10.12.98.0 255.255.255.0 Tunnel0
ip route 0.0.0.0 0.0.0.0 192.168.144.1
access-list 101 permit udp any any gt 1024
access-list 101 permit udp any any eq snmp
access-list 101 permit udp any any eq snmptrap
access-list 101 permit tcp any any gt 1024
access-list 101 permit tcp any any eq 162
access-list 101 permit tcp any any eq www
```

```
access-list 101 permit icmp any any
!
snmp-server community public RO
snmp-server community 21smra RW
!
line con 0
 exec-timeout 0 0
 password mudd799
line aux 0
 transport input all
line vty 0 4
 password mudd799
 login
!
end
```

Configuration File for Caird-side Local Router with a Tunnel

This is a complete configuration for the Caird side of the tunnel:

```
!
version 12.0
service timestamps debug uptime
service timestamps log uptime
no service password-encryption
!
hostname Router_X
!
enable secret 5 $1$i6wF$mk3xB6ldSrQo.vBPw2wJo0
!
no ip subnet-zero
!
!
process-max-time 200
!
interface Tunnel0
 ip address 172.16.1.6 255.255.255.252
 tunnel source Ethernet0/1
 tunnel destination 172.31.1.10
!
```

```
interface Ethernet0/0
 ip address 10.12.98.0 255.255.255.0
 no ip directed-broadcast
!
interface Ethernet0/1
 ip address 10.100.100.5 255.255.255.252
 no ip directed-broadcast

!
ip classless
ip route 0.0.0.0 0.0.0.0 10.100.100.6
ip route 192.168.1.0 255.255.255.0 Tunnel0
snmp-server community public RO
!
!
line con 0
 password mudd799
 transport input none
line aux 0
line vty 0 4
 password mudd799
 login
!
no scheduler allocate
end
```

Conclusion

Network management is important in today's high tech world. Caird has a great idea in what it is trying to do with its management center. The problem right now is that there is no good solution to the duplicate IP address problem. While the tunnel solution proposed above might seem pretty cool, it is a temporary solution at best. Caird cannot afford to keep buying more and more management systems if it expects to be profitable.

This design will become more complex as Caird moves forward, adding new services. In our basic design, we've kept an eye on ease of growth and the relative simplicity of adding clients. Basically, each client addition should be largely the same.

This design should last a couple of years, but it will need to be modified as Caird's service offerings change. Once you can convince a client to let you drop a Frame Relay link into the network, there are hundreds of useful things you can do for that client. In essence, Caird has now become an extension of that client's network.

This design should provide a decent base on which Caird can build its management services business. Where the design goes in the next two years will depend largely on how the network management market develops. Caird is moving into a relatively new market, and it will be interesting to see how it all turns out. For now, we have created a management WAN infrastructure that should allow Caird enough flexibility and expandability to handle whatever the market throws its way.

 NOTE At some point, Caird will need to add backup capabilities in case it loses a frame link.

Case Study 6: A Large Network Infrastructure

A billion-dollar national corporation wishes to upgrade its existing core network infrastructure. The current infrastructure looks like Figure 14.13. This design was done about 10 years ago and has served the corporation well. However, FDDI is much less popular than it used to be, and it is becoming harder and harder to find FDDI equipment. Also, the hubs that service the user segments are starting to fail. With this in mind, a large amount of money has been budgeted to upgrade the infrastructure.

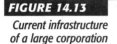

FIGURE 14.13

Current infrastructure of a large corporation

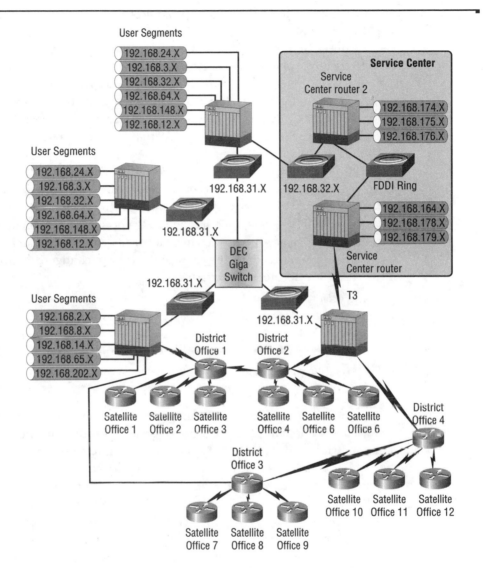

Setting the Stage

The existing regional and satellite WAN connections will remain largely the same. In Figure 14.13, you can see that each district office has two paths back to the main office. All communication lines are running at T1 speed. The one change that we will make is to phase out RIP as the routing protocol and replace it with EIGRP. We've chosen EIGRP because it looks similar to RIP to configure and it can handle IPX and IP. Because the environment will be all Cisco equipment, the fact that EIGRP is a Cisco-proprietary protocol is not an issue. EIGRP will significantly reduce the amount of overhead traffic involved in maintaining the environment. Also, since EIGRP stores backup routes in its routing database, it will switch to the backup links in the network much more quickly than RIP. In addition, the incremental SAP feature of EIGRP will be used to reduce the considerable IPX SAP traffic that is currently traversing the WAN links.

EIGRP allows for incremental SAP updates. The router can send only incremental changes across slower links while providing normal, periodic SAP updates on the faster local links. We can do this by configuring the router to send only incremental SAPs on the WAN interface, then setting EIGRP not to send incremental SAPs on the LAN interfaces. The sending of incremental SAP updates is set on an interface-by-interface basis. You would use the commands below to configure the router to send incremental SAP updates on interface serial 0:

```
sparky(config)#int s0
sparky(config-if)#ipx sap-incremental eigrp 55
```

 NOTE The 55 value is the autonomous system in which serial 0 is located.

This configuration saves a significant amount of bandwidth because SAPs are only sent when they need to be. There is no reason to repeat the same information every 60 seconds across the WAN link. Typically, on LAN interfaces it is easiest to allow the router to process SAP via the default method of broadcasting every 60 seconds. This way, we don't need to worry whether other network devices that need to see the SAPs can deal with a decreased SAP update interval or with incremental SAPs. Things are very straightforward when only routers are involved. When you get to the local environment, however, the router administrator tends to lose some control over what happens on the network. For this reason, and because LAN links are typically at least 10 times faster than WAN links, I don't modify the SAP behavior on interfaces connecting to LAN segments.

Normal IPX RIP SAP updates are still required to be run on segments populated by Novell servers. Across WAN links, however, we can run only EIGRP, which will significantly reduce the amount of overhead on the link. The router sends out normal RIP SAP updates on the LAN port, but only sends changes and periodic keep-alive packets for SAP traffic across the more expensive bandwidth on the WAN links. This configuration is shown in Figure 14.14.

FIGURE 14.14

Incremental SAP update can significantly reduce overhead on links

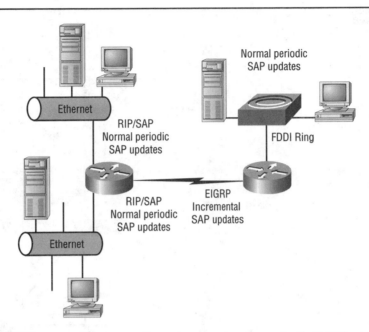

Using EIGRP means that you really end up having to run both EIGRP and IPX RIP for segments with Novell servers on them. Compared to RIP, the amount of overhead caused by EIGRP is insignificant. If you can take IPX RIP off of even one segment, you come out ahead. For this design, selective LAN segments run IPX RIP, while all of the WAN links run only EIGRP. Although this is slightly more difficult to configure, it saves a lot of bandwidth that would otherwise be wasted by IPX RIP traffic.

NOTE RIP is needed on local segments with Novell servers because Novell servers think they are routing devices. These servers really do not understand any IPX routing protocol other than RIP, and static IPX routing is not an option. Basically, NetWare listens to the RIP updates to figure out how to get to other IPX networks.

The existing building infrastructure is pretty well set up. A large amount of fiber runs from the computer room into each communications closet. There is fiber running between the communication closets themselves. Figure 14.15 shows the fiber layout for one floor of the main building. Currently, some servers are attached to the FDDI ring and serviced at 100Mb, while others are located on 10Mb segments.

FIGURE 14.15

Typical floor fiber layout

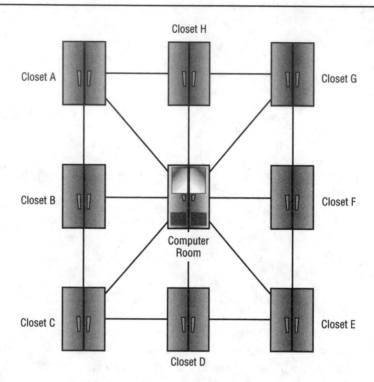

As you saw in Figure 14.15, redundancy is a major concern. The service center is required to operate around the clock. In redesigning the network, it is important that the service center will be at least as fault tolerant as it is in the current configuration.

Identifying a Solution

The current environment has a core speed of 100Mbps and connections to the desktop at 10Mbps. We need to come up with a design that offers at least this much speed. During the design process, we deduced that the DEC Giga Switch represented a single point of failure for the core environment. This was unacceptable; whatever solution we propose must address this issue.

Upgrading the Wiring Closets

The price differential between hubs and switches is small enough that all hubs can be replaced with Cisco switches. We've chosen Cisco 2924 and 4000 switches to populate the closets. The typical closet will look like the one shown in Figure 14.16.

FIGURE 14.16

Typical closet configuration

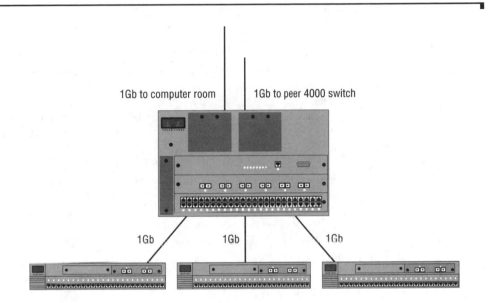

1Gb to computer room | 1Gb to peer 4000 switch

1Gb   1Gb   1Gb

In the figure, you can see that a Catalyst 4003 and three Catalyst 2924XL switches are used to populate a closet. The 2924XLs are connected to the 4003 via a 1Gb Ethernet fiber link. The 4003 is then connected to the computer room via a 1Gb Ethernet fiber link. The final fiber connection ties the 4003 in this closet to another 4003. This is done to add redundancy to the design. The port that connects the two peer 4000s is generally port 2/2, which will be configured to have a higher port cost (less preferred route) than the other ports on the switch. This insures that, during normal operations, the link between the two 4003 switches is placed in the blocking state by Spanning Tree. Fifty was selected for the port cost of this link because it is high enough to make it less preferential than any other port in the switch. To set the port cost, you would execute the following command:

```
set spantree portcost 2/2 50
```

All of the 10/100 ports in the switches are locked into a 10Mbps half-duplex configuration, which prevents auto-negotiation. Not all of the client systems have NICs that will support 100Mbps, so we've chosen 10Mbps. This choice has the additional benefit of preventing oversubscription. Also, in order to get the Novell client to work properly, we've done the following:

- Enabled `spanningtree portfast` all client ports
- Disabled channel negotiation
- Reduced the forwarding delay to 4 seconds

 NOTE The Novell client must see a response back from a server within *x* seconds upon booting. The Spanning Tree process takes too long to put the port into a forwarding state. This causes the Novell client to give up. To fix this, modify the way the STP algorithm gets to the forwarding state. Enabling `portfast` significantly reduces the amount of time the port takes to get to the forwarding state. By enabling `portfast`, you are basically telling the switch, "There is no loop on this port, so don't worry about checking for topology loops; start forwarding data as soon as the port comes up." The delay caused by Spanning Tree negotiation causes problems with both Novell and Microsoft NT networks.

Figure 14.17 shows the peer-to-peer closet connection. If switch A's link to the computer room dies, the Spanning Tree protocol (STP) will bring up the link to switch B, and the devices connected to switch A can use the path to B to get back to the computer room. This provides a redundant link back to the computer room in case the fiber to the computer room happens to fail.

FIGURE 14.17

Peer-to-peer 4000 connection

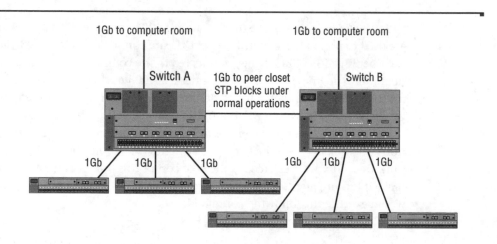

Core Infrastructure

After taking care of the closets, we need to focus on the core. The FDDI equipment and Giga switch will be replaced with two Catalyst 6509 switches with the *multilayer switch feature card* (MSFC). The MSFC allow us to run a routing engine within the switch. The 6509 is a layer 3 switch with a 33Gbps backplane, so it should be an ample replacement for the DEC Giga Switch and FDDI rings.

Four Gigabit Ethernet ports are used on each switch to connect the switches together. The circuits are configured in full-duplex mode, so these ports are trunked to let the switch use the combined circuits as one 4Gb link, for an effective throughput of 8Gb. This link is then configured as a trunk link for all VLANs that the two 6509s know about. Figure 14.18 displays this configuration.

FIGURE 14.18

Trunk configuration for 6509s

4 x 1Gb ethernet port channeled
together and configured as a trunk

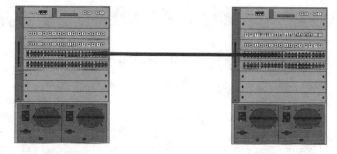

The 6509 switches are configured as Virtual Trunk protocol (VTP) servers; all of the other switches in the environment are set to VTP transparent mode. Because it was felt that support staff would be confused by the complexity of sending VLAN information out to the closet, all closest switches have their ports configured in VLAN 1. Since VLAN information is stripped from the frame as it leaves a nontrunk port, having all the closet switches with their ports in VLAN 1 is not a problem. This is kind of like having a hub cascade off the 6509 switch ports. The closet switch does not know which VLAN it is connected to on the 6509; it only knows that it has this 1Gb port that is in VLAN 1, and it treats all frames accordingly. Basically, the closet switches are not segregated into multiple VLANs, so a device hanging off any port can talk to any other device connected to the closet switch. You end up with a very simple switch configuration for the 4000 switches in the communication closets.

NOTE The fact that the all the closet switches have all of their ports in VLAN 1 does cause one problem, though. Cisco Discovery Protocol (CDP) version 2, which is the default on the shipping version of Catalyst software, shares native VLAN information with the CDP neighbor device. When these VLANs are mismatched, as is the case in this design, an error message is logged about every half hour. In order to fix this, we must upgrade the CAT4000 switches to revision 5.4 and set CDP to run at version 1. Revisions 5.2 and 5.3 run CDP version 2 and don't let you change the version.

Once this problem with the CDP version is addressed, the configuration of the closet switches is simple. The closet switch configuration can be reduced to a simple process where the only variables are the system name and the IP address of the switch. The main part of the network configuration is done in the 6509 switches. The 6509s really end up controlling the network, with the 4003 and 2924xl switches performing very simple switching tasks.

Cisco Discovery Protocol (CDP)

CDP is a Cisco-proprietary protocol developed by Cisco which runs on all Cisco devices. What CDP does is to allow Cisco devices to exchange certain information among each other. CDP communicates via a layer 2 multicast with an address of 01-00-0C-CC-CC. Because it is a layer 2 multicast, CDP information will only be exchanged on the local network segment and will not be routed. This allows Cisco devices to learn about all their neighboring Cisco devices.

CDP is both media- and protocol-independent. Media independence means that CDP does not care whether it runs across FDDI, ATM, Token Ring, Ethernet, and so on. Because CDP is also protocol-independent, two hosts running different protocols can talk CDP; they need not support a common protocol. Thus, a router supporting IP can talk CDP to another router that is using another protocol, such as IPX or AppleTalk, or even to a Catalyst switch that is only performing layer 2 switching. This can be very useful in verifying connectivity. If a router can see its CDP neighbor across a link, then obviously there is some sort of a connection between the two devices allowing CDP information to pass.

Continued

CONTINUED

To see the Cisco devices a router knows about via CDP, use the following command:

```
MO_rtr#sh cdp neighbors
Capability Codes: R - Router, T - Trans Bridge, B - Source Route Bridge
        S - Switch, H - Host, I - IGMP, r - Repeater


Device ID    Local Intrfce   Holdtme  Capability Platform Port ID
MMAGH        Eth 0    140       R     2500    Eth 0
BOS_r        Ser 0    120       R     3600    Ser 0
```

You can see that this router has two neighbors. One is a Cisco 2500-series router with a hostname of MMAGH connected off the Ethernet port. The other is the BOS_r router connected off the serial 0 port. Under the Capability heading, you can see what capabilities the device actually has. Since both of the CDP neighbors are routers, we get an R to signify router. The possible capability codes are displayed before the actual CDP output.

You can gain even more information using the detail option with the show cdp neighbors command, like this:

```
KAH_RTR#show cdp neighbors detail
---------------
Device ID: MMAGH
Entry address(es):
 IP address: 10.1.1.3
Platform: cisco 2500, Capabilities: Router
Interface: Ethernet0, Port ID (outgoing port): Ethernet0
Holdtime : 130 sec


Version :
Cisco Internetwork Operating System Software
IOS (tm) 2500 Software (C2500-IO-L), Version 12.0(8), RELEASE SOFTWARE
(fc1)
Copyright (c) 1986-1999 by cisco Systems, Inc.
Compiled Mon 29-Nov-99 16:22 by kpma
```

Continued

CONTINUED

You can see that the neighbor device is MMAGH, and it is a Cisco 2500 router with an IP addresses of 10.1.1.3. The router learned about MMAGH via Ethernet 0. You can also see the IOS version the neighbor is running. In this case, it's C2500-IO-L version 12.0(8).

Cisco has recently added some enhancements to the CDP protocol and release CDP version 2. CDP version 2 can now exchange the following:

- VTP management domain information
- Native port VLAN information for devices that support 802.1Q
- Port duplex configuration (full or half)

At the switch level, in the 6509s a single Gigabit Ethernet is assigned for each user segment that previously existed as a router interface. This VLAN is named after the segment address. For example, 192.168.3.x would be VLAN 3. Segment 31 is moved to the 10/100 ports held in the 6509s, with servers populated evenly between the two switches. These ports are placed in VLAN 31 and run at 100Mbps full duplex, since the servers are directly connected to the switch.

The routing engine of the switch is a pretty straightforward configuration. EIGRP is used as the routing protocol for IP, and IPX RIP is used within the core environment because the Novell servers need to see IPX RIP and SAP traffic. Figure 14.19 shows a typical redundant segment.

As you can see, we are using secondary IP addresses on the VLAN interfaces. This allows any of the devices on either switch to have a segment 8 or 3 address. So, from the router's perspective, it looks like one big segment supporting two class C subnets. This allows us to have the multiple paths we need. It makes it a little hard to comprehend that VLAN 3 can also support traffic for segment 8 because of its secondary address of 192.168.8.253, but that is no big deal. The fact that segment 3 and segment 8 actually exist as the same layer 2 segment does not cause any problems. In general, users on the two segments will not talk to each other but instead will be accessing the servers hanging off segment 31, anyway. User systems on these segments will be configured with two gateway statements:

- One to the primary router interface
- One to the secondary interface on the segment's peer router port

FIGURE 14.19

Redundant segments

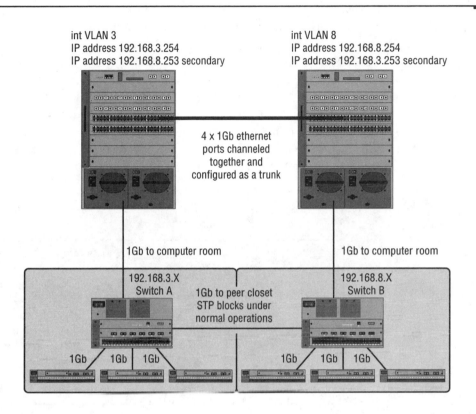

The configuration shown in Figure 14.19 is repeated over and over until all the segments within the main office are taken care of. To handle the redundancy required by the service center, this same design concept will be carried out for the communications in the data closets in that building. Because the service center has fewer users, however, we'll use Catalyst 6506 switches.

The connection between the two buildings will be modified. We already have fiber runs connecting the two buildings. These will be used at gigabit speed to provide the primary connection to the service center. Each 6509 switch will use two gigabit ports Etherchanneled together to connect to the service center. While these two ports will be Etherchanneled together, we will not configure VTP or pass VLAN information along the circuit. Instead, we will use the MSFC's routing functionality to handle data across this link. By using a routed circuit, we will achieve better traffic isolation of broadcast and multicast traffic, thus improving performance across the link.

The existing T3 connection will remain for redundancy. Because all of the fiber between the buildings runs in the same bundle, it is very unlikely that just one pair of fibers would be cut. The two buildings are about 15 miles apart, so we cannot really assume that the fiber will not be touched. The T3 gives us a completely separate communication path on different media, so we can handle a fiber cut. The distance between buildings also forces us to use the high-power Gigabit Ethernet Converters (GBICs) for the Catalyst 6509 to insure that our power budget is above 0. During implementation, we discovered that the high-power GBICs were too powerful, so we added 10db attenuators to the transmit side of each GBIC to get the links to function properly. Figure 14.20 shows what the service center connection will look like.

FIGURE 14.20

Service center redundant connection

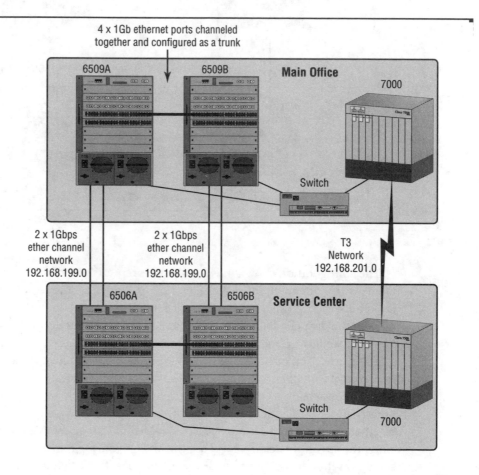

NOTE In Figure 14.20, all unlabeled links are 1Gbps.

The client has a full class B address, which it is using in class C blocks, so it is not necessary to do any variable-length subnetting, even though we are wasting a lot of addresses on the point-to-point links. Since we are running EIGRP, which uses bandwidth as one of its metrics, the T3 link will not be chosen as the best path unless all the fiber links die. This means that the T3 ends up being a very expensive backup link. Because of the way the service center is tied into the business, however, the T3 is a necessary insurance policy. We simply cannot afford to lose connectivity to the service center, and the T3 is there to guarantee that connectivity will not be lost. Besides, this link is already in place, so we have not asked them to add another T3 link.

Sample Configurations

Rather than showing you the entire switch configuration files, which are each between 8 and 20 pages long, I am including only the commands you'll need to configure them.

Sample 4000 Switch Configuration Commands

Commands used on the 4000 switch:

```
set boot system flash bootflash:cat4000_5-4-1.bin pre
set snmp community read-write gulliver
set snmp community read-write-all agh11
set vtp mode transparent
set cdp version v1
set interface sc0 192.168.32.1 255.255.255.0
set ip route default 192.168.32.254
set port host 3/1-48
set port speed 3/1-48 10
set port duplex 3/1-48 half
set logging server enable
set logging server 192.168.31.174
set span 1 3/48
set spantree portcost 2/2 50
set system name closet1
```

Sample 6509 Switch Configuration Commands

Commands used on the 6509 switch:

```
set vtp domain Worsley
set vlan 31 5/1-48
set vlan 8 3/1
set vlan 14 3/2
set vlan 24 3/3
set vlan 32        4/1
set vlan 65 4/2
set vlan 148 4/3
set port channel 3/7-8,4/7-8 on
set trunk 3/7 on isl 1-1005
set interface sc0 31 192.168.31.4 255.255.255.0
set ip route default 192.168.31.1
set snmp community read-write gulliver
set snmp community read-write-all agh11
set logging server enable
set logging server 192.168.31.174
```

Sample 6509 Route Engine Configuration

This is a complete configuration for the 6509 route engine:

```
!
version 12.0
no service pad
service timestamps debug uptime
service timestamps log uptime
no service password-encryption
!
hostname 6509_RTR
!
boot system flash bootflash:c6msfc-js-mz_120-3_XE2.bin
boot system sup-slot0:c6msfc-js-mz_120-3_XE2.bin
boot system flash bootflash:c6msfc-is-mz.120-3.XE1
logging buffered 4096 debugging
enable secret 5 $1$aOdH$/1ucEA2FlkVVOFdSQ8Y71/
!
ip subnet-zero
no ip domain-lookup
```

```
!
ip cef
!
ipx routing 0030.80f7.9080
ipx internal-network 11001982
!
interface Vlan8
 description T1A1 connection
 ip address 192.168.3.253 255.255.255.0 secondary
 ip address 192.168.8.254 255.255.255.0
 no ip directed-broadcast
 ipx input-sap-filter 1000
 ipx network 11001021
 ipx output-sap-filter 1000
 ipx output-gns-filter 1003
!
interface Vlan12
 description T1B3 connection
 ip address 192.168.202.253 255.255.255.0 secondary
 ip address 192.168.12.254 255.255.255.0
 no ip directed-broadcast
 ipx network 11001012
!
interface Vlan24
 description T1E1 connection
 ip address 192.168.2.253 255.255.255.0 secondary
 ip address 192.168.24.254 255.255.255.0
 no ip directed-broadcast
 ipx input-sap-filter 1000
 ipx network 11001002
 ipx output-gns-filter 1003
!
interface Vlan31
 ip address 192.168.31.249 255.255.255.0
 no ip directed-broadcast
 ipx network 11001025
!
interface Vlan32
 description T1E4
```

```
     ip address 192.168.14.253 255.255.255.0 secondary
     ip address 192.168.32.254 255.255.255.0
     ip helper-address 192.168.31.185
     no ip directed-broadcast
     ipx network 11001060
     ipx output-gns-filter 1003
    !
   interface Vlan65
    description T2B1 connection
    ip address 192.168.64.253 255.255.255.0 secondary
    ip address 192.168.65.254 255.255.255.0
    no ip directed-broadcast
    ipx input-sap-filter 1000
    ipx network 11001014
    ipx output-sap-filter 1000
    ipx output-gns-filter 1003
    !
   interface Vlan148
    description TLF1
    ip address 192.168.148.254 255.255.255.0
    no ip directed-broadcast
    ipx input-sap-filter 1000
    ipx network 11001020
    ipx output-sap-filter 1000
    ipx output-gns-filter 1003
    !
   router eigrp 64533
    network 192.168.2.0
    network 192.168.3.0
    network 192.168.8.0
    network 192.168.12.0
    network 192.168.14.0
    network 192.168.24.0
    network 192.168.31.0
    network 192.168.32.0
    network 192.168.64.0
    network 192.168.65.0
    network 192.168.148.0
    network 192.168.202.0
```

```
!
!
ip classless
no ip http server
!
logging 192.168.31.174
access-list 1000 deny FFFFFFFF 47
access-list 1000 deny FFFFFFFF 4B
access-list 1000 deny FFFFFFFF 1DA
access-list 1000 deny FFFFFFFF 30C
access-list 1000 deny FFFFFFFF 363
access-list 1000 deny FFFFFFFF 3C4
access-list 1000 deny FFFFFFFF 580
access-list 1000 deny FFFFFFFF 8002
access-list 1000 deny FFFFFFFF 9000
access-list 1000 permit FFFFFFFF 130
access-list 1000 permit FFFFFFFF 0
access-list 1003 deny 11001846.0000.0000.0001
access-list 1003 deny 11001845.0000.0000.0001
access-list 1003 deny 11001840.0000.0000.0001
access-list 1003 deny 11001839.0000.0000.0001
access-list 1003 deny 11001838.0000.0000.0001
access-list 1003 deny 11001837.0000.0000.0001
access-list 1003 deny 11001836.0000.0000.0001
access-list 1003 deny 11001833.0000.0000.0001
access-list 1003 deny 11001832.0000.0000.0001
access-list 1003 deny 11001831.0000.0000.0001
access-list 1003 deny 11001820.0000.0000.0001
access-list 1003 deny 11001819.0000.0000.0001
access-list 1003 deny 11001812.0000.0000.0001
access-list 1003 deny 11001811.0000.0000.0001
access-list 1003 deny 11001810.0000.0000.0001
access-list 1003 deny 11001809.0000.0000.0001
access-list 1003 deny 11001765.0000.0000.0001
access-list 1003 deny 11001764.0000.0000.0001
access-list 1003 deny 11001763.0000.0000.0001
access-list 1003 deny 11001762.0000.0000.0001
access-list 1003 deny 11001767.0000.0000.0001
access-list 1003 deny 11001854.0000.0000.0001
```

```
access-list 1003 deny 11001853.0000.0000.0001
access-list 1003 deny 11001852.0000.0000.0001
access-list 1003 deny 11001851.0000.0000.0001
access-list 1003 deny 11001868.0000.0000.0001
access-list 1003 deny 11001867.0000.0000.0001
access-list 1003 deny 11001866.0000.0000.0001
access-list 1003 deny 11001807.0000.0000.0001
access-list 1003 deny 11001875.0000.0000.0001
access-list 1003 deny 11001874.0000.0000.0001
access-list 1003 deny 11001872.0000.0000.0001
access-list 1003 deny 11001871.0000.0000.0001
access-list 1003 deny 11001886.0000.0000.0001
access-list 1003 deny 11001887.0000.0000.0001
access-list 1003 deny 11001800.0000.0000.0001
access-list 1003 deny 11001801.0000.0000.0001
access-list 1003 deny 11001791.0000.0000.0001
access-list 1003 deny 11001798.0000.0000.0001
access-list 1003 deny 11001790.0000.0000.0001
access-list 1003 deny 11001784.0000.0000.0001
access-list 1003 deny 11001789.0000.0000.0001
access-list 1003 deny 11001865.0000.0000.0001
access-list 1003 deny 11001850.0000.0000.0001
access-list 1003 deny 11001793.0000.0000.0001
access-list 1003 deny 11001841.0000.0000.0001
access-list 1003 deny 11001826.0000.0000.0001
access-list 1003 deny 11001843.0000.0000.0001
access-list 1003 deny 11001842.0000.0000.0001
access-list 1003 deny 11001877.0000.0000.0001
access-list 1003 deny 11001813.0000.0000.0001
access-list 1003 deny 11001804.0000.0000.0001
access-list 1003 deny 11001856.0000.0000.0001 4
access-list 1003 deny 11001783.0000.0000.0001 4
access-list 1003 deny 11001782.0000.0000.0001 4
access-list 1003 deny 11001786.0000.0000.0001 4
access-list 1003 deny 11001864.0000.0000.0001 4
access-list 1003 deny 11001863.0000.0000.0001 4
access-list 1003 deny 11001862.0000.0000.0001 4
access-list 1003 deny 11001861.0000.0000.0001 4
access-list 1003 deny 11001860.0000.0000.0001 4
```

```
access-list 1003 deny 11001859.0000.0000.0001 4
access-list 1003 deny 11001858.0000.0000.0001 4
access-list 1003 deny 11001855.0000.0000.0001 4
access-list 1003 deny 11001857.0000.0000.0001 4
access-list 1003 deny 11001898.0000.0000.0001
access-list 1003 deny 4000204.0000.0000.0001
access-list 1003 deny 11001869.0000.0000.0001
access-list 1003 permit FFFFFFFF
!
!
ipx router eigrp 64533
 network 11001002
 network 11001020
 network 11001021
 network 11001012
 network 11001060
 network 11001014
!
!
snmp-server engineID local 000000090200000021000000
snmp-server community public RO
snmp-server community gulliver RW
snmp-server community private RW
snmp-server host 192.168.8.230 private snmp
!
line con 0
 password roger
 transport input none
line vty 0 4
 password roger
 login
!
end
```

Satellite Router

This router is configured for EIGRP and incremental SAP updates on the WAN link, and IPX RIP and normal periodic SAP updates on the LAN interface.

```
!
version 11.3
service timestamps debug uptime
```

```
service timestamps log datetime msec
service password-encryption
!
hostname Satellite6
!
enable secret 5 $1$n7LRsdsujWdzm8SpO3KoCwWEe/
enable password 7 070C28344D0648
!
!
ipx routing 0010.7b5c.6a00
ipx internal-network 444993
!
!
interface Ethernet0/0
 ip address 192.168.55.253 255.255.255.0
 ip helper-address 192.168.17.212
 ipx network 4005
!
interface Serial0/0
 ip address 192.168.54.253 255.255.255.0
 encapsulation ppp
 no ip mroute-cache
 ipx network 1111
 ipx sap-incremental eigrp 64533
!
interface Serial0/1
 no ip address
 shutdown
 no cdp enable
!
router eigrp 64533
 redistribute connected
 network 192.168.54.0
 network 192.168.55.0

!
ip classless
!
!
```

```
ipx router eigrp 64533
 network 1111
 network 4005
!
ipx router rip
 no network 1111
!
logging buffered 4096 debugging
dialer-list 1 protocol ip permit
dialer-list 1 protocol ipx permit
!
!
snmp-server community public RO
snmp-server community private RW
snmp-server host 192.168.8.230 traps private snmp
!
!

line con 0
 exec-timeout 0 0
line aux 0
line vty 0 4
 password 7 03077404025E
 login
 transport preferred none
!
no scheduler allocate
end
```

Regional Router

This router is configured for EIGRP and Incremental SAP updates on the WAN links, and IPX RIP and normal periodic SAP updates on the LAN interface.

```
!
version 11.3
service timestamps log datetime msec
service password-encryption
service udp-small-servers
service tcp-small-servers
```

```
!
hostname North_region
!
enable secret 5 $1$jmo5$xfarocksVtP9D7Ej538./B1
enable password 7 070C2344D0648
!
!
ipx routing 0000.0c18.709e
ipx internal-network 440995
!
interface Ethernet0
 ip address 192.168.142.254 255.255.255.0 secondary
 ip address 192.168.17.252 255.255.255.0
 media-type 10BaseT
 ipx network 4012

!
interface Ethernet1
 no ip address
 shutdown
!
interface Serial0
 description Satellite6 T1 serial
 ip address 192.168.54.254 255.255.255.0
 encapsulation ppp
 bandwidth 694
 ipx network 1111
 ipx sap-incremental eigrp 64533
 no fair-queue
 mop enabled

!
interface Serial1
 description Satellite2 56kb serial
 ip address 192.168.76.254 255.255.255.0
 encapsulation ppp
 bandwidth 56
 ipx network 1122
 ipx sap-incremental eigrp 64533
```

```
!
interface Serial2
 no ip address
 shutdown
!
interface Serial3
 description Connection to main office T1 serial
 ip address 192.168.26.253 255.255.255.0
 bandwidth 1544
 ipx network 99
 ipx sap-incremental eigrp 64533
 ipx output-sap-filter 1000
 mop enabled

!
router eigrp 64533
 network 192.168.17.0
 network 192.168.26.0
 network 192.168.54.0
 network 192.168.76.0
 network 192.168.142.0
 !
no ip classless
 !
ipx router eigrp 64533
 network 99
 network 1111
 network 1122
 network 4012
 !
ipx router rip
 no network 99
 no network 1111
 no network 1122
 !

logging buffered
access-list 1000 deny FFFFFFFF 47
access-list 1000 deny FFFFFFFF 4B
```

```
access-list 1000 deny FFFFFFFF 1DA
access-list 1000 deny FFFFFFFF 23F
access-list 1000 deny FFFFFFFF 30C
access-list 1000 deny FFFFFFFF 363
access-list 1000 deny FFFFFFFF 3C4
access-list 1000 deny FFFFFFFF 8002
access-list 1000 deny FFFFFFFF 9000
access-list 1000 permit FFFFFFFF 130
access-list 1000 permit FFFFFFFF 0
!
!
snmp-server community public RO
snmp-server community private RW
snmp-server host 192.168.8.230 private snmp

line con 0
line aux 0
line vty 0 4
 password 7 1HIF343KATHY81AGH5A
 login
 transport preferred none
!
end
```

Conclusion

This case study covers a very involved infrastructure upgrade. The most important thing with this new design is redundancy. If you look over the design carefully, you will notice that in almost all cases the new infrastructure is more fault-tolerant than what it is replacing.

Now that the network will run at speeds about 10 times faster through the core environment, the performance bottlenecks will shift to some place other than the network. There is no way that the current systems on this network can come anywhere close to maxing out the bandwidth that has been deployed with this design.

This design was developed with an eye to fault tolerance and manageability. There are certainly other ways to accomplish the design goals. What we ended up with, though, is a network that should need minimal attention to function properly—and isn't that the goal of network engineering? As exciting as working in this field can be, you probably don't enjoy the kind of excitement generated by 2:00 A.M. pages when the network is down. This design should help to minimize that unwelcome occurrence.

Summary

In this chapter, we looked at a variety of network designs, ranging from simple point-to-point links all the way up to large infrastructures. If you are currently designing your own infrastructure, you should be able to pull a few tricks and ideas from these case studies.

In the next chapter, we'll discuss Cisco certification and other ways to pursue Cisco and IOS education.

CHAPTER 15

Getting Cisco Certified

It's possible that you're one of those people who like to understand hot technologies, and that you picked up this book for fun and personal growth. It's more likely, however, that you read it for work- or business-related purposes. Whatever your reasons for wanting to master Cisco technology, there may be a day when you'd like to quantify what you know, both for yourself and, perhaps more importantly, for potential employers. Cisco's program of certifications can help you do that in a way that is immediately recognized by the technical and business communities. This chapter is designed to give you an overview of the Cisco Career Certifications program.

 NOTE All descriptions of exams, fees, and training from Cisco are subject to change. To be sure that you have the most up-to-date information about Cisco Career Certifications, see the Cisco Web site at www.cisco.com.

The Brief History of Cisco Certifications

You don't have to be very old to remember the days when the network administrator for a small-to-medium business might be the person whose desk was closest to the printer. Or maybe the office manager's son was "into computers" and had taught her a few tricks. But as internetworking became more complex and required increasingly sophisticated equipment and design, it became obvious that the business world needed a labor pool of qualified technicians whose knowledge and skills were up to date with the technology. Vendors of computer software and hardware started to develop certification programs in order to insure that customers could find reliable people to help implement their products.

The first certification offered by Cisco was the CCIE (Cisco Certified Internetworking Engineer), a notoriously difficult level of certification that often required (and still does require) years of experience, thousands of dollars' worth of training, a torturous lab practical, and multiple attempts at the exam in order to pass. Given the rigorous nature of the exam, very few CCIE candidates actually passed. (Of course, those who did were properly worshipped.) Eventually, Cisco developed intermediate levels of certification for those who were not quite ready to tackle the daunting CCIE exam, but who still had an interest in identifying themselves as Cisco-knowledgeable. This system of certifications became known as Cisco Career Certifications.

The Cisco Career Certifications program arose from a need to insure that if businesses were going to invest in expensive technology, they could find qualified employees to implement and care for their investment. And they needed to insure that once found, those candidates could actually do the job. Perhaps one of the reasons that Cisco products have dominated the market is that the very successful certification program helps to designate talented people who can manage, implement, and troubleshoot the networks built on cutting-edge Cisco products.

Why Get Certified?

It should not come as news that there are more tech-related jobs out there than there are people to fill them. A quick survey of the employment-related Internet sites will tell you that companies are suffering from a shortage of qualified computer professionals. Human Resources departments are having to employ creative strategies in order to hire and retain desirable candidates. A great deal of this wealth of employment opportunities can be attributed to the need for businesses to "get wired," or Internet- and intranet-connected. The Bureau of Labor Statistics' *Occupational Outlook Handbook* specifically designates businesses' growing demand for "networking" as a major factor in the proliferation of computer-related jobs.

From the Bureau of Labor Statistics' *Occupational Outlook Handbook*:

"The demand for 'networking' to facilitate the sharing of information, the expansion of client/server environments, and the need for specialists to use their knowledge and skills in a problem solving capacity will be a major factor in the rising demand for systems analysts. Falling prices of computer hardware and software should continue to induce more businesses to expand computerized operations and integrate new technologies. In order to maintain a competitive edge and operate more cost effectively, firms will continue to demand computer professionals who are knowledgeable about the latest technologies and able to apply them to meet the needs of businesses."

A college degree—in any field—does not guarantee a job, nor does it guarantee that the person holding the diploma is capable of doing the job. Perhaps you know someone with an advanced degree who is underemployed, or even unemployed altogether. Many of the people working in the technical field have traditional college degrees in Computer Science or a related field, but with the constantly shifting nature of internetworking technology, the knowledge gained while obtaining a four-year degree could theoretically be obsolete by graduation day.

Certifications in computer-related industries are specifically designed to convey to employers that potential candidates or clients know what they're doing in a real-world setting using the most current technology. The "shorthand" of being able to attach a meaningful acronym to your resume is helpful because Human Resources administrators, who do not necessarily have technical backgrounds, often do much of the initial screening. As desperate as companies may be for qualified network administrators, it's a waste of time and money to hire someone who doesn't have the skills and knowledge needed to work in a practical environment.

While almost every major tech company offers certification programs centered around its products, all certifications are not created equal. Cisco has worked very hard to make sure that its certifications retain their worth in the marketplace. All told, the Cisco Career Certifications program is among the most respected in the field.

For that reason, Cisco certification exams are constantly being updated to keep up with product and design advances. Within a few months of this book's printing, beta exams for new CCNA (Cisco Certified Network Associate) and CCNP (Cisco Certified Network Professional) certifications will be released, with the older exams scheduled for retirement by July 2000. Cisco has also raised the scores required to pass in some instances (much to the frustration of those whose score ends up being above the old passing score but below the new one). The program is constantly undergoing revision to insure that Cisco certifications maintain their acknowledged industry authority.

 NOTE Chat rooms dedicated to computer certification are filled with people complaining about "paper" certifications—that veritable alphabet soup that follows a person's name that may have no real value in determining just what that person can do in a practical setting. However, very few people in those same chat rooms complain about how easy the CCNA (Cisco's initial certification level) exam is, and the idea of a "paper" CCIE is ridiculous.

While the Cisco certification exams are focused primarily on the use of Cisco products, there is enough theoretical content that employers can assume candidates have a good general internetworking knowledge. Thus, a Cisco certification still retains its significance even if a potential employer is one of the odd 18 percent or so of the market that does not use Cisco technology. Employers also can infer that a certified individual has shown the dedication it takes to master a given subject, a skill that bodes well for any type of technical work.

NOTE Current estimates put Cisco's market share at around 80 percent, and Cisco's 1999 annual report puts net sales at over $12 billion.

The payoff for completing a certification program is manifold, and the possibilities include

- Salary increases and higher consulting fees demanded
- Prestigious job titles
- Demarcation from those job candidates without recognized credentials
- Peer recognition
- Self-confidence that you have the skills to work with Cisco technology authoritatively
- Increased job security obtained by attaching your skills to a specific vendor that currently enjoys 80 percent of the market share
- Demonstration to potential employers that you are interested in staying current with the latest technology, and that you take both your career and your training seriously

Certification Levels

Cisco Career Paths are specifically developed toward skill level and specialty. The system is divided into two tracks:

- Network Support
- Network Design

Each track has a gradual set of steps designed to reflect the candidate's level of skill and knowledge.

 NOTE Since the title of this book is *Mastering Cisco Routers*, the information for the exams comes from Cisco's Routing and Switching program, which is the most popular flavor of Cisco certifications. The other available specialty, WAN Switching, follows the same certification tracks as described here, but the exams are different. See the sidebar at the end of this section for information on the WAN Switching specialty.

The Network Support Track

The Cisco Network Support certification track is intended for those who are working with Cisco-based networks using LAN and WAN routers and LAN switches. Within this track, shown in Figure 15.1, there are three levels of certification:

- CCNA (Cisco Certified Network Associate)
- CCNP (Cisco Certified Network Professional)
- CCIE (Cisco Certified Internetworking Expert)

FIGURE 15.1

The Cisco Career Certification Network Support track

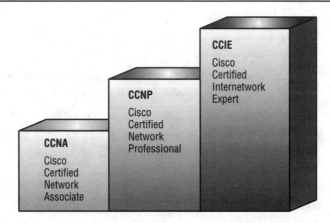

 NOTE The CCNA is a prerequisite for the CCNP certification level. However, neither the CCNA nor the CCNP is a specific prerequisite for taking the CCIE exam, although both are useful stepping stones toward the industry's top level. Theoretically, a person could start his or her certification with the CCIE, however unlikely or unwise that might be.

In general, the Network Support track is concerned with evaluating the following skills:

- Installing and configuring networks
- Maximizing network performance through various means
- Improving network security
- Creating a global intranet
- Providing application-oriented solutions

CCNA: Cisco Certified Network Associate

The CCNA is the first step in Cisco certification, and is a required prerequisite for the CCNP and CCDP certification levels. It consists of a 100-question, multiple-choice exam, #604-507, whose questions center around the candidate's understanding of implementing and configuring simple routed LANs and WANs and switched LANs. Cisco's list of simple networks includes

- Access lists
- AppleTalk
- Ethernet
- Frame Relay
- EIGRP
- IP
- IP RIP
- IPX
- IPX RIP
- Serial
- VLANs

All of these subjects have been touched on in this book. You are already well on your way to having the required skills to pass your CCNA exam.

 NOTE 604-507 is the number of the exam for the CCNA 2.0 certification, which is in beta testing as this book is being written. Exam 604-407 (CCNA 1.0) will be retired on July 31, 2000, and the 2.0 versions should be in full use.

CCNP: Cisco Certified Network Professional

The next level up on the Network Support track is the Cisco Certified Network Professional, designed for those who are able to install, configure, operate, and troubleshoot complex routed LANs, routed WANs, switched LAN networks, and Dial Access Services. In addition to those listed under CCNA, Cisco designates complex networks as the following:

- 802.10
- Async routing

- BGP
- DDR
- Extended access lists
- FDDI
- ISDN
- ISL
- OSPF
- PPP
- PSTN
- Route redistribution
- Route summarization
- Transparent and translational bridging
- VLANs
- VLSM
- X.25

You should already feel comfortable with about half of these technologies. Subjects like extended access lists, VLSM, route redistribution, and summarization have been covered in detail in this book. This means that you only have to fill in a few blanks before testing for your CCNP certification.

In order to obtain a CCNP certification, you must possess CCNA certification, and then pass an additional series of exams designed to demonstrate mastery of four specific areas:

- Routing
- Switching
- Remote access
- Support

In the 1.0 certification path, these different exams were designated by various confusing acronyms; in version 2.0, they are simply named after the subject matter.

 NOTE   Since the 2.0 versions of the exams should be in use shortly after the publication of *Mastering Cisco Routers,* information on this chapter is based primarily on the new exams.

FIGURE 15.2

*The CCNP 2.0
exam path*

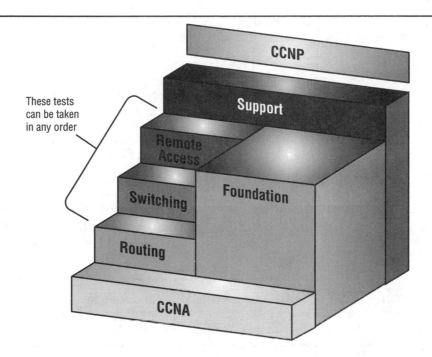

These tests
can be taken
in any order

You'll notice in Figure 15.2 that there are actually two exam paths you can follow to achieve CCNP status. One path involves four separate 100-question exams, one for each subject concentration. The other, the Foundation exam path, has an option for taking one 200-page exam in place of the subject exams for Routing, Switching and Remote Access. For those who prefer one long exam to three shorter ones this might be the preferable option. You can also save money this way, because the cost of the Foundation exam is the same as two of the subject tests, so you save the $100 you would've spent on the third one.

 TIP Some suggest that taking the Foundation exam allows you to "hide" your weak areas by counting on your strengths to give you the majority of your right answers.

A person choosing the CCNP certification can also choose one of six areas of specialization (by taking another exam!):

- Security
- Voice access

- SNA/IP integration
- LAN ATM
- SNA/IP network management

CCIE (Cisco Certified Internetwork Expert)

With estimates in the range of 75–80 percent market share for Cisco equipment, there are tens of thousands of people working on Cisco Networks every day. Of that large pool, only around 4,500 individuals have attained CCIE status. In order to achieve CCIE certification, one must first pass the 100-question qualification exam. Those who can successfully jump that hurdle get the privilege of attempting to complete the certification through a two-day lab practical at one of a handful Cisco CCIE testing labs worldwide. A notoriously high number of people have failed the qualification exam. And of those who do pass, many go on to fail the lab practical.

 NOTE In one newsgroup, in the place where contributors usually sign off with their certification acronyms attached, one writer designated himself as "passed CCIE written," feeling that would be recognized as an accomplishment in itself.

It should be sufficient to say that the potential CCIE candidate should have at least two years' experience in a Cisco network environment and a thorough knowledge of every conceivable aspect of internetworking. Given the high failure rate and expense of taking the exam—$200 per attempt for the written and $1,000 for the lab—nerves of steel wouldn't hurt, either. The blueprint for the CCIE exam includes the following major subject areas:

- Cisco device operation: Commands, infrastructure, operations
- General networking theory: OSI model, general routing concepts, protocol theory and mechanics
- Bridging and LAN switching
- Internet Protocol (IP)
- IP routing protocols
- Desktop protocols
- Performance management
- WAN addressing, signaling, and framing
- LAN: Data-Link layer, Ethernet, Token Ring, FDDI

- Network security
- Multiservice, including voice and video

 NOTE The CCIE has other concentrations possible in addition to the Routing and Switching and WAN Switching options offered at the lower levels. You can also take the ISP-Dial or SNA-IP specializations at the CCIE level, and beta exams for other specialties, including Network Design, are coming soon.

The Network Design Track

The Cisco Network Design certification track is intended for those who are designing networks using Cisco-predominant LAN and WAN routers and LAN switches. The Design track has three levels of certification, as shown in Figure 15.3 below:

- CCDA (Cisco Certified Design Associate)
- CCNA (the same Cisco Certified Network Associate described in the "Network Support Track" section)
- CCDP (Cisco Certified Design Professional)

FIGURE 15.3

The Cisco Career Certification Network Design track

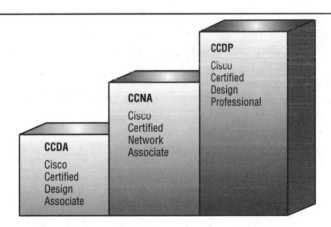

CCDA: Cisco Certified Design Associate

Those hoping to attain CCDA status are expected to be able to design simple routed LAN, routed WAN, and switched LAN networks. They should also have the prerequisite knowledge and skills to install, configure, and operate those networks. The

Design track was created to appeal to network design engineers, especially CCNAs, CCNPs, and CCIEs wanting to perform design tasks or to move to a design-oriented role in their careers.

In the process of studying for the CCDA, you will need to make sure that you have solid knowledge of the following:

- Filtering with access lists
- Network layer addressing
- Network sizing
- VLAN use and propagation

These are subjects that we have touched on in this book. In fact, the CCDA exam is very similar to the case studies we looked at in Chapters 13 and 14. For most questions, you are presented with a network design problem and asked how to resolve specific issues.

CCDP: Cisco Certified Design Professional

Building on the base level of technical knowledge acquired by obtaining the two prerequisite certifications, CCDPs must demonstrate proficiency in

- Addressing the Network layer in a hierarchical environment
- Managing network traffic with access lists and hierarchical network design
- Using VLANs and propagation
- Determining required hardware and software, switching engines, and memory requirements to maximize performance
- Employing various strategies to minimize costs

Like the CCNP path, the CCDP also has the option of taking the Foundation exam, instead of the three specific subject exams, as shown in Figure 15.4. However, the CCDP has two prerequisite certifications, the CCDA and the CCNA, and CCDPs take the CID (Cisco Internetworking Design) rather than the Support exam taken by CCNPs.

FIGURE 15.4

The CCDP exam path

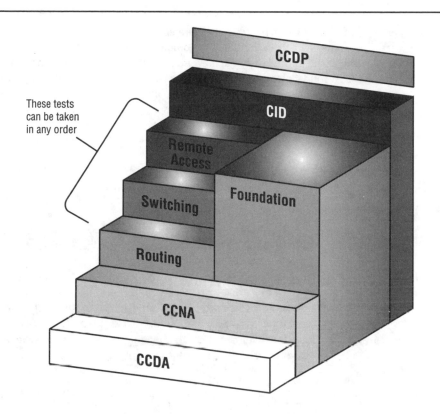

NOTE The Routing, Switching, and Remote Access exams do not have to be taken in any particular order.

You'll notice that the center "steps" of the CCNP and CCDP exam paths are the same; these overlapping requirements allow expedited cross-certification. This means that a CCNP with CCNA and CCDA certification can take the missing CID exam to achieve CCDP status. And a CCDP only need take the Support exam from the CCNP track to achieve the CCNP level.

NOTE Cisco's pyramid structure can be confusing; it appears from Cisco's literature that the CCDP and the CCIE are comparable levels, when actually the CCDP is meant to reflect the same level of achievement as the other Professional-level certification, the CCNP. (And it gets more confusing when they suggest that CCIEs may want to take the CCDP, and vice versa.) Perhaps this will become clearer when Cisco releases the upcoming CCIE-Design option, giving both tracks a visible Associate, Professional, and Expert progression. Or it may just get more confusing.

Aside from the specializations analogous to those in the Network Support track, the CCDP also has a specialization for SNA/IP Integration as it relates to Network Design.

WAN Switching Option

Although most people reading this book (and most people in general) are more likely to choose the Routing and Switching route, Cisco does offer a WAN Switching specialization, as mentioned earlier. Due to the unique features of switched WAN environments, this exam specifically tests the following areas:

- Media and telephony transmission techniques
- Error detection
- Time Division Multiplexing (TDM)
- Knowledge of Frame Relay and ATM
- Knowledge of Cisco-specific technologies, including WAN switch platforms/applications/architectures and interfaces
- Knowledge of service provider technology, including packet encapsulation and network-to-network interconnections

Four WAN Switching certifications are available, covering the Associate (CCNA-WAN Switching), Professional (CCNP-WAN Switching and CCDP-WAN Switching), and Expert (CCIE-WAN Switching) levels. One warning: Since the WAN Switching test is less popular, you may find fewer resources for self- or directed study. For exam path specifics for this option, see the Cisco Web site.

Certification Requirements

Cisco certifications consist primarily of multiple-choice exams (except for the Lab portion of the CCIE, described later) that are composed of 100 or so questions from real-world scenarios. The one other exception is the Foundation exam in either of the CC*x*P paths, which combines the subject matter from the three 100-question subject exams into one 200-question test. Generally, a score of somewhere around 75 percent is required to pass, although Cisco sets the bar where Cisco sees fit.

 WARNING The threshold is not going down. The definition of a passing score depends on statistical analysis and is therefore always changing. You'll find out when you take the test what the current passing score is.

As mentioned earlier, the CCIE exam is structured differently than the others are. Candidates are required to pass a 100-question written exam just to qualify to take the lab portion. The hands-on practical is a two-day event in which candidates are required first to demonstrate their familiarity with complex configuring of Cisco networking equipment, and then, on the second day, to troubleshoot an intentionally problematic network (meaning that Cisco engineers have deliberately introduced problems that you have to find and fix).

 NOTE Aside from taking the exams, you will need to sign two agreements from Cisco to complete certification. The first is a confidentiality agreement that must be signed before each exam you take. The second is the Cisco Career Certification Agreement, which you must sign one time during your active certification process. For more information on the content of these documents, you can download PDFs at http://www.cisco .com/warp/public/10/wwtraining/certprog/testing/agreement.htm.

Preparing for the Tests

The best way to pass the exams on the first try is to be prepared. Although you get a great start from the material in this book, at $100 a shot, you neeed to know going in that you are ready to pass. Given the popularity of the Cisco certification program, there are many resources available for making yourself ready.

Experience

Like most things in life, there is no substitute for experience when it comes to Cisco exams. Part of the reason Cisco certifications are so respected is that they are intended to reflect more than book learning. Cisco recommends one year of on-the-job experience before attempting the CCNA (although if there is one exam that can be passed without extensive experience, this is it). For CCIE hopefuls, they recommend at least two years of network experience, thus giving you an opportunity to encounter by chance more of the kinds of problems that you're likely to see in the lab test.

NOTE Especially when it comes to CCIE certification, you must be current on the documentation for Cisco products. Up-to-date documentation for Cisco products and systems can be found at http://www.cisco.com/univercd/cc/td/doc/product/index.htm.

Self-Study Resources

Many people prefer self-study as their primary means of preparation for Cisco exams. There are books for each level of certification available from many of the major publishers, including Cisco Press. Aside from the popular CCNA Study Guide, (the second edition of which will be published at the end of May 2000), Sybex also has study guides for many of the other tests, as well as a line of Exam Notes based on the Study Guides designed to offer a portable, concise tool for review. Coriolis has a popular "Exam Cram" series, as well, but be warned: Cisco certification exams are not designed to reflect cramming ability, but real-world experience. The Cisco Web site has a recommended reading list for each level of certification.

Books vary in quality and usefulness for the exams, so you may want to find out other people's recommendations before you invest the $50 or so. One place to check out what other candidates think is Amazon.com's Certification Central. (Just follow the links from Amazon's home page to Books to the Computers & Internet section, then to Certification Central.) Chat rooms and bulletin boards can also be a source of information for discovering which books have been the most helpful to those who have actually passed. Other newsgroups and Web sites can give you a good idea of which books are recommended by your peers.

Preparing for the CCNA with Sybex

Reading this book can't hurt, and if you'd like a book geared specifically toward the CCNA exam, pick up a copy of Todd Lammle's acclaimed *CCNA: Cisco Certified Network Associate Study Guide*. Todd's book was designed specifically to help readers pass the test, and if you listen to the majority of study-group chat room participants and Amazon reviewers, it works to its intended purpose.

Sybex also has a *CCNA: Virtual Lab e-Trainer*, which turns your computer in to a simulated network environment with three routers and a switch, so that you can get the necessary hands-on training. The e-trainer was designed to be used in concert with the *CCNA Study Guide*, but it can definitely contribute to any study program.

Classes and Training Seminars

Cisco provides specifically tailored training programs for each exam, the information for which can be obtained at the Cisco Web site. There is also a multitude of private companies offering classes to help students study for these popular certifications. Additionally, Cisco has partnered with many high schools and junior colleges to create the Cisco Networking Academy, where students earn course credit as they train for certification exams.

E training

If you don't have time to travel to an in-person seminar, there are a number of e-training programs available also. Cisco has several e-learning courses available through Cisco Learning Partners, where busy professionals can keep up with the technology from the convenience of their laptop. As is the case with bricks-and-mortar classroom training, there are also numerous private companies offering training seminars over the Internet.

 WARNING Check out the Web sites and chat rooms where Cisco certification students discuss the pros and cons of various seminars, virtual labs, and books. Some of these products can be very expensive, and you should make sure that you are making a wise investment.

Web Resources

There are a variety of Web sites with FAQs, study groups, bulletin boards, and interesting articles on the Cisco certification process. These are good places to gain insider insight into the exams, and often you can find practice questions here, as well. Here is a list of some useful sites:

TCP Mag.com This site, specifically designated for Cisco networking professionals, has an abundance of information about training for certification, including firsthand articles about the certification process. The site has polls and forums where certification pursuers exchange knowledge, and plenty of links to companies providing certification training.

Cramsession.com "Everything you needed to know about IT certification," this site has good general coverage on certification from a variety of vendors. The Cisco certification section is just in its burgeoning stage, but that's bound to change.

Networkstudyguides.com Primarily a vendor of Cisco Study Guides, this site has good information on the Cisco tests and a Members area for information exchange.

Boson.com You can download free demo versions of this site's relatively inexpensive practice tests for most of the Cisco Exams, then upgrade later.

Netcerts.com This site offers certification resources specifically for networkers. It also has a good Cisco certs bulletin board where you can get candid opinions on the difficulty of the exams, as well as the value of different study guides and practice materials.

Practice Labs

Practice, practice, practice is a crucial element of training for these tests, which are specifically designed to test your practical knowledge. Not getting enough exposure at work? Here are some options:

Network simulators Many companies are now selling software that allows your comupter to simulate a network environment, so that you can get the hands-on practice of a network without the cost of setting up a home lab.

Online labs You can sign up to connect to an online lab to practice with different configurations, troubleshooting senarios, and so on.

Home-based labs While it can obviously be expensive, some people do set up at-home labs to practice on. Some suggest buying used equipment at online auctions in order to set up at reduced cost.

Practice labs for CCIE There are a few labs across the country that are purposely designed to simulate the CCIE Lab Exam environment. Sometimes, their availablity is limited to those who have already passed the written qualification exam. The price range hovers around $500 per day, with a recommended two-day reservation.

Taking the Tests

The multiple-choice written exams are given by Sylvan Prometric at centers around the world. You can register to take the exam online at Sylvan's registration Web site at www.2test.com or by calling Sylvan at 1-800-829-NETS (inside the US and Canada) and 1-408-525-NETS internationally. The Web site also has information on fees, test schedules, required materials, and testing center locations.

 TIP Since Cisco is often updating the exams, check the Web site for beta exams offered for free or at reduced cost.

The registration fee for the exams at the CCNA, CCDA, CCNP, and CCDP levels is generally $100 per exam. Taking the Foundation exam found in the CCxP path (which costs $200) is actually a cost savings of $100 over taking each of the subject exams separately. The written part of the CCIE is also $200, and the fee for the lab exam is $1,000. (Since there only a handful of Cisco CCIE Exam Labs in the world, chances are you'll have to add transportation and lodging expenses to your budget for taking the practical.)

 WARNING If your plans change, you must either cancel your lab 28 days before your exam appointment or forfeit the full $1,000.

Of course, the usual advice for taking exams applies: Get plenty of rest, eat healthily in the days leading up to the test, and stay relaxed!

Summary

The Cisco Career Certifications program offers a way for networking professionals to test, challenge, and quantify their networking knowledge, both for their own sense of self-worth and for a shorthand way to convey to potential employers that they are up to date on the most recent technology. Ultimately, there is no substitute for experience, and that probably holds true in the job market, as well. No certification alone will open doors for you, but it won't hurt your résumé, either. Perhaps you, too, can some day be one of those legendary CCIEs with your choice of six-figure job offers. Certainly, by tying your knowledge and skills to this industry leader, you're putting yourself in a prime position to rise above the networking throng.

GLOSSARY

A

A&B bit signaling

Used in T1 transmission facilities and sometimes called "24th channel signaling." Each of the 24 T1 subchannels in this procedure uses one bit of every sixth frame to send supervisory signaling information.

AAL

ATM Adaptation Layer: A service-dependent sublayer of the Data-Link layer that accepts data from other applications and brings it to the ATM layer in 48-byte ATM payload segments. CS and SAR are the two sublayers that form AALs. Currently, the four types of AAL recommended by the ITU-T are AAL1, AAL2, AAL3/4, and AAL5. AALs are differentiated by the source-destination timing they use, whether they are CBR or VBR, and whether they are used for connection-oriented or connectionless mode data transmission. *See also: AAL1, AAL2, AAL3/4, AAL5, CS, and SAR, ATM, and ATM layer.*

AAL1

ATM Adaptation Layer 1: One of four AALs recommended by the ITU-T, it is used for connection-oriented, time-sensitive services that need constant bit rates, such as isochronous traffic and uncompressed video. *See also: AAL.*

AAL2

ATM Adaptation Layer 2: One of four AALs recommended by the ITU-T, it is used for connection-oriented services that support a variable bit rate, such as voice traffic. *See also: AAL.*

AAL3/4

ATM Adaptation Layer 3/4: One of four AALs (a product of two initially distinct layers) recommended by the ITU-T, supporting both connectionless and connection-oriented links. Its primary use is in sending SMDS packets over ATM networks. *See also: AAL.*

AAL5

ATM Adaptation Layer 5: One of four AALs recommended by the ITU-T, it is used to support connection-oriented VBR services primarily to transfer classical IP over ATM and LANE traffic. This least complex of the AAL recommendations uses SEAL, offering lower bandwidth costs and simpler processing requirements but also providing reduced bandwidth and error-recovery capacities. *See also: AAL.*

AARP

AppleTalk Address Resolution Protocol: The protocol in an AppleTalk stack that maps data-link addresses to network addresses.

AARP probe packets

Packets sent by the AARP to determine whether a given node ID is being used by another node in a nonextended AppleTalk network. If the node ID is not in use, the sending node appropriates that node's ID. If the node ID is in use, the sending node will select a different ID and then send out more AARP probe packets. *See also: AARP.*

ABM

Asynchronous Balanced Mode: When two stations can initiate a transmission, ABM is an HDLC (or one of its derived protocols) communication technology that supports peer-oriented, point-to-point communications between both stations.

ABR

Area Border Router: An OSPF router that is located on the border of one or more OSPF areas. ABRs are used to connect OSPF areas to the OSPF backbone area.

access list

A set of test conditions kept by routers that determines "interesting traffic" to and from the router for various services on the network.

access method

The manner in which network devices approach gaining access to the network itself.

access server

Also known as a "network access server," it is a communications process connecting asynchronous devices to a LAN or WAN through network and terminal emulation software, providing synchronous or asynchronous routing of supported protocols.

acknowledgment

Verification sent from one network device to another signifying that an event has occurred. May be abbreviated as ACK. *Contrast with: NAK.*

ACR

allowed cell rate: A designation defined by the ATM Forum for managing ATM traffic. Dynamically controlled using congestion control measures, the ACR varies between the minimum cell rate (MCR) and the peak cell rate (PCR). *See also: MCR and PCR.*

active monitor

The mechanism used to manage a Token Ring. The network node with the highest MAC address on the ring becomes the active monitor and is responsible for management tasks such as preventing loops and ensuring tokens are not lost.

address mapping

By translating network addresses from one format to another, this methodology permits different protocols to operate interchangeably.

address mask

A bit combination descriptor identifying which portion of an address refers to the network or subnet and which part refers to the host. Sometimes simply called the mask. *See also: subnet mask.*

address resolution

The process used for resolving differences between computer addressing schemes. Address resolution typically defines a method for tracing Network layer (Layer 3) addresses to data-link layer (Layer 2) addresses. *See also: address mapping.*

adjacency

The relationship made between defined neighboring routers and end nodes, using a common media segment, to exchange routing information.

administrative distance

A number between 0 and 225 that expresses the value of trustworthiness of a routing information source. The lower the number, the higher the integrity rating.

administrative weight

A value designated by a network administrator to rate the preference given to a network link. It is one of four link metrics exchanged by PTSPs to test ATM network resource availability.

ADSU

ATM Data Service Unit: The terminal adapter used to connect to an ATM network through an HSSI-compatible mechanism. *See also: DSU.*

advertising

The process whereby routing or service updates are transmitted at given intervals, allowing other routers on the network to maintain a record of viable routes.

AEP

AppleTalk Echo Protocol: A test for connectivity between two AppleTalk nodes where one node sends a packet to another and receives an echo, or copy, in response.

AFI

Authority and Format Identifier: The part of an NSAP ATM address that delineates the type and format of the IDI section of an ATM address. *See also: IDI and NSAP.*

AFP

AppleTalk Filing Protocol: A presentation-layer protocol, supporting AppleShare and Mac OS File Sharing, that permits users to share files and applications on a server.

AIP

ATM Interface Processor: Supporting AAL3/4 and AAL5, this interface for Cisco 7000 series routers minimizes performance bottlenecks at the UNI. *See also: AAL3/4 and AAL5.*

algorithm

A set of rules or process used to solve a problem. In networking, algorithms are typically used for finding the best route for traffic from a source to its destination.

alignment error

An error occurring in Ethernet networks, in which a received frame has extra bits; that is, a number not divisible by eight. Alignment errors are generally the result of frame damage caused by collisions.

all-routes explorer packet

An explorer packet that can move across an entire SRB network, tracing all possible paths to a given destination. Also known as an all-rings explorer packet. *See also: explorer packet, local explorer packet, and spanning explorer packet.*

AM

Amplitude Modulation: A modulation method that represents information by varying the amplitude of the carrier signal. *See also: modulation.*

AMI

Alternate Mark Inversion: A line-code type on T1 and E1 circuits that shows zeros as "01" during each bit cell, and ones as "11" or "00," alternately, during each bit cell. The sending device must maintain ones density in AMI but not independently of the data stream. Also known as binary-coded, alternate mark inversion. *Contrast with: B8ZS. See also: ones density.*

amplitude

An analog or digital waveform's highest value.

analog transmission

Signal messaging whereby information is represented by various combinations of signal amplitude, frequency, and phase.

ANSI

American National Standards Institute: The organization of corporate, government, and other volunteer members that coordinates standards-related activities, approves U.S. national standards, and develops U.S. positions in international standards organizations. ANSI assists in the creation of international and U.S. standards in disciplines such as communications, networking, and a variety of technical fields. It publishes over 13,000 standards for engineered products and technologies ranging from screw threads to networking protocols. ANSI is a member of the IEC and ISO. *See also: IEC and ISO.*

anycast

An ATM address that can be shared by more than one end system, allowing requests to be routed to a node that provides a particular service.

AppleTalk

Currently in two versions, the group of communication protocols designed by Apple Computer for use in Macintosh environments. The earlier Phase 1 protocols support one physical network with only one network number that resides in one zone. The later Phase 2 protocols support more than one logical network on a single physical network, allowing networks to exist in more than one zone. *See also: zone.*

Application layer

Layer 7 of the OSI reference network model, supplying services to application procedures (such as electronic mail or file transfer) that are outside the OSI model. This layer chooses and determines the availability of communicating partners along with the resources necessary to make the connection, coordinates partnering applications, and forms a consensus on procedures for controlling data integrity and error recovery.

ARA

AppleTalk Remote Access: A protocol for Macintosh users establishing their access to resources and data from a remote AppleTalk location.

area

A logical, rather than physical, set of segments (based on either CLNS, DECnet, or OSPF) along with their attached devices. Areas are commonly connected to others using routers to create a single autonomous system. *See also: autonomous system.*

ARM

Asynchronous Response Mode: An HDLC communication mode using one primary station and at least one additional station, in which transmission can be initiated from either the primary or one of the secondary units.

ARP

Address Resolution Protocol: Defined in RFC 826, the protocol that traces IP addresses to MAC addresses. *See also: RARP.*

ASBR

Autonomous System Boundary Router: An area border router placed between an OSPF autonomous system and a non-OSPF network that operates both OSPF and an additional routing protocol, such as RIP. ASBRs must be located in a non-stub OSPF area. *See also: ABR, non-stub area, and OSPF.*

ASCII

American Standard Code for Information Interchange: An eight-bit code for representing characters, consisting of seven data bits plus one parity bit.

ASN.1

Abstract Syntax Notation One: An OSI language used to describe types of data that is independent of computer structures and depicting methods. Described by ISO International Standard 8824.

ASP

AppleTalk Session Protocol: A protocol employing ATP to establish, maintain, and tear down sessions, as well as sequence requests. *See also: ATP.*

AST

Automatic Spanning Tree: A function that supplies one path for spanning explorer frames traveling from one node in the network to another, supporting the automatic resolution of spanning trees in SRB networks. AST is based on the IEEE 802.1 standard. *See also: IEEE 802.1 and SRB.*

asynchronous transmission

Digital signals sent without precise timing, usually with different frequencies and phase relationships. Asynchronous transmissions generally enclose individual characters in control bits (called start and stop bits) that show the beginning and end of each character. *Contrast with: isochronous transmission and synchronous transmission.*

ATCP

AppleTalk Control Program: The protocol for establishing and configuring AppleTalk over PPP, defined in RFC 1378. *See also: PPP.*

ATDM

Asynchronous Time-Division Multiplexing: A technique for sending information, it differs from normal TDM in that the time slots are assigned when necessary rather than preassigned to certain transmitters. *Contrast with: FDM, statistical multiplexing, and TDM.*

ATG

Address Translation Gateway: The mechanism within Cisco DECnet routing software that enables routers to route multiple, independent DECnet networks and to establish a user-designated address translation for chosen nodes between networks.

ATM

Asynchronous Transfer Mode: The international standard, identified by fixed-length 53-byte cells, for transmitting cells in multiple service systems, such as voice, video, or data. Transit delays are reduced because the fixed-length cells permit processing to occur in the hardware. ATM is designed to maximize the benefits of high-speed transmission media, such as SONET, E3, and T3.

ATM ARP server

A device that supplies logical subnets running classical IP over ATM with address-resolution services.

ATM endpoint

The initiating or terminating connection in an ATM network. ATM endpoints include servers, workstations, ATM-to-LAN switches, and ATM routers.

ATM Forum

The international organization founded jointly by Northern Telecom, Sprint, Cisco Systems, and NET/ADAPTIVE in 1991 to develop and promote standards-based implementation agreements for ATM technology. The ATM Forum broadens official standards developed by ANSI and ITU-T and creates implementation agreements before official standards are published.

ATM layer

A sublayer of the Data-Link layer in an ATM network that is service independent. To create standard 53-byte ATM cells, the ATM layer receives 48-byte segments from the AAL and attaches a 5-byte header to each. These cells are then sent to the Physical layer for transmission across the physical medium. *See also: AAL.*

ATMM

ATM Management: A procedure that runs on ATM switches, managing rate enforcement and VCI translation. *See also: ATM and VCI*

ATM user-user connection

A connection made by the ATM layer to supply communication between at least two ATM service users, such as ATMM processes. These communications can be uni- or bidirectional, using one or two VCCs, respectively. *See also: ATM layer and ATMM.*

ATP

AppleTalk Transaction Protocol: A transport-level protocol that enables reliable transactions between two sockets, where one requests the other to perform a given task and to report the results. ATP fastens the request and response together, assuring a loss-free exchange of request-response pairs.

attenuation

In communication, weakening or loss of signal energy, typically caused by distance.

AURP

AppleTalk Update-based Routing Protocol: A technique for encapsulating AppleTalk traffic in the header of a foreign protocol that allows the connection of at least two noncontiguous AppleTalk internetworks through a foreign network (such as TCP/IP) to create an AppleTalk WAN. The connection made is called an AURP tunnel. By exchanging routing information between exterior routers, the AURP maintains routing tables for the complete AppleTalk WAN. *See also: AURP tunnel and exterior router.*

AURP tunnel

A connection made in an AURP WAN that acts as a single, virtual link between AppleTalk internetworks separated physically by a foreign network such as a TCP/IP network. *See also: AURP.*

authority zone

A portion of the domain-name tree associated with DNS for which one name server is the authority. *See also: DNS.*

automatic call reconnect

A function that enables automatic call rerouting away from a failed trunk line.

autonomous confederation

A collection of self-governed systems that depend more on their own network accessibility and routing information than on information received from other systems or groups.

autonomous switching

The ability of Cisco routers to process packets more quickly by using the CiscoBus to switch packets independently of the system processor.

autonomous system (AS)

A group of networks under mutual administration that share the same routing methodology. Autonomous systems are subdivided by areas and must be assigned an individual 16-bit number by the IANA. *See also: area and IANA.*

autoreconfiguration

A procedure executed by nodes within the failure domain of a Token Ring, wherein nodes automatically perform diagnostics, trying to reconfigure the network around failed areas.

B

B8ZS

Binary 8-Zero Substitution: A line-code type, interpreted at the remote end of the connection, that uses a special code substitution whenever eight consecutive zeros are transmitted over the link on T1 and E1 circuits. This technique assures ones density independent of the data stream. Also known as bipolar 8-zero substitution. *Contrast with: AMI. See also: ones density.*

backbone

The basic portion of the network that provides the primary path for traffic sent to and initiated from other networks.

back end

A node or software program supplying services to a front end. *See also: client, front end, and server.*

bandwidth

The gap between the highest and lowest frequencies employed by network signals. More commonly, it refers to the rated throughput capacity of a network protocol or medium.

baseband

A feature of a network technology that uses only one carrier frequency; for example, Ethernet. Also named "narrowband." *Compare with: broadband.*

baud

Synonymous with bits per second (bps), if each signal element represents one bit. It is a unit of signaling speed equivalent to the number of separate signal elements transmitted per second.

B channel

Bearer channel: A full-duplex, 64Kbps channel in ISDN that transmits user data. *Compare with: D channel, E channel, and H channel.*

beacon

An FDDI device or Token Ring frame that points to a serious problem with the ring, such as a broken cable. The beacon frame carries the address of the station thought to be down. *See also: failure domain.*

BECN

Backward Explicit Congestion Notification: BECN is the bit set by a Frame Relay network in frames moving away from frames headed into a congested path. A DTE that receives frames with the BECN may ask higher-level protocols to take necessary flow control measures. *Compare with: FECN.*

BGP4

BGP Version 4: Version 4 of the interdomain routing protocol most commonly used on the Internet. BGP4 supports CIDR and uses route-counting mechanisms to decrease the size of routing tables. *See also: CIDR.*

binary

A two-character numbering method that uses ones and zeros. The binary numbering system underlies all digital representation of information.

BIP

Bit Interleaved Parity: A method used in ATM to monitor errors on a link, sending a check bit or word in the link overhead for the previous block or frame. This allows bit errors in transmissions to be found and delivered as maintenance information.

BISDN

Broadband ISDN: ITU-T standards created to manage high-bandwidth technologies such as video. BISDN presently employs ATM technology along SONET-based transmission circuits, supplying data rates between 155Mbps and 622Mbps and beyond. Contrast with N-ISDN. *See also: BRI, ISDN, and PRI.*

bit-oriented protocol

Regardless of frame content, the class of data-link layer communication protocols that transmits frames. Bit-oriented protocols, as compared with byte-oriented, supply more efficient and trustworthy, full-duplex operation. *Compare with: byte-oriented protocol.*

border gateway

A router that facilitates communication with routers in different autonomous systems.

BPDU

Bridge Protocol Data Unit: A Spanning Tree protocol initializing packet that is sent at definable intervals for the purpose of exchanging information among bridges in networks.

BRI

Basic Rate Interface: The ISDN interface that facilitates circuit-switched communication between video, data, and voice; it is made up of two B channels (64Kbps each) and one D channel (16Kbps). *Compare with: PRI. See also: BISDN, ISN.*

bridge

A device for connecting two segments of a network and transmitting packets between them. Both segments must use identical protocols to communicate. Bridges function at the Data-Link layer, Layer 2 of the OSI reference model. The purpose of a bridge is to filter, send, or flood any incoming frame, based on the MAC address of that particular frame.

broadband

A transmission methodology for multiplexing several independent signals onto one cable. In telecommunications, broadband is classified as any channel with bandwidth greater than 4kHz (typical voice grade). In LAN terminology, it is classified as a coaxial cable on which analog signaling is employed. Also known as wideband. *Contrast with: baseband.*

broadcast

A data frame or packet that is transmitted to every node on the local network segment (as defined by the broadcast domain). Broadcasts are known by their broadcast address, which is a destination network and host address with all the bits turned on. *Also called "local broadcast." Compare with: directed broadcasts.*

broadcast domain

A group of devices receiving broadcast frames initiating from any device within the group. Because they do not forward broadcast frames, broadcast domains are generally surrounded by routers.

broadcast storm

An undesired event on the network caused by the simultaneous transmission of any number of broadcasts across the network segment. Such an occurrence can overwhelm network bandwidth, resulting in time-outs.

buffer

A storage area dedicated to handling data while in transit. Buffers are used to receive/store sporadic deliveries of data bursts, usually received from faster devices, compensating for the variations in processing speed. Incoming information is stored until everything is received prior to sending data on. Also known as an information buffer.

bus topology

A linear LAN architecture in which transmissions from various stations on the network are reproduced over the length of the medium and are accepted by all other stations. *Compare with: ring, star, and tree topologies.*

bus

Any physical path, typically wires or copper, through which a digital signal can be used to send data from one part of a computer to another.

BUS

broadcast and unknown servers: In LAN emulation, the hardware or software responsible for resolving all broadcasts and packets with unknown (unregistered) addresses into the point-to-point virtual circuits required by ATM. *See also: LEC, LECS, LES, and LANE.*

BX.25

AT&T's use of X.25. *See also: X.25.*

bypass mode

An FDDI and Token Ring network operation that deletes an interface.

bypass relay

A device that enables a particular interface in the Token Ring to be closed down and effectively taken off the ring.

byte-oriented protocol

Any type of data-link communication protocol that, in order to mark the boundaries of frames, uses a specific character from the user character set. These protocols have generally been superseded by bit-oriented protocols. *Compare with: bit-oriented protocol.*

C

cable range

In an extended AppleTalk network, the range of numbers allotted for use by existing nodes on the network. The value of the cable range can be anywhere from a single to a sequence of several touching network numbers. Node addresses are determined by their cable range value.

CAC

Connection Admission Control: The sequence of actions executed by every ATM switch while connection setup is performed in order to determine if a request for connection is violating the guarantees of QoS for established connections. Also, CAC is used to route a connection request through an ATM network.

call admission control

A device for managing of traffic in ATM networks, determining the possibility of a path containing adequate bandwidth for a requested VCC.

call priority

In circuit-switched systems, the defining priority given to each originating port; it specifies in which order calls will be reconnected. Additionally, call priority identifies which calls are allowed during a bandwidth reservation.

call set-up time

The length of time necessary to effect a switched call between DTE devices.

CBR

Constant Bit Rate: An ATM Forum QoS class created for use in ATM networks. CBR is used for connections that rely on precision clocking to guarantee trustworthy delivery. *Compare with: ABR and VBR.*

CD

Carrier Detect: A signal indicating that an interface is active or that a connection generated by a modem has been established.

CDP

Cisco Discovery Protocol: Cisco's proprietary protocol that is used to tell a neighbor Cisco device about the type of hardware, software version, and active interfaces that the Cisco device is using. It uses a SNAP frame between devices and is not routable.

CDVT

Cell Delay Variation Tolerance: A QoS parameter for traffic management in ATM networks specified when a connection is established. The allowable fluctuation levels for data samples taken by the PCR in CBR transmissions are determined by the CDVT. *See also: CBR and PCR.*

cell

In ATM networking, the basic unit of data for switching and multiplexing. Cells have a defined length of 53 bytes, including a 5-byte header that identifies the cell's data stream and 48 bytes of payload. *See also: cell relay.*

cell payload scrambling

The method by which an ATM switch maintains framing on some medium-speed edge and trunk interfaces (T3 or E3 circuits). Cell payload scrambling rearranges the data portion of a cell to maintain the line synchronization with certain common bit patterns.

cell relay

A technology that uses small packets of fixed size, known as cells. Their fixed length enables cells to be processed and switched in hardware at high speeds, making this technology the foundation for ATM and other high-speed network protocols. *See also: cell.*

Centrex

A local exchange carrier service, providing local switching that resembles that of an on-site PBX. Centrex has no on-site switching capability. Therefore, all customer connections return to the CO. *See also: CO.*

CER

Cell Error Ratio: The ratio in ATM of transmitted cells having errors to the total number of cells sent in a transmission within a certain span of time.

channelized E1

Operating at 2.048Mpbs, an access link that is sectioned into 29 B-channels and one D-channel, supporting DDR, Frame Relay, and X.25. *Compare with: channelized T1.*

channelized T1

Operating at 1.544Mbps, an access link that is sectioned into 23 B-channels and 1 D-channel of 64Kbps each, where individual channels or groups of channels connect to various destinations, supporting DDR, Frame Relay, and X.25. *Compare with: channelized E1.*

CHAP

Challenge Handshake Authentication Protocol: Supported on lines using PPP encapsulation, it is a security feature that identifies the remote end, helping keep out unauthorized users. After CHAP is performed, the router or access server determines whether a given user is permitted access. It is a newer, more secure protocol than PAP. *Compare with: PAP.*

checksum

A test for ensuring the integrity of sent data. It is a number calculated from a series of values taken through a sequence of mathematical functions, typically placed at the end of the data from which it is calculated, and then recalculated at the receiving end for verification. *Compare with: CRC.*

choke packet

When congestion exists, it is a packet sent to inform a transmitter that it should decrease its sending rate.

CIDR

Classless Interdomain Routing: A method supported by classless routing protocols, such as OSPF and BGP4, based on the concept of ignoring the IP class of address, permitting route aggregation and VLSM that enable routers to combine routes in order to minimize the routing information that needs to be conveyed by the primary routers. It allows a group of IP networks to appear to other networks as a unified, larger entity. In CIDR, IP addresses and their subnet masks are written as four dotted octets, followed by a forward slash and the numbering of masking bits (a form of subnet notation shorthand). *See also: BGP4.*

CIP

Channel Interface Processor: A channel attachment interface for use in Cisco 7000 series routers that connects a host mainframe to a control unit. This device eliminates the need for an FBP to attach channels.

CIR

Committed Information Rate: Averaged over a minimum span of time and measured in bps, a Frame Relay network's agreed-upon minimum rate of transferring information.

Cisco FRAD

Cisco Frame-Relay Access Device: A Cisco product that supports Cisco IPS Frame Relay SNA services, connecting SDLC devices to Frame Relay without requiring an existing LAN. May be upgraded to a fully functioning multiprotocol router. Can activate conversion from SDLC to Ethernet and Token Ring, but does not support attached LANs. *See also: FRAD.*

CiscoFusion

Cisco's name for the internetworking architecture under which its Cisco IOS operates. It is designed to "fuse" together the capabilities of its disparate collection of acquired routers and switches.

Cisco IOS software

Cisco Internet Operating System software. The kernel of the Cisco line of routers and switches that supplies shared functionality, scalability, and security for all products under its CiscoFusion architecture. *See also: CiscoFusion.*

CiscoView

GUI-based management software for Cisco networking devices, enabling dynamic status, statistics, and comprehensive configuration information. Displays a physical view of the Cisco device chassis and provides device-monitoring functions and fundamental troubleshooting capabilities. May be integrated with a number of SNMP-based network management platforms.

classical IP over ATM

Defined in RFC 1577, the specification for running IP over ATM that maximizes ATM features. Also known as CIA.

CLP

Cell Loss Priority: The area in the ATM cell header that determines the likelihood of a cell being dropped during network congestion. Cells with CLP = 0 are considered insured traffic and are not apt to be dropped. Cells with CLP = 1 are considered best-effort traffic that may be dropped during congested episodes, delivering more resources to handle insured traffic.

CLR

Cell Loss Ratio: The ratio of discarded cells to successfully delivered cells in ATM. CLR can be designated a QoS parameter when establishing a connection.

CO

Central Office: The local telephone company office where all loops in a certain area connect and where circuit switching of subscriber lines occurs.

collapsed backbone

A nondistributed backbone where all network segments are connected to each other through an internetworking device. A collapsed backbone can be a virtual network segment at work in a device such as a router, hub, or switch.

collision

The effect of two nodes sending transmissions simultaneously in Ethernet. When they meet on the physical media, the frames from each node collide and are damaged. *See also: collision domain.*

collision domain

The network area in Ethernet over which frames that have collided will spread. Collisions are propagated by hubs and repeaters, but not by LAN switches, routers, or bridges. *See also: collision.*

configuration register

A 16-bit configurable value stored in hardware or software that determines how Cisco routers function during initialization. In hardware, the bit position is set using a jumper. In software, it is set by specifying specific bit patterns used to set startup options, configured using a hexadecimal value with configuration commands.

congestion

Traffic that exceeds the network's ability to handle it.

congestion avoidance

To minimize delays, the method an ATM network uses to control traffic entering the system. Lower-priority traffic is discarded at the edge of the network when indicators signal it cannot be delivered, thus using resources efficiently.

congestion collapse

The situation that results from the retransmission of packets in ATM networks where little or no traffic successfully arrives at destination points. It usually happens in networks made of switches with ineffective or inadequate buffering capabilities combined with poor packet discard or ABR congestion feedback mechanisms.

connectionless

Data transfer that occurs without the creating of a virtual circuit. No overhead, best-effort delivery, not reliable. *Contrast with: connection-oriented. See also: virtual circuit.*

connection-oriented

Data transfer method that sets up a virtual circuit before any data is transferred. Uses acknowledgments and flow control for reliable data transfer. *Contrast with: connectionless. See also: virtual circuit.*

control direct VCC

One of three control connections defined by Phase I LAN Emulation; a bi-directional virtual control connection (VCC) established in ATM by an LEC to an LES. *See also: control distribute VCC.*

control distribute VCC

One of three control connections defined by Phase 1 LAN Emulation; a unidirectional virtual control connection (VCC) set up in ATM from an LES to an LEC. Usually, the VCC is a point-to-multipoint connection. *See also: control direct VCC.*

convergence

The process required for all routers in an internetwork to update their routing tables and create a consistent view of the network, using the best possible paths. No user data is passed during a convergence time.

cost

Also known as path cost, an arbitrary value, based on hop count, bandwidth, or other calculation, that is typically assigned by a network administrator and used by the routing protocol to compare different routes through an internetwork. Routing protocols use cost values to select the best path to a certain destination: the lowest cost identifies the best path. Also known as path cost. *See also: routing metric.*

count to infinity

A problem occurring in routing algorithms that are slow to converge where routers keep increasing the hop count to particular networks. To avoid this problem, various solutions have been implemented into each of the different routing protocols. Some of those solutions include defining a maximum hop count (defining infinity), route poising, poison reverse, and split horizon.

CPCS

Common Part Convergence Sublayer: One of two AAL sublayers that is service-dependent, it is further segmented into the CS and SAR sublayers. The CPCS prepares data for transmission across the ATM network; it creates the 48-byte payload cells that are sent to the ATM layer. *See also: AAL and ATM layer.*

CPE

Customer Premises Equipment: Items such as telephones, modems, and terminals installed at customer locations and connected to the telephone company network.

crankback

In ATM, a correction technique used when a node somewhere on a chosen path cannot accept a connection setup request, blocking the request. The path is rolled back to an intermediate node, which then uses GCAC to attempt to find an alternate path to the final destination.

CRC

cyclical redundancy check: A methodology that detects errors, whereby the frame recipient makes a calculation by dividing frame contents with a prime binary divisor and compares the remainder to a value stored in the frame by the sending node. *Contrast with: checksum.*

CSMA/CD

Carrier Sense Multiple Access with Collision Detection: A technology defined by the Ethernet IEEE 802.3 committee. Each device senses the cable for a digital signal before transmitting. Also, CSMA/CD allows all devices on the network to share the same cable, but one at a time. If two devices transmit at the same time, a frame collision will occur and a jamming pattern will be sent; the devices will stop transmitting, wait a predetermined amount of time, and then try to transmit again.

CSU

channel service unit: A digital mechanism that connects end-user equipment to the local digital telephone loop. Frequently referred to along with the data service unit as CSU/DSU. *See also: DSU.*

CTD

Cell Transfer Delay: For a given connection in ATM, the time period between a cell exit event at the source user-network interface (UNI) and the corresponding cell entry event at the destination. The CTD between these points is the sum of the total inter-ATM transmission delay and the total ATM processing delay.

cut-through frame switching

A frame-switching technique that flows data through a switch so that the leading edge exits the switch at the output port before the packet finishes entering the input port. Frames will be read, processed, and forwarded by devices that use cut-through switching as soon as the destination address of the frame is confirmed and the outgoing port is identified.

D

data direct VCC

A bidirectional point-to-point virtual control connection (VCC) set up between two LECs in ATM and one of three data connections defined by Phase 1 LAN Emulation. Because data direct VCCs do not guarantee QoS, they are generally reserved for UBR and ABR connections. *Compare with: control distribute VCC and control direct VCC.*

datagram

A logical collection of information transmitted as a Network layer unit over a medium without a previously established virtual circuit. IP datagrams have become the primary information unit of the Internet. At various layers of the OSI reference model, the terms *cell, frame, message, packet,* and *segment* also define these logical information groupings.

Data-Link control layer

Layer 2 of the SNA architectural model, it is responsible for the transmission of data over a given physical link and compares somewhat to the Data-Link layer of the OSI model.

Data-Link layer

Layer 2 of the OSI reference model, it ensures the trustworthy transmission of data across a physical link and is primarily concerned with physical addressing, line discipline, network topology, error notification, ordered delivery of frames, and flow control. The IEEE has further segmented this layer into the MAC sublayer and the LLC sublayer. Also known as the link layer. Can be compared somewhat to the Data-Link control layer of the SNA model. *See also: Application layer, LLC, MAC, Network layer, Physical layer, Presentation layer, Session layer, and Transport layer.*

DCC

Data Country Code: Developed by the ATM Forum, one of two ATM address formats designed for use by private networks. *Compare with: ICD.*

DCE

data communications equipment (as defined by the EIA) or data circuit-terminating equipment (as defined by the ITU-T): The mechanisms and links of a communications network that make up the network portion of the user-to-network interface, such as modems. The DCE supplies the physical connection to the network, forwards traffic, and provides a clocking signal to synchronize data transmission between DTE and DCE devices. *Compare with: DTE.*

D channel

1. Data channel: A full-duplex, 16Kbps (BRI) or 64Kbps (PRI) ISDN channel. *Compare with: B channel, E channel, and H channel.*
2. In SNA, anything that provides a connection between the processor and main storage with any peripherals.

DDP

Datagram Delivery Protocol : Used in the AppleTalk suite of protocols as a connection-less protocol that is responsible for sending datagrams through an internetwork.

DDR

dial-on-demand routing: A technique that allows a router to automatically initiate and end a circuit-switched session per the requirements of the sending station. By mimicking keepalives, the router fools the end station into treating the session as active. DDR permits routing over ISDN or telephone lines via a modem or external ISDN terminal adapter.

default route

The static routing table entry used to direct frames whose next hop is not spelled out in the dynamic routing table.

delay

The time elapsed between a sender's initiation of a transaction and the first response they receive. Also, the time needed to move a packet from its source to its destination over a path. *See also: latency.*

demarc

The demarcation point between the customer premises equipment (CPE) and the telco's carrier equipment.

demodulation

A series of steps that return a modulated signal to its original form. When receiving, a modem demodulates an analog signal to its original digital form (and, conversely, modulates the digital data it sends into an analog signal). *See also: modulation.*

demultiplexing

The process of converting a single multiplex signal, comprising more than one input stream, back into separate output streams. *See also: multiplexing.*

designated bridge

In the process of forwarding a frame from a segment to the route bridge, the bridge with the lowest path cost.

designated router

An OSPF router that creates LSAs for a multiaccess network and is required to perform other special tasks in OSPF operations. Multiaccess OSPF networks that maintain a minimum of two attached routers identify one router that is chosen by the OSPF Hello protocol, which makes possible a decrease in the number of adjacencies necessary on a multiaccess network. This in turn reduces the quantity of routing protocol traffic and the physical size of the database.

destination address

The address for the network devices that will receive a packet.

directed broadcast

A data frame or packet that is transmitted to a specific group of nodes on a remote network segment. Directed broadcasts are known by their broadcast address, which is a destination subnet address with all the bits turned on. *Compare with: local broadcasts.*

discovery mode

Also known as dynamic configuration, this technique is used by an AppleTalk interface to gain information from a working node about an attached network. The information is subsequently used by the interface for self-configuration.

distance vector routing algorithm

In order to find the shortest path, this group of routing algorithms repeats on the number of hops in a given route, requiring each router to send its complete routing table with each update, but only to its neighbors. Routing algorithms of this type tend to generate loops, but they are fundamentally simpler than their link state counterparts. *See also: link state routing algorithm and SPF.*

DLCI

Data Link Connection Identifier: Used to identify virtual circuits in a Frame Relay network.

DNS

Domain Name System: Used to resolve host names to IP addresses.

DSAP

Destination Service Access Point: The service access point of a network node, specified in the destination field of a packet. *See also: SSAP and SAP.*

DSR

Data Set Ready: When a DCE is powered up and ready to run, this EIA/TIA-232 interface circuit is also engaged.

DSU

data service unit: This device is used to adapt the physical interface on a data terminal equipment (DTE) mechanism to a transmission facility such as T1 or E1 and is also responsible for signal timing. It is commonly grouped with the channel service unit and referred to as the CSU/DSU. *See also: CSU.*

DTE

data terminal equipment: Any device located at the user end of a user-network interface serving as a destination, a source, or both. DTE includes devices such as multiplexers, protocol translators, and computers. The connection to a data network is made through data channel equipment (DCE) such as a modem, using the clocking signals generated by that device. *See also: DCE.*

DTR

data terminal ready: An activated EIA/TIA-232 circuit communicating to the DCE the state of preparedness of the DTE to transmit or receive data.

DUAL

Diffusing Update Algorithm: Used in Enhanced IGRP, this convergence algorithm provides loop-free operation throughout an entire route's computation. DUAL grants routers involved in a topology revision the ability to synchronize simultaneously, while routers unaffected by this change are not involved. *See also: Enhanced IGRP.*

DVMRP

Distance Vector Multicast Routing Protocol: Based primarily on the Routing Information Protocol (RIP), this Internet gateway protocol implements a common, condensed-mode IP multicast scheme, using IGMP to transfer routing datagrams between its neighbors. *See also: IGMP.*

DXI

Data Exchange Interface: Described in RFC 1482, DXI defines the effectiveness of a network device such as a router, bridge, or hub to act as an FEP to an ATM network by using a special DSU that accomplishes packet encapsulation.

dynamic routing

Also known as adaptive routing, this technique automatically adapts to traffic or physical network revisions.

E

E1

Generally used in Europe, a wide-area digital transmission scheme carrying data at 2.048Mbps. E1 transmission lines are available for lease from common carriers for private use.

E.164

1. Evolved from the standard telephone numbering system, the standard recommended by ITU-T for international telecommunication numbering, particularly in ISDN, SMDS, and BISDN.
2. Label of field in an ATM address containing numbers in E.164 format.

E channel

Echo channel: A 64Kbps ISDN control channel used for circuit switching. Specific description of this channel can be found in the 1984 ITU-T ISDN specification, but was dropped from the 1988 version. *See also: B, D, and H channels.*

edge device

A device that enables packets to be forwarded between legacy interfaces (such as Ethernet and Token Ring) and ATM interfaces based on information in the Data-Link and Network layers. An edge device does not take part in the running of any Network layer routing protocol; it merely uses the route description protocol in order to get the forwarding information required.

EEPROM

Electronically Erasable Programmable Read-Only Memory: Programmed after their manufacture, these nonvolatile memory chips can be erased if necessary using electric power and reprogrammed. *See also: EPROM, PROM.*

EFCI

Explicit Forward Congestion Indication: A congestion feedback mode permitted by ABR service in an ATM network. The EFCI may be set by any network element that is in a state of immediate or certain congestion. The destination end-system is able to carry out a protocol that adjusts and lowers the cell rate of the connection based on value of the EFCI. *See also: ABR.*

EIGRP

See: Enhanced IGRP.

EIP

Ethernet Interface Processor: A Cisco 7000 series router interface processor card, supplying 10Mbps AUI ports to support Ethernet Version 1 and Ethernet Version 2 or IEEE 802.3 interfaces with a high-speed data path to other interface processors.

ELAN

Emulated LAN: An ATM network configured using a client/server model in order to emulate either an Ethernet or Token Ring LAN. Multiple ELANs can exist at the same time on a single ATM network and are made up of an LAN emulation client (LEC), an LAN Emulation Server (LES), a Broadcast and Unknown Server (BUS), and an LAN Emulation Configuration Server (LECS). ELANs are defined by the LANE specification. *See also: LANE, LEC, LECS, and LES.*

ELAP

EtherTalk Link Access Protocol. In an EtherTalk network, the link-access protocol constructed above the standard Ethernet Data-Link layer.

encapsulation

The technique used by layered protocols in which a layer adds header information to the protocol data unit (PDU) from the layer above. As an example, in Internet terminology, a packet would contain a header from the Physical layer, followed by a header from the Network layer (IP), followed by a header from the Transport layer (TCP), followed by the application protocol data.

encryption

The conversion of information into a scrambled form that effectively disguises it to prevent unauthorized access. Every encryption scheme uses some well-defined algorithm, which is reversed at the receiving end by an opposite algorithm in a process known as decryption.

Enhanced IGRP

Enhanced Interior Gateway Routing Protocol: An advanced routing protocol created by Cisco, combining the advantages of link state and distance vector protocols. Enhanced IGRP has superior convergence attributes, including high operating efficiency. *See also: IGP, OSPF, and RIP.*

enterprise network

A privately owned and operated network that joins most major locations in a large company or organization.

EPROM

Erasable Programmable Read-Only Memory: Programmed after their manufacture, these nonvolatile memory chips can be erased if necessary using high-power light and reprogrammed. *See also: EEPROM, PROM.*

ESF

Extended Superframe: Made up of 24 frames with 192 bits each, with the 193rd bit providing other functions including timing. This is an enhanced version of SF. *See also: SF.*

Ethernet

A baseband LAN specification created by the Xerox Corporation and then improved through joint efforts of Xerox, Digital Equipment Corporation, and Intel. Ethernet is similar to the IEEE 802.3 series standard and, using CSMA/CD, operates over various types of cables at 10Mbps. *Also called: DIX (Digital/Intel/Xerox) Ethernet. See also: 10BaseT, Fast Ethernet, and IEEE.*

EtherTalk

A data-link product from Apple Computer that permits AppleTalk networks to be connected by Ethernet.

excess rate

In ATM networking, traffic exceeding a connection's insured rate. The excess rate is the maximum rate less the insured rate. Depending on the availability of network resources, excess traffic can be discarded during congestion episodes. *Compare with: maximum rate.*

expansion

The procedure of directing compressed data through an algorithm, restoring information to its original size.

expedited delivery

An option that can be specified by one protocol layer, communicating either with other layers or with the identical protocol layer in a different network device, requiring that identified data be processed faster

explorer packet

An SNA packet transmitted by a source Token Ring device to find the path through a source-route-bridged network.

F

failure domain

The region in which a failure has occurred in a Token Ring. When a station gains information that a serious problem, such as a cable break, has occurred with the network, it sends a beacon frame that includes the station reporting the failure, its NAUN, and everything between. This defines the failure domain. Beaconing then initiates the procedure known as autoreconfiguration. *See also: autoreconfiguration and beacon.*

fallback

In ATM networks, this mechanism is used for scouting a path if it isn't possible to locate one using customary methods. The device relaxes requirements for certain characteristics, such as delay, in an attempt to find a path that meets a certain set of the most important requirements.

Fast Ethernet

Any Ethernet specification with a speed of 100Mbps. Fast Ethernet is ten times faster than 10BaseT, while retaining qualities like MAC mechanisms, MTU, and frame format. These similarities make it possible for existing 10BaseT applications and management tools to be used on Fast Ethernet networks. Fast Ethernet is based on an extension of IEEE 802.3 specification (IEEE 802.3u). *Compare with: Ethernet. See also: 100BaseT, 100BaseTX, and IEEE.*

fast switching

A Cisco feature that uses a route cache to speed packet switching through a router. *Contrast with: process switching.*

FDM

Frequency-Division Multiplexing: A technique that permits information from several channels to be assigned bandwidth on one wire based on frequency. *See also: TDM, ATDM, and statistical multiplexing.*

FDDI

Fiber Distributed Data Interface: An LAN standard, defined by ANSI X3T9.5 that can run at speeds up to 200Mbps and uses token-passing media access on fiber-optic cable. For redundancy, FDDI can use a dual-ring architecture.

FECN

Forward Explicit Congestion Notification: A bit set by a Frame Relay network that informs the DTE receptor that congestion was encountered along the path from source to destination. A device receiving frames with the FECN bit set can ask higher-priority protocols to take flow-control action as needed. *See also: BECN.*

FEIP

Fast Ethernet Interface Processor: An interface processor employed on Cisco 7000 series routers, supporting up to two 100Mbps 100BaseT ports.

firewall

A barrier purposefully erected between any connected public networks and a private network, made up of a router or access server or several routers or access servers, that uses access lists and other methods to ensure the security of the private network.

flash memory

Developed by Intel and licensed to other semiconductor manufacturers, it is non-volatile storage that can be erased electronically and reprogrammed, physically located on an EEPROM chip. Flash memory permits software images to be stored, booted, and rewritten as needed. Cisco routers and switches use flash memory to hold the IOS by default. *See also: EPROM, EEPROM.*

flooding

When traffic is received on an interface, it is then transmitted to every interface connected to that device with exception of the interface from which the traffic originated. This technique can be used for traffic transfer by bridges and switches throughout the network.

flow control

A methodology used to ensure that receiving units are not overwhelmed with data from sending devices. Pacing, as it is called in IBM networks, means that when buffers at a receiving unit are full, a message is transmitted to the sending unit to temporarily halt transmissions until all the data in the receiving buffer has been processed and the buffer is again ready for action.

FRAD

Frame Relay Access Device: Any device affording a connection between a LAN and a Frame Relay WAN. *See also: Cisco FRAD, FRAS.*

fragment

Any portion of a larger packet that has been intentionally segmented into smaller pieces. A packet fragment does not necessarily indicate an error and can be intentional. *See also: fragmentation.*

fragmentation

The process of intentionally segmenting a packet into smaller pieces when sending data over an intermediate network medium that cannot support the larger packet size.

frame

A logical unit of information sent by the Data-Link layer over a transmission medium. The term often refers to the header and trailer, employed for synchronization and error control, that surround the data contained in the unit.

Frame Relay

A more efficient replacement of the X.25 protocol (an unrelated packet relay technology that guarantees data delivery). Frame Relay is an industry-standard, shared-access, best-effort, switched data-link layer encapsulation that services multiple virtual circuits and protocols between connected mechanisms

Frame Relay bridging

Defined in RFC 1490, this bridging method uses the identical spanning–tree algorithm as other bridging operations but permits packets to be encapsulated for transmission across a Frame Relay network.

FRAS

Frame Relay Access Support: A feature of Cisco IOS software that enables SDLC, Ethernet, Token Ring, and Frame Relay-attached IBM devices to be linked with other IBM mechanisms on a Frame Relay network. *See also: FRAD.*

frequency

The number of cycles of an alternating current signal per time unit, measured in hertz (cycles per second).

FSIP

Fast Serial Interface Processor: The Cisco 7000 routers' default serial interface processor, it provides four or eight high-speed serial ports.

FTP

File Transfer Protocol: The TCP/IP protocol used for transmitting files between network nodes, it supports a broad range of file types and is defined in RFC 959. *See also: TFTP.*

full duplex

The capacity to transmit information between a sending station and a receiving unit at the same time. *See also: half duplex.*

full mesh

A type of network topology where every node has either a physical or a virtual circuit linking it to every other network node. A full mesh supplies a great deal of redundancy but is typically reserved for network backbones because of its expense. *See also: partial mesh.*

G

GNS

Get Nearest Server: On an IPX network, a request packet sent by a customer for determining the location of the nearest active server of a given type. An IPX network client launches a GNS request to get either a direct answer from a connected server or a response from a router disclosing the location of the service on the internetwork to the GNS. GNS is part of IPX and SAP. *See also: IPX and SAP.*

GRE

Generic Routing Encapsulation: A tunneling protocol created by Cisco with the capacity for encapsulating a wide variety of protocol packet types inside IP tunnels, thereby generating a virtual point-to-point connection to Cisco routers across an IP network at remote points. IP tunneling using GRE permits network expansion across a single-protocol backbone environment by linking multiprotocol subnetworks in a single-protocol backbone environment.

guard band

The unused frequency area found between two communications channels, furnishing the space necessary to avoid interference between the two.

H

half duplex

The capacity to transfer data in only one direction at a time between a sending unit and receiving unit. *See also: full duplex.*

handshake

Any series of transmissions exchanged between two or more devices on a network to ensure synchronized operations.

H channel

High-speed channel: A full-duplex, ISDN primary rate channel operating at a speed of 384Kbps. *See also: B, D, and E channels.*

HDLC

High-level Data Link Control: Using frame characters, including checksums, HDLC designates a method for data encapsulation on synchronous serial links and is the default encapsulation for Cisco routers. HDLC is a bit-oriented synchronous data-link layer protocol created by ISO and derived from SDLC. However, most HDLC vendor implementations (including Cisco's) are proprietary. *See also: SDLC.*

helper address

The unicast address specified, which instructs the Cisco router to change the client's local broadcast request for a service into a directed unicast to the server.

hierarchical addressing

Any addressing plan employing a logical chain of commands to determine location. IP addresses are made up of a hierarchy of network numbers, subnet numbers, and host numbers to direct packets to the appropriate destination.

HIP

HSSI Interface Processor: An interface processor used on Cisco 7000 series routers, providing one HSSI port that supports connections to ATM, SMDS, Frame Relay, or private lines at speeds up to T3 or E3.

holddown

The state a route is placed in so that routers can neither advertise the route nor accept advertisements about it for a defined time period. Holddown is used to surface bad information about a route from all routers in the network. A route is generally placed in holddown when one of its links fails.

hop

The movement of a packet between any two network nodes. *See also: hop count.*

hop count

A routing metric that calculates the distance between a source and a destination. RIP employs hop count as its sole metric. *See also: hop and RIP.*

HSCI

High-Speed Communication Interface: Developed by Cisco, a single-port interface that provides full-duplex synchronous serial communications capability at speeds up to 52Mbps.

HSRP

Hot Standby Router Protocol: A protocol that provides high network availability and provides nearly instantaneous hardware fail-over without administrator intervention. It generates a Hot Standby router group, including a lead router that lends its services to any packet being transferred to the Hot Standby address. If the lead router fails, it will be replaced by any of the other routers—the standby routers— that monitor it.

HSSI

High-Speed Serial Interface: A network standard physical connector for high-speed serial linking over a WAN at speeds of up to 52Mbps.

I

ICD

International Code Designator: Adapted from the subnetwork model of addressing, this assigns the mapping of Network layer addresses to ATM addresses. HSSI is one of two ATM formats for addressing created by the ATM Forum to be utilized with private networks. *See also: DCC.*

ICMP

Internet Control Message Protocol: Documented in RFC 792, it is a Network layer Internet protocol for the purpose of reporting errors and providing information pertinent to IP packet procedures.

IEEE

Institute of Electrical and Electronics Engineers: A professional organization that, among other activities, defines standards in a number of fields within computing and electronics, including networking and communications. IEEE standards are the predominant LAN standards used today throughout the industry. Many protocols are commonly known by the reference number of the corresponding IEEE standard.

IEEE 802.1

The IEEE committee specification that defines the bridging group. The specification for STP (Spanning Tree protocol) is IEEE 802.1d. The STP uses SPA (spanning-tree algorithm) to find and prevent network loops in bridged networks. The specification for VLAN trunking is IEEE 802.1q. *Compare to: ISL.*

IEEE 802.3

The IEEE committee specification that defines the Ethernet group, specifically the original 10Mbps standard. Ethernet is a LAN protocol that specifies Physical layer and MAC sublayer media access. IEEE 802.3 uses CSMA/CD to provide access for many devices on the same network. FastEthernet is defined as 802.3u, and Gigabit Ethernet is defined as 802.3q. *See also: CSMA/CD.*

IEEE 802.5

IEEE committee that defines Token Ring media access.

IGMP

Internet Group Management Protocol: Employed by IP hosts, the protocol that reports their multicast group memberships to an adjacent multicast router.

IGP

Interior Gateway Protocol: Any protocol used by the Internet to exchange routing data within an independent system. Examples include RIP, IGRP, and OSPF.

ILMI

Integrated (or Interim) Local Management Interface. A specification created by the ATM Forum, designated for the incorporation of network-management capability into the ATM UNI. Integrated Local Management Interface cells provide for automatic configuration between ATM systems. In LAN emulation, ILMI can provide sufficient information for the ATM end station to find an LECS. In addition, ILMI provides the ATM NSAP (Network Service Access Point) prefix information to the end station.

in-band management

In-band management is the management of a network device "through" the network. Examples include using Simple Network Management Protocol (SNMP) or Telnet directly via the local LAN. *Compare with: out-of-band management.*

insured burst

In an ATM network, it is the largest, temporarily permitted data burst exceeding the insured rate on a PVC and not tagged by the traffic policing function for being dropped if network congestion occurs. This insured burst is designated in bytes or cells.

interarea routing

Routing between two or more logical areas. Contrast with: intra-area routing. *See also: area.*

interface processor

Any of several processor modules used with Cisco 7000 series routers. *See also: AIP, CIP, EIP, FEIP, HIP, MIP, and TRIP.*

Internet

The global "network of networks," whose popularity has exploded in the last few years. Originally a tool for collaborative academic research, it has become a medium for exchanging and distributing information of all kinds. The Internet's need to link disparate computer platforms and technologies has led to the development of uniform protocols and standards that have also found widespread use within corporate LANs. *See also: TCP/IP and MBONE.*

internet

Before the rise of the Internet, this lowercase form was shorthand for "internetwork" in the generic sense. Now rarely used. *See also: internetwork.*

Internet protocol

Any protocol belonging to the TCP/IP protocol stack. *See also: TCP/IP.*

internetwork

Any group of private networks interconnected by routers and other mechanisms, typically operating as a single entity.

internetworking

Broadly, anything associated with the general task of linking networks to each other. The term encompasses technologies, procedures, and products. When you connect networks to a router, you are creating an internetwork.

intra-area routing

Routing that occurs within a logical area. *Contrast with: interarea routing.*

Inverse ARP

Inverse Address Resolution Protocol: A technique by which dynamic mappings are constructed in a network, allowing a device such as a router to locate the logical network address and associate it with a permanent virtual circuit (PVC). Commonly used in Frame Relay to determine the far-end node's TCP/IP address by sending the Inverse ARP request to the local DLCI.

IP

Internet Protocol: Defined in RFC 791, it is a Network layer protocol that is part of the TCP/IP stack and allows connectionless service. IP furnishes an array of features for addressing, type-of-service specification, fragmentation and reassembly, and security.

IP address

Often called an Internet address, this is an address uniquely identifying any device (host) on the Internet (or any TCP/IP network). Each address consists of four octets (32 bits), represented as decimal numbers separated by periods (a format known as "dotted-decimal"). Every address is made up of a network number, an optional sub-network number, and a host number. The network and subnetwork numbers together are used for routing, while the host number addresses an individual host within the network or subnetwork. The network and subnetwork information is extracted from the IP address using the subnet mask. There are five classes of IP addresses (A–E), which allocate different numbers of bits to the network, subnetwork, and host portions of the address. *See also: CIDR, IP, and subnet mask.*

IPCP

IP Control Program: The protocol used to establish and configure IP over PPP. *See also: IP and PPP.*

IP multicast

A technique for routing that enables IP traffic to be reproduced from one source to several endpoints or from multiple sources to many destinations. Instead of transmitting only one packet to each individual point of destination, one packet is sent to a multicast group specified by only one IP endpoint address for the group.

IPX

Internetwork Packet Exchange: Network layer protocol (Layer 3) used in Novell NetWare networks for transferring information from servers to workstations. Similar to IP and XNS.

IPXCP

IPX Control Program: The protocol used to establish and configure IPX over PPP. *See also: IPX and PPP.*

IPXWAN

Protocol used for new WAN links to provide and negotiate line options on the link using IPX. After the link is up and the options have been agreed upon by the two end-to-end links, normal IPX transmission begins.

ISDN

Integrated Services Digital Network: Offered as a service by telephone companies, a communication protocol that allows telephone networks to carry data, voice, and other digital traffic. *See also: BISDN, BRI, and PRI.*

isochronous transmission

Asynchronous data transfer over a synchronous Data-Link, requiring a constant bit rate for reliable transport. *Compare with: asynchronous transmission and synchronous transmission.*

ITU-T

International Telecommunication Union Telecommunication Standardization Sector: This is a group of engineers that develops worldwide standards for telecommunications technologies.

L

LAN

Local Area Network: Broadly, any network linking two or more computers and related devices within a limited geographical area (up to a few kilometers). LANs are typically high-speed, low-error networks within a company. Cabling and signaling at the physical and Data-Link layers of the OSI are dictated by LAN standards. Ethernet, FDDI, and Token Ring are among the most popular LAN technologies. *Compare with: MAN and WAN.*

LANE

LAN emulation: The technology that allows an ATM network to operate as a LAN backbone. To do so, the ATM network is required to provide multicast and broadcast support, address mapping (MAC-to-ATM), SVC management, in addition to an operable packet format. Additionally, LANE defines Ethernet and Token Ring ELANs. *See also: ELAN.*

LAN switch

A high-speed, multiple-interface transparent bridging mechanism, transmitting packets between segments of data links, usually referred to specifically as an Ethernet switch. LAN switches transfer traffic based on MAC addresses. Multilayer switches are a type of high-speed, special-purpose, hardware-based router. *See also: multilayer switch, cut-through packet switching, and store-and-forward packet switching.*

LAPB

Link Accessed Procedure, Balanced: A bit-oriented data-link layer protocol that is part of the X.25 stack and has its origin in SDLC. *See also: SDLC and X.25.*

LAPD

Link Access Procedure on the D channel. The ISDN data-link layer protocol used specifically for the D channel and defined by ITU-T Recommendations Q.920 and Q.921. LAPD evolved from LAPB and is created to comply with the signaling requirements of ISDN basic access.

latency

Broadly, the time it takes a data packet to get from one location to another. In specific networking contexts, it can mean either 1) the time elapsed (delay) between the execution of a request for access to a network by a device and the time the mechanism actually is permitted transmission, or 2) the time elapsed between when a mechanism receives a frame and the time that frame is forwarded out of the destination port.

Layer-3 switch

See also: multilayer switch.

LCP

Link Control Protocol: The protocol designed to establish, configure, and test data link connections for use by PPP. *See also: PPP.*

leaky bucket

An analogy for the basic cell rate algorithm (GCRA) used in ATM networks for checking the conformance of cell flows from a user or network. The bucket's "hole" is understood to be the prolonged rate at which cells can be accommodated, and the "depth" is the tolerance for cell bursts over a certain time period. *See also: GCRA.*

learning bridge

A bridge that transparently builds a dynamic database of MAC addresses and the interfaces associated with each address. Transparent bridges help to reduce traffic congestion on the network.

LE ARP

LAN Emulation Address Resolution Protocol: The protocol providing the ATM address that corresponds to a MAC address.

LEC

LAN Emulation Client: Software providing the emulation of the link layer interface that allows the operation and communication of all higher-level protocols and applications to continue. The LEC client runs in all ATM devices, which include hosts, servers, bridges, and routers. The LANE client is responsible for address resolution, data transfer, address caching, interfacing to the emulated LAN, and driver support for higher-level services. *See also: ELAN and LES.*

LECS

LAN Emulation Configuration Server: An important part of emulated LAN services, providing the configuration data that is furnished upon request from the LES. These services include address registration for Integrated Local Management Interface (ILMI) support, configuration support for the LES addresses and their corresponding emulated LAN identifiers, and an interface to the emulated LAN. *See also: LES and ELAN.*

LES

LAN Emulation Server: The central LANE component that provides the initial configuration data for each connecting LEC. The LES typically is located on either an ATM-integrated router or a switch. Responsibilities of the LES include configuration and support for the LEC, address registration for the LEC, database storage and response concerning ATM addresses, and interfacing to the emulated LAN *See also: ELAN, LEC, and LECS.*

link state routing algorithm

A routing algorithm that allows each router to broadcast or multicast information regarding the cost of reaching all its neighbors to every node in the internetwork. Link state algorithms provide a consistent view of the network and are therefore not vulnerable to routing loops. However, this is achieved at the cost of somewhat greater difficulty in computation and more widespread traffic (compared with distance vector routing algorithms). *See also: distance vector routing algorithm.*

LLAP

LocalTalk Link Access Protocol: In a LocalTalk environment, the data link-level protocol that manages node-to-node delivery of data. This protocol provides node addressing and management of bus access, and it also controls data sending and receiving to assure packet length and integrity.

LLC

Logical Link Control: Defined by the IEEE, the higher of two data-link layer sublayers. LLC is responsible for error detection (but not correction), flow control, framing, and software-sublayer addressing. The predominant LLC protocol, IEEE 802.2, defines both connectionless and connection-oriented operations. *See also: Data-Link layer and MAC.*

LMI

An enhancement to the original Frame Relay specification. Among the features it provides are a keepalive mechanism, a multicast mechanism, global addressing, and a status mechanism.

LNNI

LAN Emulation Network-to-Network Interface: In the Phase 2 LANE specification, an interface that supports communication between the server components within one ELAN.

local explorer packet

In a Token Ring SRB network, a packet generated by an end system to find a host linked to the local ring. If no local host can be found, the end system will produce one of two solutions: a spanning explorer packet or an all-routes explorer packet.

LocalTalk

Utilizing CSMA/CD, in addition to supporting data transmission at speeds of 230.4Kbps, LocalTalk is Apple Computer's proprietary baseband protocol, operating at the data link and Physical layers of the OSI reference model.

LSA

link state advertisement: Contained inside of link state packets (LSPs), these advertisements are usually multicast packets, containing information about neighbors and path costs, that are employed by link state protocols. Receiving routers use LSAs to maintain their link state databases and, ultimately, routing tables.

LUNI

LAN Emulation User-to-Network Interface: Defining the interface between the LAN Emulation Client (LEC) and the LAN Emulation Server, LUNI is the ATM Forum's standard for LAN Emulation on ATM networks. *See also: LES and LECS.*

M

MAC

media access control: The lower sublayer in the Data-Link layer, it is responsible for hardware addressing, media access, and error detection of frames. *See also: Data-Link layer and LLC.*

MAC address

A data-link layer hardware address that every port or device needs in order to connect to a LAN segment. These addresses are used by various devices in the network for accurate location of logical addresses. MAC addresses are defined by the IEEE standard and their length is six characters, typically using the burned-in address (BIA) of the local LAN interface. Variously called hardware address, physical address, burned-in address, or MAC layer address.

MacIP

In AppleTalk, the Network layer protocol encapsulating IP packets in Datagram Delivery Protocol (DDP) packets. MacIP also supplies substitute ARP services.

MAN

Metropolitan-Area Network: Any network that encompasses a metropolitan area; that is, an area typically larger than a LAN but smaller than a WAN. *See also: LAN and WAN.*

Manchester encoding

A method for digital coding in which a mid-bit–time transition is employed for clocking, and a 1 (one) is denoted by a high voltage level during the first half of the bit time. This scheme is used by Ethernet and IEEE 802.3.

maximum burst

Specified in bytes or cells, the largest burst of information exceeding the insured rate that will be permitted on an ATM permanent virtual connection for a short time and will not be dropped even if it goes over the specified maximum rate. *Compare with: insured burst. See also: maximum rate.*

maximum rate

The maximum permitted data throughput on a particular virtual circuit, equal to the total of insured and uninsured traffic from the traffic source. Should traffic congestion occur, uninsured information may be deleted from the path. Measured in bits or cells per second, the maximum rate represents the highest throughput of data the virtual circuit is ever able to deliver and cannot exceed the media rate. *Compare with: excess rate. See also: maximum burst.*

MBS

Maximum Burst Size: In an ATM signaling message, this metric, coded as a number of cells, is used to convey the burst tolerance.

MBONE

multicast backbone: The multicast backbone of the Internet, it is a virtual multicast network made up of multicast LANs, including point-to-point tunnels interconnecting them.

MCDV

Maximum Cell Delay Variation: The maximum two-point CDV objective across a link or node for the identified service category in an ATM network. The MCDV is one of four link metrics that are exchanged using PTSPs to verify the available resources of an ATM network. Only one MCDV value is assigned to each traffic class.

MCLR

Maximum Cell Loss Ratio: The maximum ratio of cells in an ATM network that fail to transit a link or node compared with the total number of cells that arrive at the link or node. MCDV is one of four link metrics that are exchanged using PTSPs to verify the available resources of an ATM network. The MCLR applies to cells in VBR and CBR traffic classes whose CLP bit is set to zero. *See also: CBR, CLP, and VBR.*

MCR

Minimum Cell Rate: A parameter determined by the ATM Forum for traffic management of the ATM networks. MCR is specifically defined for ABR transmissions and specifies the minimum value for the allowed cell rate (ACR). *See also: ACR and PCR.*

MCTD

Maximum Cell Transfer Delay: In an ATM network, the total of the maximum cell delay variation and the fixed delay across the link or node. MCTD is one of four link metrics that are exchanged using PNNI topology state packets to verify the available resources of an ATM network. There is one MCTD value assigned to each traffic class. *See also: MCDV.*

MIB

management information base: Used with SNMP management software to gather information from remote devices. The management station can poll the remote device for information, or the MIB running on the remote station can be programmed to send information on a regular basis.

MIP

Multichannel Interface Processor: The resident interface processor on Cisco 7000 series routers, providing up to two channelized T1 or E1 connections by serial cables connected to a CSU. The two controllers are capable of providing 24 T1 or 30 E1 channel groups, with each group being introduced to the system as a serial interface that can be configured individually.

mips

millions of instructions per second: A measure of processor speed.

MLP

Multilink PPP: A technique used to split, recombine, and sequence datagrams across numerous logical data links.

MMP

Multichassis Multilink PPP: A protocol that supplies MLP support across multiple routers and access servers. MMP enables several routers and access servers to work as a single, large dial-up pool with one network address and ISDN access number. MMP successfully supports packet fragmenting and reassembly when the user connection is split between two physical access devices.

modem

modulator-demodulator: A device that converts digital signals to analog and vice-versa so that digital information can be transmitted over analog communication facilities, such as voice-grade telephone lines. This is achieved by converting digital signals at the source to analog for transmission and reconverting the analog signals back into digital form at the destination. *See also: modulation and demodulation.*

modem eliminator

A mechanism that makes possible a connection between two DTE devices without modems by simulating the commands and physical signaling required.

modulation

The process of modifying some characteristic of an electrical signal, such as amplitude (AM) or frequency (FM), in order to represent digital or analog information. *See also: AM.*

MOSPF

Multicast OSPF: An extension of the OSPF unicast protocol that enables IP multicast routing within the domain. *See also: OSPF.*

MPOA

Multiprotocol over ATM: An effort by the ATM Forum to standardize how existing and future network-layer protocols such as IP, Ipv6, AppleTalk, and IPX run over an ATM network with directly attached hosts, routers, and multilayer LAN switches.

MTU

maximum transmission unit: The largest packet size, measured in bytes, that an interface can handle.

multicast

Broadly, any communication between a single sender and multiple receivers. Unlike broadcast messages, which are sent to all addresses on a network, multicast messages are sent to a defined subset of the network addresses; this subset has a group multicast address, which is specified in the packet's destination address field. *See also: broadcast, directed broadcast.*

multicast address

A single address that points to more than one device on the network by specifying a special non-existent MAC address specified in that particular multicast protocol. Identical to group address. *See also: multicast.*

multicast send VCC

A two-directional point-to-point virtual control connection (VCC) arranged by an LEC to a BUS, it is one of the three types of informational link specified by phase 1 LANE. *See also: control distribute VCC and control direct VCC.*

multilayer switch

A highly specialized, high-speed, hardware-based type of LAN router, the device filters and forwards packets based on their Layer 2 MAC addresses and Layer 3 network addresses. It's possible that even Layer 4 can be read. *Sometimes called a Layer 3 switch. See also: LAN switch.*

multiplexing

The process of converting several logical signals into a single physical signal for transmission across one physical channel. *Contrast with: demultiplexing.*

N

NAK

negative acknowledgment: A response sent from a receiver, telling the sender that the information was not received or contained errors. *Compare with: acknowledgment.*

NAT

network address translation: An algorithm instrumental in minimizing the requirement for globally unique IP addresses, permitting an organization whose addresses are not all globally unique to connect to the Internet, regardless, by translating those addresses into globally routable address space.

NBP

Name Binding Protocol: In AppleTalk, the transport-level protocol that interprets a socket client's name, entered as a character string, into the corresponding DDP address. NBP gives AppleTalk protocols the capacity to discern user-defined zones and names of mechanisms by showing and keeping translation tables that map names to their corresponding socket addresses.

neighboring routers

Two routers in OSPF that have interfaces to a common network. On networks with multiaccess, these neighboring routers are dynamically discovered using the Hello protocol of OSPF.

NetBEUI

NetBIOS Extended User Interface: An improved version of the NetBIOS protocol used in a number of network operating systems including LAN Manager, Windows NT, LAN Server, and Windows for Workgroups, implementing the OSI LLC2 protocol. NetBEUI formalizes the transport frame not standardized in NetBIOS and adds more functions. *See also: OSI.*

NetBIOS

Network Basic Input/Output System: The API employed by applications residing on an IBM LAN to ask for services, such as session termination or information transfer, from lower-level network processes.

NetView

A mainframe network product from IBM, used for monitoring SNA (Systems Network Architecture) networks. It runs as a VTAM (Virtual Telecommunications Access Method) application.

NetWare

A widely used NOS created by Novell, providing a number of distributed network services and remote file access.

Network layer

In the OSI reference model, it is Layer 3—the layer in which routing is implemented, enabling connections and path selection between two end systems. *See also: Application layer, Data-Link layer, Physical layer, Presentation layer, Session layer, and Transport layer.*

NFS

Network File System: One of the protocols in Sun Microsystems' widely used file system protocol suite, allowing remote file access across a network. The name is loosely used to refer to the entire Sun protocol suite, which also includes RPC, XDR (External Data Representation), and other protocols.

NHRP

Next Hop Resolution Protocol: In a nonbroadcast multiaccess (NBMA) network, the protocol employed by routers in order to dynamically locate MAC addresses of various hosts and routers. It enables systems to communicate directly without requiring an intermediate hop, thus facilitating increased performance in ATM, Frame Relay, X.25, and SMDS systems.

NHS

Next Hop Server: Defined by the NHRP protocol, this server maintains the next-hop resolution cache tables, listing IP-to-ATM address maps of related nodes and nodes that can be reached through routers served by the NHS.

NIC

network interface card: An electronic circuit board placed in a computer. The NIC provides network communication to a LAN.

NLSP

NetWare Link Services Protocol: Novell's link state routing protocol, based on the IS-IS model.

NMP

Network Management Processor: A Catalyst 5000 switch processor module used to control and monitor the switch.

non-stub area

In OSPF, a resource-consuming area carrying a default route, intra-area routes, inter-area routes, static routes, and external routes. Non-stub areas are the only areas that can have virtual links configured across them and exclusively contain an anonymous system boundary router (ASBR). *Compare with: stub area. See also: ASBR and OSPF.*

NRZ

Nonreturn to Zero: One of several encoding schemes for transmitting digital data. NRZ signals sustain constant levels of voltage with no signal shifting (no return to zero-voltage level) during a bit interval. If there is a series of bits with the same value (1 or 0), there will be no state change. The signal is not self-clocking. *See also: NRZI.*

NRZI

Nonreturn to Zero Inverted: One of several encoding schemes for transmitting digital data. A transition in voltage level (either from high to low or vice-versa) at the beginning of a bit interval is interpreted as a value of 1; the absence of a transition is interpreted as a 0. Thus, the voltage assigned to each value is continually inverted. NRZI signals are not self-clocking. *See also: NRZ.*

NVRAM

Non-Volatile RAM: Random-access memory that keeps its contents intact while power is turned off.

O

OC

Optical Carrier: A series of physical protocols, designated as OC-1, OC-2, OC-3, and so on, for SONET optical signal transmissions. OC signal levels place STS frames on a multimode fiber-optic line at various speeds, of which 51.84Mbps is the lowest (OC-1). Each subsequent protocol runs at a speed divisible by 51.84. *See also: SONET.*

100BaseT

Based on the IEEE 802.3u standard, 100BaseT is the Fast Ethernet specification of 100Mbps baseband that uses UTP wiring. 100BaseT sends link pulses (containing more information than those used in 10BaseT) over the network when no traffic is present. *See also: 10BaseT, Fast Ethernet, and IEEE 802.3.*

100BaseTX

Based on the IEEE 802.3u standard, 100BaseTX is the 100Mbps baseband Fast Ethernet specification that uses two pairs of UTP or STP wiring. The first pair of wires receives data; the second pair sends data. To ensure correct signal timing, a 100BaseTX segment cannot be longer than 100 meters.

ones density

Also known as pulse density, this is a method of signal clocking. The CSU/DSU retrieves the clocking information from data that passes through it. For this scheme to work, the data needs to be encoded to contain at least one binary 1 for each eight bits transmitted. *See also CSU and DSU.*

OSI

Open System Interconnection: International standardization program designed by ISO and ITU-T for the development of data networking standards that make multi-vendor equipment interoperability a reality.

OSI reference model

Open System Interconnection reference model: A conceptual model defined by the International Organization for Standardization (ISO), describing how any combination of devices can be connected for the purpose of communication. The OSI model divides the task into seven functional layers, forming a hierarchy with the applications at the top and the physical medium at the bottom, and it defines the functions each layer must provide. *See also: Application layer, Data-Link layer, Network layer, Physical layer, Presentation layer, Session layer, and Transport layer.*

OSPF

Open Shortest Path First: A link state, hierarchical IGP routing algorithm derived from an earlier version of the IS-IS protocol, whose features include multipath routing, load balancing, and least-cost routing. OSPF is the suggested successor to RIP in the Internet environment. *See also: enhanced IGRP, IGP, and IP.*

out-of-band management

Management "outside" of the network's physical channels. For example, using a console connection not directly interfaced through the local LAN or WAN or a dial-in modem. *Compare to: in-band management.*

out-of-band signaling

Within a network, any transmission that uses physical channels or frequencies separate from those ordinarily used for data transfer. For example, the initial configuration of a Cisco Catalyst switch requires an out-of-band connection via a console port.

P

packet

In data communications, the basic logical unit of information transferred. A packet consists of a certain number of data bytes, wrapped or encapsulated in headers and/or trailers that contain information about where the packet came from, where it's going, and so on. The various protocols involved in sending a transmission add their own layers of header information, which the corresponding protocols in receiving devices then interpret.

packet switch

A physical device that makes it possible for a communication channel to share several connections, its functions include finding the most efficient transmission path for packets.

packet switching

A networking technology based on the transmission of data in packets. Dividing a continuous stream of data into small units—packets—enables data from multiple devices on a network to share the same communication channel simultaneously but also requires the use of precise routing information. *Contrast with: circuit switching.*

PAP

Password Authentication Protocol: In Point-to-Point Protocol (PPP) networks, a method of validating connection requests. The requesting (remote) device must send an authentication request, containing a password and ID, to the local router when attempting to connect. Unlike the more secure CHAP (Challenge Handshake Authentication Protocol), PAP sends the password unencrypted and does not attempt to verify whether the user is authorized to access the requested resource; it merely identifies the remote end. *See also: CHAP.*

parity checking

A method of error-checking in data transmissions. An extra bit (the parity bit) is added to each character or data word so that the sum of the bits will be either an odd number (in odd parity) or an even number (even parity).

partial mesh

A type of network topology in which some network nodes form a full mesh (where every node has either a physical or a virtual circuit linking it to every other network node), but others are attached to only one or two nodes in the network. A typical use of partial-mesh topology is in peripheral networks linked to a fully meshed backbone. *See also: full mesh.*

PCR

Peak Cell Rate: As defined by the ATM Forum, the parameter specifying, in cells per second, the maximum rate at which a source may transmit.

PDN

Public Data Network: Generally for a fee, a PDN offers the public access to computer communication network operated by private concerns or government agencies. Small organizations can take advantage of PDNs, aiding them creating WANs without investing in long-distance equipment and circuitry.

PGP

Pretty Good Privacy: A popular public-key/private-key encryption application offering protected transfer of files and messages.

Physical layer

The lowest layer—Layer 1—in the OSI reference model, it is responsible for converting data packets from the Data-Link layer (Layer 2) into electrical signals. Physical-layer protocols and standards define, for example, the type of cable and connectors to be used, including their pin assignments and the encoding scheme for signaling 0 and 1 values. *See also: Application layer, Data-Link layer, Network layer, Presentation layer, Session layer, and Transport layer.*

Ping

packet Internet groper: A Unix-based Internet diagnostic tool, consisting of a message sent to test the accessibility of a particular device on the IP network. The acronym (from which the "full name" was formed) reflects the underlying metaphor of submarine sonar. Just as the sonar operator sends out a signal and waits to hear it echo ("ping") back from a submerged object, the network user can ping another node on the network and wait to see if it responds.

pleisochronous

Nearly synchronous, except that clocking comes from an outside source instead of being embedded within the signal as in synchronous transmissions.

PLP

Packet Level Protocol: Occasionally called X.25 Level 3 or X.25 Protocol, a network-layer protocol that is part of the X.25 stack.

PNNI

Private Network-Network Interface: An ATM Forum specification for offering topology data used for the calculation of paths through the network, among switches and groups of switches. It is based on well known link state routing procedures and allows for automatic configuration in networks whose addressing scheme is determined by the topology.

point-to-multipoint connection

In ATM, a communication path going only one way, connecting a single system at the starting point, called the "root node," to systems at multiple points of destination, called "leaves." *See also: point-to-point connection.*

point-to-point connection

In ATM, a channel of communication that can be directed either one way or two ways between two ATM end systems. *See also: point-to-multipoint connection.*

poison reverse updates

These update messages are transmitted by a router back to the originator (thus ignoring the split-horizon rule) after route poisoning has occurred. Typically used with DV routing protocols in order to overcome large routing loops and offer explicit information when a subnet or network is not accessible (instead of merely suggesting that the network is unreachable by not including it in updates). *See also: route poisoning.*

polling

The procedure of orderly inquiry, used by a primary network mechanism, to determine if secondary devices have data to transmit. A message is sent to each secondary, granting the secondary the right to transmit.

POP

1. Point Of Presence: The physical location where an interexchange carrier has placed equipment to interconnect with a local exchange carrier.
2. Post Office Protocol (currently at version 3): A protocol used by client e-mail applications for recovery of mail from a mail server.

PPP

Point-to-Point Protocol: The protocol most commonly used for dial-up Internet access, superseding the earlier SLIP. Its features include address notification, authentication via CHAP or PAP, support for multiple protocols, and link monitoring. PPP has two layers: the Link Control Protocol (LCP) establishes, configures, and tests a link; and then any of various Network Control Programs (NCPs) transport traffic for a specific protocol suite, such as IPX. *See also: CHAP, PAP, and SLIP.*

Presentation layer

Layer 6 of the OSI reference model, it defines how data is formatted, presented, encoded, and converted for use by software at the Application layer. *See also: Application layer, Data-Link layer, Network layer, Physical layer, Session layer, and Transport layer.*

PRI

Primary Rate Interface: A type of ISDN connection between a PBX and a long-distance carrier, which is made up of a single 64Kbps D channel in addition to 23 (T1) or 30 (E1) B channels. *See also: ISDN.*

priority queuing

A routing function in which frames temporarily placed in an interface output queue are assigned priorities based on traits such as packet size or type of interface.

process switching

As a packet arrives on a router to be forwarded, it's copied to the router's process buffer, and the router performs a lookup on the Layer 3 address. Using the route table, an exit interface is associated with the destination address. The processor forwards the packet with the added new information to the exit interface, while the router initializes the fast-switching cache. Subsequent packets bound for the same destination address follow the same path as the first packet.

PROM

programmable read-only memory: ROM that is programmable only once, using special equipment. *Compare with: EPROM.*

propagation delay

The time it takes data to traverse a network from its source to its destination.

protocol

In networking, the specification of a set of rules for a particular type of communication. The term is also used to refer to the software that implements a protocol.

protocol stack

A collection of related protocols.

PSE

Packet Switch Exchange: The X.25 term for a switch.

PSN

packet-switched network: Any network that uses packet-switching technology. Also known as packet-switched data network (PSDN). *See also: packet switching.*

PSTN

Public Switched Telephone Network: Colloquially referred to as "plain old telephone service" (POTS). A term that describes the assortment of telephone networks and services available globally.

PVC

permanent virtual circuit: In a Frame-Relay network, a logical connection, defined in software, that is maintained permanently. *Compare with: SVC. See also: virtual circuit.*

PVP

permanent virtual path: A virtual path made up of PVCs. *See also: PVC.*

PVP tunneling

permanent virtual path tunneling: A technique that links two private ATM networks across a public network using a virtual path; wherein the public network transparently trunks the complete collection of virtual channels in the virtual path between the two private networks.

Q

QoS

Quality of Service: A set of metrics used to measure the quality of transmission and service availability of any given transmission system.

queue

Broadly, any list of elements arranged in an orderly fashion and ready for processing, such as a line of people waiting to enter a movie theater. In routing, it refers to a backlog of information packets waiting in line to be transmitted over a router interface.

R

RARP

Reverse Address Resolution Protocol: The protocol within the TCP/IP stack that maps MAC addresses to IP addresses. *See also: ARP.*

rate queue

A value, assigned to one or more virtual circuits, that specifies the speed at which an individual virtual circuit will transmit data to the remote end. Every rate queue identifies a segment of the total bandwidth available on an ATM link. The sum of all rate queues should not exceed the total available bandwidth.

RCP

Remote Copy Protocol: A protocol for copying files to or from a file system that resides on a remote server on a network, using TCP to guarantee reliable data delivery.

redistribution

Command used in Cisco routers to inject the paths found from one type of routing protocol into another type of routing protocol. For example, networks found by RIP can be inserted into an IGRP network.

redundancy

In internetworking, the duplication of connections, devices, or services that can be used as a backup in the event that the primary connections, devices, or services fail.

reload

An event or command that causes Cisco routers to reboot.

RIF

Routing Information Field: In source-route bridging, a header field that defines the path direction of the frame or token. If the Route Information Indicator (RII) bit is not set, the RIF is read from source to destination (left to right). If the RII bit is set, the RIF is read from the destination back to the source, so the RIF is read right to left. It is defined as part of the Token Ring frame header for source-routed frames, which contains path information.

ring

Two or more stations connected in a logical circular topology. In this topology, which is the basis for Token Ring, FDDI, and CDDI, information is transferred from station to station in sequence.

ring topology

A network logical topology comprising a series of repeaters that form one closed loop by connecting unidirectional transmission links. Individual stations on the network are connected to the network at a repeater. Physically, ring topologies are generally organized in a closed-loop star. *Compare with: bus topology and star topology.*

RIP

Routing Information Protocol: The most commonly used interior gateway protocol in the Internet. RIP employs hop count as a routing metric. *See also: Enhanced IGRP, IGP, OSPF, and hop count.*

routed protocol

Routed protocols (such as IP and IPX) are used to transmit user data through an internetwork. By contrast, routing protocols (such as RIP, IGRP, and OSPF) are used to update routing tables between routers.

route poisoning

Used by various DV routing protocols in order to overcome large routing loops and offer explicit information about when a subnet or network is not accessible (instead of merely suggesting that the network is unreachable by not including it in updates). Typically, this is accomplished by setting the hop count to one more than maximum. *See also: poison reverse.*

route summarization

In various routing protocols, such as OSPF, EIGRP, and IS-IS, the consolidation of publicized subnetwork addresses so that a single summary route is advertised to other areas by an area border router.

router

A network-layer mechanism, either software or hardware, using one or more metrics to decide on the best path to use for transmission of network traffic. Sending packets between networks by routers is based on the information provided on Network layers. Historically, this device has sometimes been called a gateway.

routing

The process of forwarding logically addressed packets from their local subnetwork toward their ultimate destination. In large networks, the numerous intermediary destinations a packet might travel before reaching its destination can make routing very complex.

routing domain

Any collection of end systems and intermediate systems that operate under an identical set of administrative rules. Every routing domain contains one or several areas, all individually given a certain area address.

routing metric

Any value that is used by routing algorithms to determine whether one route is superior to another. Metrics include such information as bandwidth, delay, hop count, path cost, load, MTU, reliability, and communication cost. Only the best possible routes are stored in the routing table, while all other information may be stored in link state or topological databases. *See also: cost.*

routing protocol

Any protocol that defines algorithms to be used for updating routing tables between routers. Examples include IGRP, RIP, and OSPF.

routing table

A table kept in a router or other internetworking mechanism that maintains a record of only the best possible routes to certain network destinations and the metrics associated with those routes.

RP

Route Processor: Also known as a supervisory processor, a module on Cisco 7000 series routers that holds the CPU, system software, and most of the memory components used in the router.

RSP

Route/Switch Processor: A processor module combining the functions of RP and SP used in Cisco 7500 series routers. *See also: RP and SP.*

RTS

Request To Send: An EIA/TIA-232 control signal requesting permission to transmit data on a communication line.

S

sampling rate

The rate at which samples of a specific waveform amplitude are collected within a specified period of time.

SAP

Way to inform network clients of resources and services availability on network, using routers and servers. See also: IPX.

SCR

Sustainable Cell Rate: An ATM Forum parameter used for traffic management, it is the long-term average cell rate for VBR connections that can be transmitted.

SDLC

Synchronous Data Link Control: A protocol used in SNA data-link layer communications. SDLC is a bit-oriented, full-duplex serial protocol that is the basis for several similar protocols, including HDLC and LAPB. *See also: HDLC and LAPB.*

seed router

In an AppleTalk network, the router that is equipped with the network number or cable range in its port descriptor. The seed router specifies the network number or cable range for other routers in that network section and answers to configuration requests from nonseed routers on its connected AppleTalk network, permitting those routers to affirm or modify their configurations accordingly. Every AppleTalk network needs at least one seed router physically connected to each network segment.

server

Hardware and software that provide network services to clients.

Session layer

Layer 5 of the OSI reference model, responsible for creating, managing, and terminating sessions between applications and overseeing data exchange between Presentation layer entities. *See also: Application layer, Data-Link layer, Network layer, Physical layer, Presentation layer, and Transport layer.*

SF

super frame: A super frame (also called a D4 frame) consists of 12 frames with 192 bits each, and the 193rd bit providing other functions including error checking. SF is frequently used on T1 circuits. A newer version of the technology is Extended Super Frame (ESF), which uses 24 frames. *See also: ESF.*

signaling packet

An informational packet created by an ATM-connected mechanism that wants to establish connection with another such mechanism. The packet contains the QoS parameters needed for connection and the ATM NSAP address of the endpoint. The endpoint responds with a message of acceptance if it is able to support the desired QoS, and the connection is established. *See also: QoS.*

silicon switching

A type of high-speed switching used in Cisco 7000 series routers, based on the use of a separate processor (the Silicon Switch Processor, or SSP). *See also: SSE.*

sliding window

The method of flow control used by TCP, as well as several data-link layer protocols. This method places a buffer between the receiving application and the network data flow. The "window" available for accepting data is the size of the buffer minus the amount of data already there. This window increases in size as the application reads data from it and decreases as new data is sent. The receiver sends the transmitter announcements of the current window size, and it may stop accepting data until the window increases above a certain threshold.

SLIP

Serial Line Internet Protocol: An industry standard serial encapsulation for point-to-point connections that supports only a single routed protocol, TCP/IP. SLIP is the predecessor to PPP. *See also: PPP.*

SMDS

Switched Multimegabit Data Service: A packet-switched, datagram-based WAN networking technology offered by telephone companies that provides high speed.

SMTP

Simple Mail Transfer Protocol: A protocol used on the Internet to provide electronic mail services.

SNA

System Network Architecture: A complex, feature-rich, network architecture similar to the OSI reference model but with several variations; created by IBM in the 1970s and essentially composed of seven layers.

SNAP

Subnetwork Access Protocol: SNAP is a frame used in Ethernet, Token Ring, and FDDI LANs. Data transfer, connection management, and QoS selection are three primary functions executed by the SNAP frame.

socket

1. A software structure that operates within a network device as a destination point for communications.
2. In AppleTalk networks, an entity at a specific location within a node; AppleTalk sockets are conceptually similar to TCP/IP ports.

SONET

Synchronous Optical Network: The ANSI standard for synchronous transmission on fiber-optic media, developed at Bell Labs. It specifies a base signal rate of 51.84Mbps and a set of multiples of that rate, known as Optical Carrier levels, up to 2.5Gbps.

SP

Switch Processor: Also known as a CiscoBus controller, it is a Cisco 7000 series processor module acting as governing agent for all CxBus activities.

span

A full-duplex digital transmission line connecting two facilities.

SPAN

Switched Port Analyzer: A feature of the Catalyst 5000 switch, offering freedom to manipulate within a switched Ethernet environment by extending the monitoring ability of the existing network analyzers into the environment. At one switched segment, the SPAN mirrors traffic onto a predetermined SPAN port, while a network analyzer connected to the SPAN port is able to monitor traffic from any other Catalyst switched port.

spanning explorer packet

Sometimes called limited-route or single-route explorer packet, it pursues a statically configured spanning tree when searching for paths in a source-route bridging network. *See also: all-routes explorer packet, explorer packet, and local explorer packet.*

spanning tree

A subset of a network topology within which no loops exist. When bridges are interconnected into a loop, the bridge, or switch, cannot identify a frame that has been forwarded previously, so there is no mechanism for removing a frame as it passes the interface numerous times. Without a method of removing these frames, the bridges continuously forward them—consuming bandwidth and adding overhead to the network. Spanning trees prune the network to provide only one path for any packet. *See also: Spanning Tree protocol and spanning-tree algorithm.*

spanning-tree algorithm (STA)

An algorithm that creates a spanning tree using the Spanning Tree protocol (STP). *See also: spanning tree and Spanning Tree protocol.*

Spanning Tree protocol (STP)

The bridge protocol (IEEE 802.1d) that enables a learning bridge to dynamically avoid loops in the network topology by creating a spanning tree using the spanning-tree algorithm. Spanning-tree frames called bridge protocol data units (BPDUs) are sent and received by all switches in the network at regular intervals. The switches participating in the spanning tree don't forward the frames; instead, they're processed to determine the spanning-tree topology itself. Cisco Catalyst series switches use STP 802.1d to perform this function. *See also: BPDU, learning bridge, MAC address, spanning tree, and spanning-tree algorithm.*

SPF

Shortest Path First algorithm: A routing algorithm used to decide on the shortest-path spanning tree. Sometimes called Dijkstra's algorithm and frequently used in link state routing algorithms. *See also: link state routing algorithm.*

SPID

Service Profile Identifier: A number assigned by service providers or local telephone companies and assigned by administrators to a BRI port. SPIDs are used to determine subscription services of a device connected via ISDN. ISDN devices use SPID when accessing the telephone company switch that initializes the link to a service provider.

split horizon

Useful for preventing routing loops, a type of distance vector routing rule where information about routes is prevented from leaving the router interface through which that information was received.

spoofing

1. In dial-on-demand routing (DDR), where a circuit-switched link is taken down to save toll charges when there is no traffic to be sent, spoofing is a scheme used by routers that causes a host to treat an interface as if it were functioning and supporting a session. The router pretends to send "spoof" replies to keepalive messages from the host in an effort to convince the host that the session is up and running. *See also: DDR.*

2. The illegal act of sending a packet labeled with a false address, in order to deceive network security mechanisms such as filters and access lists.

spooler

A management application that processes requests submitted to it for execution in a sequential fashion from a queue. A good example is a print spooler.

SPX

Sequenced Packet Exchange: A Novell NetWare transport protocol that augments the datagram service provided by Network layer (Layer 3) protocols, it was derived from the Switch-to-Switch Protocol of the XNS protocol suite.

SQE

Signal Quality Error: In an Ethernet network, a message sent from a transceiver to an attached machine that the collision-detection circuitry is working.

SRB

Source-Route Bridging: Created by IBM, the bridging method used in Token-Ring networks. The source determines the entire route to a destination before sending the data and includes that information in route information fields (RIF) within each packet. *Contrast with: transparent bridging.*

SRT

source-route transparent bridging: A bridging scheme developed by IBM, merging source-route and transparent bridging. SRT takes advantage of both technologies in one device, fulfilling the needs of all end nodes. Translation between bridging protocols is not necessary. *Compare with: SR/TLB.*

SR/TLB

source-route translational bridging: A bridging method that allows source-route stations to communicate with transparent bridge stations aided by an intermediate bridge that translates between the two bridge protocols. Used for bridging between Token Ring and Ethernet. *Compare with: SRT.*

SSAP

Source Service Access Point: The SAP of the network node identified in the Source field of the packet. *See also: DSAP and SAP.*

SSE

Silicon Switching Engine: The software component of Cisco's silicon switching technology, hard-coded into the Silicon Switch Processor (SSP). Silicon switching is available only on the Cisco 7000 with an SSP. Silicon-switched packets are compared to the silicon-switching cache on the SSE. The SSP is a dedicated switch processor that offloads the switching process from the route processor, providing a fast-switching solution, but packets must still traverse the backplane of the router to get to the SSP and then back to the exit interface.

star topology

A LAN physical topology with endpoints on the network converging at a common central switch (known as a hub) using point-to-point links. A logical ring topology can be configured as a physical star topology using a unidirectional closed-loop star rather than point-to-point links. That is, connections within the hub are arranged in an internal ring. *See also: bus topology and ring topology.*

startup range

If an AppleTalk node does not have a number saved from the last time it was booted, then the node selects from the range of values from 65280 to 65534.

static route

A route whose information is purposefully entered into the routing table and takes priority over those chosen by dynamic routing protocols.

statistical multiplexing

Multiplexing in general is a technique that allows data from multiple logical channels to be sent across a single physical channel. Statistical multiplexing dynamically assigns bandwidth only to input channels that are active, optimizing available bandwidth so that more devices can be connected than with other multiplexing techniques. Also known as statistical time-division multiplexing or stat mux.

STM-1

Synchronous Transport Module Level 1. In the European SDH standard, one of many formats identifying the frame structure for the 155.52Mbps lines that are used to carry ATM cells.

store-and-forward packet switching

A technique in which the switch first copies each packet into its buffer and performs a cyclical redundancy check (CRC). If the packet is error-free, the switch then looks up the destination address in its filter table, determines the appropriate exit port, and sends the packet.

STP

1. Shielded Twisted Pair: A two-pair wiring scheme, used in many network implementations, that has a layer of shielded insulation to reduce EMI.
2. Spanning Tree protocol.

stub area

An OSPF area carrying a default route, intra-area routes, and interarea routes, but no external routes. Configuration of virtual links cannot be achieved across a stub area, and stub areas are not allowed to contain an ASBR. *See also: non-stub area, ASBR, and OSPF.*

stub network

A network having only one connection to a router.

STUN

Serial Tunnel: A technology used to connect an HDLC link to an SDLC link over a serial link.

subarea

A portion of an SNA network made up of a subarea node and its attached links and peripheral nodes.

subarea node

An SNA communications host or controller that handles entire network addresses.

subchannel

A frequency-based subdivision that creates a separate broadband communications channel.

subinterface

One of many virtual interfaces available on a single physical interface.

subnet

See: subnetwork.

subnet address

The portion of an IP address that is specifically identified by the subnet mask as the subnetwork. *See also: IP address, subnetwork, and subnet mask.*

subnet mask

Also simply known as mask, a 32-bit address mask used in IP to identify the bits of an IP address that are used for the subnet address. Using a mask, the router does not need to examine all 32 bits, only those selected by the mask. *See also: address mask and IP address.*

subnetwork

1. Any network that is part of a larger IP network and is identified by a subnet address. A network administrator segments a network into subnetworks in order to provide a hierarchical, multilevel routing structure, and at the same time protect the subnetwork from the addressing complexity of networks that are attached. Also known as a subnet. *See also: IP address, subnet mask, and subnet address.*
2. In OSI networks, the term specifically refers to a collection of ESs and ISs controlled by only one administrative domain, using a solitary network connection protocol.

SVC

switched virtual circuit: A dynamically established virtual circuit, created on demand and dissolved as soon as transmission is over and the circuit is no longer needed. In ATM terminology, it is referred to as a switched virtual connection. *See also: PVC.*

switch

1. In networking, a device responsible for multiple functions such as filtering, flooding, and sending frames. It works using the destination address of individual frames. Switches operate at the Data-Link layer of the OSI model.
2. Broadly, any electronic/mechanical device allowing connections to be established as needed and terminated if no longer necessary.

switched LAN

Any LAN implemented using LAN switches. *See also: LAN switch.*

synchronous transmission

Signals transmitted digitally with precision clocking. These signals have identical frequencies and contain individual characters encapsulated in control bits (called start/stop bits) that designate the beginning and ending of each character. *See also: asynchronous transmission and isochronous transmission.*

T

T1

Digital WAN that uses 24 DS0s at 64K each to create a bandwidth of 1.536Mbps, minus clocking overhead, providing 1.544Mbps of usable bandwidth.

T3

Digital WAN that can provide bandwidth of 44.763Mbps.

tag switching

Based on the concept of label swapping, where packets or cells are designated to defined-length labels that control the manner in which data is to be sent, tag switching is a high-performance technology used for forwarding packets. It incorporates data-link layer (Layer 2) switching and Network layer (Layer 3) routing and supplies scalable, high-speed switching in the network core.

tagged traffic

ATM cells with their cell loss priority (CLP) bit set to 1. Also referred to as discard-eligible (DE) traffic. Tagged traffic can be eliminated in order to ensure trouble-free delivery of higher priority traffic, if the network is congested. *See also: CLP.*

TCP

Transmission Control Protocol: A connection-oriented protocol that is defined at the Transport layer of the OSI reference model. Provides reliable delivery of data.

TCP/IP

Transmission Control Protocol/Internet Protocol. The suite of protocols underlying the Internet. TCP and IP are the most widely known protocols in that suite. *See also: IP and TCP.*

TDM

time division multiplexing: A technique for assigning bandwidth on a single wire, based on preassigned time slots, to data from several channels. Bandwidth is allotted to each channel regardless of a station's ability to send data. *See also: ATDM, FDM, and multiplexing.*

TE1

A device with a four-wire, twisted-pair digital interface is referred to as terminal equipment type one. Most modern ISDN devices are of this type.

TE

terminal equipment: Any peripheral device that is ISDN-compatible and attached to a network, such as a telephone or computer.

telco

A common abbreviation for the telephone company.

Telnet

The standard terminal emulation protocol within the TCP/IP protocol stack. Method of remote terminal connection, enabling users to log in on remote networks and use those resources as if they were locally connected. Telnet is defined in RFC 854.

10BaseT

Part of the original IEEE 802.3 standard, 10BaseT is the Ethernet specification of 10Mbps baseband that uses two pairs of twisted-pair, Category 3, 4, or 5 cabling—using one pair to send data and the other to receive. 10BaseT has a distance limit of about 100 meters per segment. *See also: Ethernet and IEEE 802.3.*

terminal adapter

A hardware interface between a computer without a native ISDN interface and an ISDN line. In effect, a device to connect a standard async interface to a non-native ISDN device, emulating a modem.

terminal emulation

The use of software, installed on a PC or LAN server, that allows the PC to function as if it were a "dumb" terminal directly attached to a particular type of mainframe.

TFTP

Trivial File Transfer Protocol. Conceptually, a stripped-down version of FTP, it's the protocol of choice if you know exactly what you want and where it's to be found. TFTP doesn't provide the abundance of functions that FTP does. In particular, it has no directory browsing abilities; it can do nothing but send and receive files.

token

A frame containing only control information. Possessing this control information gives a network device permission to transmit data onto the network. *See also: token passing.*

token bus

LAN architecture that is the basis for the IEEE 802.4 LAN specification and employs token passing access over a bus topology. *See also: IEEE.*

token passing

A method used by network devices to access the physical medium in a systematic way based on possession of a small frame called a token. *Contrast with: circuit switching. See also: token.*

Token Ring

IBM's token-passing LAN technology. It runs at 4Mbps or 16Mbps over a ring topology. Defined formally by IEEE 802.5. *See also: ring topology and token passing.*

transparent bridging

The bridging scheme used in Ethernet and IEEE 802.3 networks, it passes frames along one hop at a time, using bridging information stored in tables that associate end-node MAC addresses within bridge ports. This type of bridging is considered transparent because the source node does not know it has been bridged, because the destination frames are sent directly to the end node. *Contrast with: SRB.*

Transport layer

Layer 4 of the OSI reference model, used for reliable communication between end nodes over the network. The Transport layer provides mechanisms used for establishing, maintaining, and terminating virtual circuits, transport fault detection and recovery, and controlling the flow of information. *See also: Application layer, Data-Link layer, Network layer, Physical layer, Presentation layer, and Session layer.*

TRIP

Token Ring Interface Processor: A high-speed interface processor used on Cisco 7000 series routers. The TRIP provides two or four ports for interconnection with IEEE 802.5 and IBM media with ports set to speeds of either 4Mbps or 16Mbps set independently of each other.

TTL

time to live: A field in an IP header, indicating the length of time a packet is valid.

TUD

Trunk Up-Down: A protocol used in ATM networks for the monitoring of trunks. Should a trunk miss a given number of test messages being sent by ATM switches to ensure trunk line quality, TUD declares the trunk down. When a trunk reverses direction and comes back up, TUD recognizes that the trunk is up and returns the trunk to service.

tunneling

A method of avoiding protocol restrictions by wrapping packets from one protocol in another protocol's packet and transmitting this encapsulated packet over a network that supports the wrapper protocol. *See also: encapsulation.*

U

UDP

User Datagram Protocol: A connectionless Transport layer protocol in the TCP/IP protocol stack that simply allows datagrams to be exchanged without acknowledgments or delivery guarantees, requiring other protocols to handle error processing and retransmission. UDP is defined in RFC 768.

unnumbered frames

HDLC frames used for control-management purposes, such as link startup and shutdown or mode specification.

V

VBR

Variable Bit Rate: A QoS class, as defined by the ATM Forum, for use in ATM networks that is subdivided into real-time (RT) class and non-real-time (NRT) class. RT is employed when connections have a fixed-time relationship between samples. Conversely, NRT is employed when connections do not have a fixed-time relationship between samples, but still need an assured QoS.

VCC

Virtual Channel Connection: A logical circuit that is created by VCLs. VCCs carry data between two endpoints in an ATM network. Sometimes called a virtual circuit connection.

VIP

1. Versatile Interface Processor: An interface card for Cisco 7000 and 7500 series routers, providing multilayer switching and running the Cisco IOS software. The most recent version of VIP is VIP2.
2. Virtual IP: A function making it possible for logically separated switched IP workgroups to run Virtual Networking Services across the switch ports of a Catalyst 5000.

virtual circuit

Abbreviated VC, a logical circuit devised to assure reliable communication between two devices on a network. Defined by a virtual path connection (VPC)/virtual path identifier (VCI) pair, a virtual circuit can be permanent (PVC) or switched (SVC). Virtual circuits are used in Frame Relay and X.25. Known as virtual channel in ATM. *See also: PVC and SVC.*

virtual ring

In an SRB network, a logical connection between physical rings, either local or remote.

VLAN

Virtual LAN: A group of devices on one or more logically segmented LANs (configured by use of management software), enabling devices to communicate as if attached to the same physical medium, when they are actually located on numerous different LAN segments. VLANs are based on logical instead of physical connections and thus are tremendously flexible.

VLSM

variable-length subnet mask: Helps optimize available address space and specify a different subnet mask for the same network number on various subnets. *Also commonly referred to as "subnetting a subnet."*

W

WinSock

Windows Socket Interface: A software interface that makes it possible for an assortment of applications to use and share an Internet connection. The WinSock software consists of a Dynamic Link Library (DLL) with supporting programs such as a dialer program that initiates the connection.

workgroup switching

A switching method that supplies high-speed (100Mbps) transparent bridging between Ethernet networks as well as high-speed translational bridging between Ethernet and CDDI or FDDI.

X

X.25

An ITU-T packet-relay standard that defines communication between DTE and DCE network devices. X.25 uses a reliable data-link layer protocol called LAPB. X.25 also uses PLP at the Network layer. X.25 has mostly been replaced by Frame Relay.

Z

ZIP

Zone Information Protocol: A session-layer protocol used by AppleTalk to map network numbers to zone names. NBP uses ZIP in the determination of networks containing nodes that belong to a zone. *See also: ZIP storm and zone.*

ZIP storm

A broadcast storm occurring when a router running AppleTalk reproduces or transmits a route for which there is no corresponding zone name at the time of execution. The route is then forwarded by other routers downstream, thus causing a ZIP storm. *See also: broadcast storm and ZIP.*

zone

A logical grouping of network devices in AppleTalk. *See also: ZIP.*

INDEX

Note to the Reader: Throughout this index **boldfaced** page numbers indicate primary discussions of a topic. *Italicized* page numbers indicate illustrations.

CISCO® STUDY GUIDES
FROM SYBEX™

- **Prepare for Cisco certification with the experts**
- **Full coverage of each exam objective**
- **Hands-on labs and hundreds of sample questions**

ISBN 0-7821-2381-3
768 pp; 7½" x 9"; $49.99
Hardcover

ISBN 0-7821-2403-8
832 pp; 7½" x 9"; $49.99
Hardcover

ISBN 0-7821-2571-9
704 pp; 7½" x 9"; $49.99
Hardcover

**CCDA™: Cisco® Certified Design
Associate Study Guide**
ISBN: 0-7821-2534-4; 800 pp; 7½" x 9"
$49.99; Hardcover; CD

**CCNP™: Cisco® Internetwork
Troubleshooting Study Guide**
ISBN 0-7821-2536-0; 704 pp; 7½ x 9
$49.99; Hardcover; CD

**CCNP™: Configuring, Monitoring, and
Troubleshooting Dial-Up Services
Study Guide**
ISBN 0-7821-2544-1; 704 pp; 7½" x 9"
$49.99; Hardcover; CD

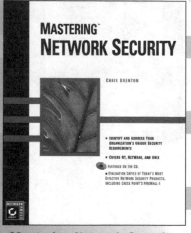

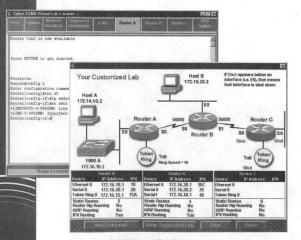